Microsoft Visual Basic 2013 Step by Step

Michael Halvorson

Published with the authorization of Microsoft Corporation by:
O'Reilly Media, Inc.
1005 Gravenstein Highway North
Sebastopol, California 95472

ISBN: 978-0-7356-6704-4

1 2 3 4 5 6 7 8 9 LSI 8 7 6 5 4 3

Printed and bound in the United States of America.

Microsoft Press books are available through booksellers and distributors worldwide. If you need support related to this book, email Microsoft Press Book Support at mspinput@microsoft.com. Please tell us what you think of this book at *http://www.microsoft.com/learning/booksurvey.*

Acquisitions and Developmental Editor: Russell Jones

Production Editor: Kristen Brown

Editorial Production: Zyg Group, LLC

Technical Reviewer: Tim Patrick

Copyeditor: Richard Carey

Indexer: Bob Pfahler

Cover Design: Twist Creative • Seattle

Cover Composition: Randy Comer

Illustrator: Rebecca Demarest

Contents at a glance

Contents

What do you think of this book? We want to hear from you!

Microsoft is interested in hearing your feedback so we can continually improve our books and learning resources for you. To participate in a brief online survey, please visit:

microsoft.com/learning/booksurvey

PART V MICROSOFT WINDOWS PHONE PROGRAMMING

Introduction

Microsoft Visual Basic 2013 is an important upgrade and enhancement of the popular Visual Basic programming language and compiler, a technology that enjoys an installed base of millions of programmers worldwide. Visual Basic 2013 is not a stand-alone product but a key component of Microsoft Visual Studio 2013—a comprehensive development system that allows you to create powerful applications for Microsoft Windows 8.1, the Windows desktop, the web, Windows Phone 8, and a host of other environments.

Whether you purchase one of the commercial editions of Visual Studio 2013 or you download Visual Basic Express 2013 for a free test-drive of the software, you are in for an exciting experience. The latest features of Visual Basic will increase your productivity and programming prowess, especially if you enjoy using and integrating information from databases, entertainment media, webpages, and websites. In addition, an important benefit of learning Visual Basic and the Visual Studio Integrated Development Environment (IDE) is that you can use many of the same tools to write programs for Microsoft Visual C# 2013, Microsoft Visual C++ 2013, HTML5 and JavaScript, and other popular languages.

Microsoft Visual Basic 2013 Step by Step is a comprehensive introduction to Visual Basic programming using the Visual Basic 2013 software and Windows 8.1. I've designed this practical, hands-on tutorial with a variety of skill levels in mind. In my opinion, the best way to master a complex technology like Visual Basic is to follow the premise that programmers learn by doing. Therefore, by reading this book and working through the examples, you'll learn essential programming techniques through carefully prepared tutorials that you can complete on your own schedule and at your own pace.

Although I have significant experience with college teaching and corporate project management, this book is not a dry textbook or an "A to Z" programmer's reference; instead, it is a practical hands-on programming tutorial that puts *you* in charge of your learning, developmental milestones, and achievements. By using this book, programmers who are new to this topic will learn Visual Basic software development fundamentals in the context of useful, real-world applications; and intermediate Visual Basic programmers can quickly master the essential tools and techniques offered in the Visual Basic 2013 and Windows 8.1 upgrades.

I've taken a multiplatform approach in this book, so in addition to learning Visual Basic programming skills you'll learn to create a wide variety of applications, including Windows Store apps, Windows Forms (Windows desktop) apps, console apps, web apps

(ASP.NET), and Windows Phone 8 apps. Each of these application types has a place and a purpose in real-world development.

To complement this comprehensive approach, the book is structured into 5 topically organized parts, 21 chapters, and dozens of step-by-step exercises and sample programs. By using this book, you'll quickly learn how to create professional-quality Visual Basic 2013 applications for the Windows operating system, Windows Phone 8 platform, and a variety of web browsers. You'll also have fun!

Who should read this book

This is a step-by-step programming tutorial for readers who enjoy learning to do new things by doing them. My assumption is that you already have some experience with programming, possibly even an earlier version of Visual Basic, and that you are ready to learn about the Visual Studio 2013 product in the context of building applications that you can market in the Windows Store, Windows Forms (Windows desktop) for personal and enterprise purposes, web (ASP.NET) applications that run in browsers, and apps for the Windows Phone 8 platforms.

This book's content will supply you with concrete Visual Basic coding techniques as well as a broad overview of programming strategies suitable for Visual Basic development. The book's extensive collection of step-by-step exercises has a broad focus; they are written for technical people who understand programming and are not simply targeted toward hobbyists or absolute beginners. In addition, you will learn about the capabilities of the Windows 8.1 operating system and the specific design guidelines that Microsoft recommends for Windows 8.1 and Windows Phone 8 applications.

Assumptions

This book is designed to teach readers how to use the Visual Basic programming language. You will also learn how to use the Visual Studio 2013 IDE and development tools. This book assumes no previous experience with Visual Studio 2013, but it is written for readers who understand programming and are not absolute beginners. I assume that you are familiar with programming basics or have studied some version of BASIC or Visual Basic in the past and are now ready to move beyond elementary skills to platform-specific techniques.

If you have no prior knowledge of programming or Visual Basic, you might want to fill in some of the gaps with my introduction to Visual Basic 2012 and Windows Store development, *Start Here! Learn Visual Basic 2012* (Microsoft Press, 2012). From time to time, I will refer to the exercises in that book to give you additional resources for your learning.

Microsoft Visual Basic 2013 Step by Step also assumes that you have acquired and are running the Windows 8.1 operating system and that you want to learn how to create applications for the Windows Store platform and other environments. To make the most of your programming practice, you will need to know a little about how to perform common tasks in Windows 8.1, how to customize the Start page and user interface, how to work with information on the web, and how to adjust basic system settings. If you also have Windows 8.1 installed on a tablet or touchpad device, all the better, because a fundamental design emphasis of Windows 8.1 is to make touch and gestures a natural way to manipulate content. You can build your applications on a laptop or desktop running Visual Studio 2013 and Windows 8.1 and then test out the applications on your tablet or touchpad.

In terms of the Visual Studio software, I assume that you are using one of the full, retail versions of Visual Studio 2013, such as Visual Studio Professional, Premium, or Ultimate. This will enable you to create the full range of application types that I describe in this book, including Windows Store apps, Windows Forms (Windows desktop) apps, console apps, Web Forms (ASP.NET) apps, and Windows Phone 8 apps.

If you don't have access to a full, retail version of Visual Studio 2013, you can experiment with the Visual Studio 2013 software by downloading free versions of the suite designed for specific platforms. These limited-feature or "Express" versions of Visual Studio 2013 are called Express for Windows, Express for Windows Desktop, Express for Windows Phone, and Express for Web. The Visual Studio website (*http://www.microsoft.com/visualstudio*) provides access to the retail and Express versions of Visual Studio, and it explains the differences among all of the available versions.

Who should not read this book

You might be disappointed with this book if you are already a knowledgeable Visual Basic programmer and are just looking to explore the new features of Visual Studio 2013. The *Step By Step* series is targeted toward readers who are professional developers but who have little to no previous experience with the topic at hand. If you are an advanced Visual Basic developer, you are likely to grow weary of the step by step exercises that introduce essential features such as decision structures, XAML markup, data access strategies, or using the .NET Framework.

Developers who have a lot of experience will feel that I'm exploring the obvious—but what is obvious to experienced programmers often isn't obvious at all to someone who is learning to use a new development platform. If Windows Store or Windows Phone programming with Visual Basic is a new concept for you, this is the place to start.

Organization of this book

This book is divided into five sections, each of which focuses on a different aspect or technology within the Visual Studio software and the Visual Basic programming language. Part I, "Introduction to Visual Studio development," provides an overview of the Visual Studio 2013 IDE and its fundamental role in .NET application creation and then moves into step-by-step development walkthroughs on the Windows Store and Windows Forms (Windows desktop) platforms.

Part II, "Designing the user interface," continues the focus on application creation in the Visual Studio IDE, emphasizing the construction of Windows Store apps, Windows Forms (Windows desktop) apps, and console apps. In particular, you'll learn how to work with XAML markup, XAML styles, important controls, and new Windows 8.1 design features, including command bar, flyout, tiles on the Windows Start page, and touch input.

Part III, "Visual Basic programming techniques," covers core Visual Basic programming skills, including managing data types, using the .NET Framework, structured error handling, working with collections and generics, data management with LINQ, and fundamental object-oriented programming skills.

Part IV, "Database and web programming," introduces data management techniques in Windows desktop and Windows Store applications, including binding data to controls and working with XML documents and Microsoft Access data sources. You'll also get an overview of ASP.NET web development strategies, along with a complete walkthrough of web development on the Web Forms (ASP.NET) platform.

Finally, Part V, "Microsoft Windows Phone programming," provides an overview of the features and capabilities presented by the Windows Phone 8 platform. You'll identify key hardware characteristics in the Windows Phone ecosystem, the marketing opportunities tendered by the Windows Phone Store, and you'll create a complete Windows Phone 8 app step by step.

Finding your best starting point in this book

This book is designed to help you build skills in a number of essential areas. You can use it if you're new to programming, switching from another programming language, or upgrading from Visual Studio 2010 or Visual Basic 2012. Use the following table to find your best starting point in this book.

If you are ...	Follow these steps
New to Visual Basic programming	1. Install the sample projects as described in the section "Installing the code samples," later in this Introduction. 2. Learn essential skills for using Visual Studio and Visual Basic by working sequentially from Chapter 1 through Chapter 21. 3. Use the companion book *Start Here! Learn Microsoft Visual Basic 2012* for additional instruction as your level of experience dictates.
Upgrading from Visual Basic 2010 or 2012	1. Install the sample projects as described in the section "Installing the code samples." 2. Read Chapter 1, skim Chapters 2 through 4, and complete Chapters 5 through 21.
Interested primarily in creating Windows Store apps for Windows 8.1	1. Install the sample projects as described in the section "Installing the code samples." 2. Complete Chapters 1 through 3, Chapter 5, Chapters 7 through 16, and Chapter 18.
Interested primarily in creating Windows Forms (Windows desktop) apps for Windows 8.1, Windows 8, or Windows 7	1. Install the sample projects as described in the section "Installing the code samples." 2. Complete Chapters 1 through 2, Chapter 4, Chapter 6, Chapter 10, and Chapters 11 through 17.

Conventions and features in this book

This book presents information using the following conventions designed to make the information readable and easy to follow:

- Each exercise consists of a series of tasks, presented as numbered steps (1, 2, and so on) listing each action you must take to complete the exercise.

- The names of all program elements—controls, objects, methods, functions, properties, classes, variable names, and so on—appear in *italics*.

- As you work through steps, you'll occasionally see tables with lists of properties that you'll set in Visual Studio. Text properties appear within quotes, but you don't need to type the quotes.

- Boxed elements with labels such as "Note" provide additional information or alternative methods for completing a step successfully.

- Text that you type (including some code blocks) appears in **bold**.

- A plus sign (+) between two key names means that you must press those keys at the same time. For example, "Press Alt+Tab" means that you hold down the Alt key while you press the Tab key.

- A vertical bar between two or more menu items (for example, File | Close) means that you should select the first menu or menu item, then the next, and so on.

System requirements

You will need the following hardware and software to work through the examples in this book:

- The Windows 8.1 operating system. (Depending on your Windows configuration, you might also require Local Administrator rights to install or configure Visual Studio 2013.) Note that while the full versions of Visual Studio 2013 do support earlier versions of Windows, such as Windows 8 and Windows 7 SP1, the features described in this book require Windows 8.1, and the screen shots will all show this environment.

- A full retail edition of Visual Studio 2013, required for completing all of the exercises in this book (Visual Studio 2013 Professional, Premium, or Ultimate). The Visual Studio website (*http://www.microsoft.com/visualstudio*) explains the differences among these versions. Alternatively, you can experiment with the Visual Studio 2013 software by downloading free versions of the suite designed for specific platforms. The limited-feature versions of Visual Studio 2013 are called Express for Windows, Express for Windows Desktop, Express for Windows Phone, and Express for Web. You will need to download all four of these Express versions to get the necessary software to complete the book's exercises. (However, even with these Express editions, there will be a few gaps; for example, you will be unable to complete Chapter 10, "Creating console applications.")

- An Internet connection to view Visual Studio help files, try out the Windows Store and Windows Phone Store, and download this book's sample files.

- A computer with 1.6 GHz or faster processor.

- 1 GB RAM (32-bit) or 2 GB RAM (64-bit).

- 16 GB available hard disk space (32-bit) or 20 GB (64-bit) for Windows 8.1.

- DirectX 9 graphics device with WDDM 1.0 or higher driver.

- 1024 × 768 minimum screen resolution.

If you want to use touch for user input, you'll need a multitouch-capable laptop, tablet, or display. A multitouch-capable device is optional for the exercises in this book, although one is useful if you want to understand what such devices are capable of. Typically, a programmer will develop software on a desktop or laptop computer and then test multitouch functionality on a multitouch-capable device.

Although this book develops applications for Windows Phone 8, a Windows Phone is not required to complete the book's step-by-step exercises.

Code samples

Most of the chapters in this book include step-by-step exercises that let you interactively try out new material learned in the main text. All sample projects can be downloaded from the following page:

http://aka.ms/VB2013_SbS/files

Follow the instructions to download the Visual_Basic_2013_SBS_Sample_Code.zip file.

Installing the code samples

Follow these steps to install the code samples on your computer so that you can use them with the exercises in this book:

1. Unzip the Visual_Basic_2013_SBS_Sample_Code.zip file that you downloaded from the book's website. (Name a specific directory along with directions to create it, if necessary.) I recommend My Documents\Visual Basic 2013 SBS for the files.

2. If prompted, review the displayed end user license agreement. If you accept the terms, select the accept option, and then click Next.

Using the code samples

The code samples .zip file for this book creates a folder named Visual Basic 2013 SBS that contains 19 subfolders—one for each of the chapters in the book that have exercises. To find the examples associated with a particular chapter, open the appropriate chapter folder. You'll find the examples for that chapter in separate subfolders. The subfolder names have the same names as the examples in the book. For example, you'll find an example called Music Trivia in the My Documents\Visual Basic 2013 SBS\Chapter 02 folder on your hard drive. If your system is configured to display file extensions of the Visual Basic project files, look for .sln as the file extension. Depending on how your system is configured, you might see a Documents folder rather than a My Documents folder.

Acknowledgments

This book is a very substantial revision of an earlier Visual Basic Step by Step book published by Microsoft Press. In fact, in almost every way, it is an entirely new book, and it is the first programming title that I have written specifically to be a multiplatform guidebook, covering Visual Basic development on the Windows Store, Windows Forms, Web Forms, and Windows Phone platforms. I am very grateful to the many talented programmers and editors who offered their ideas and contributions to this volume.

At Microsoft Press, I would like to thank Devon Musgrave for his early enthusiasm for the project and for connecting me to team members in the Visual Studio product group. At O'Reilly Media, I would like to thank again Russell Jones, who discussed many of the topics in this book with me and offered technical and practical suggestions for completing the work on schedule. I am also grateful to Tim Patrick, a technical reviewer and experienced author and developer, who worked on both this Step by Step volume and the companion book, *Start Here! Learn Microsoft Visual Basic 2012*. (Perhaps we will work on a history book someday as well, Tim!)

Within the editorial group at O'Reilly Media, I would like to thank Kristen Brown, for scheduling the editorial review and answering questions about the design; and Richard Carey, for his skillful copy editing and managing all style and localization issues that arose. (It is good to work with you again, Richard!) I would also like to thank Rebecca Demarest, Kim Burton-Weisman, and Linda Weidemann for their important artistic, editorial, and technical contributions.

I am also most grateful to the Microsoft Visual Studio 2013 development team for providing me with the preview and release candidate software to work with. In addition, I would like to thank the Microsoft Windows 8.1 team for their support and offer my special thanks to the many MSDN forum contributors who asked and answered questions about Visual Basic and Windows programming.

Finally, I offer thanks and admiration to my immediate family for their continued support of my writing projects and various academic pursuits. Once again I was able to involve my son, Henry Halvorson, with the creation of electronic music and artwork, and his contributions appear in Chapters 3, 4, 5, and 9.

Errata & book support

We've made every effort to ensure the accuracy of this book and its companion content. Any errors that have been reported since this book was published are listed on our Microsoft Press site at oreilly.com:

http://aka.ms/VB2013_SbS/errata

If you find an error that is not already listed, you can report it to us through the same page.

If you need additional support, email Microsoft Press Book Support at *mspinput@ microsoft.com.*

Please note that product support for Microsoft software is not offered through the addresses above.

We want to hear from you

At Microsoft Press, your satisfaction is our top priority, and your feedback is our most valuable asset. Please tell us what you think of this book at:

http://www.microsoft.com/learning/booksurvey

The survey is short, and we read every one of your comments and ideas. Thanks in advance for your input!

Stay in touch

Let's keep the conversation going! We're on Twitter: *http://twitter.com/MicrosoftPress.*

You can also learn more about Michael Halvorson's books and ideas at *http://michaelhalvorsonbooks.com.*

PART I

Introduction to Visual Studio development

CHAPTER 1

Visual Basic 2013 development opportunities and the Windows Store

After completing this chapter, you will be able to

■ Describe the development opportunities provided by Microsoft Visual Basic 2013.

■ Understand requirements for distributing applications in the Windows Store.

Are you ready to start working with Microsoft Visual Basic 2013? In this chapter, you'll get an overview of the features and capabilities of the Microsoft Visual Studio 2013 development system and the different editions of Visual Studio that you can purchase or download for *free*. You'll learn about emerging hardware and software platforms and their uses and the impressive range of applications that you can create for these platforms, including Windows Store apps for Windows 8.1; Windows desktop apps for Windows 7, Windows 8, and Windows 8.1; Windows Phone 8 apps; web apps; console apps; and much more.

You'll also learn about the Windows Store, an exciting new distribution point for apps designed especially for Windows 8.1. You'll review a checklist of planning tasks to consider before you begin building a Windows Store application, and you'll learn the procedures for selling and distributing apps through the Windows Store. After you have a clear list of the Windows Store requirements and program features in mind, you'll be ready to build your own programs, including Windows Store apps that you can distribute to millions of potential customers worldwide.

Before we begin, a word about terminology. This book has been designed and tested using the Windows 8.1 operating system. The Windows Store apps that you create will run under Windows 8.1 and will target the .NET Framework version 4.5.1. You will also learn to create Visual Basic programs using the Windows Forms and console app models, which run on what is now known as the "Windows desktop." These types of apps will run under Windows 8.1, Windows 8, Windows 7, and earlier versions of Windows, provided that the Windows installation has the proper .NET Framework files installed.

Yet another type of application you will create in this book, using Visual Studio and a technology called ASP.NET, are Web Forms apps. These apps run in a web browser, such as Internet Explorer. Finally, you'll create mobile phone apps during the course of this book, using Visual Studio and the Windows Phone SDK 8.0. These apps run on the Windows Phone 8 platform.

Visual Basic 2013 products and opportunities

I'm going to assume that you have purchased this book because you want to learn how to program in Visual Basic. In fact, my underlying assumption is that you might already have some development experience—perhaps even with an earlier version of Visual Basic—and that you are ready to learn about the Visual Studio 2013 product in the context of the Windows Store, Windows Forms, Windows Phone, and Web Forms platforms. Enhancing your Visual Basic development skills is an excellent choice; there are over four million Visual Basic programmers in the world developing innovative solutions, and Microsoft's newest operating system, Windows 8.1, presents many amazing opportunities for Visual Basic programmers.

"Visual Basic" essentially has two meanings in the software development marketplace. In a narrower engineering sense, Visual Basic is the name of a programming language with specific syntax rules and logical procedures that must be followed when a developer creates code for a compiler with the goal of making an executable program or *application*. However, Visual Basic is also used in a more comprehensive product-related sense to describe the collection of tools and techniques that developers use to build Windows-based applications with a particular software suite. In the past, developers could purchase a stand-alone version of Visual Basic, such as Microsoft Visual Basic .NET 2003 Professional Edition, but these days Visual Basic is sold only as a component within the Visual Studio software suite, which also includes Microsoft Visual C#, Microsoft Visual C++, and other development tools.

The Visual Studio 2013 development suite is distributed in several different product configurations, including Professional, Premium, and Ultimate, along with a subset of Visual Studio tools designed for test engineers, known as Visual Studio 2013 Test Professional. In addition to these retail products, you can experiment with the Visual Studio 2013 software by downloading free versions of the suite designed for specific development platforms. These limited-feature or "Express" versions of Visual Studio 2013 are called Express for Windows, Express for Windows Desktop, Express for Windows Phone, and Express for Web.

The full retail versions of Visual Studio 2013 have different prices and feature sets, with Ultimate being the most comprehensive (and expensive) development package. The Visual Studio website (*http://www.microsoft.com/visualstudio*) explains the differences among all of these versions. Typically, the full retail versions of Visual Studio are also available for a 30-day free trial period that can be extended to 90 days. These trial versions are more feature-rich than the Express products. In addition, the faculty, staff, and students of recognized academic institutions can download full editions of Visual Studio 2013 through the Microsoft DreamSpark program, and these free downloads don't expire.

I wrote this book to highlight the features and development opportunities provided by Visual Studio 2013 Professional and Visual Studio 2013 Premium. If you are using Visual Studio Ultimate, you will also have what you need to complete the exercises in this book—and then some. The extra features included in Visual Studio Ultimate primarily relate to larger team development projects and enterprise-computing scenarios that go beyond the scope of this book.

You can also complete most of the exercises in this book if you install *all four* of the Express editions of Visual Studio 2013, and then switch among them as directed. (That is, you can complete most of the exercises in this book if you install Visual Studio 2013 Express for Windows, Visual Studio 2013 Express for Windows Desktop, Visual Studio 2013 Express for Web, and Visual Studio 2013 Express for Windows Phone 8.) I will let you know which Express product is necessary for each chapter and when the individual Express products have limitations that will restrict your ability to compete the exercises. Occasionally, the instructions in this book will apply only to the full retail editions of Visual Studio 2013, such as Chapter 10, "Creating console applications."

Collectively, the chapters in this volume are designed to open up an exciting new world of technical and business opportunities to Visual Basic 2013 programmers. The book's extensive collection of step-by-step exercises has a broad focus, and they are written for technical people who understand programming and are not simply hobbyists or absolute beginners. In short, the exercises in this book will give you a taste of real-world programming practices and experiences. If you have no prior knowledge of Visual Basic or Visual Studio, you might want to fill in some of the gaps with my comprehensive introduction to Visual Basic 2012 and Windows 8 development, *Start Here! Learn Visual Basic 2012* (Microsoft Press, 2012). From time to time, I will refer to the exercises in that book to give you additional resources for your learning.

An impressive range of development opportunities and platforms

How has Visual Basic programming evolved over time, and what opportunities are available now to Visual Basic 2013 programmers? Before we start writing code, let's briefly examine some of the recent trends in software development and Windows programming.

Microsoft released Visual Basic 1.0 in 1991. From its initial announcement at Windows World, the product impressed software developers because it innovatively combined an advanced Visual Basic language compiler with an Integrated Development Environment (IDE) that allowed programmers to build Windows applications by visually arranging controls on a Windows form and then customizing the controls with property settings and Visual Basic code. From these modest beginnings, Visual Basic grew into a powerful development tool that was closely aligned with Windows programming, capable of creating fast and efficient Windows-based applications that could run on a variety of hardware platforms.

In the early 2000s, Visual Basic programmers were concerned primarily with creating applications for Windows that helped businesses manage data effectively. Visual Basic's ability to graphically display information and provide access to it with powerful user interface controls gained many supporters for the product, and the installed base grew into the millions. Over the past decade, the leading Visual Basic applications have been database front-ends, inventory management systems, web applications and utilities, purchasing tools, CAD programs, scientific applications, and games.

However, in the 2010s, the explosion of Internet connectivity and online commerce has dramatically changed the landscape for software developers. In the past, most applications for Windows ran on a server or a desktop PC. Today, laptops, tablet devices, and smartphones are everywhere, and often the same person owns three or four device types. Consumers need to move applications and information seamlessly across these devices, and software developers need the tools that will allow them to create applications that work on multiple platforms or that can be ported easily from one device to the next.

The Visual Studio 2013 product team took the challenge of coding for diverse platforms seriously, and they have created a software suite that allows developers to leverage their existing work while also letting them target a variety of different application models. The following list highlights the major development platforms and opportunities for Visual Basic programmers (some of which are supported only by the full retail versions of Visual Studio 2013):

- **Windows 8.1**   Visual Basic developers can create Windows Store apps for Windows 8.1 that run on a wide range of devices, including desktop PCs, laptops, and Microsoft Surface tablets. (Note: To create new Windows Store apps for Windows 8, you need to use Microsoft Visual Studio 2012.)

- **Windows 8, Windows 7, and Windows Server**   Visual Basic developers can create desktop applications for earlier versions of Windows and distribute them in a variety of ways. You can create desktop applications using the Windows Forms ("Win forms") model or the Windows Presentation Foundation (WPF) model.

- **Windows Phone 8**   Using Visual Studio 2013, Visual Basic programmers can create applications that run on the Windows Phone 8 platform and take advantage of its unique features. You will learn to write mobile phone apps for Windows Phone devices in Chapter 20, "Introduction to Windows Phone 8 development," and Chapter 21, "Creating your first Windows Phone 8 application."

- **Web development**   Developers can use Visual Basic, HTML5, CSS3, or JavaScript to create applications that will run on the web and look great in a variety of browsers. A technology known as ASP.NET allows Visual Basic programmers to build websites, web applications, and web services quickly without knowing all the details about how the information will be stored on the web. The full list of options is explored in Chapter 19, "Visual Studio web development with ASP.NET."

- **Console applications and device drivers**   Visual Basic programmers can write applications that run in command-line mode, which is sometimes called the Windows text console or DOS window. While console apps primarily handle "behind the scenes" calculations, they can also use libraries in the .NET Framework. I describe console programming in Chapter 10.

- **Office applications**   Visual Basic programmers can still build macros and other tools that enhance the functionality of Microsoft Office applications, such as Excel, Word, Access, and PowerPoint.

- **Xbox 360**   Visual Basic programmers can write games for the Xbox using Visual Studio and Microsoft XNA Game Studio (version 4.0 and later).

- **Windows Azure applications for web servers and the cloud**   Visual Basic is powerful enough to write applications that will be used on sophisticated web servers, distributed data centers, and a version of Windows designed for cloud computing known as Windows Azure.

This is an amazing list of application types! Although this list might seem daunting at first, the good news is that the fundamental Visual Basic programming skills that you will explore here remain the same from platform to platform, and there are numerous tools and techniques that help you to port work easily between them. This book provides a solid introduction to many of the core skills that you will use, and especially the new tools provided by Visual Studio 2013 to help you develop your solution for Windows 8.1, the Windows desktop, and Windows Phone 8. However, after you master the core Visual Basic programming skills, you can move on to specific platforms by acquiring materials specifically related to those markets.

Taking a multiplatform approach to learning Visual Basic

As you have probably discovered by now, applications for Windows 8.1 are often called Windows Store apps. Yes, the connection between Windows 8.1 and the Windows Store is *that* direct. However, Microsoft understands that not all developers are prepared to write applications *only* for Windows 8.1 because developers still need to support earlier versions of Windows, and many developers are designing apps for web browsers, which must be run on a variety of platforms. For this reason, I am describing Visual Basic programming techniques for a wide range of programming platforms in this book. You will learn how to create Windows Store apps, Windows desktop apps, console apps, Web apps, and Windows Phone apps.

In some cases, I will discuss Visual Basic programming techniques related to a specific platform in a chapter, such as Chapter 3, "Creating your first Windows Store application." In other cases, I move back and forth between the platforms, showing how the Visual Basic language, or Visual Studio features related to different platforms, might be adapted to unique situations. An example of this approach is Chapter 14, "Using arrays, collections, and generics to manage data," in which I provide data management instruction using examples from both the Windows Store and the Windows desktop (Windows Forms) platforms.

I have taken this comprehensive approach in *Microsoft Visual Basic 2013 Step by Step* because Visual Studio 2013 Professional has been designed to support all of these application types. The current reality is that Visual Basic programming is a multiplatform endeavor, and intermediate Visual Basic programmers need exposure to many environments as they expand and enhance their development skills. At the same time, Windows Store programming is quite new, so I spend a little more time exploring this platform than the others.

Evaluating the Windows Store

Because the Windows Store provides a new and potentially profitable way of selling and distributing apps to a wide audience, I want to begin this book with a description of what the Windows Store is and how you can use it to reach potential customers. In addition to providing a strong *business* incentive to developing Windows Store apps, I want you to become familiar with the technical requirements of the Windows Store before you begin this type of development so that you know what you will need to do before you get too far along in a big Windows Store project. Microsoft recommends this "up-front education" too, because teams that are creating apps for the Windows Store can be most productive when they know all the certification requirements in advance.

What is the Windows Store?

The Windows Store is an electronic marketplace that allows consumers to search for and acquire applications for Windows. The Windows Store is designed to distribute apps for Windows 8 and Windows 8.1, much like Apple's Mac App Store allows consumers to download Mac software, and the Windows Phone Store allows consumers to download products for devices running Windows Phone 8.

 Note The Windows Phone Store is described in detail in Chapter 20.

The Windows Store allows developers to reach a global marketplace in ways that have been difficult or impossible in the past. Through the Windows Store, Windows-based apps can be monetized, either by charging for an application or by including advertising in the application. Programs downloaded from the Windows Store are certified and ready to run; after you meet the requirements for preparing an app for the marketplace, the details about downloading and deploying the application are handled by the Store.

Throughout this book, you will learn how to create apps to run on Windows 8.1 by using Visual Basic and Visual Studio 2013. At this point, you just need to learn how products are bought and sold in the Windows Store, and to review a Windows Store checklist that identifies which features are necessary for certification and distribution to the global marketplace.

Accessing the Windows Store

If you are running Windows 8.1 on your computer, you will see a Windows Store tile on the Windows Start page, which is the gateway to accessing the Windows Store. If you are not currently running Windows 8.1, you can learn *about* the Windows Store at *http://www.windowsstore.com/*, but you won't be able to access the Windows Store itself, because it is designed for use only within Windows 8.1.

The following illustration shows what the Windows Store looks like when you first access it. Because the list of featured products is always changing, your screen will look different.

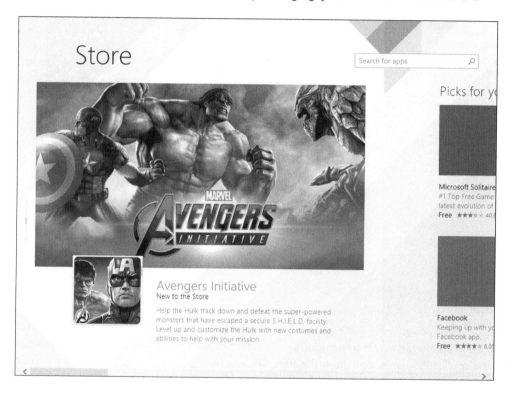

If you right-click in the Windows Store, you'll see a navigation pane that allows you to browse for the top paid and the top new Windows Store apps. In addition, you'll see useful product categories, such as Games, Social, Entertainment, Photo, Music & Video, Sports, and Books & Reference. When you select a category and an item, you'll see an app listing page similar to the following screen:

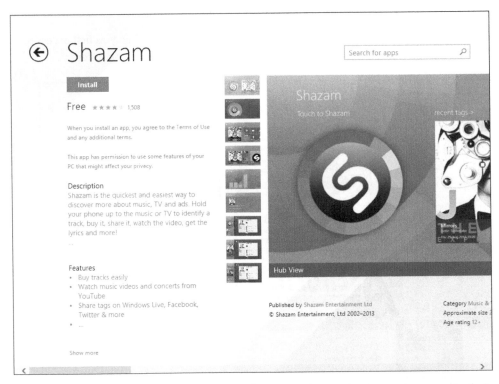

The app listing page is the place where software vendors get a chance to promote their products and describe app benefits. It is tremendously important to present your app in the best possible light here. The application name, description, feature list, age rating, price, and screen shots are all significant factors in making a good impression on your audience. As people purchase or download your app, the rating system (based on five possible stars for the highest level of customer satisfaction) is also an important factor in drawing people to your app.

Installing an app from the Windows Store is extremely simple; you just click the Install button, and within moments, the app will be deployed on your Start page and available for use. A reliable Internet connection is required to download the app and (often) to feed the app data as the program runs.

Sales information and price tiers

Windows-based apps can be distributed free via the Windows Store, or they can be sold for a price. A setting called a *price tier* sets the fee for the app that you plan to sell. You can set the price tier that you like; tiers start at 1.49 USD and move up in increments of 0.50 USD to 4.99 USD, with higher product prices available.

If you plan to sell apps via the Windows Store, it is important to understand a little about how that process might work, even before you begin development. For the first 25,000 USD of an app's sales, you will receive 70% of the revenues that Microsoft receives for the product. If and when an application receives more than 25,000 USD in sales, you will receive 80% of the revenues over 25,000 USD. Keep in mind that your product will be sold internationally, and in some countries, the amount that Microsoft receives will be reduced to account for taxes required by local laws.

It is also required that you register to be a Windows Store developer before you can sell products through Microsoft's new electronic marketplace. The initial annual cost for a developer account in the United States was 49 USD for an individual and 99 USD for a company. You will also need to complete some registration paperwork containing contact information and other details.

Or your application could be free...

Of course, it is not necessary that you sell your application. You can also offer it as a free download to users all over the world. This might be useful if you want to provide general information or a public service or if you want to draw attention to your company or make its products or services more usable. For example, you might want to create a Windows Store app that presents the menu and other services provided by a restaurant, or publish news highlights and photos from an information service.

Within these free applications, you could then decide to use online advertising tools to generate revenue, or you could simply distribute information and know that you had fostered communication about your product throughout the world. The Windows Store has a special marketing category for free apps, as shown in the following illustration:

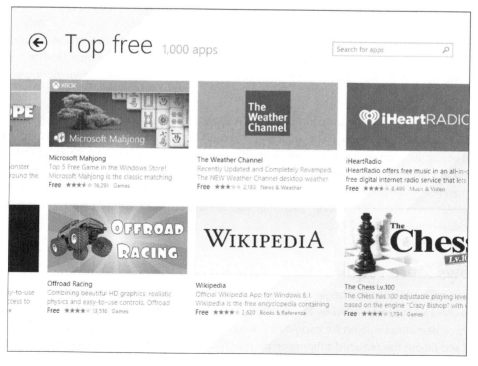

Whether you sell or distribute your app for free is up to you and the needs of your business and your customers!

Planning ahead for certification

Before you begin serious development on your project, Microsoft recommends that you review the certification requirements carefully for Windows Store apps so that you aren't surprised by the necessary steps. For the most part, these steps are simply good development practices that will make your programs robust and high quality. Microsoft is enforcing high standards so that customers come to trust the Windows Store and all of the software distributed through it. We all have a lot riding on the success of the Windows Store.

The Visual Studio Professional IDE contains a Store submenu on the Project menu, with eight commands pertaining to the Windows Store, as shown in the following illustration:

Before you begin serious development on a project that you intend to submit to the Windows Store, you should run the first three commands on the Windows Store submenu. The Open Developer Account command will get you signed up with Microsoft as an individual or a company. This enables the submission process and allows you to get more information. The Reserve App Name command lets you reserve a name for your application within the store. You want to do this before you get too far along (and then learn that you need to change the name). The Acquire Developer License command lets you get a temporary developer license, which you might have already done during your work in Visual Studio.

A helpful blog for developers preparing for the Windows Store is available at *http://blogs.windows.com/windows/b/appbuilder/.* Here you'll find Microsoft employees and other industry experts explaining key application concepts and answering pertinent questions. For example, in addition to the Windows Store checklist shown in Table 1-1 in this chapter, you'll need to fill out a complete package manifest for your project and practice other safe programming practices. You can also find useful information in the MSDN article "Take your app to market" at *http://msdn.microsoft.com/en-us/library/windows/apps/br230836.aspx.*

Windows Store requirements checklist

The formal certification process begins when you upload your app to the Windows Store. Table 1-1 contains a checklist recommended by Microsoft for developers who are creating apps for the Store. Most of these items are required for certification and will be evaluated when you register with Microsoft and fill out the required submission pages online. The certification requirements can be updated periodically, but this checklist will help you get started. The point is that you need to do some preparation before you get online and submit your app for certification. You should have the necessary information ready, and be sure that it has been proofread carefully.

TABLE 1-1 Windows Store submission checklist

Submission page	Field name	Description
Name	App Name	Provide a name for your app that is 256 characters or less. Pick a name that will capture your customers' attention. It is best to keep this name short.
Selling Details	Price Tier	Prepare to specify a selling price for your app (or set the price to "free").
	Free Trial Period	Allow your customer to download the app for a free trial period. If the customer does not buy it in the set period of time, it will stop working.
	Countries/Regions	Identify the market for your product.
	Release Date	Set the app's release date.
	Category	Assign a category for your app so that customers can find it in the Windows Store. There is a helpful list of predefined categories to choose from.
	Accessible App	If your app has been designed to meet Microsoft's accessibility guidelines, indicate that here.
	Minimum DirectX Feature Level	Indicate the video and hardware requirements for your application.
	Minimum System RAM	Indicate how much RAM your app requires. You might want to double-check the basic system requirements for the devices that your app will run on.
Advanced Features	In-App Offers	Provide information about products that users can purchase from within your app, including what the customer must pay and how long the purchased feature can be used.
Ratings	Age Rating	Specify an appropriate age rating for your app, using the levels provided.
	Rating Certificates	If you are selling a game, you might need to provide a rating certificate from a ratings board, depending on where you plan to sell your app.
Cryptography	Question 1	Indicate whether your app makes use of cryptography or encryption.
	Question 2	Verify that any use of cryptography is within the allowable limits imposed by the Bureau of Industry and Security in the United States Department of Commerce.
Packages	Package Upload Control	Provide the path to your app's completed package.

Submission page	Field name	Description
Description	Description	Provide clear and concise marketing copy that describes your application, its features, and its benefits. Review this information carefully before posting. It must be 10,000 characters or less.
	App Features	(Optional) Provide up to 20 features of your app. (Each feature must be 200 characters or fewer.)
	Keywords	(Optional) Provide up to seven concise keywords describing your app.
	Description of Update	Provide a description of how this new version of your app updates the previous version. (Leave blank for the first release of your app.)
	Copyright and Trademark Info	Provide a brief copyright notice, 200 characters or fewer.
	Additional License Items	(Optional) Provide 10,000 characters or fewer.
	Screenshots	Up to 8 quality screen shots of your app as it is running. Each can have a description of up to 200 words. The minimum size of the image must be 1366 × 766 pixels. You can capture these screens using the Store | Capture Screenshots command in Visual Studio.
	Promotional Images	(Optional) Provide other promotional images for your app (up to four).
	Recommended Hardware	(Optional) Provide up to 11 notes about the hardware requirements for your app.
	App Website	Provide the website URL for your product.
	Support Contact	Provide a contact URL for customers so that they can get support or ask additional questions. Prepare to be very responsive to customer questions and feedback.
	Privacy Policy	Prepare an appropriate statement about your privacy policy regarding data collected about users.
	In-App Offer Description	Provide information about products that users can purchase from within your app, including what the customer must pay and how long the purchased feature can be used. (This field was indicated above as well. Use the same information.)
Notes to Testers	Notes	Give the evaluators at Microsoft additional information about your app so that they can test its functionality. For example, describe hidden features or provide user name and password information if needed.

It's all in the details

The value of the preceding checklist becomes apparent when you look again at the content for Windows Store apps within the Windows Store. The more you know about your customers and your product's central features before you get started, the easier it will be to make design and layout decisions as you create your application. In the following screen illustration, notice how important the ratings, description, and features categories are for the featured app, as well as the value of the screen shot that visually describes the product.

The Details page (not shown, but accessible via the Details link) presents additional information, including release notes, supported processors, supported languages, and application permissions. The Reviews page (also not shown) contains comments from actual customers.

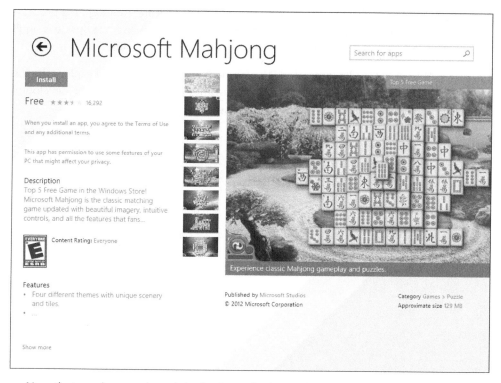

Now that you have reviewed the basic marketing and distribution mechanisms for apps in the Windows Store, it is time to get started building Visual Basic apps in Visual Studio. Although many of the apps that you will create in this book will be demonstration programs designed to teach discrete elements of the Visual Basic programming language, you should always keep an eye on the end-goal of your learning—creating software that other people can *use*.

Summary

Each chapter in this book concludes with a Summary section that offers a review of what the chapter has presented. You can use these sections to quickly recap what you have learned in each chapter before you move on to the one that follows.

This chapter has introduced development opportunities for Visual Basic programmers, including the many opportunities available to users of Visual Studio 2013. You've learned about the application types that you can create with Visual Studio 2013 and about the specific tools and platforms that are described by this book. You've also learned about the Windows Store, an incredible distribution point and marketing opportunity for software developers who want to sell or freely distribute their products. You've learned how the Windows Store operates and about some of the requirements you'll need to satisfy to distribute apps for Windows 8.1 via the Windows Store. Although the process will require some up-front planning, as well as technical and marketing expertise, the upside is significant. The Windows Store has the potential to reach millions of customers worldwide.

In Chapter 2, "The Visual Studio Integrated Development Environment," you'll explore the Visual Studio 2013 IDE, including how to run and test Visual Basic programs, how to use the development tools in the IDE, and how to adjust important compiler settings.

The Visual Studio Integrated Development Environment

After completing this chapter, you will be able to

- Use the Visual Studio 2013 Integrated Development Environment.

- Load and run Windows Store apps.

- Work with XAML markup in the Designer.

- Use the Properties windows to change property settings.

- Organize Visual Studio programming windows and tools.

- Configure the IDE for step-by-step exercises.

This chapter gives you the skills you need to get up and running with the Visual Studio 2013 Integrated Development Environment (IDE)—the place where you will write Microsoft Visual Basic programs. My assumption is that you have written programs before in some earlier version of Visual Basic and that you need only a refresher on how the main IDE tools work. However, I plan to cover some essential IDE skills here, including a few things about how Visual Studio 2013 works in relation to XAML markup and Windows Store programming.

This chapter begins with a review of essential Visual Studio menu commands and programming procedures. You'll open and run a simple Windows Store app named Music Trivia; you'll change a property setting; and you'll practice moving, sizing, docking, and hiding tool windows. You'll also learn how to configure the IDE to match this book's step-by-step instructions. This final exercise is especially important, because the programming exercises that follow will rely on those specific settings.

Before you begin this chapter, you need to install Visual Studio 2013. For more information about that process and the options available to you, see the Introduction and Chapter 1, "Visual Basic 2013 development opportunities and the Windows Store."

Not enough beginning material here? Keep in mind that this is a book for programmers who have used some version of Visual Basic or Visual Studio in the past. As a book in the Microsoft Press Developer Step by Step series, this tutorial is designed to inform new-to-topic programmers and teach fundamental techniques and features. Although I do review essential techniques such as setting properties and moving around tool windows, you'll find a lot more introductory tips, tricks, and techniques in my companion book *Start Here! Learn Microsoft Visual Basic 2012* (Microsoft Press, 2012).

Getting started

To boot up Visual Studio and get working in the IDE, complete the following steps. Depending on the edition of Visual Studio that you have, you will use slightly different commands and see slightly different things, but the differences will not be substantial. (In the screen shots that follow, you will see Visual Studio 2013 Professional.)

Start Visual Studio 2013

1. On the Windows Start page, click Visual Studio 2013.

   If this is the first time you are starting Visual Studio, the program will take a few moments to configure the environment. You might be prompted to get a developer license for Windows, which typically requires that you create a Windows Live account or enter existing account information. At the time of this writing, developer licenses were free and valid for a month before they needed to be renewed. You will likely encounter a similar registration scenario.

2. If you are prompted to identify your programming preferences, select Visual Basic Development Settings, as shown in the following screen:

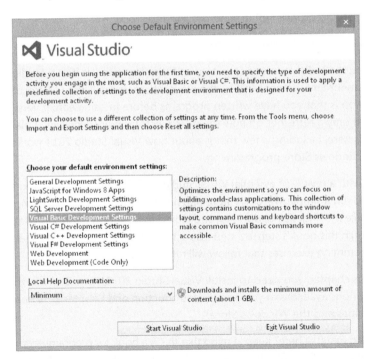

3. Click Start Visual Studio in the Choose Default Environment Settings dialog box.

   When Visual Studio starts, you see the IDE on the screen with its familiar menus, tools, and component windows. You also should see a Start page containing a set of tabs with links, learning resources, news, and project options.

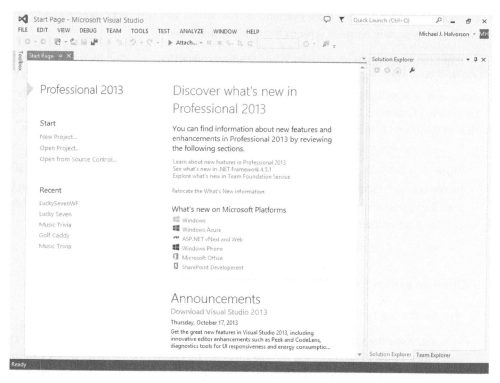

The screen shown here offers a typical Visual Studio Professional setup. I captured the screen at a resolution of 1024 × 768, which might be smaller than you are using on your computer, but I wanted you to see the content as clearly as possible. In the e-book versions of this text, you will see the images in color.

You have a number of display options when you work in Visual Studio 2013. For visual clarity, I chose the Light color theme for my work, primarily because it produces the clearest screen illustrations in a printed book. However, when you first open Visual Studio, you might see the Dark color theme, which displays white text on a dark background. Although the Dark color theme is restful and emphasizes the code and user interface elements of your program, you might want to change it if matching my screens is important to you.

If you see the Dark color theme and want to change it, do so now by choosing the Options command on the Tools menu, click General in the Environment category, select Light in the Color Theme drop-down list box, and click OK. This first screen illustration depicts the Light theme.

The Visual Studio development environment

In the Visual Studio IDE, you can open a new or existing Visual Studio project or you can explore the many online resources available to you for Visual Basic programming. In the 2013 product, one of the first new features that you might see is your login name in the upper-right corner of the IDE. By signing in to Visual Studio each time that you start the IDE, you can save your Visual Studio settings to the cloud and have them move from machine to machine as you work on projects in different locations. You'll see my sign-in name in screens throughout the book.

Right now, let's open an existing Visual Studio project that I created for you, entitled Music Trivia, which asks a trivia question about a musical instrument and then displays an answer to the question along with a digital photo of the instrument. All of the Windows Store apps that I create in this book target the Windows 8.1 operating system. (The Windows Forms and console apps will run on any version of Windows 7, Windows 8, or Windows 8.1.)

 Note The following steps ask you to open and run a Windows Store app in the IDE. If you haven't downloaded this book's sample files yet, you should do so now, because you'll be asked to open a specific program on your hard disk. The Introduction explains how to locate and download what you need.

Open an existing Visual Studio project

1. On the Start page, on the left side of the screen, click the Open Project link.

   You'll see the Open Project dialog box. (You can also display this dialog box by clicking the Open Project command on the File menu or by pressing Ctrl+Shift+O.) As you probably know by now, the Open Project dialog box is straightforward because it resembles the familiar Open dialog box in many other Windows applications.

 Tip In the Open Project dialog box, you see a number of storage locations along the left side of the window. The Projects folder under Microsoft Visual Studio 2013 is particularly useful. By default, Visual Studio saves your programming projects in this Projects folder, giving each project its own subfolder. However, this book uses a different Projects folder to organize your programming coursework, the My Documents\Visual Basic 2013 SBS folder.

2. Browse to the My Documents\Visual Basic 2013 SBS folder on your hard disk.

   This folder is the default location for the book's extensive sample file collection, and you'll find the files there if you followed the instructions in "Code samples" in the Introduction. Again, if you didn't copy the sample files, close this dialog box and copy them now.

   If you click the Chapter 02 folder, your Open Project dialog box will look like this. The number "12" in the Music Trivia icon indicates that the project was created with the 12th version of Visual Basic, or Visual Basic 2013.

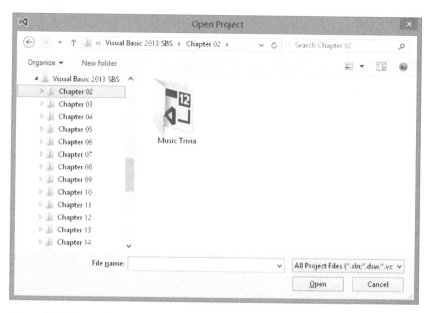

3. Open the Chapter 02\Music Trivia folder, and then double-click the Music Trivia solution file. (If your system shows file name extensions, this file will end with .sln.)

4. Visual Studio loads the Music Trivia page, properties, and program code for the solution, which is a Windows Store app designed for Windows 8.1. Solution Explorer, a tool window on the right side of the screen, lists some of the files in the solution.

Visual Studio provides a special option named Always Show Solution to control several options related to solutions within the IDE. The option's check box is located on the Projects And Solutions | General tab of the Options dialog box, which you open by clicking the Options command on the Tools menu. If the check box is selected (the default position), a subfolder is created for each new solution, placing the project and its files in a separate folder beneath the solution.

If you keep the default selection for Always Show Solution, a few options related to solutions appear in the IDE, such as commands on the File menu and a solution entry in Solution Explorer. If you like creating separate folders for solutions and seeing solution-related commands and settings, I suggest that you keep the default (selected) option for this check box. You'll learn more about these options at the end of the chapter.

Project and solution terminology

In Visual Studio, programs under development are typically called projects or solutions because they contain many individual components, not just one file. Visual Basic 2013 programs include a project file (.vbproj), a solution file (.sln), and several supporting files organized into various subfolders. A Windows Store app will also have one or more markup files (.xaml) and an Assets folder.

A *project* contains files and other information specific to a single programming undertaking. A *solution* contains all the information for one or more projects. Solutions are therefore useful mechanisms to manage multiple related projects. The samples included with this book typically have a single project for each solution, so opening the project file (.vbproj) has the same effect as opening the solution file (.sln). But for a multiproject solution, you will want to open the solution file.

Important tools in the IDE

Take some time now to identify the programming tools and windows in the Visual Studio 2013 IDE. If you've written Visual Basic programs before, you'll recognize most of these programming tools. Collectively, these features are the components that you use to construct, organize, and test your Visual Basic programs. A few of the programming tools also help you learn more about the resources on your system, including the larger world of databases and website connections available to you.

My assumption is that you've used Visual Studio, Word, and other Windows-based applications enough to know quite a bit about menus, toolbars, the Help system, and familiar commands such as New Project, Close Project, Start Debugging, and Save All. You can see the full list of toolbars at any time by right-clicking any toolbar in the IDE.

The Help menu is especially useful in Visual Studio, and you can also access an extensive collection of Visual Studio and Visual Basic programming resources online at *http://msdn.microsoft.com/.* You'll often be asked to reference online topics on the Microsoft Developer Network (MSDN) as you use this book.

The following illustration shows some of the tools and windows in the Visual Studio Professional IDE. Don't worry that this illustration looks different from your current development environment view. You'll learn more about these elements (and how you adjust your views) as you work through the chapter.

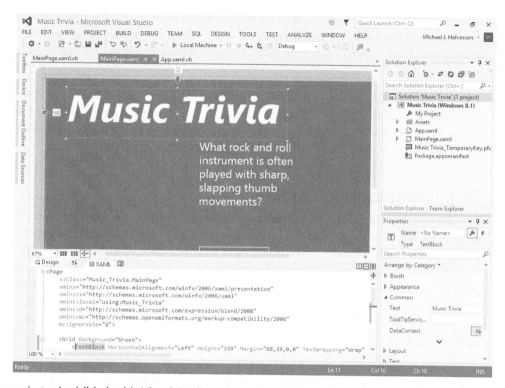

The main tools visible in this Visual Studio IDE are the Designer, the Solution Explorer, the Properties window, and the Extensible Application Markup Language (XAML) tab of the Code Editor. You might also see more specialized tools such as the Toolbox, Document Outline window, Device window, Data Sources window, Server Explorer, and Object Browser; alternatively, these tools might appear as tabs within the IDE. Because no two developers' preferences are exactly alike, it is difficult to predict what you'll see if your Visual Studio software has already been used. (What I show is essentially the fresh-download, or out-of-the-box, view with the Designer displaying a sample application in development.)

Note Note that from time to time, the menus in the IDE change based on what you are doing in Visual Studio.

A new feature in Visual Studio 2013 is the Feedback button, which appears as a "thought bubble" or smile icon at the top of the screen, to the left of the Quick Launch text box. You can use the Feedback button to let Microsoft know about the features in Visual Studio that you like or do not like. You can also use the button to access MSDN Forums and report a bug in the software.

If a tool isn't visible and you want to see it, click the View menu and then select the tool. Because the View menu has expanded steadily over the years, Microsoft has moved some of the less frequently used View tools to a submenu called Other Windows. Check there if you don't see what you need.

A few new Visual Studio 2013 features that you can see now include more colorful icons in the toolbars and Solution Explorer (folder icons are now yellow), and the scroll bar in the Code Editor contains a "caret position" indicator, which shows the relative position of the insertion point in the open document.

Organizing tools in the IDE

Your IDE might not look exactly like the image I've shown because the exact size and shape of the tools and windows in the IDE depend on how your particular development environment has been configured. With Visual Studio, you can align and attach, or *dock*, windows to make visible only the elements that you want see. You can also partially conceal tools as tabbed documents along the edge of the development environment and then switch back and forth between documents quickly. For example, if you click the Toolbox label on the left side of the screen, the Toolbox panel will fly out, ready for use. If you click another tool or window in the IDE, the Toolbox panel will return to its concealed position.

Your development environment will probably look best if you set your monitor and Windows desktop settings so that they maximize your screen space, but even then, things can get a little crowded. In fact, many professional Visual Studio programmers use two monitors to display different views of the software.

The purpose of all this tool complexity is to add many new and useful features to the IDE while providing clever mechanisms for managing the clutter. These mechanisms include features such as docking, autohiding, floating, and a few other window states that I'll describe later. Visual Studio 2013 also hides rarely used IDE features until you begin to use them, which has also helped to clean up the IDE workspace.

If you're just writing your first Windows Store app with Visual Studio, the best way to deal with feature overload is to hide the tools that you don't plan to use often to make room for the important ones. The crucial windows and tools for intermediate Visual Basic programming tasks—the ones you'll start using right away in this book—are the Designer window, the Properties window, Solution Explorer, and the Toolbox. You won't use the Document Outline, Server Explorer, Data Sources, Class View, Object Browser, Device, or Debug windows until later in the book, so feel free to hide them by clicking the Close button on the title bar of any window that you don't want to see.

In the following exercises, you'll review the behavior of the essential tools in the Visual Studio IDE. You'll also learn about XAML markup, the design language used to define the user interface in Windows Store apps.

The Designer and XAML markup

If you completed the previous exercise ("Open an existing Visual Studio project"), the Music Trivia project is loaded in the Visual Studio development environment. However, the user interface, or page, for the project might not yet be visible in Visual Studio. (More sophisticated projects might contain several pages, but this first example program needs only one.) To make the page of the Music Trivia project visible in the IDE, you display it by using Solution Explorer.

> **Note** If you don't currently have the Music Trivia project loaded, go back to and complete the exercise in this chapter titled "Open an existing Visual Studio project."

Display the Designer window

1. Locate the Solution Explorer window near the upper-right corner of the Visual Studio development environment. If you don't see Solution Explorer, click the View menu and then select Solution Explorer to display it.

> **Note** From here on in this book, you'll sometimes see a shorter method for describing menu choices. For example, "Choose View | Solution Explorer" means "Click the View menu and then select Solution Explorer."

When the Music Trivia project is loaded, Solution Explorer looks like this:

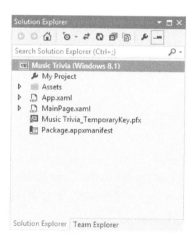

Like most basic Windows Store applications, this Visual Basic solution contains an App.xaml file that holds global project settings and resources; an Assets folder that contains an assortment of logo files and a splash screen for the project; a certificate file containing temporaries keys; a *deployment package manifest*, containing build and distribution settings for your file; and one or more user interface windows, or *pages*, which you can identify because they have the extension .xaml.

Near the top of Solution Explorer, the Music Trivia program is identified as a Windows 8.1 project. This means that it is designed for the Windows 8.1 platform and uses features within the Windows 8.1 operating system.

In Visual Studio 2012, there was also a Common folder that was visible in Windows Store projects, containing common classes and XAML styles, but those items are now hidden from view.

2. Click the expansion arrow to the left of the MainPage.xaml file in the Solution Explorer window.

With the MainPage.xaml file expanded, Solution Explorer looks like this:

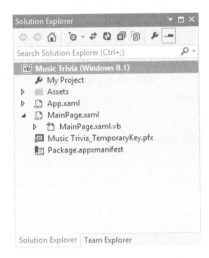

In this Windows Store project, the main page of the Music Trivia program is defined by the MainPage.xaml file.

You can open MainPage.xaml in Design view so that you can examine and modify the user interface with graphical design tools, or you can open the file in the Code Editor, where you can modify the user interface with XAML, the user interface definition language designed for Windows Store apps and other computer programs.

Tip If you've created Windows Presentation Foundation (WPF) apps in an earlier version of Visual Studio, this is the same XAML markup language (with some important updates) that you might already have worked with to create the user interface for Visual Basic applications. Essentially, Windows Store apps are a successor to WPF-style apps.

Below the MainPage.xaml file, you will see a second file, named MainPage.xaml.vb. This file is also associated with the user interface of the Music Trivia project. MainPage.xaml.vb is called a code-behind file because it contains a listing of the Visual Basic program code connected to the user interface defined by MainPage.xaml. As you learn how to create Windows Store apps using Visual Basic and Visual Studio, you'll become very adept at customizing this file.

Solution Explorer is the gateway to working with the various files in your project—it is an essential tool. When you double-click a file in Solution Explorer, it opens the file in an appropriate editor, if direct editing of the file is allowed.

3. Double-click the MainPage.xaml file in Solution Explorer to display the project's user interface in the Designer window, if it is not already visible. If necessary, use the vertical scroll bar to adjust your view of the user interface.

The Music Trivia page is displayed in the Designer, as shown here:

Notice that a tab with the file name MainPage.xaml is visible near the top of the Designer window, along with additional tab names. You can click a tab at any time to display the contents of the various open files.

As noted earlier, the MainPage.xaml file is the visual representation of the program's user interface. However, you can readily examine the XAML markup used to define the user interface by double-clicking the XAML tab of the Code Editor at the bottom of the Designer window.

Because you can't see the entire user interface now, you might want to resize the Designer so that you can see more of the program.

4. Move the pointer to the right edge of the Designer window (the outside edge of the scroll bar) until the pointer changes to a double-headed arrow (the resizing pointer). Then drag the window's edge to the right to enlarge the window.

The Designer window will get larger, and the Solution Explorer and Properties windows will get smaller. Your screen will look something like this:

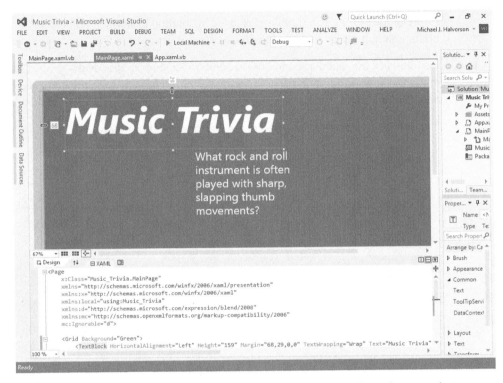

Now you'll examine the XAML markup that defines the user interface elements that you are looking at in the Designer.

5. Return the Designer to its original size, and then double-click the XAML tab to display the XAML markup for the page in the Code Editor.

6. Scroll to the top of the window to see the entire document.

You'll see the following:

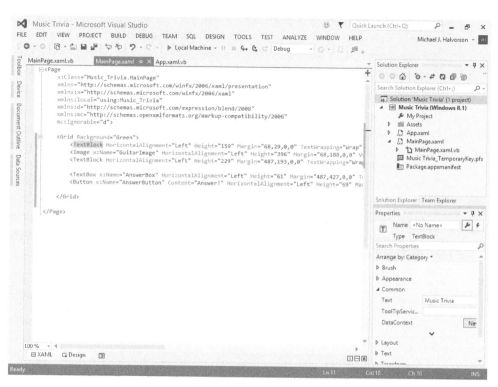

The XAML contents of MainPage.xaml appear in the Code Editor, and it is this structured information that controls how Visual Studio and Windows will display the application's user interface and graphics. If you know some WPF or HTML, this should look somewhat familiar. XAML contains markup—instructions whose primary purpose is to tell a program how to display things on the screen. The XAML markup shown here is displayed between <Page> and </Page> tags and is further indented to make the information readable. (Windows Phone apps also use XAML markup to define the user interface.)

The first seven lines below <Page> define the resources used to create the user interface. Below these lines, the <Grid> ... </Grid> section defines the objects in the user interface. This XAML content defines two *TextBlock* controls, one *Image* control, one *TextBlock* control, and one *Button* control. If you look at the screen illustration of the Designer again, you can see how many of these elements appear visually. (Two of them are currently hidden, so those are not visible.) You can even see specific property settings for the objects being assigned through individual property names (like *HorizontalAlignment*) and values (like Left).

You'll learn a lot more about XAML markup in later chapters. For now, you should know that the Designer window allows you to see both a *preview* of the user interface and the XAML markup that defines the specific characteristics of objects that appear on the preview page. Visual Studio programmers often want to see both panes of information side by side as they work on a program. In fact, if you've built an HTML application in the past for the web, this whole concept might seem a little familiar, because a number of web design tools also display page layout at the top of the screen while showing HTML code at the bottom.

 Tip There are some handy buttons along the bottom of the Designer window and Code Editor that allow you significant control over the split-screen behavior of these elements. At the lower left of the Designer window are XAML and Design tabs, as well as a handy Document Outline button that opens a separate window to display the objects within the user interface organized by type. At the lower right of the Designer window are Vertical Split, Horizontal Split, and Expand Pane/Collapse Pane buttons, which control how the Designer window and Code Editor are arranged. Expand Pane/Collapse Pane is especially useful; it is a toggle that allows you to view the windows one at a time or side by side.

7. Click the Design tab to display the project's main page in the Designer window again.

8. Click the Expand Pane button to display the XAML markup that renders the page in a window below the Designer window.

Now you'll try running this simple program within Visual Studio.

Running and testing Windows Store apps

Music Trivia is a simple Windows Store app written in Visual Basic 2013. I created it to familiarize you with the programming tools in Visual Studio. The page you see now has been customized with five objects, and I've added three lines of program code to a code-behind file to make the program ask a simple question and display the appropriate answer. You'll learn more about creating objects like these and adding Visual Basic code to a code-behind file in Chapter 3, "Creating your first Windows Store application." For now, try running the program in the Visual Studio IDE.

Run the Music Trivia program

1. Click the Start button (the right-facing arrow next to the words Local Machine) on the Standard toolbar to run the Music Trivia program in Visual Studio.

 Tip You can also press F5 or click the Start Debugging command on the Debug menu to run a program in the Visual Studio IDE.

Visual Studio loads and compiles the project into an *assembly*, an EXE file that contains data and code in a form that can be used by the computer. This particular assembly also contains information that is useful for testing, or *debugging*, which is a fundamental part of the software development process. If the compilation is successful, Visual Studio runs the program in the IDE. (This is known as running the program on a *local machine*, as opposed to running on a remote computer somewhere on the web or in a software simulator of some kind.)

While the program is running, an icon for the program appears on the Windows taskbar. After a moment, you will see the Music Trivia user interface running as any application would under Windows 8.1. (You might also see some numbers along the top edge of the screen that are used for debugging purposes; I've removed these from the book's screen shots for clarity.)

Otherwise, the program looks just like the preview version did within the Visual Studio Designer:

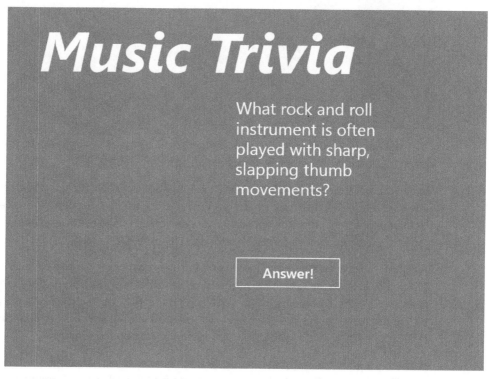

Music Trivia now asks you a question: What Rock And Roll Instrument Is Often Played With Sharp, Slapping Thumb Movements?

2. Click the Answer! button to reveal the solution to the question, and the program displays the answer (The Bass Guitar) below the question. A photo of a bass player also appears on the page.

3. Close the app by dragging the title bar (or top portion of the screen) to the bottom of the screen (or however you normally terminate an app).

When you move the mouse cursor to the top edge of the screen, it changes to a hand, which provides some visual feedback as you drag the title bar to the bottom of the screen to terminate the program. After the application closes, you can press the Windows key or click the Visual Studio program icon on the desktop to activate the IDE again.

The Music Trivia application might continue to run for a moment or two as the Visual Studio IDE catches up with the terminate-program request that you just issued. (For example, you might see the phrase Running in the Visual Studio title bar, which indicates that a program in the IDE is still executing.) You can force an immediate stop to any running application in the Visual Studio IDE by clicking the Stop Debugging button on the toolbar.

After the program has stopped running, you will notice a few changes in the IDE. For example, you will likely see an Output window at the bottom of the IDE with information about how the assemblies in the application were compiled and executed. This is the expected behavior within Visual Studio after a program has been compiled and run. The Output window provides a fairly detailed listing of what happened during compilation, a process that involves several stages and the loading of a number of files and resources called *libraries*. This record of the process is especially valuable when the compilation fails due to an unforeseen programming mistake or error.

4. After you've reviewed the content of the Output window, click its Close button to hide it.

You won't read much more about the Output window in the early chapters of this book, but if you encounter an inadvertent error as you write your own programs, you'll find this tool useful. Most of the time, you can simply close the window to allow more room for examining your code.

Working with the Properties window

Like earlier versions of Visual Studio, Visual Studio 2013 has a Properties window in the IDE to allow you to change the characteristics, or *property settings*, of one or more user interface elements on a page. A property setting is a quality of one of the objects in your program, such as its position on the screen, its size, the text displayed on it, and so on. For example, you can modify the text block object that asks the question about musical instruments by specifying a different font or font size using property settings.

The Properties window contains a list of the properties for the object that is currently selected in the Designer window. For example, if a button object is selected in the Designer, the properties for the object will be visible in the Properties window. The first property listed at the top of the Properties window is the *Name* property, and you will use this property to name your objects if you plan to customize them using Visual Basic code. (By default, all new XAML objects are unnamed.) Although there are a lot of properties for each object on a page, Visual Studio assigns default values for most of them, and you can quickly find the properties that you want to set by arranging them using the Arrange By drop-down box at the top of the Properties window.

You can change property settings from the Properties window while you are working on a page, you can modify a property setting by editing the XAML markup for a page, and you can add Visual Basic code to a page's code-behind file to instruct Windows to change one or more property settings while a program is running.

As you'll learn later, you can also customize the event handlers for objects on a page by using the Event Handlers button (which looks like a lightning bolt) near the top of the Properties window. Event handlers are custom Visual Basic routines that run when the user interacts with the objects on a page by clicking, tapping, dragging, and other actions.

Use the following exercise to review how to set properties. You'll modify the text in the button object and change the font weight and style of the first text block object. (If you don't need a property setting review, skip ahead to the section "Organizing the programming tools.")

Change properties

1. Click the Answer button on the page that is currently loaded in the Designer window.

To work with an object on a page, you must first select the object. When you select an object, the property settings for the object are displayed in the Properties window.

2. Press F4 to display the Properties window, if it is not currently visible.

   The Properties window might or might not be visible in Visual Studio, depending on how it has been configured and used on your system. It usually appears below Solution Explorer on the right side of the IDE.

   You'll see a window similar to the following:

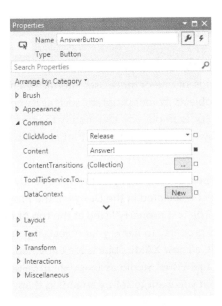

   The Properties window lists all the property settings for the selected button object, which I named AnswerButton while creating the program. Properties are listed in nested groups, and the default view displays the properties alphabetically by category. (*Brush* is first, *Appearance* is second, *Common* is third, and so on.) When you expand the property groups, the property names are generally listed on the left side, and the property values are listed on the right. Some property settings, like *Brush*, are updated by selecting color values with a design tool, so there are a variety of ways to set properties—not just entering text via the keyboard.

3. In the Common property group (containing the most typical properties for a button object), see that the *Content* property is set to Answer!

   Answer! is the text that currently appears on the page's main button, and you can change it to whatever you would like using the Properties window. Remove the exclamation point now to practice changing a property.

4. Click after Answer! in the Content text box, remove the exclamation mark (!), and then press Enter.

   The Content property setting is changed to Answer in three places: within the Properties window, on the page in the Designer window, and within the XAML markup in the Code Editor.

> **Tip** Instead of pressing the Enter key to change a property setting, you can simply click another location in the Properties window. (For example, click in another text box.) Just be careful not to inadvertently adjust another property setting by clicking around.

Now you'll change the font style of the text block object to remove the bold and italic. The text block object currently contains the text Music Trivia.

5. Click the Music Trivia text block object on the page. A text block object is an excellent way to display descriptive text on a page.

6. In the Properties window, click the Text property group (not the *Text* property in the Common group that is currently visible).

7. Click the Bold button to remove the bold formatting.

8. Click the Italic button to remove the italic formatting.

Visual Studio records your changes and adjusts the property settings accordingly. Your screen should look like this:

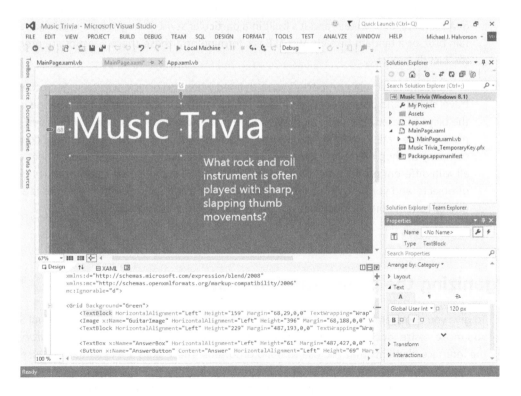

You've just updated three properties, and the process is very similar to earlier versions of Visual Studio, although in this case you are adjusting XAML properties related to a Windows Store app. Keep this fundamental skill in mind—you'll have numerous font, color, and style options to choose from as you complete this book.

Objects and properties: A terminology review

Here are some things to keep in mind as you work with objects and properties in a Visual Basic program. First, remember that each user interface element in a program (including the page itself) has a set of definable properties. You can set properties at design time by using the Properties window or by editing properties in the XAML markup for the page that defines one part the program's user interface.

Properties can also be set or referenced in Visual Basic code to make changes to program elements while the application runs. (User interface elements that receive input often use properties to receive information into the program.) Property settings are easy to grasp if you view them in terms of something from everyday life. Consider the following bicycle analogy I've used for several years to describe object and property terminology.

A bicycle is an object that you might use to ride from one place to another. Because a bicycle is a physical object, it has several inherent characteristics. It has a brand name, a color, gears, brakes, and wheels, and it's built in a particular style. (It might be a road bike, a mountain bike, or a tandem bike.) In Visual Basic terminology, these characteristics are *properties* of the bicycle object.

Most of the bicycle's properties were defined when the bicycle was built. But others (tires, travel speed, and options such as reflectors and mirrors) are properties that change while the bicycle is used. The bike might even have intangible (that is, invisible) properties, such as manufacture date, current owner, value, or rental status. And to add a little more complexity, a company or shop might own one bicycle or (the more likely scenario) an entire fleet of bicycles, all with different properties. As you work with Visual Basic, you'll set the properties of a variety of objects, and you'll organize them in very useful ways. Working with properties is a fundamental task in object-oriented programming and Visual Studio 2013.

Organizing the programming tools

To give you complete control over the shape and size of the elements in the IDE, Visual Studio lets you move, resize, dock, and automatically hide when not needed (a feature called *autohide*) most of the interface elements that you use to build programs. These skills are essential, because they will be used over and over in this book. If you want to review how the tools are used, read the following sections and practice the techniques. If you already feel up to speed, skip ahead to the section "Configuring the IDE for step-by-step exercises."

Moving and docking tools

To move one of the tool windows in Visual Studio, simply click its title bar and drag the window to a new location. If you position the window somewhere in the middle of the IDE and let go, it will *float* over the surface of Visual Studio, unattached to other tool windows. If you drag a window along the edge of another window, it attaches to that window, or *docks* itself.

Dockable windows are advantageous because they always remain visible. (They don't become hidden behind other windows.) If you want to see more of a docked window, simply drag one of its borders to view more content.

If you want to completely close a window, click the Close button in the upper-right corner of the window. You can always open the window again later by clicking the appropriate command on the View menu.

Autohide

If you want an option somewhere between docking and closing a window, you might try *autohiding* a tool window at the side, top, or bottom of the Visual Studio IDE by clicking the tiny Auto Hide push-pin button on the right side of the tool's title bar. This action removes the window from the docked position and places the title of the tool at the edge of the development environment on an unob-trusive tab. When you autohide a window, you'll notice that the tool window remains visible as long as you keep the mouse pointer in the area of the window. When you click another part of the IDE (or move the mouse away), the window slides out of view.

To restore a window that you have autohidden, click the tool tab at the edge of the development environment. (You can recognize a window that is autohidden because the pushpin in its title bar is pointing sideways.) By clicking the tool tab repeatedly at the edge of the IDE, you can use the tools in what I call *peekaboo mode*—that is, to quickly display an autohidden window, click its tab, check or set the information you need, and then click its tab again to make it disappear. If you ever need the tool displayed permanently, click the Auto Hide pushpin button again so that the point of the pushpin faces down, and the window then remains visible.

Tabbed documents, manual docking, and docking guides

Another useful capability of Visual Studio is the ability to dock the Code Editor or the Designer win-dows as tabbed documents. A tabbed document is a window with a tab handle that partially hides behind other windows. This is the default way that document windows are displayed.

You can also manually dock programming tools such as the Properties window where you would like by dragging the tool and using the docking guides that appear as tiny squares on the perimeter of the IDE. A centrally located guide diamond will also help you manually dock tool windows by giv-ing you a preview of where the tool will go.

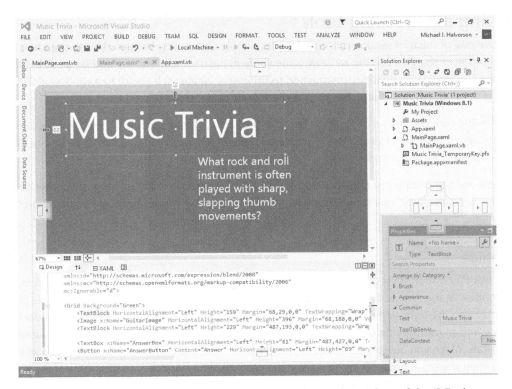

The docking guides are changeable icons that appear on the surface of the IDE when you move a window or tool from a docked position to a new location. Because the docking guides are associated with shaded, rectangular areas of the IDE, you can preview the results of your docking maneuver before you actually make it. Your window orientation changes will not stick until you release the mouse button.

Mastering the docking and autohiding techniques might take some practice when you are first using them, so you might want to experiment a little.

Hiding tool windows

To hide a tool window, click the Auto Hide pushpin button on the right side of the title bar to conceal the window beneath a tool tab on the edge of the IDE, and click it again to restore the window to its docked position. You can also use the Auto Hide command on the Window menu (or right-click a title bar and select Auto Hide) to autohide a tool window. Use the following procedure when you need to use autohide.

Use the Auto Hide feature

1. Locate the Auto Hide pushpin button on the title bar of the Properties window.

   The pushpin is currently in the down, or pushed-in, position, meaning that the Properties window is "pinned" open and autohide is disabled.

2. Click the Auto Hide button on the Properties window title bar, and the Properties window slides off the screen and is replaced by a small tab named Properties.

 Note The benefit of enabling autohide is that the process frees up additional work area in Visual Studio. But the hidden window is also quickly accessible.

3. Click the Properties tab, and the Properties window should immediately reappear.

4. Click the mouse elsewhere within the IDE, and the window disappears again.

5. Finally, display the Properties window again, and then click the pushpin button on the Properties window title bar. The Properties window returns to its familiar docked position, and you can use it without worrying about it sliding away.

Spend some time moving, resizing, docking, and autohiding tool windows in Visual Studio now to create your version of the perfect work environment. As you work through this book, you'll want to adjust your window settings periodically to adapt your work area to the new tools you're using.

Configuring the IDE for step-by-step exercises

Like the tool windows and other environment settings within the IDE, the compiler and personal settings within Visual Studio 2013 are highly customizable. It is important to review a few of these settings now so that your version of Visual Studio is configured in a way that is compatible with the step-by-step programming exercises that follow. You will also learn how to customize Visual Studio generally so that as you gain programming experience, you can set up Visual Studio in the way that is most productive for you.

If you just installed Visual Studio, you are ready to start this book's programming exercises. But if your installation of Visual Studio has been on your machine for a while or if your computer is a shared resource used by other programmers who might have modified the default settings (perhaps in a college computer lab), complete the following steps to verify that your settings related to projects, solutions, and the compiler match those that I use in the book.

Adjust project and compiler settings

1. Click the Options command on the Tools menu to display the Options dialog box.

   The Options dialog box is your window to many of the customizable settings within Visual Studio. To assist you in finding the settings that you want to change, Visual Studio organizes the settings by category.

2. Expand the Projects And Solutions category, and then click the General item within it.

   This group of check boxes and options configures the Visual Studio project and solution settings.

3. So that your software matches the settings used in this book, adjust your settings to match those shown in the following dialog box:

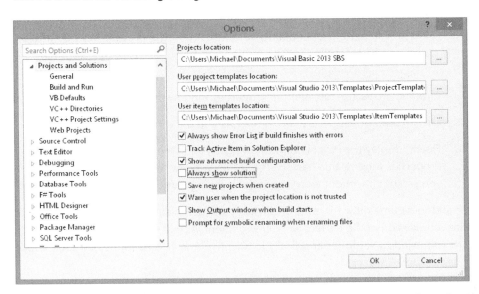

In particular, I recommend that you clear the check marks (if you see them) from the Always Show Solution and Save New Projects When Created check boxes. The first option, when selected, shows additional solution commands in the IDE, which is not necessary for solutions that contain only one project (the situation for most programs in this book).

Clearing the second option causes Visual Studio to postpone saving your project until you click the Save All command on the File menu and provide a location for saving the file. This delayed-save feature allows you to create a test program, compile and debug the program, and even run it without actually saving the project on disk—a useful feature when you want to create a quick test program that you might want to discard instead of saving. (An equivalent situation in word-processing terms is when you open a new Word document, enter an address for a mailing label, print the address, and then exit Word without saving the file.) With this setting cleared, the exercises in this book prompt you to save your projects after you create them, although you can also save your projects in advance by selecting the Save New Projects When Created check box.

You'll also notice that I have browsed to the location of the book's sample files (Visual Basic 2013 SBS) in the top text box on the form to indicate the default location for this book's sample files. Most of the projects that you create will be stored in this folder, and they will have a "My" prefix to distinguish them from the completed project I provide for you to examine. (Be sure to change this path to the location of the book's sample files on your computer.)

After you have adjusted these settings, you're ready to check the Visual Basic compiler settings.

4. Click the VB Defaults item in the expanded Projects And Solutions section.

Visual Studio displays a list of four compiler settings: Option Explicit, Option Strict, Option Compare, and Option Infer. Your screen likely looks like this:

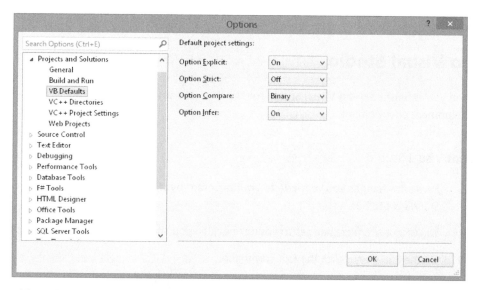

Although a detailed description of these settings is beyond the scope of this chapter, you'll want to verify that Option Explicit is set to On and Option Strict is set to Off—the default settings for Visual Basic programming within Visual Studio. Option Explicit On is a setting that requires you to declare a variable before using it in a program—a very good programming practice that I want to encourage. Option Strict Off allows variables and objects of different types to be combined under certain circumstances without generating a compiler error. (For example, a number can be assigned to a text box object without error.) Although this is a potentially worrisome programming practice, Option Strict Off is a useful setting for certain types of demonstration programs.

Option Compare determines the comparison method when different text strings are compared and sorted. For more information about comparing strings and sorting text, see Chapter 14, "Using arrays, collections, and generics to manage data," and Chapter 15, "Innovative data management with LINQ."

Option Infer was a new setting in Visual Basic 2008. When you set Option Strict to Off and Option Infer to On, you can declare variables without explicitly stating a data type. Or rather, if you make such a declaration, the Visual Basic compiler will infer (or take an educated guess about) the data type based on the initial assignment you made for the variable. You'll learn more about the feature in Chapter 11, "Mastering data types, operators, and string processing."

As a general rule, I recommend that you set Option Infer to Off to avoid unexpected results in how variables are used in your programs. I have set Option Infer to Off in most of the sample projects included in the sample files.

5. Feel free to examine additional settings in the Options dialog box related to your programming environment and Visual Studio. When you're finished, click OK to close the Options dialog box.

You're ready to exit Visual Studio and start programming.

Exiting Visual Studio

When you're finished using Visual Studio for the day, save any projects that are open and close the development environment.

Exit Visual Studio

1. Save any changes you've made to your program by clicking the Save All button on the Standard toolbar.

   You've made a few changes to your project, so you should save your changes now.

2. On the File menu, click the Exit command.

   The Visual Studio program closes. You are now ready to create a program from scratch in Chapter 3.

Summary

This chapter introduced you to Visual Studio 2013 and the IDE that you use to open and run Visual Basic programs. You can create applications for the various Windows platforms by opening new or existing projects in Visual Studio and then adding to the project with the assorted programming tools. In this chapter, you learned how to display the user interface of a Windows Store app, how to examine XAML objects on the page, and how to change property settings.

As you toured the Visual Studio IDE, you reviewed how to open and run an application, how to examine XAML markup in the Code Editor, and how to manipulate tool windows in the IDE. You also learned how to customize settings in Visual Studio by using the Options command on the Tools menu.

The Visual Studio IDE is a busy place, and I have reviewed a few essential IDE techniques so that you will be able to complete the step-by-step programming exercises that follow. However, there is much more to learn. If you would like more information, consult my companion tutorial for Visual Basic programming entitled *Start Here! Learn to Program in Visual Basic 2012* (Microsoft Press, 2012).

In the next chapter, you'll create your first Windows Store application from scratch, a lucky number slot machine game.

CHAPTER 3

Creating your first Windows Store application

After completing this chapter, you will be able to

- Design the user interface for a Windows Store app.

- Use XAML controls in the Toolbox.

- Work with random numbers, digital photos, and sound effects.

- Write Visual Basic program code for an event handler.

- Create a splash screen for your Windows Store app.

- Save, test, and build a Windows Store app.

As you learned in Chapter 2, "The Visual Studio Integrated Development Environment," the Microsoft Visual Studio 2013 IDE is ready to help you build your Visual Basic applications. In this chapter, you'll dive right in and create a Visual Basic program for the Windows Store. As a complete walkthrough exercise, this chapter describes the essential steps that you will complete each time that you create a Visual Basic application in the Visual Studio 2013 IDE. In future chapters, you'll learn more about the diversity of application types that you can create with Visual Studio, including apps for the Windows Store, the Windows desktop, the console, the web, and Windows Phone. After you learn the core Visual Basic programming skills, you'll find that all of these application types have much in common.

In this chapter, you'll learn how to create a Las Vegas-style slot machine for the Windows Store. You'll design the user interface for the program with XAML controls in the Toolbox, and you'll adjust property settings and resize objects on the page with tools in the IDE. As part of the process, you'll use the *TextBlock* control to display random numbers, the *Image* control to insert a digital photograph, and the *MediaElement* control to play a sound effect when the user spins the number 7. To create the core functionality of the Windows Store app, you'll write Visual Basic program code for an event handler. Finally, you'll create a splash screen for the app, save and test the app in the IDE, and build an executable file that can be launched from the Windows Start page.

Lucky Seven: A Visual Basic app for the Windows Store

The Windows Store app that you're going to construct is Lucky Seven, a game program that simulates a lucky number slot machine. Lucky Seven has a simple user interface and can be created and compiled in just a few minutes by using Visual Studio 2013. Here's what your program will look like when it's finished:

Programming step by step

The Lucky Seven user interface contains one button, three text block objects to display lucky numbers, a digital photo depicting cash winnings, and a text block containing the title "Lucky Seven." I produced these elements by creating five visible objects on the Lucky Seven page and then changing several properties for each object. I also added a *MediaElement* control to the page, which is not visible at runtime, to play a special sound effect when the user wins the game.

After I designed the basic user interface, I added program code for the Spin button to process the user's button clicks and to display random numbers on the page. Finally, I created a splash screen for the app and prepared it for distribution by using tools in the Visual Studio IDE.

To re-create Lucky Seven, you'll follow five essential programming steps that will be the same for most of the projects that you create with Visual Studio. You'll design the user interface with Toolbox controls, adjust important property settings, write Visual Basic code, prepare a splash screen and other required elements, test the program, and build an executable file.

Designing the user interface

In this exercise, you'll start building Lucky Seven by first creating a new project and then using XAML controls for Windows Store apps to construct the user interface.

Create a new project

1. Start Visual Studio 2013.

2. On the Visual Studio File menu, click New Project.

   The New Project dialog box opens, as shown here:

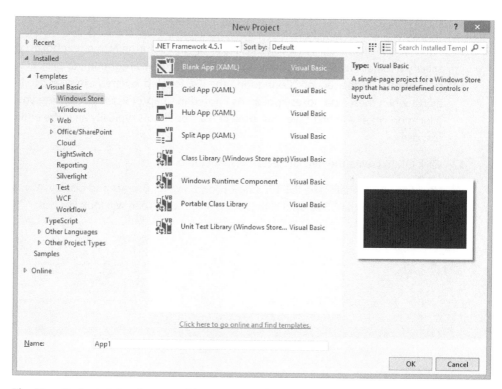

The New Project dialog box provides access to the major template types available for creating applications with Visual Studio. On the left side of the dialog box is a list of the many template types available. Because the most recent language selection I made in this dialog box was Visual Basic, the Visual Basic templates are currently visible, but other programming templates and resources are also offered, including those for Visual C#, Visual C++, and JavaScript.

3. In the Visual Basic template group, click the Blank App (XAML) project if it is not already selected.

   When you use the Blank App template, Visual Studio will create a basic Windows Store app project with default tiles, splash screen, manifest, and startup code, but no predefined controls or layout. Note that other app types are available (which we'll get to later), including Windows (that is, Windows desktop), Web, and Windows Phone.

4. In the Name text box, type **My Lucky Seven**.

   Visual Studio assigns the name My Lucky Seven to your project. (You'll specify a folder location for the project later.)

 Important I'm recommending the "My" prefix here so that you don't confuse your new app with the Lucky Seven project I've created for you on disk. However, you'll see that I don't use the "My" prefix myself in the instructions, sample projects, or screen shots in the book—I am leaving that for your use.

   If the New Project dialog box contains Location and Solution Name text boxes, you need to specify a folder location and solution name for your new programming project now. Refer to Chapter 2, in the section "Configuring the IDE for step-by-step exercises," to learn how to adjust when these text boxes appear. As I noted in Chapter 2, I will be asking you to specify a location when you first save your project—a step that is typically near the end of each exercise.

5. Click OK to create the new project in Visual Studio.

   Visual Studio prepares the IDE for a new programming project and displays Visual Basic code associated with the blank application template. Your screen will look like this:

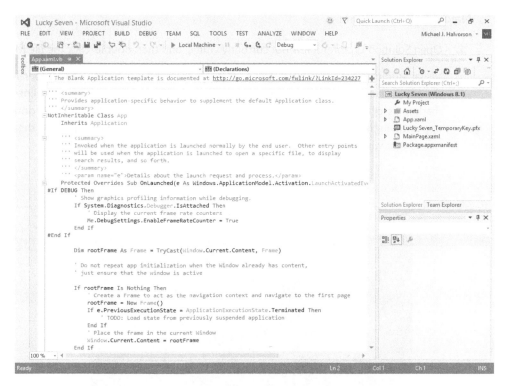

What you see here is standard startup code for a Windows Store app created in Visual Studio 2013, and the code is stored in the file App.xaml.vb within the project. Although each project contains an App.xaml file, your work in this chapter will begin with the app's user interface, which is stored in the MainPage.xaml file.

Note The section beginning *#If DEBUG Then* near the center of this illustration displays debugging information on the screen when the Windows Store app is executed in debugging mode, and it is designed for testing purposes. This code was present in the final Visual Studio 2013 software release and displays information about how long various tasks are taking during the execution of the Visual Studio app, including the frame rate for the user interface thread and how long it took (in milliseconds) to load the user interface. If you want to suppress the debugging information, remove the code between the *#If DEBUG* and *#End If* statements. For more information about the meaning of the debugging counters that appear at the top of the screen during testing, see *EnableFrameRateCounter* on *http://msdn.microsoft.com*.

You'll display that user interface now in the Designer and enhance it with Toolbox controls.

Navigate the Designer

1. Open Solution Explorer if it is not currently visible, and then double-click the file MainPage.xaml.

   Visual Studio opens MainPage.xaml in a Designer window and shows the upper-left corner of the app's main page. Below this page, you'll see the Code Editor with several lines of XAML markup associated with the user interface page in the Designer. As you add controls to the app page in the Designer, the Code Editor reflects the changes by displaying the XAML statements that will create the user interface. Your screen should look like this:

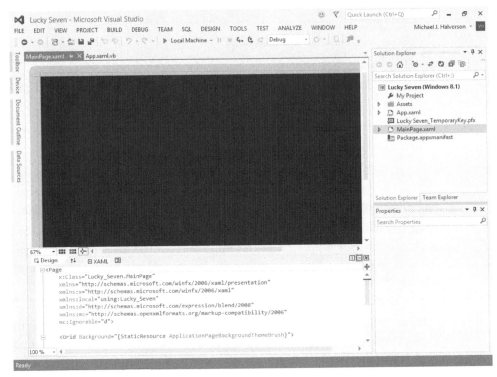

   Each time that you create a Windows Store app with Visual Basic and Visual Studio, you'll use Toolbox controls and XAML markup to design the user interface. This technique will be new to Visual Basic programmers who have primarily created Windows applications by using the technology known as Windows Forms. (You will have used the Toolbox but not XAML markup.) However, XAML will be somewhat familiar to programmers who have created Windows applications using Windows Presentation Foundation (WPF) or Windows Phone.

   Now let's review how the Designer works.

2. Click the scroll box in the Designer's vertical scroll bar, and drag it down.

   When you drag a scroll box in the Designer window, you can see more of the user interface you are working on.

3. Click the scroll box in the Designer's horizontal scroll bar, and drag it right. (Likewise, when you drag a horizontal scroll box, you can see hidden parts of the user interface.)

Near the lower-left corner of the Designer, you'll see a Zoom tool, which allows you to zoom in on the current application page (to see more detail) or zoom out (to see more of the page). The current value of the Zoom tool is 67%. You can select a different value by clicking the Zoom tool's drop-down button.

4. Click the Zoom drop-down button, and then click Fit All.

The entire application page now fits within the Designer. Depending on your screen resolution and the amount of screen space you have designated for the other IDE tools, you'll see a somewhat smaller version of the page.

 Tip If your mouse has a mouse wheel, you can move quickly from one zoom setting to the next by holding down the Ctrl key and rotating the mouse wheel. This feature works whenever the Designer is active.

It is important to be able to quickly view different parts of the application page in different sizes while you build it. Sometimes you want to see the entire page to consider the layout of controls or other elements, and sometimes you need to view portions of the page up close. It's up to you to adjust the Designer window so that you can see the user interface clearly as you work with it.

Now set the Designer to its full-size setting.

5. Click the Zoom drop-down button, and then click 100%.

6. Adjust the Designer's vertical and horizontal scroll bars so that you can see the upper-left edge of the page.

Seeing the edge of the page will help you orient yourself to the application window that the user sees.

Now you'll add a Toolbox control to the page.

Open the Toolbox and use the *TextBlock* control

1. If the Toolbox is not currently visible, click the Toolbox tab or click the Toolbox command on the View menu.

The Toolbox window contains a large collection of user interface controls that you can add to your application. Because you are building a Windows Store app for Windows 8.1, the types of controls that are displayed in the Toolbox are so-called XAML controls—that is, structured elements that control the look and feel of an application and can be successfully organized on a page by the XAML parser within Visual Studio.

There are also other collections of Toolbox controls for other types of applications (Windows Forms controls, HTML controls for web applications, Windows Phone controls, and so on), but you don't have to worry about that now—Visual Studio automatically loads the proper controls into the Toolbox when you open a new solution.

Your screen should look like this:

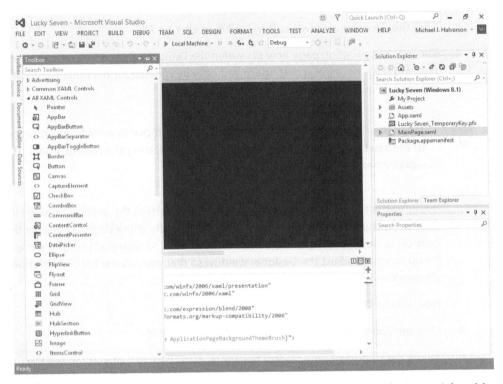

For convenience, the Toolbox controls have been organized into several groups: Advertising, Common XAML Controls (those controls that appear in many applications), and All XAML Controls (a list of all the XAML controls for Windows Store apps that are configured for use with Visual Studio).

Remember that the Toolbox window is like any other tool window in the Visual Studio IDE. You can move it, resize it, or pin it as needed. You can choose to keep the Toolbox open while you add controls to a new page (pinning it to the side of the IDE), or you can choose to use the Toolbox window's autohide feature so that the Toolbox collapses after each control has been selected.

2. Click the *TextBlock* control in the Toolbox, and move the mouse pointer to the Designer window.

The mouse pointer changes to crosshairs. The crosshairs are designed to help you draw the rectangular shape of the *TextBlock* control on the page. You can also create a *TextBlock* with the default size by double-clicking the control in the Toolbox.

3. Click and drag to create a large rectangle-sized text block object that fills the top-left corner of the page.

   When you release the mouse button, Visual Studio creates a XAML text block object. *TextBlock* is designed to display text on your page and, in this case, can create a welcoming banner for your Windows Store app. You can update the text stored in the *TextBlock* object on your page by setting the *Text* property, either with the Properties window, XAML markup, or program code.

4. In the Properties window, change the *Text* property of the text block object to **Lucky Seven** and press Enter.

   Visual Studio displays "Lucky Seven" in the Properties window and in the Designer window. Now you'll increase the point size of the title and apply other formatting effects.

5. In the Properties window, in the *Text* category, click the Font Size text box, type **98**, and press Enter.

   The Font Size text box offers a variety of font sizes up to 72, but in this case, you're typing a larger number to create a big impact on the screen.

> **Tip** At any time, you can delete an object and start over again by selecting the object on the page and then pressing Delete. Feel free to create and delete objects to practice creating your user interface.

6. In the Properties window, in the *Brush* category, click the *Foreground* property, if it is not already selected.

   The *Foreground* property controls the color of the text in the text block.

7. Click the Solid Color Brush button.

   The Solid Color Brush button is the second tile from the left near the top of the dialog box. (This button might also be the default selection, but it will cause no harm if you click it again.)

   When the Solid Color Brush button is selected, you'll see the Color Resources editor.

8. If you'd like more room to see the content of the Properties window, enlarge the window or configure the tool as a floating window so that you can see the Color Resources editor clearly.

9. Near the bottom of the editor, select the number containing the pound (#) sign.

   This eight-digit number is known as a hexadecimal color value—that is, a number expressed in base-16 arithmetic that specifies color by using RGBA values. When you specify a new color for text, you can specify individual values for red, green, and blue (R, G, and B), or you can use a standardized name, such as Red, DarkRed, White, Black, Purple, Lime, or Aquamarine.

10. Type **DarkRed** and press Enter.

Note that after you press Enter in the Color Resources editor, Visual Studio converts "DarkRed" to the hexadecimal value #FF8B0000, as shown in the following screen:

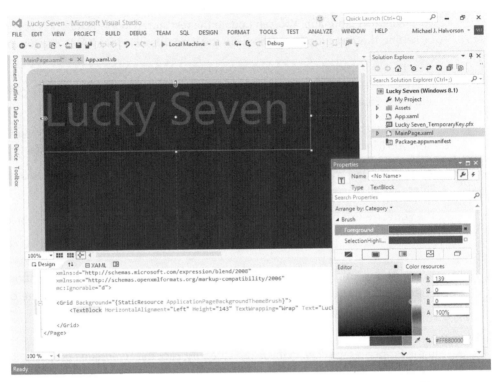

11. Return the Properties window to its docked position if you moved or enlarged it.

Now you'll add three *TextBlock* controls below the Lucky Seven banner to display the randomly chosen numbers in the game. Each time that the user clicks Lucky Seven's Spin button, three new numbers will appear in these text blocks. If one of the numbers is a 7, the user wins and a sound is played.

Add text blocks for the random numbers

1. Double-click the *TextBlock* control in the Toolbox.

Visual Studio creates a text block object on the page. In this case, the text block object is quite small, but you can resize it.

2. In the Properties window, click the *Text* category, click the *FontSize* box, type **72**, and then press Enter.

Visual Studio expands the text block object to accommodate text in 72-point font.

3. In the Properties window, click the *Common* category, click the Text box, type **0**, and press Enter.

   0 will be an initial value for the first lucky number in the program.

4. At the top of the Properties window, change the *Name* property of the text block object to **FirstNum**.

   It is not required that all objects be named in your user interface, but it is important to name objects that will be referenced in program code. Because you'll be controlling the value of this lucky number in a Visual Basic event handler, you'll give it the name *FirstNum* here.

5. Drag the *FirstNum* text block object below the "u" in Lucky Seven.

   Your page should look something like this:

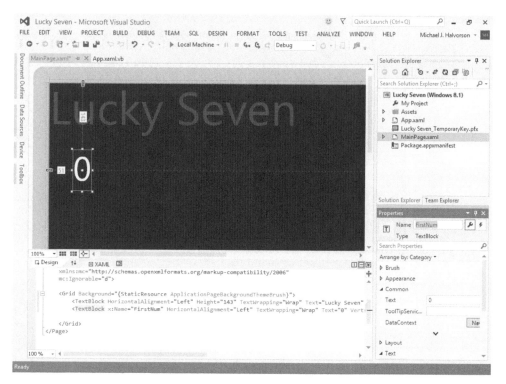

6. Double-click the *TextBlock* control in the Toolbox to create another text block object.

   This object will hold the second lucky number on the page.

7. Using the Properties window, set the *Name* property of the object to **SecondNum**, set the *FontSize* property to **72**, and set the *Text* property to **0**.

8. Move the new *SecondNum* object to the right of the *FirstNum* object, directly below the "y" in Lucky Seven.

   Now you'll create the third lucky number for the page.

9. Double-click the *TextBlock* control in the Toolbox to create the last text block object.

10. Using the Properties window, set the *Name* property of the object to **ThirdNum**, set *FontSize* to **72**, and set *Text* to **0**.

11. Move the *ThirdNum* object to the right of the *SecondNum* object, directly below the first "e" in Lucky Seven.

    When you've finished, your four text block objects should look like those in this screen shot. (You can move your objects if they don't look quite right.)

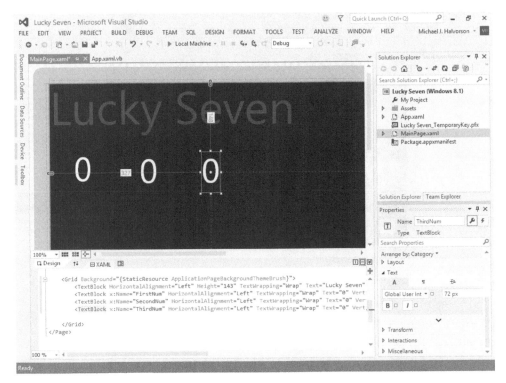

Now you'll add a button control to the page.

Add a button control

1. Click the *Button* control in the Toolbox, and then move the mouse pointer over the application page.

2. Drag the pointer down and to the right. Release the mouse button to complete the button.

3. In the Properties window, in the *Common* category, change the *Content* property to **Spin** and press Enter.

   Note that a button object's contents are set via the *Content* property, rather than *Text* (like a text block object), because buttons can contain artwork and other data.

4. In the Properties window, change the button object's *Name* property to **SpinButton**.

5. In the Properties window, in the *Text* category, change the *FontSize* property to **24**.

6. Resize the *SpinButton* object so that it is 81 pixels high and 95 pixels wide.

7. Move the button object so that it is to the right of the third lucky number on the page. Snap lines will appear again as you move the object, and the top edge of the button will snap to the top edge of the three numbers when aligned.

   Your screen should look like this:

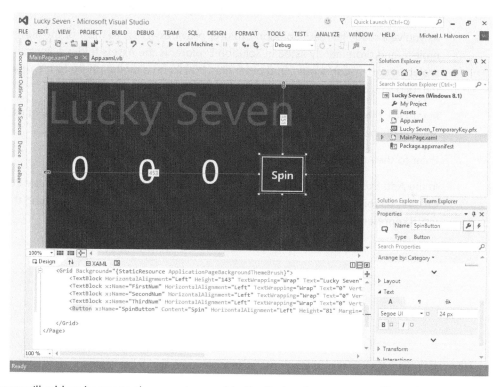

Now you'll add an image to the page to graphically display the payout you'll receive when you draw a 7 and hit the jackpot. An *Image* control is designed to display bitmaps, icons, digital photos, and other artwork—a major design feature of most Windows Store apps. One of the most common uses for an *Image* control is to display a PNG or JPEG file.

Add an image

1. Click the *Image* control in the Toolbox.

2. Using the control's drawing pointer, create a large rectangular box below the lucky numbers and the Spin button on the page.

3. If necessary, adjust the Zoom setting in the Designer window so that you can see more of the page in the Designer. For example, a Zoom setting of 50% might be useful.

    It would be good if the image object covered most of the remaining area of the page below the numbers and the Spin button. Sometimes it is useful to reduce the size of a page in the Designer with the Zoom control to make these types of operations easier.

    Now you'll add a suitable photo to the project by using Solution Explorer and the Assets folder, a special container for resource files in your project.

4. If Solution Explorer is not visible now, open it by clicking Solution Explorer on the View menu.

    As you've already learned, Solution Explorer provides access to most of the files in your project, and prominently listed in Solution Explorer is the Assets folder, a container for your project's logo, splash screen, and other files. You'll add a digital photo to the Assets folder in the following step, which will make it available to your program.

5. Right-click the Assets folder in Solution Explorer to display a shortcut menu of useful Visual Studio commands.

6. Point to the Add command, and then click Existing Item.

7. In the Add Existing Item dialog box, browse to the My Documents\Visual Basic 2013 SBS\ Chapter 03 folder and click Coins.jpg, a JPEG file containing coins from around the world—a visual representation of winnings in the Lucky Seven app.

8. Click Add to add the photo to your project in the Assets folder.

Visual Studio inserts the file, and it appears now in Solution Explorer under Assets, as shown in the following illustration:

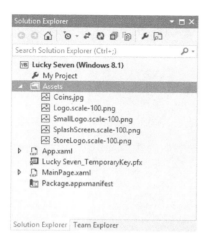

When a file has been added to the Assets folder, it becomes part of the project you are working on, and it can be referenced via the Properties window. Most importantly, it becomes part of the project when the project is compiled for distribution—there is no need to remember where the file was originally located on your hard disk, because a copy will now travel with the project.

9. Select the image object (if it is not already selected) so that its properties are visible in the Properties windows.

10. In the Properties window, in the Common category, click the *Source* text box, and then click Coins.jpg.

You might need to expand the Properties window a little to see the drop-down list box arrow in the Source text box.

After the file has been selected, a photo of coins from around the world fills the image object in the Designer.

11. Adjust the spacing of the image so that it takes up much of the left side of the page in the Designer.

When you've finished, your page should look like this:

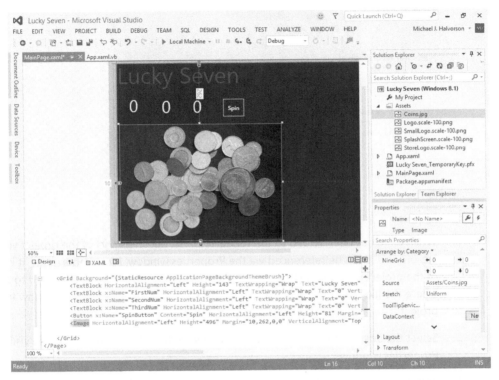

12. In the Properties window, change the *Name* property of the image object to **CoinImage**.

Naming the image object is an important step, because you'll be referring to this object in Visual Basic code. Often you'll see me include the name of the control at the end of an object name so that its object type is clear.

Now you'll add a sound effect to the program so that the game plays a sound when the user spins a 7. You'll add this sound effect with the *MediaElement* control, which plays audio and video files in a Windows Store app. The sound you'll play is stored in a short WAV file named ArcadeRiff, created by Henry Halvorson.

Play audio media with the *MediaElement* control

1. In the Toolbox, expand the All XAML Controls category and double-click the *MediaElement* control.

    Visual Studio places a new media player object in the upper-left corner of the page. Like other new objects in the Designer, you can now move the object to a new location and customize it with property settings. However, the *MediaElement* control is essentially a behind-the-scenes tool; it is not visible to the user unless the control is displaying a video clip. For now, you can leave the media element object where it is.

    The *Source* property of the *MediaElement* control specifies the name of the media file that will be loaded into the control for playback. Before you can assign this property, you need to add a valid media file to the Assets folder, just as you did for the image control.

2. Right-click the Assets folder in Solution Explorer to display the shortcut menu.

3. Point to the Add command, and then click Existing Item.

4. In the Add Existing Item dialog box, browse to the My Documents\Visual Basic 2013 SBS\ Chapter 03 folder and click ArcadeRiff.wav.

5. Click Add to add the music file to your project in the Assets folder.

    Visual Studio inserts the file, and it appears now in Solution Explorer under Assets.

    Now you're ready to name the media element object and assign it a music asset by using the *Source* property.

6. Click the media element object in the Designer window. (Zoom in on the Designer if necessary—remember that the object is invisible but it can be selected. You can always find it by clicking the *MediaElement* entry in the XAML tab of the Code Editor.)

7. In the Properties window, change the *Name* property to **CoinSound**.

8. Expand the *Media* category, scroll down to the *Source* property, and click the Source list box.

    Your new media file (ArcadeRiff.wav) appears in the list.

    Click the ArcadeRiff.wav file to link it to the *CoinSound* object.

    Your screen will look like this (notice the entries in Solution Explorer and the Properties window):

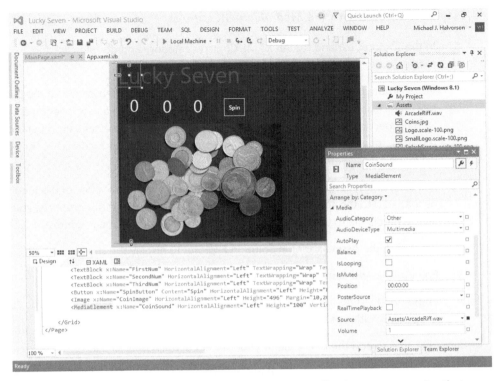

The Properties window exposes a few other important media element properties that you can examine and adjust if desired.

For example, the AutoPlay check box is enabled by default, which directs the media control to automatically play the specified media file when the page loads. Because you don't want the sound to play until it is needed, disable that now.

9. Remove the check mark from the AutoPlay check box.

There are some other options you might notice now (but not adjust). The *Position* property specifies the location within the media file where playback will begin; this option is very useful if there is a specific place in the song or video where you want to start.

The *IsLooping* property is a Boolean value that allows you to run the media file over and over again if you like. Finally, *Volume* allows you to set an initial volume level for the media playback, which you can adjust with property settings in an event handler while the program is running.

Final property settings and adjustments

Your Lucky Seven page is almost complete. You just need to make a few final property settings, write the Visual Basic code, and design a splash screen that runs when your project starts.

Before you begin these tasks, let's think a little more specifically about how the program will operate when it runs. The game starts when the user opens the program and clicks the Spin button. When the Spin button is clicked, the app generates three random numbers and displays them in text block objects on the page. If and when the player hits the jackpot (that is, when at least one 7 appears in the text block objects), the object containing the photo of coins appears, and then the media element control plays a "celebration" sound.

Although the flow of events is pretty straightforward, the program needs to continue operating after the first "win." So, when the user clicks the Spin button, the coins image needs to disappear and remain hidden until another 7 appears, at which point the image is displayed again and the sound effect also run.

To get this behavior to work correctly, you need to find a mechanism to make the image object visible and invisible when you want. That can be accomplished by setting the image object's *Visibility* property, which is assigned *Visible* or *Collapsed* (invisible) values as needed. In fact, most objects in a Windows Store app can be made visible or invisible if you set this property—it is a built-in tool to control what appears on the screen. Give it a try here.

Set the *Visibility* property

1. Click the image object on the page.

2. In the Properties window, click the *Appearance* category, and then click the *Visibility* property.

3. In the drop-down list box that appears, click the *Collapsed* property.

    The image object on the page disappears. Don't worry—this is the desired effect. The object is not gone, it is just currently invisible. You'll make it reappear by using program code in an event handler.

Now you'll adjust the background color for the page. The default color value for Windows Store apps is Black, but a more colorful value can make the game more appealing. You can adjust this color by selecting the *Grid* object on the page and adjusting values in the *Brush* category by using the Properties window.

Set the page's background color

1. Select the *Grid* object by clicking the background page in the Designer (not one of the objects that you've just added).

    You can tell when you've selected the *Grid* object because its properties will fill the Properties window.

    As you'll learn in Chapter 7, "XAML markup step by step," each of the objects in a Windows Store app is defined by XAML markup codes and data that can be entered or adjusted in the Code Editor. The *Grid* object is the base layout element for a page, and all of the elements on a page are nested within this *Grid* object. In addition to serving as a useful container for objects, the *Grid* object also has settings that you can adjust, such as the background color that appears for your app. You'll set this now.

2. Click the *Brush* category, click the *Background* property, and then click the Solid Color Brush button.

3. Near the bottom of the Color Resources editor, select the number containing the pound (#) sign, replace the contents with **Green**, and press Enter.

    The alphanumeric value for green (#FF0080000) appears in the text box, and the background color of the *Grid* object changes to green. Feel free to experiment with other color values if you like.

    OK—that's it for the user interface design walkthrough. Save your work now, before you write the program code.

Save changes

1. Click the Save All command on the File menu to save all your additions to the Lucky Seven project.

    The Save All command saves everything in your project—the project file, the pages, the code-behind files, the assets, the package manifest, and other related components in your application. Because this is the first time that you have saved your project, the Save Project dialog box opens, prompting you for the name and location of the project. (If your copy of Visual Studio is configured to prompt you for a location when you first create your project, you won't see the Save Project dialog box now—Visual Studio just saves your changes.)

2. Browse and select a location for your files. I recommend that you use the My Documents\ Visual Basic 2013 SBS\Chapter 03 folder (the location of the book's sample files), but the location is up to you. Because you used the "My" prefix when you originally opened your project, this version won't overwrite the practice file that I built for you on disk.

3. Clear the Create Directory For Solution check box.

   When this check box is selected, it creates a second folder for your program's solution files, which is not necessary for solutions that contain only one project (the situation for most programs in this book).

4. Click Save to save your files.

 Tip If you want to save just the item you are currently working on (the page, the code module, or something else), you can use the Save command on the File menu. If you want to save the current item with a different name, you can use the Save As command.

Writing the code

Now you're ready to write the code for the Lucky Seven program. Because most of the objects you've created already "know" how to work when the program runs, they're ready to receive input from the user and process it. The inherent functionality of objects is one of the great strengths of Visual Studio and Visual Basic—after objects are placed on a page and their properties are set, they're ready to run without any additional programming.

However, the "meat" of the Lucky Seven game—the code that actually calculates random numbers, displays them in boxes, and detects a jackpot—is still missing from the program. This computing logic can be built into this Windows Store app only by using program statements—code that clearly spells out what the program should do at each step of the way. Because the Spin button drives the program, you'll associate the code for the game with an event handler designed for that button.

In the following steps, you'll enter the Visual Basic code for Lucky Seven in the Code Editor.

Use the Code Editor

1. In the Visual Studio Designer, click the *SpinButton* object.

2. Open the Properties window, and close the *Brush* category.

3. Near the top of the Properties window and to the right of the *Name* property and the Properties button, click the Event Handler button (a square button displaying a lightning bolt icon).

   A collection of actions or events that a button object can respond to fills the Properties window. Typical events that a button might recognize include *Click* (a mouse click), *DragOver* (an object being dragged over a button), Tapped (a button being touched by a finger), and *Drop* (an object being dragged over and dropped on a button).

Because Visual Basic is, at its core, an event-driven programming language, much of what you do as a software developer is create user interfaces that respond to various types of input from the user, and then you write event handlers that manage the input. Most of the time, you will need to write event handlers only for a few events associated with the objects in your programs. (However, the list of events is quite comprehensive to give you many options.)

To create an event handler for a particular event, you double-click the text box next to the event in the Properties window. Because you want to generate three random numbers each time that the user clicks the Spin button in your program, you'll write an event handler for the button's *Click* event.

4. Double-click the text box next to the *Click* event in the Properties window.

Visual Studio inserts an event handler named *SpinButton_Click* in the Click text box, and opens the MainPage.xaml.vb code-behind file in the Code Editor. Your screen should look like this:

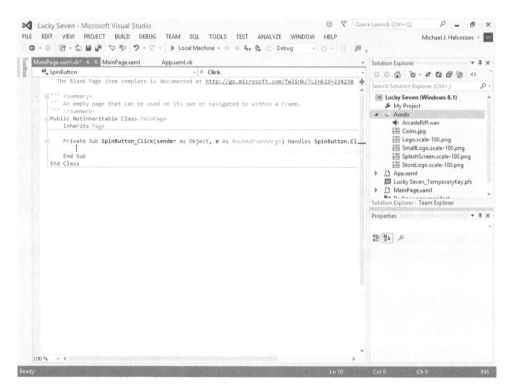

Inside the Code Editor are program statements associated with the *MainPage* template that you opened when you started this project. This is Visual Basic program code, and you might notice right away that some of the code is organized into concise units, known as *procedures*. Near the bottom of the file is a new event handler procedure that you just created, called *SpinButton_Click*.

The *Sub* and *End Sub* keywords designate a procedure, and the keywords *Protected* and *Private* indicate how the procedure will be used. You'll learn more about these keywords later.

When you double-clicked the Click text box in the Properties window, Visual Studio automatically added the first and last lines of the *SpinButton_Click* event procedure, as the following code shows. (Your event procedure will not wrap as this one does. In print, I need to respect the book's margins.)

```
Private Sub SpinButton_Click(sender As Object, e As RoutedEventArgs) Handles SpinButton_
Click

End Sub
```

The body of a procedure fits between these lines and is executed whenever a user activates the interface element associated with the procedure. In this case, the event is a mouse click, but as you'll see later in the book, it could also be a different type of event. Programmers refer to this sequence as "triggering" or "firing" an event.

> **Tip** You might also notice lines of text with green type in the Code Editor. In the default settings, green type indicates that the text is a *comment*, or an explanatory note written by the creator of the program, so that it might be better understood or used by others. The Visual Basic compiler does not execute, or *evaluate*, program comments.

5. Type the following program code, and press the Enter key after the last line:

```
Dim generator As New Random
CoinImage.Visibility = Windows.UI.Xaml.Visibility.Collapsed

FirstNum.Text = generator.Next(0, 9)
SecondNum.Text = generator.Next(0, 9)
ThirdNum.Text = generator.Next(0, 9)

If (FirstNum.Text = "7") Or (SecondNum.Text = "7") Or
    (ThirdNum.Text = "7") Then
    CoinImage.Visibility = Windows.UI.Xaml.Visibility.Visible
    CoinSound.Play()
End If
```

As you enter the program code, Visual Studio formats the text and displays different parts of the code in color to help you identify the various elements. When you begin to type the name of an object property, Visual Basic also displays the available properties for the object that you're using in a list box, so you can click the property or keep typing to enter it yourself.

Your screen should now look like this:

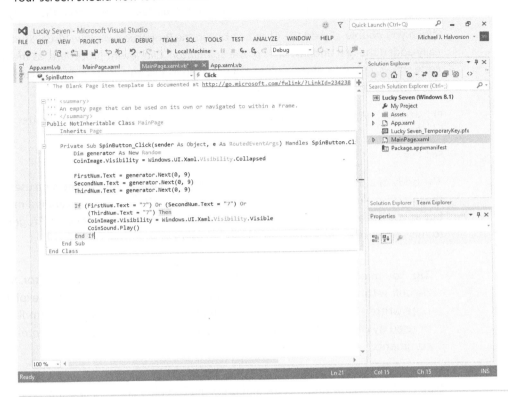

Note If Visual Basic displays an additional error message, you might have misspelled a program statement. Check the offending line against the text in this book, make the necessary correction, and continue typing. (You can also delete a line and type it again from scratch.)

In Visual Studio, program statements can be composed of keywords, properties, object names, variables, numbers, special symbols, and other values. As you enter these items in the Code Editor, Visual Studio uses a feature known as IntelliSense to help you write the code. With IntelliSense, as Visual Studio recognizes language elements, it will automatically complete many expressions.

6. Click the Save All button to save your changes.

A look at the *SpinButton_Click* event handler

The *SpinButton_Click* event handler is executed when the user clicks the Spin button on the page. Essentially, the event handler performs four main tasks:

1. It declares a random number generator named *generator* in the program.

2. It hides the digital photo.

3. It creates three random numbers and displays them in text block objects.

4. It displays the Coins.jpg photo and plays a sound when the number 7 appears.

Let's look at each of these steps individually.

The random number generator is declared by this line of code:

```
Dim generator As New Random
```

You've probably declared and used variables before in programs. But notice the variable type here—the generator is declared using the type *Random*, which has been specifically designed to support the creation of so-called "pseudo-random" numbers—that is, numbers that don't follow a particular pattern and appear in a specific range. You'll use random numbers often in this book, and you'll learn much more about data types and conversion in Chapter 11, "Mastering data types, operators, and string processing."

Hiding the photo is accomplished by the following line:

```
CoinImage.Visibility = Windows.UI.Xaml.Visibility.Collapsed
```

As you learned earlier, the *Visibility* property determines whether or not an object on a page is visible. This specific syntax uses the objects in the .NET Framework to collapse (or hide) the photo of the coins. (This line is designed to restore the program to a neutral state if a previous spin had displayed the coins.)

The next three lines handle the random number computations. Does this concept sound strange? You can actually make Visual Basic generate unpredictable numbers within specific guidelines—that is, you can create random numbers for lottery contests, dice games, or other statistical patterns. The *generator* instance's *Next* method in each line creates a random number between 0 and 9—just what you need for this particular slot machine application.

```
FirstNum.Text = generator.Next(0, 9)
SecondNum.Text = generator.Next(0, 9)
ThirdNum.Text = generator.Next(0, 9)
```

The last group of statements in the program checks whether any of the random numbers is 7. If one or more of them is, the program displays the graphical depiction of a payout and plays the sound effect to announce the winnings.

```
If (FirstNum.Text = "7") Or (SecondNum.Text = "7") Or
    (ThirdNum.Text = "7") Then
    CoinImage.Visibility = Windows.UI.Xaml.Visibility.Visible
    CoinSound.Play()
End If
```

Each time the user clicks the Spin button, the *SpinButton_Click* event handler is executed, or called, and the program statements in the handler are run again. However, if you click the Spin button many times in rapid succession, you might miss one or more of the sound effects, because the media element object can play only one sound effect at a time.

Running Windows Store apps

Congratulations! You're ready to run your first Windows Store app. To run a Visual Basic program from the IDE, you can do any of the following:

- Click Start Debugging on the Debug menu.

- Click the Start Debugging button on the Standard toolbar. (You'll typically see "Local Machine" next to this button, because you debug on the local computer by default.)

- Press F5.

Try running your Lucky Seven program now. If Visual Basic displays an error message, you might have a typing mistake or two in your program code. Try to fix it by comparing the printed version in this book with the one you typed, or load Lucky Seven from your hard disk and run it.

 Note I assume that you have named your project My Lucky Seven, but the instructions and screen shots below will show Lucky Seven because you might be running the sample project that I created.

Run the Lucky Seven program

1. Click the Start Debugging button on the Standard toolbar.

   The Lucky Seven program compiles and runs. After a few seconds, the user interface appears, just as you designed it.

2. Click the Spin button.

   The program picks three random numbers and displays them in the labels on the page. When a 7 appears, your screen will look like this:

The presence of a 7 also triggers the sound effect, which lasts a few seconds and sounds a bit like an electronic slot machine. You win!

3. Click the Spin button 15 or 16 more times, watching the results of the spins in the number text blocks.

   About half the time you spin, you hit the jackpot—pretty easy odds. (The actual odds are about 2.8 times out of 10; you're just lucky at first.) Later on, you might want to make the game tougher by displaying the photo only when two or three 7s appear, or by creating a running total of winnings.

4. When you've finished experimenting with your new creation, close the Windows Store app.

   The program stops, and the IDE reappears on your screen. Click the Stop Debugging button on the toolbar to end the program. Now you'll add a splash screen to the project.

Creating a splash screen for your app

A *splash screen* is a transitional image that appears when your app first launches. Every Windows Store app must have a splash screen, which consists of an image (or text) and a surrounding background color. The splash screen is stored in the Assets folder within Solution Explorer, and every new Windows Store app has a basic splash screen that is created by default. You'll also see tile images in the Assets folder, which you'll learn to customize in Chapter 9, "Exploring Windows 8.1 design features: Command bar, flyout, tiles, and touch."

Although you can create a splash screen with Microsoft Paint or another third-party graphics program, you can also create a simple splash screen within Visual Studio. Just remember that a splash screen appears very briefly when you first launch your app. Accordingly, this is not the place to put elaborate program instructions or copyright information. You'll want to avoid placing advertisements or version information on a splash screen.

Instead, use the splash screen to offer a preview of the functionality of your app in some unique way. Consider an image or photo that will be easily adapted to other countries and cultures (that is, easily *localizable*) and that can be displayed effectively in different screen resolutions. Notice that Portable Network Graphics (.png) format is used because this file type is capable of displaying alpha transparency and 24-bit color images. When part of an image is formatted as transparent, the background color will be displayed behind it. (You'll see this in most splash screens and tiles in Windows Store and Windows Phone apps.)

Create a Lucky Seven splash screen

1. In Solution Explorer, open the Assets folder, and then double-click the file SplashScreen.scale-100.png.

2. This action opens the Image Editor Designer in Visual Studio, and loads the SplashScreen.scale-100.png file into the editor. Your screen looks like this:

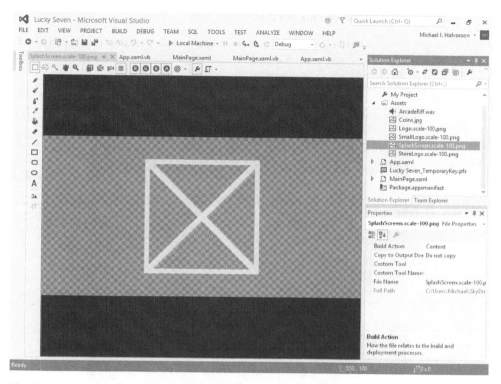

The Solution Explorer and Properties windows are still visible. However, the Image Editor is active, and the design canvas is surrounded by graphics editing tools. The "X" shape in the center of the canvas is simply the default image for the SplashScreen.scale-100.png file. This is the image that you want to replace now.

3. Click the Selection tool in the upper-left corner of the Image Editor, select the entire "X" shape, and press Delete.

You now have a blank canvas on which to create your splash screen image. The alpha checkerboard pattern that you see is a color scheme that allows you to more easily see the transparent portions of your image—that is, what you see displayed as the checkerboard now will be replaced by the background when your splash screen is actually displayed on the screen.

4. Click the Ellipse tool on the left side of the Designer, and then create a circle shape in the middle of the splash screen.

You can use the X- and Y-axis indicators in the lower-right corner of the screen to create your circle if you like. You can also use the Selection tool to move your shape to the center of the screen if you like.

Your Image Editor will look like this:

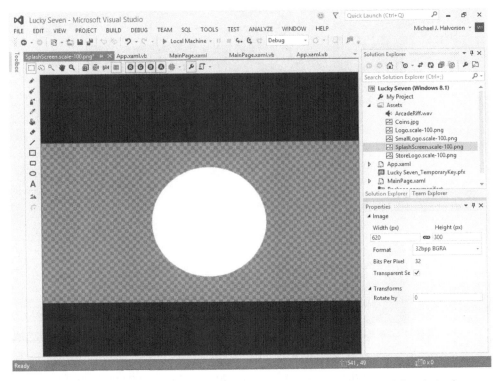

5. Use the Ellipse tool to add four or five smaller circles around the edge of the circle that you have created.

Typical splash screens show simple geometric shapes like this. Consider using a simplified version of your company logo.

Your simple splash screen now looks like this:

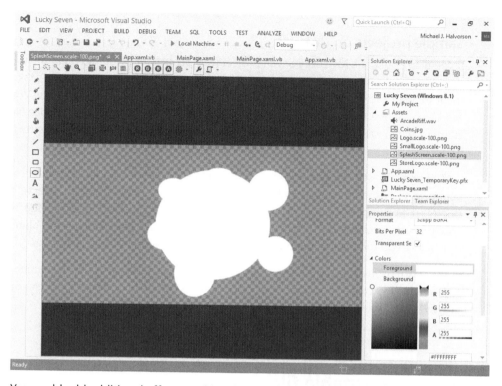

You could add additional effects to this splash screen, embellishing it with colors, images, text, or animation. However, for this first walkthrough, you have something that will work just fine.

6. Click the Save All command on the File menu to save your changes.

7. Press F5 to run the project, and examine your splash screen.

   Notice that the splash screen comes and goes in just a few moments. Did you notice the ellipse shapes and the black background color?

8. Close the program, and then close the Image Editor Designer.

Now your project is complete—it is time to test and deploy the app by adding it to the Windows Start page on your local computer. However, note that if this were a commercial Windows Store app being prepared for distribution to other users via the Windows Store, you would now add additional items to your app as described in Table 1-1. For more information, see Chapter 1, "Visual Basic 2013 development opportunities and the Windows Store."

Sample projects on disk

If you didn't build the My Lucky Seven project from scratch (or if you did build the project and want to compare what you created to what I built for you as I wrote the chapter), take a moment to open and run the completed Lucky Seven project, which is located in the Visual Basic 2013 SBS\Chapter 03 folder on your hard disk (the default location for the practice files for this chapter). If you need a refresher course on opening projects, see the detailed instructions in Chapter 2.

This book is a step-by-step tutorial, so you will benefit most from building the projects on your own and experimenting with them. But after you have completed the projects, it is often a good idea to compare what you have with the practice file "solution" that I provide, especially if you have unexpected results. To make this easy, I will give you the name of the solution files on disk before you run the completed program in most of the step-by-step exercises.

After you have compared the My Lucky Seven project to the Lucky Seven solution files on disk, reopen My Lucky Seven and prepare to compile it as an executable file. If you didn't create My Lucky Seven, use my solution file to complete the exercise.

Building an executable file

Your last task in this chapter is to complete the development process and create an application for Windows, or an *executable file*. Windows applications created with Visual Studio have the file name extension .exe and can be run on any system that contains Windows and the necessary support files. If you end up distributing your application via the Windows Store, the complete deployment package will be posted securely in the Store and made available to customers who would like to download it. However, you can also deploy your application to individual computers running Windows directly from within Visual Studio.

Because you just created a Windows Store app that targets the Windows 8.1 operating system, you need to be running Windows 8.1 to run this particular program. You won't post the sample app to the Windows Store yet, because it has not been registered or thoroughly tested. But you can deploy the app on your own computer, which does not have as many registration requirements as the Windows Store interface.

To assist in the testing and compilation process, Visual Studio allows you to create two types of executable files for your Windows application project: a *debug build* and a *release build*.

Debug builds are created automatically by Visual Studio when you create and test your program. They are stored in a folder called bin\Debug within your project folder. The debug executable file contains debugging information that makes the program run slightly slower.

Release builds are optimized executable files stored in the bin\Release folder within your project. To customize the settings for your release build, you click the *ProjectName* Properties command on the Project menu, and then click the Compile tab, where you'll see a list of compilation options that looks like the following screen. The Solution Configurations drop-down list box on the Standard Visual Studio toolbar indicates whether the executable is a debug build or a release build.

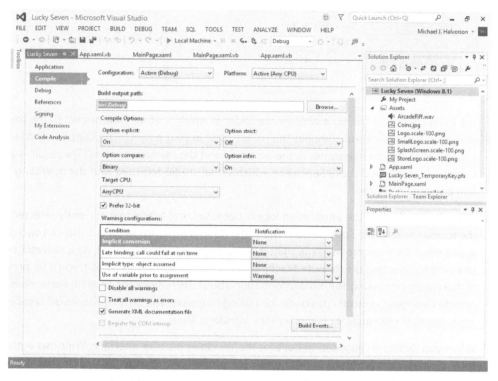

The process of preparing an executable file for a specific computer is called *deploying the application*. As noted, when you deploy an application with Visual Studio, the IDE handles the process of copying all the executable and support files that you will need to register the program with the operating system and run it. Visual Studio allows you to deploy applications *locally* (on the computer you are using) or *remotely* (on a computer attached to the network or Internet).

In the following steps, you'll deploy a release build for the My Lucky Seven application locally and create an application icon for the program on the Windows Start page.

Deploy a release build for the Lucky Seven app

1. Click the Solution Configurations drop-down list box on the Standard toolbar, and then click the Release option. Visual Studio will prepare your project for a release build, with the debugging information removed. The build output path is set to bin\Release\.

2. On the Build menu, click the Deploy Lucky Seven command.

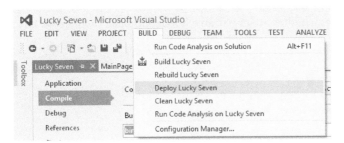

The Build command creates a bin\Release folder in which to store your project (if the folder doesn't already exist) and compiles the source code in your project. The Output window appears to show you milestones in the assembly and deployment process. The result is an executable file named Lucky Seven.exe, which Visual Studio registers with the operating system on your computer.

Visual Studio deploys the application locally because Local Machine is currently selected on the toolbar next to the Start button. This is the desired behavior here, but you can also deploy applications on a remote machine (that is, a computer attached to yours via a network or the Internet) by selecting the Remote Machine option. If you select this option, you'll be presented with a dialog box asking for more information about the remote connection. Remember that remote deploying is mostly designed for testing purposes. The best way to install completed applications via the Internet is through the Windows Store.

When you deploy an application built for the Windows 8.1 user interface, Windows automatically creates a new program icon for the application on the Start page. You can use this icon to launch the program whenever you want to run it. Try running My Lucky Seven now from the Start page on your computer.

3. Open the Windows Start page, and browse to the list of applications that are currently installed.

4. There are two possible locations for your new app: the main Start page, or the secondary Start page containing a longer list of app tiles. (This is where my Windows 8.1 system put the new Lucky Seven program.)

Because you didn't create a colorful Start page tile for your app, the default (gray) tile is shown. Your screen will look similar to this (note the Lucky Seven app in the second column):

5. Click the Lucky Seven application icon, and the Lucky Seven program will load and run in Windows.

6. Test the application again, clicking Spin several times and building up a few wins. When you are finished, close the app.

7. Return to Visual Studio, and close the Output window and the Lucky Seven properties page. Note that you can view and change compilation options whenever you want—the properties page is always available.

8. On the File menu, click Exit to close Visual Studio and the My Lucky Seven project.

9. Click Save if you are prompted to, and the Visual Studio IDE will close.

Congratulations on completing your first Windows Store app!

Summary

This chapter described how to create a Windows Store app named Lucky Seven by using Visual Studio 2013. The development process has much in common with earlier versions of Visual Basic and Visual Studio. You add Toolbox controls to a page, set properties, write program code, test the application, and prepare it for deployment. However, the XAML Toolbox for Windows Store apps is significantly different than the Toolbox used to create Windows Forms apps for the Windows desktop. In this chapter, we reviewed how to use XAML controls step by step. In the next chapter, you'll review how to use the Windows Forms Toolbox to create a desktop application for Windows 8.1, Windows 8, or Windows 7.

While creating the Lucky Seven slot machine game, you practiced using the *TextBlock* control, the *Button* control, the *Image* control, the *MediaElement* control, and setting the *Grid* control's background color. You also learned how to create a splash screen with the Visual Studio Image Editor. Finally, you tested and deployed your application to the Windows Start page. With a little more work, you'll also be able to deploy applications like Lucky Seven to the Windows Store.

CHAPTER 4

Windows desktop apps: A walkthrough using Windows Forms

After completing this chapter, you will be able to

- Create a Windows desktop app using Windows Forms.

- Build a user interface using the Windows Forms Designer.

- Use controls in the Windows Forms Toolbox.

- Write Visual Basic code for event handlers.

- Run, test, and deploy a Windows desktop app.

Chapter 3, "Creating your first Windows Store application," offered step-by-step instructions for building a Windows Store app using Visual Basic and the Visual Studio 2013 IDE. Windows Store apps represent a major new business opportunity for software developers, and as the platform grows, you will be well positioned to benefit from the improved functionality of Windows as well as the impressive reach of the Windows Store's global distribution system.

However, there are additional factors to consider as you choose development platforms for your Visual Basic applications. For example, you might work in an organization that continues to support earlier versions of Windows while also transitioning into Windows Store app development. Or you might work in a shop that has significant source code investments in earlier versions of Visual Basic, such as user interfaces designed for Windows Forms or Windows Presentation Foundation (WPF). That is, although the Windows Store might represent the future of application programming, current software platforms and technologies are equally important. This chapter introduces the support for earlier versions of Windows and Visual Basic that is built into Visual Studio 2013.

First, you'll learn how to create Windows desktop apps for Windows 8.1, Windows 8, and Windows 7 using an efficient Visual Studio technology known as *Windows Forms*. The term "Windows desktop app" is simply a new term for what Windows programmers have long described as "Windows-based applications"—that is, fully functional programs that run in a frame on the Windows desktop and that contain title bars, menus, dialog boxes, buttons, and other controls. In this chapter, you'll revisit the Lucky Seven slot machine that you built in Chapter 3, but this time you'll build the project as a Windows desktop app in Visual Studio 2013.

You'll construct the user interface for the slot machine game using controls in the Windows Forms Toolbox, and you'll build the application window or *form* by using the Windows Forms designer in the IDE. Next, you'll customize the form and its controls by using property settings, and you'll generate the random numbers and special effects by adding Visual Basic code to two event handlers. You'll also play music using the *My.Computer.Audio* object in the .NET Framework. As you create this application, I'll point out the similarities and differences between Windows desktop apps and Windows Store apps and how to switch back and forth between the two platforms as you need to. In Part II, "Designing the user interface," you'll see plenty of coding examples for both platforms.

This chapter will be especially helpful to programmers who have had previous experience with Visual Basic. Fundamentally, you'll learn that you can quickly translate your existing development skills to the Visual Studio 2013 IDE. If you have been using Windows Forms, you'll see that you can maintain your existing programs rather easily, while benefiting from the new improvements to the Visual Studio 2013 product. And throughout the book, you'll learn what is new and improved about the Visual Basic language.

Inside Windows desktop apps

What *is* a Windows desktop app, actually? As noted in the preceding section, a Windows desktop app is essentially a Windows application designed to run under Windows 8.1, Windows 8, or Windows 7. These "traditional" apps present their features using *chrome,* or visible and persistent user interface elements, including a title bar, menu bar, toolbars, menu commands, buttons, dialog boxes, scroll bars, status bars, and other user interface elements. Although the design guidelines for Windows Store apps require developers to minimize or eliminate many of these traditional user interface elements (screen space is at a premium in tablets and mobile devices), Microsoft recognizes that thousands of popular Windows-based apps use these features and that customers want to run these apps now and in the future.

Windows desktop apps are also structured in different ways than Windows Store apps; they use different controls and components, make use of different features in the Windows Runtime, and have different installation and security requirements. To integrate Windows desktop apps into the Windows 8.1 operating system, Windows 8.1 provides a separate operating environment for the programs to run in and a distinctive Desktop tile on the Windows Start page to open the environment and allow for easy interaction between Windows 8.1 and the Windows desktop.

The following illustration shows the Windows version 8.1 Start page with the Desktop tile visible near the upper-left corner of the screen. (The Desktop tile contains the image of clouds and a mountain top.) Windows desktop apps run in this environment under Windows 8.1, Windows 8, or on the traditional Windows desktop in Windows 7.

Visual Basic and Windows desktop apps

Within Visual Studio 2013 Professional, Premium, and Ultimate, the Windows Forms project type provides a proven model upon which to build Windows desktop apps. Because this program type is essentially the original user interface model for Visual Basic applications, the Visual Studio IDE is well-suited to creating Windows Forms apps and offers a Windows Forms Designer and Windows Forms Toolbox that are mature, feature-rich, and easy to use.

From a technical point of view, Windows Forms is the smart-client component of the .NET Framework, a set of managed libraries that enable common application tasks such as reading and writing to the file system. In Visual Studio, a Windows Forms app is built on classes from the *System.Windows.Forms* namespace.

When you create a Windows desktop app with Windows Forms technology, you are using controls, objects, properties, and events that have been available since Visual Studio 2005 and earlier. However, because you are using the most recent version of Visual Studio, you receive the feature updates and improvements related to Windows 8.1, the .NET Framework version 4.5.1, and the extended Visual Basic programming language, which continues to evolve with each new version. As a result, you can use your existing Windows Forms programming skills to create or maintain a Windows desktop app in Visual Studio 2013, and as you support your code and add new features, you'll receive additional benefits simply by using newer technology.

You can also use Windows Presentation Foundation (WPF) for the user interface and features of your Windows desktop app in Visual Studio 2013. This mature technology (first introduced in Visual Studio 2008) allows you to create the user interface for your program by using XAML markup and efficient WPF controls. However, because using Visual Basic and WPF is similar to creating Windows Store apps with Visual Basic 2013 (especially in relation to using XAML and WPF-style controls), I will be emphasizing Windows Store app development in this book and, as an alternative, Windows Forms app development for the Windows desktop.

 Note To create a Windows desktop app in this chapter, you'll need Visual Studio 2013 Professional, Premium, or Ultimate, which includes templates for Windows desktop apps. The Microsoft Visual Studio Express 2013 for Windows application does not include support for Windows desktop apps. However, if you don't have Visual Studio 2013 Professional or Ultimate, you can download the Microsoft Visual Studio Express 2013 for Windows Desktop application for free via the Microsoft Visual Studio website (*http://www.microsoft.com/visualstudio/*). Use it to complete the exercises in this chapter and elsewhere when Windows Forms programming is discussed.

In the following sections, you'll create the Lucky Seven Windows desktop app shown in the following illustration. Although the user interface looks somewhat different in this version of the program than it did under Windows 8.1, the Visual Basic program code that drives each application is very similar. This correspondence is a fundamental emphasis of this chapter—although user interface technologies vary from platform to platform, the underlying application logic often looks very similar because it draws on the same Visual Basic language structures and vocabulary.

Creating a Windows desktop app

In this exercise, you'll start building Lucky Seven by first creating a new Windows desktop app project and then using controls in the Windows Forms Toolbox to construct the user interface.

Create a new project

1. Start Visual Studio 2013.

2. On the Visual Studio File menu, click New Project.

 Tip You can also start a new programming project by clicking the blue New Project link on the Start page.

The New Project dialog box opens, with project templates listed by category on the left side of the dialog box. As discussed in Chapter 3, the Visual Basic templates are listed by type, along with the templates for other languages, such as Visual C#, Visual C++, and JavaScript.

Near the top of the New Project dialog box, you'll also notice a drop-down list box. This feature allows you to specify the version of the Microsoft .NET Framework that your application will target. This feature is sometimes called *multitargeting*, meaning that through it you can select the target environment that your program will run on. For example, if you retain the default selection of .NET Framework 4.5.1, any computer that your application will run on must have .NET Framework 4.5.1 installed. (It would typically be a computer running Windows 8.1.) Unless you have a specific need, you can usually leave this setting the way it is. However, if you want to support earlier versions of Windows (and therefore an earlier version of the Framework), you can specify a different version.

> **Note** Visual Studio Express 2013 for Windows Desktop does not include the multitargeting list box, and the product offers a smaller selection of available templates. But you'll be just fine completing the steps in this chapter.

3. Click the Windows category under Visual Basic in the Templates area of the dialog box.

The New Project dialog box looks like this:

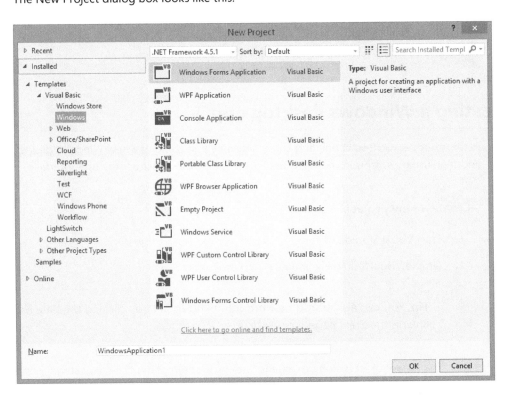

4. Click the Windows Forms Application item in the central Templates area of the dialog box, if it is not already selected.

   Visual Studio prepares the development environment for your Visual Basic Windows desktop app.

5. In the Name text box, type **MyLuckySevenWF**.

   Visual Studio assigns the name MyLuckySevenWF to your project. (You'll specify a folder location for the project later.) As noted in Chapter 3, I'm recommending the "My" prefix here so that you don't confuse your new application with the LuckySevenWF project I've created for you on disk.

   I've added the "WF" suffix to the project name to indicate "Windows Forms" for clarity. (However, Windows Forms apps don't need any special naming scheme.)

6. Click OK to create the new project in Visual Studio.

   Visual Studio cleans the slate for a new programming project and displays a blank Windows form in the Designer that you can use to build your user interface.

Now you'll enlarge the form and create two buttons in the interface.

Create the user interface

1. Point to the lower-right corner of the form in the Designer until the mouse pointer changes to a resizing pointer, and then drag to increase the size of the form to make room for the objects in your program.

   As you resize the form, scroll bars might appear in the Designer to give you access to the entire form you're creating. Depending on your screen resolution and the Visual Studio tools you have open, you might not be able to see the entire form at once.

   Size your form so that it is about the size of the form shown in the following illustration. If you want to match my example exactly, you can use the width and height dimensions (560 pixels × 375 pixels) shown in the lower-right corner of the screen.

   To see the entire form without obstruction, you can resize or close the other programming tools, as you learned in Chapter 2, "The Visual Studio Integrated Development Environment." (Return to Chapter 2 if you have questions about resizing windows or tools.)

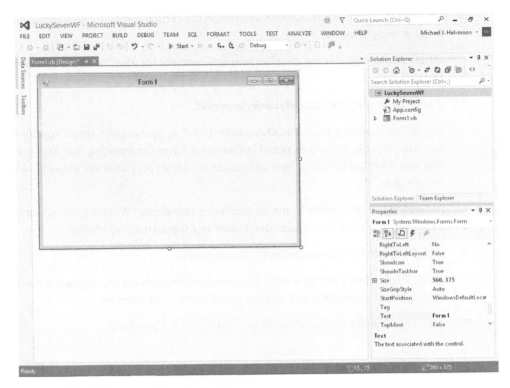

Now you'll add a button object to the form.

2. Click the Toolbox tab to display the Windows Forms Toolbox window in the IDE.

This Toolbox contains different controls than the ones that you used in Chapter 3. Rather than controls for Windows Store apps, this Toolbox contains controls for Windows Forms apps. Not only are the items named differently, they have different underlying properties and events. The Windows Forms controls are organized by category, and there are several controls visible—a testament to how long this style of programming has been around.

3. In the All Windows Forms category, double-click the *Button* control in the Toolbox, and then move the mouse pointer away from the Toolbox.

Visual Studio creates a default-sized button object on the form and hides the Toolbox, as shown here:

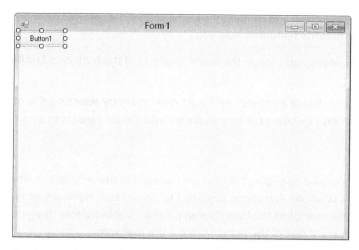

The button is named *Button1* because it is the first button in the program. The new button is selected and enclosed by resize handles. When Visual Basic is in *design mode* (that is, when you are creating a program and not executing it), you can move objects on the form by dragging them with the mouse, and you can resize them by using the resize handles. However, while a program is running, the user can't move user interface elements unless you've changed a property in the program to allow this.

4. Using the Properties window, change the *Name* property of the button object to **SpinButton**.

The *Name* property is listed near the top of the Properties window. Giving each object a name in your user interface will make the objects more recognizable in program code. As noted in Chapter 3, I recommend including the name of the control in the object name if you have the space for it.

Now you'll add a second button to the form, below the first button.

Add a second button

1. Click the Toolbox tab to display the Toolbox.

2. Click the *Button* control in the Toolbox (single-click this time), and then move the mouse pointer over the form.

The mouse pointer changes to crosshairs and a button icon. The crosshairs are designed to help you draw the rectangular shape of the button on the form, and you can use this method as an alternative to double-clicking to create a control of the default size.

3. Click and drag the pointer down and to the right. Release the mouse button to complete the button.

4. Resize the button object so that it is the same size as the first button.

5. Move the two buttons down and to the right a little so that they are not right on the edge of the form. (Use the snapline feature to help you.)

6. Use the Properties window to change the Name property of the button to **EndButton**.

> **Tip** At any time, you can delete an object and start over again by selecting the object on the form and then pressing Delete. Feel free to create and delete objects to practice creating your user interface.

Now you'll add the labels used to display the random numbers in the program. A *label* is a special user interface element in a Windows Forms app designed to display text, numbers, or symbols when the program runs. When the user clicks the Lucky Seven program's Spin button, three random numbers appear in the label boxes. If one of the numbers is a 7, the user wins.

Add the number labels

1. Double-click the *Label* control in the Toolbox.

   Visual Studio creates a label object on the form. The label object is just large enough to hold the text contained in the object (it is rather small now), but it can be resized.

2. Drag the *Label1* object to the right of the two button objects.

   Your form looks something like this (note also the position of the two buttons):

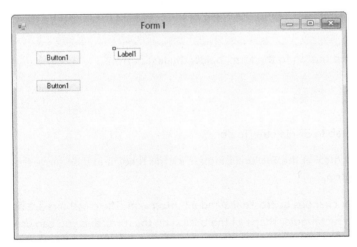

3. Double-click the *Label* control in the Toolbox to create a second label object.

   This label object will be named *Label2* in the program.

4. Double-click the *Label* control again to create a third label object.

5. Move the second and third label objects to the right of the first one on the form.

   Allow plenty of space between the three labels because you will use them to display large numbers when the program runs.

   Now you'll use the *Label* control to add a descriptive label to your form. This will be the fourth and final label in the program.

6. Double-click the *Label* control in the Toolbox.

7. Drag the *Label4* object below the two command buttons.

   When you've finished, your four labels should look like those in the following screen shot. (You can move your label objects if they don't look quite right.)

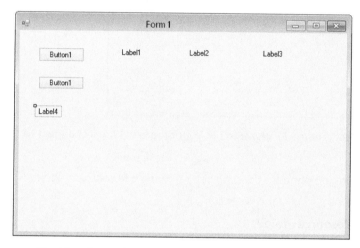

Now you'll add a picture box to the form to graphically display the payout you'll receive when you draw a 7 and hit the jackpot. A *picture box* is designed to display bitmaps, icons, digital photos, and other artwork in a Windows Forms program. One of the best uses for a picture box is to display a JPEG image file. You'll use the same image that you used in Chapter 3—a photo of coins from around the world on a dark background.

Add a picture

1. Click the *PictureBox* control in the Toolbox.

   The *PictureBox* control has been a part of the Windows Forms Toolbox since Visual Basic version 1. However, recall that when you created the Windows Store app in Chapter 3, you used the *Image* control to display the photo on the page. As you switch back and forth between the two toolboxes, keep in mind that you'll be using different controls and that these controls contain different property settings and respond to different events.

2. With the *PictureBox* control selected, use the pointer to create a large rectangular box below the second and third labels on the form.

   Leave a little space below the labels for their size to grow. When you've finished, your picture box object looks similar to this:

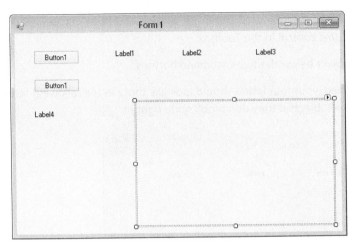

   Currently, the object is named *PictureBox1* in your program. (You'll change it to *CoinImage* later.)

Now you'll add the Coins.jpg photo to the project by creating a Resources folder.

Add a photo to the Resources folder

1. If Solution Explorer is not visible now, open it by clicking Solution Explorer on the View menu.

   As you've already learned, Solution Explorer provides access to most of the files in your project. In Chapter 3, you practiced using the Assets folder in a Windows Store project to customize your project's logo, splash screen, and other files. However, the Assets folder is something unique to Windows Store apps; it is not supplied by default in a Windows desktop app. Instead, you can create a Resources folder in Solution Explorer, which lets you access important files and store them with the project.

   The easiest way to create a Resources folder now is to use the smart tag provided by the picture box object.

2. Select the picture box object on the form if it is not selected already.

   If you look carefully at the picture box's border now, you'll notice a tiny shortcut arrow called a *smart tag* near its upper-right corner. A smart tag is a context-sensitive button that you can use to quickly change common settings.

3. Click the smart tag in the picture box object to display the shortcut menu of commands.

4. Click Choose Image to display the Select Resource dialog box.

5. Click Project Resource File, and then click the Import button to create a new Resources folder and place a file in the folder.

6. Double-click Coins.jpg in the My Documents\Visual Basic 2013 SBS\Chapter 04 folder.

   Visual Studio inserts the file, and it appears in the Select Resource dialog box, as shown in the following illustration:

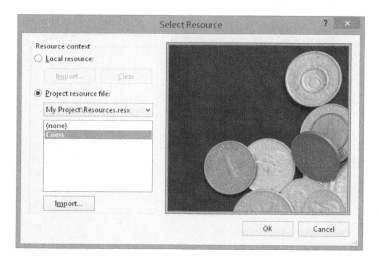

After an image or file has been added to a project, it becomes part of the application that you are working on, and it can be referenced via the Solution Explorer and Properties window. It is also gathered in as part of the application when the final project is compiled for distribution—obviating the need to track the file or recall where the file was originally located on your hard disk.

7. Click OK.

   In Solution Explorer a Resources folder now appears with the file Coins.jpg in it.

8. In the Picture Box Tasks menu, click Stretch Image in the Size Mode list box.

   A photo of coins from around the world fills the picture box object in the Designer.

9. Adjust the spacing of the image so that it takes up much of the right side of the form in the Designer.

Your screen should look like this (notice especially the Resources folder in Solution Explorer).

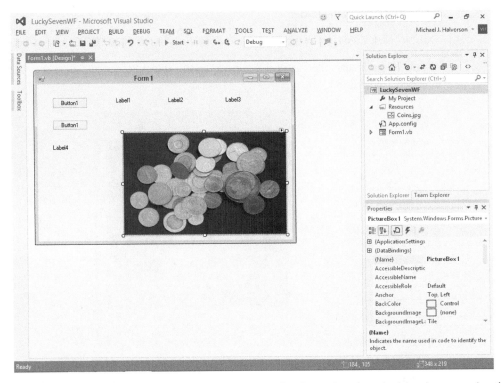

Now you'll add a sound file to the Resources folder so that it can be played when the user wins the game. This time, you'll add the resource by using the Visual Studio Project Properties Designer.

Add a .wav file to the Resources folder

1. Click the LuckySevenWF Properties command on the Project menu.

   The Project Properties Designer appears in the IDE with project settings for twelve categories.

2. Click the Resources category.

   The Coins.jpg file appears in the Designer. In the upper-left corner of the Designer is a drop-down list box containing six resource categories, and currently Images is specified. Rather than list all of the project resources together, the six categories give you a chance to organize your project assets.

3. Click the Audio category in the drop-down list box.

   The list is currently empty. Now you'll add the ArcadeRiff.wav file to the project. This is the same electronic music file that you used in Chapter 3 to play an electronic arcade sound effect.

4. Click the drop-down arrow next to the Add Resource command, and then click Add Existing File.

5. Browse to the My Documents\Visual Basic 2013 SBS\Chapter 04 folder, click the ArcadeRiff.wav file, and then click Open.

    The ArcadeRiff.wav file appears in the Resources window and is now ready for use in the program. You'll reference this resource later when you write your event handler code.

6. Click the Save All button on the Standard toolbar.

7. Specify My Documents\Visual Basic 2013 SBS\Chapter 04 for the location, and then click Save.

8. Click Yes To All if you are prompted to save or reload the project after the inclusion of the new resources.

9. Close the Project Properties Designer.

Now you're ready to further customize the program's user interface by setting some more properties.

Setting properties

As you reviewed in Chapters 2 and 3, you can change an object's properties by selecting the object on the page (or the form) and then setting properties in the Properties window. You'll do this now in your Windows desktop app by changing settings for the two buttons on the form.

Set the button properties

1. Click the first button (SpinButton) on the form.

    The button is selected and is surrounded by resize handles.

2. At the top of the Properties window, click the Categorized button.

3. Resize the Properties window (if necessary) so that there is plenty of room to see the property names and their current settings.

    These properties include settings for the background color, text, font height, and width of the button. Your Properties window should look something like this:

4. If it is not already visible, scroll in the Properties window until you see the *Text* property located in the Appearance category.

5. Double-click the *Text* property in the first column of the Properties window.

    The current *Text* setting ("Button1") is highlighted in the Properties window.

6. Type **Spin**, and then press Enter.

    The *Text* property changes to "Spin" in the Properties window and on the button on the form. Now you'll change the *Text* property of the second button to "End."

7. Open the Object list at the top of the Properties window.

    A list of the interface objects in your program appears in a drop-down list box.

8. Click EndButton (the second button) in the list box.

    The property settings for the second button appear in the Properties window, and Visual Studio highlights the button on the form.

9. Delete the contents of the *Text* property, type **End**, and press Enter.

    The text of the second button changes to "End."

> **Tip** Using the Object list is a handy way to switch between objects in your program. You can also switch between objects on the form by clicking each object.

Now you'll set the properties for the labels in the program. The first three labels will hold the random numbers generated by the program and will have identical property settings. (You'll set most of them as a group.) The descriptive label settings will be slightly different.

Set the number label properties

1. Click the first number label (*Label1*), hold down the Shift key, click the second and third number labels, and then release the Shift key. (If the Properties window is in the way, move it to a new place.)

   A selection rectangle and resize handles appear around each label you click. You'll change the *TextAlign, BorderStyle,* and *Font* properties now so that the numbers that will appear in the labels will be centered, boxed, and identical in font and font size. (All these properties are located in the Appearance category of the Properties window.) You'll also set the *AutoSize* property to False so that you can change the size of the labels according to your precise specifications. (The *AutoSize* property is located in the Layout category.)

> **Note** When more than one object is selected, only those properties that can be changed for the group are displayed in the Properties window.

2. Click the *AutoSize* property in the Properties window, and then click the arrow that appears in the second column.

3. Set the *AutoSize* property to False so that you can size the labels manually.

4. Click the *TextAlign* property, and then click the arrow that appears in the second column.

   A graphical assortment of alignment options appears in the list box; you can use these settings to align text anywhere within the borders of the label object.

5. Click the center option (MiddleCenter).

   The *TextAlign* property for each of the selected labels changes to MiddleCenter.

6. Click the *BorderStyle* property, and then click the arrow that appears in the second column.

   The valid property settings (None, FixedSingle, and Fixed3D) appear in the list box.

7. Click FixedSingle in the list box to add a thin border around each label.

8. Click the *Font* property, and then click the ellipsis button (the button with three dots that's located next to the current font setting).

   The Font dialog box opens.

9. Change the font to Segue UI, the font style to SemiBold, and the font size to 24, and then click OK.

   The label text appears in the font, style, and size you specified.

   Now you'll set the text for the three labels to the number 0—a good "placeholder" for the numbers that will eventually fill these boxes in your game. (Because the program produces the actual numbers, you could also delete the text, but putting a placeholder here gives you something to base the size of the labels on.)

10. Click a blank area on the form to remove the selection from the three labels, and then click the first label.

11. Double-click the *Text* property, type **0**, and then press Enter.

    The text of the *Label1* object is set to 0. You'll use program code to set this property to a random "slot machine" number later in this chapter.

12. Change the text in the second and third labels on the form to **0** also.

13. Resize the three labels so that you can see the number 0 in each label.

14. Move and adjust the final spacing among the labels so that they look proportional.

    Your form should now look something like this:

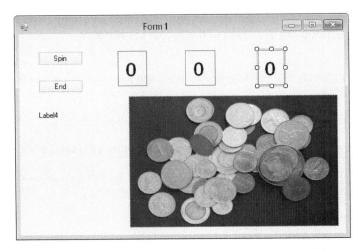

Now you'll change the *Text, Font,* and *ForeColor* properties of the fourth label.

Set the descriptive label properties

1. Click the fourth label object (*Label4*) on the form.

2. Change the *Text* property in the Properties window to **Lucky Seven**.

3. Click the *Font* property, and then click the ellipsis button.

4. Use the Font dialog box to change the font to Segoe UI, the font style to SemiBold, and the font size to 18. Then click OK.

    The font in the *Label4* object is updated, and the label is resized automatically to hold the larger font size because the object's *AutoSize* property is set to True.

5. Click the *ForeColor* property in the Properties window.

6. Type **DarkRed** in the *ForeColor* property, and then press Enter.

   Visual Studio changes the color of the Lucky Seven label (*Label4*) to DarkRed (139,0,0), which is the same color you used in the Lucky Seven Windows Store app in Chapter 3.

Now you'll change the *Text* property for the form so that "Lucky Seven" appears on the app's title bar.

Set the form's title bar text

1. Click the form in the Designer (not any specific object on the form).

2. In the Properties window, change the *Text* property to **Lucky Seven** and press Enter.

   Your form now looks like this:

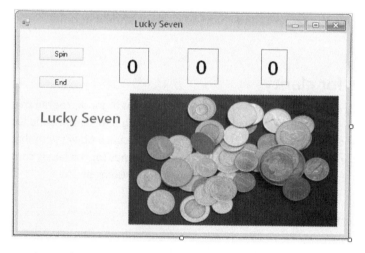

Now you're ready to set the properties for *PictureBox1*, the last object on the form.

The picture box properties

When the person playing your game hits the jackpot (that is, when at least one 7 appears in the number labels on the form), the picture box object will display an image (in .jpg format) of coins from around the world. I have supplied you with this digitized image in the book's sample files, but you can substitute your own image if you like.

Earlier in this chapter, you set the *SizeMode* property of the *PictureBox1* object to accurately position the picture in the frame, and you set the *Image* property to indicate the name of the JPEG file that you are displaying on the form. Now you need to set the *Visible* property, which specifies the picture state when the app starts running. (You don't always need to make objects visible on the form; as this app runs, you will toggle the image between visible and invisible settings, based on the numbers displayed.)

Set the *Visible* picture box property

1. Click the picture box object on the form.

2. Click the *Visible* property in the Behavior category of the Properties window, and then click the arrow in the second column.

   The valid settings for the *Visible* property appear in a list box.

3. Click False to make the coins image invisible when the program starts.

   Setting the *Visible* property to False affects the picture box when the program runs but not now, while you're designing it.

> **Tip** You can also double-click property names that have True and False settings (so-called Boolean properties), to toggle back and forth between True and False. Default Boolean properties are shown in regular type, and changed settings appear in bold.

Naming objects for clarity

Earlier in this chapter, you named the button objects on the form as a good programming practice. I recommend that you name all of the objects that you will be using in program code to avoid any confusion. You can name objects by setting the *Name* property for each object with the Properties window. In the following exercise, you'll add a few more object names for the labels containing lucky numbers. You'll also name the picture box object that contains the Coins photo.

Set the *Name* property

1. Click the *Label1* object on the form (the first lucky number window), and then change the object's *Name* property to **FirstNum**.

   You might want to list the property settings alphabetically so that the *Name* property appears near the top of the list.

2. Click the *Label2* object on the form (the second lucky number window), and then change the object's *Name* property to **SecondNum**.

3. Click the *Label3* object on the form, and then change the object's *Name* property to **ThirdNum**.

4. Click the *PictureBox1* object on the form, and then change the picture box's *Name* property to **CoinImage**.

5. You are finished setting properties for now, so if your Properties window is floating, hold down the Ctrl key and double-click its title bar to return it to the docked position.

Writing the code

Now you're ready to write the code for the Lucky Seven Windows desktop app. As you learned in Chapter 3, you enter and edit Visual Basic code by using the Code Editor. Although the controls used to create the user interface for this Windows Form app are different than the ones you used to create a Windows Store app, the program code is much the same. This is because the underlying Visual Basic programming language is identical between the two platforms. The only differences you'll encounter will be the names of objects and properties and, occasionally, the classes that you use in the .NET Framework. The core Visual Basic language elements are essentially the same.

Complete the following steps to enter the Lucky Seven Windows desktop app code using the Code Editor.

Use the Code Editor

1. Double-click the End button on the form.

   The Code Editor appears as a tabbed document window in the center of the Visual Studio IDE, as shown here:

   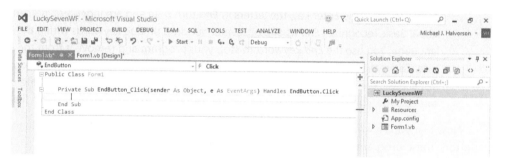

   Inside the Code Editor are program statements associated with the current form. Program statements in a Windows Forms app are always grouped in one or more procedures. There are three types of procedures that you'll see in Visual Basic code: *Sub* procedures, *Function* procedures, and *Property* procedures.

   EndButton_Click is a *Sub* procedure that is being declared to handle the event that occurs when the user clicks the End button in the program. This *Sub* procedure begins with the *Sub* keyword and concludes with the *End Sub* keywords.

   In the Windows Forms paradigm, such a procedure is also called an *event handler*. This particular handler is executed when the *Click* event takes place (or fires), but no value is returned to the calling routine by the procedure. (*Function* and *Property* procedures often do return values, as you'll see later in the book.)

When you double-clicked the End button in the IDE, Visual Studio automatically added the first and last lines of the *EndButton_Click* event handler and associated those lines with the button's *Click* event, as the following code shows. You might notice other bits of code in the Code Editor (words like *Public* and *Class*), which Visual Studio has added to define important characteristics of the form. I will describe them more fully later.

```
Private Sub EndButton_Click(sender As Object, e As EventArgs) Handles Button2.Click

End Sub
```

The body of a procedure fits between the preceding lines and is executed whenever a user triggers the action associated with the event handler. In this case, the event is a mouse click, but it could also be a different type of event.

2. Type **End**, and then press the Enter key.

   Visual Studio recognizes *End* as a unique reserved word or *keyword* and displays it in a list box with Common and All tabs. Microsoft calls this interactive assistance feature *IntelliSense* because it tries to intelligently help you write code, and you can browse through various Visual Basic keywords and objects alphabetically. (In this way, the language is partially discoverable through the IDE itself.)

   After you press the Enter key, the letters in *End* turn blue and are indented, indicating that Visual Basic recognizes *End* as one of several hundred unique keywords within the Visual Basic language. You use the *End* keyword to stop your program and remove it from the screen. In this case, *End* is also a complete program statement, a self-contained instruction recognized by the Visual Basic compiler, the part of Visual Studio that processes, or *parses,* each line of Visual Basic source code, combining the result with other resources to create an executable file.

Now that you've written the code associated with the End button, you'll write code for the Spin button. These program statements will be a little more extensive.

Write code for the Spin button

1. Click the Form1.vb [Design] tab near the top of the Code Editor to display the form again.

   When the Code Editor is visible, you won't be able to see the form you're working on. However, it is easy to switch back and forth between the Windows Forms designer and the Code Editor by clicking the tabs near the top of each window.

2. Double-click the Spin button on the form.

   The Code Editor appears, and an event handler associated with the Spin button appears.

   Although you changed the text of this button to "Spin," recall that its name in the program is *SpinButton*. The *SpinButton_Click* event handler executes each time that the user clicks the Spin button.

3. Type the following program lines between the *Private Sub* and *End Sub* statements. Press Enter after each line, and press Tab to indent. As you enter the program code, the IDE formats the text and displays different parts of the program in color to help you identify the various elements.

```
Dim generator As New Random
CoinImage.Visible = False

FirstNum.Text = generator.Next(0, 9)
SecondNum.Text = generator.Next(0, 9)
ThirdNum.Text = generator.Next(0, 9)

If (FirstNum.Text = "7") Or (SecondNum.Text = "7") Or
    (ThirdNum.Text = "7") Then
    CoinImage.Visible = True
    My.Computer.Audio.Play(My.Resources.ArcadeRiff, AudioPlayMode.Background)
End If
```

When you've finished, the Code Editor looks as shown in the following screen shot:

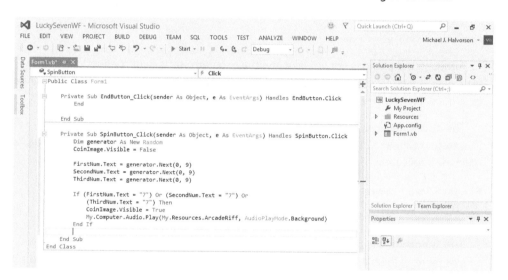

4. Click the Save All command on the File menu to save your additions to the program.

Behind the scenes in the *SpinButton_Click* event handler

The *SpinButton_Click* event handler is executed when the user clicks the Spin button on the form. The *Handles* keyword in the first line of the *Sub* procedure is the statement that links the button on the form to the event handler.

The work this routine does is very similar to the Visual Basic code you used in Chapter 3 to drive the Lucky Seven game designed for the Windows Store. Essentially, the event handler performs four main tasks:

1. It declares a random number generator named *Random* in the program.

2. It hides the digital photo of coins.

3. It creates three random numbers and displays them in text block objects.

4. It displays the Coins photo and plays music when the number 7 appears.

As you've learned, the random number generator is initialized by the following statement:

```
Dim generator As New Random
```

This line declares a random number generator that can be used to calculate single digits that follow no particular numeric pattern. The *generator* identifier is used later in the procedure.

Hiding the photo is accomplished by the following line:

```
CoinImage.Visible = False
```

Although the photo is not visible when the program starts (you changed the image's *Visible* property in an earlier exercise to accomplish this), this line of code handles the situation when the user has won the game and needs to have the image hidden again.

The next three lines handle the random number computations. The *generator* object in each line is used to create a random number between 0 and 9—just what you need for this particular slot machine application. These lines are identical to the code in Chapter 3.

```
FirstNum.Text = generator.Next(0, 9)
SecondNum.Text = generator.Next(0, 9)
ThirdNum.Text = generator.Next(0, 9)
```

The last group of statements in the program checks whether any of the random numbers is 7. If one or more of them is, the program displays the graphical depiction of a payout and plays an electronic arcade sound to announce the winnings.

```
If (FirstNum.Text = "7") Or (SecondNum.Text = "7") Or
    (ThirdNum.Text = "7") Then
    CoinImage.Visible = True
    My.Computer.Audio.Play(My.Resources.ArcadeRiff, AudioPlayMode.Background)
End If
```

The sound is created by the same .wav audio file that you used in Chapter 3. However, because there is no *MediaElement* control in the Windows Forms Toolbox, I've played the sound using the *My.Computer.Audio* object provided by the .NET Framework. This object offers the *Play* method, which I've used to play a sound resource in the project's Resources folder. The *AudioPlayMode.Background* property used in the call to the *Play* method rings the sound in the background while the program does its work.

Each time that the user clicks the Spin button, the *SpinButton_Click* event handler is executed, or *called*, and the program statements in the procedure are run again.

Running the Lucky Seven desktop app

Perfect—you're ready to run your new Windows desktop app. As you learned in Chapter 2, you can run an application by clicking the Start button on the Standard toolbar.

Follow these steps to run—and more importantly, *test*—the MyLuckySevenWF program.

> **Note** If you didn't build the MyLuckySevenWF project from scratch or if you want to compare what you created to what I built for you, take a moment now to open and run the completed LuckySevenWF project, which is located in the My Documents\Visual Basic 2013 SBS\Chapter 04 folder on your hard disk (the default location for the practice files for this chapter).

Run the LuckySevenWF program

1. Click the Start button on the Standard toolbar.

   The Lucky Seven program compiles and runs. After a few seconds, the user interface appears, just as you designed it.

2. Click the Spin button several times until you draw one or more 7s.

   Each time that you click Spin, the program picks three random numbers and displays them in labels on the form. When you win, your screen will look something like this:

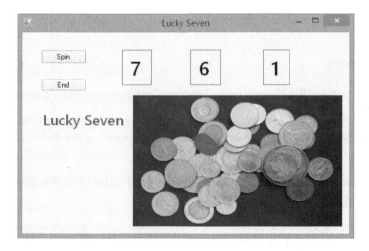

Because a 7 appears in the first label box, the digital photo depicting the payoff appears, and the computer plays an arcade sound. You win!

3. Click the Spin button a dozen or more times, watching the results of the spins in the number boxes.

This is the time to give the program some careful attention. Is the program working correctly? Does the sound effect work correctly every time? Does the coin image always go away when you spin again? Do the numbers always look right—and does the spinning pattern look *random*—in the spinner windows?

It seems like about half of the time that you spin, you will hit the jackpot. However, in mathematical terms, the odds are not actually that good. The actual probability of a win is about 2.8 times out of 10.

4. When you've finished experimenting with your new creation, click the End button.

The Windows desktop app stops, and the IDE reappears on your screen.

Building an executable file

Your last task in this chapter is to complete the development process and create a final Windows desktop app for your computer. Windows desktop apps created with Visual Studio 2013 have the file name extension .exe and can be run on any system that contains Windows and the necessary support files. One of the crucial system libraries that Visual Studio programs need is the .NET Framework. However, this is present on virtually all Windows 8.1, Windows 8, and Windows 7 installations.

As you learned in Chapter 3, you can create two types of executable files for your project at this point: a debug build or a release build. The Solution Configurations drop-down list box on the Standard Visual Studio toolbar indicates whether the executable is a debug build or a release build.

Try creating a release build named LuckySevenWF.exe now.

Create an executable file

1. On the Standard toolbar, click Release in the Solution Configurations drop-down list box.

This will prepare Visual Studio to create a release build of your Windows desktop app that does not contain debugging information. The build will be stored in the Bin\Release folder for your project.

2. On the Build menu, click the Build LuckySevenWF command. (Your project might have the "My" prefix in front of the project name.)

The Build command compiles the source code in your project. The result is an executable file of the Windows desktop app type named LuckySevenWF.exe.

Now try running this program outside the Visual Studio IDE within the Windows desktop. (The next command depends on the version of Windows you're using.)

3. If you have Windows 8 or Windows 8.1, click the Search charm, type **run** in the Search (apps) text box, and Press Enter to open the Run dialog box.

   If you have Windows 7 or Windows Vista, type **run** in the Search text box and press Enter to open the Run dialog box.

4. Click Browse, and then navigate to the My Documents\Visual Basic 2013 SBS\Chapter 04\MyLuckySevenWF\Bin\Release folder.

5. Click the MyLuckySevenWF.exe application icon, click Open, and then click OK.

   The LuckySevenWF program loads and runs in the Windows desktop area.

   Because this is a simple test application and it does not possess a formal publisher certificate that emphasizes its reliability or authenticity, you might see the following message: "The publisher could not be verified. Are you sure you want to run this software?"

   If this happens, click Yes to run the program anyway. (Creating such certificates is beyond the scope of this chapter, but this program is quite safe—unless you spend a lot of time gambling!)

6. Click Spin a few times to verify the operation of the game, and then click End.

 Tip You can also run Windows-based applications, including compiled Visual Basic programs, by opening Windows Explorer and double-clicking the executable file.

Publishing a Windows desktop app

As you learned in Chapter 3, a Windows Store app is designed to be sold and distributed online via the Windows Store. Although Windows desktop apps cannot currently be distributed in this manner, it is simple to distribute or *publish* a Windows desktop app using ClickOnce Security and Deployment. ClickOnce assembles your project files into a package that can be located on a web server, a file share, the local computer (your PC or laptop), or removable media such as a CD-ROM or DVD-ROM.

Complete the following steps to publish a Windows desktop app. (Publish the MyLuckySevenWF project now, or keep these steps handy for future reference.)

Publish with ClickOnce deployment

1. Click the *ProjectName* Properties command (LuckySevenWF or other) on the Project menu.

   The Project Properties Designer opens, with its many tabs and options related to the application and its features.

2. Click the Publish tab, where you'll see a list of deployment options like those shown on the following screen:

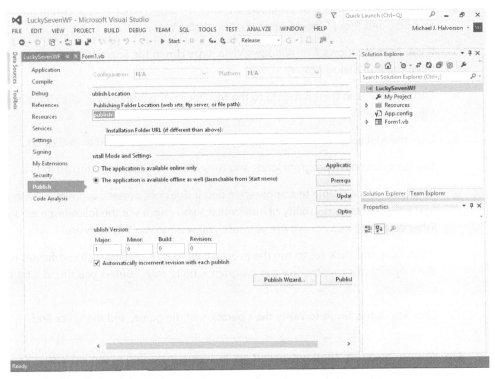

3. In the Publishing Folder Location text box, specify the name of a web server, file server, or path name to a location on your local computer where you would like to place the setup package that Visual Studio will create for you.

Note This is not the location for the final, installed application; it is the location for the setup files that your user will use to install the new Windows desktop app. That is, you are specifying here a location for users to get the setup package that they need. (For this reason, a web server makes a lot of sense.)

4. Optionally, click the ellipses box next to the Publishing Folder Location text box if you want to browse to the deployment location.

   If you click this helpful tool, the Open Web Site dialog box appears, which lets you browse to a folder in your computer's file system, an Internet Information Services (IIS) location, an FTP site, or another web location.

   Alternatively, you can click the Publish Wizard button, and a wizard will step you through a series of questions about what you want to deploy and where you want to deploy it.

5. When you're finished, click the Publish Now button at the bottom of the properties page.

6. Visual Studio will copy a convenient setup package for the application to the location you specified. The user can then install the application on their system.

 Tip To learn more about security considerations and deploying Windows desktop applications, click the Security tab on the Project Properties Designer. You can learn about security issues and adjust security settings as appropriate for your application.

Congratulations! You've created a Windows desktop app from scratch by using Windows Forms and Visual Basic. Save your changes now, and exit Visual Studio.

7. Click the Save All button on the Standard toolbar to save your changes.

8. Close the project properties page by clicking the X on the page's tab.

9. On the File menu, click Exit to close Visual Studio and the LuckySevenWF project.

The Visual Studio development environment closes.

Summary

This chapter describes how to build a Windows desktop app named LuckySevenWF, using Visual Basic and the Windows Forms programming model. The development process is similar to what you accomplished in Chapter 3 with the Windows Store programming model, and the same program (a lucky number arcade game) was deliberately chosen so that you could compare and contrast the two methods of creating a Visual Basic 2013 application.

Windows Forms continues to be an important technology for writing Windows-based applications with Visual Basic. There is a substantial code base in the marketplace that was created using Windows Forms, and in addition to the practical necessities of maintaining this code, the Windows Forms Designer and Toolbox are easy to use and mature in ways that the Windows Presentation Foundation and Windows Store App tools currently are not.

In this chapter, you worked with the *Button*, *Label*, and *PictureBox* controls and customized them on a form using original artwork and property settings. You learned how to write program code in the Code Editor and how to publish an application using ClickOnce Security and Deployment. In Chapter 6, "Working with Windows Forms controls," you will learn more about Windows Forms Toolbox controls and many essential features for Windows desktop apps, including menus and toolbars.

The major limitation of Windows Forms is that its graphics routines are somewhat slower than equivalent WPF and Windows Store apps, and Windows Forms does not fully support the redesigned Windows 8 and Windows 8.1 operating systems. The advantage of these platforms consists in security, reliability, broader support for touch-based devices, and, of course, a new user interface. We are simply in an era of transition, and professional Visual Basic programmers will need to acquire skills worthy of the terrain we currently find ourselves in. This means learning more than one development platform and finding creative ways to migrate code from model to model.

Fortunately, Visual Studio makes this dynamic interchange more than possible. In fact, as Chapter 3 and this chapter have demonstrated, you can build two user interfaces with different tools and still maintain the same application logic in Visual Basic code. I will continue to emphasize this similarity throughout the book, extending the Visual Basic language parallels to web-based (HTML) apps and Windows Phone 8 apps.

In the next chapter, you'll return to Windows Store development and some of the essential controls in the Windows Store Toolbox.

PART II

Designing the user interface

CHAPTER 5

Working with Windows Store app controls

After completing this chapter, you will be able to

- Use the *TextBox* control to manage text input tasks.

- Use the *FlipView* control to display a series of images or photos.

- Use the *MediaElement* control to play entertainment media.

- Use the *WebView* control to display live web content.

You create the user interface for your Windows Store app by using Toolbox controls such as *Image*, *ListBox*, *WebView*, and *DatePicker*. In Chapter 3, "Creating your First Windows Store application," you learned the basics of using the *Button*, *TextBlock*, and *Image* controls, and you reviewed how to adjust property settings and build event handlers. In this chapter, you'll learn to use four additional Windows Store app controls. The process will deepen your understanding of the Windows 8.1 user interface and help you establish a foundation for your own programs.

First, you'll learn how to use the *TextBox* control to gather lines and paragraphs of textual input from the user, store them in variables, check spelling, and process the text in interesting ways. Next, you'll use the *FlipView* control to display a collection of graphical images on the screen, which you can easily navigate through by using touch input or mouse clicks. Because audio and video content make Windows Store apps fun to use, you'll learn more about using the *MediaElement* control to play entertainment media. Finally, you'll learn to use the *WebView* control to display content from one or more webpages on the surface of your app.

Tip In addition to this chapter and the exercises in later chapters, you can learn much more about essential Windows Store app controls in my companion book *Start Here! Learn Microsoft Visual Basic 2012* (Microsoft Press, 2012). For example, in that book, in Chapter 3, "Using Controls," I describe how to use the *Ellipse*, *TextBlock*, *CheckBox*, and *RadioButton* controls. In Chapter 4, "Designing Windows 8 Applications with Blend for Visual Studio," I demonstrate how to use Blend to add controls to a page and customize them with animation effects.

Understanding Windows Store app controls

Windows Store app controls are interactive elements that a developer can place on the surface of a Windows 8.1 app to communicate with the user or manage essential tasks, such as displaying text or images, launching a video, or browsing a website. Like other programmable controls, Windows Store app controls typically have the ability to be selected or to *receive the focus* while a program is running, and they are manipulated by the familiar input mechanisms of the Windows 8.1 operating system, such as mouse, keyboard, stylus, touch, and gestures.

All Windows Store app controls come from the *Windows.UI.Xaml.Controls* namespace, a hierarchical library of classes that provides a unique definition and list of programmable features for each control. Many of the Windows Store app controls share common attributes and capabilities, and in this way, they work together to enable the rich user experience that is at the heart of Windows 8.1.

When you create a new Windows Store app in Visual Studio 2013, the IDE automatically loads a collection of Windows Store app controls (also called *XAML controls*) into the Toolbox, and organizes them by category. When you use one of these controls to create an object in your application, you are creating a specific *instance* of the control definition on the page within your program. Each instance of the control is unique, so it maintains its own name, content, size, shape, event handlers, and other defining characteristics.

For example, if you use the *Button* control in the Toolbox to create three button objects on a page in your Windows Store app, each button object will have its own name, dimensions, and programmable functionality. Although these buttons inherit their default characteristics from the *Windows.UI.Xaml.Controls.Button* class, you can customize each object individually in the program. This is one of the core features and advantages of object-oriented programming with Visual Studio and Visual Basic. Another useful feature is that you can share event handlers among controls.

Roots in Windows Presentation Foundation and XAML

Windows Store app controls have their roots in Windows Presentation Foundation (WPF) controls and Extensible Application Markup Language (XAML), an XML-based language used to define and link various elements in the user interface of a Windows-based application. WPF was added to the Visual Studio 2008 product as an option for rendering user interfaces, and since 2008 it has supplied a popular alternative to the Windows Forms programming model. At that time, Microsoft also introduced a rudimentary WPF Designer and a Toolbox with XAML controls into the Visual Studio IDE.

Although the original WPF Designer and Toolbox were somewhat limited, over time the Visual Studio components related to WPF have improved. A number of Visual Basic programmers who have wanted to add cutting-edge graphics, video, and animation features to their applications have used WPF to prepare applications for the .NET platform. (In fact, WPF was especially designed to support DirectX, a hardware-accelerated graphics API that is often used in cutting-edge computer games.)

Microsoft also used a subset of WPF to create Microsoft Silverlight, an application framework for creating Internet applications that is similar in some ways to Adobe Flash. The Silverlight framework is also associated with Windows Phone development, although in Windows Phone 8 the term Silverlight is no longer used. However, when you write Windows Phone applications, you still use an optimized version of XAML controls for the Phone user interface. Windows Phone programming is covered more fully in Chapter 20, "Introduction to Windows Phone 8 development," and Chapter 21, "Creating your first Windows Phone 8 application."

Designing for Windows 8.1

When Microsoft planned the release of Windows 8, an ambitious new operating system designed to operate on a very broad spectrum of devices, they chose to base user interface development on XAML-style controls, including the controls used in WPF and Windows Phone applications. Accordingly, many of the Windows Store app controls have the same names as WPF controls, and controls in the two platforms also share many of the same properties and events. In addition, there are some controls (such as *ProgressRing*) that support the unique features of the Windows 8 and Windows 8.1 user interface.

Windows Store app controls continue to support high-performance graphics cards and animation features, and they also use XAML markup to build the user interface so that it can be customized for different platforms and devices. In this way, Windows 8.1 and Visual Studio 2013 have carried forward earlier technologies (WPF, Silverlight, and Windows Forms) and combined them in new ways to support advancements in user interface design, connectivity, and security. On the Windows 8.1 platform, Visual Studio 2013 adds support for the *CommandBar* and *Flyout* controls in Windows Store apps, which are discussed in Chapter 9, "Exploring Windows 8.1 design features: Command bar, flyout, tiles, and touch."

If you have previous experience using WPF or Silverlight controls, this chapter will show you how some of the essential controls have changed. You'll also see how the features of Windows 8.1 have been integrated into the controls and how they have been modified for applications that will be sold in the Windows Store.

If you have previous experience with Windows Forms, many of these controls will be new to you, but the essential software development techniques will not be that different from what you have learned in the past. You'll still build your applications by adding Toolbox controls to a page, setting essential properties, writing event handlers, and then compiling and testing your work.

Let's begin with the *TextBox* control.

Using the *TextBox* control to receive input

The *TextBox* control makes it easy to gather basic, textual input from the user and to put it to work in your Windows Store app. In addition, *TextBox* controls can be used to display information quickly on a page, such as the results of a calculation or the content returned from a database query. Although most *TextBox* controls are designed to be just one line long, you can also create multiline *TextBox* controls following the same basic procedure and then use them to gather input or display a paragraph or more of text.

In the following exercises, you'll learn how to receive input using a *TextBox* control, assign the information to a variable, create a multiline *TextBox* control, and check the spelling in a *TextBox*. Later in this chapter, you'll learn how to transfer data from a *TextBox* control to a *ListBox* control.

Use a *TextBox* control for basic input

1. Start Visual Studio 2013.

2. On the Visual Studio File menu, click New Project.

    The New Project dialog box opens.

3. In the Visual Basic template group, click Windows Store and then the Blank App (XAML) project.

    Visual Studio prepares the IDE for a basic Windows Store app with no predefined layout.

4. In the Name text box, type **My Text Input**.

    Visual Studio assigns the name My Text Input to your project. As noted in Chapter 3, I'm recommending the "My" prefix here so that you don't confuse your new application with the Text Input project I've created for you in the book's sample files.

5. Click OK to create the new project in Visual Studio.

    Visual Studio opens a new programming project and displays the Visual Basic code associated with the blank application template.

6. Open Solution Explorer in the IDE if it is not currently visible, and then double-click the file MainPage.xaml.

    Visual Studio opens MainPage.xaml in the Designer window.

7. If the Toolbox is not currently visible, click the Toolbox tab or click the Toolbox command on the View menu.

8. This Toolbox contains Windows Store app (XAML) controls.

9. Click the *TextBox* control in the Toolbox, move the mouse pointer to the Designer window, and then drag right and down to create a small, rectangular box on the page.

    You'll find the *TextBox* control in both the Common XAML Controls and the All XAML Controls categories. When you release the mouse button, Visual Studio creates a text box object on the page.

    In the XAML tab of the Code Editor, notice that XAML markup for the text box object now appears, with several properties already assigned, based on the size and shape of the text box. The Properties window also displays several of these properties.

10. Click the *TextBox* control in the Toolbox again, and then create a second text box object below the first one.

11. Resize the text box so that it is the same size and shape as the first one.

    Now you'll create a button object on the form as well.

12. Click the *Button* control in the Toolbox, and then create a small button object below the two text boxes.

13. Click the *Zoom* control in the Designer, and then select 100% zoom to see a bit more of the application page.

    Your IDE will now look something like this:

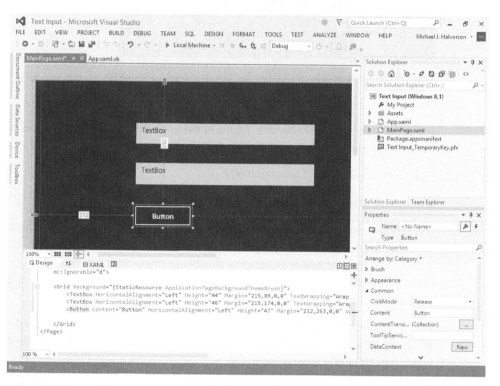

14. Enlarge the Properties window so that you have plenty of room to make some adjustments to the new objects' properties.

15. Change the *Name* property of the first text box to **InputString**, and delete contents of the object's *Text* property.

16. Change the *Name* property of the second text box to **Output**, and delete contents of the object's *Text* property.

17. Change the *Name* property of the button object to **TestButton**, and change the *Content* property of the button to **Click To Test**.

Your screen should look like this:

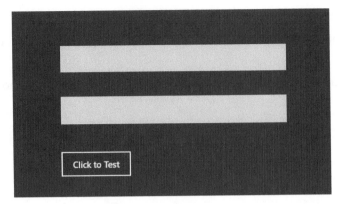

Now you'll create an event handler for the button on the page.

18. Double-click the button object.

The *TestButton_Click* event handler opens in the Code Editor, and the insertion point blinks between the *Sub* and *End Sub* statements.

19. Type the following line of program code:

```
Output.Text = InputString.Text.Length
```

This program statement examines the *Text* property of the first text box on the page (*InputString*) and uses the *Length* property to determine how many characters have been entered into the text box. It assigns this number to the second text box (*Output*). The point of the demonstration program is simply to show how text boxes can be used to gather and display textual information in a program.

The *Length* property is one of several methods and properties that can be used with textual (or *String*) data. You'll learn more about the *String* data type in Chapter 11, "Mastering data types, operators, and string processing."

Now run the program to see how the sample project and its text boxes operate.

20. Click the Start Debugging button on the Standard toolbar.

The Text Input program runs, and the Windows Store app you created appears on the screen.

21. Type **You can do this!** in the first text box, and then click the Click To Test button.

Visual Basic counts 16 characters in the user input you entered and then displays the following results:

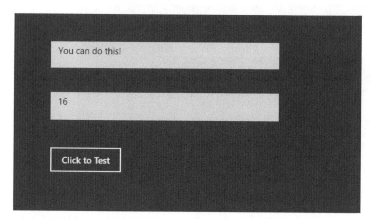

22. Notice that the *Length* property counted blank spaces and punctuation, as well as the letters that you typed. Give it another try.

> **Tip** Does the top line of your output screen contain debugging information? Recall from Chapter 3 that you might see a few sets of numbers at the top of your screen when your app runs in Debugging mode. These numbers summarize how long various tasks take during the execution of your Visual Studio app, including the frame rate for the user interface thread and how long it took to load the user interface. These numbers will not appear in the Release build for your application, and you can suppress them in Debugging mode by removing the code between the *#If DEBUG* and *#End If* statements in the App.xaml.vb file. To avoid distraction, I will not show the debugging numbers in the screen shots in this book.

23. Remove You Can Do This! from the first text box, and then type **Microsoft Visual Basic 2013 programming**.

24. Click the Click To Test button.

25. Visual Basic counts all the characters that you typed and displays the number 39 in the second text box. Your screen looks like this:

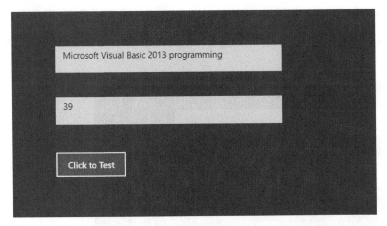

You've demonstrated how to use the *TextBox* control to manage basic input and output tasks.

26. Experiment further if you like, and when you're finished, close the application.

27. Click the Save All command on the File menu to save your project, and specify *the* My Documents\Visual Basic 2013 SBS\Chapter 05 folder.

Now you'll store the contents of a *TextBox* control in a string variable.

Assigning *TextBox* contents to a variable

A *variable* is a temporary store location for data in a program. As you probably already know, you can use one or more variables in your code to store words, numbers, dates, and other values. I'll spend much more time talking about the advanced uses of variables and operators in Chapter 11, but while we are looking at the *TextBox* control, it is worth noting that you can assign the contents of the *Text* property to a variable when you are using *TextBox* for input.

Traditionally, programmers will use the *TextBox* control's *Text* property to manage string input—that is, textual information such as words, letters, symbols, and so on. You can also use implicit variable declaration to create variables of other types as well. You'll be using the *Dim* keyword to declare the variable in code, which reserves room in memory for the variable when the program runs. Give it a try now.

Use a string variable to hold *TextBox* input

1. Open the *TestButton_Click* event handler in the Code Editor.

You'll modify the event handler for the button object so that it stores the data entered in the first text box in a variable named *SampleText*. Then you'll use the *ToUpper* property to change the letters in the text string to uppercase, and you'll display the contents of the variable in the second text box.

2. Replace the line *Output.Text = InputString.Text.Length* with the following code:

```
Dim sampleText As String
sampleText = InputString.Text
Output.Text = sampleText.ToUpper
```

3. Run the revised program.

4. In the first text box, type **happy new year.**

Your screen looks like this:

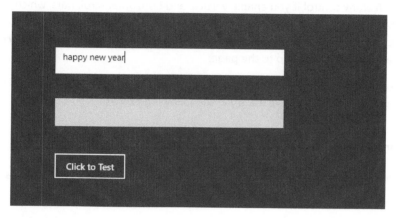

5. Click the Click To Test button.

Visual Basic changes the text from lowercase to uppercase. You'll see the following screen:

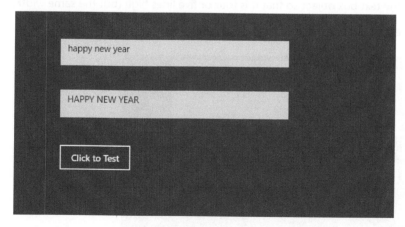

6. You've demonstrated one of the most fundamental tasks of processing user input—receiving information in a *TextBox* control and assigning it to a variable. With a variable in memory, you can perform any number of tasks with the information.

7. When you're finished, close the application.

8. Click the Save All command on the File menu to save your changes.

Now you'll practice managing multiline input with a *TextBox* control.

Multiline *TextBox* controls

A multiline *TextBox* control is simply a *TextBox* control that has been sized so that it is capable of displaying more than one line of information. You can also provide access to information beyond the edges of your *TextBox* control if you enable vertical and horizontal scroll bars, which are controlled by an instance of the *ScrollViewer* class that is exposed to container controls like *TextBox*. The *ScrollViewer* class and properties such as *VerticalScrollBarVisibility* and *HorizontalScrollBarVisibility* are easiest to set by adding XAML markup to the page.

When you're using a multiline *TextBox* control, a single variable of type *String* can also be used to handle an entire paragraph of text. Give it a try in the following exercise.

Manage a paragraph of text with a *TextBox* control

1. Display the user interface for your Windows Store app (MainPage.xaml) in the Designer.

   The text box object that you'll enlarge is the top one on the page.

2. Hold the mouse over the top border of the text box object until the pointer becomes a resizing tool.

3. Expand the text box object so that it is four or five lines high (but the same width).

   Your screen should look like this:

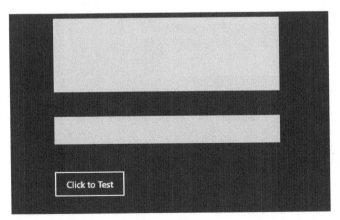

   Now you'll add a vertical scroll bar to the text box object by setting the *VerticalScrollBarVisibility* property using XAML markup. As you learned in Chapter 2, "The Visual Studio Integrated Development Environment," and in Chapter 3, "Creating your first Windows Store application,"

the XAML tab of the Code Editor shows the XAML markup that is associated with each object in the user interface as you create a page for your Windows Store application.

When you add a new control to a page, a new line of XAML is added to the Code Editor, and you can edit this markup directly as an alternative to manipulating objects on the page or setting properties in the Properties window. In this case, you'll edit the XAML markup for the *InputString* text box directly.

4. In the XAML tab of the Code Editor, below the Designer, locate the XAML markup for the *InputString* text box control. (The first text box on the page.)

5. After the markup *x:Name="InputString"*, enter the following property setting:

```
ScrollViewer.VerticalScrollBarVisibility="Visible"
```

6. Press the Spacebar after you finish typing, to create a blank space between the property setting you just added and the *HorizontalAlignment* property setting on the same line.

You're using the *VerticalScrollBarVisibility* property of the *ScrollViewer* class to add a vertical scroll bar to the text box object when the user moves the mouse pointer over the text box. Note that the scroll bar will be visible only when the application is running and the user hovers the mouse pointer over it. The Windows 8.1 design guidelines seek to minimize unused "chrome" (or user interface features) on the screen and displays them only when they are needed.

Your screen should look like this:

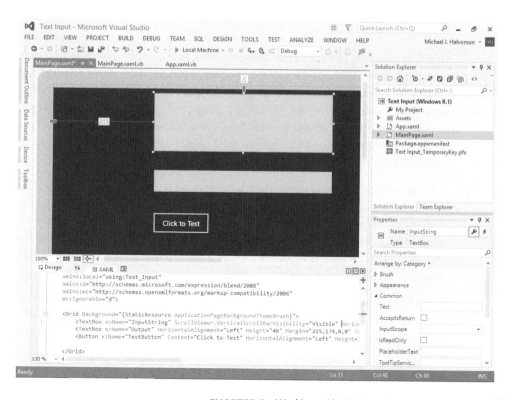

Now you'll add some Visual Basic code to assign a new paragraph of text to a variable and check it for keywords.

7. Click the MainPage.xaml.vb tab in the IDE to display the Visual Basic code-behind file in the Code Editor.

8. You'll see the following three lines of program code in the *TestButton_Click* event handler:

```
Dim sampleText As String
sampleText = InputString.Text
Output.Text = sampleText.ToUpper
```

9. Keep the first two lines, but replace the last program statement with the following code block:

```
If sampleText.Contains("River") Then
    Output.Text = "The string 'River' was found"
Else
    Output.Text = "The string 'River' was not found"
End If
```

Your Code Editor should look like this:

```
Private Sub TestButton_Click(sender As Object, e As RoutedEventArgs) Handles TestButton.Click
    Dim sampleText As String
    sampleText = InputString.Text
    If sampleText.Contains("River") Then
        Output.Text = "The string 'River' was found"
    Else
        Output.Text = "The string 'River' was not found"
    End If
End Sub
```

The four new lines of code comprise an *If...Then...Else* decision structure that determines whether the word "River" is located in the first text box on the page. The first text box is considered a multiline text box because it has been resized to hold more than one line. (The change was automatic; in Windows Forms programming, you had to specify multiline with a property setting.) With the larger text box, there is now plenty of room for the user to enter a long paragraph of text, and scroll bars will permit content to go well beyond the physical dimensions of the object.

The key method here is *Contains*, which determines whether the specified string ("*River*") occurs in the current string (*sampleText*, a variable that holds a copy of the text in the first text box). If the string "*River*" is found in *SampleText*, the message "The string 'River' was found" is copied into the second text box. If the string "*River*" is not found (and note that this would include any capitalization variation, such as "*river*"), the message "The string 'River' was not found" is copied into the second text box.

You'll learn more about useful *If...Then...Else* code blocks in Chapter 12, "Creative decision structures and loops."

10. Now run the revised Windows Store app.

11. In the first text box on the page, type the following sample paragraph:

I hope to travel one day to a land with a beautiful, shimmering lake, or perhaps a famous body of water—like Loch Ness. Or, perhaps travel on a wine-dark sea and sail for adventure and discovery. If not, I would be happy to fish for trout in the Yellowstone River.

As you type, notice that the vertical scroll bars appear on the text box and allow you to scroll if necessary. These scroll bars are visible now because you set the *VerticalScrollBarVisibility* property to True. When the first text box has the focus or when you hover the mouse pointer over the text box, the scroll bars will appear.

12. Click the Click To Test button.

Your screen will look like this:

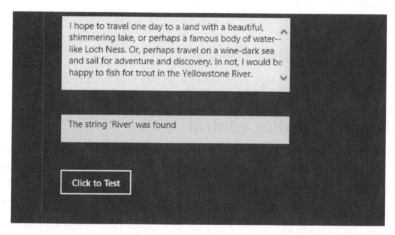

Everything is working correctly. The word "River" was in the last sentence you typed, so the appropriate message has appeared in the second text box.

13. Now remove the last sentence from the first text box. The last words visible there should be "adventure and discovery."

14. Click the Click To Test button.

Because the word "River" is no longer present, the other message is displayed in the second text box. Your screen looks like this:

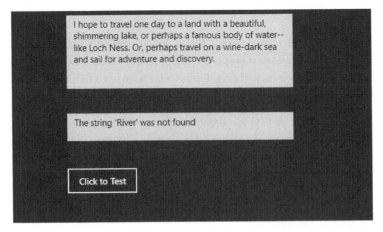

I hope to travel one day to a land with a beautiful, shimmering lake, or perhaps a famous body of water-- like Loch Ness. Or, perhaps travel on a wine-dark sea and sail for adventure and discovery.

The string 'River' was not found

Click to Test

You have successfully tested both cases in the *If...Then...Else* code block.

15. Close the application.

16. Click the Save All button to save your changes.

Well done! But before we move on, let's experiment with one final feature of the *TextBox* control.

Check spelling in a *TextBox* control

One of the most helpful features of Microsoft Office applications is that they can check your spelling as you type. Although I have written dozens of books about computer software and historical subjects, a day does not go by when I fail to spell check some text that I have written or edited.

A similar capability is available in Windows Store applications, and you can add it to many container-type Visual Studio controls that are designed to manage text. In this section, you'll learn how to enable the spell checker in the *TextBox* control. If you use the *TextBox* control in a commercial application, your users will appreciate the convenience.

Use the *IsSpellCheckEnabled* property

1. Click the MainPage.xaml tab to display the Designer window in the IDE.

2. Select the first text box on the page (*InputString*) so that its properties are visible in the Properties window.

3. Open the Properties windows, expand the second half of the Common category, and add a check mark to the *IsSpellCheckEnabled* check box.

   When set to True, the *IsSpellCheckEnabled* property activates a spell checker in the *TextBox* control so that unidentified words are flagged with an underline feature. As with Microsoft Office and other Windows programs, if you right-click a misspelled word, a list of potential fixes will appear and you can select a correction.

Add a check mark to the AcceptsReturn check box in the Common category.

Enabling this property will allow the user to enter a carriage return in the check box, which can help format text.

Your Properties window should look like this:

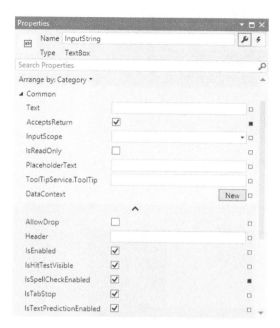

Now try running the program again.

4. Click Start Debugging on the Standard toolbar.

5. In the first text box, type the following text:

Whan that aprill with his shoures soote

The droghte of march hath perced to the roote,

Weary students of medieval English literature might recognize these as the opening lines of the Prologue of Geoffrey Chaucer's *Canterbury Tales*. However, the Visual Studio 2013 spell checker is not fully acquainted with this text and identifies several words for a closer look, as noted in the following screen shot:

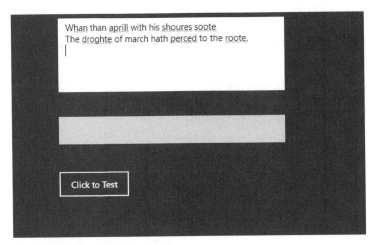

6. Right-click the third word in the text box ("aprill"), and see what sort of correction is suggested by the spell checker.

The pop-up box on my system looked like this:

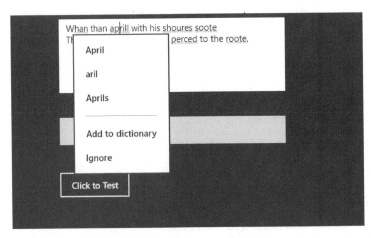

For "aprill," the spelling checker suggests that we consider "April," "aril," or "Aprils." Alternatively, we can ignore the correction (to preserve Chaucer's medieval English) or add the word to the dictionary so that future spell checks recognize the word.

7. Click "April" to make a change and to see how spelling corrections are made in a *TextBox* control.

Visual Studio deletes the old word and inserts a new one, as shown in the following screen shot:

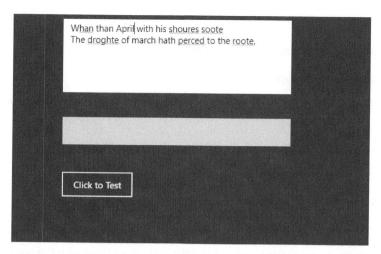

Spelling corrections work essentially as they do in Microsoft Office and most mainstream applications for Windows. You've added a useful, professional grade feature to your list of *TextBox* skills and techniques. You'll learn how to add a pop-up box to your user interface with the *Flyout* control in Chapter 9.

8. Close the Text Input program.

9. Click Save All to save your final changes.

10. Click Close Project on the File menu to close the Text Input application.

It's time to move on to another Windows Store app control.

Using the *FlipView* control to display a series of images

Applications for Windows 8.1 are designed to be content-rich and visually interesting, with graphic elements, photographs, video clips, and other special effects that engage the user and help them to quickly focus on the task at hand. The *FlipView* control is one such design tool. It allows you to present a collection of images to the user that is stunningly beautiful and easy to navigate through.

In this section, you'll learn how to use the use *FlipView* control in a Windows Store app to display a series of photographs that fill up the entire screen. To prepare images for the control, you'll add six test images that I've created for you to the Assets folder in a Visual Studio project, and then you'll create a large *FlipView* control on the page to display the photos.

Add images to the Assets folder

1. On the Visual Studio File menu, click New Project.

   The New Project dialog box opens.

2. In the Visual Basic template group, click Windows Store, and then click the Blank App (XAML) project.

   Visual Studio prepares the IDE for a basic Windows Store app.

3. In the Name text box, type **My Image Gallery**.

   Visual Studio assigns the name My Image Gallery to the project.

4. Click OK to create the new project in Visual Studio.

   Visual Studio opens a new project and displays the code associated with the blank application template.

5. Open Solution Explorer in the IDE if it is not currently visible.

6. In Solution Explorer, right-click the Assets folder, select Add | Existing Item, and browse to the My Documents\Visual Basic 2013 SBS\Chapter 05 folder.

   You'll see the following Add Existing Item dialog box:

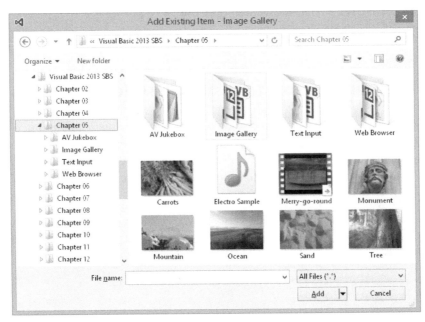

As you learned in Chapter 3, the Assets folder in Solution Explorer allows you to include resources in a project so that they can be referenced easily in XAML markup and Visual Basic code. An additional benefit is that the asset files will be added to the project automatically when it is distributed.

7. Hold down the Ctrl key, and then click the six files entitled Carrots, Monument, Mountain, Ocean, Sand, and Tree.

 Tip You can select contiguous or noncontiguous files by holding down the Ctrl key and clicking the desired files.

8. These are images of natural objects and an architectural detail, which I have taken over the past few years—the type of full screen images that look really good in a *FlipView* control.

9. Click Add to add the selected items to the Assets folder.

Visual Studio adds the selected images. Now you'll create a *FlipView* control on the page to display the images.

Add a *FlipView* control to the page

1. Double-click the MainPage.xaml file in Solution Explorer to open the main application page in the Designer window.

2. Click the Zoom tool in the Designer, and then click the Fit All option so that you can see the entire page in the Designer.

3. Open the Toolbox, and find the *FlipView* control.

   Although you could use this control now to create the flip view object you'll use, I'm going to direct you to create the object using XAML markup. This step allows you to set more precise dimensions for the *FlipView* frame, and you can also use XAML markup to nest the images nicely within the *FlipView* control.

   Learning to nest a child control (*Image*) within a parent control (*FlipView*) is an important skill that you'll practice often in this book.

4. Close the Toolbox, and open the XAML tab of the Code Editor, which should be open now beneath the Designer window.

5. After the line of markup that includes the keywords *Grid Background*, enter the following XAML markup to define the *FlipView* control and six *Image* controls within it:

```
<FlipView Height="750" Width="1000">
    <Image Source="Assets/Tree.jpg" />
    <Image Source="Assets/Carrots.jpg" />
    <Image Source="Assets/Mountain.jpg" />
    <Image Source="Assets/Sand.jpg" />
    <Image Source="Assets/Ocean.jpg" />
    <Image Source="Assets/Monument.jpg" />
</FlipView>
```

Notice how you are placing each new image definition on its own new line, and at the top of the markup, you set the height and width of the *FlipView* control. While you are entering this markup, Visual Studio's IntelliSense feature helps you by supplying some of the keywords, quotation marks, and indents. (Note that the indenting here is just for clarity; you could also enter all of the markup on one line in the Code Editor.)

I chose the dimensions 750×1000, measured in pixels, so that the *FlipView* control would fill up most of the screen on my computer display. However, if you are using a higher resolution display setting, the control might not fill up your screen entirely. You can adjust this by specifying a larger *FlipView* height and width if you like.

The Designer and IDE will look like this when you are finished:

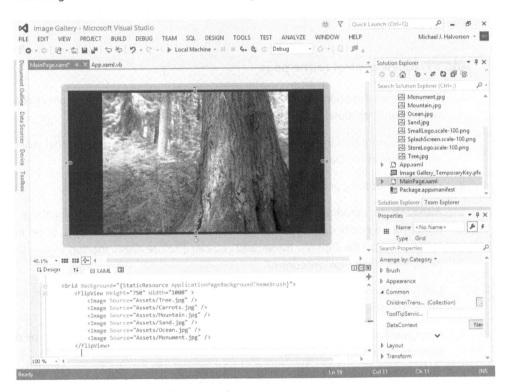

Your Image Gallery program is now ready to run.

6. Click Start Debugging on the Standard toolbar.

The program runs, and the first image appears on the page, as shown in the following screen shot. This photo is of a giant Douglas fir tree in a Washington State forest.

Notice the small arrow pane or Next button on the right side of the image, which appears when you first move the mouse or touch the screen. This is a scrolling feature that allows you to move to the next image in the collection. You can also move forward or backward in the image collection by swiping or using the direction keys.

7. Move the mouse pointer to the right side of the page, and click the Next button.

A second image appears of carrots for sale at a farmer's market in Cambridge, England.

8. Click through the remaining images until the final photo appears, a time-worn stone bust of a princely figure on the side of a building in London, England.

Your screen will look like the following screen shot. Because this is the last image in the *FlipView* control, only the Back button appears on the left side of the image.

9. Feel free to scroll back through the images, and then move forward again.

   As you can see, the *FlipView* control allows you rapid access to a series of photos, and you can scroll through them with minimal visual distractions (no scroll bars, buttons, or toolbars to look at). This graphics-centered content is at the heart of the Windows 8.1 user interface, and you'll find FlipView to be very helpful when you are designing a photo sorting program, music catalog tool, or any type of Windows Store app where a large number of images need to be displayed quickly.

10. Close the application when you have finished examining the photos.

11. Save your changes, specify the My Documents\Visual Basic 2013 SBS\Chapter 05 folder for the project, and then click the Close Project command on the File menu.

    Visual Studio save your files and then closes the project.

You're finished with the *FlipView* control for now. However, keep in mind that you worked with the *FlipView* control in this chapter without adding any Visual Basic program code at all. You can enhance your program by adding an event handler for the *SelectionChanged* event so that each time you click the Next or Back buttons, you perform some additional action, such as playing a sound effect or displaying information in a *TextBox* on the page.

You can experiment with these additional features another time. In the next section, you'll learn how to play entertainment media in a Windows Store app, such as audio clips or a short video file.

Using the *MediaElement* control to play entertainment media

In addition to the colorful images that you can display with the *FlipView* control, a Windows Store app can be enhanced by the inclusion of entertainment media, such as music or sound effects, video footage, commercials, or other A/V media. You experimented a little bit with this feature in Chapter 3 when playing a musical sound effect for the Lucky Seven program.

The procedure for integrating entertainment media involves adding the media file or files to the Assets folder in your Visual Studio project and then adding a *MediaElement* control to the page to run the media file when it is needed. The *MediaElement* control is located in the Windows Store app Toolbox, and when you add it to a page, it has no visible interface. (However, you'll learn how to add its interface later in this chapter.) In addition to the basic playback features that you might expect in a media control, *MediaElement* offers several features that will allow you to customize how the audio or video media is controlled and displayed.

In this section, you'll learn the basics of the *MediaElement* control and its essential features. You should note that audio and video files are stored electronically in a variety of formats and that some of the proprietary ones (such as Apple's iTunes) are not supported by the *MediaElement* control. However, popular media formats like MP3, WAV, AVI, and MPEG-4 are all supported and will provide you with plenty of content choices for your applications. There are also software tools available that will allow you to create media files, edit them, and translate them from one format to another.

First, you'll play an electronic music file in your Windows Store application. In the next section, you'll learn how to manage video playback on a page.

Play music with the *MediaElement* control

1. On the Visual Studio File menu, click New Project.

    The New Project dialog box opens.

2. In the Visual Basic template group, click Windows Store, and the Blank App (XAML) project.

3. In the Name text box, type **My AV Jukebox.**

4. Click OK to create the new project in Visual Studio.

    Visual Studio opens the new project with a blank application template.

5. Double-click the file MainPage.xaml in Solution Explorer.

    Visual Studio opens MainPage.xaml in the Designer window.

6. Open the Toolbox, open the All XAML Controls category, and double-click the *MediaElement* control.

Visual Studio places a new media player object in the upper-left corner of the application page. You can set various property settings for *MediaElement*. However, you will be able to see the *MediaElement* control only while you are designing your project. When the program runs, the *MediaElement* control remains hidden, unless the control is displaying a video clip.

The *Source* property of the *MediaElement* control specifies the name of the media file that will be loaded into the control for playback. The best way to supply a media file is to add the file via the *Assets* folder in your application.

You'll add an electronic music file to this folder now.

7. Right-click the Assets folder in Solution Explorer to display the shortcut menu of commands.

8. Point to the Add command, and then click Existing Item.

9. In the Add Existing Item dialog box, browse to the My Documents\Visual Basic 2013 SBS\ Chapter 05 folder and click Electro Sample, an MP3 file containing electronic music. This file was created by my son, Henry Halvorson.

 Tip You might also be able to locate additional audio files on your system in the Libraries category, in the *My Music* folder.

10. Click Add to add the music file to your project in the Assets folder.

Visual Studio inserts the file, and it appears now in Solution Explorer under Assets.

Now you're ready to assign this music asset to the *Source* property of the media element object.

11. Click the media element object in the Designer window, and then open the Properties window.

12. Change the *Name* property to **MediaTool.**

13. Expand the *Media* category, scroll down to the *Source* property, and click the Source list box.

Your new media file (Electro Sample.mp3) appears in the list.

14. Click the media file to link it to the media element object.

Your Properties window will look like this:

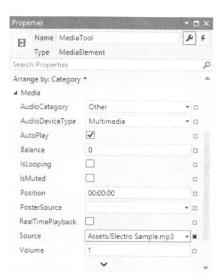

Now you're ready to save and run the project.

15. Click the Save All command on the File menu to save your project, and specify the My Documents\Visual Basic 2013 SBS\Chapter 05 folder.

16. Click Start Debugging on the toolbar.

The My AV Juke Box application runs, and the selected music starts playing. Because the *MediaElement* control has no user interface to interact with, you'll see only a blank screen. The "Electro Sample" music track runs until it is complete (a little less than a minute), and then the program waits for you to terminate it. (This is electronic music created with the Ableton Live 8 software suite.)

Now you'll close the program and add a few buttons to the page to control the playback as a typical music-sampling program might.

17. Close the My AV Jukebox program.

In the following exercise, you'll add Play, Pause, Stop, and Mute buttons to the Windows Store app.

Control playback with buttons

1. Change the Designer's Zoom setting to 100%.

2. Use the *Button* control in the Toolbox to add four *Button* controls to the left side of the page in the Designer.

3. Set the *Name* properties for the button objects to **PlayButton**, **PauseButton**, **StopButton**, and **MuteButton**, respectively.

4. Set the *Content* properties for the button objects to **Play**, **Pause**, **Stop**, and **Mute**, respectively.

The following screen shot shows how your new button objects should look on the page when you're finished. (Note also the *MediaElement* control and the XAML markup for the object in the Designer.)

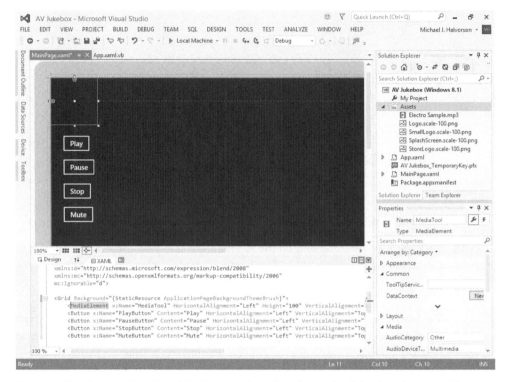

Now you'll write one-line Visual Basic event handlers for each of the four button objects.

5. Click the *PlayButton* object, open the Properties window, and then click the Event Handler (lightning bolt) button to see the list of event handlers for the *Button* control.

6. Double-click the text box next to the *Click* event to create a new event handler.

7. Enter the following line of Visual Basic program code:

```
MediaTool.Play()
```

This line uses the *Play* method of the *MediaElement* control to play the loaded media file at the current play position. If the media file has been paused, the *Play* method will cause it to resume. If the media file has been stopped, the *Play* method will cause it to start again at the beginning.

Now you'll repeat similar steps with each of the remaining buttons, creating event handlers with appropriate methods or properties for each action.

8. Return to the Designer, and click the Pause button.

9. In the Properties window, double-click the text box next to the *Click* event and type the following line of code into the *PauseButton_Click* event handler:

```
MediaTool.Pause()
```

This line uses the *Pause* method to pause the loaded media file at the current play position. This feature can be used to give users some control as they listen to music or watch video.

10. Return to the Designer, and click the Stop button.

11. In the Properties window, double-click the text box next to the *Click* event and type the following line of code into the *StopButton_Click* event handler:

```
MediaTool.Stop()
```

This line uses the *Stop* method to end audio or video playback. Different from the *Pause* method, which temporarily stops playback but retains the current position in the track, the *Stop* method ends playback. If you execute the *Play* method after the *Stop* method, playback will begin again, but at the start of the media file.

12. Return to the Designer, and click the Mute button.

13. In the Properties window, double-click the text box next to the *Click* event and type the following code:

```
MediaTool.IsMuted = Not MediaTool.IsMuted
```

This line uses the *Boolean IsMuted property* to mute or unmute audio playback. The statement uses the *Not* operator to switch, or toggle, the current value of *IsMuted*. If playback is currently muted, the statement will remove the muting effect. If playback is currently unmuted, the statement will mute playback.

14. Click the Save All command on the File menu to save your changes.

Now you'll run the program again to see how the four playback controls work.

15. Click Start Debugging on the toolbar.

The My AV Jukebox application runs, and the selected audio file begins to play. Your screen should look like this:

16. After a few moments of electronic music, click the Pause button.

    The song pauses at the current playback position.

17. Click the Play button.

    Audio playback resumes right where you left off.

18. Click the Mute button.

    The music is muted (volume is temporarily set to 0), but playback continues.

19. After a few moments, click the Mute button again.

    The original volume setting is restored, and you'll be able to hear music again. However, you might notice that the song has advanced, and if you wait too long, the song will end. That is, the Mute button is different from the Pause button.

20. Click the Stop button.

    Audio playback terminates.

21. Click the Play button.

    The electronic music file begins again, but at the beginning of the song.

22. Continue experimenting with the playback controls you just created. When you're finished, quit the program.

As you can see, the *MediaElement* control not only allows you to play audio files, but it provides you with interesting methods and properties to control what happens during playback. You can create buttons and other features that let the user control what is happening, or you can control playback behind the scenes in event handlers—playing audio tracks only when you want them to be played.

In the next section, you'll modify the My AV Jukebox app so that it plays a video file rather than a music file.

Play videos using the *MediaElement* control

1. Display Solution Explorer, and then right-click the Assets folder to display the shortcut menu.

2. Point to the Add command, and then click Existing Item.

3. In the Add Existing Item dialog box, browse to the My Documents\Visual Basic 2013 SBS\ Chapter 05 folder and click Merry-go-round, a video file in WAV format created for this book by Henry Halvorson.

   You might also be able to locate valid video files on your system in the Libraries category, in the *Videos* folder.

4. Click Add to add the video file to the project's Assets folder.

   Visual Studio inserts the file. All you need to do now is replace the reference to the music file from the last exercise with the video file that you just added.

5. Click the media player element again in the Designer, and then open the Properties window and click the Properties button.

6. Expand the Media category, scroll down to the *Source* property, and click the Source list box.

7. Click the video you just added to link it to the media element object.

   Your video file is ready to run. However, for best results, you'll want to resize your media element object so that it is larger, because the current playback window is a bit small. The window size you set is up to you, but keep in mind that a variety of devices might need to run your program (all with different screen dimensions), so pick a size that makes sense for your application.

8. In the Designer window, move the media element object to the right of the four button objects.

9. Increase the size of the media element object so that it takes up about one-third of the screen.

   You can fine-tune the size after you run the program and get a sense for how big the video window is. Your Designer will look like this (note the selected media element object on the page):

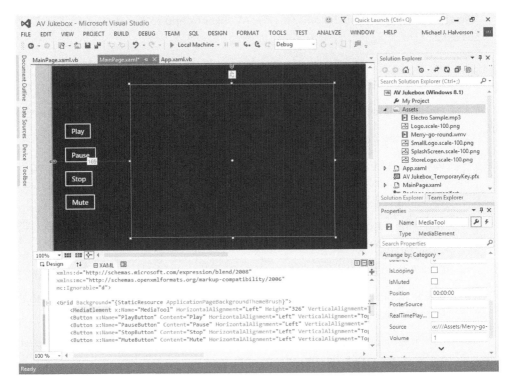

Now you're ready to test the application.

10. Click the Save All command on the File menu to save the changes to your project.

11. Click Start Debugging on the toolbar.

The My AV Jukebox app runs, and the selected video file begins to play in the window you moved and resized. The media playback controls you created will work just as they did for the audio file, with the caveat that now you'll have both video and audio. This merry-go-round is at a local park by my house.

Your screen should look something like this:

12. Experiment with the Pause, Play, Stop, and Mute buttons in the project.

The *MediaElement* control is designed to work with both audio and video files, so the program's event handlers manage your playback requests with no code changes. This particular media file was edited with Windows Movie Maker.

13. When you're finished, quit the Windows Store app.

If you like, you can go back into the project and experiment with additional audio or video files on your computer. Just be careful not to insert files that are too large, because they can be cumbersome when it comes time to distribute your app!

14. When you're finished working with the program, close the Visual Studio project.

Use the *WebView* control to display live web content

Windows Store apps are designed to be sold and installed over the Internet and to take advantage of information that resides on the web in a variety of ways. One of the simplest ways to access web data in a Windows Store app is simply to open a browser window on your application page and to allow the user to access a website directly. Visual Studio allows you to do this programmatically with the *WebView* control in the Windows Store app Toolbox.

The *WebView* control is not a full-featured web browser like Internet Explorer. However, it was added to the Windows Store app toolbox so that programmers would have an easy way to display live web content if they needed to in a Windows Store application. In the following section, you'll explore this feature and some of its practical uses.

Create a simple browser with the *WebView* control

1. On the Visual Studio File menu, click New Project.

   The New Project dialog box opens.

2. In the Visual Basic template group, click Windows Store, and then click the Blank App (XAML) project.

3. In the Name text box, type **My Web Browser.**

4. Click OK to create the new Visual Studio project.

   Visual Studio opens the new project template.

5. Double-click the file MainPage.xaml in Solution Explorer.

   Visual Studio opens the app's user interface in the Designer.

   This program will feature a *TextBox* control to hold the web address, a *Button* control to navigate to the web address, and a *WebView* control to display the specified webpage. Create these items now.

6. At the upper-left corner of the page, create a long, single-line text box object, using the *TextBox* control in the Toolbox.

7. Use the Properties window to set the text box's *Name* property to **URL**, and set the text box's *Text* property to **http://michaelhalvorsonbooks.com**.

8. At the top of the page, to the right of the new text box object, create a small button object, using the *Button* control in the Toolbox.

9. Use the Properties window to set the button object's *Name* property to **NavigateButton**, and set the button's *Content* property to **Open**.

10. Click the *WebView* control in the Toolbox. (You'll find it in the All XAML Controls section.)

11. Using the control's drawing pointer, create a very large rectangular box on the page below the text box and button objects.

    In this simple test app, the goal will be to display as much of the web browser as possible so that the user will not need to use scroll bars to examine information that is beyond the edge of the *WebView* control window. So make the *WebView* control really big, taking up all the remaining real estate on the page.

12. After you create the object, you might want to close the Toolbox window and adjust the amount of zoom magnification in the Designer window to make as much of the page visible in the IDE as possible. (The Zoom tool's Fit All setting will help you do this.)

13. Use the Properties window to set the web view object's *Name* property to **Browser**, and set the *HorizontalAlignment* and *VerticalAlignment* properties to Center.

The alignment-related properties are located in the Layout category, and they center-align content in the browser window.

Your final user interface should now look similar to the following screen shot. (Again, note that the XAML markup for the *WebView* control has been added to the Code Editor.)

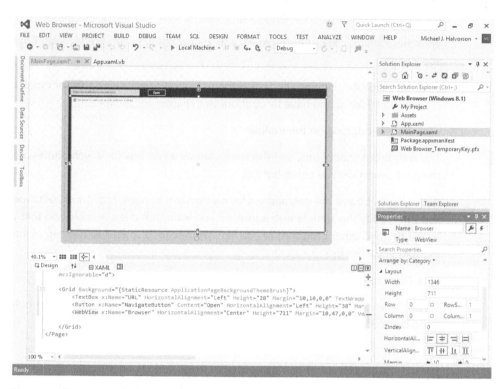

Now you'll create a short event handler for the button object to load the web view control with a web address or URL when the program runs. To quickly create an event handler for an object's default event (typically *Click*), you can double-click the object on the page to open the event handler in the Code Editor.

14. Double-click the button object in the Designer.

The *NavigateButton_Click* event handler opens in the Code Editor, and the insertion point blinks between the *Sub* and *End Sub* statements. *Click* is the default event for button objects.

15. Type the following line of program code:

```
Browser.Navigate(New Uri(URL.Text))
```

This mighty line of Visual Basic code has a lot packed into it! The *Navigate* method of the *Browser* object directs the *WebView* control to load the specified webpage. The webpage is listed in the *URL* text box that you created at the top of the user interface. The other important syntax here are the keywords *New Uri*, which put the web address into a format that is standard for web browsers, the so-called *uniform resource indicator* (URI) format.

Because this is a test program, I assume that you will type in a web address in the proper format. However, if you don't use proper syntax (if you misspell the address), the page won't load and you will receive only minimal feedback from the program that something went wrong. Obviously, a more sophisticated program would make the error condition clearer and instruct the user about how to fix it, but we won't spend time creating the error handler now. (For more about that topic, see Chapter 13, "Trapping errors by using structured error handling.")

With these limitations out in the open, you're now ready to run the My Web Browser application.

16. Click the Save All command on the File menu to save the changes to your project. Specify the Chapter 05 folder as you have throughout this chapter for the location.

17. Click Start Debugging on the toolbar.

   The Web Browser app runs, and the screen shows a text box for a web address at the top of the page, along with an Open button.

   Within the text box is the web address for my own author page, *http://michaelhalvorsonbooks.com*. You can modify this sample web address if you want, but it is a reliable one that you can use to test this and other programs as you like. (You might also find something of interest there, including new books!)

18. Click Open to open the webpage.

   Visual Studio loads the web address into the *WebView* control. Your screen should look something like this:

Yes, that's me on the screen! And, you'll find that the *WebView* control is also scrollable, so you can use touch input, mouse wheel, or the direction keys to move up and down as you like. Web links and other content are also "live" on this page, so you can navigate to additional pages as you like. Beyond the actual links in the website, there are few navigation controls in this demonstration program. However, you can create your own navigation buttons and controls if you would like, by programming the events, properties, and methods provided by the *WebView* control.

19. Type another web address in the text box, and then click Open.

Visual Studio loads the new page, and you can explore that website as well.

But...what if you encounter an error condition while loading webpages?

Actually, if you encounter any type of error while loading a webpage when using the *WebView* control, the Visual Studio IDE will display an error message in a text box asking you whether or not you want to continue, or whether you want additional information about what happened. Often these problems will simply be Internet script errors or other warning messages, because various websites have their own ways of sending information to the different web browsers on the market.

You can suppress such "noise" in the Visual Studio IDE by closing the application and then clicking Tools | Options | Debugging | Just-In-Time. Remove the check mark from the Script check box, and then run the program again. Just be careful to use the Tools | Options | Debugging command again to put the check mark back when you're done. (There are possible security issues associated with having your users browse to unknown or untrusted websites.)

Error handling is something that you will get to a little later in the book. For now, consider how easy it is to launch an Internet browser from within a Visual Studio application. You have made an excellent start with a collection of very useful Windows Store controls.

20. When you're finished, quit the My Web Browser program.

You're finished working with Windows Store app controls for this chapter.

21. On the File menu, click the Close Project command, and then exit Visual Studio.

Summary

In this chapter, you experimented with some of the most useful controls in the Visual Studio Toolbox. Specifically, you worked with Windows Store app (XAML) controls that are designed for Windows 8.1-based applications. You learned how to use the *TextBox* control to manage a variety of text input tasks, the *FlipView* control to display a series of interesting photos, the *MediaElement* control to play audio and video files, and the *WebView* control to display content from a webpage.

These controls manage information and allow the user to access interesting media within Windows Store applications. I will continue to discuss common Windows Store app controls and their uses in this book. If you want to see a complete list, you can examine the "controls" entry in the Index of this book to find all the controls that I discuss listed alphabetically. You might also want to consult my book *Start Here! Learn Microsoft Visual Basic 2012,* (Microsoft Press), which provides a thorough introduction to the basic Windows Store app controls, including *Button, Ellipse, TextBlock, CheckBox, RadioButton,* and much more.

In Chapter 6, "Working with Windows Forms controls," you'll continue learning about controls, but this time in relation to the Windows Forms controls that a Visual Studio programmer uses when they create a Windows desktop application. As you learned in Chapter 4, "Windows desktop apps: A walkthrough using Windows Forms," Windows desktop apps utilize a different Toolbox and have different requirements for the way that controls are used within applications and the user interface. Chapter 6 introduces what I consider the essential Windows desktop app controls, such as *DateTimePicker, CheckBox, RadioButton, ListBox, MenuStrip, ToolStrip,* and *OpenFileDialog.*

Working with Windows Forms controls

After completing this chapter, you will be able to

■ Use the *DateTimePicker* control to display calendars and choose dates.

■ Use *CheckBox, RadioButton, GroupBox*, and *ListBox* controls to process user input.

■ Add menus to your Windows desktop app by using the *MenuStrip* control.

■ Add toolbars and buttons by using the *ToolStrip* control.

■ Add standard dialog boxes to your programs, including *OpenFileDialog* and *ColorDialog*.

A s you learned in earlier chapters, Microsoft Visual Studio 2013 controls are the graphical tools you use to build the user interface of a Visual Basic app. Controls are located in the IDE's Toolbox, and you use controls to create objects on a page or a form. You customize them with property settings and event handlers. The controls that load into the Visual Studio Toolbox will depend on the type of application that you are creating.

If you open a new Windows desktop application project, you'll see Windows Forms controls in the Toolbox, and you received some basic exposure to the *Label, Button*, and *PictureBox* controls in Chapter 4, "Windows desktop apps: A walkthrough using Windows Forms." In this chapter, you'll continue working with Windows desktop apps, and you'll learn how to manage information using the *DateTimePicker, CheckBox, RadioButton, ListBox*, and *GroupBox* controls. You'll also learn how to create menus, toolbars, and dialog boxes in a Windows desktop app by using the *MenuStrip, ToolStrip*, and *OpenFileDialog* controls.

These common controls are what I consider the essential user interface tools and design features for a Windows desktop (Windows Forms) application, and they will be useful to you as you prepare programs for that environment. However, keep in mind that Windows Forms controls are not easily copied to Windows Store apps; typically, you need to use completely separate controls for Window Store apps, which necessitates the multiplatform approach I am discussing in this book. In this chapter, I will present some of the Windows Forms controls that you should be familiar with if you are going to create Windows desktop apps using Visual Basic 2013. This information will also be useful for Visual Studio developers who are moving back and forth between the two platforms.

Using the *DateTimePicker* control

As you learned in earlier chapters, some Visual Studio controls display information, and others gather information from the user or process data behind the scenes. In this opening exercise, you'll work with a simple Windows Forms control called *DateTimePicker*, which can be placed on a form and will prompt the user for a date or time using a graphical calendar. Although your use of the control will be rudimentary at this point, experimenting with *DateTimePicker* will familiarize you with how Windows Forms controls work and how much work many controls do on their own, with little programmatic involvement.

The Birthday program uses a *DateTimePicker* control and a *Button* control to prompt the user for the date of his or her birthday. It then displays that information by using a pop-up window called a *message box*, which is a common feature of Windows desktop applications. Give it a try now.

Gather information from a calendar with *DateTimePicker*

1. Start Visual Studio 2013.

2. On the Visual Studio File menu, click New Project.

   The New Project dialog box opens, with project templates listed by category on the left side of the dialog box. Because you are now creating a Windows desktop (Windows Forms) app, you want to be sure to select the Windows template, rather than the Windows Store template you used in Chapter 5, "Working with Windows Store app controls."

3. Click the Windows category under Visual Basic in the Templates area of the dialog box.

   The New Project dialog box looks like this:

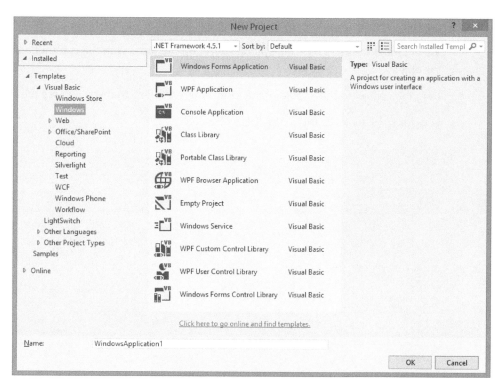

4. Click the Windows Forms Application icon in the central Templates area of the dialog box, if it is not already selected.

Visual Studio prepares the development environment for Visual Basic Windows desktop app.

5. In the Name text box, type **My Birthday**.

Visual Studio assigns the name My Birthday to your project. (You'll specify a folder location for the project later.)

6. Click OK to create the new project in Visual Studio.

Visual Studio cleans the slate for a new programming project and displays a blank Windows form in the Designer for your user interface. Remember that, by convention, a window in a Windows Store app is called a *page*, and a window in a Windows desktop app is called a *form*, and I'll recognize these distinctions in this book.

7. Open the Toolbox in the IDE, and examine the various controls provided for Windows desktop (Windows Forms) apps.

You'll find the most typical controls in the Common Controls category of the Toolbox. All Windows Forms is also a very useful category.

8. Double-click the *DateTimePicker* control in the Common Controls category of the Toolbox.

   Visual Studio creates a date time picker object on the form, with the current date displayed in the object.

9. Drag the control to the middle of the form, and resize it so that you can see the entire date.

   Your form will look like this in the IDE:

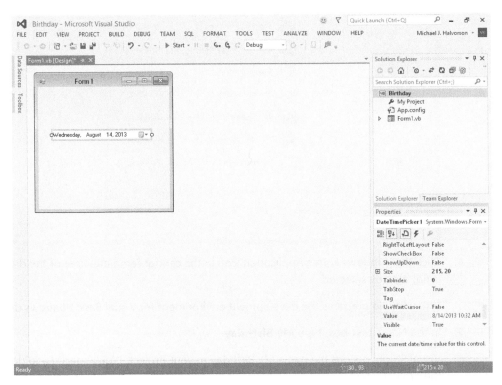

By default, the date/time picker object displays the current date, but you can adjust the current setting by changing the object's *Value* property. Displaying the date is a handy design guide—it lets you size the date/time picker object appropriately when you're creating it.

10. Double-click the *Button* control in the Toolbox to add a button object to the form, and then drag it below the date time picker.

    You'll use this button to display your own birth date and to test that the control is working properly.

11. In the Properties window, change the *Text* property of the button object to **Show My Birthday**, and if necessary, resize the button object to display all of the text.

12. Change the *Name* property of the button object to **DateButton**.

13. Click the form object itself (the background of the form anywhere within the *Form1* window frame), and then display the form's *Text* property in the Properties window.

14. Change the *Text* property of the form object to **Date Time Picker Example**.

As you learned in Chapter 4, you can change the *Text* property of the form to modify the words that appear at the top of this window's frame when the program runs. Making this change makes your program's purpose clearer and more interesting visually than the default "Form1."

Now you'll add a few lines of Visual Basic code to an event handler associated with the button object.

15. Double-click the button object on the form to display its default event handler, and then type the following statements between the *Private Sub* and *End Sub* in the *DateButton_Click* event handler:

```
MsgBox("Your birth date was " & DateTimePicker1.Text)
MsgBox("Day of the year: " & DateTimePicker1.Value.DayOfYear.ToString())
```

These program statements display two message boxes (small dialog boxes) with information from the date time picker object. The first line uses the *Text* property of date time picker to display the birth date information that you select when using the object at run time. The *MsgBox* function displays the string value *"Your birth date was"* in addition to the textual value held in the date time picker's *Text* property. These two pieces of information are joined together by the string concatenation operator (&).

The statement *DateTimePicker1.Value.DayOfYear.ToString()* uses the date time picker object to calculate the day of the year in which you were born, counting from January 1. This is accomplished by the *DayOfYear* property and the *ToString* method, which converts the numeric result of the date calculation to a textual value that's more easily displayed by the *MsgBox* function.

Methods, like *ToString* in the preceding example, are elements in Visual Basic code that perform an *action* or a *service* for a particular object, such as converting a number to a string or adding items to a list box. Methods differ from *properties*, which manage a value, and *event handlers*, which execute or *fire* when a user manipulates an object. You'll see that numerous methods are shared among objects so that when you learn how to use a particular method, you'll be able to use it again in different circumstances.

After you enter the code for the *DateButton_Click* event handler, the Code Editor looks similar to this:

16. Click the Save All button to save your changes to disk, and specify My Documents\Visual Basic 2013 SBS\Chapter 06 as the folder location.

Now you're ready to run the simple Windows desktop app.

Run the Birthday program

1. Click the Start Debugging button on the toolbar.

   The Birthday program starts to run. The current date is displayed in the date time picker.

2. Click the arrow in the date time picker to display the object in Calendar view.

   Your form looks like the following screen shot, but most likely with a different month and date.

3. Click the Left scroll arrow to look at previous months on the calendar.

   Notice that the text box portion of the object also changes as you scroll the date. However, the Today value at the bottom of the calendar doesn't change.

   Although you can scroll all the way back to your exact birthday, you might not have the patience to scroll month by month. To move to your birth year faster, select the year value in the date time picker text box and enter a new year.

Tip To move even faster to previous (or future years), click the month title at the top of the picker to zoom out and display the entire year. Click again to zoom out to a list of years, and click once more to zoom out to a decade.

4. Select the four-digit year in the date time picker text box.

    When you select the date, the date time picker closes.

5. Type your birth year in place of the year that's currently selected, and then click the arrow again.

    The calendar reappears in the year of your birth.

6. Click the scroll arrow again to locate the month in which you were born, and then click the exact day on which you were born.

    If you didn't know the day of the week on which you were born, now you can find out!

    When you select the final date, the date time picker closes, and your birth date is displayed in the text box. You can click the button object to see how this information is made available to other objects on your form.

7. Click the Show My Birthday button.

    Visual Basic executes your program code and displays a message box containing the day and date of your birth. Notice how the two dates shown in the two boxes match:

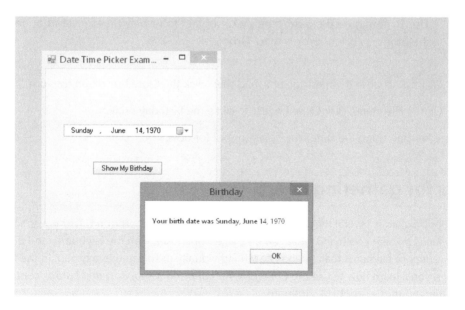

8. Click OK in the message box.

   A second message box appears, indicating the day of the year on which you were born—everything is working as planned.

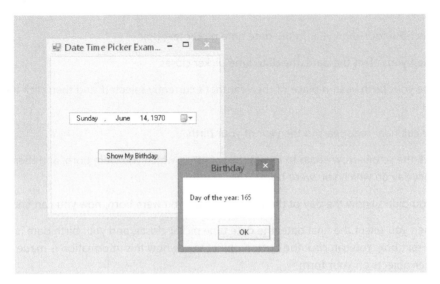

You'll find this control to be quite capable—not only does it remember the new date or time information that you enter but it also keeps track of the current date and time, and it can display this date and time information in a variety of useful formats.

 Tip To configure the date/time picker object to display times instead of dates, set the object's *Format* property to **Time**.

9. Click OK to close the message box, and then click the Close button on the form.

10. On the File menu, click Close Project to close the Birthday project.

You're finished using the *DateTimePicker* control for now.

Controls for gathering input

Visual Basic provides several mechanisms for gathering input in a program. *Text boxes* accept typed input, *menus* present commands that can be clicked or chosen with the keyboard, and *dialog boxes* offer a variety of elements that can be chosen individually or selected in a group. In the following exercises, you'll learn how to use the *CheckBox, RadioButton, GroupBox, and ListBox* controls to help you gather input in a variety of situations.

Using the *CheckBox* control

Your first task will be to experiment with the *CheckBox* control in the Toolbox. You'll use *CheckBox* to explore how basic user input is processed in a Windows desktop app.

Create a *CheckBox* control

1. On the File menu, click New Project.

   The New Project dialog box opens.

2. Create a new Windows Forms application named **My CheckBox**.

   The new project is created, and a blank form appears in the Designer.

3. Enlarge the form substantially so that it takes up about half of the screen and is in a rectangular shape that is wider than it is high.

4. Click the *CheckBox* control in the Toolbox, and then create a check box object near the bottom of the form.

   A new check box appears on the form much like other objects in a Windows desktop app. You can name, move, and resize this check box, as well as adjust features such as font name and font style.

5. Use the Properties window to change the check box's *Name* property to DisplayImageCheckBox.

6. Set the check box's *Text* property to **Display Bird Image**.

7. Set the check box's *Checked* property to True.

   The *Checked* property specifies whether or not a check mark appears in the check box. You are setting the *Checked* property to True now because you want the check box to be selected when the user first opens the program.

   Now you'll create a large picture box object above the check box.

8. Click the *PictureBox* control in the Toolbox, and then create a substantial, rectangular picture box object above the check box.

   By default, the picture box is named *PictureBox1*.

9. Set the *Name* property of the picture box object to **BirdPhoto**.

   Now you'll add a swan photo to the picture box by using the picture box's smart tag feature. As you learned in Chapter 4, a smart tag is a context-sensitive button attached to the upper-right corner of the picture box frame. You can use the smart tag to quickly adjust common settings.

10. Click the picture box object's smart tag to display the shortcut menu of commands.

11. Click Choose Image to display the Select Resource dialog box.

12. Click Project Resource File, and then click the Import button to create a new Resources folder and place a file in the folder.

    A Resources folder is perfect for art and photo files, and it will allow the images to travel with the project as you move and distribute it.

13. Double-click Swan.jpg in the My Documents\Visual Basic 2013 SBS\Chapter 06 folder.

    Visual Studio inserts the photo of a swan swimming, and it appears in the Select Resource dialog box. Your dialog box will look like this:

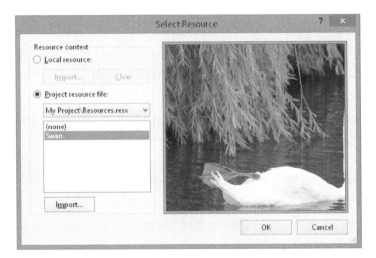

14. Click OK.

    In Solution Explorer, a Resources folder now appears with the file Swan.jpg in it.

15. In the smart tag's Picture Box Tasks menu, click StretchImage in the Size Mode list box.

    A photo of a swan swimming in a lake fills the picture box object in the Designer.

16. Adjust the spacing of the image so that it takes up about the amount of space on the form as shown in the following illustration:

Now you'll adjust the words that appear on the title bar of the Windows desktop app when it runs.

17. Click the form's background (not an object on the form), and then use the Properties window to set the form's *Text* property to **Check Box Sample**.

Now you're ready to create a simple event handler to process the check box selection that the user can make on the form. The *If...Then...Else* decision structure shown here can be expanded to handle any number of tasks, so you can use the event handler as a model as you use check boxes in your own Windows desktop apps. The code tests the *Checked* property, which is set to True if the user selects the check box.

18. Double-click the check box object on the form to open the *DisplayImageCheckBox_CheckedChanged* event handler in the Code Editor.

19. Enter the following program code:

```
If DisplayImageCheckBox.CheckState = CheckState.Checked Then
    BirdPhoto.Visible = True
Else
    BirdPhoto.Visible = False
End If
```

The *DisplayImageCheckBox_CheckedChanged* event handler runs only if the user clicks in the check box while the program is running. The event handler uses an *If...Then...Else* decision structure to complete its work, which I will discuss more fully in Chapter 12, "Creative decision structures and loops." In this case, the rather simple routine is quite easy to understand.

The *If* statement begins by checking the current status, or *state*, of the check box on the form, which you have named *DisplayImageCheckBox*. If a check mark is present (that is, the check box is selected), the comparison with the *CheckState.Checked* enumeration will result in a value of True, and the bird photo will be displayed.

The fourth line also makes use of the *Visible* property, but in this case it hides the Swan photo if a check box has been cleared from the check box. Finally, all multiline *If...Then...Else* decision structures conclude with an *End If* statement.

Typically, you'll want to add an event handler like this for each check box object that you place on a form. Because this project contains only one check box, you just need the one event handler.

20. Click the Save All button on the Standard toolbar to save your changes, specifying the My Documents\Visual Basic 2013 SBS\Chapter 06 folder as the location.

Run the CheckBox program

1. Click the Start Debugging button on the Standard toolbar.

Visual Basic runs the program in the IDE. A Swan appears in a picture box on the form, and the check box is selected. Your form will look like this:

2. Click the Display Bird Image check box to clear the check mark.

   Visual Basic removes the Swan image, and your form looks like this:

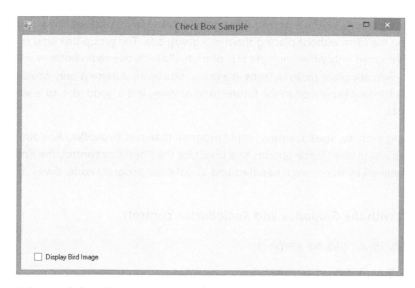

3. Select and clear the check box several times to see how the image appears and disappears in connection with the check box. Your event handler has linked these two user interface elements. The component is immediately recognizable as a standard user interface feature of a Windows-based application.

4. Click the Close button on the form to terminate the program.

5. On the File menu, click Close Project to close the CheckBox project.

You're ready to move on to another input mechanism in a Windows Forms application.

Using group boxes and radio buttons

The *RadioButton* control is another tool that you can use to receive input in a Windows desktop app, and you'll find it located on the Common Controls tab of the Windows Forms Toolbox. Radio buttons get their name from the old push-button car radios of the 1950s and 1960s, when people pushed or "selected" one button on the car radio and the rest of the buttons clunked back to the unselected position. Only one button could be selected at a time, because (it was thought) the driver should listen to only one thing at a time.

In Visual Studio, you can also offer mutually exclusive options for a user on a form, allowing them to pick one (and only one) option from a group. The procedure is to use the *GroupBox* control to create a frame on the form and then to use the *RadioButton* control to place the desired number of radio buttons in the frame. (Because the *GroupBox* control is not used that often, it is located on the Containers tab of the Toolbox.)

Note also that your form can have more than one *group* of radio buttons, each operating independently of one another. For each group that you want to construct, simply create a group box object first and then add radio buttons one by one to the group box.

There is one caveat to note: If a form requires only one set of radio buttons, the buttons can be placed directly on the form without placing them in a group box. The group box (and other containers) are actually required only when multiple sets of mutually exclusive radio buttons are used on one form. However, I typically place radio buttons in a group box (even if there is only one set per form) because it allows for easy expansion in the future. (And anyway, it is a good idea to learn to use the *GroupBox* control.)

In the following exercise, you'll create a simple program that uses *GroupBox, RadioButton*, and *PictureBox* controls to present three options to a user. Like the *CheckBox* control, the *RadioButton* control is programmed by using event handlers and Visual Basic program code. Give it a try now.

Gather input with the *GroupBox* and *RadioButton* controls

1. On the File menu, click New Project.

   The New Project dialog box opens.

2. Create a new Visual Basic Windows Forms Application project named **My Radio Button**.

   The new project is created, and a blank form appears in the Designer.

3. Enlarge the form a little so that you have a little more room to create a collection of controls and a picture box object.

4. In the Toolbox, open the Containers tab and click the *GroupBox* control.

5. Create a medium-sized group box on the top half of the form.

6. Return to the Toolbox, scroll up to the Common Controls tab, and click the *RadioButton* control.

7. Create three radio button objects in the group box.

   It is handy to double-click the *RadioButton* control to create radio buttons. Notice that each radio button gets its own number, which you can use to set properties. Your form should look similar to this:

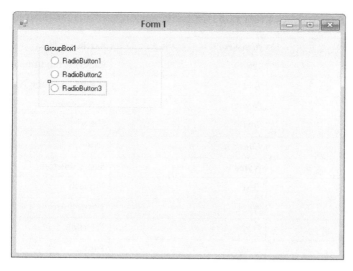

8. Using the *PictureBox* control, create one rectangular picture box object beneath the group box on the form.

9. Click the picture box object's smart tag to display the shortcut menu.

10. Click Choose Image to display the Select Resource dialog box.

11. Click Project Resource File, and then click the Import button to create a new Resources folder in the project.

   Now you'll add three photos to the project so that you can display them on the form.

12. Browse to the My Documents\Visual Basic 2013 SBS\Chapter 06 folder, hold down the Ctrl key, and then click Fern.jpg, Squash.jpg, and Thistle.jpg.

   You can select more than one file at once if you hold down the Ctrl key. In this case, you are selecting three files at once.

 Tip To select a contiguous range of file names in this dialog box, you can hold down the Shift key and click the first and last file names in the range.

13. Click the Open button to add the files to the Select Resource dialog box.

14. Click the Fern.jpg file in the list box to make it the default image for the picture box object.

15. Click OK.

   In Solution Explorer, a Resources folder now appears with the files Fern.jpg, Squash.jpg, and Thistle.jpg in it.

16. Set the following properties for the group box, radio button, and picture box objects:

Object	Property	Setting
Form1	Text	Radio Button Sample
GroupBox1	Text	"Select an Image Type"
RadioButton1	Name	FernButton
	Text	"Fern"
	Checked	True
RadioButton2	Name	SquashButton
	Text	"Squash"
RadioButton3	Name	ThistleButton
	Text	"Thistle"
PictureBox1	Image	Fern
	Name	PlantPictureBox
	SizeMode	StretchImage

The initial radio button state is controlled by the *Checked* property. Notice that the Fern radio button now appears selected in the IDE. Your IDE and form now look like this:

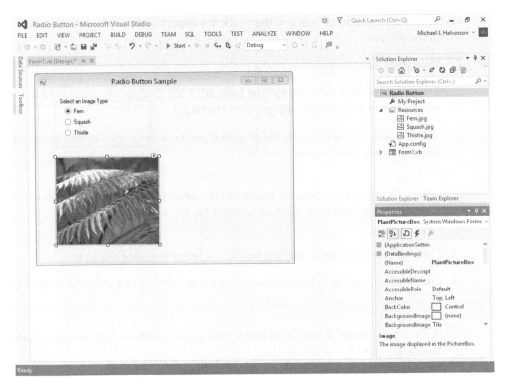

Now you'll add some program code to make the radio buttons switch among the photos you've added when the program runs.

17. Double-click the first radio button object (*FernButton*) on the form to open the Code Editor.

The *CheckedChanged* event handler for the *FernButton* object appears in the Code Editor. This procedure is run each time the user clicks the first radio button. Because you want to change the picture box image when this happens, you'll add a line of program code to accomplish that.

18. Type the following program code:

```
If (FernButton.Checked) Then PlantPictureBox.Image = My.Resources.Fern
```

This program statement checks the state of the *FernButton* radio button and then displays the fern image if the radio button has been selected. The image is displayed by copying the Fern.jpg file from the project's Resources folder into the picture box object's *Image* property. A similar statement will be attached to each button so that the appropriate photos will appear in the picture box as the different buttons are selected.

This copying task is made simple because you have already loaded the images into the project's Resource folder. The "My" namespace is used again here, a rapid access feature first introduced in Chapter 4 when you accessed the *My.Computer.Audio* object to play a sound. The *My* namespace is designed to simplify accessing the .NET Framework to perform common tasks, such as using your application's resources and adjusting settings on your computer. The *My* namespace is organized as a hierarchy, which you can use and explore using IntelliSense and Visual Studio's object-oriented terminology.

19. Switch back to the Designer, double-click the second radio button object on the form, and type the following program code:

```
If (SquashButton.Checked) Then PlantPictureBox.Image = My.Resources.Squash
```

20. Switch back to the Designer, double-click the third radio button object on the form, and type the following program code:

```
If (ThistleButton.Checked) Then PlantPictureBox.Image = My.Resources.Thistle
```

21. Click the Save All button on the toolbar to save your changes, specifying the My Documents\ Visual Basic 2013 SBS\Chapter 06 folder as the location.

Run the Radio Button program

1. Click the Start Debugging button on the Standard toolbar.

Visual Basic runs the program in the IDE. The fern photograph appears in a picture box on the form, and the first radio button is selected.

2. Click the second radio button (Squash).

Visual Basic displays the image, as shown here:

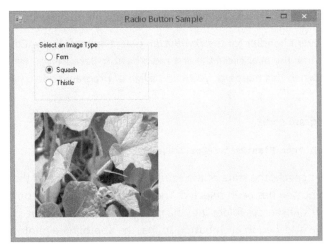

3. Click the third radio button (Thistle).

   A photo of a garden Thistle appears.

4. Click the first radio button (Fern).

   The image of a fern plant appears again.

5. Continue testing the program to verify that each of the *CheckedChanged* event handlers is loading the proper images into the picture box.

6. When you're finished, click the Close button on the form to end the program.

7. On the File menu, click Close Project to close the Radio Button project.

Well done! You're finished working with *GroupBox* and *RadioButton* controls for now. But can you imagine how you might use them in a Windows desktop app of your own? Presenting visual choices to the user is one exciting way to request and receive input from the user—what you display depends only on your creativity!

Processing input with list boxes

In addition to check boxes and radio buttons, a useful mechanism for gathering input in a Windows desktop app is the *ListBox* control, a scrollable container used to present a list of items and allow the user to select one or more items. List boxes are created in Visual Studio 2013 apps by selecting the *ListBox* control in the Windows Forms Toolbox and then adding the control to a form. A list box can expand or contract while a program is running, and you can use a list box to present a variable number of items. In addition, you can add scroll bars to a list box, if the number of items is greater than you can display at once.

Unlike a set of radio buttons, the items in a list box can be rearranged while a program is running, while radio buttons typically stay in the same order. You can also add a *collection* of items to a list box at design time by setting the *Items* property of the list box, which you will find under the *Data* category in the Properties window.

The key property associated with the *ListBox* control is *SelectedIndex*, which returns to the program the item number selected in the list box. (List box lists are numbered starting with zero.) Also useful is the *Add* method, which allows you to add items to a list box in an event handler or any other block of code. In the following exercise, you'll experiment with both of these features.

Create a list box and process a user's selections

1. On the File menu, click New Project, and create a new Windows Forms Application project named **My ListBox**.

   The new project is created, and a blank form appears in the Designer.

2. Enlarge the default form so that you have more room to create a list box and a picture box.

   You'll work with the four images you used earlier in this chapter.

3. In the Toolbox, click the *ListBox* control, and then create a medium-sized list box object on the top half of the form.

4. Use the *PictureBox* control to create a rectangular picture box object beneath the list box object on the form.

5. Click the picture box object's smart tag to display the shortcut menu.

6. Click Choose Image to display the Select Resource dialog box.

7. Click Project Resource File, and then click the Import button to create a new Resources folder in the project.

   Now you'll add four photos to the project so that you can display them on the form.

8. Browse to the My Documents\Visual Basic 2013 SBS\Chapter 06 folder, click Fern.jpg, hold down the Shift key, click Thistle.jpg, and then click Open.

   Four images are added to the Select Resource dialog box, including Fern.jpg, Squash.jpg, Swan.jpg, and Thistle.jpg.

9. Click OK.

   In Solution Explorer, a Resources folder is visible with four files to choose from.

10. Set the following properties for the list box and picture box objects on the form:

Object	Property	Setting
Form1	*Text*	"List Box Sample"
ListBox1	*Name*	PhotosListBox
PictureBox1	*Name*	PhotosPictureBox
	Image	(none)
	SizeMode	StretchImage

Your form now will look like this. (Notice that no photo is currently visible, because you selected (none) for the picture box object's *Image* property.)

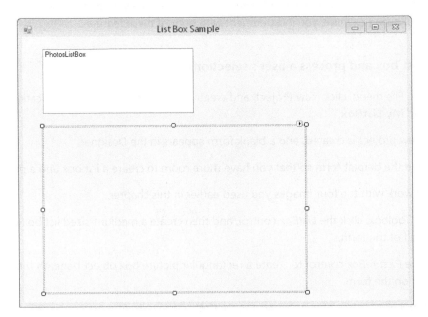

Now you'll add the necessary Visual Basic code to fill the list box object with valid selections, and you'll also create an event handler to process each selection that the user makes.

11. Double-click the list box object (*PhotosListBox*) to open the Code Editor.

The *SelectedIndexChanged* event handler for the *PhotosListBox* object appears in the Code Editor. This procedure runs each time the user clicks an item in the list box object. We need to update the image in the picture box object named *PhotosPictureBox* when a selection is made, and you'll handle the task by creating a decision structure known as a *Select Case* code block.

12. Type the following program code:

```
Select Case PhotosListBox.SelectedIndex
    Case 0
        PhotosPictureBox.Image = My.Resources.Fern
    Case 1
        PhotosPictureBox.Image = My.Resources.Squash
    Case 2
        PhotosPictureBox.Image = My.Resources.Swan
    Case 3
        PhotosPictureBox.Image = My.Resources.Thistle
End Select
```

The routine that you typed is called a *Select Case* decision structure, which explains to the compiler how to process the user's selection in the list box. The important identifier that begins this decision structure is *PhotosListBox.SelectedIndex*, which is read as "the *SelectedIndex* property of the list box object named *PhotosListBox*."

Recall that the *SelectedIndex* property returns a number to the program corresponding to the placement of the item that the user selected in the list box. In the current program, there are four items in the list box. These will be numbered 0, 1, 2, and 3 (from top to bottom).

If list item 0 is selected, the *Case 0* section of the structure is executed and the rest of the lines are skipped over. The program statement uses the *My* namespace to load a picture from the Resources folder.

If item 1 is selected, the *Case 1* section will be executed instead. This program statement also causes a photo to appear in the picture box, but it is a different photo. Likewise, if item 2 or item 3 is selected, the third or fourth *Case* clauses will process those selections.

You'll learn about more *Select Case* syntax in Chapter 12, "Creative decision structures and loops". There are a number of interesting options available, and they apply equally to Windows Store and Windows desktop applications.

Now you need to add some program code to create the initial entries in the list box object. To do this, we'll add some Visual Basic code to the *Form1_Load* event handler in the Code Editor, which is run when the program first starts and the *Form1* class instance is loaded.

13. Switch back to the Designer, and double-click the form (*Form1*) to display the *Form1_Load* event handler in the Code Editor.

   The *Form1_Load* event handler appears. This program code is executed each time the ListBox program is loaded into memory. (That is, each time that the application creates an instance of the form.) Windows Forms programmers put program statements in this special procedure when they want them executed every time a form loads. (Your Windows desktop app can display more than one form, or none at all, but the default behavior is that Visual Basic loads one initial form each time the user runs the program, which in turn executes the form's load event handler.) Often, as in the ListBox program, these statements define an aspect of the user interface that couldn't be created easily by using the controls in the Toolbox or the Properties window.

14. Type the following program code:

```
'Add items to a list box like this:
PhotosListBox.Items.Add("Fern")
PhotosListBox.Items.Add("Squash")
PhotosListBox.Items.Add("Swan")
PhotosListBox.Items.Add("Thistle")
```

   The first line is simply a comment offering a reminder about what the code accomplishes. The next three lines add items to the list box (*PhotosListBox*) in the program. The words in quotes will appear in the list box when it appears on the form. The important portion in these statements is *Add*, a handy method that adds items to list boxes or other items. Remember that in the *ListBox1_SelectedIndexChanged* event handler, these items will be identified as 0, 1, 2, and 3 because they appear at positions 0 through 3 in the list box.

15. Click the Save All button on the toolbar to save your changes, specifying the My Documents\ Visual Basic 2013 SBS\Chapter 06 folder as the location.

Run the ListBox program

1. Click the Start Debugging button on the Standard toolbar.

   Visual Studio launches the program. The four items appear in the list box, but because no item is currently selected, nothing appears yet in the picture box object.

2. Click the first item in the list box (Fern).

   Visual Basic displays a photograph of a green fern, as shown here:

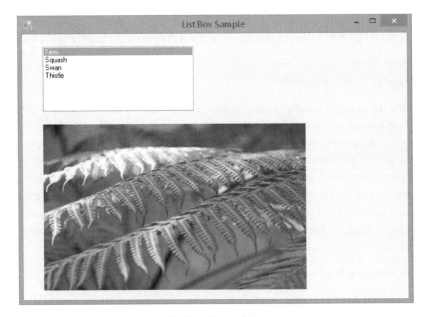

3. Click the second item in the list box (Squash).

   The green plant with yellow fruit appears on the screen.

4. Click the third item in the list box (Swan).

5. Click the fourth item in the list box (Thistle).

   The photo of a purple thistle plant appears, as shown in the following illustration:

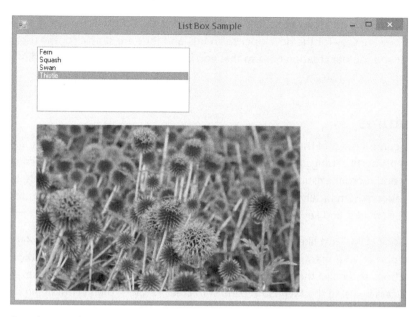

Good. Everything seems to be working properly in the list box and in the event handlers. However, keep testing the program for a while, clicking items in a different order, using the directional keys on the keyboard, using touch gestures, and so on—until you've tested every possible input pattern that a user might also try. As you test the seaworthiness of your own programs, be sure that you investigate all possible input scenarios. Yes, it is good to be finished with your work. But it is better to find a problem now than to have your users find it later.

6. When you're finished experimenting, click the Close button on the form to end the program.

7. Click Close Project on the File menu to unload the project from memory.

You're finished working with list boxes for now. If you like, you can broaden your learning by investigating the *ComboBox* and *CheckedListBox* controls on your own, too. These operate similar to the tools that you have been using in the last few exercises.

When you're ready to move on, use the following sections to learn how to add menu commands and toolbars to a Windows desktop application.

Adding menus by using the *MenuStrip* control

In Windows Store applications, menus and toolbars have been pushed to the sidelines. Because the goal is to support a variety of platforms—some with very small visual interfaces—the recommendation is to display menus and toolbars only occasionally and, in a general sense, to minimize "chrome" in applications (that is, persistent user interface features like toolbars and menu bars).

However, in Windows desktop apps there is still a need to support these venerable user interface features. They are easy for the developer to create, and they are simple for the user to operate. I'll review menu and toolbar creation here so that you can learn how to build and maintain these features.

Menu features

The *MenuStrip* control is a tool that adds menus to your Windows desktop programs, which you can customize with property settings using the Properties window. With *MenuStrip*, you can add new menus, modify and reorder existing menus, and delete old menus. You can also create a standard menu configuration automatically, and you can enhance your menus with useful features such as access keys, check marks, and keyboard shortcuts.

The menus look solid—just like a traditional Windows desktop application—but *MenuStrip* creates only the *visible* part of your menus and commands. You still need to write event handlers that process the menu selections and make the commands perform useful work. In the following exercise, you'll explore the process by using the *MenuStrip* control to create a Clock menu containing commands that display the current date and time.

Create a menu

1. On the File menu, click New Project.

   The New Project dialog box opens.

2. Create a new Windows Forms Application project named **My Menu**.

3. Click the *MenuStrip* control on the Menus & Toolbars tab of the Toolbox, and then draw a menu control on your form.

   Don't worry about the location—Visual Studio will move the control and resize it automatically. Your form looks like the one shown here:

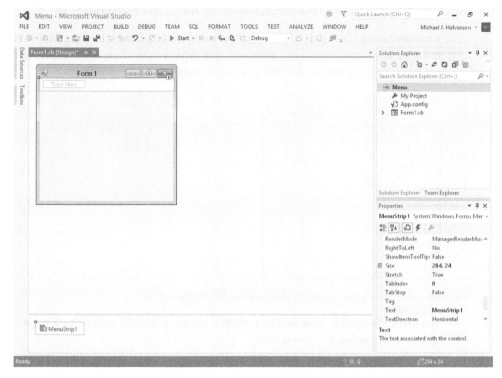

The menu strip object doesn't appear on your form, but below it. Non-visible objects, such as menus and timers, are displayed in the IDE in a separate pane named the *component tray*, and you can select them, set their properties, or delete them from this pane.

In addition to the menu strip object in the component tray, Visual Studio displays a visual representation of the menu that you created at the top of the form. The *Type Here* tag encourages you to click the tag and enter the title of your menu. After you enter the first menu title, you can enter submenu titles and other menu names by pressing the Arrow keys and typing additional names. Best of all, you can come back to this in-line Menu Designer later and edit what you've done or add additional menu items—the menu strip object is fully customizable, and with it, you can create an exciting menu-driven user interface like the ones you've seen in the best Windows desktop applications.

4. Click the *Type Here* tag, type **Clock**, and then press Enter.

The word *Clock* is entered as the name of your first menu, and two additional *Type Here* tags appear, with which you can create submenu items below the new Clock menu or additional menu titles. The submenu item is currently selected.

5. Type **Date** to create a Date command for the Clock menu, and then press Enter.

Visual Studio adds the Date command to the menu and selects the next submenu item.

6. Type **Time** to create a Time command for the menu, and then press Enter.

   You now have a Clock menu with two menu commands, Date and Time. You could continue to create additional menus or commands, but what you've done is sufficient for this example program. Your form looks like the one shown here:

7. Click the form's background to close the Menu Designer.

   The Menu Designer closes, and your form is visible in the IDE with a Clock menu. You're ready to start customizing the menu now.

Adding access keys to menu commands

With most Windows desktop applications, you can access and execute menu commands by using the keyboard. For example, in Visual Studio, you can open the File menu by pressing the Alt key and then pressing the F key. When the File menu is open, you can start a new project by pressing the P key and then Enter. The key that you press in addition to the Alt key is called an *access key*. You can identify the access key of a menu item because it's either underlined or, in some Windows 7-based applications, it appears in a small, handy box on the menu.

Visual Studio makes it easy to provide access key support. To add an access key to a menu item, activate the Menu Designer, and then type an ampersand (&) before the appropriate letter in the menu name. When you open the menu at run time (when the program is running), your program automatically supports the access key.

Menu conventions

A convention in many Windows desktop apps is that each menu title and menu command in a Windows desktop app has an initial capital letter. On occasion, you will see some variation in this style—for example, Visual Studio 2012 and Visual Studio 2013 use all capital letters for menu titles. File and Edit are often the first two menu names on the menu bar, and Help is usually the last. Other common menu names are View, Format, and Window.

No matter what menus and commands you use in your applications, take care to be clear and consistent with them. Menus and commands should be easy to use and should have as much in common as possible with those in other Windows-based applications. As you create menu items, use the following guidelines:

- Use short, specific captions consisting of one or two words at most.

- Assign each menu item an access key. Use the first letter of the item if possible, or the access key that is commonly assigned (such as *x* for Exit).

- Menu items at the same level should have a unique access key. (If they don't, the user can move between them by pressing the access key and will then need to press Enter to run the command.)

- If a command is used as an on/off toggle, place a check mark to the left of the item when it's active. You can add a check mark by setting the *Checked* property of the menu command to True in the Properties window.

- Place an ellipsis (...) after a menu command that requires the user to enter more information before the command can be executed. The ellipsis indicates that you'll open a dialog box if the user selects this item.

Note By default, most newer versions of Windows don't display the underline or small box for access keys in a program until you press the Alt key for the first time. In Windows 8.1, Windows 8, and Windows 7, you can adjust this option by clicking the Appearance And Personalization option in Control Panel, clicking Ease Of Access Center, clicking Make The Keyboard Easier To Use, and then selecting Underline Keyboard Shortcuts And Access Keys.

Try adding access keys to the Clock menu now.

Add access keys

1. Click the Clock menu name on the form, pause a moment, and then click it again.

    The menu name is highlighted, and a blinking I-beam (text-editing cursor) appears at the end of the selection. With the I-beam, you can edit your menu name or add the ampersand character (&) for an access key. (If you double-clicked the menu name, the Code Editor might have opened. If that happened, close the Code Editor and repeat step 1.)

2. Press the left arrow key five times to move the I-beam to just before the Clock menu name.

    The I-beam blinks before the letter C in *Clock.*

3. Type **&** to define the letter C as the access key for the Clock menu.

    An ampersand appears in the text box in front of the word *Clock.*

4. Click the Date command in the menu list, and then click Date a second time to display the I-beam.

5. Type **&** before the letter *D.*

    The letter *D* is now defined as the access key for the Date command.

6. Click the Time command in the menu list, and then click the command a second time to display the I-beam.

7. Type **&** before the letter *T.*

    The letter *T* is now defined as the access key for the Time command.

8. Press Enter.

    Pressing Enter locks in your text-editing changes. Your form looks like this:

Now you'll practice using the Menu Designer to switch the order of the Date and Time commands on the Clock menu. Changing the order of menu items is an important skill because at times you'll think of a better way to define your menus.

Change the order of menu items

1. Click the Clock menu on the form to display its menu items, if they are not already visible.

   To change the order of a menu item, simply drag the item to a new location on the menu. Try it now.

2. Drag the Time menu on top of the Date menu, and then release the mouse button.

   Dragging one menu item on top of another menu item means that you want to place the first menu item ahead of the second menu item on the menu. As quickly as that, Visual Studio moves the Time menu item ahead of the Date item.

You've finished creating the user interface for the Clock menu. Now you'll use the menu event handlers to process the user's menu selections in the program.

> **Tip** To delete a menu item from a menu, click the unwanted item in the menu list, and then press the Delete key. (If you try this now, remember that Visual Studio also has an Undo command, located on both the Edit menu and the Standard toolbar, so you can reverse the effects of the deletion.)

Processing menu choices

After menus and commands are configured by using the menu strip object, they also become new objects in your program. To make the menu objects do meaningful work, you need to write event handlers for them. Menu event handlers typically contain program statements that display or process information on the form and modify one or more menu properties. If more information is needed from the user to process the selected command, you can write your event handler so that it displays a dialog box and one or more of the input controls you used earlier in the chapter.

In the following exercise, you'll add a label object to your form to display the output of the Time and Date commands on the Clock menu.

Add a label object to the form

1. Click the *Label* control in the Toolbox.

2. Create a label in the middle of the form.

   The label object appears on the form and displays the name *Label1* in the program code.

3. Set the following properties for the label:

Object	Property	Setting
Label1	*Name*	ClockOutput
	AutoSize	False
	BorderStyle	FixedSingle
	Font	Microsoft Sans Serif, Bold, 24-point
	Text	(empty)
	TextAlign	MiddleCenter

4. Resize the label object so that it is much larger (it will be holding clock and date values), and position it in the center of the form. Your form should look similar to the following:

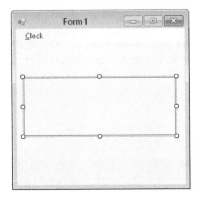

5. Use the Properties window to change the *Text* property of the *Form1* object to **Menu Samples**.

Now you'll add program statements to the Time and Date event handlers to process the menu commands.

Edit the menu event handlers

1. Click the Clock menu on the form to display its commands.

2. Double-click the Time command on the menu to open an event handler for the command in the Code Editor.

The *TimeToolStripMenuItem_Click* event handler appears in the Code Editor. The name *TimeToolStripMenuItem_Click* includes the name "Time" that you gave this menu command. The concatenated words in *ToolStripMenuItem* indicate that in its underlying technology, the *MenuStrip* control is related to the *ToolStrip* control. (We'll see further examples of that later in this chapter.) By convention, the *_Click* syntax means that this is the event handler that runs when a user clicks the menu item.

3. Type the following program statement:

```
ClockOutput.Text = TimeString
```

This program statement displays the current time (from the system clock) in the *Text* property of the label object (*ClockOutput*), replacing the previous contents of the label (if any). *TimeString* is a property that contains the current time formatted for display or printing. You can use *TimeString* in your Visual Basic Windows desktop programs to display the time accurately, down to the second.

> **Tip** You can set the system time by using the Clock, Language, and Region category in the Control Panel in Windows 8.1, Windows 8, or Windows 7.

4. Press Enter.

5. Click the View Designer button in Solution Explorer, and then double-click the Date command on the Clock menu.

   The *DateToolStripMenuItem_Click* event handler appears in the Code Editor. This event handler is executed when the user clicks the Date command on the Clock menu.

6. Type the following program statement:

```
ClockOutput.Text = DateString
```

This program statement displays the current date (from the system clock) in the *Text* property of the label object, replacing the previous text. The *DateString* property is also available for general use in your Windows desktop apps written in Visual Basic. Assign *DateString* to the *Text* property of an object whenever you want to display the current date on a form.

> **Tip** The Visual Basic *DateString* property returns the current system date. You can set the system date by using the Clock, Language, and Region category in the Control Panel of Windows 8.1, Windows 8, or Windows 7.

7. Press Enter to complete the line.

Your screen looks similar to this:

You've finished building the Menu program. Now you'll save your changes to the project, and run it.

8. Click the Save All button on the Standard toolbar, and then specify the My Documents\Visual Basic 2013 SBS\Chapter 06 folder as the location.

Run the Menu program

1. Click the Start Debugging button on the Standard toolbar.

The Menu program runs in the IDE.

2. Click the Clock menu on the menu bar.

The contents of the Clock menu appear.

3. Click the Time command.

The current system time appears in the label box, as shown here:

Notice that the clock is showing what is sometimes referred to as "military time" in North America—that is, a 24-hour clock.

Now you'll try displaying the current date by using the access keys on the menu.

4. Press and release the Alt key, and then press the C key.

   The Clock menu opens, and the first item on it is highlighted.

5. Press the D key to display the current date.

   The current date appears in the label box, as shown in the following illustration:

If the label you created is not big enough to fully display the date, the value might be truncated. If this happens, you'll need to resize the label object so that it can fully display the information. Stop the program, resize the label, and try it again.

6. When you're finished experimenting, click the Close button on the program's title bar to stop the program.

Congratulations! You've created a working program that uses menus and access keys. In the next exercise, you'll learn how to use toolbars.

System clock properties and methods

You can use various properties and methods to retrieve chronological values from the system clock. You can use these values to create custom calendars, clocks, and alarms in your programs. Table 6-1 lists a few of the most useful system clock properties and methods.

TABLE 6-1 System clock properties and methods

Property or method	Description
TimeString	This property sets or returns the current time from the system clock.
DateString	This property sets or returns the current date from the system clock.
Now	This property returns an encoded value representing the current date and time. This property is most useful as an argument for other system clock functions.
Hour (date)	This method extracts the hour portion of the specified date/time value (0 through 23).
Minute (date)	This method extracts the minute portion of the specified date/time value (0 through 59).
Second (date)	This method extracts the second portion of the specified date/time value (0 through 59).
Month (date)	This method extracts a whole number representing the month (1 through 12).
Year (date)	This method extracts the year portion of the specified date/time value.
Weekday (date)	This method extracts a whole number representing the day of the week (1 is Sunday, 2 is Monday, and so on).

Adding toolbars with the *ToolStrip* control

Parallel to the *MenuStrip* control, you can use the Visual Studio *ToolStrip* control to quickly add toolbars to a Windows desktop app's user interface. The *ToolStrip* control is placed on a Visual Basic form but resides in the component tray in the IDE, just like the *MenuStrip* control. You can also add a variety of features to your toolbars, including labels, combo boxes, text boxes, and split buttons. Toolbars look especially useful when you add them, but remember, as with menu commands, that you must write an event handler for each button that you want to use in your program. Still, it is amazing how much toolbar configuring the Visual Studio 2013 IDE does for you.

In the following exercise, you'll add a toolbar to the Menu project you've been building.

Create a toolbar

1. Display the form that you are creating in the Designer.

2. Click the *ToolStrip* control on the Menus & Toolbars tab of the Toolbox, and then draw a tool-bar control on your form.

   Don't worry about the location—Visual Studio will create a toolbar on your form automatically and extend it across the window. The tool strip object itself appears below the form in the component tray. On the form, the default toolbar contains one button. Now you'll use a special shortcut feature to populate the toolbar automatically.

3. Click the tiny smart tag in the upper-right corner of the new toolbar.

   The smart tag points to the right and looks similar to the smart tag we used with the *PictureBox* control earlier in the chapter. When you click the tag, a ToolStrip Tasks window opens that includes a few of the most common toolbar tasks and properties, as shown here. You can configure the toolbar quickly with these commands.

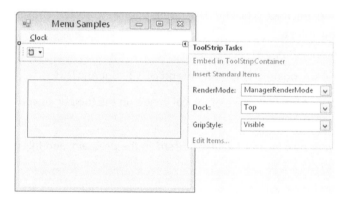

4. Click Insert Standard Items.

   Visual Studio adds a collection of standard toolbar buttons to the toolbar, including New, Open, Save, Print, Cut, Copy, Paste, and Help. Your form looks similar to the following screen shot:

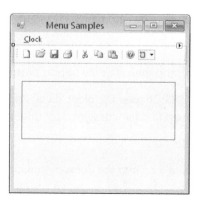

It is not necessary for you to start with a full toolbar of buttons as I have done here—I'm merely demonstrating one of the useful "automatic" features of Windows Forms programming in Visual Studio 2013. You could also create the buttons on your toolbar one by one, using the *ToolStrip* editing commands, as I'll demonstrate shortly. But for many applications, clicking Insert Standard Items is a timesaving feature. However, remember that although these toolbar buttons look professional, they are not functional yet. They need individual event handlers to make them work.

5. Click the Add ToolStripButton arrow on the right side of the new toolbar, and then click the Button item.

    Add ToolStripButton allows you to add more items to your toolbar, such as buttons, labels, split buttons, text boxes, combo boxes, and other useful user interface elements. You've now created a custom toolbar button; by default, it displays a mountain-and-sun scene.

 Tip If you need additional room on your toolbar for new buttons, simply widen the form window, and you'll be able to see the tool strip items. This might be important in the following step, because you'll be expanding your new button considerably to fit in some descriptive text.

6. Right-click the new button, point to DisplayStyle, and click ImageAndText.

    Your new button displays both text and a graphical image on the toolbar. (If you don't see the new button, widen your form now.)

    Visual Studio names your new button *ToolStripButton1* in the program, and this name appears by default on the toolbar.

7. Select the *ToolStripButton1* object, if it is not already selected.

8. In the Properties window, change the *ToolStripButton1* object's *Text* property to **Color**, which will be the name of your button on the form.

    The Color button appears on the toolbar. You'll use this button later in the program to change the color of text on the form. Now insert a custom bitmap for your button.

9. Right-click the Color button, and then click the Set Image command.

    The Select Resource dialog box appears.

10. Click Local Resource (if it is not already selected), and then click the Import button.

11. Browse to the My Documents\Visual Basic 2013 SBS\Chapter 06 folder, if you are not already there, and then select the ColorButton.bmp bitmap file that I designed for this exercise.

12. Click Open, and then click OK to finalize your selection.

    Visual Studio loads the pink, blue, and yellow paint icon into the Color button, as shown in the following screen shot:

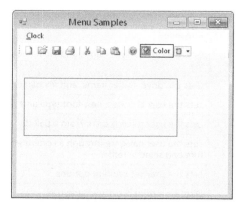

Your new button is complete, and you have learned how to add your own buttons to the toolbar. Now you'll learn how to delete and rearrange toolbar buttons.

Move and delete toolbar buttons

1. Drag the new Color button to the left side of the toolbar.

   Visual Studio lets you rearrange your toolbar buttons by using simple drag movements.

2. Right-click the second button in the toolbar (New), and then click the Delete command.

   The New button is removed from the toolbar. With the Delete command, you can delete unwanted buttons, which makes it easy to customize the standard toolbar buttons provided by the *ToolStrip* control.

3. Delete the Save and Print buttons, but be sure to keep the Color and Open buttons.

Now you'll learn how to program a toolbar button so that it displays a dialog box with useful controls and commands.

Using dialog box controls

Visual Studio 2013 contains eight standard dialog box controls for Windows desktop apps on the Dialogs and Printing categories of the Toolbox. These dialog boxes are ready-made, so you don't need to create your own custom dialog boxes for the most common tasks in Windows desktop apps, such as opening, saving, and printing files. In many cases, you'll still need to write the event handler code that connects these dialog boxes to your program, but the user interfaces are built for you and conform to the design standards for traditional Windows desktop apps.

The eight standard dialog box controls available to you are listed in Table 6-2. Note that the *PrintPreviewControl* and *PrintDocument* controls aren't listed here, but you'll find them useful if you use the *PrintPreviewDialog* control.

TABLE 6-2 Standard dialog box controls

Control	Purpose
OpenFileDialog	Gets the drive, folder name, and file name for an existing file
SaveFileDialog	Gets the drive, folder name, and file name for a new file
FontDialog	Lets the user choose a new font type and style
ColorDialog	Lets the user select a color from a palette
FolderBrowserDialog	Lets the user navigate through a computer's folder structure and select a folder
PrintDialog	Lets the user set printing options
PrintPreviewDialog	Displays a print preview dialog box
PageSetupDialog	Lets the user control page setup options, such as margins, paper size, and layout

In the following exercises, you'll practice using the *OpenFileDialog* and *ColorDialog* controls. The *OpenFileDialog* control lets your program locate bitmap files, and the *ColorDialog* control enables your program to change the color of the clock output. You'll connect these dialog boxes to the toolbar that you just created, although you could just as easily connect them to menu commands.

Add *OpenFileDialog* and *ColorDialog* controls

1. Click the *OpenFileDialog* control on the Dialogs tab of the Toolbox, and then click the form.

   An open file dialog box object appears in the component tray.

2. Click the *ColorDialog* control on the Dialogs tab of the Toolbox, and then click the form again.

   The component tray now looks like this:

Just like the menu strip and tool strip objects, the open file dialog box and color dialog box objects appear in the component tray, and they can be customized with property settings.

Now you'll create a picture box object on the form. Although you've used the *PictureBox* control several times in this chapter, this time you'll create a live picture box object that allows you to browse to items and display them using your new dialog box object.

Add a picture box object

1. Enlarge the form a little so that there is room for the new picture box object.

2. Click the *PictureBox* control in the Toolbox, and then draw a large, square picture box object on the form, below the label.

3. Change the picture box object's *Name* property to **OpenImage**.

4. Use the smart tag in the picture box object to set the *SizeMode* property of the picture box to StretchImage.

Now you'll create event handlers for the Color and Open buttons on the toolbar.

Event handlers that manage common dialog boxes

After you create a dialog box object, you can use the dialog box in a program by doing the following:

- If necessary, set one or more dialog box properties with the Properties window or by using program code before opening the dialog box.

- To open the dialog box, type the dialog box name with the *ShowDialog* method in an event handler associated with a toolbar button or menu command.

- Use program code to respond to the user's dialog box selections after the dialog box has been manipulated and closed.

Although all the possibilities for a Windows desktop application cannot be demonstrated here, in the following exercise you'll get your feet wet by writing the code for an *OpenToolStripButton_Click* event handler, a routine that runs when the Open command is clicked. You'll set the *Filter* property in the *OpenFileDialog1* object to define the file type in the Open common dialog box. (You'll specify JPEG files so that you can use the photographs you've been working with in this chapter.)

Next, you'll use the *ShowDialog* method to display an Open dialog box in your program. After the user has selected a file and closed this dialog box, you'll display the file that he or she selected in a picture box by setting the *Image* property of the picture box object to the file name the user selected.

Edit the Open button event handler

1. Double-click the Open button on your form's toolbar.

   The *OpenToolStripButton_Click* event handler appears in the Code Editor.

2. Type the following program statements in the event handler. Be sure to type each line exactly as it's printed here, and press the Enter key after each line.

```
OpenFileDialog1.Filter = "JPEG (*.jpg)|*.jpg"
If OpenFileDialog1.ShowDialog() = Windows.Forms.DialogResult.OK Then
    OpenImage.Image = System.Drawing.Image.FromFile _
        (OpenFileDialog1.FileName)
End If
```

The first three statements in the event handler refer to three different properties of the open file dialog box object. The first statement uses the *Filter* property to define a list of valid files. (In this case, the list has only one item: *.jpg.) This is important for the Open dialog box because a picture box object can display a number of file types, including the following:

- Joint Photographic Experts Group (JPEG) format (.jpg and .jpeg files)

- Bitmaps (.bmp files)

- Windows metafiles (.wmf files)

- Icons (.ico files)

- Portable Network Graphics (PNG) format (.png files)

- Graphics Interchange Format (.gif files)

To add additional items to the *Filter* list, you can type a pipe symbol (|) between items. For example, the following program statement allows both JPEG and Windows metafiles to be chosen in the Open dialog box:

```
OpenFileDialog1.Filter = "JPEG (*.jpg)|*.jpg|Metafiles (*.wmf)|*.wmf"
```

The second statement in the event handler displays the Open dialog box in the program. The *ShowDialog* method returns a result named *DialogResult*, which indicates the button on the dialog box that the user clicked. To determine whether the user clicked the Open button, an *If...Then* decision structure is used to check whether the returned result equals *DialogResult.OK*. If it does, a valid .jpg file path should be stored in the *FileName* property of the open file dialog box object.

The third statement uses the file name selected in the dialog box by the user. When the user selects a drive, folder, and file name and then clicks Open, the complete path is passed to the program through the *OpenFileDialog1.FileName* property. The *System.Drawing.Image.FromFile* method, which loads electronic artwork, is then used to copy the specified photo file into the picture box object. (I wrapped this statement with the line continuation character (_) because it was rather long.)

Now you'll write an event handler for the Color button that you added to the toolbar.

Write the Color button event handler

1. Display the form again, and then double-click the Color button on the toolbar that you added to the form.

    An event handler named *ToolStripButton1_Click* appears in the Code Editor. The object name includes *Button1* because it was the first nonstandard button that you added to the toolbar. (You can change the name of this object to something more intuitive, such as *ColorToolStripButton*, by clicking the button on the form and changing the *Name* property in the Properties window.)

2. Type the following program statements in the event handler:

```
ColorDialog1.ShowDialog()
ClockOutput.ForeColor = ColorDialog1.Color
```

The first program statement uses the *ShowDialog* method to open the color dialog box. *ShowDialog* is the method you use to open any form as a dialog box, including a form created by one of the standard dialog box controls that Visual Studio provides. The second statement in the event handler will assign the color that the user selects in the dialog box to the *ForeColor* property of the label object (*ClockOutput*). You should remember *ClockOutput* from earlier in this chapter—it's the label box you used to display the current time and date on the form. You'll use the color returned from the color dialog box to set the color of the text in the label.

Note that the color dialog box can be used to set the color of any user interface element that supports color in a Windows Forms app. Other possibilities include the background color of the form, the colors of shapes on the form, and the foreground and background colors of objects.

3. Click the Save All button on the Standard toolbar to save your changes.

Controlling color choices by setting color dialog box properties

If you want to further customize the color dialog box, you can control what color choices the dialog box presents to the user when the dialog box opens. You can adjust these color settings by selecting the *ColorDialog1* object and using the Properties window, or by setting properties by using program code before you display the dialog box with the *ShowDialog* method. Table 6-3 describes the most useful properties of the *ColorDialog* control. Each property should be set with a value of True to enable the option or False to disable the option.

TABLE 6-3 *ColorDialog* control properties

Property	Meaning
AllowFullOpen	Set to True to enable the Define Custom Colors button in the dialog box.
AnyColor	Set to True if the user can select any color shown in the dialog box.
FullOpen	Set to True if you want to display the Custom Colors area when the dialog box first opens.
SolidColorOnly	Set to True if you want the user to select only solid colors (dithered colors—those that are made up of pixels of different colors—are disabled).

Now you'll run the Menu program and experiment with the menus and dialog boxes you've created.

Run the Menu program

1. Click the Start Debugging button on the Standard toolbar.

   The program runs, and the Clock menu and the toolbar appear at the top of the screen.

2. On the form's toolbar, click Open.

   The Open dialog box opens. It looks great, doesn't it? (That is, it looks just like a regular Windows desktop app.) Notice the JPEG files (*.jpg) entry in the dialog box. You defined this entry with the following statement in the *OpenToolStripButton_Click* event handler:

   ```
   OpenFileDialog1.Filter = "JPEG (*.jpg)|*.jpg"
   ```

   The first part of the text in quotes—JPEG (*.jpg)—specifies which items are listed in the Files Of Type box. The second part—*.jpg—specifies the file name extension of the files that are to be listed in the dialog box.

3. Open a folder on your system that contains JPEG images. I'm using the Swan photo I've used in this chapter (located in My Documents\Visual Basic 2013 SBS\Chapter 06), but you can display any .jpg file accessible via your computer.

4. Select the JPEG file in the Open dialog box, and then click the Open button.

   A picture of the photo appears in the picture box. My form looks like this:

   Now you'll practice using the Color dialog box.

5. On the Clock menu, click the Time command.

   The current time appears in the label box.

6. Click the Color button on the toolbar.

The Color dialog box opens, as shown here:

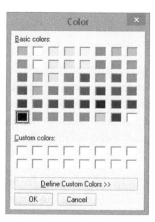

The Color dialog box contains elements that you can use to change the color of the clock text in your program. The current color setting, black, is selected.

7. Click one of the blue color boxes, and then click OK.

The Color dialog box closes, and the color of the text in the clock label changes to blue. (That's not significantly visible in the printed version of this book, alas, but you'll see it on the screen and in e-book versions.)

8. On the Clock menu, click the Date command.

The current date is displayed in blue type. Now that the text color has been set in the label, it remains blue until the color is changed again or until the program closes.

9. Close the Menu Samples program.

    The application terminates, and the Visual Studio IDE appears.

10. Close Visual Studio.

    You're finished working with Windows desktop apps for now.

Very well done! You've reviewed dozens of useful techniques for processing user input in a Windows desktop application. Although all of the Toolbox controls that manage this input are unique to Windows Forms applications and the Windows desktop, there will be ample opportunity to put these skills to work for the foreseeable future. Windows desktop apps are popular and useful in a variety of corporate and business settings, and these programs will need maintenance and, in many cases, further development.

In Part III, "Visual Basic programming techniques," you'll see both the Windows Forms and Windows Store platforms used. I can use this multiplatform approach because the Visual Basic language is independent of the operating environment upon which application programs are run. In this way, Windows Store apps and Windows desktop apps coexist very nicely, and you should know how to create each application type.

Summary

In this chapter, you reviewed several important Toolbox controls for Windows Forms applications that run on the Windows desktop. These controls have been available in Visual Studio for several releases, and they continue to provide excellent utility for Visual Basic programmers who are creating or maintaining traditional Windows desktop applications that run under Windows 8.1, Windows 8, or Windows 7.

Through numerous demonstration programs, you reviewed how to manage user input using the *DateTimePicker*, *CheckBox*, *RadioButton*, *ListBox*, and GroupBox controls. You also learned how to create menus, toolbars, and dialog boxes in a Windows desktop app using the *MenuStrip*, *ToolStrip*, and *OpenFileDialog* controls. Along the way, you learned about the *My* namespace, gained additional experience with the *Label* and *PictureBox* controls, and added artwork to a project's Resources folder so that it could be used easily throughout the application. Moving forward, you can use these essential tools and techniques to build Windows desktop apps with efficient and attractive user interfaces. Chapters 11-16 will teach fundamental Visual Basic programming techniques using Windows Forms apps alongside Windows Store apps.

In the next chapter, we return again to the user interface of Windows Store applications and examine in greater detail the opportunities presented by XAML, an advanced markup language that allows you to take greater control over the way that your user interface is constructed and compiled. You'll learn important conceptual terminology and more about how XAML markup is structured so that you can edit your user interfaces directly and create a number of exciting graphics effects.

CHAPTER 7

XAML markup step by step

After completing this chapter, you will be able to

- Describe the core features of a XAML document.

- Examine the XAML project files App.xaml and MainPage.xaml.

- Edit XAML elements and properties using the XAML tab of the Code Editor.

- Use XAML markup to add *ToggleButton*, *Image*, and *Canvas* objects to a Windows Store app.

This chapter provides a thorough introduction to XAML (pronounced *zammel*) and what you'll need to know about XAML markup to create Windows Store apps in Visual Studio 2013. You'll learn about the structure of XAML elements and tags, how to work with XAML markup in the Code Editor, and how to use XAML elements to create interesting features in a Windows Store app.

As you learned in Chapter 3, "Creating your first Windows Store application," XAML is a type of structured text that controls how Windows will display your application's user interface and graphics when the program runs. This structured text, or *markup*, is organized into a hierarchy of named *tags* and *attributes* (elements between the characters < and >). If you know something about the layout of HTML, the structure and content of XAML files will be somewhat familiar to you.

Within Visual Studio, XAML markup is created automatically for you when you use XAML Toolbox controls to create the user interface for a Windows Store app. This structured text is stored in various document files in your project, including App.xaml and MainPage.xaml—and you can examine and modify these files by using the XAML markup editing tools. Although most XAML documents function perfectly well without any additional editing from the software developer, it is helpful to know how XAML documents are organized, because there are times when modifying a XAML document directly is faster and more efficient than by using the Visual Studio Designer. There are also Windows Store app features that can be added only by editing XAML elements manually.

This chapter will help you learn the basics of XAML markup. In Chapter 8, "Using XAML styles," you'll learn timesaving XAML features that will help you set styles and reuse them for a consistent appearance across multiple controls.

Introduction to XAML

XAML is an abbreviation for Extensible Application Markup Language, an open Microsoft specification related to Extensible Markup Language (XML) and HyperText Markup Language (HTML). XAML documents are essentially text files that use tags to define how objects will be created in a Windows application's user interface. Microsoft introduced XAML as a design tool for the user interface of Windows Presentation Foundation (WPF) apps in Visual Studio 2008. Since that time, XAML has gained momentum as a design alternative to Windows Forms, the popular development platform we explored in Chapter 4, "Windows desktop apps: A walkthrough using Windows Forms," and Chapter 6, "Working with Windows Forms controls."

Although the Windows Forms designer in Visual Studio is well-established and easy to use, a key benefit of XAML is that you can define user interface elements with *markup tags*, either manually with the XAML tab of the Code Editor or using a design tool like the Visual Studio designer or Blend for Visual Studio. XAML tags are nested in a XAML document so that the objects on the page have a hierarchical, or *tree*, relationship. The location and characteristics of each object are precisely defined, and it is easy to adjust the size and shape of objects by entering specific values in the markup. In a typical design session, you might create several of the objects in the user interface with a design tool and then add additional objects and features by using XAML markup in the Code Editor. How much you use a design tool and how much you directly enter XAML markup is up to you.

Another benefit of XAML-based platforms is that Visual Studio separates the XAML markup used to define the user interface from the run-time logic that controls how the program works. As you've already learned, the run-time logic is stored in Visual Basic code-behind files that have the extension .vb in a project. These files are distinct from XAML markup files that have the extension .xaml in a project. The file separation means that one developer can work on the user interface for a project (using a design tool and XAML), and another developer can create the code-behind files (using Visual Basic or another Visual Studio language). When the completed project is assembled, the two sets of files (known to programmers as *partial class definitions*) are joined to form a finished Windows application. You'll learn more about partial classes in the section "Examining XAML project files."

In Visual Studio 2013, XAML is the required user interface model for Visual Basic programmers who are creating Windows Store apps or Windows Phone apps. WPF also uses XAML for user interface design, and it has been updated in Visual Studio 2013. (You can use WPF to create Windows Desktop apps and Web browser apps, but not Windows Store apps.) But as I have already mentioned, XAML is not a part of the Windows Forms programming model, so the information in this chapter does not apply to the construction of Windows Forms apps.

XAML in the Visual Studio IDE

When you create the user interface for a Windows Store app in the Visual Studio designer, you are building a XAML document that describes the objects, styles, and layout for your program's user interface. If you are running the Visual Studio IDE in Split view (with both Design and XAML views visible), you can see XAML markup at the bottom of the screen, as shown in the following illustration:

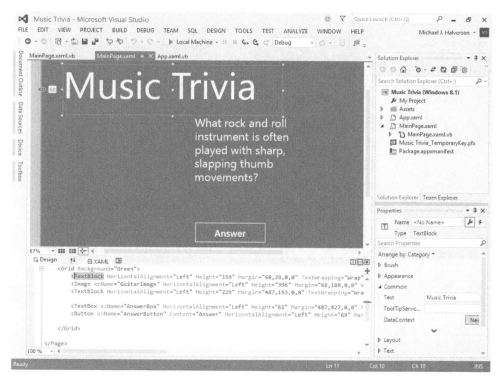

As this screen indicates, XAML documents are basically tagged text files that define the arrangement of panels, buttons, and objects on the page for a Windows app. These documents appear in Solution Explorer as .xaml files. To help you identify the various elements, the Code Editor displays the objects, properties, and strings in different colors.

XAML in Blend for Visual Studio

The Visual Studio designer is not the only tool that you can use to create XAML tags and documents. You can also use Blend for Visual Studio 2013, a Windows-based application that is distributed with Visual Studio 2013 Professional, Premium, and Ultimate editions, as well as Visual Studio Express 2013 for Windows. Blend is a stand-alone program that has several advanced design features; it contains tools and controls that are compatible with the Visual Studio IDE but are in some cases easier and more powerful to use. For example, you can use Blend's *Artboard* to create controls and dynamic, artistic effects; and you can build *storyboards* in Blend that animate the visual and audio elements of your design.

The following illustration shows Blend for Visual Studio when the Music Trivia project from Chapter 2 is loaded and displayed in Split view, with both the Design and XAML panes visible. Using this view, you can edit the user interface by using both Blend's tools and XAML markup in the Code Editor. For more information about using Blend to create Windows Store apps, see Chapter 4, "Designing Windows 8 Applications with Blend for Visual Studio," in my companion book *Start Here! Learn Microsoft Visual Basic 2012* (Microsoft Press, 2012).

XAML elements

Here is what a typical XAML definition looks like in the Visual Studio Code Editor for a text box object named *AnswerBox* from the Music Trivia project:

```
<TextBox x:Name="AnswerBox" HorizontalAlignment="Left" Height="61" Margin="487,427,0,0"
TextWrapping="Wrap" VerticalAlignment="Top" Width="333" Visibility="Collapsed"/>
```

This XAML markup defines a text box that will be left-aligned, have a height of 61 pixels, have a location on the page 487 pixels from the left margin and 427 pixels from the top margin, is formatted for text wrapping and top vertical alignment, will have a width of 333 pixels, and is temporarily invisible. (The text box appears only when the user clicks the Answer button.)

When the program is run and the user clicks Answer, an event handler makes the text box visible and places the string The Bass Guitar in the text box. Within the context of the Music Trivia program, the text box object looks like this:

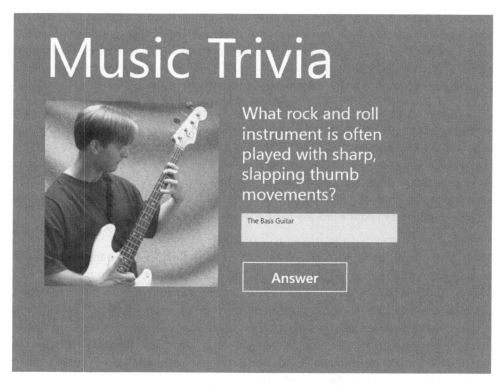

Although the XAML markup that creates the text box object actually appears on one line in the Code Editor, I've broken it into two lines in the book because the markup is fairly long. Visual Studio can handle very long lines, but to allow for easier reading in books, writers will often break long statements over several lines, as shown here:

```
<TextBox x:Name="AnswerBox"
         HorizontalAlignment="Left"
         Height="61"
         Margin="487,427,0,0"
         TextWrapping="Wrap"
         VerticalAlignment="Top"
         Width="333"
         Visibility="Collapsed"/>
```

The preceding two text box definitions are exactly the same, except for the extra carriage returns and the indentation at the start of each line in the second example. Notice that in both cases, the markup begins with the < tag and ends with the /> tag. This is an important syntax rule for XAML documents—all XAML object definitions that do not contain child elements begin with an opening angle bracket (<), indicate the class of the object (in this case, *TextBox*), and end with a forward slash and a closing bracket (/>).

A *child element* is an item (typically a control) that is nested within a parent control. For example, the XAML file defining a program's user interface contains a top-level *Grid* control, and beneath the *Grid* control are additional child elements (such as *TextBlock* and *Image*) that are nested under the *Grid* control and share a special relationship with it. You'll learn more about child elements in the procedure titled "Edit XAML markup in MainPage.xaml," later in this chapter.

You might also have noticed that each line in the XAML definition we are discussing sets a *property* for the text box object. The first such setting assigns a value to the *Name* property, and the process continues until the final property, *Visibility*, is assigned a value of "Collapsed." Note that each property assignment contains an equal sign (=) and a value in quotation marks. You've already been making property assignments like this with the Properties windows in the Visual Studio IDE, and you should know that you can also make them manually within the XAML tab of the Code Editor. In fact, many Visual Basic programmers find the process to be a lot faster in the Code Editor.

Note In some books about XML and XAML, you will see the property names for objects referred to as *attributes* instead of properties. This is also a correct way to describe them. Do not be confused by the different terminologies; the disparate terms simply have their roots in separate programming languages and traditions. I use the term *properties* in this book because of my roots as a Visual Basic programmer, where the term has long been current. But someone with a WPF or XAML background will likely use the term *attributes*. The two terms are actually connected—XAML attributes are essentially used to control object properties within a Windows Store application.

Namespaces in XAML markup

The *Name* property is a special case in XAML object definitions. In the XAML for the preceding text box, the *Name* definition is prefaced by the characters *x:*, as in the following markup:

```
<TextBox x:Name="AnswerBox"
```

In this case, *x:Name* indicates that a *namespace* is being assigned to the text box object and that the text box will be referred to as *AnswerBox* in the program. This syntax is based on XML, because all namespaces in XAML conform to the rules for XML namespaces. An XML namespace allows you to have one set of tagged elements that serve multiple purposes, each purpose represented by a different namespace, including the default namespace (where no namespace is specified). You'll learn more about the difference between XAML namespaces and .NET Framework namespaces in the next section.

Examining XAML project files

To get started with XAML, it is helpful to open a new Visual Basic Windows Store app and examine the default XAML documents that Visual Studio creates for you automatically. If you select the Visual Basic Blank App (XAML) template, you'll receive two XAML files, App.xaml and MainPage.xaml. Each file contains default XAML definitions for your application and user interface, and as you add to the project, the XAML files will expand. You'll also see two Visual Basic files in the project, App.xaml.vb and MainPage.xaml.vb. These files are the Visual Basic code-behind files, and although the XAML files and the Visual Basic files are related and linked together, they are written in separate languages. As you've already seen, .xaml files contain XAML markup, and .vb files contain Visual Basic code.

The following exercises step through these files and show you more about them. You'll also learn how to edit XAML files directly to change the content of your application.

Create a new Windows Store app and examine *App.xaml*

1. Start Visual Studio, and click New Project to open a new Visual Studio application.

2. Choose Visual Basic/Windows Store under Templates, and then verify that the Blank App (XAML) template is selected.

3. Type **My XAML Features** in the Name text box.

4. Click OK to open and configure the new project.

   Visual Studio opens, and a new project is created with the appropriate files. After a moment, you'll see the App.xaml.vb code-behind file for the Blank App template in the Code Editor, as shown in the following screen shot:

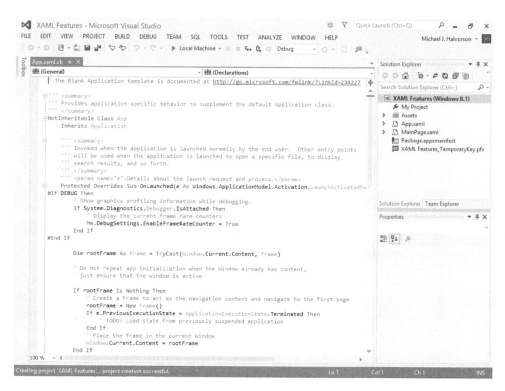

The App.xaml.vb file contains boilerplate code that defines the *Application* class and indicates what actions should take place when the program launches, as well as what to do when it is suspended. This is not XAML markup, but Visual Basic code, and in most cases you do not need to modify this default code listing. However, it is useful to examine the instructions in all new template files, and when you open other, more substantial Visual Basic templates, you'll see that there is more code to examine and more areas for you to complete.

Now you'll open the App.xaml file in the Code Editor.

5. In Solution Explorer, right-click the file App.xaml, and then click the View Designer command.

6. A new tab opens in the Code Editor, and the file App.xaml is loaded into it. (Notice that the code-behind file, App.xaml.vb, is still open and represented by a tab.) Your screen should look like this:

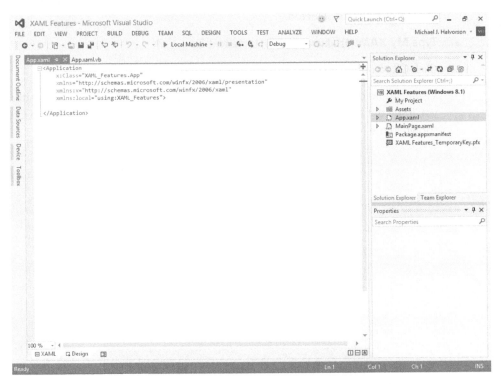

Now you'll see a few more items that you'll want to become familiar with.

First, in every XAML document, there is a core definition, or *root element*, that acts like a master container for the file. In App.xaml, the root element is *Application* (the core definition for this programming project), so the App.xaml file begins with the tag *<Application>* and, near the bottom, ends with the tag *</Application>*.

Within this core definition are the various classes and namespaces that collectively mold and shape the project. These lines are typically included at the top of a XAML file. In App.xaml, they include the following:

```
x:Class="XAML_Features.App"
xmlns="http://schemas.microsoft.com/winfx/2006/xaml/presentation"
xmlns:x="http://schemas.microsoft.com/winfx/2006/xaml"
xmlns:local="using:XAML_Features">
```

The first line defines a new *partial class* associated with the application name you've selected—in this case, *XAML_Features.App*. A partial class is a class whose definition can be split into multiple pieces, either across multiple files or within a single source file. The pieces of a partial class are merged when your Visual Basic project is compiled so that the resulting class is equivalent to a class specified in one location.

 Note If you specified a different application name when you created the project, that name will appear here instead. I am assuming that you've added the *My* prefix to your files to keep them separate from mine.

In this case, the statement connects the code-behind file, App.xaml.vb, to the XAML file, App. xaml, when the project is compiled. Each of these files holds a partial class definition, but when the project is compiled, the files form a complete class.

The second, third, and fourth lines declare XAML namespaces in the project that define default elements in the user interface. It is necessary to reference the definitions in specific documents because there are many XAML elements that have the same name, and Visual Studio needs to know which definition to use when there is a conflict. The second and third lines are standard XAML features: core namespaces that will appear in each XAML document that you create in Visual Studio or Blend. The *x* prefix, which is used here in the third line after the colon, is an *alias*, or shorthand way to refer to the classes in the namespace.

As you get deeper into Visual Studio programming terminology, you will see the term *namespace* being used in two ways. In Visual Basic code, a namespace is a hierarchical library of classes in the .NET Framework organized under a unique name, such as *Windows.UI*. You can reference individual namespaces of this type by placing an *Imports* statement at the top of a Visual Basic code-behind file.

However, a *XAML namespace* is used in XAML markup to differentiate between multiple vocabularies that can appear together in one XML document, or to indicate portions of an XML document that serve a specific purpose. The files App.xaml and MainPage.xaml both have default XAML namespace definitions of this type.

That's all that you'll see in this file—that is, if you're running Visual Studio 2013. However, if you had some experience with Visual Studio 2012, you would have noticed another section named *<Application.Resources>* in the App.xaml file for Visual Studio 2012 projects. Microsoft included a reference to the resource dictionary StandardStyles.xaml in *<Application.Resources>*, but that reference and resource dictionary are now located deeper within the Visual Studio 2013 product. So the default App.xaml file is a little shorter now in the default Visual Studio 2013 project.

Now you'll examine the markup in MainPage.xaml, the file where the features of your user interface are defined. You'll also make some changes to the file.

Edit XAML markup in MainPage.xaml

1. Right-click the MainPage.xaml file in Solution Explorer, and then select View Designer.

    Visual Studio loads MainPage.xaml into the Designer. If your IDE is set for Split view (the XAML designer's default orientation), you'll see a blank page near the top of the screen and the XAML markup associated with the Blank App template near the bottom of the screen.

    Tip If the Designer is not in Split view now, switch to Split view by clicking the Horizontal Split button near the lower-right corner of the Designer.

    Your screen will look like this:

    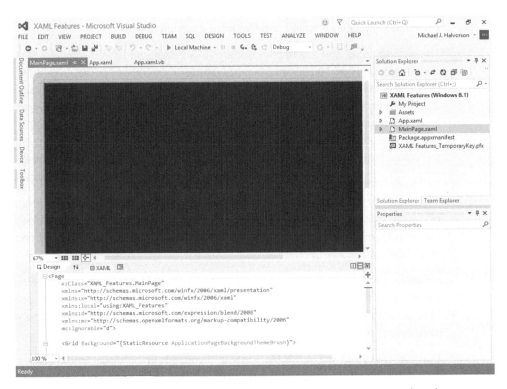

    The XAML document at the bottom begins with the root element *Page*, rather than *Application*, the core container discussed in the last example. In XAML, a *Page* element organizes a selection of user interface content that you want Visual Studio to display or navigate to; that is, it is a container for part or all of your application's user interface. Note that you can have more than one user interface page in a program, as long as each page is given a unique name.

New pages like this also require the core namespace definitions that you learned about in the App.xaml file previously. In addition to these namespaces, the file also includes a namespace associated with Blend, as well as one related to the Microsoft Office Open XML format, as indicated by "openxmlformats.org."

2. Scroll down the XAML tab of the Code Editor to display the lines beginning with *Grid* in the MainPage.xaml file. You'll see the following markup:

```
<Grid Background="{StaticResource ApplicationPageBackgroundThemeBrush}">

</Grid>
```

The *Grid* element is the default user interface element that appears within the root element of MainPage.xaml. It is also the fundamental layout control that will hold the other controls that appear on a page. Note that each XAML file contains only one top-level *Grid* control, but it can contain other, nested controls known as child elements. The way that controls on a page are nested within a structured hierarchy defines their relationship to one another and, ultimately, how they are displayed in the user interface.

It might be useful for you to think of this *Grid* element as a direct reference to a .NET Framework class named *Grid* in the *Windows.UI.Xaml.Controls* namespace. That is, elements in XAML markup are directly related to objects that you can use in Visual Basic program code. In an application created for Windows 8.1 in Visual Studio 2013, XAML elements and Visual Basic objects are two sides of the same coin.

Currently, the grid on this blank page contains no other objects, and its gridlines are not even visible on the screen. (A grid is more of a layout and design feature than a visible element of your user interface.) However, the grid's background color and texture are now being set via the *Background* property for the grid and the system resource setting *ApplicationPageBackgroundThemeBrush*.

Depending on which version of Visual Basic you are using, you may see either the name "ThemeResource" or "StaticResource" before the setting *ApplicationPageBackgroundThemeBrush*. ThemeResource was inserted into the default MainPage.xaml file in the final release of the Visual Studio 2013 software.

One way to adjust the *Background* property of the grid is to use the Properties window in the IDE. If you select the page itself in the Designer (not a specific object on the page), you can open the Properties window, click the *Brush* category, adjust the *Background* property, and see the XAML markup updated automatically to match your selection.

However, you've already had plenty of experience adjusting properties with the Properties window. Instead, you'll now try adjusting the *Background* property by editing XAML markup in the XAML tab of the Code Editor.

3. Click after the equal sign in the phrase <Grid Background=" and then delete the characters in the line following the equal sign.

4. Now change the background color to orange by typing **"Orange">** after the equal sign.

Your grid definition should look like this in the Code Editor:

```
<Grid Background="Orange">

</Grid>
```

Notice that as soon as you type the closing bracket (>), the page's background color changes to orange. In addition, the IntelliSense feature offers you different color options in a drop-down list box while you type in the color name. You've now seen a major reason why it is useful to edit XAML documents from within Visual Studio—the IDE actually helps you compose your XAML by supplying useful properties, elements, and resources.

5. Select File | Save All to save your changes. Specify My Documents\Visual Basic 2013 SBS\ Chapter 07 as the folder.

You're off to a very good start with XAML documents and definitions. Now you'll add a few more controls to the grid and experiment with more useful XAML-editing techniques in the Code Editor.

Adding XAML elements using the Code Editor

Each of the XAML controls in the Visual Studio Toolbox can be added to a page by using the XAML tab of the Code Editor. You have the freedom to type in the markup for the controls directly, or you can add the controls by using Blend or the Visual Studio Designer and then modify the elements by using XAML markup.

As you work with various elements in XAML markup, you need to be mindful of the hierarchy of objects on the page that you are constructing. So far in this book, you've added a few dozen controls to pages as you've experimented with Visual Studio tools and features. But as you write more complex programs, the way that different objects are organized becomes central. You can group items together by placing child elements within parent elements. You can also use special container controls, such as *Canvas* and *StackPanel*, that are designed to organize child elements and display them as a group. Within XAML markup, such relationships are defined through the careful nesting of tags, and the relationships are also highlighted through indentation patterns, which make the markup easier to read.

In the following exercises, you'll get some additional practice adding XAML Toolbox controls to a grid and editing the resulting objects on the XAML tab of the Code Editor. You'll also create an event handler for a *ToggleButton* control, and you'll use the *Canvas* control to organize a group of child elements on the page to display a complex drawing.

Add *ToggleButton* and *Image* controls to the grid

1. With the My XAML Features project still loaded in Visual Studio, open the Toolbox and double-click the *ToggleButton* control.

    Visual Studio creates a toggle button object at the top of the application page. (The page is blank but formatted with orange color.)

    The *ToggleButton* control, introduced here for the first time, is a useful user interface feature for collecting input when the desired response is *Boolean* in nature—that is, either *yes* or *no* (or more precisely, either *true* or *false*). An example of this type of control in human life is a light switch that has only *on* or *off* (true or false) settings. In a computer program, you can use such an input tool to indicate different true or false states, such as whether or not an image should be displayed on the page. In this way, the *ToggleButton* control has a lot in common with the *CheckBox* control.

    Your screen should now look like this:

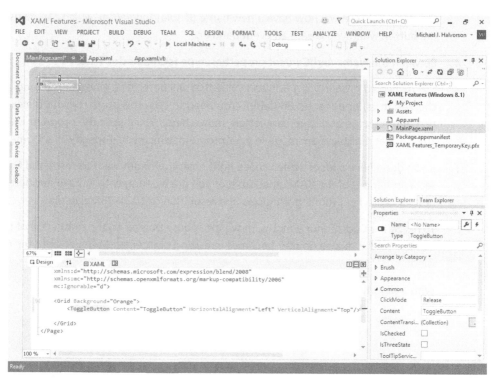

    Although the toggle button object on the page is interesting, I want you to focus on the XAML markup for the object that has now appeared on the XAML tab of the Code Editor. Notice that the following definition has appeared:

    ```
    <ToggleButton Content="ToggleButton" HorizontalAlignment="Left" VerticalAlignment="Top"/>
    ```

The *ToggleButton* object derives its core definition from the *ToggleButton* class and is delimited by start and end tags. It currently has three property settings: *Content*, *HorizontalAlignment*, and *VerticalAlignment*.

You'll adjust the *Content* property now and add two new property settings.

2. In the Code Editor, change the *Content* property from "ToggleButton" to "Display Picture."

    This property sets the text that is displayed in the button on the screen. After you finish typing the new value, it is also updated in the Designer.

3. Move the insertion point before the *Content* property name, and then type **x:Name="DisplayToggleBtn"**.

    Notice that at the moment you type the equal sign, the quotation marks that follow will be inserted by Visual Studio, so you don't need to type them. This might take a little getting used to—the Visual Studio IDE is trying to be helpful, but the IntelliSense feature can also lead to coding errors if you are not careful.

    The toggle button will now have a new name (*DisplayToggleBtn*), which can be used to identify the button when you create an event handler.

4. Between the *Name* and *Content* properties, type **IsChecked="True"**.

    The *IsChecked* property is a Boolean value that will determine whether the toggle button is checked (true) or not checked (false). (You need to type this property with the exact combination of uppercase and lowercase letters shown here.) You'll start the program with a value of *True* so that it displays an image in your program, which you'll specify in a moment.

5. If you don't have a lot of screen space right now, you might want to resize the Code Editor to see a little more of the XAML markup that you are working with. (I have decided to do this now, because I am running Windows at a resolution of 1024×768 pixels.)

    To resize the Code Editor window, move the mouse pointer to the right edge of the Code Editor until the mouse pointer becomes a resizing pointer, and then enlarge the Code Editor window.

    With a slightly bigger Code Editor, my XAML markup now looks like this:

Now you'll create an *Image* control on the page to display the photo of a relaxing mountain setting as your program starts. However, before you create the control, add a file containing the photograph to your project in the Assets folder.

6. Resize the Code Editor window so that it is in its original (smaller) shape.

7. In Solution Explorer, display the Assets folder, which contains the default images for your project.

8. Right-click the Assets folder, point to the Add submenu, and then click Existing Item.

9. In the Add Existing Item dialog box, browse to the My Documents\Visual Basic 2013 SBS\ Chapter 07 folder, select the AutumnField.bmp file, and then click Add.

   Visual Studio adds the AutumnField.bmp file to the Assets folder in your project. Now it is ready to be used anywhere in your program, and it will automatically be included with your project's files when the application is compiled and packaged for distribution.

   Now you'll add an *Image* control to your page using XAML markup to display the photo.

10. Return to the XAML tab of the Code Editor, and place the insertion point on the blank line beneath the definition of the toggle button object.

11. Type the following line of markup:

```
<Image x:Name="AutumnImage" Height="600" HorizontalAlignment="Left"
       Source="Assets/AutumnField.bmp" VerticalAlignment="Center" Width="800" />
```

   You can type the markup all on one line, or you can break the definition into multiple lines, as long as you do not attempt to break a line in the middle of a property assignment.

   When you finish entering the image object definition, a new image object appears on the page; however, you won't see the photo yet in the Designer.

   The new image object is named *AutumnImage* so that it can be used in an event handler. The *Source* property of the image contains a reference to the Assets folder, which contains a copy of the AutumnField.bmp file.

12. Select File | Save All to save your changes.

Congratulations—you've learned how to modify the properties of an object in the Code Editor and also how to type in a new control definition from scratch. Now you'll add some code to a Visual Basic event handler to toggle the autumn photo *on* or *off* when the program runs.

Create an event handler for the toggle button object

1. Load the Properties windows with the settings for the toggle button object by clicking the line containing the toggle button markup in the Code Editor.

   When the insertion point is in a line of markup in the Code Editor, the Properties window will contain the properties of that object. You want to display the properties now, because you are going to use the Properties window to create a new event handler.

2. In the Properties window, click the Event Handler button (the lightning bolt) near the *Name* text box.

The Event Handler button displays the events that the toggle button can respond to. The list of events in the Properties window looks like this:

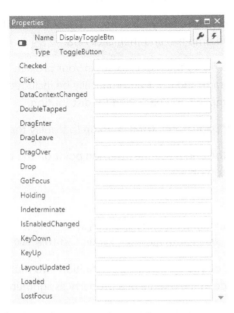

Recall that you can create an event handler for a particular event by double-clicking the text box next to the event in the Properties window. In this case, you'll write an event handler for the *Click* event because you want to examine the state of the toggle button object each time the user clicks the button. If the button is checked after a click, you want to display the photograph on the page, or make it *visible*. If the button is not checked after a click (indicating that the toggle has been unselected or set to *false*), you want to collapse the image on the page, or make it *invisible*.

3. Double-click next to the *Click* event in the Properties window.

Visual Studio inserts an event handler named *DisplayToggleBtn_Click* in the *Click* text box and opens the MainPage.xaml.vb code-behind file in the Code Editor.

4. Type the following Visual Basic statements in the Code Editor, between the *Private Sub* and *End Sub* statements:

```
If DisplayToggleBtn.IsChecked Then
    AutumnImage.Visibility = Windows.UI.Xaml.Visibility.Visible
Else
    AutumnImage.Visibility = Windows.UI.Xaml.Visibility.Collapsed
End If
```

Your Code Editor will look like this:

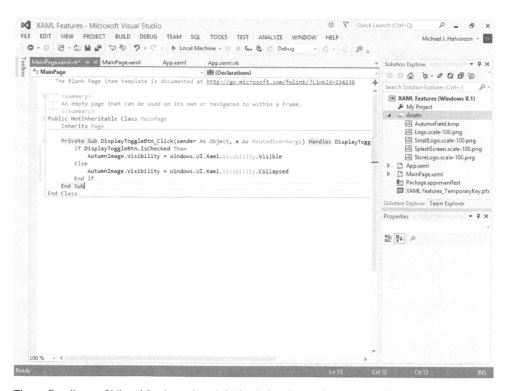

These five lines of Visual Basic code might look familiar—they use an *If...Then...Else* decision structure, similar to what you used in Chapters 3 and 6 to respond to user input. The event handler runs each time the user clicks the Display Picture button on the page. If the toggle button is checked (that is, if it appears selected or highlighted in the manner of apps in the Windows 8.1 user interface), the image will be made visible by a call to *Windows.UI.Xaml.Visibility*. This particular feature is made available as part of the XAML namespace and the basic functionality of *Image* controls in the .NET Framework.

However, if the toggle button moves from a checked state to a cleared (unchecked) state, the *Else* clause of the decision structure is executed and the image is collapsed or made invisible. The photo is not totally gone, but it is temporarily hidden until the next time the user clicks the toggle button.

Now you'll save and run the program to see how your new toggle button feature works.

5. Select File | Save All to save your changes.

6. Click the Start Debugging button on the Standard toolbar.

   The program compiles and runs in the IDE. The image of brown grass and a bare tree appears on the page along with the toggle button, which is displayed in a selected, or checked, state. The image is from the state of Montana in autumn. Your screen should look like this:

7. Click the Display Picture button.

   Visual Studio toggles the button (removing the selection effect) and then fires the *DisplayToggleBtn_Click* event procedure. The photo is then made invisible.

8. Click the Display Picture button again.

   The button is selected again, and the landscape photo reappears.

   The XAML markup should display the user interface correctly, and the Visual Basic event procedure should function as you designed it. You can use this strategy to make a wide range of objects on your page visible or invisible, depending on various program conditions, including user input.

9. Experiment with the toggle button a few more times, and then close the program.

10. Select File | Close Project to close the project.

Nice work with XAML and Visual Basic! Now you'll create a second Windows Store app project, and you'll practice using the *Canvas* control to create some more sophisticated images on a page.

Add a *Canvas* control and fill it with shapes

1. Select File | New Project to open a new Visual Studio project.

2. Choose Visual Basic/Windows Store under Templates, and verify that Blank App (XAML) template is selected.

3. Type **My XAML Box Art** in the Name text box.

4. Click OK to open the new project.

   Visual Studio opens and loads the default template files.

5. In Solution Explorer, right-click the file MainPage.xaml, and then click View Designer.

   The Designer appears with the blank page and grid of the Blank App template. XAML markup for the page is also visible in the Code Editor.

   Now practice the new skill you learned in changing the *Background* color for page. This time, you'll specify the custom color *DarkKhaki*.

6. Move the insertion pointer to the Code Editor and scroll down to the line that defines the grid background color.

7. Click after the equal sign in the phrase *<Grid Background="*, and then delete the characters in the line following the equal sign.

8. Change the background color to green by typing **"DarkKhaki">** after the equal sign.

   Your grid definition should look like this in the Code Editor:

   ```
   <Grid Background="DarkKhaki">

   </Grid>
   ```

   In the Designer, the page turns a dark khaki (or tan) color, as you specified.

   Now you'll add a XAML container called a *Canvas* to the page and fill it with shape controls that collectively create an animal's face. Within the *Canvas* container, you'll create several rectangle and ellipse shapes to build the drawing. The following XAML markup shows how you can accomplish this task.

9. Move the insertion point to the line between the *<Grid Background="DarkKhaki">* and *</Grid>* tags, and then type the following lines in the Code Editor. Feel free to use the Visual Studio IntelliSense feature as you type, and indent using the pattern shown here for clarity and readability. (In XAML markup listings, each level of indentation typically indicates that one or more child elements are being nested within a parent element.)

```
<Canvas Margin="224,194,0,0">
    <Rectangle Width="220"
               Height="220"
               Stroke="Black"
               Fill="Pink"
               StrokeThickness="2" />
    <Rectangle Fill="Black"
               Width="139"
               Height="75"
               Canvas.Left="-87"
               Canvas.Top="-15" />
    <Rectangle Fill="Black"
               Width="139"
               Height="75"
               Canvas.Left="179"
               Canvas.Top="-30" />
    <Ellipse Fill="Chocolate"
             Width="20"
             Height="20"
             Canvas.Left="130"
             Canvas.Top="60" />
    <Ellipse Fill="Chocolate"
             Width="20"
             Height="20"
             Canvas.Left="70"
             Canvas.Top="60" />
    <Ellipse Fill="Black"
             Width="46"
             Height="35"
             Canvas.Left="87"
             Canvas.Top="98" />
    <Path Stroke="Black"
          StrokeThickness="5"
          Data="M 30,120 S 80,230 180,140" />
</Canvas>
```

10. If you notice a syntax error, you might need to retype one or more lines of markup.

Typically, you'll find that it is pretty easy to forget to add closing tags at the end of each object definition. It is also a little tricky at first to avoid typing the quotation marks, as the Visual Studio IntelliSense feature tries to enter them for you.

If you place the insertion point on the last line ("</Canvas>") when you are finished typing, the entire selection of objects on the canvas will be selected. Your screen should look like the following:

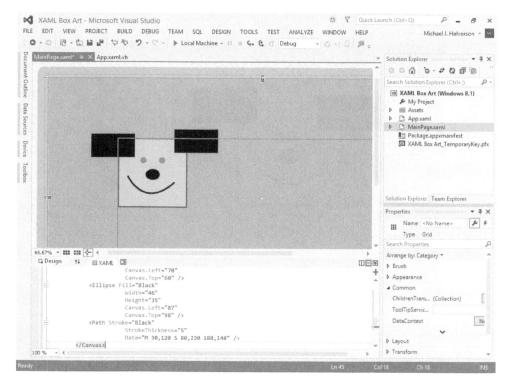

The XAML you entered creates a smiling face made up of three shaded rectangles, three shaded ellipses, and one pen drawing. The seven shapes comprise the face, eyes, ears, nose, and mouth of the drawing, and they were created using *Rectangle*, *Ellipse*, and *Path* elements, with property settings for fill color, height, width, and location on the canvas. The *Path* element used for the smile includes property settings for stroke (color), pen thickness (in pixels), and various points on a line specified in pixels.

Notice how all of the elements and property settings are carefully nested within the *Canvas*, *Grid*, and *Page* elements. Proper nesting is the key to establish proper parent element and child element relationships in XAML markup.

Now you'll save and run the program to see how your drawing looks.

11. Select File | Save All to save your changes. Specify My Documents\Visual Basic 2013 SBS\ Chapter 07 as the location.

12. Click the Start Debugging button on the Standard toolbar.

The program compiles and runs in the IDE. The image of the smiling face with big ears appears on the page, brushed with vibrant colors. (I think that the image looks a little bit like a happy dog coming to greet you.) Your screen should look like this:

Congratulations on creating several interesting effects with XAML and Visual Studio! The *Canvas* control, in particular, offers an excellent way to group elements together and apply one effect (like transformation) to all of the elements at once. You can try similar approaches with *StackPanel* and other group container controls.

13. Exit the My XAML Box Art program, and then select File | Exit to close the project and exit Visual Studio.

You now have the essential skills necessary to work with XAML markup in your projects and to fine-tune settings in the user interface. As you continue to develop rich applications for the Windows Store, you can use any combination of user interface design tools that make sense for your project, including the XAML tab of the Code Editor, the Visual Studio Designer, and Blend. Best of all, if you want to copy XAML markup from one project to the next, it is as easy as using a cut-and-paste operation to transfer the desired XAML markup. Give it a try!

Summary

In this chapter, you explored the content and structure of XAML, a markup language used to define the user interface in Windows Store and Windows Phone applications. XAML documents control the appearance and functionality of a user interface by applying and using a hierarchy of named tags and attributes. Within Visual Studio, XAML documents contain .xaml file extensions and are displayed in Solution Explorer. You can edit XAML documents by inserting and deleting text in the Code Editor. Any changes that you make to the document are immediately reflected on the page in the Visual Studio Designer.

You used XAML in several exercises to manipulate the appearance of Windows Store apps. You set the background color, explored App.xaml and MainPage.xaml, and created *ToggleButton*, *Image*, and *Canvas* controls with XAML markup. In the XAML Box Art project, you used the *Canvas* control to create a piece of custom artwork on the page, and you also learned how you can nest parent and child elements on a grid. You also learned about Blend for Visual Studio, a design tool that lets you customize applications with XAML markup.

In the next chapter, you'll continue working with XAML to customize the user interface of a Windows Store app. That chapter is designed especially to enhance your productivity: you'll learn to use styles to organize groups of properties into named resources and then reuse them for a consistent look-and-feel across multiple controls.

CHAPTER 8

Using XAML styles

After completing this chapter, you will be able to

- Understand how XAML styles are used to build attractive-looking user interfaces.

- Define reusable styles in the App.xaml project file.

- Reference new styles by using the *Style* property for controls on the page.

- Build new styles from existing styles using inheritance and the *BasedOn* property.

This chapter continues your exploration of XAML markup by investigating how XAML styles are used to format controls with a consistent and attractive appearance across the user interface. So far in this book, you've created controls individually and customized them with a variety of property settings. However, you can also define new, reusable styles in a project that will help you format objects automatically. This sophisticated design feature allows you to save time and build a consistent and professional-looking user interface in Windows Store apps.

You'll begin by creating a new Windows Store application, and then you'll define a new style resource in the App.xaml file, so that it can be referenced throughout the project. You'll define the new style with XAML markup, identifying the control that you want to configure with the *TargetType* property. You'll then assign specific properties to the style by defining one or more *Setter* elements for the control. Finally, you'll open the MainPage.xaml file and create XAML Toolbox controls on the page that will take advantage of the new styles you've defined. You'll also extend your expertise by using the *BasedOn* property, which allows you to build new styles from existing styles. In object-oriented programming terminology, this mechanism is known as *inheritance*—you assign the features and properties of one resource to another resource.

Introduction to XAML styles

Most programmers dislike *reinventing the wheel*, or completing the same basic task over and over again. If there is a simple way to automate a bit of formatting or programming, software developers will usually go out of their way to do it, especially if automating the task helps them save time and avoid potential coding mistakes down the road.

XAML styles are one useful coding mechanism that allows Visual Studio developers to automate the construction of the user interface. XAML styles enable the Windows programmer to set various properties for controls and then reuse those settings to build a consistent visual appearance across the application. Each XAML style that you create is designed for a particular XAML Toolbox control. For example, you might create a new style named *FramedPhoto* that is meant to assign a collection of standard display properties to one or more *Image* controls in the user interface of a Windows Store app. Of course, you could assign these properties *individually* to each *Image* control that you wanted to look a particular way, but a simpler method would be to create a new style resource that could be assigned to all of the *Image* controls. Such an approach would have the advantage of saving you development time, but it would also produce more consistent formatting results across the objects in the user interface. When you use styles, you are less likely to forget a crucial property setting when you are formatting a collection of similar objects.

An additional advantage of custom styles is that you can make broad formatting changes in an existing project very quickly. When you modify an existing style resource in App.xaml or a resource dictionary associated with the project, all of the objects that reference that particular style will automatically reflect the change.

Where did StandardStyles.xaml go?

In Visual Studio 2012, a style resource dictionary named StandardStyles.xaml was automatically created for each new Windows Store project and stored in the Common folder in Solution Explorer. This file contained a vast collection of predefined styles that you could use in your programs, and it was possible to modify the file to customize the basic styles that Microsoft supplied. StandardStyles.xaml was integral to Windows Store app development in Visual Studio 2012 because it defined user interface elements that closely followed Microsoft's design principles for Windows 8.

The following screen shot shows the default reference to StandardStyles.xaml in a Visual Studio 2012 project designed for the Windows Store. This reference appears in the App.xaml file in the project. I mention it now because you might still see this reference in projects that have been migrated to Visual Studio 2013 from Visual Studio 2012.

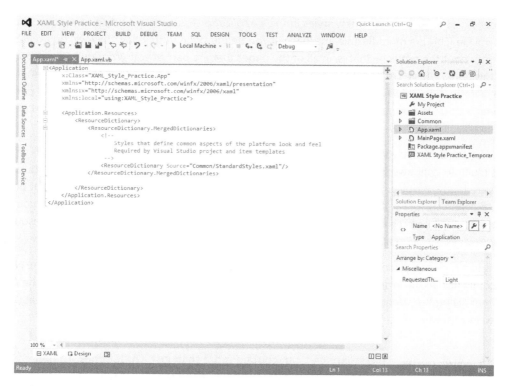

However, in Visual Studio 2013, StandardStyles.xaml file is no longer created automatically in a Windows Store project, and in the App.xaml file the entire *<Application.Resources>* section has been deleted. You also won't see the Common folder in Solution Explorer that once held StandardStyles. xaml. Instead, the Windows Store platform automatically supports Windows 8.1 control styling, and it is no longer necessary to edit StandardStyles.xaml directly. You can reference predefined styles by using the *StaticResource* extension in XAML markup when you work with controls.

Creating new XAML styles

When you are ready to create your own XAML styles in a project, you have some options about where you place the markup that defines the styles. First, you can create a style for an individual page by adding the style definition to the *<Page.Resources>* section of the page's XAML file. If your Windows Store app has only one page in it, this file will be named MainPage.xaml by default. (You've been using MainPage.xaml throughout this book to define the user interface for your app.) However, if you define new styles in this way, they can be referenced only by objects located on the page where you defined the style. This type of declaration is called a *page-level* resource definition.

Second, you can create your new styles in the *<Application.Resources>* section of your project's App.xaml file. This is a more flexible approach; if you define styles in this way, they will be available for use throughout the project—that is, in all of the pages that are part of your Windows Store app. So far in this book, you've created demonstration programs that use just one page to process input and display information. However, more sophisticated "real world" programs often utilize several pages to manage input and output. For this reason, it is best to get comfortable defining new styles in the App.xaml file.

Third, you can also create new styles in a stand-alone XAML resource dictionary file that is shared across multiple Windows Store apps. This is a useful programming strategy if you find that you are always creating controls on the page that have the same base characteristics and if you find it bother-some to define custom styles in the App.xaml file of each new project that you start. In fact, you can create more than one resource dictionary file in Visual Studio, and you can assign multiple resource dictionary files to your applications.

To add a resource dictionary file to your project, open the project in Visual Studio, click the New Item command on the Project menu, and double-click the Resource Dictionary template in the Add New Item dialog box. Define your new styles in this template, and add it to other projects that you want to incorporate the custom styles.

Note XAML resource dictionary files can contain more than just XAML styles. To find out more about resource dictionaries and their uses, search for "ResourceDictionary class (Windows)" at *http://msdn.microsoft.com.*

Considering the scope of a style

As your Visual Studio projects begin to fill up with custom styles, a new question might suddenly occur to you: How do the various style definitions coexist in a project if the styles are defined in more than one file location?

The answer to this question depends on where the new styles were defined and the way in which they are used. That is, issues related to the accessibility context or *scope* of the new styles. Page-level styles are available only to the objects that exist on the same page where the styles are defined. However, if styles with the same name are defined in both the project-wide App.xaml file and on an individual page like MainPage.xaml, the local style on MainPage.xaml *overrides* (or takes priority over) the resource in App.xaml. Likewise, a style defined in App.xaml overrides a style of the same name in a resource dictionary file that has been added to the project.

Thinking about the scope of styles, variables, namespaces, and other definitions in a Windows Store app is important to do because there are often times when the same names are used. You'll learn more about these issues in Part III of this book, "Visual Basic programming techniques."

Sample markup for a new XAML style

How is a new style definition created?

Styles should be defined in the XAML file that gives the style resource the broadest scope without forcing you to maintain files that you would not otherwise be using. As noted earlier in this chapter, most of the time you should be defining styles in App.xaml or a resource dictionary. Inside the files, you define each new style between *<Style>* and *</Style>* tags, and you must define the styles after any resources that contain information pertinent to the styles. (For example, it is important to define new styles after any *MergedDictionary* entries that you see, because new styles often make use of standard styles that are included in these entries.)

For a page-level definition in a file such as MainPage.xaml, place the style under the *<Page.Resources>* tag. For a project-level definition in the App.xaml file, place the style under the *<Application.Resources>* tag. In a resource dictionary file, place the style under the *<ResourceDictionary>* tag.

In the style definition itself, you use the *x:Key* property to give the style a unique name, and you use the *TargetType* property to identify the control that you are customizing or *styling*. You then assign individual property settings using one or more *Setter* properties. Each *Setter* assignment must include a property name and a value that is defined using XAML markup. These property assignments must be compatible with the control you are styling. If you assign a property or value to a style that does not match the control definition you are referencing, an error will occur.

The following XAML markup sample shows the elements of a new style definition in an App.xaml file, which will make the style resource available through the application. The new style is named *FramedPhoto,* and it appears in a new *<Application.Resources>* section in the file. The new style resource has been formatted in bold type.

The style will set the *Height, Width,* and *Stretch* properties for any *Image* control in the project that references the style. Note that I am including some of the boilerplate markup in App.xaml so that you can see where the new style is located. In particular, it is necessary to place the new style definition between the *<Application.Resources>* and *</Application.Resources>* tags. The style itself is defined between the *<Style>* and *</Style>* tags.

```
<Application
    x:Class="XAML_Style_Practice.App"
    xmlns="http://schemas.microsoft.com/winfx/2006/xaml/presentation"
    xmlns:x="http://schemas.microsoft.com/winfx/2006/xaml"
    xmlns:local="using:XAML_Style_Practice">
    <Application.Resources>
        <Style x:Key="FramedPhoto" TargetType="Image">
            <Setter Property="Height" Value="240"/>
            <Setter Property="Width" Value="320"/>
            <Setter Property="Stretch" Value="Fill"/>
        </Style>
    </Application.Resources>
</Application>
```

Referencing a style

To use or *reference* a new style in the XAML markup for an object in the user interface, you use the *Style* property.

The following markup shows how you might reference the new *FramedPhoto* style defined in the preceding section. There are four lines highlighted in bold type (lines 2–5) that I want to direct your attention to—these define an image object on the page that will be styled by the *FramedPhoto* style resource. Notice in particular how the *FramePhoto* name is used along with the *StaticResource* markup extension, quotation marks, and a pair of curly brackets.

```
<Grid Background="{StaticResource ApplicationPageBackgroundThemeBrush}">
        <Image Style="{StaticResource FramedPhoto}"
            HorizontalAlignment="Left"
            Margin="522,176,0,0"
            VerticalAlignment="Top"/>
        <Image HorizontalAlignment="Left"
            Margin="346,75,0,0"
            VerticalAlignment="Top"/>
</Grid>
```

What results does this XAML markup produce? Even though the new style is being used to set some of the properties for the first image object on the page (*Height*, *Width*, and *Stretch*), several remaining properties are set by markup associated with the image object's own definition (*HorizontalAlignment*, *Margin*, and *VerticalAlignment*). As a result, the image object is defined with a height of 240 pixels, a width of 320 pixels, a *Stretch* property set to Fill, a horizontal alignment set to Left, and so on. Because none of the property settings overlap, there are no scope or override issues, but you can see how such overlaps might occur. As I noted earlier, Visual Studio will resolve them by giving priority to the style with the most local scope.

There is also a second image object defined in this sample markup. Note that this image has no particular style associated with it, so it will *not* be formatted by the *FramedPhoto* style. I defined two image objects in this sample simply to clarify that you don't need to style every object the same way if you don't want to.

Using explicit and implicit styles

When you define a new style as a resource in your project, there are actually two ways to work with the style in XAML markup. First, you can define and use the new style *explicitly*, as shown earlier in this chapter, by identifying a specific *x:Key* property for the style and then referencing the style *by name* when you format controls on the page.

Alternatively, you can define and use styles *implicitly* (that is, without giving the style a specific name), by omitting the *x:Key* property when you define the style and then letting Visual Studio assign the style automatically to every control that matches the style's *TargetType*. Implicit styling is the best way to get *all* of the objects of a particular type to be styled the same way in a project. It works because Visual Studio takes the *TargetType* (control name) from the style definition and assigns it to the *x:Key* property for the style.

If implicit styling sounds a little confusing, here's a simple example that explains how implicit styling works and why it might be useful. Consider the following page-level definition for a new XAML style that formats a text box control. At the top of the sample is a style definition between the *<Page.Resources>* and *</Page.Resources>* tags that defines the new style. It sets the *Background* property of a *TextBox* control to the color green and changes the control's *FontSize* property to 24 point. Notice that there is no *x:Key* property, but *TargetType* is set to TextBox, making the style implicit for all of the text box objects in the project that do not have a specific style name. (If a text box object does have a specific style associated with it, it would be exempt from the implicit styling.)

```
<Page.Resources>
    <Style TargetType="TextBox">
        <Setter Property="Background" Value="Green"/>
        <Setter Property="FontSize" Value="24"/>
    </Style>
</Page.Resources>

<Grid Background="{StaticResource ApplicationPageBackgroundThemeBrush}">
    <TextBox
        HorizontalAlignment="Left"
        Height="136"
        Margin="346,75,0,0"
        Text="Green Text Box"
        Width="263" />
</Grid>
```

The bottom portion of the XAML code defines a text box object within the main grid on the page. A collection of properties are set by the markup; in addition to these, Visual Studio uses the implicit style definition to format the background color of the text box to green and to set the font size to 24-point. This is the recommended strategy you should follow when using implicit styles—define a handful of essential properties with the implicit style, and then further customize individual objects in the project with additional styles that are needed. You should become familiar with both explicit and implicit styling strategies to managing the look and feel of objects in your user interface.

Practicing XAML styles

Complete the following steps to create a new Windows Store app named My XAML Style Practice. In this exercise, you will create three button objects on the page, and you will format two of them with an explicit style named *GradientButton*.

GradientButton is a custom style resource that you will define in App.xaml so that it can be used throughout the program. It formats the buttons that reference it with a blended, gradient effect that transitions gradually from black to white. Because the formatting effect involves some rather complex brush formatting, it is a good candidate for a new style resource that can be used over and over again in a project. The gradient effect will look great on the screen or in an e-book. (It will be more subtle in the printed version of this book.)

Create a new style in App.xaml

1. Start Visual Studio, and click New Project to open a new Visual Studio application.

2. Choose Visual Basic/Windows Store under Templates, and then verify that the Blank App (XAML) template is selected.

3. Type **My XAML Style Practice** in the Name text box.

4. Click OK to open and configure the project.

   Visual Studio creates a new Windows Store app with the appropriate supporting files. After a moment, you'll see the App.xaml.vb code-behind file for the Blank App template in the Code Editor.

   Now you'll open the App.xaml file so that you can add a new style definition to it.

   In Solution Explorer, right-click the file App.xaml, and then click the View Designer command.

5. A new tab opens in the Code Editor, and the App.xaml file is loaded into it. Your screen should look like this:

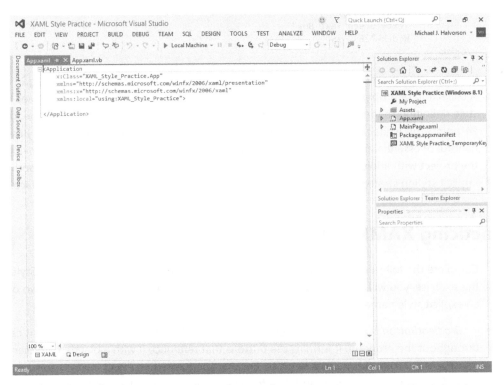

   The root element in the App.xaml file is *Application*, so the XAML document is defined between the *<Application* and *</Application>* tags. You'll create an *<Application.Resources>* section here with room for several *<Style>* definitions.

6. Move the insertion point below the line containing *xmlns:local="using:XAML_Style_Practice">*, press Enter, and then type the following markup to define a new style named *GradientButton*:

```xml
<Application.Resources>
    <Style x:Key="GradientButton" TargetType="Button">
        <Setter Property="FontSize" Value="28"/>
        <Setter Property="Background" >
            <Setter.Value>
                <LinearGradientBrush EndPoint="0.5,1" StartPoint="0.5,0">
                    <GradientStop Color="Black"/>
                    <GradientStop Color="White" Offset="1"/>
                </LinearGradientBrush>
            </Setter.Value>
        </Setter>
    </Style>
</Application.Resources>
```

Your Code Editor should now look like this:

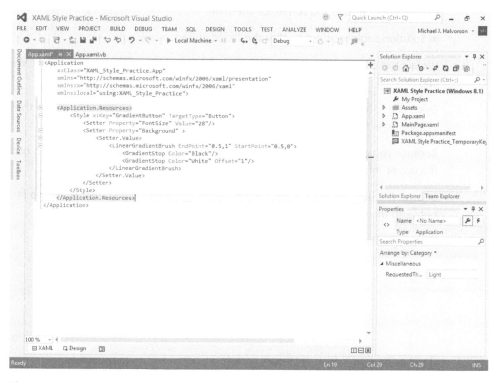

The *<Application.Resources>* tag indicates that a collection of application-scoped resources is being defined in the App.xaml file, which will be valid (or have *scope*) throughout the entire project. Although you will be adding only styles to this collection, you could also add templates or brushes to it as well. Note that this resource collection is XAML-based and not something that is stored in the Assets folder, which you have used to store artwork and media files.

The *<Style>* tag indicates that a new style resource is being added to the XAML resource collection. The style is given a name through the *x:Key* tag, and the control type is set to "Button" using the *TargetType* property. Two additional properties are now added to the style using the *Setter* property. The first assigns a value of 28 to the *FontSize* property, increasing the default font size for a button object to 28-point. This is a straightforward use of the *Setter* property that we have seen several times in the standard syntax for a new style definition.

However, the *Background* property assignment for the button is a little more complex. Because *Background* can be assigned a collection of property settings, I've used the *<Setter.Value>* tag to allow for several values, including *LinearGradientBrush*, *EndPoint*, *StartPoint*, *GradientStop*, and *Color*. These values collectively create a transitional gradient effect that moves from solid black to white on the button's surface. (If you were setting these properties using the Properties window, you would fill out a property page that contains numerous settings and values.)

Now it's time to test this new explicit style. Complete the following steps to add some buttons to the user interface and reference the style.

7. In Solution Explorer, double-click the file MainPage.xaml.

   Visual Studio opens MainPage.xaml in the Designer, the primary page in your Windows Store app.

8. Open the Toolbox, and double-click the *Button* control three times to create three button unique objects on the page.

   Because you didn't specify a location, the buttons will be stacked one on top of the other in the upper-left corner of the page.

9. Enlarge the buttons and position them on the page in a row so that there is a little space between them. However, don't adjust the default *FontSize* property.

   Your page should now look something like this:

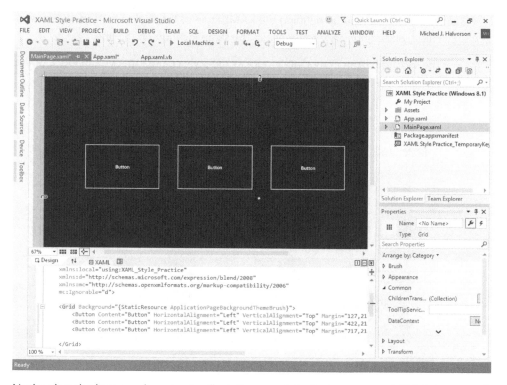

Notice that the buttons do not yet reflect the new style that you created. This is because the *GradientButton* style is explicit and must be referenced specifically in the XAML markup for the button objects. You'll reference the style name now for two of the three buttons to see how the process works.

10. Move the insertion pointer to the XAML tab of the Code Editor, and place the pointer between the *Button* object name and the *Content* property setting for the first button.

11. Type the following markup to assign the *GradientButton* style to the button:

```
Style="{StaticResource GradientButton}"
```

This XAML uses the *StaticResource* keyword to let Visual Studio know that you are using a named resource in the project. Be sure to include the curly brackets and quotes, which are used to identify a resource in the project. When you move the insertion pointer to a new line, the button on the page displays the gradient formatting effect and the size of the type in the button is also enlarged.

12. Add the same markup defining the XAML style to the second button object in the Code Editor, placing the *Style* reference in the same location on the line.

The second button immediately reflects the style change that you made, a reference to the explicit style defined in App.xaml. Your screen will look like this:

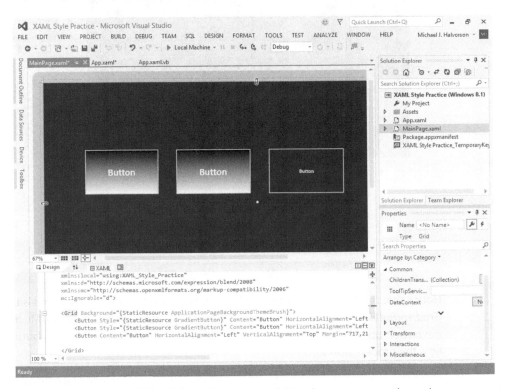

Basically, because you defined the style as an explicit style, you can use the style resource on whichever button you prefer in the project. Only the buttons that refer to *GradientButton* by name will be formatted according to the new style.

13. Save your project and specify the My Documents\Visual Basic 2012 SBS\Chapter 08 folder as the location.

14. Now run the project to see how the buttons look when they are part of a demonstration program running under Windows 8.1.

The program begins, and the buttons appear on screen as they did in the Visual Studio Designer. You'll see something like the following illustration:

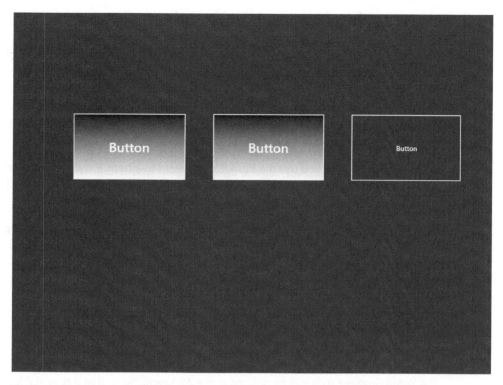

The buttons aren't truly functional now, of course—you haven't defined event handlers that do anything when the user clicks the buttons. But you've learned important lessons about how XAML styles can be used to create consistent and interesting formatting effects, which will save you considerable time as you tackle larger development projects.

15. Close the My XAML Style Practice app.

The IDE reappears with the page you've been configuring in the Designer.

Now you're ready to learn another important technique related to XAML styles and user interface construction.

Building new styles from existing styles

After you create a style, you can use it as a model for additional styles in a project through a process known as style *inheritance*. This means that the features and properties of one style can be used as the basis for another style. The only requirement is that the new styles are based on an existing style of the same control type. For example, after you have defined a button style named *GradientButton* in your project, you can create a new style based on *GradientButton* that might do additional formatting to buttons—but the style can be applied only to button controls in the project.

At the XAML markup level, you use the *BasedOn* property to inherit a style within a new style definition. The new style is assigned a name through the *x:Key* property, as you have already learned. If a property is not set in the new style, it is inherited from the base style.

The following exercise demonstrates the process using the My XAML Style Practice app. You'll create a new button style named *YellowGradient* that inherits its gradient formatting characteristics from the *GradientButton* style. The new style adds yellow color formatting in two places—presumably something that you might want for some, but not all, of the buttons in a user interface.

Use the *BasedOn* property to inherit a style

1. Click the App.xaml document tab at the top of the Designer.

   The *YellowGradient* style will be defined in the App.xaml file so that it is available throughout the Windows Store app.

2. Move the insertion point below the *GradientButton* style you just defined (between the *</Style>* and *</Application.Resources>* tags), and enter the following XAML markup to define the new style:

   ```
   <Style x:Key="YellowGradient" TargetType="Button"
          BasedOn="{StaticResource GradientButton}">
          <Setter Property="BorderBrush" Value="Yellow"/>
          <Setter Property="Foreground" Value="Yellow"/>
   </Style>
   ```

   Your Code Editor should look like this:

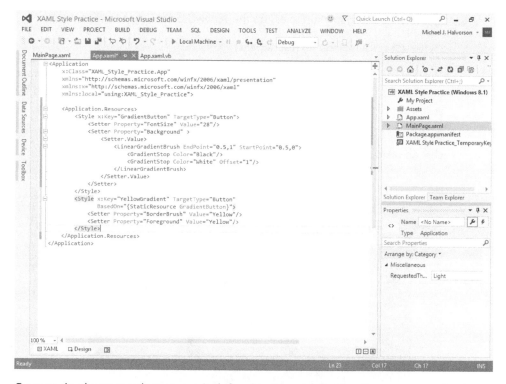

Once again, the new style resource is defined in the *<Application.Resources>* section between *<Style>* and *</Style>* tags. You'll recognize most of the markup used for this new resource, with the exception of the *BasedOn* property, used here for the first time. *BasedOn* allows you to inherit the characteristics of the *GradientButton* style and use them as the basis of the new style. Because the *GradientButton* is a project resource, it is also referred to using the *StaticResource* keyword.

The style is assigned a name using the *x:Key* tag. Two *Setter* properties apply yellow formatting to the button border and the type displayed in the button. However, in other respects, the button simply inherits the property settings and characteristics of the *GradientButton* style.

3. Click the MainPage.xaml tab at the top of the Designer.

Now you'll reference the *YellowGradient* style in the markup for the third button on the page.

4. Move the insertion pointer to the Code Editor, and place the pointer between the *Button* and *Content* property settings for the third button.

5. Type the following markup to assign the *YellowGradient* style to the button:

```
Style="{StaticResource YellowGradient}"
```

The familiar *StaticResource* keyword is used again to reference the style you want to use. The third button's design will be based on the style model for the first and second buttons, with yellow formatting added via the new *YellowGradient* style.

As soon as you move the insertion point off the third button's XAML markup, the formatting change takes place. Your screen will look like this:

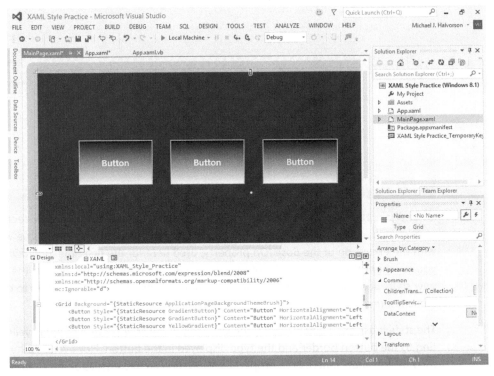

6. Save your changes to the project, and then run the program to see what the new button looks like.

The Windows Store app starts and the three buttons appear on the screen. You'll see something like the following illustration. Note that the color yellow in the third button will be distinctive only on the screen in front of you and in the e-book version of this title. The printed book won't show the yellow formatting.

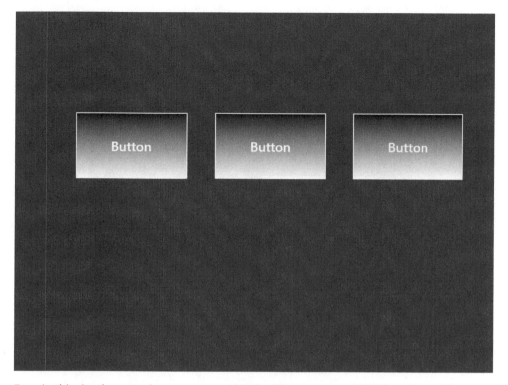

Even in this simple example, you can see the significant power of XAML styles and how one style design can be used as the basis for addition styles.

7. Exit the My XAML Style Practice application, and display the IDE again.

IDE shortcuts for applying styles

A useful shortcut for applying XAML styles like the ones that you have created in this chapter is to right-click an object on the page that you want to format with a new style and apply the style name from a list in a pop-up window. When you apply XAML styles in this way, using only commands in the IDE, Visual Studio updates the XAML markup for you automatically. You won't need to manually enter the style using the XAML *Style* property in the Code Editor.

Give this shortcut a try now.

Apply a XAML style using the IDE

1. In the Designer, right-click the first button on the page.

2. In the pop-up menu that appears, click Edit Template | Apply Resource | YellowGradient.

3. Your screen will look this as you are making your style resource selection:

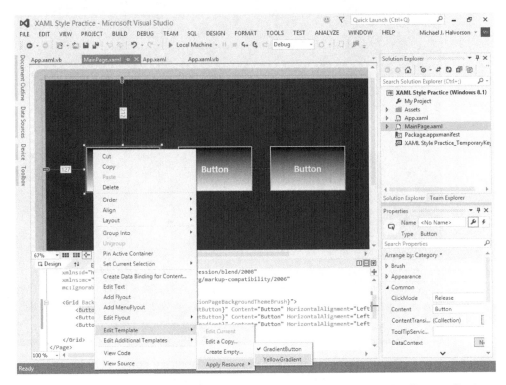

The two styles that you added to the App.xaml file (*GradientButton* and *YellowGradient*) are now ready for you to use at the click of a button.

After you select the *YellowGradient* style, Visual Studio applies it to the object selected in the Designer and updates the *Style* property for the object in the XAML markup and Code Editor.

That's all there is to it! You've learned another useful way to take advantage of style resources in a Visual Studio project!

4. Save your changes, and exit Visual Studio.

You're finished working with XAML styles in this chapter. Be sure to use them as you design Windows Store apps, and return to this chapter for a refresher course when you start building larger projects—styles become incredibly useful in larger, team-development efforts.

Summary

In this chapter, you learned how to create and use XAML styles in your Windows Store apps. XAML styles allow you to set a wide range of formatting properties for controls and then reuse those settings to build a more consistent user interface. I recommend that you create your first styles in a project's App.xaml file so that you can use them throughout the program. As you learn more about styles and develop favorites that you want to use often, I recommend that you place them in a resource dictionary that you can share across multiple applications.

In the exercises in this chapter, you learned the syntax necessary to create XAML styles, how to use explicit and implicit styles, and how to build new styles from existing styles through the process of style inheritance. You also learned shortcuts in the Visual Studio IDE for applying styles to objects on the page.

In the next chapter, you'll continue designing the user interface of Windows Store apps. In particular, you'll learn how to use some essential Windows 8.1 design features for applications, including the new *CommandBar* and *Flyout* controls, how to customize "live" tiles on the Windows Start page, planning for touch and gestures in Windows Store apps, and using the Manifest Designer to set program permissions and capabilities.

CHAPTER 9

Exploring Windows 8.1 design features: Command bar, flyout, tiles, and touch

After completing this chapter, you will be able to

■ Create a *CommandBar* with buttons to manage common tasks.

■ Use the *Flyout* control to collect input and display information.

■ Design a custom tile for your Windows Store app on the Start page.

■ Plan for touch input and gestures in a Windows Store app.

■ Use the Manifest Designer to set program permissions and capabilities.

I n this chapter, you'll continue examining the user interface of Windows Store apps, and you'll learn more about the features of programs distributed via the Windows Store. In particular, you'll learn more about the user experience (UX) design guidelines for the Windows 8.1 operating system. You'll learn how to create an interactive command bar in your project that uses buttons to launch commands and how to use the XAML *Flyout* control to display and receive information with a tap or a click. These tools are new features in Visual Studio 2013 designed for Windows Store apps.

Windows Store applications need to have a consistent design from start to finish. Accordingly, this chapter describes how to create a custom Start page tile for your Windows Store app and how to plan for touch input and gestures in a program that runs on touch-enabled devices. In addition, you'll learn how to edit the Package.appxmanifest file by using the Manifest Designer to control important permissions and capabilities for users of your software. This last step will ensure that your customers can accomplish the work that they need to without endangering the system or the sensitive information stored on it.

The following techniques apply specifically to Windows Store apps that run under Windows 8.1. In some circumstances, the full implementation of these features will require a little advanced work that is beyond the scope of this chapter— for example, creating live tiles that respond to a variety of input scenarios. However, the topics introduced here will lay the groundwork for Windows Store projects and prepare you for your own explorations and team development efforts.

Creating a command bar to manage common tasks

The Windows 8.1 design guidelines encourage software developers to present users with a minimum of "chrome," or persistent user interface features, in a Windows Store app. This means that you should minimize the use of static title bars, menu bars, toolbars, and buttons that are always on the screen in the manner of traditional Windows desktop apps. Instead, rich user content is to be at the center of the Windows 8.1 computing experience. Information is to be presented graphically when possible, preferably in tiles or panels containing beautiful text, striking photographs, and original art.

An excellent resource for Windows 8.1 design information is the Microsoft user experience (UX) guidelines, prepared to help developers think about the way that software is used and the emotions and perceptions of consumers as they work with Windows Store apps. These guidelines are introduced in the article "Designing UX for apps," on MSDN, and I recommend the resource to you. (See *http://msdn.microsoft.com/en-us/library/windows/apps/hh779072.aspx.*)

So, if the developer needs to replace traditional menu bars and toolbars with another mechanism for issuing commands and managing tasks, what tool or tools should they use?

Part of the answer to this question involves really thinking about the user content in your application and the ways that the user needs to work with it. Within the XAML Toolbox for a Windows Store application, there are numerous user interface tools to choose from, and you have already surveyed several in this book, including *Image*, *TextBlock*, *WebView*, *MediaElement*, *TextBox*, and *FlipView*.

However, there are times when it is useful to display a palette of commands for the user to choose from. In the Visual Studio 2012 product, one way to accomplish this was via the XAML *AppBar* control, which displays a pop-up window of common commands at the top or the bottom of the app. While *AppBar* is still available to Windows Store applications, much of the same functionality is now offered in Visual Studio 2013 with the *CommandBar*, *AppBarButton*, and *AppBarToggleButton* controls located in the XAML Toolbox. The following illustration shows the Microsoft Calendar app with a command bar at the bottom of the page and five buttons in the command bar.

July 2014

Sunday	Monday	Tuesday	Wednesday	Thursday	Friday	Saturday
29	30	1 · 9a Group plann...	2	3	4 · Independence D...	5
6	7	8	9	10	11	12
13	14 · 9a Product Rele...	15	16	17	18	19
20	21	22	23 · 9a Team Review	24	25	26
27	28	29	30	31	1	2

Day · Week · Month · Today · New

Command bar features

CommandBar is useful because it provides an automatic layout of common command buttons that appears at the top or bottom of the application windows whenever the user right-clicks the mouse, swipes from the edge of the screen to the center, or presses Windows+Z. The bar is further organized into a primary panel on the right side and a secondary panel on the left side.

The Windows 8.1 design guidelines require application windows to be resizable, which means that the content within applications needs to be adjusted dynamically if the user chooses to resize or reorient the application workspace. The *CommandBar* control handles this resizing automatically, and if necessary, *CommandBar* will be displayed in a special compact state, which can also be set programmatically if you change the control's *IsCompact* property setting to True.

A *CommandBar* control is typically created in a Windows Store app by adding XAML markup to the MainPage.xaml file inside the *<Page>* tag for the file. Individual buttons in the *CommandBar* are creating using the *AppBarButton* control, which is also new in Visual Studio 2013 and available in the XAML Toolbox for Windows Store applications. The *AppBarButton* control has *Icon* and *Label* properties that collectively determine which button shapes are displayed in the bar and the text label that is used to describe the button. You then "wire up" each of the command buttons to event handlers that perform the work of the button via Visual Basic code. Typically, a separate event handler is used to handle each button click or tap.

This is what the XAML looks like for a *CommandBar* control that contains three *AppBarButton* controls. The XAML is specified near the top of the *Page* control (before the *Grid* control is defined), and the *BottomAppBar* identifier indicates that the bar will be attached to the bottom of the page. (Use *TopAppBar* to create a command bar at the top of the page.)

```
<Page.BottomAppBar>
    <CommandBar>
        <AppBarButton Icon="Play" Label="Play" Click="PlayButton_Click"/>
        <AppBarButton Icon="Pause" Label="Pause" Click="PauseButton_Click"/>
        <AppBarButton Icon="Stop" Label="Stop" Click="StopButton_Click"/>
    </CommandBar>
</Page.BottomAppBar>
```

The buttons are named Play, Pause, and Stop. Notice how each button calls a separate event handler when they are clicked via the *Click* property. (The Visual Basic code for the event handlers is not provided here—that will be part of the exercise that follows.) By default, buttons appear in the lower-right corner of the command bar.

Button names identified by the *Icon* property are loaded from a Visual Studio styles file containing valid button symbols for Windows Store apps. You can examine the impressive list of symbols available by examining the following documentation file on MSDN: *http://msdn.microsoft.com/nl-nl/library/windows/apps/windows.ui.xaml.controls.symbol.aspx*.

If the button you want is actually a *toggle button* with distinct on and off states, you can make such an image appear on the command bar by specifying *AppBarToggleButton* instead of *AppBarButton* in the XAML for the control. (You'll see an example of this technique in the exercise later in this chapter.) The text in the *Label* property for each button specifies the name that will appear beneath the icon on the command bar when the bar is made visible. It is only coincidence that in this example the *Icon* and *Label* properties contain exactly the same information.

Designing your command bar

You'll want to take some time designing your command bars so that they display the needed icons and commands in a predictable way. For example, use a command bar on the bottom of the page to display commands relevant to the user's current context, such as items that are selected and might require editing or deleting. A command bar at the top of the page is typically used to display navigational elements and is sometimes known as the navigation bar. Here you'll see elements such as a forward or back button, or a selector that allows you to change the page.

Keeping with the goal to reduce chrome, command bars are not visible by default. They appear only when a user right-clicks or swipes a finger from the top or bottom edge of the screen. However, you can also make a command bar appear programmatically by using Visual Basic code.

When you design your command bar, begin by placing typical default commands on the right side of the command bar. If there are only a few relevant command buttons for the task at hand, you might end up showing just one or two on the right side. (That's OK and something typical in the Windows 8.1 environment.) However, if there are a larger number of commands to show, separate the button in sets on the right and left sides of the bar to balance out the application workspace and make the commands ergonomically accessible.

Some command buttons are very typical and appear in many Windows Store apps. To create consistency and emphasize ease of use, follow Microsoft's lead in how the buttons are organized on typical applications like Internet Explorer, Calendar, Mail, and Store. That way, your users will leverage their own knowledge and become familiar with the placement of common buttons. For example, a New button should usually be the rightmost button on a command bar at the bottom of the page.

Should you use a charm instead?

When possible, in addition to command bars, you should try to use the standard charms on the Windows *charm bar* to handle common tasks, such as searching within your application, sharing data from your application with others, and adjusting common settings in your application. Charms are universal buttons that appear on the right side of the screen in Windows 8 and Windows 8.1 when you swipe in from the right or hold the mouse pointer in the upper-right corner of the screen. The charms can be used to provide the following features to your users, which should not be duplicated by buttons on the command bar in your app:

- **Search** Allows your app to be a data provider for searches by any user on the system. If your program has lots of data to use and share, the Search charm can be a great gateway to your program's data for others.

- **Share** Allows users to share content from your app with other users or Windows Store programs.

- **Devices** Allows users to send audio, video, or pictures from your app to other devices attached to your computer or network.

- **Settings** Allows users to manage common application settings in your Windows Store app by using the same tool that they are familiar with in Windows.

Charms are built into Windows 8 and Windows 8.1—they are a core usability feature of the operating system that can be accessed by software developers. To interact with a charm and use it to provide application-specific information, you establish a *contract* with the charm, which involves declaring the charm that you want to use in the Package.appxmanifest file (discussed later in this chapter) and then accessing the charm using Visual Basic code in your app.

The most common Windows charm to use is Search, which can allow users to extract valuable information from your app. For more information about using the Search charm, see "Quickstart: Adding search to an app (Windows Store apps using C#/VB/C++ and XAML)" at *http://msdn.microsoft.com/en-us/library/windows/apps/hh868180.aspx*.

Command bar practice step by step

Let's try some sample code that creates a new *CommandBar* control in a Windows Store app and uses it to execute simple commands. The sample program will play music with the *MediaElement* control that you learned to use in Chapter 5, "Working with Windows Store app controls." The command bar in the program provides five media-related button commands: Loop Track, Mute, Play, Pause, and Stop. You need to be running Windows 8.1 to create this project.

Use a *CommandBar* control to manage media playback

1. Start Visual Studio 2013, and create a new Windows Store app using Visual Basic and the Blank App (XAML) template.

2. In the Name text box, type **My Command Bar Demo**.

3. Click OK to create the new project in Visual Studio.

    Visual Studio opens the new project with a blank application template.

4. Double-click the file MainPage.xaml in Solution Explorer.

5. Open the Toolbox's All XAML Controls category, and double-click the *MediaElement* control.

    Visual Studio places a new media player object in the upper-left corner of the application page. Recall that you can see the outline of this control while your project is in design mode, but that it will be invisible when the program runs. For this reason, you will use the *CommandBar* control to provide some useful playback features.

    Now you'll add a media file to the project.

6. Right-click the Assets folder in Solution Explorer to display the shortcut menu of commands.

7. Point to the Add command, and then click Existing Item.

8. In the Add Existing Item dialog box, browse to the My Documents\Visual Basic 2013 SBS\ Chapter 09 folder and click Electro Sample, the same MP3 file containing electronic music that you used in Chapter 5.

9. Click Add to add the music file to your project in the Assets folder.

    Now you're ready to assign this music asset to the *Source* property of the media element object.

10. Click the media element object in the Designer window, and then use the Properties window to change the *Name* property to **MediaTool**.

11. Expand the *Media* category, scroll down to the *Source* property, and click the Source list box.

    The media file you added to the project appears in the list.

12. Click Electro Sample.mp3 to add the music file.

Now you're ready to add a *CommandBar* control to the project. You'll add the bar using XAML markup, which is much more efficient than using the Toolbox and Properties window in this instance.

13. Open the MainPage.xaml file in the XAML pane of the Code Editor.

At the top of the file, you'll see the *<Page>* header followed by seven lines of XAML that define namespaces and other important objects in the project.

14. Beneath these lines (but above the *Grid* header), type the following markup:

```
<Page.BottomAppBar>
    <CommandBar>
        <AppBarButton Icon="Play" Label="Play" Click="PlayButton_Click"/>
        <AppBarButton Icon="Pause" Label="Pause" Click="PauseButton_Click"/>
        <AppBarSeparator/>
        <AppBarButton Icon="Stop" Label="Stop" Click="StopButton_Click"/>

        <CommandBar.SecondaryCommands>
            <AppBarToggleButton Icon="RepeatAll" Label="Loop Track"
                                Click="LoopButton_Click"/>
            <AppBarToggleButton Icon="Mute" Label="Mute"
                                Click="MuteButton_Click"/>
        </CommandBar.SecondaryCommands>
    </CommandBar>
</Page.BottomAppBar>
```

Like the sample markup shown earlier, this XAML creates a command bar attached to the bottom of the page. The command bar contains five buttons: Play, Pause, Stop, RepeatAll, and Mute. The last two buttons are created with the *AppBarToggleButton* control and are also so-called "secondary commands," meaning that they are listed on the left side of the command bar.

The Stop button is created on the far right of the command bar and separated from the others with a thin line that has been added purely for stylistic purposes. Notice that each of the five buttons has its own unique event handler, which you will define in the following steps by using Visual Basic *Sub* procedures.

15. Open the MainPage.xaml.vb code behind file in the Code Editor.

16. Type the following Visual Basic code beneath the *Inherits Page* statement in the file:

```
Sub StopButton_Click()
    MediaTool.Stop()
End Sub

Sub PlayButton_Click()
    MediaTool.Play()
End Sub
```

```
Sub PauseButton_Click()
    MediaTool.Pause()
End Sub

Sub LoopButton_Click()
    MediaTool.IsLooping = Not MediaTool.IsLooping
End Sub

Sub MuteButton_Click()
    MediaTool.IsMuted = Not MediaTool.IsMuted
End Sub
```

These five single-line event handlers use properties and methods in the *MediaElement* control to manage playback of the music asset loaded into the project. If you completed Chapter 5 in this book, you saw several of these methods already. The *IsLooping* property is used here for the first time, which determines whether the song will return to the beginning and play again after it finishes. The statement uses the *Not* Boolean operator to switch, or toggle, the current value of *IsLooping*.

17. Click the Save All command on the File menu to save your changes.

18. Specify the My Documents\Visual Basic 2013 SBS\Chapter 09 folder for the location.

Now you'll run the program again to test the command bar you've created.

19. Click Start Debugging on the toolbar.

The application runs, and the selected audio file begins to play. A feature of the *MediaElement* control is that it runs automatically by default. However, the screen is blank.

20. After a few moments of electronic music, open the command bar by clicking the right mouse button, pressing Windows+Z, or (if you have a touch screen) swiping up from the bottom edge of the screen.

You'll see the following command bar:

21. Click the Pause button.

The song pauses at the current playback position.

22. Click the Play button.

Audio playback resumes where you left off.

23. Click the Mute button.

The music is muted (volume is temporarily set to 0), but playback continues. Because Mute is a toggle button, the icon is filled with a white background color.

24. After a few moments, click the Mute button again.

The original volume setting is restored, and you'll be able to hear music again. You will notice that the song has advanced (and will complete if you wait too long).

25. Click the Stop button.

Audio playback terminates.

26. Click the Play button again.

The electronic music file begins again but at the beginning of the song.

27. Click the Loop Track button.

The toggle button is filled with a white background color and prepares the *MediaElement* control for looping. When the track ends, it will run again (and again) until you close the program or toggle the button.

 Note As you might have noticed, there was no specific "looping" button available in the collection of symbols supplied by Microsoft for Windows Store apps, so I used the RepeatAll button for this project (it has a similar look and feel). You can usually get away with this type of substitution, as long as the button you use is not well-known for another function.

28. Continue experimenting with the command bar controls that you just created. You can also open and close the command bar, playing with it for a while, and then closing it when it is no longer needed. The entire purpose of this bar is to be nonexistent when it is not needed.

29. When you're finished, quit the program and close the project. (But keep Visual Studio open.)

You've learned how to use the *CommandBar*, *AppBarButton*, and *AppBarToggleButton* controls to define a command bar and associate command buttons with event handlers that perform useful work.

Using the *Flyout* control to collect input and display information

Visual Basic 2013 also introduces a new control named *Flyout* for Windows Store apps that allows you to temporarily display a dialog box on the surface of your application. The proposed use for the *Flyout* control is to allow for quick pop-up messages or input in a situation when a complete page of information is not required, such as a message asking you to confirm a deletion or disconnection request. A flyout should be used in response to a user tap or click on the screen; like a command bar, it is quickly dismissed when the user clicks a button within the flyout, clicks outside the flyout, or presses the Esc key.

Flyouts are typically used in combination with button objects on the page in a Windows Store app. For example, consider the following screen shot of the Microsoft Calendar program, a Windows Store app that allows users to manage pending events on a shareable calendar.

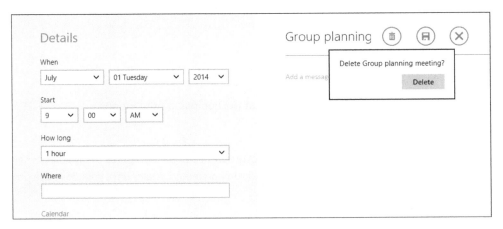

On the screen, the user has just clicked the Delete button in the upper-right corner of the page to delete a pending event. However, rather than simply removing the planning meeting—an action that will result in calendar data loss—the program uses a flyout to confirm the deletion. In particular, the flyout asks the user to confirm the removal by clicking Delete or canceling the action by pressing Esc or clicking outside the flyout.

Microsoft recommends that developers use flyouts for several actions in a Windows Store app, including the following:

- **Gathering data**   Use a flyout when you want to collect additional information from a user that is beyond the scope of typical input. For example, you might use text boxes and radio buttons on a page to gather typical customer information but then use a flyout for supplemental data or to remind the user that a required field has been left empty.

- **Warning messages**   Use a flyout to warn the user that data is about to be lost as a result of a command or action that they have just taken in the application. This is easy to do if you attach a flyout to a button on the page, because buttons have the built-in ability to display flyouts.

- **Selecting one option from many**   Microsoft recommends that you use flyouts in combination with command bars to display menus when a button has more than one option to choose from.

- **Additional context information**   Flyouts can be very helpful if you want to display additional information about something in your user interface. Microsoft recommends that you reduce the clutter or "chrome" on the screen. A flyout can be a good choice when you want to display informative text related to an action or feature, but only some of the time.

In Visual Studio 2013, the XAML *Button* control has a new *Flyout* property to make it easy to open a flyout on the page. Another technique for using *Flyout* controls (not discussed in this chapter) involves attaching a flyout to an object on the page by using the *FlyoutBase.AttachedFlyout* property and then handling the event that calls the flyout by creating a custom property in Visual Basic to respond to the interaction. (You'll learn more about creating properties and base classes in Chapter 16, "Object-oriented programming techniques.")

The following exercise shows you how to use the *Flyout* control to display a confirmation message when the user clicks a Display Photo button in a Windows Store application named Flyout Demo. The program is a revision of the Command Bar Demo program that you created earlier in the chapter. However, I have saved the project with a new name and added a few features to prepare it for the *Flyout* control practice that you will try.

Use the *Flyout* control to confirm an action

1. Open the Flyout Demo app, located in the My Documents\Visual Basic 2013 SBS\Chapter 09 folder on your hard disk.

    Flyout Demo is a Visual Studio 2013 app, containing controls that are not available in Visual Studio 2012. If you are currently running the Visual Studio 2012 software, you will not be able to open this project. (The app also requires that you are using Windows 8.1.)

2. Open the MainPage.xaml file.

    This program also has a very minimal user interface. Like Command Bar Demo, it contains a *MediaElement* control that plays music, and there is a command bar with buttons to let you control the playback of one electronic music file.

    The changes that I have made to the page include adding a button object containing the text "Display Photo" and adding an image object that displays a color photograph of my Seattle-based cover band, American Standard. (That's right, I don't only write computer books!)

    The photo is loaded into the Assets folder in the project, and it has been linked to the image object via the object's *Source* property. I have set the *Stretch* property for the image to Uniform, and I have hidden the image by setting the object's *Visibility* property to Collapsed. That's why you can't see the photo on the page right now.

    In the following steps, you will use XAML to attach a *Flyout* control to the *Button* object defined in MainPage.xaml.

3. Using the Code Editor, scroll down in the MainPage.xaml file to display the XAML defining the *Grid* and the *Button* objects.

4. Below the *Button* object's *Width* property, you'll notice the following markup:

```
<Button.Flyout>
<Flyout>
<StackPanel>
<TextBlock>You have requested a photo to be displayed. Do you want to continue?
</TextBlock>
<Button Click="DisplayPhoto_Click">Yes, display the photo</Button>
</StackPanel>
</Flyout>
</Button.Flyout>
```

> **Note** To allow the markup to appear on the printed page without line breaks, I have not indented the XAML in the book. However, in the Code Editor, you should feel free to accept the indents that Visual Studio recommends to show the nesting of elements.

Your IDE will look like this:

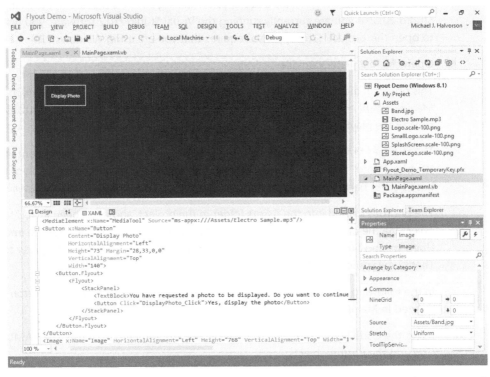

The new XAML attaches the *Flyout* control to the *Button* object and defines the content of the flyout using *StackPanel*, *TextBlock*, and *Button* controls. These are simply the user inter-face tools that I thought would make a good flyout—you can use any combination of XAML controls that you want in a flyout. Just try to be relatively simple here, because a flyout is not supposed to be as full-featured as a regular page in your user interface.

You should also notice the inner button used in the flyout. This markup specifies the text that will be displayed in the button ("Yes, display the photo") and also the event handler that will run when the user clicks the button (*DisplayPhoto_Click*).

Now you'll see the contents of the event handler in the Visual Basic code-behind file.

5. Open MainPage.xaml.vb in the Code Editor.

6. Scroll to the bottom of the file, and locate the following *Sub* procedure, which will make the image on the page visible when the user clicks the Display Photo button:

```
Sub DisplayPhoto_Click()
    Image.Visibility = Windows.UI.Xaml.Visibility.Visible
End Sub
```

This event handler simply sets the *Visibility* property. The long setting is simply a reference to the *Windows.UI.Xaml* namespace, which has more options available for visibility than simply True or False.

 Tip If you want Visual Studio to close the flyout programmatically after the Yes, Display The Photo button has been clicked, add the statement *Button.Flyout.Hide()* to the bottom of the *DisplayPhoto_Click* event handler. You can either close the flyout with program code or let the user click outside the flyout to close the pop-up window.

Now you'll run the program.

7. Click the Start button.

The familiar electronic music begins its progression in the Windows Store app, starting automatically when the program launches.

8. Click the Display Photo button.

The button launches the flyout, which displays a confirmation message in a temporary box near the button, asking whether you want to continue loading the photo.

9. Click Yes, Display The Photo.

The program confirms the request and loads the cover band photo. However, the flyout stays open until you press Esc or click outside the flyout.

Your screen looks like this:

The flyout text reads: "You have requested a photo to be displayed. Do you want to continue?" with a button "Yes, display the photo"

10. Click the page outside the flyout.

The flyout disappears and the image remains.

11. Right-click the mouse button, or sweep up from the bottom edge of the page.

The command bar appears, showing the controls that you can use to manage the playback of the music file.

12. Experiment a little more with the command bar buttons to ensure that they are still working as expected.

You created this same command bar in the previous exercise in this chapter, of course.

13. When you're finished experimenting, close the program.

That's all there is to it! You've learned how to display information and manage input using a *Flyout* control. You'll find this to be a helpful addition to your collection of Windows Store user interface tools. Like the command bar, flyouts help you reduce screen clutter, and they also fit the user experience (UX) guidelines that Microsoft recommends for solid user interface design. In the next section, you'll learn about another distinctive feature of Windows 8.1—the tile-based layout of the Start page—and how to prepare the necessary logos for the Start page and the Windows Store.

Designing custom tiles for your app

The Start page presents a collection of colorful, customizable application tiles that are used to launch programs and to provide visual feedback about events taking place in Windows Store applications, such as the current weather in the city you are in. Although Start page tiles can be simple, static images (containing nothing but a basic logo and the application name), you can also create dynamic "live tiles" containing additional images or textual content that is updated periodically by the application or a trusted web service.

In this section, you'll learn how application tiles are created in a Windows Store project, beginning with static tiles and then moving on to live tiles. What you design will be compatible with Windows Store apps sold via the Windows Store. However, you follow a similar process when designing tiles for Windows Phone 8 devices and Microsoft Xbox.

The Assets folder

Application tiles, or *logos*, are part of the distribution package for a Windows Store application. You will see them listed in Solution Explorer in the Assets folder for a project. Default "empty" tiles containing nothing but an "X" on a dark background are included automatically as placeholders for your app when you create a new Windows Store project. You can modify these images or replace them completely with your own custom image files. The tiles must be in PNG or JPEG format, and the images must fit exactly the required dimensions and specification. (See the next section of this chapter for details.) I recommend the PNG format, because that file type is better suited for transparency.

The names for your tiles are stored individually in the Package.appxmanifest file in your project, and you will find them all listed under the Application UI category when you edit the Package.appxmanifest file by using the Manifest Designer. (You can double-click the Package.appxmanifest file in Solution Explorer to open this editor.)

In addition to the tile names, you will see other helpful settings under the Application UI category, including the URI template location where tiles can receive live updates, the foreground and background colors used for the tiles (be sure to make these consistent), and the application name that appears on the tiles in the Windows Start page and in other locations. You can either embed the application name in your tile or have Visual Studio display a text overlay with the name on the tile. I recommend the second approach in your Windows Store apps. If you go this route, you can create the text overlay using the Short Name text box in the Application UI category of the Package.appxmanifest file.

Required tiles and uses

Because application tiles are used in different ways by Windows, there are several images required for each Windows Store application. The requirements that I'll discuss here apply to Windows 8.1.

For a Windows Store app that runs under Windows 8.1, three tile images are required, and two additional images are optional (but recommended). The major differentiating feature among all of these tiles is that they are different sizes. For the best possible display results, the designers of Windows 8.1 recommend that you don't simply "scale" one tile to fit the various required sizes; this often produces fuzzy images that don't look as good as they might.

The tiles for a Windows Store app can be created using third-party image-editing software, or you can use the Image Editor that is included with Visual Studio, which you first encountered in Chapter 3, "Creating your first Windows Store application," when you created a splash screen. (If you didn't complete the Windows Store app walkthrough in Chapter 3, you might want to check out those instructions before you complete this section. You will use the Image Editor in the upcoming exercise.

The three required tiles sizes for a Windows Store app in Windows 8.1 are 150×150 pixels for the basic Start page logo, 30×30 pixels for a small version of the logo suitable for search results and use on the secondary Start page or "Apps By Name" panel, and 50×50 pixels for an image that can be used for marketing purposes in the Windows Store. Optionally, you can also create two supplemental tiles for Windows Store apps: a 310×150 pixels "wide" image for the Start page (which contains a little more real estate for live data and other goodies), and a tiny 24×24 pixels image for *badge notification* that appears on the Windows Lock screen and in other situations.

In terms of design, you'll want to avoid loading down your tiles with unwieldy text and overly complicated artwork. Consider using an image or photo that can easily be adapted to other countries and cultures (that is, easily localizable), and use a background color that is attractive and complementary with the tiles a user would typically see on the Start page, such as those provided in the default installation of Windows 8.1.

The following illustration shows the five tile images described above for the Microsoft Weather application that is shipped with most retail versions of Windows 8.1. (Weather is also available as a free application download in the Windows Store.)

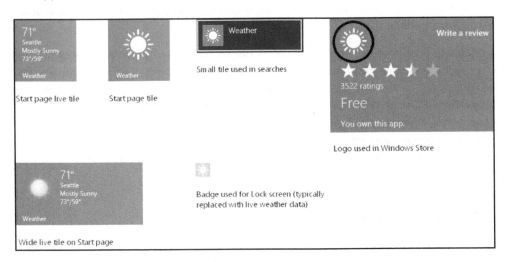

Notice how similar the Weather logos are within the sample tiles shown here, although they are actually different sizes in all but one case. The most obvious difference that you will see here is that two of the Weather tiles are dynamic "live tiles" containing weather updates that are downloaded periodically from a web server. The user can disable a live tile like Weather by right-clicking the tile on the Start page, and then selecting the Turn Live Tile Off command. By the way, the first tile in the preceding illustration (top left) shows the live tile version of the Weather application; the second image (top, second from the left) shows the Weather tile with live updates disabled.

Although the software developer must take responsibility for designing the different tiles shown here for certification in the Windows Store, most users will not realize that each image is a unique file. (And of course, as noted earlier, you are not required to create a live tile if you don't want to right now.) This is not the place for time-saving shortcuts. For example, simply scaling the tile (that is, using an image editor to expand or shrink the tile programmatically) is not a good way to speed up the logo design process, because the results can look "jaggy" and not as crisp as the tiles created by your competitors! In short, your tiles should resemble as closely as possible professional tiles, because this feature is one that is very prominently displayed on the Start page and in the Windows Store.

With this introduction to tiles, try creating one now by completing the following steps. You can repeat the process whenever you need to design a custom tile for your Windows Store application. The project that you have open for this exercise does not matter—I will keep using the Flyout Demo app, but you can use whatever Windows Store project that you want. The focus of the instruction is on the steps you need to complete rather than on the specific design you create.

Design a custom tile for a Windows Store app

1. Open a valid Windows Store project designed for Windows 8.1, such as Flyout Demo, the project that you just worked on earlier in this chapter.

   If you use a Visual Studio 2012 project designed for Windows 8, the steps are similar, but the names of the logo files are different. (They were updated for Windows 8.1.)

2. In Solution Explorer, expand the Assets folder for the project, and then double-click the file Logo.scale-100.png.

   This action opens the Image Editor in Visual Studio and loads the Logo.scale-100.png file into the editor. This is the basic logo tile that appears on the full-sized Windows Start page for your application. Your screen looks like this:

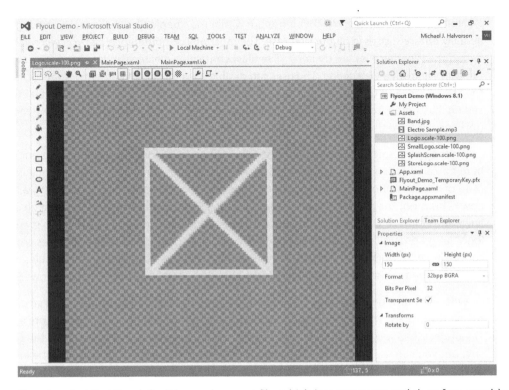

Keep in mind that the default image is a .png file, which is transparent and therefore capable of showing a background color behind it. (That's a good thing; Windows 8 tiles and Windows 8.1 tiles take advantage of this feature.)

In Visual Studio now, the Solution Explorer and Properties windows are still visible. The Image Editor is surrounded by various graphics editing tools. The "X" shape in the center of the canvas is simply the default image for the Start page tile. This is the image that you want to replace now.

3. Click the Selection tool in the upper-left corner of the Designer, select the entire "X" shape, and press Delete.

You now have a blank canvas to create your Start page tile. On my system, the default background for the canvas is a green "alpha" checkerboard pattern that makes it easy for you to see the background behind transparent tiles. (If you see the checkerboard pattern, that means that you can see the background through the tile.) If you see something different and would like to see what I see, adjust the background setting by using the tool labeled Show Or Hide The Alpha Checkerboard Pattern, located on the top of the canvas.

4. Click the Rectangle tool on the left side of the Image Editor, and then create a series of rectangles in the middle of the screen. Design the rectangles so that they are equally spaced apart and ascending in height so that the last rectangle is taller than the first.

By default, Rectangle and the other tools will create images in white, which will look especially good on the Windows Start page. Your Designer should look something like this:

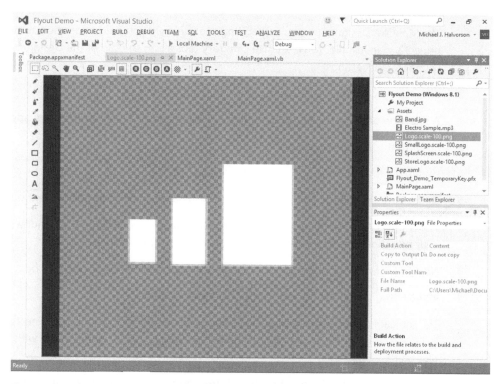

If you are unhappy with the way that the rectangles look, simply select one or more rectangles with the selection tool, press Delete, and start over again. Or you can create a design that better fits the application that you are creating.

Although you might be tempted to add some text now using the Text tool, I recommend that you create a text overlay using the Manifest Designer, which you'll do in the next exercise. Try to add little, if any, text to your actual tile file.

Tip Ready for more features? The Image Editor tool has many useful editing tools that you can check out. The basic shape tools work much like Microsoft Paint, but there are also sophisticated design features related to color channels and transparency that you can learn about via the online help resource, "Image Editor," at *http://msdn.microsoft.com/en-us/library/vstudio/hh315744*.

5. When you're finished designing, click the Save All command on the File menu to save your changes.

Now you'll open the Visual Studio Manifest Designer and set the title and background color for your new tile.

Adjust tile options in the Manifest Designer

1. Double-click the Package.appxmanifest file in Solution Explorer.

    The Manifest Designer opens. This editing tool will help you adjust common settings in the project's manifest file. You'll see five category tabs along the top of the Designer to help you with different settings.

2. Click the Application UI category if it is not already visible.

    A selection of general items that control the appearance of the user interface appears.

3. Scroll to the Visual Assets section.

4. Under Tile Images and Logos, click Square 150x150 Logo.

5. Under Title, type **Flyout** (or another application name) in the Short Name text box.

    This is the content of the text overlay that will appear on your tile in the Windows Start page. Your title should be short and unique to your application, if possible.

6. Next to Show Name, place a check mark in the Square 150x150 Logo check box.

7. In the Foreground Text list box, verify that Light is selected.

    This indicates that light color (typically white) will be the color for the text. The actual color will match the Light Windows color scheme and will therefore be consistent with the other tiles on the Start page.

8. In the Background Color text box, type **blue**, and click somewhere else in the Manifest Designer.

    You can specify a color value by using a Hex value, as you can throughout Visual Studio when assigning colors, but a large selection of color names are also recognized.

    Visual Studio records each tile-related formatting option as you make it and loads a preview of the new tile in the Scaled Assets area of the Manifest Designer. Your screen will look like this:

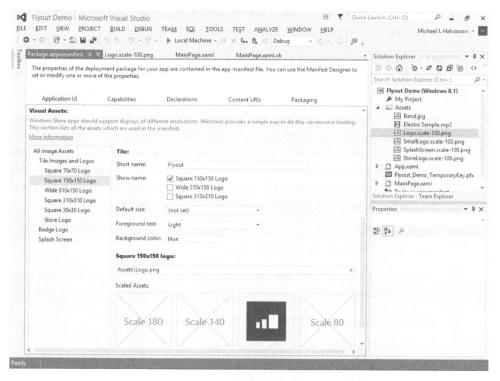

9. Click the Save All button to save your changes.

10. On the Build menu, click Build Flyout Demo.

   Building a project will deploy the new tile on the Apps By Name panel, a secondary Start page connected to the Windows Start page via a Down Arrow button. Users of Visual Studio 2012 and Windows 8 will notice a change here. In Visual Studio 2012, the Build command deployed the application directly on the Start page, but that has changed.

11. Click Start to run the Windows Store app.

   The Flyout Demo program starts, and the familiar music plays. (If you built a tile for another application, that program will appear instead.)

12. Close the application.

   Now you'll examine the tile on the Start page.

13. Click the Start button to display the Windows Start page.

14. Click the Down Arrow button on the left side of the screen, near the bottom of the Start page, to display the secondary Start page or Apps By Name panel.

As you complete these steps, carefully notice the tiles that you see. The main Windows Start page has the standard application tiles that are 150×150 pixels in size—that is, the format that you have just created. (You'll also see some wide 310×150 live tiles here.)

When you display the secondary Start page (the Apps By Name panel), you'll see the smaller tiles. These are the 30×30 images defined by the SmallLogo.scale-100.png file in a Windows Store app's Assets folder. You should see your application tile here (Flyout or whatever project that you are using), but because you didn't create a 30×30 image in the preceding exercise, your tile will continue to show the default "X" design. However, you'll move the Flyout tile to the Start page now and see what your 150×150 logo looks like.

15. Locate the 30×30 application tile in the Apps By Name panel, right click the tile, and then select Pin To Start on the command bar.

This command will display your tile on the Start page and load the 150×150 pixel image that you just created.

16. Enlarge the Flyout tile on the Start page. (Select Medium size.)

Your tile will look like this on the Start page:

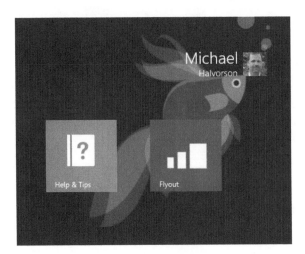

I've shown another tile on the page too, so you can see how the image and colors compare. What you have looks similar to a professional Windows Store app tile, and it just took a few moments to create!

By switching between the two Start pages you can now see how Windows actually *does* use different tile sizes to represent Windows Store apps in diverse locations. This is the reason that three tile sizes are required and also why you might want to create the optional sizes while you're at it—there are a variety of ways that your application tiles will be represented by the operating system.

17. Return to Visual Studio.

You're done creating tiles now, but you'll use the Manifest Designer again in a few minutes.

By exploring the Image Editor and Manifest Designer in this section, you've received some fundamental training on how Visual Studio tools for Windows Store development can support Visual Basic programmers.

Programming live tiles

A *live tile* is an application tile that receives periodic updates from a Window Store app or a web server. Live tiles can be used to notify the user of an important event in the program, such as the arrival of email, or to send some sort of teaser information to get the user to activate the app, such as a juicy news headline.

Because the application tile is the front door to your Windows Store app, adding dynamic live content to your tile can be an important programming activity. It can draw users to your program and increase their satisfaction with the app. The following illustration shows the Windows 8.1 Start page with several active live tiles, including Contacts, Finance, Weather, Photos, and Travel:

In Windows programming terminology, the arrival of new content to a Start page tile is called a *notification*. There are four ways that a live tile can receive a notification:

- **Local** A Windows Store app can initiate a notification while the program is running by using one or more methods in the *TileUpdateManager* class. The way that you actually update a tile is to modify an XML template file that is connected to the live tile and represents its content by using nodes. For example, a running music app might update its tile to contain the text "Now Playing" while a song is playing in the program.

- **Scheduled** Your app can schedule a notification *in advance* that will be sent to the app tile at the appropriate time. This process is similar to sending direct notification to a tile by using the *TileUpdateManager* class, but you also use the *ScheduleTileNotification* object to schedule the event so that it happens at the desired time. For example, a calendar app might update its live tile to show a pending afternoon meeting.

- **Periodic** You can connect your application's tile to a cloud service that will send periodic updates to the tile. This notification is initiated by the Windows Store app, which identifies the URL of a cloud location that Windows will poll for tile updates and how often the URL should be checked. For example, a ski school app might update its tile every hour to show recent snowfall amounts at a specified ski resort. However, note that in this periodic scenario the app can only arrange for updates while the program is running.

- **Push** A live tile can also receive updates from a cloud service when the Windows Store app is *not* running. This is called a push notification because you arrange for the occasional updates using the Windows Push Notification Service (WNS). The procedure involves composing an HTTP POST request, authenticating the cloud server you are using, creating XML content to define the notification, and arranging to send the needed content from the server to the app. Rather than *periodic* updates from the cloud, push updates happen *immediately* when the desired information becomes available, meaning that the live content will arrive somewhat unpredictably. For example, a sports app might update its tile when emerging sports data arrives, probably based on some criteria established by the cloud service.

If you choose to create a live tile for your app, you will probably find that local notification methods work just fine for most scenarios. However, the choice is really up to you, and the method or methods chosen really depend on the type of information that you are delivering. (In many situations, you won't even need a live tile to please your customers.)

Just don't get too crazy. Microsoft recommends that you update live tile content no more than once every 30 minutes or so. If you decide to go the scheduled notification route, you can also arrange for the notification to expire after some period of time by using the *ScheduledTileNotification.ExpirationTime* method. Finally, be sure that you don't use live tiles to display advertisements, irrelevant information, or spam of any kind. Microsoft will not take kindly to this use of the live tile gateway, and the company has threatened to remove apps from the Windows Store for such behavior.

Creating live tiles is a pretty advanced topic, and the procedure requires some programming techniques that we haven't covered yet. It is especially involved to create live tiles with push notification, although the rewards are great as well. To learn more about this topic and the best way to approach it, see the section "Tiles, badges, and notifications (Windows Store apps)" in the Windows Store app section of MSDN, located at *http://msdn.microsoft.com/en-us/library/windows/apps/hh779725.aspx*.

Planning for touch input

As you have learned throughout this book, Windows Store apps should be designed so that they can receive input in a variety of ways, including mouse, keyboard, touch, and so on. Traditional desktop computers are naturally a major platform for Windows Store apps, but so are emerging touch-based devices, such as Microsoft Surface tablets and touch-enabled laptops. In fact, to be fully certified by the Windows Store for distribution, a Windows Store app needs to offer support for mouse, keyboard, *and* touch input—something that will take a little thought if developers are to create programs that are ergonomic, fast, and fluid.

Although some of the features in touch-based devices do require specific calls to the .NET Framework and Windows Runtime API to make them operate, much of the support for touch is provided automatically to Windows Store apps by Windows 8.1 and Visual Studio 2013. When you create a Windows Store app by using XAML controls and Visual Studio, basic touch and gesture support is included by default to the extent that it is supported by the hardware device that you are using. So, when you run a new Windows Store app on a Surface tablet or touch-enabled laptop, touch input will work automatically to the extent that your device supports touch and gestures.

Of course, the computer industry is going through a transition right now in terms of support for touch input and user expectations about how hardware and software should be used. When Microsoft released Windows 8, it announced that touch input should become a standard feature of Windows applications, and this commitment to touch has continued with Windows 8.1. However, traditional mouse and keyboard input is also important and not going away. As a developer, you need to think about adding support not only for touch-based devices but also for enhanced traditional features, such as the right button and tilt wheel on a mouse, or interesting third-party devices like the pen or stylus.

As you move beyond the basics of mouse and keyboard input in a Visual Basic program, you'll want to consider carefully the value of touch input and how you might innovatively use touch capabilities for Windows users. Although much of the support for touch and gestures comes automatically in Windows Store apps, there are important considerations about design that you should think about as you write programs for the Windows Store.

In the following section, you'll learn the basics about touch input and some of the pitfalls to avoid when designing apps for Windows 8.1 that support touch and gestures.

XAML controls handle touch automatically

Touch is a considered a primary mode of interaction in Windows 8.1, so Visual Studio 2013 has been optimized to make touch input straightforward, precise, and trouble free. The XAML controls in the Visual Studio Toolbox have been designed to support touch input as well as traditional mouse and keyboard interaction. The built-in support for touch input in XAML controls includes gestures such as tap, slide, swipe, press and hold, pinch, and stretch. Also included is support for useful touch procedures such as panning, zoom, rotating, and dragging. Not all controls support touch equally, but in areas where touch functionality is useful, you'll find that most of the support for this type of input is already enabled in the software. The *CommandBar* and *Flyout* controls that you have already used in this chapter provide evidence of this.

In addition, the event handlers for controls that support touch have built-in events that support touch interaction, such as *Tapped*. Most XAML controls also have property settings that are related to touch input and gesture support.

Common gestures

The most fundamental touch input is the *tap* gesture, shown in the following illustration. Tapping on a screen element should always invoke its primary action in touch-enabled user interfaces; for example, a user might tap a photograph to enlarge it or open it for editing in a graphics program. Keep in mind that while a mouse or a pen might offer very precise on-screen input, fingers typically are not as accurate, so your screen elements should be large enough to support tap gestures and other touch input.

Another foundational gesture in a Windows Store app is the panning movement, or *slide*, shown in the following illustration. A slide is a one-finger motion that moves the page right or left and often supports moving items from one location to another. This gesture is typically equivalent to scrolling with the mouse or using the arrow keys on a keyboard. You can also use a slide gesture in moving, drawing, or writing operations.

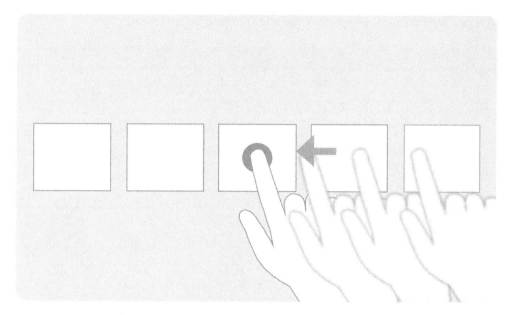

Input gestures often involve using two or even three fingers to manipulate objects in a Windows Store app. The on-screen objects in the following illustrations help to demonstrate the zoom-in or *stretch* gesture, a technique used to increase the magnification of the page so that objects can be examined more clearly. The opposite of this gesture is called a *pinch*, which produces the opposite visual effect: a zoom-out.

On this touch-enabled screen, notice what the objects look like before zooming:

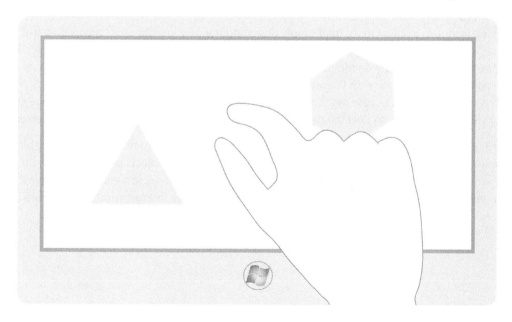

And notice what the same objects look like after zooming (or stretching):

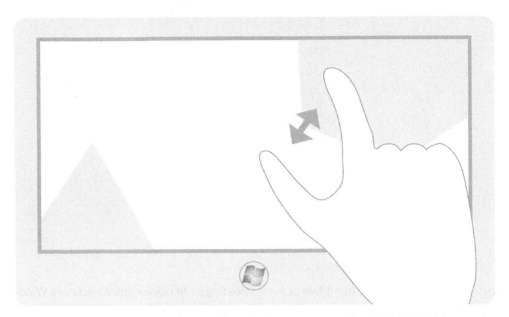

Programmers can also use the stretch or pinch gestures to allow individual objects to be resized on a page. Note that some objects can be resized. Resizing capability depends on what the programmer wants to allow the user to do.

Usability considerations

Designing for touch involves more than simply designing the user interface for finger input and touch gestures. It also requires thinking about how the touch-enabled device will be held by the user. For example, if the device is held on the user's lap, the user can have both hands free to manipulate the objects on the screen. However, if the user is holding the device in two hands, the lower parts of the screen will likely be partially obscured by the hands, and only the top half of the device will be completely visible. Depending on how the device is held, some types of input will be harder or easier.

Furthermore, because most people are right-handed, they will tend to hold the touch-enabled device with their left hand and touch it with their right. Accordingly, objects placed on the right side of the screen will be easier to touch than objects on the left. In addition, some users might have motor impairments or other disabilities that can influence how they interact with touch-enabled devices.

Even as you work to consider how touch input and gestures might be best used in an application, don't forget about traditional input devices and how users might innovatively use them in a Windows Store app. For example, consider adding support for the right mouse button or a tilt wheel in your application. These are very common input features and are commonly used in Windows-based applications; users will often expect to see them supported. Visual Studio and the Windows Runtime API offer support for an amazing array of input devices and input techniques, so be sure to add these features to your applications as you write more sophisticated programs.

Finally, although it is possible to create Windows Store apps on a computer that is not touch enabled, it is important for you to get some hands-on experience with touch-enabled devices before you get too far along in the development process. Learning the tap, slide, pinch, and stretch techniques should become a priority, as well as understanding how Windows interacts with the various visual elements on the screen. The same is true with Windows Phone 8 programming, which you'll learn more about in Chapter 20, "Introduction to Windows Phone 8 development," and Chapter 21, "Creating your first Windows Phone 8 application."

Some useful online materials are available on the web to help with touch and gesture support. For more information about planning for touch in your applications, visit *http://msdn.microsoft.com* and search for the topics "Touch interaction design" and "Responding to user interaction."

Security and permissions settings

When you write programs for your own use, you can be trusted to use the applications appropriately and for the purposes that they were intended. But when you are creating applications that will be distributed commercially via the Windows Store, you can't always be so trusting. Accordingly, it is important to control the permissions and capabilities that users receive when they operate programs that you have created. Visual Studio gives you this control via Package.appxmanifest, the settings file that you just used to configure your Start page tile.

Each Windows Store app runs in a security container with limited access to the computer's hardware, the network, and the file system. Using the Capabilities category of Package.appxmanifest, you can control the various permissions that an application receives, establishing an appropriate level of system security. For example, you can control whether the user can access the computer's built-in web camera or microphone through your app, or whether the user can have the ability to browse the computer's music or picture libraries.

Table 9-1 describes the important security and permissions settings that can be set in the Capabilities category of the Package.appxmanifest file.

TABLE 9-1 Useful security and permissions settings

Capability	Description
Enterprise Authentication	Allows an app to connect to intranet resources that require domain credentials.
Internet (Client)	Allows your app to access the Internet and public networks. Most apps that require Internet access should use this capability.
Internet (Client & Server)	Allows your app to access the Internet and public networks and allows incoming connections from the Internet to your app. This is a superset of the Internet (Client) capability. You do not need to declare both.
Location	Allows your app to access the user's current location.
Microphone	Allows your app to access the user's microphone.
Music Library	Allows your app to access the user's music library and to add, change, or delete files. It also allows access to music libraries on HomeGroup computers and to music file types on locally connected media servers.
Pictures Library	Allows your app to access the user's picture library and to add, change, or delete files. It also allows access to picture libraries on HomeGroup computers and to picture file types on locally connected media servers.
Private Networks (Client & Server)	Allows access to connected home or intranet networks that have the property authentication.
Proximity	Allows your app to access the user's near-field communication (NFC) device.
Removable Storage	Allows your app to access removable storage devices, such as an external hard drive or USB flash drive, and to add, change, or delete files. Your app can access only file types that it has declared in the manifest. Your app can't access removable storage devices on HomeGroup computers.
Shared User Certificates	Allows your app to access software and hardware certificates, such as smart card certificates.
Videos Library Access	Allows your app to access the user's video library and to add, change, or delete files. It also allows access to video libraries on HomeGroup computers and to video file types on locally connected media servers.
Webcam	Allows your app to access the user's camera.

In the following exercise, you'll use the Manifest Designer to edit permissions in the Package.appx-manifest file for the Flyout Demo project. You can use another project if you like.

Set permissions and capabilities for your app

1. Open the Flyout Demo project now if it is not already open. You'll find the project in the My Documents\Visual Basic 2013 SBS\Chapter 09 folder.

2. When we last used Visual Studio, the Manifest Designer was open. If it is not open now, access it by double-clicking Package.appxmanifest in Solution Explorer.

3. Click the Capabilities tab.

   You'll see the following page, which includes a list of the permissions and capabilities that you can control in a Windows Store app:

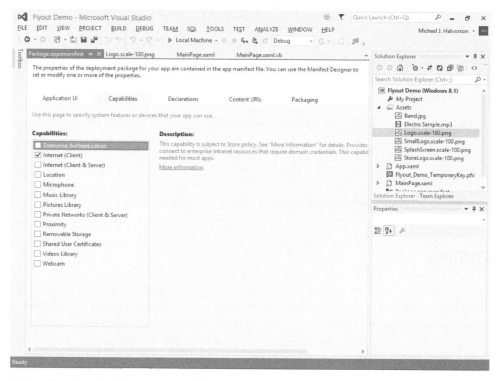

Notice that the check boxes containing permissions and capabilities are in the same order as they are in Table 9-1. You can learn additional information about each setting by clicking the item and reading information in the Description field on the page.

Currently, this application allows only client Internet access; the user is allowed basic Internet access if you provide it via controls in the application user interface. To remove this capability, you would remove the check mark from the Internet (Client) check box. Some capabilities require that you configure additional settings on the Declarations tab of the Manifest Designer.

4. Read about the various permission and capabilities, and keep them in mind as you create apps for Windows 8.1.

Visual Studio developers often adjust these settings early in the programming process so that they apply to testing scenarios. However, they can be adjusted as necessary throughout the development process.

For example, in the Flyout Demo app, it would be appropriate for you to allow access to the Music Library on the user's computer. That way the program could be expanded so that additional songs could be loaded from the user's computer and played using the existing controls.

5. Return the permissions and capabilities in this project back to the original (default) settings if you changed them.

   In addition to considering important security issues, you've learned another valuable use for the Package.appxmanifest file. Remember that this file travels with the project and informs the operating system about the capabilities and settings for your app.

6. Save your changes, and then choose File | Close Project to close the application.

   You're finished with the Flyout Demo program.

7. Close Visual Studio.

You're finished building Windows Store apps in this chapter. Nice work!

Summary

This chapter has focused on several design features unique to Windows Store applications, including the *CommandBar* and *Flyout* controls, live tiles on the Start page, support for touch input, and controlling security and permissions. The material expanded upon the XAML programming skills that you learned in Chapter 5, "Working with Windows Store app controls," Chapter 7, "XAML markup step by step," and Chapter 8, "Using XAML styles."

Windows Store app programming is a relatively new paradigm for software developers. However, from the perspective of the Visual Basic programmer, many of the fundamental coding techniques and concerns are the same in Windows 8.1 as they are in a Windows Forms environment. The goal of this chapter has been to introduce some of the newest tools and techniques that you will need to write Windows Store apps for the Windows 8.1 operating system. These programs have the potential to revolutionize how consumer applications are created, purchased, and used. Windows Store apps shine when rich user content and information is at the center of the computing experience, presented visually with beautiful text, photos, original art, and tiles.

In the next chapter, you'll strike a new chord completely by creating a fascinating program-type that typically has *no graphical user interface at all*—the console application. Console apps run in a text-based Command window sometimes called the Windows text console. However, despite the minimal user interface, Visual Basic console apps are full .NET applications with lightning-fast access to the .NET Framework and a variety of Windows services. To make the task fun, you'll write some old-fashioned computation games involving probability.

CHAPTER 10

Creating console applications

After completing this chapter, you will be able to

- Understand console applications and their uses.

- Learn to use the Console Application template in Visual Studio 2013.

- Work with modules, functions, and procedures in the Visual Studio IDE.

- Explore the *Console* object and its useful properties and methods, including *WriteLine* and *ReadLine*.

- Build, publish, and run console applications.

This chapter describes how to create a console, or *command-line*, application in Visual Studio 2013. Console applications are considered a bit of an anomaly today in the world of advanced graphics user interfaces and Windows Store apps. This is because a console application has an extremely minimal user interface—the only interaction you get between a console application and the user is character-based monitor output and the keyboard. However, console applications are extremely useful as a tool for teaching Visual Basic programming, and they are also used today by system administrators who are designing setup and maintenance programs, as well as by programmers who have no particular need for a graphical user interface. For this reason, a discussion of console applications usefully rounds out our discussion of user interface design techniques in Part II and paves the way for Part III, "Visual Basic programming techniques."

You'll begin in this chapter by creating a new console application for Windows in Visual Studio 2013. You'll learn to use the Console Application template and how to edit a code module in the Visual Studio IDE. You'll learn how to use the *Console* object in a console application with its useful methods and properties, including *Title*, *WriteLine*, *Readline*, and *ReadKey*. You'll also learn how to start a console application from the Windows command prompt and interact with console applications by using the keyboard. The programs that you create will demonstrate math operations, gaming strategies, and important Visual Basic language elements, including decision structures, loops, and math functions in the .NET Framework.

 Note Console applications are supported in Visual Studio 2013 Professional, Premium, and Ultimate versions, but not in Visual Studio Express 2013 for Windows.

Console applications in Visual Studio

A Visual Studio console application is a Windows program that runs in the text-based *Command window*, sometimes also called the Windows text console or DOS window. Console applications are full .NET applications with access to the .NET Framework, a comprehensive, object-oriented class library that offers a variety of Windows features and services.

The fact that console applications exist might come as a surprise to some Visual Studio programmers who, for good reason, might assume that only graphics-based Windows programs are supported by Windows 8.1 and the Visual Studio product line. But the historic roots of Windows in the world of MS-DOS programming means that command-line applications (what we now call console applications) have a long history with PCs. This command-line application support continues with Visual Studio 2013, and Visual Studio recently added support for UTF 16 encoding with surrogates in console applications, an enhanced Unicode standard that allows for the representation (potentially) of over one million distinct characters in the Command window. That's right—you're not limited to the basic range of ASCII characters, but you can display symbols in a variety of languages.

You can run console applications from within the Visual Studio IDE or directly from the Windows command prompt. You can also run console apps in Windows PowerShell, a task-based command-line shell and scripting language that is included with Windows 8 and Windows 8.1. Windows PowerShell is built on the .NET Framework and is designed especially for system administrators. The tool helps IT professionals and power users control and automate system-level tasks within Windows. Although the features and commands of Windows PowerShell go well beyond the scope of this book (and I'll be using the Windows text console for testing), you can experiment with the Windows PowerShell tool by searching for "Windows PowerShell" with the Windows Search charm.

What type of user interface will you see in console applications? Traditionally, the only output that users experience in console apps are text strings displayed within the confines of the character-based Command window. User input is usually limited to the keyboard. However, developers are not actually limited to these input and output mechanisms. For example, you could add a reference to the *System.Windows.Forms* assembly and use a tool like *MessageBox* to interact with the user outside of the console window. But this sort of activity is rarely done. The simple beauty of console applications is that in some cases you simply don't need a fancy user interface to interact with the user. If what you need is the Visual Basic language, access to the .NET Framework, and lots of power and speed—but not impressive graphics or Windows Store app features—you might find that a basic console app is just the tool for you.

Creating a console application

To create a console application, open the Console Application template in the Visual Basic/Windows category of the New Project dialog box. Console applications have a somewhat smaller electronic footprint than Windows Store apps, but there are still an assortment of project files associated with a console apps, including project and solution files, various setting and resource files, an assembly file, and the /bin and /obj folders for the executable images. You can also create setup and installation files for a console application in Visual Studio.

Try building a sample console application now, using the following steps.

Open the Console Application template

1. Start Visual Studio, and click New Project to open a new Visual Studio application.

2. Choose Visual Basic/Windows under Templates, and then select the Console Application template.

   The New Project dialog box looks like this when Console Application is selected:

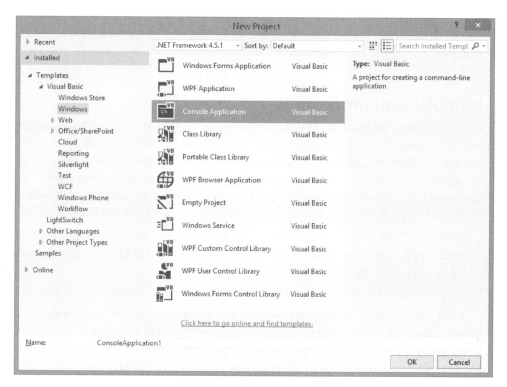

3. Type **My-Temp-Conversion** in the Name text box.

4. Click OK to configure the project and load it in the IDE.

   Visual Studio creates a new console application with the appropriate supporting files. After a moment, you'll see the Code Editor and an empty Visual Basic code module, the place where you will type in your Visual Basic code for the program. There is no user interface designer for the console application nor is there any XAML markup to manage.

Your IDE will look like this:

Modules and procedures

As you can see in the preceding illustration, a standard feature of the console application is the *module* component (Module1.vb) with its *Sub Main()* and *End Sub* keywords. A module is a named storage container designed to hold program code in a Visual Studio application. A module is a little like a code-behind file, such as MainPage.xaml.vb. However, modules are not associated with the user interface specifically. Instead, modules typically contain global variable declarations and *Sub* and *Function* procedures. You can include a module in any Visual Basic application.

Note You'll learn more about global variable declarations in Chapter 11, "Mastering data types, operators, and string processing."

A module file has a .vb file name extension and is visible in Solution Explorer as part of a Visual Studio project. The first module in a program is named Module1.vb by default, but you can change the name by right-clicking the file in Solution Explorer, selecting Rename, and typing a new name. Modules are optional in Windows Store applications (although they are often very useful), but they are required in console applications. You can add additional modules to a Visual Studio project by clicking the Add New Item command on the Project menu and selecting the Module template.

A code module in a Visual Basic application typically contains groups of *Sub* and *Function* procedures. These entities are a lot like the event handlers that you have been using so far in this book. (And in fact, an event handler is just an ordinary *Sub* procedure that has been associated with a particular event.) *Sub* and *Function* procedures contain Visual Basic source code, and they are designed to be *called* and perform useful work in an application. Here are a few things that make *Sub* and *Function* procedures distinct:

- *Function* procedures are called by name from event handlers or other procedures, and they can also receive *arguments*, or a list of values in a specific data type separated by commas. Functions also return a value using the *Return* statement.

- *Sub* procedures are also called by name from event handlers and other procedures. They can receive a list of arguments and pass back modified values through the arguments if they are passed by reference. However, unlike functions, *Sub* procedures don't always return one or more values. Instead of computing new information, *Sub* procedures are typically used to process user input, display repetitive output, or set standard properties.

Although *Sub* and *Function* procedures can also be defined in code-behind files, if you define them in a module they have scope (or validity) throughout the entire project. (You'll see an example of this later in this chapter.) In object-oriented programming terminology, *Sub* and *Function* procedures are essentially the same as methods, and some Visual Basic programming books simply call *Sub* and *Function* procedures methods.

The *Sub Main()* procedure

Each console application always starts with the same *Sub* procedure, which in Visual Basic programs is named *Main()*. The empty parentheses after the name *Main* indicate that the procedure has no arguments associated with it. Each console application needs a *Main()* procedure so that Windows and Visual Studio know where to begin execution. You can also define additional *Sub* or *Function* procedures in the Module1.vb file if you like. However, in the following sample program, additional procedures will not be necessary.

Enter the Visual Basic code for a console application now that converts a temperature in Fahrenheit to a temperature in Celsius. The exercise demonstrates how to manage input and output, declare variables, and use the *Math* class in the .NET Framework.

Build a console application that converts temperature values

1. In the Code Editor, move the insertion point to the blank line between the *Sub Main()* and *End Sub* statements.

2. Type the following Visual Basic program code:

```
'Display an informative title in the Command window
Console.Title = "Fahrenheit to Celsius Conversion"

'Declare 3 variables for Fahrenheit temp, Celsius temp, and city name
'The Single data type allows the temps to contain decimal values
Dim fahrenheitTemp As Single, celsiusTemp As Single
Dim cityName As String

'Ask the user for the name of a city that they have weather data for
Console.Write("Enter the name of a city: ")
cityName = Console.ReadLine()

'Ask the user for the temperature in Fahrenheit...
Console.Write("Enter the temperature in {0} (Fahrenheit): ", cityName)
fahrenheitTemp = Console.ReadLine
```

```
'Convert Fahrenheit temp to Celsius & round to nearest tenth of a degree
'The Math.Round method rounds the temp to the nearest 0.1
celsiusTemp = Math.Round((fahrenheitTemp + 40) * 5 / 9 - 40, 1)

'Display the city name and temperatures using replaceable parameters
Console.WriteLine("The temperature in {0} is {1} Fahrenheit and {2} Celsius.",
    cityName, fahrenheitTemp, celsiusTemp)

'Pause until the user presses a key, which closes the Command window
Console.ReadKey()
```

The Comment character (') allows you to enter descriptive text that explains what the program statements in a routine are doing. In this case, I use comments liberally to explain how variables are declared, input and output are managed, and a Fahrenheit temperature is converted to Celsius.

In a console application, the *Console* object provides useful methods and properties for managing information in a Command window. This routine begins by using the *Console.Title* property to set the text that appears in the Command window title bar. Three variables are defined using syntax that will be described more fully in Chapter 11. In this program, note that I am using the camel-casing style when declaring variables—that is, using an initial lowercase letter to differentiate variables from properties, methods, and keywords (for example, the string variable *cityName*).

The *Console.Write* method is used to display a line of text in the Command window, prompting the user to enter the name of a city where they know the temperature. I use both the *Console.Write* and the *Console.WriteLine* methods in this program to display text in the Command window. The difference is that *Write* leaves the cursor at the end of the line that it displays, while *WriteLine* adds carriage return and line feed characters to the end of the line. (The *Write* method is typically used right before user input so that the cursor blinks in the appropriate location.)

The *Console.ReadLine()* method is used to receive user input in a program and assign it to a variable, such as *cityName* (a string variable) or *fahrenheitTemp* (a single-precision floating point variable). Near the bottom of the program, I also use the *Console.ReadKey()* method to wait for input until a key is pressed. This essentially keeps the Command window open after the program has finished its work. (If you don't include this statement, the Command window will close immediately after the program finishes—at least if it is running as a stand-alone console app under Windows.)

The actual mathematical conversion from Fahrenheit to Celsius is achieved by the following Visual Basic program statement:

```
CelsiusTemp = Math.Round((fahrenheitTemp + 40) * 5 / 9 - 40, 1)
```

This line computes the result using a standard conversion formula, mathematical operators, and the *FahrenheitTemp* variable. The result is rounded to the nearest tenth using the *Round* method in the *Math* class of the .NET Framework, a powerful feature that is available to all Visual Studio applications. In this example, I thought a tenth of a point was an appropriate level of granularity for the result; however, this value can be adjusted by replacing the 1 argument near the end of the line with another value. If you changed this to a 2, for example, the result would round to two decimal places.

> **Note** For more information about mathematical formulas and the .NET Framework, see Chapter 11.

Finally, I want to draw your attention to the three *replaceable parameters* that are used in the following statement near the end of the routine:

```
Console.WriteLine("The temperature in {0} is {1} Fahrenheit and {2} Celsius.",
    CityName, FahrenheitTemp, CelsiusTemp)
```

A replaceable parameter is a value between curly brackets corresponding to the arguments that follow in the *WriteLine* statement. The {0} parameter corresponds to the *cityName* variable, the {1} parameter corresponds to the *fahrenheitTemp* value, and so on. The program essentially ends after these three values have been displayed with an explanatory sentence in the Command window. (Note that I divided this line into two lines so that it could be easily typed and printed in the book. But you can also type it all on one line.)

Your screen will look like this:

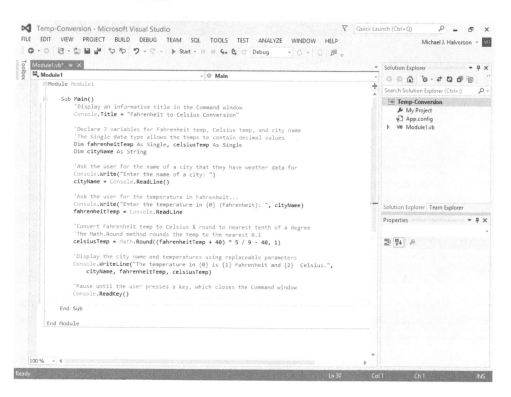

3. Save your project, and specify the My Documents\Visual Basic 2013 SBS\Chapter 10 folder as the location.

   Now run the project to see how the console application uses the Command window for its input and output.

4. Click the Start button on the Standard tool bar.

   The program begins, and a Command window opens on top of the IDE. The text Fahrenheit To Celsius Conversion appears in the window's title bar. You'll see something like the following illustration:

5. Type **Paris** and press Enter.

6. The application prompts you for the temperature in Paris (or the city you specified). The program used a *Console.Write* method and a replaceable parameter to display the city in question. The program specifically requests a temperature in Fahrenheit.

7. Because you used a single-precision data type for the *fahrenheitTemp* variable, you can enter your temperature with or without a decimal point. However, it is important that you do enter a number here and don't simply press Enter. If you do so now, the program will halt execution or crash because you will have improperly assigned information to the *fahrenheitTemp* variable. Because this is a short demonstration program, we won't fix the problem now, but I'll show you how to make this program more robust in Chapter 12, "Creative decision structures and loops."

8. Type **55** and press Enter.

   The program converts 55 degrees Fahrenheit to 12.8 degrees Celsius and displays the result. Your screen will look like this:

Notice that the final *Console.ReadKey()* method in the code causes the Command window to stay open after the final result is displayed.

9. Press Enter to close the Command window.

The Visual Studio IDE returns. Feel free to run the program again if you like, and this time, try out a different city name and temperature. Test the program carefully to be sure that it is working as expected.

10. Save any changes that you have made, and close the Temp-Conversion project.

Congratulations—you've created a simple—and useful—console application in Visual Studio. Let's try another example that uses more sophisticated variables, a decision structure, and an interesting random number generator from the .NET Framework.

Interactive math games

Back in the days of command-line applications, there were numerous math games that programmers would play for hours on their computers, using numbers and complex formulas but rarely much in the way of a user interface. Math games like this are still diverting, and they can be good resources for learning to write Visual Studio console applications.

Find the number

In the following exercise, you are asked to build a console app that finds a hidden number from 1 through 100. The program uses a random number generator in the .NET Framework to pick a random number for you, and then it is your job (or rather, the user's job) to guess the number using a variety of hints. The program is relatively simple, but it can be easily adapted to pick a random number within a variety of ranges. (For example, you can edit the program so that it picks a hidden number between 1 and 10 or between 1 and 10,000.) An interesting question in guessing games like this is how many selections it should probably take the user (on average) to find the hidden number. Are there a maximum number of guesses you might reasonably be expected to use? Does this number depend entirely on the range of numbers you draw from? Or from the strategy you take to find the hidden number? As you experiment with the console application, you'll want to give this some thought.

In addition to the use of random numbers, the Find-The-Number program demonstrates how to use the *Console* class, and in particular the *Write*, *WriteLine*, and *ReadKey* methods. The game also introduces the *ForegroundColor* property, which changes the color of the text displayed in the Command window. The guessing logic is handled by a *Do...Until Loop* and a *Select Case* decision structure, which work together to provide clues about the hidden number—and eventually a message of congratulations when the number is actually found. You'll learn more about *Do* loops and *Select Case* decision structures in Chapter 12.

Find the hidden number

1. Click New Project on the File menu to create a new Visual Studio application.

2. Choose Visual Basic/Windows under Templates, and then select the Console Application template.

   Because you just used the Console Application template, it should still be highlighted in the New Project dialog box.

3. Type **My-Find-The-Number** in the Name text box.

4. Click OK to configure the project and load it in the IDE.

   As you've already learned, a console application has no user interface designer. Instead, you enter the Visual Basic code for the app into a module, between the *Sub Main()* and *End Sub* statements.

5. Type the following program code:

```
'Set app title in Command window and explain the game
Console.Title = "Find the Hidden Number: A Game of Chance and Skill"
Console.WriteLine("I'm thinking of a number from 1 through 100.")
Console.WriteLine("Can you guess what it is?")
Console.WriteLine()

Dim generator As New Random 'declare generator as source for random numbers
'Pick a random number from 1-101 (not including 101) and assign to RandNum
Dim randNum As Integer = generator.Next(1, 101)
Dim guesses As Integer = 0
Dim guess As Integer

Do   'This Do Loop repeats over and over again until user gets the answer
        Console.Write("Guess: ")
        guess = Console.ReadLine 'read in a number and assign to guess variable
        Select Case guess 'Select Case structure evaluates guess variable
            Case randNum   'if correct number found, congratulate user
                Console.ForegroundColor = ConsoleColor.DarkYellow
                Console.WriteLine("That's Right!")
                Console.ForegroundColor = ConsoleColor.Gray
```

```
        Case Is < randNum 'but if guess is too small, ask for bigger number
            Console.WriteLine("Try a bigger number")
        Case Is > randNum 'or if guess is too big, ask for smaller number
            Console.WriteLine("Try a smaller number")
    End Select
    Console.WriteLine()
    guesses = guesses + 1 ' increment guesses, which tracks num of guesses
Loop Until guess = randNum 'continue looping until user chooses correctly

'After looping complete, display number of guesses it took user to find num
Console.Write("You found the hidden number in {0} guesses.", guesses)
Console.ReadKey() 'pause until user presses a key
```

The hidden number for the game is selected at random each time the program runs, so you'll get a new hidden number each time. The selection of the hidden number is handled by the program statement:

```
Dim randNum As Integer = generator.Next(1, 101)
```

You might recall this program logic from Chapter 3, "Creating your first Windows Store application." When you use the *generator* variable, the *Next* method allows you to pick a new random number, which is selected according to a pseudo-random number generating algorithm within the .NET Framework. The random number must be an integer within the specified range—in this case, it must be an integer from 1 to 101. However, note that the upper bound of the range is exclusive—that is, the number will be picked from 1 to 100. If you want to specify a different range, simply adjust these values and change the opening *WriteLine* statement in the program to let the user know.

6. Save the project, and specify the My Documents\Visual Basic 2013 SBS\Chapter 10 folder as the location.

   Now run the console app to see how the guessing game operates in the Command window.

7. Click the Start button on the Standard menu bar.

   The Find-The-Number program starts, and you'll see an opening screen that looks like this:

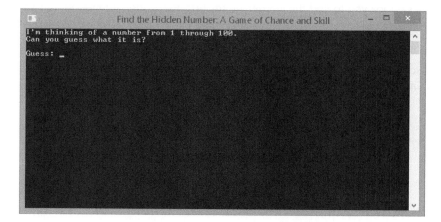

The most effective strategy in this type of hidden number guessing game is to pick a number that is midway between the high and low values in the range or *span* where the hidden number might potentially lie. In this case, the number could be anywhere between 1 and 100, so the best guess is 51. Try that number now, and keep in mind that the results you see will vary based on the number the program has selected. (The number will likely be different each time.)

8. Type **51** and press Enter.

The program compares the number you entered with the random number generated, and the *Select Case* decision structure displays a message with appropriate feedback. When I ran the program, I received the result Try A Smaller Number, as shown in the following screen:

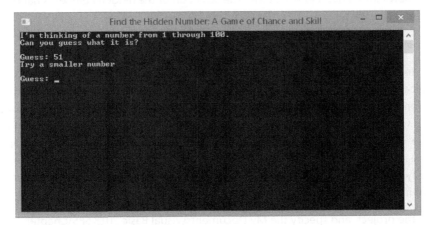

Asked to guess a smaller number, I determined that the hidden value was somewhere between 1 and 50, so I guessed the number 26. Consider following the same logic for your guess, although the guessing pattern that you follow will depend on the hints you are given.

9. Enter a second guess, and continuing guessing until you find the hidden number.

When you finish the game, you'll receive a message from the program and the number of guesses it took you to find the integer. (In my test, the hidden number was 11.) Notice that the program changes the color of the text when the winning message appears—this is the *ForegroundColor* property at work.

Your screen will look similar to the following. Just keep in mind that in most cases you'll receive a different result than the one shown.

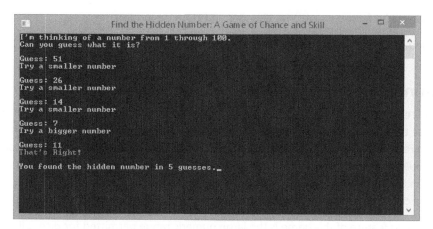

10. Press Enter to close the Command window.

The Visual Studio IDE returns. Now run the program several more times to see how long it takes you on average to find the hidden number. Develop new guessing strategies to find the number, and also intentionally make poor guesses as a way of testing the program's logic. What is your personal best for lowest number of guesses?

You might also wish to modify the random number selection range so that there are more (or fewer) hidden numbers to pick from. Test the modified version of Find-The-Number to be sure that it is working correctly. You'll find that it takes more guesses to find a hidden number in a larger range. If you start to make a number of guesses, you can expand the Command window or use the window's scroll bars to see information that scrolls off the screen.

Here is what the program looks like if you change the range from 1-101 to 1-1001:

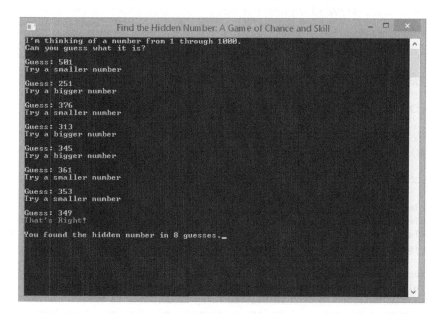

11. When you're finished, save your changes and close the project.

Would you like to try another math-oriented console application?

Simulating dice

Another interesting game involving mathematics and random numbers is to simulate rolling dice. Random dice throws can be handled quite easily in a Visual Studio application by using the *Next* method in a routine that has a defined random number generator. In the following console application, you'll build a dice game in which the user rolls a pair of virtual dice a set number of times. The program asks the user for what number they are looking for (a dice roll between 2 and 12, inclusively), and then the game rolls the dice and displays the results.

An interesting feature of this game is the large numeric range permitted for dice rolls. You can specify a number of dice rolls anywhere between 1 and just over 2.1 billion—that is, the upper bound of a 32-bit Integer variable, which the program uses to store the number of rolls and number of wins. Most of the time, you'll simply want to roll the dice 10, 100, or 1000 times, which a typical computer can process almost instantaneously. However, it is interesting to see what happens when you try a larger number. (I show you what happens with a test case of 2 billion rolls in our game—the program worked just fine, but the result took about 5 minutes to calculate on my computer.)

Complete the following steps to create a new console application named Roll-The-Dice.

Roll the dice

1. Click New Project on the File menu to create a new Visual Studio application.

2. Choose Visual Basic/Windows under Templates, and then select the Console Application template.

3. Verify that the Console Application template is highlighted in the New Project dialog box.

4. Type **My-Roll-The-Dice** in the Name text box.

5. Click OK to configure the project and load the new program in the IDE.

   Now you'll enter the code for the dice game in the program's *Main* module, between the *Sub Main()* and *End Sub* statements.

6. Type the following program code:

```
Console.Title = "Roll the Dice"
Console.WriteLine("This game determines how many times a lucky dice roll appears.")
Console.WriteLine("Pick a lucky number for a two dice roll (2-12) & times to throw.")
Console.WriteLine()

Dim luckyNumber As Integer ' declare lucky number variable
Dim rolls As Integer       ' declare variable for number of rolls
Dim wins As Integer = 0    ' initialize lucky number hits to zero
Dim counter As Integer     ' declare counter variable for For...Next loop
```

```
Dim die1 As Integer          ' declare variables to store dice rolls
Dim die2 As Integer
Dim generator As New Random ' use Random class to create random rolls

Console.Write("What lucky number are you trying for (2-12): ")
LuckyNumber = Console.ReadLine  ' get lucky number from user
Console.Write("How many times do you want to roll the dice? ")
rolls = Console.ReadLine  'get number of dice rolls requested

For counter = 1 To rolls  ' a loop rolls the dice the requested number of times
    die1 = Int(generator.Next(1, 7))  ' roll first die and save number
    die2 = Int(generator.Next(1, 7))  ' roll second die and save number
    If die1 + die2 = luckyNumber Then wins = wins + 1 ' add rolls / check for win
Next Counter

Console.WriteLine()  ' display number of rolls, lucky number, and wins
Console.Write("Out of {0} rolls, the number {1} came up {2} times.",
            rolls, luckyNumber, Wins)
Console.WriteLine()
Console.Write("That's a win rate of {0}%", ((wins / rolls) * 100))
Console.ReadKey()     ' pause until user presses a key
```

The program uses a *For...Next* loop to process the number of rolls requested by the user. As you'll learn in Chapter 12, a *For...Next* loop completes its work by constantly monitoring a *counter* variable and then looping a set number of times. The dice rolling is simulated by using the *generator.Next* syntax with in the loop, and the results are displayed at the end of the routine with the *Console.Write* method and three replaceable parameters.

7. Save the project, and specify the My Documents\Visual Basic 2013 SBS\Chapter 10 folder as the location.

Now run the console app to see how the dice game performs in the Command window.

8. Click the Start button on the Standard menu bar.

The Roll-The-Dice program starts, and you'll see an opening screen that looks like this:

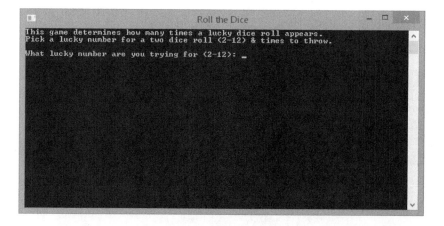

9. Type **6** and press Enter.

The program asks you how many times you would like to roll the dice.

10. Type **100** and press Enter.

The console app rolls the dice 100 times and displays the result. The number of times that the lucky number comes up varies somewhat each time that you run the program, although the basic laws of probability for dice rolls will be in effect. When I ran the program, the game rolled the number 6 eighteen times out of 100 rolls, with a win rate of 18%. My screen looked like this:

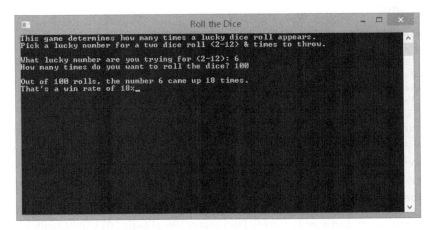

11. Press Enter (or any key) to terminate the program.

Continue testing the console application, trying the odds for more difficult (less probable) rolls.

12. Run the program again.

13. Specify **2** for the lucky number and **1000** for the number of times to roll the dice.

You'll receive output similar to the following screen:

As noted earlier, you can actually increase the number of rolls quite significantly for this program, and the console application can handle the mathematics quite easily. For example, you could try 10,000 rolls, 100,000 rolls, 10,000,000 rolls, or more! Just be aware that if you significantly increase the number of rolls, it will begin to take a little time for Visual Studio to compute the results. Further, in the Windows 8.1 multitasking environment, the processor typically devotes only about 25% of its resources to any one application so that the system runs smoothly at all times. Still, Visual Studio applications are capable of very significant mathematical tasks, and it is interesting to try larger numbers to see what kind of results you get.

If you have 2–3 minutes to wait, try the following calculations to see how the Roll-The-Dice application handles very large numbers.

14. Press Enter to end the program, and then run it again.

15. Type **7** for the lucky number, and press Enter.

16. Type **2000000000** for the number of rolls, and press Enter. (That's nine zeros after the 2.)

That's right, you've asked the computer to throw the dice 2 billion times!

The program quietly works on the problem and will continue to do so for 2–4 minutes, depending on the speed of your computer. You can continue working with your computer in other ways until the calculation is complete. When Visual Studio is finished, you'll see a Command window that looks something like the following. (The results will vary slightly each time that you run the program.)

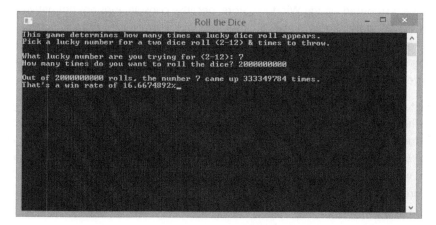

When I ran the program, the number 7 came up 333,349,784 times in 2 billion rolls, with a win rate of 16.6674892%. This is consistent with probability tables for dice rolls that indicate a 7 tends to come up about 16.67% of the time when two dice are thrown. The following table shows the basic probably for rolling two dice. You can use the following table to check how your program is functioning.

Dice Roll	Dice combinations possible	Probability
2	1	2.78%
3	2	5.56%
4	3	8.33%
5	4	11.11%
6	5	13.89%
7	6	16.67%
8	5	13.89%
9	4	11.11%
10	3	8.33%
11	2	5.56%
12	1	2.78%
Total	36	100%

17. Press Enter to terminate the program.

Building, publishing, and running console apps

Console applications can be compiled in release builds and distributed to other users via the Internet or electronic media, much like other Visual Studio applications. The only real limitation is that console apps cannot be distributed via the Windows Store, because console apps are not native applications designed for the Windows 8 or Windows 8.1 user interface. However, you can still create a tile for console applications on the Windows Start page. When you run a console app under Windows 8.1, the operating system simply opens the Desktop environment and runs the app in the Command window, as you've seen in the previous exercises.

Your final task in this chapter is to create a release build, or optimized executable program file, for the Roll-The-Dice console app that can be launched from the Windows Start page. Keep in mind that Visual Studio allows you to create two types of executable files for your projects: a *debug build* and a *release build*. Debug builds are the default executable files that are created automatically by Visual Studio when you design and test your app in the IDE. These are stored in the bin\Debug folder within your project, and they contain debugging information that is useful for testing but makes the program run slightly slower.

Release builds are optimized executable files stored in the bin\Release folder within your project. To adjust the settings for a release build, you click the *ProjectName* Properties command on the Project menu, and then click the Compile tab, where you'll see a list of adjustable compilation options for executable files. The Solution Configurations drop-down list box on the Visual Studio toolbar indicates whether the executable is a debug build or a release build. If you change the Solution Configurations setting, the path in the Build Output Path text box will also change. You might recall first learning about these options in Chapter 3.

After you've built the program in Release mode, you can launch the console app under Windows by opening File Explorer, browsing to the bin\Release folder, and double-clicking the .exe file. As you will learn in the following exercise, you can also right-click the .exe file and add it to the Windows Start page so that it is easy to launch when you need it.

If you want to distribute the console application to other users, you'll want to create a setup program for the app by using the Publish command on the Build menu. The Publish command runs a wizard that prepares a setup package and asks you where you would like to locate the final setup files. You can choose an Internet location (website or FTP server), CD-ROM, or folder on your computer system. The setup package contains everything you need to install and run the program; the user simply needs a copy of the .NET Framework on their system, which is installed automatically with most versions of Windows. (However, for Visual Studio 2013 apps that target the Windows 8.1 operating system, you need to have version 4.5.1 of the Framework installed.) After Visual Studio builds the setup package, you can run setup by double-clicking Setup.exe in File Explorer.

In the following steps, you'll compile a release build for the Roll-The-Dice application and then make an application tile for the game on the Windows Start page.

Prepare a release build for the Roll-The-Dice console app

1. Click the Solution Configurations drop-down list box on the Standard toolbar, and then click the Release option. Visual Studio will prepare your project for a release build, with the debugging information removed. The build output path is set to bin\Release\.

2. On the Build menu, click the Build Roll-The-Dice command, as shown in the following screen shot.

The Build command creates a bin\Release folder in which to store your project (if the folder doesn't already exist) and compiles the source code in your project. If configured to do so, the Output window will appear and show you milestones in the assembly and deployment process. The result is an executable file named Roll-The-Dice.exe, which Visual Studio registers with the operating system on your computer.

Now you'll examine the bin\Release folder and the executable file with File Explorer.

 Tip File Explorer, Microsoft's file manager application and navigation tool, was called Windows Explorer in earlier versions of Windows.

3. Right-click the Roll-The-Dice project in Solution Explorer, and then click Open Folder In File Explorer.

   The assorted files and folders associated with your project appear in a new File Explorer window.

4. Open the bin\Release folder.

   Several project files appear in the Release folder, including Roll-The-Dice.exe, the release build application file.

5. Right-click Roll-The-Dice at the top (or near the top) of the folder.

   There are several Roll-The-Dice files, but this one is listed as an Application type. When you right-click the file, a selection of commands appears on the shortcut menu. File Explorer will look like this:

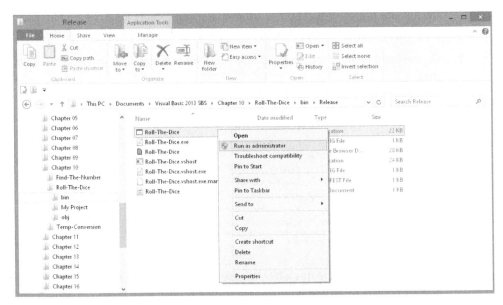

6. Click the Pin To Start command to create a tile for the game on the Windows Start page so that you have easy access to it.

7. Open the Windows Start page, and scroll to the right side of the page to see the applications that have been installed most recently.

The right side of my Windows Start page looks like this:

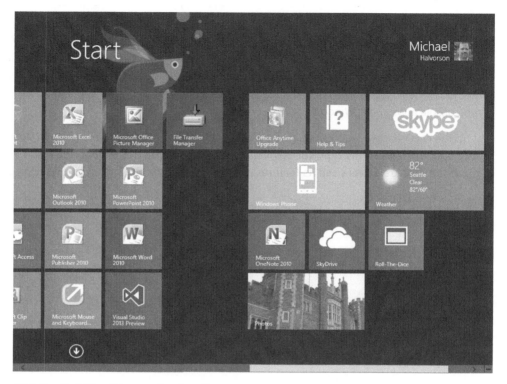

8. Click the Roll-The-Dice application tile.

   Windows opens the Windows Desktop environment and displays the opening lines of the Roll-The-Dice game in the Command window.

9. Test the console app again, picking a lucky number of the dice roll and the number of times that the dice should be thrown.

   You've demonstrated how to build and launch a console app under Windows 8.1.

10. Close File Explorer, and return to Visual Studio and close the Roll-The-Dice console app.

11. On the File menu, click Exit to close Visual Studio and the game.

You're finished working with console applications in this chapter. Continue to work with them as you build interesting games and utilities—and when you want to practice Visual Basic programming techniques. Keep in mind that many of the skills you are learning in this book apply equally well in the enchanted realm of the command prompt or "black box." The Command window is a lot of fun to work with, and even though you have very little in terms of user interface, the breadth of the .NET Framework awaits you in console apps.

Summary

In this chapter, you learned how to create console applications from scratch within Visual Studio. You learned about the basic uses for console apps, how to create a console app by using the Console Application template, and how to use code modules and the *Sub Main()* procedure. You learned important Visual Basic syntax elements within console apps, such as the *WriteLine* and *ReadLine* methods. Finally, you learned how to create a release build for a console app and how to publish and run console apps under Windows.

In the next chapter, you continue working with Visual Basic language elements in Windows Store apps and Windows Forms apps, such as data types, variables, and operators. You'll also learn more about the .NET Framework and its features related to data type conversion and string processing.

PART III

Visual Basic programming techniques

CHAPTER 11

Mastering data types, operators, and string processing

After completing this chapter, you will be able to

- Use data types, variables, and constants to manage information in a Visual Basic application.

- Master explicit and implicit variable declaration.

- Work with the XAML *ListBox* control to manage data in a Windows Store app.

- Use basic and advanced mathematical operators in formulas and event handlers.

- Convert information from one data type to another using *ToString*, *Parse*, and the *Convert* class.

- Master string-processing techniques and methods, including sorting and encryption.

Throughout this book, you've used data types and variables to store information in a program. For example, in Chapter 5, "Working with Windows Store app controls," you learned how to store the content of a *TextBox* control in a string variable and manipulate it using Visual Basic code. In Chapter 10, "Creating console applications," you also managed random number calculations with numeric variables that are helpful in mathematical games.

In this chapter, you'll go much farther with data types, mathematical operators, and the .NET Framework. You'll learn about the full range of data types provided by the .NET Framework and helpful strategies for using the *Dim* statement to declare variables in a Visual Basic application. You'll also learn how to use basic and advanced operators in formulas and mathematical calculations and how to convert data from one type to another using the *Parse* and *ToString* methods and the *Convert* class. Finally, you'll learn how to manage ASCII and Unicode values, and to use powerful string-processing techniques including combining, comparing, sorting, and encryption. Because these skills apply equally to Windows Store apps and Windows Forms apps, you'll build both types of Windows programs in this chapter.

Strategies for declaring variables and constants

A core programming task in virtually any Windows development project is managing information with data types and variables. One of my assumptions in this book is that you have written computer programs before (probably in an earlier incarnation of Visual Basic) and that you have had a basic orientation to data types, variables, and constants. The goal of this chapter is to go a little farther than the basics with variables, data types, type conversion, and operators. The first few sections offer a review of essential concepts and skills, and the later sections explore processing data with the Windows Store *ListBox* control, converting data from one type to another, and using advanced methods in the .NET Framework for string processing. You'll use the most current tools in Visual Studio 2013, and you'll build Windows Store apps and Windows Forms apps.

As you have already learned in this book, a *variable* is a temporary storage location for data in your Visual Basic application. You can use one or many variables in your event handlers and procedures, and the variables can contain words, numbers, dates, property settings, and other values. By using variables, you assign short and easy-to-remember names to each piece of data that you plan to work with in an application. Variables can hold the result of a specific calculation, information received from the user at run time, or a piece of data that you want to display on a page in the user interface. In Visual Studio, variables are defined with a specific *data type* so that the Visual Basic compiler knows how to work with the information and can manage it efficiently. As you'll see next, there are a number of useful data types available to you, and you can also create your own custom data types.

Before you can use a variable, you must set aside memory in the computer for the variable's use. I describe this process, and the venerable *Dim* statement that has long been used to *dimension* variables, in the next section.

The *Dim* statement

There are two ways to declare a variable in a Visual Basic 2013 program. You can declare the variable *explicitly*, by specifying the variable name and type after the *Dim* statement. Or you can declare the variable *implicitly*—that is, simply by using the variable without declaring it first. Implicit variable declaration is considered risky because it creates the potential for misspelled variable names and other errors, so explicit variable declaration is strongly recommended in this book and in professional programming circles. In fact, implicit variable declaration is not allowed by default; to get that style of variable declaration to work you'll need to change a setting in Visual Studio that I'll describe later in the section "Implicit variable declaration."

Explicit variable declaration

To declare a variable explicitly in Visual Basic 2013, type the variable name after the *Dim* statement. This declaration reserves room in memory for the variable when the program runs and lets Visual Basic know what type of data it should expect to see later. Although this declaration can be done at any place in the program code (as long as the declaration happens before the variable is used), most programmers declare variables in one place at the top of their event handlers or procedures.

For example, the following statement creates space for a variable named *lastName* that will hold a textual, or *string*, value:

```
Dim lastName As String
```

In addition to identifying the variable by name, note that I've used the *As* keyword to give the variable a particular type, and I've identified the type by using the keyword *String*. (You'll review the other data types later in this chapter.) A string variable contains textual information: words, letters, symbols—even numbers. I find myself using string variables a lot; they hold names, places, lines from a poem, the contents of a text box, and many other types of "wordy" data.

You might also notice the camel-casing style that I've used for the *lastName* variable here. Although the format of variable names is a matter of personal style, Microsoft currently recommends the camel-casing style as a way of formatting variables so that they are easy to read and differentiate from other objects, methods, and properties in a Visual Basic program. In camel casing, the first letter of each name is lowercase, followed by uppercase letters for each word.

Why do you need to declare variables? Visual Basic wants you to identify the name and the type of your variables in advance so that the compiler can set aside the memory the program will need to store and process the information held in the variables. Memory management might not seem like a big deal to you (after all, modern personal computers have lots of RAM and gigabytes of free hard disk space), but in some programs, memory can be consumed quickly, and it's a good practice to take memory allocation seriously even when you write simple programs. As you probably recall, different types of variables have different space requirements and size limitations.

After you declare a variable, you're free to assign information to it in your code by using the assignment operator (=). For example, the following program statement assigns the last name "Jefferson" to the *lastName* variable:

```
lastName = "Jefferson"
```

Note that I was careful to assign a textual value to the *lastName* variable because its data type is *String*. I can also assign values with spaces, symbols, or numbers to the variable, such as

```
lastName = "1313 Mockingbird Lane"
```

but the variable is still considered a string value. The number portion could be used in a mathematical formula only if it were first converted to an integer or a floating-point value by using one of a handful of conversion functions that I'll discuss later in this chapter.

After the *lastName* variable is assigned a value, it can be used in place of the name "Jefferson" in your code. For example, the assignment statement

```
TitleTextBlock.Text = lastName
```

displays "Jefferson" in a text block object named *TitleTextBlock* in a Windows Store app.

Implicit variable declaration

If you want to try implicit variable declaration—that is, simply using the variable in a statement or expression without previously declaring it using the *Dim* statement—you can place the *Option Explicit Off* statement at the very top of your page or form's program code (before any event handlers), and it will turn off the Visual Basic default requirement that variables be declared before they're used. As I mentioned earlier, I don't recommend this statement as a permanent addition to your code, but you might find it useful temporarily as you test your code or convert older Visual Basic programs to Visual Basic 2013.

Another possibility is to use the *Option Infer* statement, which was added to Visual Basic 2008 and is still useful in Visual Basic 2013. If *Option Infer* is set to On, Visual Basic will deduce, or *infer,* the type of a variable by examining the initial assignment you make. This allows you to declare variables without specifically identifying the type used, allowing Visual Basic to make the determination. For example, the expression

```
Dim attendance = 100
```

will declare the variable named *attendance* as an *Integer*, because 100 is an integer expression. That is, with *Option Infer* set to On, it is the same as typing

```
Dim attendance As Integer = 100
```

Likewise, the expression

```
Dim address = "1012 Daisy Lane"
```

will declare the variable address as type *String*, because its initial assignment was of type *String*. However, if you set *Option Infer* to Off, Visual Basic will declare the variable as type *Object*—a general (although somewhat bulky and inefficient) container for any type of data.

If you plan to use *Option Infer* to allow this type of inferred variable declaration (a flexible approach, but one that could potentially lead to unexpected results), place the following two statements at the top of the page in the Code Editor (before the *Page Class* is defined in a Windows Store app):

```
Option Explicit On
Option Infer On
```

If you are writing a Windows Forms application, you would place the statements above the *Class Form* statement for the form that you are designing.

Option Explicit Off allows variables to be declared as they are used, and *Option Infer On* allows Visual Basic to determine the type automatically. You can also set these options in new projects using the Options command on the Tools menu, as discussed in Chapter 2, "The Visual Studio Integrated Development Environment."

Defining constants

If a variable in your program contains a value that never changes (such as π, a fixed mathematical entity), you should consider declaring the value as a *constant* instead of as a variable.

A *constant* is a meaningful name that takes the place of a number or a text string that doesn't change. Constants are useful because they increase the readability of program code, they can reduce programming mistakes, and they make global changes easier to accomplish later. Constants operate a lot like variables, but you can't modify their values at run time. They are declared with the *Const* keyword, as shown in the following example:

```
Const Pi As Double = 3.14159265
```

This statement creates a constant named *Pi* that can be used in place of the value of π in the program code.

As you'll learn in the following section, a constant can be declared locally or globally. In most cases, programmers prefer to use global constant declarations so that they can be easily be referenced throughout the program.

Scope for variables and constants

By default, variables and constants are *local* to the routines that they are declared in, meaning that they have validity or scope only in the procedure in which they are dimensioned.

However, if you have more than one event handler associated with a page in the user interface, you can give your variables and constants scope throughout the page by declaring them near the top of the page's class—that is, after the *Class* statement and before any event handlers are defined. You'll see an example of this in the Data Types program later in this chapter.

If your project has more than one page or procedure in it, you can make individual variables and constants global (that is, you can give them a scope throughout the project) by declaring them in a code module and using the *Public* keyword in the declaration.

For example, if you place the statement

```
Public runningTotal As Integer
```

in a code module file (Module1.vb by default), the *runningTotal* variable will be declared publicly and maintain its value in all event handlers and procedures in the program. Likewise, a string variable named *PreferredColor* could be made global if it was declared in a code module using the following syntax:

```
Public PreferredColor As String
```

Code modules were first introduced in this book in Chapter 10, "Creating console applications." You create a code module with the Add Module command on the Project menu, and you can set the name and other characteristics of the module with settings in the Properties window. Code modules are useful tools for defining global code resources in Windows Store apps, Windows Forms apps, and Console apps.

The following screen illustration shows what a new module named *Module1* looks like in the Code Editor, with a global variable declaration for the *runningTotal* variable at the top of the module. You'll see several examples of this global variable syntax in *Visual Basic 2013 Step by Step*, and another example of a code module resource near the end of this chapter.

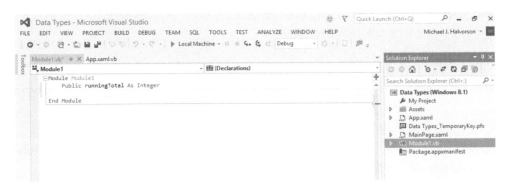

Guidelines for naming variables and constants

It is important that you give the variables and constants in your code appropriate names. Generally, you want to be as clear as possible about the function and purpose of each variable and constant so that down the road you (or a programmer on your team) can quickly understand what the identifier is used for in the program. To avoid confusion, consider the following guidelines when you name variables and constants:

- Begin each variable and constant name with a letter or underscore. This is a Visual Basic requirement. Variable and constant names can contain only letters, underscores, and numbers.

- Although variable and constant names can be virtually any length, try to keep them under 33 characters to make them easier to read. (Variable and constant names were limited to 255 characters way back in Visual Basic 6, but that's no longer a constraint.)

- Make your variable and constant names descriptive by combining one or more words when it makes sense to do so. For example, the variable name *salesTaxRate* is much clearer than *tax* or *rate*.

- Use a combination of uppercase and lowercase characters and numbers in your variables and constants. Although the style for variable names changes over time, the style that Microsoft recommends now is *camel casing* (making the first letter of a name lowercase) to distinguish variable and constant names from properties, functions, and module names, which usually begin with uppercase letters. Examples of camel casing include *dateOfBirth*, *employeeName*, and *counter*.

- Don't use Visual Basic keywords, objects, or properties as variable or constant names. If you do, you'll get an error when you try to run your program.

- Optionally, you can begin each variable and constant with a two-character or three-character abbreviation corresponding to the type of data that's stored in the identifier. For example, you could use *strName* to show that the *Name* variable contains string data. This convention, called Hungarian notation, is now falling out of favor, but it was common in earlier versions of Visual Basic and Windows, and you should learn to recognize the pattern.

Data types and the *ListBox* control

To allow for the efficient memory management of all types of data, Visual Basic provides several data types that you can use for your variables and constants. Many of these are familiar data types from earlier versions of BASIC or Visual Basic, and some of the data types were introduced more recently to allow for the efficient processing of data in newer 64-bit computers.

Table 11-1 lists the fundamental (or base) data types available in Visual Basic. These are an integral part of the Visual Basic language within Visual Studio 2013, and you can recognize them easily in the Code Editor because they are formatted in blue color as soon as you enter them. In some programming books and documentation, these language elements are called *primitive* data types.

Types in the table preceded by an *S* are designed for signed numbers, meaning that they can hold both positive and negative values. Types preceded by a *U* are unsigned data types, meaning that they cannot hold negative values. If your program needs to perform a lot of calculations, you can gain a performance advantage if you choose the most efficient data type for your variables—one with a size that's neither too big nor too small.

 Note Variable storage size is measured in bits. The amount of space required to store one standard (ASCII) keyboard character in memory is 8 bits, which equals 1 byte.

In the following exercise, you'll see how several of these data types work. You'll also learn how to use the XAML *ListBox* control, an important user-interface tool designed to process and manage data in a Windows Store application.

TABLE 11-1 Fundamental data types in Visual Basic

Data type	Size	Range	Sample usage
Short	16-bit	-32,768 through 32,767	`Dim artists As Short` `artists = 2500`
UShort	16-bit	0 through 65,535	`Dim hours As UShort` `hours = 5000`
Integer	32-bit	-2,147,483,648 through 2,147,483,647	`Dim population As Integer` `population = 375000`

Data type	Size	Range	Sample usage
UInteger	32-bit	0 through 4,294,967,295	`Dim seconds As UInteger` `seconds = 3000000`
Long	64-bit	-9,223,372,036,854,775,808 through 9,223,372,036,854,775,807	`Dim bugs As Long` `bugs = 7800000016`

ULong	64-bit	0 through 18,446,744,073,709,551,615	`Dim sandGrains As ULong`
			`sandGrains =`
			`   1800000000000000000`

Single	32-bit floating point	-3.4028235E38 through 3.4028235E38	`Dim unitCost As Single` `unitCost = 899.99`
Double	64-bit floating point	-1.79769313486231E308 through 1.79769313486231E308	`Dim pi As Double` `pi = 3.1415926535`
Decimal	128-bit	0 through +/-79,228,162,514,264, 337,593,543,950,335 (+/-7.9...E+28) with no decimal point; 0 through +/- 7.9228162514264337593543950335 with 28 places to the right of the decimal. Append "D" to the number if you want to force Visual Basic to initialize a Decimal.	`Dim debt As Decimal` `debt = 7600300.5D`
Byte	8-bit	0 through 255	`Dim retKey As Byte` `retKey = 13`
SByte	8-bit	-128 through 127	`Dim negNum As SByte` `negNum = -20`
Char	16-bit	Any Unicode symbol in the range 0–65,535. Append "c" when initializing a Char.	`Dim unicodeChar As Char` `unicodeChar = "Ä"c`
String	Usually 16-bits per character	0 to approximately 2 billion 16-bit Unicode characters	`Dim greeting As String` `greeting = "hello world"`
Boolean	16-bit	True or False. (During conversions to a Boolean value, 0 is converted to False, other values to True.)	`Dim flag as Boolean` `flag = True`
Date	64-bit	January 1, 0001, through December 31, 9999	`Dim birthday as Date` `birthday = #3/17/1900#`
Object	32-bit	Any type can be stored in a variable of type *Object*. In addition, object variables can contain defined objects in your project, like a text box object named *TextBox1*.	`Dim myControl As Object` `myControl = TextBox1`

Use fundamental data types

1. On the File menu, click Open Project.

   The Open Project dialog box opens.

2. Open the Data Types solution from the My Documents\Visual Basic 2013 SBS\Chapter 11\Data Types folder.

3. If the project's page isn't visible, double-click MainPage.xaml in Solution Explorer.

Data Types is a complete Visual Basic Windows Store app that I created to demonstrate how fundamental data types and the *ListBox* control work. You'll run the program to see what the data types look like, and then you'll look at how the variables are declared and processed with a *ListBox* control in the Visual Basic code. You'll also learn where to place variable declarations so that they're available to all the event handlers on the page.

4. Click the Start Debugging button on the Standard toolbar.

   The Data Types application opens with white user interface controls on a green background. Data Types lets you experiment with 11 data types, including integer, single-precision floating point, and date. The program displays an example of each type when you click its name in the list box. Notice how the list box functions automatically, highlighting the selected item. You can select items with the mouse, keyboard, or touch gestures (provided your device supports touch).

5. Select the *Integer* type in the list box.

   The number 37500000 appears in the Sample Data text box, as shown in the following illustration.

> **Note** With the *Short, Integer*, and *Long* data types, the default presentation does not include commas. However, you can display commas by using the *Format* function.

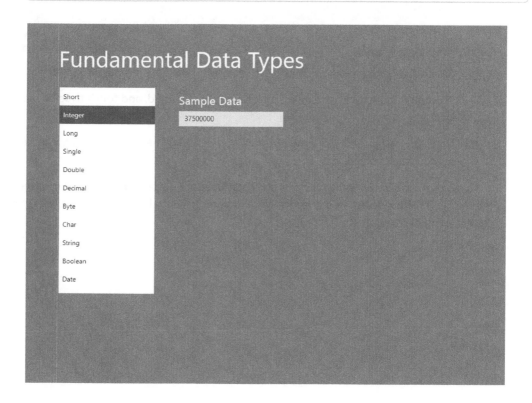

6. Select the *Date* type in the list box.

The date 11/19/1985 appears in the Sample Data box, as shown in the following screen shot:

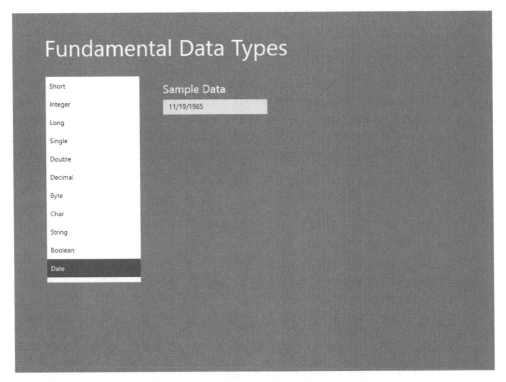

7. Select each data type in the list box to see how Visual Basic displays it in the Sample Data box.

Try using mouse clicks, the direction keys on the keyboard, and touch to select items in the list box.

8. When you're finished, close the program and redisplay the contents of the Windows Store app in the Visual Studio IDE.

Now you'll examine how the fundamental data types are declared in code and how they're used in the *DataTypeListBox_SelectionChanged* event handler. You'll also learn how to add items to a ListBox control using XAML markup.

Process data selections using the *ListBox* control

1. Open the MainPage.xaml.vb file, and enlarge the Code Editor to see more of the program code.

   The Code Editor looks like this:

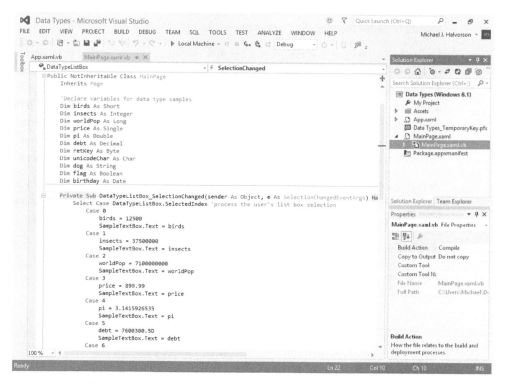

Near the top of the *MainPage* class definition in the Code Editor, you'll see a dozen or so *Dim* statements that I added to declare 11 variables in the program—one for each of the fundamental data types provided by Visual Basic. (I didn't create an example for the *SByte, UShort, UInteger,* and *ULong* types, because they closely resemble their signed or unsigned counterparts.)

By placing each *Dim* statement near the top of the main page's class initialization area, I'm ensuring that the variables will have *scope throughout* all of this page's event handlers. That way, I can set the value of a variable in one event handler and read it in another. Normally, variables are valid only in the event handler in which they're declared. To make them valid across the page, you need to declare variables at the top of your page's code.

2. Click the MainPage.xaml tab in the IDE, and examine the XAML markup that defines the list box on the page.

The XAML *ListBox* control presents a dynamic list of items on the screen and allows the user to browse the list and make a selection. Like other Windows Store controls, *ListBox* is located in the XAML Toolbox, and after you add it to a page in the user interface, you can customize its appearance with property settings. (You can use XAML markup or the Properties window to adjust the properties for the *ListBox* control.)

The items in a list box are assigned a number by Visual Studio so that you can reference them programmatically. The first item is 0, the second item is 1, the third item is 2, and so on. When the user selects an item in the list box, the *SelectionChanged* event fires for the list box and within the corresponding event handler the *SelectedIndex* property returns the number of the item selected. I typically use a decision structure to process the input that comes through a *SelectedIndex* property; for example, you can use a *Select Case* structure or an *If...Then...Else* structure to determine which item was selected and then perform the necessary action.

Within the MainPage.xaml file in the Code Editor, you'll see XAML markup for each of the objects defined in the user interface. A list box object named *DataTypeListBox* has the following markup, which defines 11 list box items representing the sample data in the program:

```
<ListBox  x:Name="DataTypeListBox"
        HorizontalAlignment="Left"
        Height="444"
        Margin="68,134,0,0"
        VerticalAlignment="Top"
        Width="206">
    <ListBoxItem Name ="List1"
            Content ="Short"
            FontSize="14"/>
    <ListBoxItem Name ="List2"
            Content ="Integer"
            FontSize="14"/>
    <ListBoxItem Name ="List3"
            Content ="Long"
            FontSize="14"/>
    <ListBoxItem Name ="List4"
            Content ="Single"
            FontSize="14"/>
    <ListBoxItem Name ="List5"
            Content ="Double"
            FontSize="14"/>
    <ListBoxItem Name ="List6"
            Content ="Decimal"
            FontSize="14"/>
    <ListBoxItem Name ="List7"
            Content ="Byte"
            FontSize="14"/>
    <ListBoxItem Name ="List8"
            Content ="Char"
            FontSize="14"/>
```

```
    <ListBoxItem Name ="List9"
            Content ="String"
            FontSize="14"/>
    <ListBoxItem Name ="List10"
            Content ="Boolean"
            FontSize="14"/>
    <ListBoxItem Name ="List11"
            Content ="Date"
            FontSize="14"/>
</ListBox>
```

If you have specific questions about how XAML markup is formatted, review the material in Chapter 7, "XAML markup step by step." Remember that XAML markup is dynamic—if you make changes to the *ListBox* markup, you'll see the changes reflected immediately in the Designer.

3. Now return to the MainPage.xaml.vb file, and examine the *DataTypeListBox_SelectionChanged* event handler.

This Visual Basic code processes the selections the user makes in the list box and looks like this:

```
Select Case DataTypeListBox.SelectedIndex 'process the user's list box selection
    Case 0
        birds = 12500
        SampleTextBox.Text = birds
    Case 1
        insects = 37500000
        SampleTextBox.Text = insects
    Case 2
        worldPop = 7100000000
        SampleTextBox.Text = worldPop
    Case 3
        price = 899.99
        SampleTextBox.Text = price
    Case 4
        pi = 3.1415926535
        SampleTextBox.Text = pi
    Case 5
        debt = 7600300.5D
        SampleTextBox.Text = debt
    Case 6
        retKey = 13
        SampleTextBox.Text = retKey
    Case 7
        UnicodeChar = "Ä"c
        SampleTextBox.Text = UnicodeChar
    Case 8
        dog = "pointer"
        SampleTextBox.Text = dog
    Case 9
        flag = True
        SampleTextBox.Text = flag
    Case 10
        birthday = #11/19/1985#
        SampleTextBox.Text = birthday
End Select
```

This routine is a *Select Case* decision structure, which you have already experimented with in this book. (You'll study *Select Case* more comprehensively in Chapter 12, "Creative decision structures and loops.") For now, notice how each section of the *Select Case* block assigns a sample value to one of the fundamental data type variables and then assigns the variable to the *Text* property of the *SampleTextBox* object on the page.

4. Scroll through the *DataTypeListBox_SelectionChanged* event handler, and examine each of the variable assignments closely.

   Try changing the data in a few of the variable assignment statements and running the program again to see what the data looks like. In particular, you might try assigning values to variables that are outside their accepted range, as shown in the data types table presented earlier. If you make such an error, Visual Basic adds a jagged line below the incorrect value in the Code Editor, and the program won't run until you change it. To learn more about your mistake, you can point to the jagged underlined value and read a short tooltip error message about the problem.

> **Tip** By default, a green jagged line indicates a warning, a red jagged line indicates a syntax error, a blue jagged line indicates a compiler error, and a purple jagged line indicates some other error.

5. If you made any changes that you want to save to disk, click the Save All button on the Standard toolbar.

6. Close the Data Types project.

   Now you'll work with some of the fundamental data types and combine them with arithmetic operators.

Operators and formulas

In this section, you'll learn about the extremely useful operators that can be used in Visual Basic programs. You'll begin by reviewing how to use the arithmetic operators to create mathematical formulas in an event handler, and then you'll learn about shortcut operators that provide similar functionality in an abbreviated form.

Remember that in Visual Basic a *formula* is just a program statement that combines numbers, variables, operators, and other keywords to create a new value. Visual Basic contains dozens of language elements designed for use in formulas, and you'll see them often in this book.

Arithmetic operators

In the following program, you'll practice working with arithmetic *operators*, the symbols used to tie together the parts of a formula. With a few exceptions, the arithmetic symbols you'll use are the ones you use in everyday life, and their operations are fairly intuitive. Visual Basic includes the arithmetic operators listed in Table 11-2.

TABLE 11-2 Arithmetic operators

Operator	Description
+	Addition
-	Subtraction
*	Multiplication
/	Division
\	Integer (whole number) division
Mod	Remainder division
^	Exponentiation (raising to a power)
&	String concatenation (combination)

The operators for addition, subtraction, multiplication, and division are pretty straightforward and can be used in any formula where numbers or numeric variables are used. The Basic Math program demonstrates how you can use them in a Windows Store app.

Build formulas using addition, subtraction, multiplication, and division

1. On the File menu, click Open Project.

2. Open the Basic Math project in the My Documents\Visual Basic 2013 SBS\Chapter 11\Basic Math folder.

3. If the project's page isn't visible, double-click MainPage.xaml in Solution Explorer.

   The Basic Math page opens in the Designer. This simple Windows Store app demonstrates how the addition, subtraction, multiplication, and division operators work with numbers that you type. It also demonstrates how you can use text box, radio button, and button objects to process user input in a program.

4. Click the Start Debugging button on the Standard toolbar.

   The Basic Math program starts. The program displays two text boxes in which you enter numeric values, a group of operator radio buttons, a box that displays results, and a button object (Calculate) to perform the math.

5. Type **100** in the first text box, and then press Tab.

   The insertion point, or *focus*, moves to the second text box.

6. Type **17** in the second text box.

   You can now apply any of the mathematical operators to the values in the text boxes.

7. Click the Addition radio button, and then click the Calculate button.

   The operator is applied to the two values, and the number 117 appears in the calculation results box, as shown in the following screen shot.

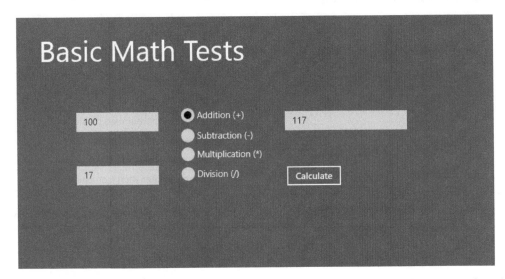

8. Practice using the subtraction, multiplication, and division operators with the two numbers in the variable boxes. (Click Calculate to calculate each formula.)

   The results appear in the result box. Feel free to experiment with different numbers in the variable text boxes. (Try a few numbers with decimal points if you like.) I used the *Double* data type to declare the variables, so you can use very large numbers.

   Now try the following test to see what happens.

9. Type **100** in the first text box, type **0** in the second text box, click the Division radio button, and then click Calculate.

   Dividing by zero is not allowed in mathematical calculations, because it produces an infinite result. Visual Basic can handle this calculation and displays a value of *Infinity* in the results text box. Being able to handle some divide-by-zero conditions is a feature that Visual Basic 2013 automatically provides.

10. When you've finished contemplating this and other tests, close the Basic Math program.

    The program terminates, and the IDE returns.

Now take a look at the program code to see how the results were calculated. Basic Math uses a few of the standard XAML controls you experimented with in Chapter 5 and an event handler that uses variables and operators to process the simple mathematical formulas. The program declares its variables at the top of the page (where the class is defined) so that they can be used in all the event handlers on the page. Although this program has only one event handler, placing the variables at the top of the page will allow for easy program expansion.

Examine the Basic Math program code

1. Double-click the Calculate button on the page.

   The Code Editor displays the *Calculate_Click* event handler. At the top of the page's code, you'll see the following statement, which declares two variables of type *Double* below the main page's class definition:

   ```
   'Declare firstNum and secondNum as double-precision variables
   Dim firstNum, secondNum As Double
   ```

   I used the *Double* type because I wanted a large, general-purpose variable type that could handle many different numbers—integers, numbers with decimal points, very big numbers, small numbers, and so on. The variables are declared on the same line by using the shortcut notation. Both *firstNum* and *secondNum* are of type *Double* and are used to hold the values input in the first and second text boxes, respectively.

2. Scroll down in the Code Editor to see the contents of the *Calculate_Click* event handler.

   The program code looks like this:

   ```
   Private Sub Calculate_Click(sender As Object, e As RoutedEventArgs) Handles Calculate.
   Click
       'Assign textbox values to variables
       firstNum = FirstTextBox.Text
       secondNum = SecondTextBox.Text

       'Determine checked button and calculate
       If Addition.IsChecked Then
           Result.Text = firstNum + secondNum
       End If
       If Subtraction.IsChecked Then
           Result.Text = firstNum - secondNum
       End If
       If Multiplication.IsChecked Then
           Result.Text = firstNum * secondNum
       End If
       If Division.IsChecked Then
           Result.Text = firstNum / secondNum
       End If
   End Sub
   ```

   The first two statements in the event handler transfer data entered in the text box objects into the *firstNum* and *secondNum* variables. The *TextBox* control handles the data transfer using the *Text* property—a property that accepts input from the user and makes it available for use in the program. (In this case, the program relies on you to enter data of the proper data type; an error will result if you type non-numeric data into the text boxes.)

After the text box values are assigned to the variables, the event handler determines which radio button has been selected, computes the mathematical formula, and displays the result in a third text box. The first radio button test looks like this:

```
'Determine checked button and calculate
If Addition.IsChecked Then
    Result.Text = firstNum + secondNum
End If
```

Only one radio button object in a group can be selected at any given time. In a Windows Store app, radio buttons are added to a group by setting the *GroupName* property of each radio button to the same name. (In this case, I set the group name to "Operator.") In the event handler, you can tell whether a radio button has been selected by evaluating the *IsChecked* property. If it's True, the button has been selected. If the *IsChecked* property is False, the button has not been selected. After this simple test, you're ready to compute the result and display it in the third text box object. That's all there is to using basic arithmetic operators.

> **Tip** You can learn more about the syntax of *If...Then* tests in Chapter 12. If you want to learn more about how XAML radio buttons work in a Windows Store app, see Chapter 3, "Using Controls," in my companion book *Start Here! Learn Microsoft Visual Basic 2012* (Microsoft Press, 2012). I also provide detailed information about how to create and use XAML *CheckBox* controls in that book, which offer a useful alternative to *RadioButton* controls.

3. On the File menu, click the Close Project button.

You're done using the Basic Math program.

Advanced arithmetic operators

In addition to the four basic arithmetic operators, Visual Basic includes four additional arithmetic operators for special-purpose calculations. These include integer division (\), remainder division (*Mod*), exponentiation (^), and string concatenation (&). The extra operators are useful in a wide range of mathematical formulas and virtually all text processing routines. The following utility (a revised version of the Basic Math program) shows how you can use each of these operators in a Windows Store app.

Explore integer division, remainder division, exponentiation, and concatenation

1. On the File menu, click Open Project, and then open the Advanced Math solution in the My Documents\Visual Basic 2013 SBS\Chapter 11\Advanced Math folder.

2. If the project's page isn't visible, double-click MainPage.xaml in Solution Explorer.

The Advanced Math user interface opens in the Designer. This program is very similar to the Basic Math app, with the exception of the operators presented by the radio buttons and the decision structures in the *Calculate_Click* event handler.

3. Click the Start Debugging button on the Standard toolbar.

   The program displays two text boxes in which you enter numeric values, a group of operator radio buttons, a text box that displays results, and a button named Calculate.

4. Type **9** in the first text box, and then press Tab.

5. Type **2** in the second text box.

   You can now apply any of the advanced operators to the values in the text boxes.

6. Click the Integer Division radio button, and then click Calculate.

   The operator is applied to the two values, and the number 4 appears in the results box, as shown here:

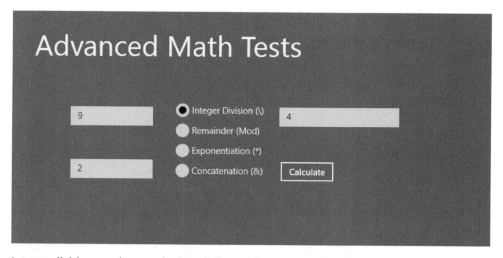

Integer division produces only the whole number result of the division operation. Although 9 divided by 2 equals 4.5, the integer division operation returns only the first part, an integer (the whole number 4). You might find this result useful if you're working with quantities that can't easily be divided into fractional components, such as the number of adults who can fit in a car.

7. Click the Remainder radio button, and then click Calculate.

   The number 1 appears in the results box. Remainder division (modulus arithmetic) returns the remainder (the part left over) after two numbers are divided. Because 9 divided by 2 equals 4 with a remainder of 1 (2 * 4 + 1 = 9), the result produced by the *Mod* operator is 1. In addition to adding an early-1970s vibe to your code, the *Mod* operator can help you track "leftovers" in your calculations, such as the amount of money left over after a financial transaction.

8. Click the Exponentiation radio button, and then click the Calculate button.

The number 81 appears in the result box. The exponentiation operator (^) raises a number to a specified power. For example, 9^2 equals 9^2, or 81. In a Visual Basic formula, 9^2 is written as 9^2.

9. Click the Concatenation radio button, and then click the Calculate button.

The number 92 appears in the results box. The string concatenation operator (&) combines two strings in a formula, but not through addition. The result is a combination of the "9" character and the "2" character. String concatenation can be performed on numeric variables—for example, if you're displaying the inning-by-inning score of a baseball game as they do in old-time score boxes—but concatenation is more commonly performed on string values or variables.

Because I declared the *firstNum* and *secondNum* variables as type *Double*, you can't combine words or letters by using the program code as written. For an example, try the following test, which causes an error and ends the program.

10. Type **birth** in the first text box, type **day** in the second text box, verify that Concatenation is selected, and then click Calculate.

Visual Basic is unable to process the text values you entered, so the program stops running, and an error message appears on the screen.

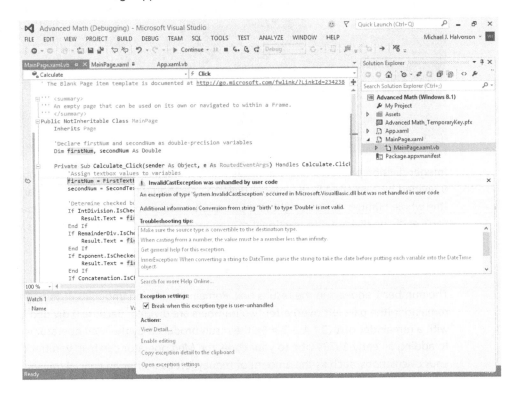

This type of error is called an *exception* or *run-time error*—a programming mistake that surfaces not during the design and compilation of the program but later, when the program is running and encounters a condition that it doesn't know how to process. The secondary message, Conversion From String 'Birth' To Type 'Double' Is Not Valid, means that the words you entered in the text boxes ("birth" and "day") could not be converted by Visual Basic to variables of the type *Double*. *Double* types can contain only numbers—period.

As I discuss later in the section "Converting data types," there are ways around such a problem, because there are specific functions in Visual Studio that allow you to convert one type of data to another. But for now, we'll move on. You have been reminded about the fickleness of data types and when not to mix them.

11. Click the Stop Debugging button on the Standard toolbar to end the program.

Your program ends and returns you to the IDE.

Now take a look at the program code to see how variables were declared and how the advanced operators were used.

12. Scroll to the code at the top of the Code Editor, if it is not currently visible.

You see the following comment and program statement:

```
'Declare firstNum and secondNum as double-precision variables
Dim firstNum, secondNum As Double
```

As you might recall from the previous exercise, *firstNum* and *secondNum* are the variables that hold numbers coming in from the *FirstTextBox* and *SecondTextBox* objects.

13. Change the data type from *Double* to *String* so that you can properly test how the string concatenation (&) operator works.

14. Scroll down in the Code Editor to see how the advanced operators are used in the program code.

You see the following code:

```
'Assign textbox values to variables
firstNum = FirstTextBox.Text
secondNum = SecondTextBox.Text

'Determine checked button and calculate
If IntDivision.IsChecked Then
    Result.Text = firstNum \ secondNum
End If
If RemainderDiv.IsChecked Then
    Result.Text = firstNum Mod secondNum
End If
If Exponent.IsChecked Then
    Result.Text = firstNum ^ secondNum
End If
If Concatenation.IsChecked Then
    Result.Text = firstNum & secondNum
End If
```

Like the Basic Math program, this program loads data from the text boxes and places it in the *firstNum* and *secondNum* variables. The program then checks to see which radio button the user checked and computes the requested formula. In this event handler, the integer division (\), remainder (*Mod*), exponentiation (^), and string concatenation (&) operators are used. Now that you've changed the data type of the variables to *String*, run the program again to see how the & operator works on text.

15. Click the Start Debugging button.

16. Type **birth** in the first text box, type **day** in the second text box, click Concatenation, and then click Calculate.

The program now concatenates the string values and doesn't produce a run-time error, as shown here:

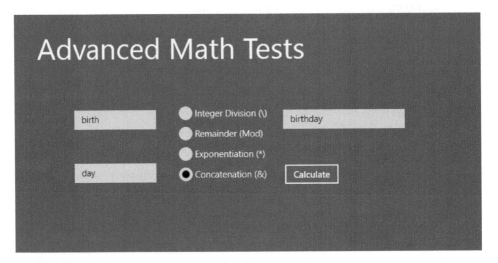

17. Close the program.

As you can see, the *String* data type has fixed the concatenation problem. However, it is not a total solution because variables of type *String* will not function correctly if you try the Integer Division, Remainder, or Exponentiation operations with them. So, if you really wanted to have your program process numbers *and* text strings interchangeably, you'd need to add some additional program logic to your code. However, for now, you're finished working with the Advanced Math program.

Note Exceptions are difficult to avoid completely—even the most sophisticated application programs, such as Microsoft Word or Microsoft Office Excel, sometimes run into error conditions that they can't handle, producing run-time errors, or *crashes*. For more information about identifying different types of errors in your code and fixing them using tools and resources in the Visual Studio IDE, see Chapter 9, "Debugging Applications," in the companion book *Start Here! Learn Microsoft Visual Basic 2012*.

Shortcut operators

A little while ago, Microsoft added a timesaving feature to the Visual Basic programming language that allows developers to use operators in a more compact way. The feature is known as a *shortcut operator*, and there are operators to choose from corresponding to most of the Visual Basic arithmetic operators. Although they have been available for a while, many programmers still don't know about them or use them, but I recommend that you take a look and consider trying them out; their compact format is clever and compelling.

Shortcut operators are primarily used for mathematical and string operations that involve changing the value of an existing variable. For example, if you combine the + symbol with the = symbol, you can add to a variable without repeating the variable name twice in the formula. Thus, you can write the formula X = X + 6 by using the syntax X += 6.

Table 11-3 shows examples of these shortcut operators. They are easy to use, as you can see from the syntax examples provided. The syntax is also reminiscent of assignment operator syntax in the C programming language.

TABLE 11-3 Shortcut operators

Operation	Long-form syntax	Shortcut syntax
Addition (+)	X = X + 6	X += 6
Subtraction (–)	X = X – 6	X -= 6
Multiplication (*)	X= X * 6	X *= 6
Division (/)	X = X / 6	X /= 6
Integer division (\)	X = X \ 6	X \= 6
Exponentiation (^)	X = X ^ 6	X ^= 6
String concatenation (&)	X = X & "ABC"	X &= "ABC"

How Visual Basic calculates formulas

In the previous exercises, you experimented with several arithmetic operators and one string operator. Visual Basic lets you mix as many arithmetic operators as you like in a formula, as long as each numeric variable and expression is separated from another by one operator. For example, this is an acceptable Visual Basic formula:

```
numberOfFish = 20000 - 750 * 20 / 3 ^ 2
```

The formula processes several values that collectively estimate the population of fish in a body of water and then assigns the result to a single-precision variable named *numberOfFish*. But how is such an expression evaluated by the Visual Basic compiler? That is, what sequence does Visual Basic follow when solving the formula? You might not have noticed, but the order of evaluation matters a great deal in this example.

Visual Basic solves this problem by establishing a specific *order of precedence* for mathematical operations. This list of rules tells Visual Basic which operator to use first, second, and so on when evaluating an expression that contains more than one operator.

Table 11-4 lists the operators from first to last in the order in which they are evaluated. (Operators on the same level in this table are evaluated from left to right as they appear in an expression.)

TABLE 11-4 How formulas are evaluated

Operator	Order of precedence
( )	Values within parentheses are always evaluated first.
^	Exponentiation (raising a number to a power) is second.
–	Negation (creating a negative number) is third.
* /	Multiplication and division (in no particular priority) are fourth.
\	Integer division is fifth.
Mod	Remainder division is sixth.
+ -	Addition and subtraction are last.

Given the order of precedence in this table, the expression

```
NumberOfFish = 20000 - 750 * 20 / 3 ^ 2
```

is evaluated by Visual Basic in the following steps (each line shows how one pair of values is computed):

```
NumberOfFish = 20000 - 750 * 20 / 9
NumberOfFish = 20000 - 15000 / 9
NumberOfFish = 20000 - 1666.67
NumberOfFish = 18333.33
```

Changing the order of precedence in a formula

You can use one or more pairs of parentheses in a formula to clarify the order of precedence or impose your own order of precedence over the standard one. For example, Visual Basic calculates the formula

```
Number = (8 - 5 * 3) ^ 2
```

by determining the value within the parentheses (–7) before doing the exponentiation—even though exponentiation is higher in order of precedence than subtraction and multiplication, according to the preceding table. You can further refine the calculation by placing nested parentheses in the formula. For example,

```
Number = ((8 - 5) * 3) ^ 2
```

directs Visual Basic to calculate the difference in the inner set of parentheses first, perform the operation in the outer parentheses next, and then determine the exponentiation. The result produced by the two formulas is different: the first formula evaluates to 49 and the second to 81. Parentheses can change the result of a mathematical operation, as well as make it easier to read.

Converting data types

As you have learned so far, it is important when using variables and constants to assign information of the proper data type to the temporary storage location that you are using in a program. The process typically begins with user input; when you receive data from the user, it is important to collect and store the data in a recognizable format so that it can be used effectively later. To accomplish this, you should pick an input control that requests the information in a structured and predictable way. For example, if you want to collect string data in a Windows Store app, you might use the XAML *TextBox* control in the Toolbox to gather the string information and then assign it to a string variable. Or alternatively, if you are designing a Windows Forms app, you might use the helpful *MaskedTextBox* control to prompt the user for input using a predefined *input mask* or pattern that collects the information in a formatted way.

If you have information stored in a variable that is *not* in the proper format, you can use one of Visual Studio's conversion methods to translate the data from one type to another, or you can *parse* (or systematically extract) the information that you need so that input or other information can be used more effectively.

In the following sections, you'll learn how to use the *ToString* method to convert numbers to text, how to use the *Parse* method to convert text to a numeric value, and how to use the *Convert* class to convert one specific data type to another. Finally, you'll review a comprehensive list of data type conversion functions that has existed in the Visual Basic language for some time. These tools supplement the *Convert* class, and you will see them in lots of Visual Basic code.

Rather than provide extensive tutorial programs in this section, I have provided the information as a reference with detailed examples so that you can return to it as you need to.

The *ToString* method

As a feature of Visual Studio's object-oriented design, most objects that represent data in some way in a program have a special *ToString* method that can be used to create a string representation of the data contained within object. This method is therefore one of the simplest methods to convert numbers or other information to text in a Visual Basic program.

The textual information returned by the *ToString* method depends on the object. For example, if you have a single-precision variable in a program that contains a numeric value with decimal point, the default use of *ToString* will return the complete number. The following sample code shows how this might work with a variable of type *Single* named *costOfFood*:

```
Dim costOfFood As Single
Dim outputString As String
costOfFood = 49.95
outputString = costOfFood.ToString
```

After these lines of code are executed by the Visual Basic compiler, the *String* variable *outputString* will contain the string value *"49.95"*. Such an operation would be useful if a number in a program needed to be put into string format for output, storage in a file, or special formatting operations.

The method works for more sophisticated objects as well, although the textual information returned by *ToString* is sometimes related to the class name of the object rather than the data held within the object. For example, the following Visual Basic code places the string value *"Windows.UI.Xaml.Controls.TextBox"* in the *outputString* variable and in a text box named *MyTextBox* on the main page:

```
Dim outputString As String
outputString = MyTextBox.ToString
MyTextBox.Text = outputString
```

This is because the namespace path and class name for the *MyTextBox* object in the program is *Windows.UI.Xaml.Controls.TextBox*. So, you can use the *ToString* method to convert variables and constants to strings but also to extract interesting (and potentially useful) information from the objects in your programs.

The *Parse* method

The Parse method allows you to convert a string in the proper format into the *Date* type or one of the fundamental numeric data types. It is very useful and has an object-oriented syntax. The only down side to the *Parse* method is that it might not always work as expected—if the string specified does not contain a number, the converted value is typically 0 (zero) or otherwise undefined.

You specify the fundamental data type along with the *Parse* method, and the valid data types are *Short, UShort, Integer, UInteger, Long, ULong, Single, Double, Decimal, Byte, SByte,* and *Boolean*. Just be sure that the string you convert can actually be stored in the type you specify. For example, the following Visual Basic code assigns the value 12345.6789 to a *String* variable named *InputString* and uses the *Double* type and the *Parse* method to convert the value from a string to a double-precision number:

```
Dim inputString As String = "12345.6789"
Dim sampleNumber As Double
sampleNumber = Double.Parse(inputString)
MyTextBox.Text = sampleNumber
```

The code also displays the new number in a text box named *MyTextBox* on the page. Just keep in mind that you can convert strings only to dates or numbers in this way.

If the conversion does not work, you will see an error message in Visual Studio. This will typically appear as a runtime error, which can result from a string that contains text and not simply a numeric value that is in string format. Or perhaps you are trying to convert a value that is simply too large to fit into the variable that you have specified. Consider the following code:

```
Dim inputString As String = "forty"
Dim sampleNumber As Double
sampleNumber = Double.Parse(inputString)
MyTextBox.Text = sampleNumber
```

Although human beings can tell that the value of the *inputString* variable is 40 in this example, the Visual Basic compiler cannot convert "*forty*" to a number as requested, and the following runtime error results when you run the program and execute this code:

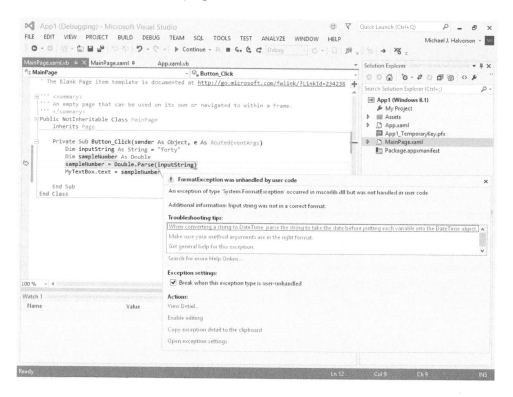

Notice, in particular, the message Input String Was Not In A Correct Format in the error message dialog box.

Likewise, the following sample code will also produce a runtime error, but for a slightly different reason:

```
Dim inputString As String = "12345.6789"
Dim sampleNumber As Integer
sampleNumber = Integer.Parse(inputString)
MyTextBox.Text = sampleNumber
```

The problem is that the large number in the *InputString* variable contains decimal places and is simply too different from an *Integer* type to be usefully converted without some closer attention. This is sometimes called an *invalid conversion*. Rather than truncate the number or make some other ad-hoc adjustment to the original value, the compiler generates a runtime error message and asks you to be more specific about the type conversion. The appropriate fix is to use a data type that is large enough and precise enough to hold the original information. Rather than use *Short* or *Integer*, it is safest to use *Double* or *Decimal* for numbers that might be large or precise.

However, despite these usage caveats, the *Parse* method is a helpful tool for string conversion and is commonly used when information is received through the *TextBox* control and prepared for use in a program. A handy companion to the *Parse* method is the *TryParse* method, which converts the string representation of a number to its double-precision floating-point number equivalent. The method returns a *Boolean* success code after the attempted conversion to help you determine whether the parse succeeded or failed.

The *Convert* class

Similar to the preceding, the *Convert* class is a part of the .NET Framework and is specifically designed to be used in Visual Studio programs for the purpose of type conversion. The *Convert* class contains dozens of methods that convert data from one type to another, complementing and extending what you can do with the *ToString* and *Parse* methods. (You'll see that virtually all of the fundamental data types are supported, and in many different size formats.) The complete list of methods is readily available via Visual Studio's IntelliSense feature when you type Convert in the Code Editor.

You will have few problems understanding how to use the *Convert* class methods when you see the basic format. The only thing you need to keep in mind is that it is sometimes advantageous to specify a specific size for the given data type when you use the *Convert* methods. For example, you can use either the *ToInt16*, *ToInt32*, or *ToInt64* method when you convert a number to the *Integer* format. These methods allocate storage in memory for 16-bit, 32-bit, and 64-bit *Integer* variables, respectively. (These sizes correspond to the *Short*, *Integer*, and *Long* data types in Visual Basic.) Depending on the potential size of your variables and the platform that you are using, you might want to be very detailed in your syntax.

The following sample code demonstrates how you can use the *ToDecimal* method in the *Convert* class. The code begins by placing the integer value 55333 into the *sampleNumber* variable. The *sampleNumber* value is converted to a decimal value in advance of a multiplication operation, and then the resulting *newDecimalNumber* variable is displayed on the page in the *MyTextBox* object. (The value displayed in the text box is 65846.27.)

```
Dim sampleNumber As Integer = 55333
Dim newDecimalNumber As Decimal
newDecimalNumber = Convert.ToDecimal(sampleNumber) * 1.19
MyTextBox.Text = newDecimalNumber.ToString
```

Older type conversion functions and their uses

Although the *Convert* class in the .NET Framework will be suitable for most type conversion scenarios, Visual Basic programmers should also be aware of older type conversion functions that exist in the Visual Basic language and still appear in a good amount of production code in the marketplace. These functions convert the information in an existing variable, constant, or literal value to a new data type. You can recognize the functions in code by looking for the *C* prefix that begins each function name. Table 11-5 lists the functions and what data type they produce.

TABLE 11-5 Visual Basic type conversion functions

Visual Basic function	Data type produced
CBool	Boolean
CByte	Byte
CChar	Char
CDate	Date
CDbl	Double
CDec	Decimal
CInt	Integer
CLng	Long
CObj	Object
CSByte	SByte
CShort	Short
CSng	Single
CStr	String
CUInt	UInteger
CULng	ULong
CUShort	UShort

For example, the following sample code declares an *Integer* variable and a *String* variable and converts the *Integer* variable to a *String* variable by using the *CStr* function:

```
Dim sampleNumber As Integer = 55333
Dim sampleString As String
sampleString = CStr(sampleNumber) 'sampleString = "55333"
```

Processing strings with the *String* class

As you learned in Chapter 10, the .NET Framework is a comprehensive, object-oriented class library that allows you to streamline a number of development tasks, including building mathematical formulas, rendering graphics, connecting to databases, and requesting system information. The .NET Framework is installed as a core component of the Windows operating system, and Microsoft Visual Studio programs rely on many of its features to load and operate.

In addition to important system-wide features, the .NET Framework also includes useful methods to help you manage string-processing tasks, such as combining strings, sorting strings, and searching strings for useful patterns. In this section, you'll experiment with the methods in the *System.String* class to help expand your knowledge of the *String* data type and its many uses.

Common tasks

The most common task you've accomplished so far with strings in this book is concatenating them by using the concatenation operator (&). For example, the following program statement concatenates three literal string expressions and assigns the result "Bring on the circus!" to the string variable *slogan*:

```
Dim slogan As String
slogan = "Bring" & " on the " & "circus!"
```

In addition to this familiar feature, you can also concatenate and manipulate strings by using methods in the *String* class of the .NET Framework library. For example, the *String.Concat* method allows equivalent string concatenation by using this syntax:

```
Dim slogan As String
slogan = String.Concat("Bring", " on the ", "circus!")
```

Visual Basic 2013 features two methods for string concatenation and many other string-processing tasks: You can use operators and functions from earlier versions of Visual Basic (*Mid, UCase, LCase,* and so on), or you can use newer methods from the .NET Framework (*Substring, ToUpper, ToLower,* and so on). There's no real penalty for using either string-processing technique, although the older methods exist primarily for compatibility purposes. (By supporting both methods, Microsoft hopes to welcome upgraders and their existing code base, allowing them to learn new features at their own pace.) In the rest of this chapter, I'll focus on the newer string-processing functions from the .NET Framework *String* class. However, you can use either string-processing feature set or a combination of both.

Table 11-6 lists several methods and one property in the *String* class that appear in subsequent exercises and their close equivalents in the Visual Basic programming language. The fourth column in the table provides sample code using the *String* class.

TABLE 11-6 Elements of the *String* class and Visual Basic equivalents

String method or property	Visual Basic function	Description	*String* example

ToUpper	*UCase*	Changes letters in a string to uppercase.	`Dim name, newName As String`
			`name = "Ace"`
			`newName = name.ToUpper`
			`'newName = "ACE"`

ToLower	*LCase*	Changes letters in a string to lowercase.	`Dim name, newName As String`
			`name = "Ace"`
			`newName = name.ToLower`
			`'newName = "ace"`

Length	*Len*	Determines the number of characters in a string.	`Dim river As String`
			`Dim size As Short`
			`river = "Columbia"`
			`size = river.Length`
			`'size = 8`

Contains	N/A	Determines whether the specified string occurs in the current string.	`Dim region As String`
			`Dim chk As Boolean`
			`region = "Brazil"`
			`chk = region.Contains("Br")`
			`'chk = True`

Substring	*Mid, Left, Right*	Returns a fixed number of characters in a string from a given starting point. (Note: The first element in a string has an index of 0.) Also generates an exception when a target set of characters doesn't exist.	`Dim cols, middle As String`
			`cols = "First Second Third"`
			`middle = cols.SubString(6, 6)`
			`'middle = "Second"`

IndexOf	*InStr*	Finds the starting point of one string within a larger string.	`Dim name As String`
			`Dim start As Short`
			`name = "Abraham"`
			`start = name.IndexOf("h")`
			`'start = 4`

Trim	*Trim, LTrim, RTrim*	Removes leading and trailing spaces from a string.	`Dim spacey, trimmed As String`
			`spacey = "   Hello   "`
			`trimmed = spacey.Trim`
			`'trimmed = "Hello"`

Remove	N/A	Removes characters from the middle of a string.	`Dim raw, clean As String`
			`raw = "Hello333 there"`
			`clean = raw.Remove(5, 3)`
			`'clean = "Hello there"`

Insert	N/A	Adds characters to the middle of a string.	`Dim old, new As String`
			`old = "Hi Roberto"`
			`new = old.Insert(3, "there")`
			`'new = "Hi there Roberto"`

String method or property	Visual Basic function	Description	*String* example
Compare	*StrComp*	Compares strings and can disregard case differences.	```Dim str1 As String = "Soccer"
Dim str2 As String = "SOCCER"
Dim match As Integer
match = String.Compare(str1,
_ str2, True)
'match = 0 [strings match]```
CompareTo	*StrComp*	Compares a string to the current string and checks for case differences.	```Dim str1 As String = "Soccer"
Dim str2 As String = "SOCCER"
Dim Match As Integer
Match = str1.CompareTo(str2)
'Match = -1 [strings do not match]```
Replace	*Replace*	Replaces all instances of a substring in a string with another string.	```Dim old, new As String
old = "*se*ll"
new = old.Replace(_
"*", "ba")
'new = "baseball"```
StartsWith	N/A	Determines whether a string starts with a specified string.	```Dim str1 As String
Dim result As Boolean
str1 = "Hi Eva"
result = str1.StartsWith("Hi")
'result = True```
EndsWith	N/A	Determines whether a string ends with a specified string.	```Dim str1 As String
Dim chk As Boolean
str1 = "Hi Eva"
chk = str1.EndsWith("Eva")
'chk = True```
Split	*Split*	Splits a string into substrings based on a specified separator and puts the substring in an array.	```Dim allText As String = _
"a*b*c*1*2*3"
Dim strArray() As String
strArray = allText.Split("*")
'strArray =
' {"a", "b", "c", "1", "2", "3"}```

Sorting text

An extremely useful skill to develop when working with textual elements is the ability to sort a list of strings. The basic concepts in sorting are simple. You draw up a list of items to sort and then compare the items one by one until the list is sorted in ascending or descending alphabetical order.

In Visual Basic, you compare one item with another by using the same relational operators that you use to compare numeric values. The tricky part (which sometimes provokes long-winded discussions among computer scientists) is the specific sorting algorithm that you use to compare elements in a list. We won't get into the advantages and disadvantages of different sorting algorithms in this chapter. (The bone of contention is usually speed, which makes a difference only when several thousand items are sorted.) Instead, we'll explore how the basic string comparisons are made in a sort.

Along the way, you'll learn the skills necessary to sort your own strings, text boxes, list boxes, and databases.

Before Visual Basic can compare one character with another in a sort, it must convert each character into a number by using one of several translation tables, including the *ASCII character set* (also called the *ANSI character set*). (The acronym ASCII stands for American Standard Code for Information Interchange. The acronym ANSI stands for American National Standards Institute.) Each of the basic symbols that you can display on your computer has a different ASCII code. These codes include the basic set of typewriter characters (codes 32 through 127) and special control characters, such as tab, line feed, and carriage return (codes 0 through 31). For example, the lowercase letter *a* corresponds to the ASCII code 97, and the uppercase letter *A* corresponds to the ASCII code 65. As a result, Visual Basic treats these two characters quite differently when sorting or performing other comparisons.

In the 1980s, IBM extended ASCII with codes 128 through 255, which represent accented, Greek, and graphic characters, as well as miscellaneous symbols. ASCII and these additional characters and symbols are typically known as the *IBM extended character set*.

The ASCII character set is still the most important numeric code for beginning programmers to learn, but it isn't the only character set. As the market for computers and application software has become more global, a more comprehensive standard for character representation called *Unicode* has emerged. Originally Unicode could display up to 65,536 symbols—plenty of space to represent the traditional symbols in the ASCII character set plus many (written) international languages and symbols.

A standards body maintains the Unicode character set and adds symbols to it periodically. In fact, Visual Studio 2012 added support for *UTF 16 encoding with surrogates*, an enhanced Unicode standard that allows for the representation (potentially) of over one million distinct characters. So, after you learn to use ASCII characters and strings, you can transfer what you know to the global world of Unicode and a vast array of languages and characters.

Working with ASCII codes

To determine the ASCII code of a particular letter, you can use the Visual Basic *Asc* function. For example, the following program statement assigns the number 122 (the ASCII code for the lowercase letter *z*) to the *ascCode* integer variable:

```
Dim ascCode As Integer
ascCode = Asc("z")
```

Conversely, you can convert an ASCII code to a letter with the *Chr* function. For example, this program statement assigns the letter *z* to the letter character variable:

```
Dim letter As Char
letter = Chr(122)
```

The same result could also be achieved if you used the *ascCode* variable just declared, as shown here:

```
letter = Chr(ascCode)
```

How can you compare one text string or ASCII code with another? You simply use one of the six relational operators Visual Basic supplies for working with textual and numeric elements. These relational operators are shown in Table 11-7.

TABLE 11-7 Visual Basic relational operators

Operator	Meaning
<>	Not equal to
=	Equal to
<	Less than
>	Greater than
<=	Less than or equal to
>=	Greater than or equal to

A character is greater than another character if its ASCII code is higher. For example, the ASCII value of the letter *B* is greater than the ASCII value of the letter *A*, so the expression:

```
"A" < "B"
```

is true, and the expression:

```
"A" > "B"
```

is false.

When comparing two strings that each contain more than one character, Visual Basic begins by comparing the first character in the first string with the first character in the second string and then proceeds character by character through the strings until it finds a difference. For example, the strings *Mike* and *Michael* are the same up to the third characters (*k* and *c*). Because the ASCII value of *k* is greater than that of *c*, the expression:

```
"Mike" > "Michael"
```

is true.

If no differences are found between the strings, they are equal. If two strings are equal through several characters but one of the strings continues and the other one ends, the longer string is greater than the shorter string. For example, the expression:

```
"AAAAA" > "AAA"
```

is true.

After you've experimented with the *Asc* function a little, you can move to the *AscW* and *ChrW* methods supplied by the *String* class of the .NET Framework. These alternatives are useful because all string values in Visual Studio .NET are based on Unicode, and these methods fully support Unicode values. The *AscW* method returns an *Integer* value representing the character code corresponding to a character. The *ChrW* method returns the character associated with the specified character code.

Sorting strings in a text box

The following exercise demonstrates how you can use relational operators, concatenation, and several string methods to sort lines of text in a Windows Forms app named Sort Text. The program also shows you how to open and close files using the *StreamReader* and *StreamWriter* classes in the .NET Framework. The Windows desktop application offers an Open command that opens an existing text file and a Close command that closes the file. There's also a Sort Text command on the File menu that you can use to sort the text currently displayed in the text box.

The *StreamReader* and *StreamWriter* classes are easy-to-use resources for working with text files in an application. Although this example demonstrates their use in a Windows Forms application, you can also use them in a Windows Store app. The *StreamReader* class is designed to facilitate reading lines of information from a standard text file. The *StreamWriter* class is a companion resource that allows you to write lines of text to a text file.

How will the Sort Text program manage its sorting activities? First, because the entire contents of a text box are stored in a single text string, the program must break the long text box string into smaller substrings. These substrings can then be sorted by using the *ShellSort Sub* procedure, a sorting routine based on an algorithm created by Donald Shell in 1959. To simplify these tasks, I created a code module for the *ShellSort Sub* procedure so that I can call it from any event handler in the project. Although you will learn to use the powerful *Array.Sort* method in Chapter 14, "Using arrays, collections, and generics to manage data," the *ShellSort* procedure is a more flexible and customizable tool. Building the routine from scratch also gives you a little more experience with processing textual values—an important learning goal of this chapter.

Another interesting aspect of this program is the routine that processes the lines in the Windows Forms text box object. I wanted the program to be able to sort a text box of any size. To accomplish this, I created the code that follows. The code uses the *Replace, EndsWith*, and *Substring* methods of the *String* class. The *Replace* method is used to replace the different newline characters (carriage return, line feed, or carriage return and line feed) with just the carriage return character. The *EndsWith* method checks for a carriage return at the very end of the text.

The *Substring* method is used to remove the last carriage return if it exists:

```
Dim sortArray() As String
Dim textString As String
Dim counter As Integer

textString = NoteTextBox.Text
'replace different new line characters with one version
textString = textString.Replace(vbCrLf, vbCr)
textString = textString.Replace(vbLf, vbCr)
'remove last carriage return if it exists
If textString.EndsWith(vbCr) Then
    textString = textString.Substring(0, textString.Length - 1)
End If

'split each line into an array
sortArray = textString.Split(vbCr)
```

This code also uses the very handy *Split* method of the *String* class. The *Split* method breaks a string down into substrings and puts each substring into an array. The breaks are based on a separator string that you specify (in this case, a carriage return). The resulting array of strings then gets passed to the *ShellSort Sub* procedure for sorting, and *ShellSort* returns the string array in alphabetical order. After the string array is sorted, it gets copied back to the text box using a *For* loop.

Run the Sort Text program

1. Open the Sort Text project located in the My Documents\Visual Basic 2013 SBS\Chapter 11\ Sort Text folder.

   Sort Text is a Windows Forms app that I designed for the Windows Desktop.

2. Click the Start Debugging button to run the program.

3. Type the following text, or some text of your own, in the text box:

   Zebra

   Gorilla

   Moon

   Banana

   Apple

   Turtle

4. Click the Sort Text command on the File menu.

The text you typed is sorted and redisplayed in the text box as follows:

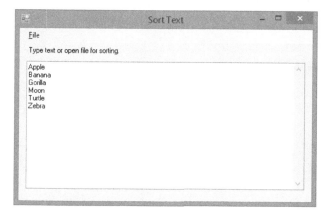

5. Click the Open command on the File menu, and then open the Abc.txt file in the My Documents\Visual Basic 2013 SBS\Chapter 11 folder, as shown here:

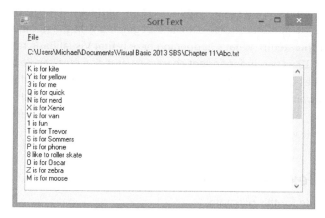

The Abc.txt file contains 36 lines of text. Each line begins with either a letter or a number from 1 through 10.

6. Click the Sort Text command on the File menu to sort the contents of the Abc.txt file.

The Sort Text program sorts the file in ascending order and displays the sorted list of lines in the text box, as shown here:

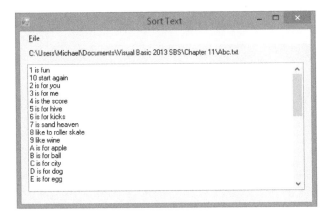

7. Scroll through the file to see the results of the alphabetical sort.

Notice that although the alphabetical portion of the sort ran perfectly, the sort produced a strange result for one of the numeric entries—the line beginning with the number 10 appears second in the list rather than tenth. What's happening here is that Visual Basic read the 1 and the 0 in the number 10 as two independent characters, not as a number. Because we're comparing the ASCII codes of these strings from left to right, the program produces a purely alphabetical sort. If you want to sort only numbers with this program, you need to prohibit textual input, modify the code so that the numeric input is stored in numeric variables, and then compare the numeric variables instead of strings.

Examining the Sort Text program code

Let's take a closer look at the code for this program.

Examine the Sort Text program

1. On the File menu of the Sort Text program, click the Exit command to stop the program.

2. Open the Code Editor for Form1, and then display the code for the *SortTextToolStripMenuItem_Click* event handler.

We've already discussed the first part of this event handler, which splits each line into an array. The remainder of the event handler calls a procedure to sort the array and displays the reordered list in the text box.

The entire *SortTextToolStripMenuItem_Click* event handler looks like this:

```
Dim sortArray() As String
Dim textString As String
Dim counter As Integer

textString = NoteTextBox.Text
'replace different new line characters with one version
textString = textString.Replace(vbCrLf, vbCr)
textString = textString.Replace(vbLf, vbCr)
'remove last carriage return if it exists
If textString.EndsWith(vbCr) Then
    textString = textString.Substring(0, textString.Length - 1)
End If

'split each line into an array
sortArray = textString.Split(vbCr)

'sort array
ShellSort(sortArray, sortArray.Length)

'then display sorted array in text box
textString = ""
For counter = 0 To sortArray.Length - 1
    textString = textString & sortArray(counter) & vbCrLf
Next counter
NoteTextBox.Text = textString
NoteTextBox.Select(0, 0)    'remove text selection
```

The *Split* method creates an array that has the same number of elements as the text box has lines of text. After the array is full of text, I call the *ShellSort* procedure located in the Module1.vb module, which I discussed earlier in this chapter. After the array is sorted, I use a *For* loop to reconstruct the lines and copy them into the text box.

3. Display the code for the Module1.vb module in the Code Editor.

This module defines the content of the *ShellSort* procedure. The *ShellSort* procedure uses an *If* statement and the <= relational operator to compare array elements and swap any that are out of order. The procedure looks like this:

```
Sub ShellSort(ByVal sort() As String, ByVal numOfElements As Integer)
    Dim temp As String
    Dim i, j, span As Integer
    'The ShellSort procedure sorts the elements of sort()
    'array in descending order and returns it to the calling
    'procedure.

    span = numOfElements \ 2
    Do While span > 0
        For i = span To numOfElements - 1
            For j = (i - span) To 0 Step -span
                If sort(j) <= sort(j + span) Then Exit For
                'swap array elements that are out of order
                temp = sort(j)
                sort(j) = sort(j + span)
```

```
                sort(j + span) = temp
            Next j
        Next i
        span = span \ 2
    Loop
End Sub
```

The method of the sort is to continually divide the main list of elements into sublists that are smaller by half. The sort then compares the tops and the bottoms of the sublists to see whether the elements are out of order. If the top and bottom are out of order, they're exchanged. The result is an array named *sort()* that's sorted alphabetically in ascending order. To change the direction of the sort, simply reverse the relational operator (change <= to >=).

Note that I've named the *For...Next* loop counter variables *i* and *j* here. Although it is usually clearer to specify longer variable names, it is common to use a single letter when you are declaring variables that will be used in nested loops. (It makes the code a little more compact and easier to read.) Since the 1960s, these loop counter variables have been named *i* and *j*, but you can use whatever name you like.

The remaining event handlers in Form1 (*OpenToolStripMenuItem_Click, CloseToolStripMenuItem_ Click, SaveAsToolStripMenuItem_Click, InsertDateToolStripMenuItem_Click*, and *ExitToolStripMenuItem_Click*) are all related to menu commands that I created; you can examine them in greater detail using the Code Editor. In particular, the Open menu command uses the *My.Computer.FileSystem* object along with the *ReadAllText* method to open a text file and display its contents within a *TextBox* control. Here is an excerpt from the important *OpenToolStripMenuItem_Click* event handler:

```
Dim allText As String = ""
OpenFileDialog1.Filter = "Text files (*.txt)|*.txt"
If OpenFileDialog1.ShowDialog() = DialogResult.OK Then 'display Open dialog box
    Try 'open file and trap any errors using handler
        allText = My.Computer.FileSystem.ReadallText(OpenFileDialog1.FileName)
        NoteLabel.Text = OpenFileDialog1.FileName 'update label
        NoteTextBox.Text = allText 'display file
```

The final three lines copy the entire contents of the file selected in the Open dialog box to the *AllText String* variable, update the label on the form to display the name of the open file, and then display the entire text file in the text box object.

Let's move on to another variation of this program that manipulates the strings in a text box or a file.

Protecting text with basic encryption

Now that you've had some experience with ASCII codes, you can begin to write simple encryption routines that shift the ASCII codes in your documents and scramble the text to hide it from intruding eyes. This process, known as *encryption*, mathematically alters the characters in a file, making them unreadable to the casual observer. Of course, to use encryption successfully, you also need to be able to reverse the process—otherwise, you'll simply be trashing your files rather than protecting them. And you'll want to create an encryption scheme that can't be easily recognized, a complicated process that's only begun by the sample programs in this chapter.

The following exercises show you how to encrypt and decrypt text strings safely. You'll run the Encrypt Text program now to see a simple encryption scheme in action. As I note at the end of this chapter, these exercises are just the tip of the iceberg for using encryption, cryptography, and file security measures—and these issues have become major areas of interest for programmers in the last decade or so. Still, even basic encryption is fun and a useful demonstration of text-processing techniques.

Encrypt text by changing ASCII codes

1. Close the Sort Text project, and then open the Windows Forms app named Encrypt Text, located in the My Documents\Visual Basic 2013 SBS\Chapter 11\Encrypt Text folder.

2. Click the Start Debugging button to run the program.

3. Type the following text, or some text of your own, in the text box:

   Here at last, my friend, you have the little book long since expected and promised, a little book on vast matters, namely, "On my own ignorance and that of many others."

   Francesco Petrarca, c. 1368

   The resulting application window and text look something like this:

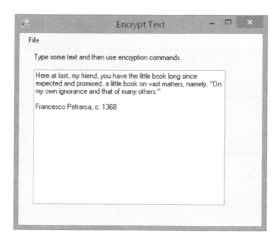

4. On the File menu, click the Save Encrypted File As command, and then save the file in the My Documents\Visual Basic 2013 SBS\Chapter 11 folder with the name **Padua.txt**.

   As you save the text file, the program scrambles the ASCII code and displays the results in the text box shown here:

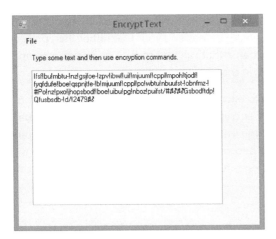

   If you open this file in Microsoft Word or another text editor, you'll see the same result—the characters in the file have been encrypted to prevent unauthorized reading.

5. To restore the file to its original form, choose the Open Encrypted File command on the File menu, and then open the Padua.txt file in the My Documents\Visual Basic 2013 SBS\Chapter 11 folder.

   The file appears again in its original form, as shown here:

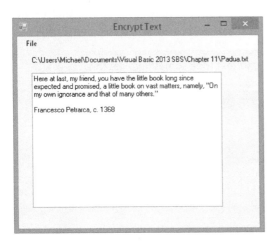

6. On the File menu, click the Exit command to end the Windows desktop program.

Examine the Encrypt Text program code

1. Open the *SaveAsItem_Click* event handler in the Code Editor to see the program code that produces the encryption that you observed when you ran the program.

   Although the effect you saw might have looked mysterious, it was a very straightforward encryption scheme. Using the *Asc* and *Chr* functions and a *For* loop, I simply incremented the ASCII code for each character in the text box by one and then saved the updated string to the specified text file.

   The entire event handler is listed here—in particular, note the items in bold:

```
Dim encrypt As String = ""
Dim letter As Char
Dim counter, charsInFile As Short

SaveFileDialog1.Filter = "Text files (*.txt)|*.txt"
If SaveFileDialog1.ShowDialog() = DialogResult.OK Then
    Try
        'save text with encryption scheme (ASCII code + 1)
        charsInFile = NoteTextBox.Text.Length
        For counter = 0 To charsInFile - 1
            letter = NoteTextBox.Text.Substring(counter, 1)
            'determine ASCII code and add one to it
            encrypt = encrypt & Chr(Asc(letter) + 1)
        Next counter
        'write encrypted text to file
        My.Computer.FileSystem.WriteAllText(SaveFileDialog1.FileName, encrypt, False)
        NoteTextBox.Text = encrypt
        NoteTextBox.Select(0, 0)    'remove text selection
        CloseItem.Enabled = True
    Catch ex As Exception
        MsgBox("An error occurred." & vbCrLf & ex.Message)
    End Try
End If
```

   Note especially the statement:

```
encrypt = encrypt & Chr(Asc(letter) + 1)
```

   which determines the ASCII code of the current letter, adds 1 to it, converts the ASCII code back to a letter, and then appends it to the *encrypt* string.

2. Now display the *OpenItem_Click* event handler in the Code Editor to see how the program reverses the encryption.

   This program code is nearly identical to that of the Save Encrypted File As command, but rather than adding 1 to the ASCII code for each letter, it subtracts 1. Here's the complete *OpenItem_Click* event handler, with noteworthy statements in bold:

```
Dim allText As String
Dim i, charsInFile As Short
Dim letter As Char
Dim decrypt As String = ""
```

```
    OpenFileDialog1.Filter = "Text files (*.txt)|*.txt"
    If OpenFileDialog1.ShowDialog() = DialogResult.OK Then 'display Open dialog box
        If My.Computer.FileSystem.FileExists(OpenFileDialog1.FileName) Then
            Try 'open file and trap any errors using handler
                allText = My.Computer.FileSystem.ReadAllText(OpenFileDialog1.FileName)
                'now, decrypt string by subtracting one from ASCII code
                charsInFile = allText.Length 'get length of string
                For i = 0 To charsInFile - 1 'loop once for each char
                    letter = allText.Substring(i, 1) 'get character
                    decrypt = decrypt & Chr(Asc(letter) - 1) 'subtract 1
                Next i 'and build new string
                NoteTextBox.Text = decrypt 'then display converted string
                NoteLabel.Text = OpenFileDialog1.FileName
                NoteTextBox.Select(0, 0)    'remove text selection
                NoteTextBox.Enabled = True 'allow text cursor
                CloseItem.Enabled = True   'enable Close command
                OpenItem.Enabled = False   'disable Open command
            Catch ex As Exception
                MsgBox("An error occurred." & vbCrLf & ex.Message)
            End Try
        End If
    End If
```

This type of simple encryption might be all you need to conceal the information in your text files. However, files encrypted in this way can easily be decoded. By searching for possible equivalents of common characters such as the space character, determining the ASCII shift required to restore the common character, and running the conversion for the entire text file, a person experienced in encryption could readily decipher the file's content. Also, this sort of encryption doesn't prevent a malicious user from physically tampering with the file—for example, opening the file up and modifying it. But if you just want to hide information quickly, this simple encryption scheme should do the trick.

Using the *Xor* operator

The preceding encryption scheme is quite safe for text files because it shifts the ASCII character code value up by just 1. However, you'll want to be careful about shifting ASCII codes more than a few characters if you store the result as text in a text file. Keep in mind that dramatic shifts in ASCII codes (such as adding 500 to each character code) won't produce actual ASCII characters that can be decrypted later. For example, adding 500 to the ASCII code for the letter *A* (65) would give a result of 565. This value couldn't be translated into a character by the *Chr* function and would generate an error. (However, you could use the *ChrW* method in this particular example, because there are plenty of Unicode characters up in that range.)

One way around this problem is to convert the letters in your file to numbers when you encrypt the file so that you can reverse the encryption no matter how large (or small) the numbers are. If you followed this line of thought, you could then apply mathematical functions—multiplication, logarithms, and so on—to the numbers as long as you knew how to reverse the results.

One tool for encrypting numeric values is already built into Visual Basic. This tool is the *Xor operator*, which performs the "exclusive or" operation, a function carried out on the bits that make up the number itself. The *Xor* operator can be observed by using a simple *MsgBox* function in a Windows Forms app. For example, the program statement:

```
MsgBox(Asc("A") Xor 50)
```

would display a numeric result of 115 in a message box in a Windows Forms app when the Visual Basic compiler executes it. Likewise, the program statement:

```
MsgBox(115 Xor 50)
```

would display a result of 65 in a message box, the ASCII code for the letter *A* (our original value). That is, the *Xor* operator produces a result that can be reversed—if the original *Xor* code is used again on the result of the first operation. This interesting behavior of the *Xor* function is used in many popular encryption algorithms. It can make your secret files more difficult to decode.

Run the Xor Encryption program now to see how the *Xor* operator works in the note-taking utility you've been building.

Encrypt text with the *Xor* operator

1. Close the Encrypt Text project, and then open the Xor Encryption project in the My Documents\Visual Basic 2013 SBS\Chapter 11\Xor Encryption folder.

    Xor Encryption is a Windows Forms app designed for the Windows Desktop, utilizing much of the code and the Toolbox controls from the previous examples.

2. Click the Start Debugging button to run the program.

3. Type the following text (or some of your own) in the encrypted text file:

    Rothair's Edict (Lombard Italy, c. 643)

    296. On Stealing Grapes. He who takes more than three grapes from another man's vine shall pay six soldi as compensation. He who takes less than three shall bear no guilt.

4. On the File menu, click the Save Encrypted File As command, and then save the file in the My Documents\Visual Basic 2013 SBS\Chapter 11 folder with the name **Oldlaws.txt**.

    The program prompts you for a secret encryption code (a number) that will be used to encrypt the file and decrypt it later. (Take note—you'll need to remember this code to decode the file.)

5. Type **500**, or another numeric code, and then press Enter.

Visual Basic encrypts the text by using the *Xor* operator and then stores it on disk as a series of numbers. You won't see any change on your screen, but rest assured that the program created an encrypted file on disk. (You can verify this with a word processor or a text editor.)

6. Click the Close command on the program's File menu to clear the text in the text box.

Now you'll restore the encrypted file.

7. On the File menu, click the Open Encrypted File command.

8. Open the My Documents\Visual Basic 2013 SBS\Chapter 11 folder, and then double-click the Oldlaws.txt file.

9. Type **500** (or the encryption code that you specified, if different) in the Xor Encryption dialog box when it appears, and then click OK.

The result is shown in the following illustration:

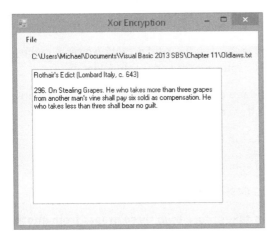

The program opens the file and restores the text by using the *Xor* operator and the encryption code you specified.

10. On the File menu, click the Exit command to end the program.

Examining the encryption program code

The *Xor* operator is used in both the *SaveAsItem_Click* and the *OpenItem_Click* event handlers. By now, these generic menu processing routines will be fairly familiar to you. The *SaveAsItem_Click* event handler consists of the following program statements (noteworthy lines in bold):

```
Dim letter As Char
Dim codeString As String
Dim i, charsInFile, code As Short
Dim streamToWrite As StreamWriter = Nothing
```

```
SaveFileDialog1.Filter = "Text files (*.txt)|*.txt"
If SaveFileDialog1.ShowDialog() = DialogResult.OK Then
    Try
        codeString = InputBox("Enter Encryption Code")
        If codeString = "" Then Exit Sub 'if cancel clicked
        'save text with encryption scheme
        code = CShort(codeString)
        charsInFile = NoteTextBox.Text.Length
        streamToWrite = My.Computer.FileSystem.OpenTextFileWriter( _
            SaveFileDialog1.FileName, False)
        For i = 0 To charsInFile - 1
            letter = NoteTextBox.Text.Substring(i, 1)
            'convert to number w/ Asc, then use Xor to encrypt
            streamToWrite.Write(Asc(letter) Xor code) 'and save in file
            'separate numbers with a space
            streamToWrite.Write(" ")
        Next
        CloseItem.Enabled = True
    Catch ex As Exception
        MsgBox("An error occurred." & vbCrLf & ex.Message)
    Finally
        If streamToWrite IsNot Nothing Then
            streamToWrite.Close()
        End If
    End Try
End If
```

In the *Write* method, the *Xor* operator is used to convert each letter in the text box to a numeric code, which is then saved to disk one number at time. The numbers are separated with spaces.

The final result of this encryption is no longer textual, but numeric—suitable to bewilder all but the nosiest snoopers. For example, the following screen shot shows the encrypted file produced by the preceding encryption routine, displayed in Notepad. (I've enabled Word Wrap so that you can see all the code.)

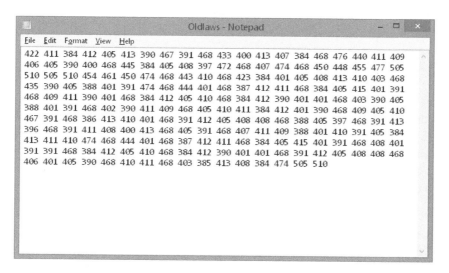

The *OpenItem_Click* event handler contains the following program statements. (Again, pay particular attention to the lines in bold.)

```
Dim allText As String
Dim i As Short
Dim ch As Char
Dim codeString As String
Dim code, number As Short
Dim numbers() As String
Dim decrypt As String = ""

OpenFileDialog1.Filter = "Text files (*.txt)|*.txt"
If OpenFileDialog1.ShowDialog() = DialogResult.OK Then 'display Open dialog box
    Try 'open file and trap any errors using handler
        codeString = InputBox("Enter Encryption Code")
        If codeString = "" Then Exit Sub 'if cancel clicked
        code = CShort(codeString)
        'read encrypted numbers
        allText = My.Computer.FileSystem.ReadAllText(OpenFileDialog1.FileName)
        allText = allText.Trim
        'split numbers in to an array based on space
        numbers = allText.Split(" ")
        'loop through array
        For i = 0 To numbers.Length - 1
            number = CShort(numbers(i)) 'convert string to number
            ch = Chr(number Xor code) 'convert with Xor
            decrypt = decrypt & ch 'and build string
        Next
        NoteTextBox.Text = decrypt 'then display converted string
        NoteLabel.Text = OpenFileDialog1.FileName
        NoteTextBox.Select(0, 0)    'remove text selection
        NoteTextBox.Enabled = True 'allow text cursor
        CloseItem.Enabled = True    'enable Close command
        OpenItem.Enabled = False    'disable Open command
    Catch ex As Exception
        MsgBox("An error occurred." & vbCrLf & ex.Message)
    End Try
End If
```

When the user clicks the Open Encrypted File command, this event handler opens the encrypted file, prompts the user for an encryption code, and displays the translated file in the text box object. The *ReadAllText* method reads the encrypted file. The *Split* method splits the numbers as strings into an array and uses the space as a separator. The *For* loop reads each numeric string in the array, converts the string to a number, and stores it in the *number* short integer variable. The *number* variable is then combined with the *code* variable by using the *Xor* operator, and the result is converted to a character by using the *Chr* function. These characters (stored in the *ch* variable of type *Char*) are then concatenated with the *decrypt* string variable, which eventually contains the entire decrypted text file, as shown here:

```
ch = Chr(number Xor code) 'convert with Xor
decrypt = decrypt & ch 'and build string
```

Encryption techniques like this are useful, and they can also be very instructional. Because encryption relies so much on string-processing techniques, it's a good way to practice a fundamental and important Visual Basic programming skill. As you become more experienced, you can also use the encryption services provided by the .NET Framework to add much more sophisticated security and cryptography services to your programs. For an introduction to these topics, search MSDN for "Cryptographic Tasks" and objects in the *System.Security.Cryptography* namespace.

Summary

In this chapter, you learned about the full range of data types provided by Visual Studio and how to declare and use variables and constants in your programs. You learned how to combine arithmetic operators with variables and numeric values to create formulas and how to convert data from one type to another using the *Parse* and *ToString* methods, and the *Convert* class. Finally, you explored the world of string processing and encryption using methods in the .NET Framework.

In the next chapter, you continue working with Visual Basic language elements, focusing on loops and decision structures that are useful in both Windows Store apps and Windows Forms apps.

CHAPTER 12

Creative decision structures and loops

After completing this chapter, you will be able to

- Use an *If...Then* statement to branch to a set of program statements based on a varying condition.

- Use the Windows Forms *MaskedTextBox* control to gather input in a specific format.

- Master *Select Case* statement syntax to manage *ListBox* control selections in a Windows Store app.

- Master *For...Next* loop syntax and learn advanced looping features.

- Build a multiline text box for output using string concatenation and formatting techniques.

- Master *Do* loops and execute code until a specific condition is met.

In the past few chapters, you used several features of Microsoft Visual Basic 2013 to process user input. You used menus, command bars, dialog boxes, and other Toolbox controls to display choices for the user, and you processed input by using property settings, variables, operators, formulas, and the Microsoft .NET Framework.

In this chapter, you'll learn more about branching conditionally to a specific area in your program based on input you receive from the user. You'll learn how to evaluate the contents of variables and properties by using conditional expressions, and then you'll execute one or more program statements based on the results. You'll also use a *For...Next* loop to execute statements a set number of times, and you'll use a *Do* loop to execute statements until a conditional expression is met. In short, you'll review and expand your knowledge of Visual Basic *decision structures* and loops, which collectively control how your program executes, or *flows*, internally.

To make your practice sessions as useful as possible, this chapter contains sample code designed for both Windows Store apps and Windows Forms apps. The rationale is eminently practical—while the syntax of basic decision structures and loops has not changed fundamentally in the last few releases of Visual Basic, the way that developers use these tools has changed a great deal. It is therefore good to see how they are used in the context of both Windows Store and Windows Forms platforms.

Event-driven programming

The programs you've written so far in this book have displayed Toolbox controls, menus, command bars, and dialog boxes on the screen, and with these programs, users could manipulate the screen elements in whatever order they saw fit. The programs put the user in charge, waited patiently for a response, and then processed the input predictably. In programming circles, this methodology is known as *event-driven programming*. You build a program by creating a group of "intelligent" objects that know how to respond to input, and then the program processes the input by using event handlers associated with the objects.

Where does this input come from? Fundamentally, of course, most input comes from the user of your program, who is typing in text boxes, clicking the mouse, using a touch input gesture, and so on. However, program input can also come from the computer system itself. For example, your program might be notified when an email arrives or when a specified period of time has elapsed on the system clock. In these situations, the computer, not the user, triggers the important events. But regardless of how an event is triggered, Visual Basic reacts by calling the event handler associated with the object that recognized the event and executes the program code in the event handler. So far, you've dealt primarily with the *Click, CheckedChanged,* and *SelectedIndexChanged* events. However, Visual Basic objects also can respond to many other types of events.

The event-driven nature of Visual Basic means that most of the computing done in your programs is accomplished by event handlers. These event-specific blocks of code process input, calculate new values, display output, and handle other tasks.

In this chapter, you'll learn how to use decision structures to compare variables, properties, and values, and how to execute one or more statements based on the results. You'll also use loops to execute a group of statements over and over until a condition is met or while a specific condition is true. Together, these powerful flow-control structures will help you build your event handlers so that they can respond to almost any situation.

Events supported by Visual Basic objects

Each object in Visual Basic has a predefined set of events to which it can respond. These events are listed when you select an object name in the Class Name list box at the top of the Code Editor and then click the drop-down arrow in the list box to the right of the Class Name list box (see following illustration). Or you will see the same events in the Properties window. (Events are visually identified in Microsoft Visual Studio by a lightning bolt icon.) You can write an event handler for any of these events, and if that event occurs in the program, Visual Basic will execute the event handler that's associated with it. For example, a XAML *TextBox* control in a Windows Store app supports more than 33 events, including *DoubleTapped, Drop, KeyUp,* and *KeyDown.* You probably won't need to write code for more than three or four of these events in your applications, but it's nice to know that you have so many choices when you create elements in your interface. The following screen shot shows a partial listing of the events for a XAML *TextBox* control in the Code Editor:

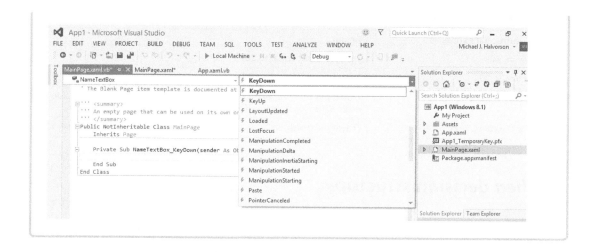

Using conditional expressions

One of the most useful tools for processing information in an event handler is a conditional expression. A *conditional expression* is a part of a complete program statement that asks a True-or-False question about a property, a variable, or another piece of data in the program code. For example, the conditional expression

```
Price < 100
```

evaluates to True if the *Price* variable contains a value that is less than 100, and it evaluates to False if *Price* contains a value that is greater than or equal to 100.

You can use the following comparison operators shown in Table 12-1 within a conditional expression.

TABLE 12-1 Visual Basic comparison operators

Comparison operator	Meaning
=	Equal to
< >	Not equal to
>	Greater than
<	Less than
>=	Greater than or equal to
<=	Less than or equal to

Table 12-2 shows some conditional expressions and their results. You'll work with conditional expressions several times in this chapter.

TABLE 12-2 Using conditional expressions

Conditional expression	Result
`10 <> 20`	True (10 is not equal to 20)
`score < 20`	True if *Score* is less than 20; otherwise False
`score = Label1.Text`	True if the *Text* property of the *Label1* object contains the same value as the *Score* variable; otherwise False
`NameTextBox.Text = "Bill"`	True if the word "Bill" is in the *NameTextBox* object; otherwise False

If...Then decision structures

When a conditional expression is used in a block of statements called a *decision structure*, it controls whether other statements in your program are executed and in what order they're executed. You can use an *If...Then* decision structure to evaluate a condition in the program and take a course of action based on the result. In its simplest form, an *If...Then* decision structure is written on a single line, where *condition* is a conditional expression and *statement* is a valid Visual Basic program statement:

```
If condition Then statement
```

Notice that I'm using italic formatting to introduce elements in the Visual Basic language that you replace with some meaningful value. This method of teaching statement syntax is also something you'll see in the Visual Studio product documentation from time to time.

For example, the following *If...Then* decision structure uses the conditional expression *score >= 20* to determine whether the program should set the *Text* property of the *MyTextBox* object to "You win!"

```
If score >= 20 Then MyTextBox.Text = "You win!"
```

If the *Score* variable contains a value that's greater than or equal to 20, Visual Basic sets the *Text* property; otherwise, it skips the assignment statement and executes the next line in the event handler. This sort of comparison always results in a True or False value. A conditional expression never results in a value of *maybe*.

Testing several conditions in an *If...Then* decision structure

More sophisticated *If...Then* decision structures include several conditional expressions. These structures will be several lines long and contain the important keywords *ElseIf, Else,* and *End If*:

```
If condition1 Then
     statements executed if condition1 is True
ElseIf condition2 Then
     statements executed if condition2 is True
[Additional ElseIf conditions and statements can be placed here]
Else
     statements executed if none of the other conditions is True
End If
```

In this structure, *condition1* is evaluated first. If this conditional expression is True, the block of statements below it is executed, one statement at a time, and then execution jumps down just past the closing *End If* statement. (For this reason, only a subset of statements within an *If...Then* decision structure are executed.) If the first condition isn't True, the second conditional expression (*condition2*) is evaluated. If the second condition is True, the second block of statements is executed, and then execution jumps down just past the closing *End If* statement. (You can add additional *ElseIf* conditions and statements if you have more conditions to evaluate.) If none of the conditional expressions is True, the statements below the *Else* keyword are executed. As I've already noted, the whole structure is closed by the *End If* keywords.

The following code shows how a multiple-line *If...Then* structure could be used to determine the amount of tax due in a hypothetical progressive tax return. (The income and percentage numbers are from the U.S. Internal Revenue Service 2012 Tax Rate Schedule for single filing status.)

```
Dim adjustedIncome, taxDue As Double
adjustedIncome = 50000
If adjustedIncome <= 8700 Then            '10% tax bracket
    taxDue = adjustedIncome * 0.1
ElseIf adjustedIncome <= 35350 Then       '15% tax bracket
    taxDue = 870 + ((adjustedIncome - 8700) * 0.15)
ElseIf adjustedIncome <= 85650 Then       '25% tax bracket
    taxDue = 4867.5 + ((adjustedIncome - 35350) * 0.25)
ElseIf adjustedIncome <= 178650 Then      '28% tax bracket
    taxDue = 17442.5 + ((adjustedIncome - 85650) * 0.28)
ElseIf adjustedIncome <= 388350 Then      '33% tax bracket
    taxDue = 43482.5 + ((adjustedIncome - 178650) * 0.33)
Else                                      '35% tax bracket
    taxDue = 112683.5 + ((adjustedIncome - 388350) * 0.35)
End If
```

 Important The order of the conditional expressions in your *If...Then* and *ElseIf* statements is critical. What happens if you reverse the order of the conditional expressions in the tax computation example and list the rates in the structure from highest to lowest? Taxpayers in the 10 percent, 15 percent, 25 percent, 28 percent, and 33 percent tax brackets are all placed in the 35 percent tax bracket because they all have an income that's less than or equal to $388,350. (This occurs because Visual Basic stops at the first conditional expression that is True, even if others are also True.) All the conditional expressions in this example test the same variable, so they need to be listed in ascending order to get the taxpayers to be placed in the right groups. Moral: When you use more than one conditional expression, consider the order carefully.

This useful decision structure tests the double-precision variable *adjustedIncome* at the first income level and subsequent income levels until one of the conditional expressions evaluates to True, and then determines the taxpayer's income tax accordingly. With some simple modifications, it could be used to compute the tax owed by any taxpayer in a progressive tax system, such as the one in the United States. Provided that the tax rates are complete and up to date and that the value in the *adjustedIncome* variable is correct, the program as written will give the correct tax owed for single

U.S. taxpayers for 2012. When the tax rates change, it's a simple matter to update the conditional expressions. With an additional decision structure to determine taxpayers' filing status, the program readily extends itself to include all U.S. taxpayers.

> **Tip** Expressions that can be evaluated as True or False are also known as *Boolean expressions*, and the True or False result can be assigned to a Boolean variable or property. You can assign Boolean values to certain object properties or Boolean variables that have been created by using the *Dim* statement and the *As Boolean* clause.

In the next exercise, you'll use an *If...Then* decision structure that recognizes users as they enter a program—a simple way to get started with writing your own decision structures. You'll also learn how to use the *MaskedTextBox* control in the Windows Forms Toolbox to receive input from the user in a specific format. The program is designed for the Windows Forms platform, because there is no masked edit control in the default Toolbox for Windows Store apps. However, you can create similar functionality using the XAML *TextBox* control.

Validate users by using *If...Then*

1. Start Visual Studio, and create a new Windows Forms application project named **My User Validation**.

   The new Windows desktop app is created, and a blank form opens in the Designer. As noted earlier, this particular program will use terms and tax data from the United States.

2. Click the form, and then set the form's *Text* property to **User Validation**.

3. Use the *Label* control in the Toolbox to create a label on your form, and use the Properties window to set the *Text* property of the object to **Enter Your Social Security Number**.

4. Use the *Button* control to create a button on your form, and set the button's *Text* property to **Sign In**.

5. Click the *MaskedTextBox* control on the Common Controls tab in the Windows Forms Toolbox, and then create a masked text box object on your form below the label.

   The *MaskedTextBox* control is similar to the *TextBox* control that you have been using, but by using *MaskedTextBox*, you can control the format of the information entered by the user into your program. You control the format by setting the *Mask* property; you can use a predefined format supplied by the control or choose your own format. You'll use the *MaskedTextBox* control in this program to require that users enter a Social Security number in the standard nine-digit format used by the U.S. Social Security Administration.

6. With the *MaskedTextBox1* object selected, click the *Mask* property in the Properties window, and then click the ellipses button in the second column.

The Input Mask dialog box opens, showing a list of your predefined formatting patterns, or *masks*.

7. Click Social Security Number in the list.

The Input Mask dialog box looks like this:

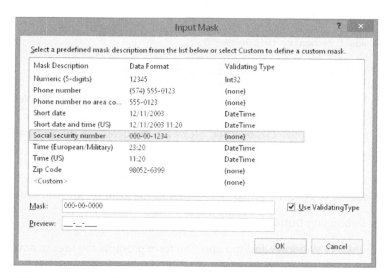

Although you won't use it now, take a moment to note the <Custom> option, which you can use later to create your own input masks using numbers and placeholder characters such as a hyphen (-).

8. Click OK to accept Social Security Number as your input mask.

Visual Studio displays your input mask in the *MaskedTextBox1* object, as shown in the following screen shot:

9. Double-click the Sign In button.

   The *Button1_Click* event handler appears in the Code Editor.

10. Type the following program statements in the event handler:

```
If MaskedTextBox1.Text = "219-09-9999" Then
    MsgBox("Welcome to the system!")
Else
    MsgBox("I don't recognize this number")
End If
```

   This simple *If...Then* decision structure checks the value of the *MaskedTextBox1* object's *Text* property, and if it equals "219-09-9999," the structure displays the message "Welcome to the system!" If the number entered by the user is some other value, the structure displays the message "I don't recognize this number." However, the beauty in this program is how the *MaskedTextBox1* object automatically filters input to ensure that it is in the correct format.

11. Click the Save All button on the Standard toolbar to save your changes. Specify the My Documents\Visual Basic 2013 SBS\Chapter 12 folder as the location for your project.

12. Click the Start Debugging button on the Standard toolbar.

   The program runs as a Windows desktop app. The form prompts the user to enter a Social Security number (SSN) in the appropriate format and displays underlines and hyphens to offer the user a hint of the format required.

13. Type **abcd** to test the input mask.

   Visual Basic prevents the letters from being displayed because letters do not fit the requested format. A nine-digit SSN is required.

14. Type **000123456** to test the input mask.

   Visual Basic displays the number 000-12-3456 in the masked text box, ignoring the 10th digit that you typed. Again, Visual Basic has forced the user's input into the proper format. Your form looks like this:

15. Click the Sign In button.

    Visual Basic displays the message "I don't recognize this number" because the SSN does not match the number the *If...Then* decision structure is looking for.

16. Click OK, delete the SSN from the masked text box, enter **219-09-9999** as the number, and then click Sign In again.

    This time the decision structure recognizes the number and displays a welcome message. You see the following message box:

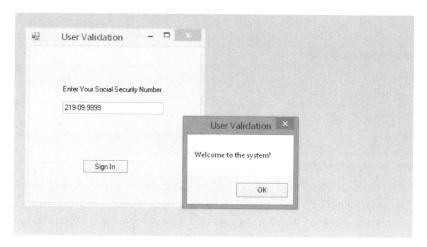

    Your code has prevented an unauthorized user from using the program, and you've learned a useful skill related to controlling input from the user.

17. Exit the program.

Using logical operators in conditional expressions

You can test more than one conditional expression in *If...Then* and *ElseIf* clauses if you want to include more than one selection criterion in your decision structure. The extra conditions are linked by using one or more of the logical operators listed in Table 12-3.

TABLE 12-3 Visual Basic logical operators

Logical operator	Meaning
And	If both conditional expressions are True, the result is True.
Or	If either conditional expression is True, the result is True.
Not	If the conditional expression is False, the result is True. If the conditional expression is True, the result is False.
Xor	If one and only one of the conditional expressions is True, the result is True. If both are True or both are False, the result is False. (*Xor* stands for *exclusive Or*.)

> **Note** When your program evaluates a complex expression that mixes different operator types, it evaluates mathematical operators first, comparison operators second, and logical operators third. In addition, the *And*, *Or*, and *Xor* operators are considered *binary* operators because they take two operands, while the *Not* operator is *unary* because it takes a single operand.

Table 12-4 lists some examples of the logical operators at work. In the expressions, it is assumed that the *Vehicle* string variable contains the value "Bike" and that the integer variable *Price* contains the value 200.

TABLE 12-4 Using logical expressions

Logical expression	Result
vehicle = "Bike" And price < 300	True (both conditions are True)
vehicle = "Car" Or price < 500	True (one condition is True)
Not price < 100	True (condition is False)
vehicle = "Bike" Xor price < 300	False (both conditions are True)

In the following exercise, you'll modify the My User Validation Windows desktop app to prompt the user for a personal identification number (PIN) during the validation process. To do this, you will add a second text box to get the PIN from the user and then modify the *If...Then* clause in the decision structure so that it uses the *And* operator to verify the PIN.

Add password protection by using the *And* operator

1. Display the User Validation form, and then add a second Windows Forms *Label* control to the user interface below the first masked text box.

2. Set the new label's *Text* property to **PIN**.

3. Add a second *MaskedTextBox* control to the form below the first masked text box and the new label.

4. Click the smart tag on the *MaskedTextBox2* object to open the MaskedTextBox Tasks list, and then click the Set Mask command to display the Input Mask dialog box.

5. Click the Numeric (5-digits) input mask, and then click OK.

   Like many PINs found online, this PIN will be five digits long. Again, if the user types a password of a different length or format, it will be rejected.

6. Double-click the Sign In button to display the *Button1_Click* event handler in the Code Editor.

7. Modify the event handler so that it contains the following code:

```
If MaskedTextBox1.Text = "219-09-9999" _
And MaskedTextBox2.Text = "54321" Then
    MsgBox("Welcome to the system!")
Else
    MsgBox("I don't recognize this number")
End If
```

The statement now includes the *And* logical operator, which requires that the user's PIN correspond with his or her SSN before the user is admitted to the system. (In this case, the valid PIN is 54321; in a real-world program, this value would be extracted along with the SSN from a secure database.) I modified the earlier program by adding a line continuation character (_) to the end of the first line and by adding the second line beginning with *And*.

8. Click the Start Debugging button on the Standard toolbar.

The Windows desktop app runs.

9. Type **219-09-9999** in the Social Security Number masked text box.

10. Type **54321** in the PIN masked text box.

11. Click the Sign In button.

The user is welcomed to the program, as shown in the following screen shot:

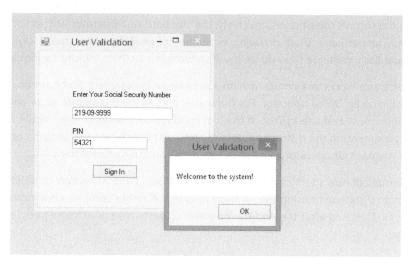

12. Click OK to close the message box.

13. Experiment with other values for the SSN and PIN.

Test the program carefully to be sure that the welcome message is not displayed when other PINs or SSNs are entered.

14. Click the Close button on the form when you're finished.

The program ends, and the development environment returns.

 Tip You can further customize this program by using the *PasswordChar* property in the masked text box objects. The *PasswordChar* property can be used to display a placeholder character, such as an asterisk (*), when the user types sensitive information. (You specify the character by using the Properties window.) Using a password character gives users additional secrecy as they enter their protected password—a standard feature of such operations.

Short-circuiting by using *AndAlso* and *OrElse*

Visual Basic offers two more logical operators that you can use in your conditional statements: *AndAlso* and *OrElse*. These operators work the same as *And* and *Or*, respectively, but offer an important subtlety in the way they're evaluated that is worth a few moments of thoughtful consideration. They are somewhat advanced, so you might not have had much experience with them in earlier programing contexts.

Consider an *If* statement that has two conditions that are connected by an *AndAlso* operator. For the statements of the *If* structure to be executed, both conditions must evaluate to True. If the first condition evaluates to False, Visual Basic skips to the next line or the *Else* statement immediately, without testing the second condition. (Conversely, the standard *And* operator will test both conditions no matter what.) The partial, or *short-circuiting*, evaluation of an *If* statement makes logical sense— why should Visual Basic continue to evaluate the *If* statement if both conditions cannot be True?

The *OrElse* operator works in a similar fashion. Consider an *If* statement that has two conditions that are connected by an *OrElse* operator. For the statements of the *If* structure to be executed, at least one condition must evaluate to True. If the first condition evaluates to True, Visual Basic begins to execute the statements in the *If* structure immediately, without testing the second condition. (But conversely, the standard *Or* operator will always test both conditions no matter what.)

Here's an example of how short-circuiting functions in Visual Basic when two conditions are evaluated in an *If* statement using the *AndAlso* operator. A rather complex conditional test (7 / humanAge <= 1) is used after the *AndAlso* operator to determine what some people call the "dog age" of a person:

```
Dim humanAge As Integer
humanAge = 7
'One year for a dog is seven years for a human
If humanAge <> 0 AndAlso 7 / humanAge <= 1 Then
    MsgBox("You are at least one dog year old")
Else
    MsgBox("You are less than one dog year old")
End If
```

As part of a larger program that determines the so-called dog age of a person by dividing his or her current age by 7, this bare-bones routine tries to determine whether the value in the *humanAge* integer variable is at least 7. (If you haven't heard the concept of "dog age" before, bear with me— following this logic, a 28-year-old person would be four dog years old. This has been suggested as an interesting way of relating to dogs, because dogs have a lifespan of roughly one-seventh that of humans.)

The code uses two *If* statement conditions and can be used in a variety of different contexts—I used it in the *Click* event handler for a button object. The first condition checks to see whether a non-zero number has been placed in the *humanAge* variable—I've assumed momentarily that the user has enough sense to place a positive age into *humanAge* because a negative number would produce incorrect results. The second condition tests whether the person is at least seven years old. If both conditions evaluate to True, the message "You are at least one dog year old" is displayed in a message box. If the person is less than seven, the message "You are less than one dog year old" is displayed.

Now imagine that I've changed the value of the *humanAge* variable from 7 to 0. What happens? The first *If* statement condition is evaluated as False by the Visual Basic compiler, and that evaluation prevents the second condition from being evaluated, thus halting, or short-circuiting, the *If* statement and saving us from a nasty "divide by zero" error that could result if we divided 7 by 0 (the new value of the *humanAge* variable). And recall that if you divide by zero in a Visual Basic program and don't catch the problem somehow, the result will be an error because division by zero isn't permitted.

In summary, the *AndAlso* and *OrElse* operators in Visual Basic open up a few new possibilities for Visual Basic programmers, including the potential to prevent run-time errors and other unexpected results. It's also possible to improve performance by placing conditions that are time-consuming to calculate at the end of the condition statement because Visual Basic doesn't perform these expensive condition calculations unless it's necessary. However, you need to think carefully about all the possible conditions that your *If* statements might encounter as variable states change during program execution.

Mastering *Select Case* decision structures

You used *Select Case* code blocks earlier in this book when you wrote event handlers to process selections in a list box. Recall that a *Select Case* structure is similar to an *If…Then…ElseIf* structure, but it's more elegant and efficient when the branching depends on one key variable, or *test case*. *Select Case* structures also make your program code more readable.

The basic syntax for a *Select Case* structure looks like this:

```
Select Case variable
    Case value1
        statements executed if value1 matches variable
    Case value2
        statements executed if value2 matches variable
    Case value3
        statements executed if value3 matches variable
```

```
    ...
    Case Else
         statements executed if no match is found
End Select
```

Select Case code blocks begin with the *Select Case* keyword and end with the *End Select* keyword. You replace *variable* with the variable, property, or other expression that is to be the key value, or test case, for the structure. You replace *value1, value2,* and *value3* with numbers, strings, or other values related to the test case being considered. If one of the values matches the variable, the statements below the *Case* clause are executed, and then Visual Basic jumps to the line after the *End Select* statement and picks up execution from there. You can include any number of *Case* clauses in a *Select Case* structure, and you can include more than one value in a *Case* clause. If you list multiple values after a case, separate them with commas.

The following example shows how a *Select Case* structure could be used to print an appropriate message about a person's age and cultural milestones in a program. Because the *age* variable contains a value of 18, the string "You can vote now!" is assigned to the *Text* property of the *AdviceTextBox* object. (You'll notice that the milestones have a U.S. slant to them; please customize freely to match your cultural setting.)

```
Dim age As Integer
age = 18
Select Case age
    Case 16
        AdviceTextBox.Text = "You can drive now!"
    Case 18
        AdviceTextBox.Text = "You can vote now!"
    Case 21
        AdviceTextBox.Text = "You can drink wine with your meals."
    Case 65
        AdviceTextBox.Text = "Time to retire and have fun!"
End Select
```

A *Select Case* structure also supports a *Case Else* clause that you can use to display a message if none of the preceding cases matches the *age* variable. Here's how *Case Else* would work in the following example—note that I've changed the value of *age* to 25 to trigger the *Case Else* clause:

```
Dim age As Integer
age = 25
Select Case age
    Case 16
        AdviceTextBox.Text = "You can drive now!"
    Case 18
        AdviceTextBox.Text = "You can vote now!"
    Case 21
        AdviceTextBox.Text = "You can drink wine with your meals."
    Case 65
        AdviceTextBox.Text = "Time to retire and have fun!"
    Case Else
        AdviceTextBox.Text = "You're a great age! Enjoy it!"
End Select
```

Using comparison operators with a *Select Case* structure

More sophisticated Select Case decision structures use comparison operators to include a range of test values. The Visual Basic comparison operators that can be used are =, <>, >, <, >=, and <=. To use the comparison operators, you need to include the *Is* keyword or the *To* keyword in the expression to identify the comparison you're making. The *Is* keyword instructs the compiler to compare the test variable to the expression listed after the *Is* keyword. The *To* keyword identifies a range of values. The following structure uses *Is, To,* and several comparison operators to test the *age* variable and to display one of five messages:

```
Select Case age
    Case Is < 13
        AdviceTextBox.Text = "Enjoy your youth!"
    Case 13 To 19
        AdviceTextBox.Text = "Enjoy your teens!"
    Case 21
        AdviceTextBox.Text = "You can drink wine with your meals."
    Case Is >= 100
        AdviceTextBox.Text = "Looking good!"
    Case Else
        AdviceTextBox.Text = "That's a nice age to be."
End Select
```

If the value of the *age* variable is less than 13, the message "Enjoy your youth!" is displayed. For the ages 13 through 19, the message "Enjoy your teens!" is displayed, and so on.

Is it clear how *Select Case* is an alternative to *If...Then...Else* in VB code? *Select Case* code blocks are typically easier to decipher, for one. But also, *Select Case* code blocks are more efficient than *If...Then...Else* structures when you're making three or more branching decisions based on one variable or property. However, when you're making two or fewer comparisons or when you're working with several different values, you'll probably want to use an *If...Then* decision structure.

In the following exercise, you'll practice using a *Select Case* structure to process input received from a list box control in a Windows Store app. You'll use the *ListBox.SelectedIndex* property to collect the input, and you'll use the *SelectionChanged* event to display a greeting in one of four languages.

Use a *Select Case* structure to process input from a list box

1. On the File menu, click New Project.

   The New Project dialog box opens.

2. Choose Visual Basic/Windows Store under Templates, and then verify that the Blank App (XAML) template is selected.

3. Type **My Select Case** in the Name text box.

4. Click OK to open and configure the new project.

    Visual Studio creates the new Windows Store project with the appropriate support files.

5. Right-click the MainPage.xaml file in Solution Explorer, and then select View Designer.

    A blank page opens in the Designer.

6. Change the magnification percentage in the Designer's Zoom box to 100%.

7. Click the XAML *TextBlock* control in the Toolbox, and then create a text label near the top of the page to display a title for the program.

8. Type **Greetings from around the World** in the text block object, and set the point size to 28-point. Set the *Name* property of the object to **PageTitle**.

9. Use the *TextBlock* control to create a second text object below the first.

    You'll use this text block as a title for the list box.

10. Type **Choose a Country** in the text block object, and set the point size to 12-point. Set the *Name* property of the object to **ListBoxTitle**.

11. Click the XAML *ListBox* control in the Toolbox, and then create a list box below the second label. Set the *Name* property of the object to **CountryListBox**.

    You'll add XAML markup to this list box object in the next procedure, which is the easiest mechanism for adding items to a list box.

12. Use the *TextBlock* control to draw a third text label below the list box.

13. Remove the text from the text block object, but set the point size to 12-point for the object. Set the *Name* property of the object to **Country**.

    The text block seems to disappear from the page, but it is still present. (You can see it listed in the XAML portion of the Code Editor.) When the program runs and the user selects a country name in the list box, that name will be copied into this text block object.

14. Use the *TextBox* control to create a rectangular output window below the third text block object.

15. Remove the text from the text box object, and set the *Name* property of the object to **GreetingTextBox**.

    When you've finished setting properties, your page and IDE will look similar to this:

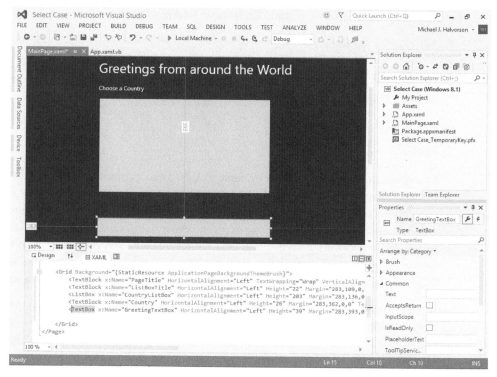

Now you'll enter the XAML markup to add items to the list box on the page. To accomplish this task, you'll edit the list box object's XAML markup in the Code Editor.

Use XAML markup to define a *ListBox*

1. Click the Swap Panes button in the Designer (a button containing two arrows—one pointing up and the other pointing down).

   The Swap Panes button gives you more room to see the XAML markup in the Code Editor.

2. Locate the *ListBox* object in the XAML markup in the Code Editor. Move the insertion pointer to the end of the line (use the scroll bar if necessary).

3. Change the markup at end of this line from "/>" to ">". (That is, remove the "/" character.)

4. You are removing the "/" character there because your *ListBox* object will now be defined by several lines of XAML markup. When you have subordinate elements for an object, the concluding "/>" is placed at the end of the tag defining the object. Subordinate elements are typically placed on their own lines and indented, but this is not a requirement. (For more information about such syntax, see Chapter 7, "XAML markup step by step.")

5. After the edit, move the insertion point to the end of the line and press Enter.

6. Type the following XAML markup to define the items in the list box:

```
<ListBoxItem Name="List1"
             Content="Australia"/>
<ListBoxItem Name="List2"
             Content="Germany"/>
<ListBoxItem Name="List3"
             Content="Italy"/>
<ListBoxItem Name="List4"
             Content="Mexico"/>
</ListBox>
```

New items are added to a list box by defining *ListBoxItem* properties for each item. Notice that in this markup I have given each item its own name, which I have specified using sequentially numbered names (*List1*, *List2*, *List3*, and *List4*). These names are arbitrary and designed here for simplicity—you can use different names for the items if you want. In addition, I have specified textual content for each item by using the *Content* property. This defines what appears in the list box on the page. Finally, notice that the entire series of items is concluded by the tag *</ListBox>*. This is necessary, as noted earlier, because the list box now contains subordinate elements.

Beyond these basic settings, you can also define *FontFamly*, *FontSize*, *FontWeight*, *Foreground*, *Height*, *Width*, and other properties for list box items. The appearance of list boxes is entirely customizable. Just be sure to give each list box item a unique *Name* property, so that it can be referred to in Visual Basic program code.

When you complete your XAML input, the Visual Studio IDE will look like this:

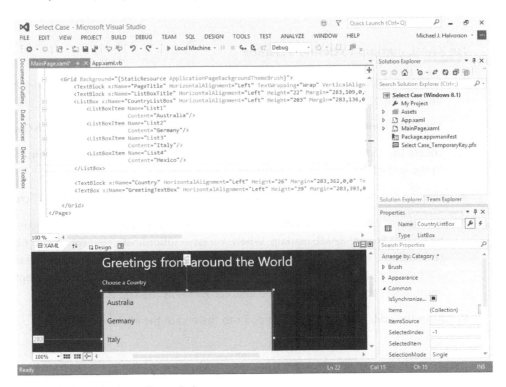

7. Click the Swap Panes button in the Designer again to move the XAML tab of the Code Editor back to the bottom of the Designer.

Now you'll enter the program code to manage the list box selections and other activities in the program.

Use Visual Basic code to process list box items

1. In the XAML tab of the Code Editor, click the line of XAML markup that begins with statement *ListBox x:Name="CountryListBox"*.

   A simple way to define an event handler for a list box is to select the list box in the Code Editor and then click the Event Handler button (the lightning bolt) in the Properties window. However, you need to be sure to select the list box object itself and not simply one of the items in the list box.

   When you click the list box, its properties are loaded into the Properties windows, and you'll see *CountryListBox* in the *Name* property.

   The event that you want to capture while the program runs is the *SelectionChanged* event, which fires whenever a list box item is selected by the user.

2. In the Properties window, click the Event Handler button near the *Name* text box.

   The Event Handler button displays the events that the list box can respond to, including *SelectionChanged*.

3. Double-click next to the *SelectionChanged* event in the Properties window.

   Visual Studio inserts an event handler named *CountryListBox_SelectionChanged* in the *SelectionChanged* text box and opens the MainPage.xaml.vb code-behind file in the Code Editor.

4. Type the following Visual Basic statements in the Code Editor between the *Private Sub* and *End Sub* statements:

```
Select Case CountryListBox.SelectedIndex
    Case 0
        Country.Text = "Australia"
        GreetingTextBox.Text = "How ya goin' programmer?"
    Case 1
        Country.Text = "Germany"
        GreetingTextBox.Text = "Hallo, programmierer"
    Case 2
        Country.Text = "Italy"
        GreetingTextBox.Text = "Ciao, programmatore"
    Case 3
        Country.Text = "Mexico"
        GreetingTextBox.Text = "Hola, programador"
End Select
```

At last we see *Select Case* at work in the heart of this Windows Store app, which displays a list of countries in a list box and uses a *Select Case* decision structure to process the user's pick. The property used for the test case is *CountryListBox.SelectedIndex*. The *SelectedIndex* property always contains the number of the item selected in the list box; the item at the top is 0 (zero), the second item is 1, the next item is 2, and so on. (A value of -1 means that there has been no selection in the list box, a situation that is not handled by this particular routine.) By using *SelectedIndex*, the *Select Case* structure can quickly identify the user's choice and display the correct greeting on the page. The greeting is displayed in the *GreetingTextBox* object, and the country name is placed in the text block named *Country*.

5. Click the Save All button on the Standard toolbar to save your changes. Specify the My Documents\Visual Basic 2013 SBS\Chapter 12 folder as the location.

    Now run the program to see how the *Select Case* statement works.

6. Click the Start Debugging button on the Standard toolbar to run the program.

7. Click each of the country names in the Choose A Country list box.

    The program displays a greeting for each of the countries listed. The following screen shot shows the greeting for Italy:

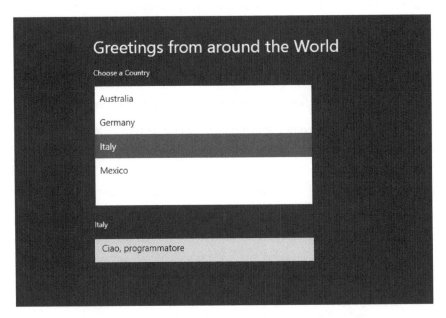

8. Close the program.

    The Windows Store app stops, and the development environment returns.

9. Click Close Project on the File menu to unload the Windows Store app.

You've finished working with *If...Then* and *Select Case* decision structures in this chapter. However, you'll have several additional opportunities to work with them in this book. They are essential decision-making mechanisms in the Visual Basic language, and you'll find that you use them in almost every program that you write.

Mastering *For...Next* loops

With a *For...Next* loop, you can execute a specific group of program statements a set number of times in an event handler or a code module. This approach can be useful if you're performing several related calculations, working with elements on the screen, or processing several pieces of user input. A *For...Next* loop is really just a shorthand way of writing out a long list of program statements. Because each group of statements in such a list does essentially the same thing, you can define just one group of statements and request that it be executed as many times as you want.

The syntax for a *For...Next* loop looks like this:

```
For variable = start To end
    statements to be repeated
Next [variable]
```

In this syntax statement, *For*, *To*, and *Next* are required keywords, as is the equal to operator (=). You replace *variable* with the name of a numeric variable that keeps track of the current loop count, and you replace *start* and *end* with numeric values representing the starting and stopping points for the loop. The *variable* after *Next* is optional, but if you include *variable* at the bottom of the loop, it must match *variable* at the top of the loop. Also note that you must declare *variable* before it's used in the *For...Next* statement and that you don't type in the brackets, which I include to indicate an optional item. The line or lines between the *For* and *Next* statements are the instructions that are repeated each time the loop is executed.

For example, the following *For...Next* loop displays the numbers "1234" in a text box object named *SampleTextBox* on the page or form in a Visual Basic app:

```
Dim i As Integer
For i = 1 To 4
    SampleTextBox.Text = SampleTextBox.Text & i
Next i
```

Each time through the loop a digit is appended to the text box because the string concatenation character (&) is used to combine the numbers. The counter variable employed in the loop is *i*, a single letter that, by convention, stands for the first integer counter in a *For...Next* loop and is declared as an *Integer* type. (You can also use a more verbose counter variable name if you like.)

Each time this particular loop is executed, the counter variable *i* is incremented by 1. The first time through the loop, the variable contains a value of 1, the value of *start*; the last time through, it contains a value of 4, the value of *end*. As you'll see in the following examples, you can use this counter variable to great advantage in your loops.

> **Tip** In loops that use counter variables, the usual practice is to use the *Integer* type for the variable declaration, as I did previously. However, you will get similar performance in Visual Basic 2013 if you declare the counter variable as type *Long* or *Decimal*.

Using a loop to fill a *TextBox* with string data

A counter variable is just like any other variable in a routine. It can be assigned to properties, used in calculations, or displayed in a program. One of the practical uses for a counter variable is to display output in a *TextBox* control in a Window Store or Windows desktop app.

Is there any trick to displaying more than one line of text in a text box? The answer is no—the XAML *TextBox* control for a Windows Store app automatically displays multiple lines of text. However, in a Windows Forms app, you do need to set the *TextBox* control's *Multiline* property to True. (You can also choose to set the *ScrollBars* property to Vertical if the Windows Forms *TextBox* will receive more lines than it can display.)

Consider the following sample *For...Next* loop that displays ten lines of text in a *TextBox* control on the page (or form) that is named *SampleTextBox*.

```
Dim i As Integer
For i = 1 To 10
    SampleTextBox.Text = SampleTextBox.Text & "Line " & i & vbCrLf
Next i
```

The code initializes a counter variable *i*, and uses a *For...Next* loop to update the contents of the text box object ten times. Each time through, a new line is added to the text box. The added content consists of the word "Line" and the current line number (which is stored in the counter variable). The *vbCrLf* constant is also used to add a carriage return and line feed to each line. Without this, all the information would be written on the same line, as it was in the previous example.

This code will work to update a *TextBox* control in either a Windows Store app or a Windows Forms app. For example, you could place it in an event handler associated with the *Click* event handler for a button object.

After the loop is executed, the text box object looks like this on the page:

```
Line 1
Line 2
Line 3
Line 4
Line 5
Line 6
Line 7
Line 8
Line 9
Line 10
```

Tip Worried about running out of room in the text box object? It will take a while if you're displaying only simple text lines. In a Windows Forms (Windows desktop) app, the maximum number of characters is specified in the *MaxLength* property for a text box. By default, *MaxLength* is set to 32,767 characters. If you need more characters, you can increase this value. If you want more formatting options, you can use the *RichTextBox* control in the Windows Forms Toolbox—a similar but even more capable control for displaying and manipulating text. (However, this control is currently available only to Windows desktop applications.)

Complex *For...Next* loops

The counter variable in a *For...Next* loop can be a powerful tool in your programs. With a little imagination, you can use it to create several useful sequences of numbers in your loops. To create a loop with a counter pattern other than 1, 2, 3, 4, and so on, you can specify a different value for *start* in the loop and then use the *Step* keyword to increment the counter at different intervals. For example, the code:

```
Dim i As Integer
For i = 5 To 25 Step 5
    SampleTextBox.Text = SampleTextBox1.Text & "Line " & i & vbCrLf
Next i
```

displays the following sequence of line numbers in a text box:

```
Line 5
Line 10
Line 15
Line 20
Line 25
```

You can also specify decimal values in a loop if you declare *i* as a floating-point type. For example, the *For...Next* loop:

```
Dim i As Single
For i = 1 To 2.5 Step 0.5
    SampleTextBox.Text = SampleTextBox.Text & "Line " & i & vbCrLf
Next i
```

displays the following line numbers in a text box named *SampleTextBox*:

```
Line 1
Line 1.5
Line 2
Line 2.5
```

In addition to displaying the counter variable, you can use the counter to set properties, calculate values, or process files. The following exercise shows how you can use the counter to assist in converting miles to kilometers. The demonstration program is a Window Store app, but you can use the same techniques for Windows Forms/Windows desktop apps.

Convert distances using a *For...Next* loop

1. On the File menu, click the New Project command.

2. Create a new Windows Store Application project named **My Miles-Kilometers.**

   When the project loads, display the MainPage.xaml file in the Designer.

3. Click the *TextBox* control in the XAML Toolbox, and then create a tall, rectangular text box object on the page.

4. Click the *Button* control, and then create a small button object on the page below the text box.

5. Set the following properties for the two objects:

Object	Property	Setting
TextBox	Name Text	DataTextBox (empty)
Button	Name	CreateButton
	Content	"Create Table"

   You'll also set an additional property for the *TextBox* object by using XAML markup in the Code Editor. The *ScrollViewer.VerticalScrollBarVisibility* property determines whether a vertical scroll bar appears in the text box. In the Properties window, it can also be set in the extended portion of the Layout category of properties. But it is good to have some practice setting properties in markup, too.

6. In the XAML pane of the Code Editor, in the line defining the *DataTextBox* object (somewhere after the *Name* property is set), type

   ```
   ScrollViewer.VerticalScrollBarVisibility="Auto"
   ```

   By setting the property to "Auto", Visual Studio will automatically add a scroll bar if there is more information in the text box than can be seen at one time. This will be the case for this particular example.

   Your page should look like this in the Designer:

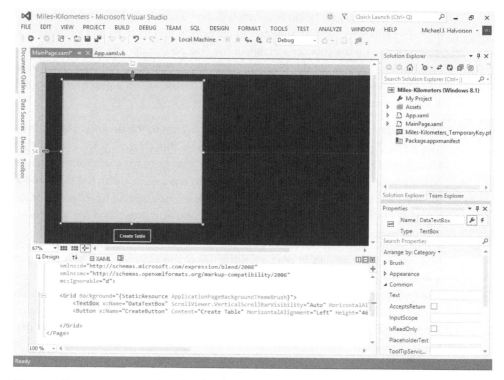

Now you'll create an event handler for the button's *Click* event and convert a series of values from miles to kilometers.

7. Double-click the Create Table button on the page.

An event handler named *CreateButton_Click* opens in the Code Editor.

8. Type the following Visual Basic code:

```
Dim miles As Single
Dim kilometers As Single
Const milesToKM As Single = 1.609344
DataTextBox.Text = "Miles" & vbTab & "Kilometers" & vbCrLf
For miles = 0.1 To 6.3 Step 0.1  'loop 63 times; display every tenth mile
    kilometers = milesToKM * miles
    'display miles and kilometers separated by a Tab character
    'format output with ToString; 1 numeric decimal place for miles
    'and 5 numeric decimal places for kilometers
    DataTextBox.Text &= miles.ToString("N1") & vbTab _
        & kilometers.ToString("N5") & vbCrLf
Next miles
```

This code begins by declaring two variables and a constant. The single-precision variables *miles* and *kilometers* will store distances corresponding to miles and kilometers, respectively. *miles* will also be the counter variable in the *For...Next* loop. The third value in this group is *milesToKM*, a constant of the single-precision type that holds the conversion value used when converting miles to kilometers. That number is 1.609344—the approximate number of kilometers in a mile.

After declaring essential values and printing a header in the text box object, the event handler uses a *For...Next* loop to create a conversion table that shows equivalencies between miles and kilometers. The loop uses the *Step* keyword to loop once for every tenth of a mile. The string concatenation shortcut operator (&=) is used to build each line in the table and append it to the previous lines. (You learned how to use the &= operator in Chapter 11, "Mastering data types, operators, and string processing.") The loop also uses the *vbTab* and *vbCrLf* constants to assist in formatting the information.

Less obvious, but equally important, is the use of the *ToString* function to convert the *miles* and *kilometers* numeric variables into strings so that they can be more easily formatted. The syntax utilizes *standard numeric format strings,* which takes the form A*xx*, where A is an alphabetic character called the *format specifier* and *xx* is an optional integer known as the *precision specifier.* The range of the precision specifier is 0 to 99; this number affects the number of formatted digits displayed by *ToString.*

I wanted to show the number of miles with one decimal digit after the decimal point, and the number of kilometers with five decimal digits after the decimal point. Without this sort of structure, the table will display numbers of different length and look uneven. I used the "N" format specifier to request a numeric value with decimal places. However, there are other options for different types of information. You can review the complete list of format specifiers if you search online for the topic "Standard Numeric Format Strings" at *http://msdn.microsoft.com.*

Finally, notice the number of iterations in the *For...Next* loop. I specified that the loop should cycle 63 times, incrementing one-tenth of a mile (by 0.1) each time through. I chose this number of iterations to create a table of values stretching from 0.1 to 6.3 miles.

9. Click the Save All button on the Standard toolbar to save your changes. Specify the My Documents\Visual Basic 2013 SBS\Chapter 12 folder as the location.

10. Click the Start Debugging button to run the program, and then click the Create Table button.

The *For...Next* loop displays the following output:

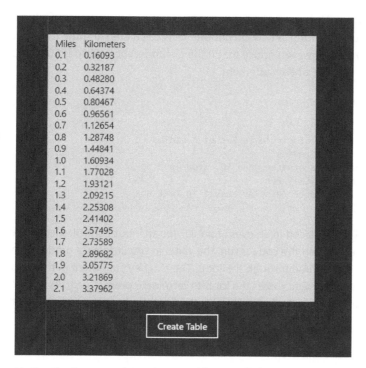

Miles	Kilometers
0.1	0.16093
0.2	0.32187
0.3	0.48280
0.4	0.64374
0.5	0.80467
0.6	0.96561
0.7	1.12654
0.8	1.28748
0.9	1.44841
1.0	1.60934
1.1	1.77028
1.2	1.93121
1.3	2.09215
1.4	2.25308
1.5	2.41402
1.6	2.57495
1.7	2.73589
1.8	2.89682
1.9	3.05775
2.0	3.21869
2.1	3.37962

Create Table

Notice the formatted numbers and how well they line up in the table. Also notice that when you move the mouse pointer into the text box, a scroll bar appears to show the information in the lower half of the table.

11. Use the vertical scroll bar to scroll down and view the remaining conversion data.

As you can see, the final values indicate that 10 kilometers is approximately equal to 6.2 miles. Long-distance runners will be well aware of this fact, because it is an internationally recognized equivalency.

12. When you're finished, close the Windows Store app.

The program stops, and the IDE returns. Modify the *For...Next* loop if you want to experiment with the number of iterations in the loop or how the table is formatted.

13. When you're finished, click Close Project on the File menu.

The *Exit For* statement

Most *For...Next* loops run to completion without incident, but now and then you'll find it useful to abort the processing of a *For...Next* loop when a particular exit condition occurs. Visual Basic allows for this possibility by providing the *Exit For* statement, which you can use to terminate the execution of a *For...Next* loop early and move execution to the first statement after the loop.

For example, the following *For...Next* loop calculates the circumference of a series of circles. (Recall that the formula for the circumference of a circle when the radius is known is 2 * pi * radius.) In the following routine, *Radius* is an integer variable that is also used as the counter variable for the loop. With each iteration through the loop, a new circumference is calculated and the result is displayed in a text box named *OutputBox*. However, notice that if the circumference exceeds 50, the looping will be stopped prematurely by the *Exit For* statement.

```
Dim circumference As Single
Dim radius As Integer
For radius = 1 To 10
    'formula for circumference of circle is 2 * pi * radius
    circumference = 2 * 3.14 * radius
    'if circle circumference is greater than 50, stop looping
    If circumference > 50 Then Exit For
    OutputBox.Text = circumference 'display result in text box
Next Radius
```

This code is designed to be placed in an event handler for an input control, such as the *Click* event handler for a button object. When the code is run, the value in *circumference* gradually increases until it exceeds 50 during the eighth time through the loop. The *If...Then* statement in the loop detects this condition, and the *Exit For* statement forces the loop to terminate prematurely. As a result, the value from the seventh iteration through the loop (43.96) is the final result displayed in the text box object.

Writing *Do* loops

As an alternative to a *For...Next* loop, you can write a *Do* loop that executes a group of Visual Basic statements until a certain condition is True. *Do* loops are valuable because often you can't know in advance how many times a loop should repeat. For example, you might want to let the user enter names in a database until the user types the word *Done* in an input control. In that case, you can use a *Do* loop to cycle indefinitely until the *Done* text string is entered.

A *Do* loop has several formats, depending on where and how the loop condition is evaluated. The most common syntax is:

```
Do While condition
    block of statements to be executed
Loop
```

For example, the following *Do* loop prompts the user for input and displays that input in a text box until the word *Done* is typed in the input box. The routine utilizes the *InputBox* function, which is available to Windows desktop apps, and also a text box object named *OutputBox*.

```
Dim inputName As String = ""
Do While inputName.ToUpper <> "DONE"
    inputName = InputBox("Enter your name or type Done to quit.")
    If inputName.ToUpper <> "DONE" And inputName <> "" Then
        OutputBox.Text = inputName
    End If
Loop
```

The conditional statement in this loop is *inputName.ToUpper* <> *"DONE"*, which the Visual Basic compiler translates to mean "loop as long as the *inputName* variable when formatted in uppercase doesn't contain the word 'DONE'." This brings up an interesting fact about this type of *Do* loop: If the condition at the top of the loop isn't True when the *Do* statement is first evaluated, the *Do* loop is never executed. Here, if the *inputName* string variable when converted to uppercase did contain the "DONE" value before the loop started (perhaps from an earlier assignment in the event handler), Visual Basic would skip the loop altogether and continue with the line below the *Loop* keyword.

If you always want the loop to run at least once in a program, put the conditional test at the bottom of the loop. For example, the loop:

```
Dim inputName As String = ""
Do
    inputName = InputBox("Enter your name or type Done to quit.")
    If inputName.ToUpper <> "DONE" And inputName <> "" Then
        OutputBox.Text = inputName
    End If
Loop While inputName.ToUpper <> "DONE"
```

is essentially the same as the previous *Do* loop, but here the loop condition is tested after a name is received from the *InputBox* function. This has the advantage of updating the *inputName* variable before the conditional test in the loop so that a preexisting *Done* value won't cause the loop to be skipped. Testing the loop condition at the bottom ensures that your loop is executed at least once.

Avoiding an endless loop

Because of the repetitive nature of *Do* loops, it's very important to design your test conditions so that each loop has a true exit point. If a loop test never evaluates to False, the loop executes endlessly, and your program might not respond to input. Consider the following example from a Visual Basic Windows desktop app:

```
Dim number as Double
Do
    number = InputBox("Enter a number to square. Type -1 to quit.")
    number = number * number
    OutputBox.Text = number
Loop While number >= 0
```

In this loop, the user enters number after number, and the program squares each number and displays it in the text box. Unfortunately, when the user has had enough, he or she can't quit because the advertised exit condition doesn't work. When the user enters –1, the program squares it, and the *number* variable is assigned the value 1. (The problem can be fixed by setting a different exit condition. The next example demonstrates how to check whether the user clicked the Cancel button and exited the loop.) Watching for endless loops is essential when you're writing *Do* loops. Fortunately, they're pretty easy to spot if you test your programs thoroughly.

Converting temperatures

The following exercise shows how you can use a *Do* loop to convert Fahrenheit temperatures to Celsius temperatures in a Windows Forms/Windows desktop app. The simple program prompts the user for input by using the *InputBox* function, converts the temperature, and displays the output in a message box using the *MsgBox* function.

Note that *InputBox* and *MsgBox* are not available in Windows Store apps, because the Windows 8.1 design guidelines discourage the overt use of pop-up boxes in Windows Store programs. This is a bit unfortunate, because *InputBox* and *MsgBox* are very easy to use, especially for testing purposes.

The closest equivalent for Windows Store apps is the *MessageDialog* class in the *Windows.UI.Popups* namespace, which supports a variety of message types and also asynchronous operations. (For more information, search for "MessageDialog Class" online at *http://msdn.microsoft.com*.) You can also use the *Flyout* control, discussed in Chapter 9, "Exploring Windows 8.1 design features: Command bar, flyout, tiles, and touch."

Convert temperatures by using a *Do* loop

1. On the File menu, click New Project.

   The New Project dialog box opens.

2. Create a new Visual Basic Windows/Windows Forms Application project named **My Celsius Conversion**.

   The new project is created, and a blank form opens in the Designer.

   In this exercise, you'll place all the code for your program in the *Form1_Load* event handler so that Visual Basic immediately prompts you for the Fahrenheit temperature when you start the application. In a Windows Forms app, the *Form_Load* event handler is typically one of the first routines to run when the program starts. Within this routine, you'll use the *InputBox* function to request the Fahrenheit data, and you'll use the *MsgBox* function to display the converted value.

3. Double-click the form.

   The *Form1_Load* event handler appears in the Code Editor.

4. Type the following program statements in the *Form1_Load* event handler:

```
Dim fahrenTemp, celsius As Single
Dim fTempInput As String
Dim prompt As String = "Enter a Fahrenheit temperature."
Do
    fTempInput = InputBox(prompt, "Fahrenheit to Celsius")
    If IsNumeric(fTempInput) Then
        fahrenTemp = CSng(fTempInput)
        celsius = Int((fahrenTemp + 40) * 5 / 9 - 40)
        MsgBox(celsius, , "Temperature in Celsius")
```

```
        End If
Loop While fTempInput <> ""
End
```

 Tip Be sure to include the *End* statement at the bottom of the *Form1_Load* event handler. When the user has had his or her fill of converting temperatures, this is how the program terminates.

This code handles the calculations for the project. The first line declares two single-precision variables, *fahrenTemp* and *Celsius*, to hold the Fahrenheit and Celsius temperatures, respectively. The second line declares a string variable named *fTempInput* that holds a string version of the Fahrenheit temperature. The third line declares a string variable named *prompt*, which will be used in the *InputBox* function, and assigns it a value. The *Do* loop repeatedly prompts the user for a Fahrenheit temperature, converts the number to Celsius, and then displays it on the screen by using the *MsgBox* function.

The value that the user enters in the input box is stored in the *fTempInput* variable. The *InputBox* function always returns a value of type *String*, even if the user enters numbers. Because we want to perform mathematical calculations on the entered value, *fTempInput* must be converted to a number. The *IsNumeric* method, introduced here for the first time, is used to determine whether the user input can be evaluated as a number. If so, the *CSng* function is used to convert a string into the *Single* data type. *CSng* is one of many conversion functions that you can use to convert a string to a different data type. (See Chapter 11 for a listing of more functions, as well as information about conversion methods and strategies.) After the conversion, the value is stored in the *fahrenTemp* variable.

The loop executes until the user clicks the Cancel button or until the user presses Enter or clicks OK with no value in the input box. Clicking the Cancel button or entering no value returns an empty string (""). The loop checks for the empty string by using a *While* conditional test at the bottom of the loop. The program statement:

```
Celsius = Int((FTemp + 40) * 5 / 9 - 40)
```

handles the conversion from Fahrenheit to Celsius in the program. This statement employs a standard conversion formula, but it uses the *Int* function to return a value that contains no decimal places to the Celsius variable. (Everything to the right of the decimal point is discarded.) This cutting sacrifices accuracy, but it helps you avoid long, unsightly numbers such as 21.11111, the Celsius equivalent to 70 degrees Fahrenheit.

5. Click the Save All button on the Standard toolbar to save your changes. Specify the My Documents\Visual Basic 2013 SBS\Chapter 12 folder as the location.

Now you'll try running the Windows desktop app.

6. Click the Start Debugging button on the Standard toolbar.

The program starts, and the *InputBox* function prompts you for a Fahrenheit temperature.

7. Type **212**.

   Your screen looks like this:

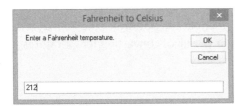

8. Click OK.

   The temperature 212 degrees Fahrenheit is converted to 100 degrees Celsius, as shown in this message box:

9. Click OK. Then type **72** in the input box, and click OK again.

   The temperature 72 degrees Fahrenheit is converted to 22 degrees Celsius.

10. Click OK, and then click Cancel in the input box.

    The program closes, and the IDE returns. You're finished working with decision structures in this chapter. You'll build on these essential techniques as you work through the book.

11. On the File menu, click Exit to exit Visual Studio.

Using the *Until* keyword in *Do* loops

The *Do* loops you've worked with so far have used the *While* keyword to execute a group of statements as long as the loop condition remains True. With Visual Basic, you can also use the *Until* keyword in *Do* loops to cycle *until* a certain condition is True. Use the *Until* keyword at the top or bottom
of a *Do* loop to test a condition, just like the *While* keyword. For example, the following *Do* loop uses
the *Until* keyword to loop repeatedly until the user enters the word *Done* in the input box:

```
Dim inputName As String = ""
Do
    inputName = InputBox("Enter your name or type Done to quit.")
    If inputName.ToUpper <> "DONE" And inputName <> "" Then
        OutputBox.Text = inputName
    End If
Loop Until inputName.ToUpper = "DONE"
```

As you can see, a loop that uses the *Until* keyword is similar to a loop that uses the *While* keyword, except that the test condition usually contains the opposite operator—in this case, the = (equal to) operator versus the <> (not equal to) operator. If using the *Until* keyword makes sense to you, feel free to use it with test conditions in your *Do* loops.

Summary

In this chapter, you explored how to use Visual Basic decision structures and loops effectively in Windows Store apps and Windows desktop apps created via the Windows Forms model. You practiced writing programs using *If...Then* and *Select Case* statements, as well as *For...Next* loops and *Do* loops.

While the syntax of these powerful Visual Basic flow control structures has not changed greatly in the last few versions of Visual Basic, the platforms and context within which you use them has changed. For this reason, you learned how to use *If...Then* with a *TextBox* and *MaskedTextBox* control in a Windows Forms app, and you learned how to use a *Select Case* statement with the *ListBox* control in a Windows Store app. You also had more practice processing data and using mathematical formulas, including routines that computed income tax, determined circumference, converted miles to kilometers, and converted Fahrenheit to Celsius.

In the next chapter, you continue working with Visual Basic language elements, focusing on trapping runtime errors using structured error-handling techniques and using *Try...Catch* code blocks.

CHAPTER 13

Trapping errors by using structured error handling

After completing this chapter, you will be able to

- Manage run-time errors and exceptions by using the *Try...Catch* error handler.

- Create an error handler that tests specific error conditions by using the *Catch* statement.

- Write complex error handlers that use the *Exception* object and the *Message* property.

- Build nested *Try...Catch* statements.

- Use error handlers in combination with defensive programming techniques.

- Leave error handlers prematurely by using the *Exit Try* statement.

Run-time errors and other program defects are a fact of life for software developers. As a Visual Basic programmer, you've undoubtedly had your share of error messages and unexpected program behaviors as you have planned and written your software. In this chapter, you'll focus on how to handle run-time errors, also referred to as *exceptions*, which occur as a result of normal operating conditions—for example, errors due to a broken Internet connection, a faulty web service, an offline printer, or a necessary image file that is missing from a DVD or flash drive. The routines that handle exceptions are called *structured error handlers* (or *structured exception handlers*), and you can use them to detect run-time errors, suppress unwanted error messages, and adjust program conditions so that your application can regain control and run again.

Visual Basic 2013 provides the powerful *Try...Catch* code block for handling errors and exceptions, a tool that has been updated to work in the multithreading, asynchronous programming environment of Windows 8.1. In this chapter, you'll learn how to trap run-time errors by using *Try...Catch* code blocks, and you'll learn how to use the *Exception* object to identify specific run-time errors. You'll learn how to use multiple *Catch* statements to write flexible error handlers, build nested *Try...Catch* code blocks, and employ the *Exit Try* statement to exit a *Try...Catch* code block prematurely. The programming techniques that you'll learn are similar to the structured error handlers provided by the most advanced programming languages, such as Java and C++. Using these skills, you will create reliable, or *robust*, Visual Basic programs that manage unforeseen circumstances and provide users with a consistent and trouble-free computing experience.

Processing errors by using the *Try...Catch* statement

A *program crash* is an unexpected problem from which a program can't recover. You might have experienced your first program crash when Visual Basic couldn't resolve a hardware problem detected in your system or when you tried a web-related operation that caused the program to stall or terminate prematurely. It's not that Visual Basic isn't smart enough to handle the glitch; it's just that the program hasn't been told what to do when something goes wrong.

Fortunately, you don't have to live with occasional errors that cause your programs to crash. You can create *structured error handlers* to manage and respond to the errors before they force the Visual Basic compiler to terminate your program. An error handler handles the run-time error by telling the program how to continue when one of its statements doesn't work. Error handlers can be placed in every event handler where there is the potential for trouble. In fact, an error handler can appear in any code module or function in a Visual Basic program.

Error handlers handle, or *trap*, a problem by using a *Try...Catch* code block and a special error-handling object named *Exception*. The *Exception* object has a *Message* property that you can use to display a description of the error. For example, if the run-time error is associated with loading a file from a flash drive that has gone missing, your error handler might display a custom error message that identifies the problem and prompts the user to insert the missing media, rather than allowing the failed operation to crash the program. Other error handlers might be more subtle, working behind the scenes (without user interaction) to retry an operation or solve a problem.

When to use error handlers

You can use error handlers in any situation where an action (either expected or unexpected) has the potential to trigger, or *throw*, an exception or produce an error that stops program execution. Typically, error handlers are used to manage error conditions related to external events—for example, exceptions caused by a failed Internet connection or web service transaction between computers, a missing flash drive or DVD, an offline printer or scanner, or a hardware problem of some sort. Table 13-1 lists potential problems that can be addressed by error handlers.

TABLE 13-1 Potential problems for error handlers

Problem	Description
Network/Internet problems	Network servers, Internet connections, web services, and other resources that fail, or *go down*, unexpectedly.
Database problems	Unable to make a database connection, a query can't be processed or times out, a database returns an error, and so on.
Drive/media problems	Unformatted or incorrectly formatted CDs, DVDs, or media that aren't properly inserted; bad sectors, CDs, DVDs, or flash drives that are full; problems with a CD or DVD drive; and so on.
File system problems	A path to a necessary file that is missing or incorrect.

Problem	Description
Printer problems	Printers that are offline, out of paper, out of memory, or otherwise unavailable.
Software not installed	A file or component that your application relies on but that is not installed on the user's computer, or an operating system incompatibility.
Security problems	An application or process that attempts to modify operating system files, use the Internet inappropriately, or modify other programs or files.
Permissions problems	User permissions that are not appropriate for performing a task.
Overflow errors	An activity that exceeds the allocated storage space.
Out-of-memory errors	Insufficient application or resource space available in the Microsoft Windows memory management scheme.
Clipboard problems	Problems with data transfer or the Windows Clipboard.
Logic errors	Syntax or logic errors undetected by the compiler and previous tests (such as an incorrectly spelled file name).

Unhandled errors or exceptions that actually cause a Visual Basic program to stop functioning are not as common as they were in earlier years, especially in the Windows Store application model, which has a little more built-in error handling than some of the earlier versions of Windows. For this reason, the sample projects in this chapter will be designed to assist Windows Forms applications that run on the Windows desktop. However, the *Try...Catch* techniques taught here are also routinely used in Windows Store programming tasks. (The syntax is the same.) Regardless of the Windows platform that you use, it is very important to take error handling seriously. Managing exceptions is not just about stopping cataclysmic program crashes but rather on setting the groundwork for a predictable computing experience that is free from distracting error messages, unanticipated delays, and confusing requests for information.

Setting the trap: the *Try...Catch* code block

To create an exception handler in code, you place the *Try* statement in a routine right before the statement you're worried about, and the *Catch* statement follows immediately with a list of the statements that you want to run if an exception actually occurs. A number of optional statements, such as *Finally*, *Exit Try*, and nested *Try...Catch* code blocks can also be included, as the examples in this chapter will demonstrate. The typical components of a *Try...Catch* exception handler are as follows:

```
Try
    Statements that might produce a run-time error
Catch
    Statements to run if a run-time error occurs
Finally
    Optional statements to run whether an error occurs or not
End Try
```

The *Try* statement identifies the beginning of an error handler in which *Try*, *Catch*, and *End Try* are the essential keywords, and *Finally* and the statements that follow are optional. Note that programmers sometimes call the statements between the *Try* and *Catch* keywords *protected code* because any run-time errors resulting from these statements won't cause the program to crash. (Instead, Visual Basic executes the error-handling statements in the *Catch* code block.)

Path name and drive errors

The following example demonstrates a common run-time error situation—a problem with a path name, flash drive, or attached peripheral device. To complete this exercise, you'll load a sample Visual Basic project for the Windows desktop that I created to show how a photograph is opened in a picture box object on a form.

To prepare for the exercise, insert a blank USB flash drive or memory stick into drive E (or equivalent), and use File Explorer to copy Road.bmp from this book's sample files to it. (I took this photograph on a recent road trip through Montana.) Alternatively, you can copy the .bmp file to a DVD or CD on drive D or to another type of removable storage media, such as a digital camera or MP3 player.

> **Note** You'll find the Road.jpg file, along with the Drive Error project, in the My Documents\Visual Basic 2013 SBS\Chapter 13 folder.

To complete the exercise, you'll need to be able to remove the flash drive or DVD as test conditions dictate, and you'll need to modify the program code with the drive letter you're using. You'll use the flash drive throughout the chapter to force run-time errors and recover from them.

Experiment with disc drive errors

1. Insert a flash drive or memory stick into the USB port on your computer, and copy the Road.jpg file to it.

    Use File Explorer or a third-party tool to copy the file to the root directory of the flash drive. Make a note of the drive letter that your system has assigned to the flash drive so that you can use it in your program code.

2. Start Visual Studio, and then open the Drive Error project, a Windows Forms application that is located in the My Documents\Visual Basic 2013 SBS\Chapter 13\Drive Error folder.

    The Drive Error project opens in the IDE.

3. If the project's form isn't visible, display it now.

    The Drive Error project is a skeleton program that displays the Road.jpg file in a picture box object when the user clicks the Check Drive button. I designed the project as a convenient way to create and trap run-time errors, and you can use it throughout this chapter to build error handlers by using the *Try...Catch* code block.

4. Double-click the Check Drive button on the form to display the *CheckButton_Click* event handler.

    You'll see the following line of program code between the *Private Sub* and *End Sub* statements:

    ```
    TestImage.Image = System.Drawing.Bitmap.FromFile("e:\road.jpg")
    ```

    In a Windows Forms program that has an active *PictureBox* control, a call to the *FromFile* method in this format will open the specified file in the picture box object. This particular call to *FromFile* opens the Road.jpg file on drive E and displays it in the picture box object on the form. However, if the flash drive is no longer in the USB port, if you are using a DVD for the file and the DVD drive door is open, or if the file is not on the flash drive or DVD at all, the statement produces a "File Not Found" error message. This is the run-time error (or exception) that we want to trap.

5. If your flash drive or attached peripheral device is using a drive letter other than E, change the drive letter in this program statement to match the letter you're using.

    For example, a DVD drive typically uses the letter *D*. USB flash drives, digital cameras, and other detachable media typically use *E*, *F*, or higher letters for the drive. It depends on what other drives you have attached or installed on your computer.

6. With your flash drive still in the USB port, click the Start Debugging button on the Standard toolbar to run the program.

    The form for the project opens, as shown here:

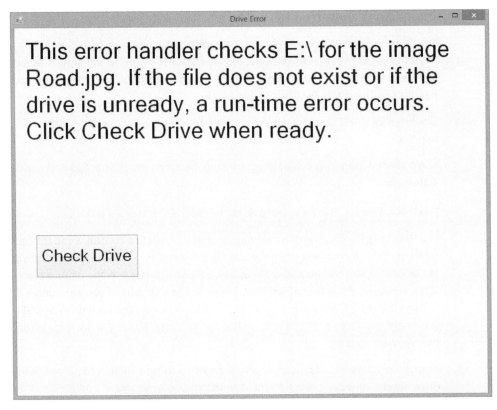

Drive Error

This error handler checks E:\ for the image Road.jpg. If the file does not exist or if the drive is unready, a run-time error occurs. Click Check Drive when ready.

Check Drive

7. Click the Check Drive button on the form.

8. The program loads the Road.jpg file from the flash drive into the picture box, as shown in the following screen shot:

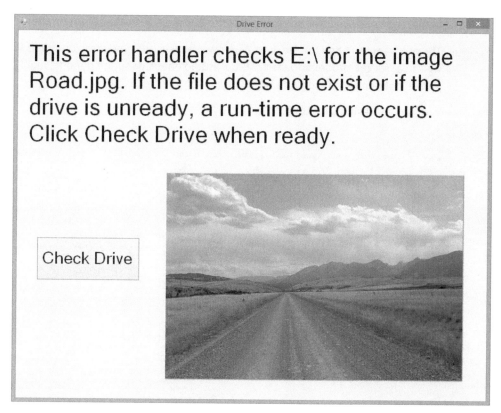

The program displays the image simply to indicate that the file-load function is working correctly. The *SizeMode* property of the picture box object is set to StretchImage, so the file fills the entire picture box.

Now see what happens when the flash drive isn't in the USB port when the program attempts to load the file.

9. Remove the flash drive from the USB port.

    If you are using a different media type, that's just fine—but remove it now.

10. In the running Drive Error program, click the Check Drive button again on the form.

The program can't find the file, and Windows issues a run-time error, or *unhandled exception*, which causes the program to crash. Visual Studio enters debugging mode, highlighting the problem statement in the Code Editor.

Your screen will look like this:

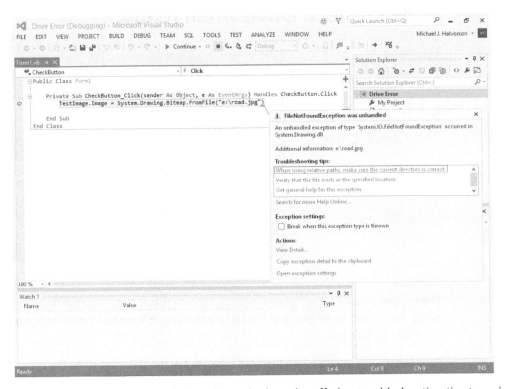

Notice how helpful Visual Studio is trying to be here, by offering troubleshooting tips to assist you in locating the source of the unhandled exception that has stopped the program. The Actions list allows you to learn even more about the specific error message that is displayed at the top of the pop-up window.

11. Click the Stop Debugging button on the Standard toolbar to close the program.

The development environment returns.

Now you'll modify the code to handle this plausible error scenario in the future, but first a word about Windows Store apps and exception handling.

Windows Store apps and built-in exception handling

The run-time error scenario that you just encountered took place in a Windows Forms (Windows desktop) app. I don't mean to pick on Windows Forms in this way, but it is easier to get a Windows desktop app to crash when loading images than it is to disable a Windows Store app. This is the case for two reasons. First, in a Windows Store app, it is customary for the images to travel with the application. Photos and other resources are placed in the project's Assets folder before they are loaded into controls. Using the Assets folder is especially important because Windows Store apps are downloaded from the Windows Store online and need to be ready for a variety of operating conditions and user scenarios. Microsoft hopes to protect apps from direct file operations in the local system as much as possible, allowing files to be loaded from the hard drive or attached media only through tools such as the File Picker. As a result, the process for loading images in a Windows Store app is a bit more involved (and safe) than doing a direct file load via a Windows Forms method like *System.Drawing.Bitmap.FromFile*.

Second, the process for loading images into a XAML *Image* control under Windows 8.1 involves using the *UriSource* and *Source* properties, which provide a little more exception handling than what you get from the *PictureBox* control in Windows Forms. If the image file being loaded into the XAML *Image* control cannot be located, the exception is handled so that there is not a program-terminating crash. Of course, this might still mean that in the Windows Store app the user will not actually see the missing image with the invalid path name—it might be that nothing appears and the program keeps on running.

If you are curious, here is the code that you would use to load the Road.jpg photo from the Assets folder in a Windows Store app into an *Image* control named *TestImage*:

```
Dim bm As BitmapImage = New BitmapImage
Bm.UriSource = New Uri("ms-appx:/Assets/Road.jpg", UriKind.Absolute)
TestImage.Source = bm
```

OK. So this process is a little more involved than using the simple *System.Drawing.Bitmap.FromFile* method that we employed in the Drive Error program to load an image. The steps here are to declare a variable of type *BitmapImage*, to build an absolute path name to the resource using the *UriSource* property, and then to locate the image in the project's Assets folder by using the string "ms-appx:/ Assets/Road.jpg". However, this code works perfectly well in a Windows Store app that has an *Image* control on the page. The only thing that you need to do before you run the program is to add the Road.jpg image to the project's Assets folder by using Visual Studio's Solution Explorer tool.

Because I wanted you to experience the hard crash that can happen when a Visual Basic program abruptly terminates, I have used the simpler Windows Forms example to help you practice your error handling skills. But the *Try...Catch* code block and basic exception handling method work the same in either a Windows Forms or a Windows Store app. Although the control names and methods are slightly different, the core Visual Basic coding skills pertaining to exception handling are the same.

Writing a flash drive error handler

The problem with the Drive Error program isn't that it somehow defies the inherent capabilities of Visual Basic to process errors. We just haven't specified what Visual Basic should do when it encounters an exception that it doesn't know how to handle. The solution to this problem is to write a *Try...Catch* code block that recognizes the error and tells Visual Basic what to do about it. You'll add this error handler now.

> **Note** Beginning with this exercise, I have saved the changes made to the Drive Error skeleton program in the Drive Handler project, which is located in the My Documents\ Visual Basic 2013 SBS\Chapter 13\Drive Handler folder. You'll see that name in the screen shots that follow. However, you can continue using the Drive Error program, adding error-handling code to it as directed. If you open up the Drive Handler project that I created, you'll see the results of all the step by step exercises in the chapter.

Use *Try...Catch* to trap the error

1. Display the *CheckButton_Click* event handler if it isn't visible in the Code Editor.

    You need to add an error handler to the event handler that's causing the problem. As you'll see in this example, you actually create the *Try...Catch* code block around the code that represents the potential source of trouble, protecting the rest of the program from the exception that it might produce.

2. Modify the event handler so that the existing *FromFile* statement fits between *Try* and *Catch* statements, as shown in the following code block:

```
Try
    TestImage.Image = System.Drawing.Bitmap.FromFile("e:\road.jpg")
Catch
    MsgBox("Please insert the flash drive in drive E!")
End Try
```

    You don't need to retype the *FromFile* statement—just type the *Try, Catch, MsgBox,* and *End Try* statements above and below it. If Visual Studio adds *Catch,* a variable declaration, or the *End Try* statement in the wrong place, simply delete the statements and retype them as shown in the book. (The Code Editor tries to be helpful, but sometimes Visual Studio's Auto Complete feature gets in the way.)

    This program code demonstrates the most basic use of a *Try...Catch* code block. It places the problematic *FromFile* statement in a *Try* code block so that if the program code produces an error, the statements in the *Catch* code block are executed. The *Catch* code block simply displays a message box asking the user to insert the required media in drive E so that the program can continue. This *Try...Catch* code block contains no *Finally* statement, so the error handler ends with the keywords *End Try.*

Again, if you are using a removable storage device or media associated with a different drive letter, you would make those changes in the statements that you just typed.

Test the error handler

1. Remove the flash drive from drive E if you did not do so in the preceding exercise, and then click the Start Debugging button to run the program.

2. Click the Check Drive button.

   Instead of stopping program execution, Visual Basic invokes the *Catch* statement, which displays the following message box:

3. Click OK, and then click the Check Drive button again.

   The program displays the message box again, asking you to insert the flash drive in drive E. Each time there's a problem loading the file, this message box appears.

4. Insert the flash drive in the USB port (drive E), wait a moment for the system to recognize the USB device (close any windows that appear when you insert the flash drive), click OK, and then click the Check Drive button again.

   The photograph appears in the picture box, as expected. The error handler has completed its work effectively—rather than the program crashing inadvertently, it's told you how to correct your mistake, and you can continue working with the application.

5. Click the Close button on the form to stop the program.

   It's time to learn some of the variations of the *Try...Catch* error handler.

Using the *Finally* clause to perform cleanup tasks

As with the syntax description for *Try...Catch* noted earlier in the chapter, you can use the optional *Finally* clause with *Try...Catch* to execute a block of statements regardless of how the application executes the *Try* or *Catch* blocks. That is, whether or not the *Try* statements produced a run-time error, there might be some code that you need to run each time an error handler is finished. For example, you might want to update variables or properties, display the results of a computation, close database connections, or perform cleanup operations by clearing variables or disabling unneeded objects on a form or on the page.

The following exercise demonstrates how the *Finally* clause works, by displaying a second message box whether or not the *FromFile* method produces a run-time error.

Use *Finally* to display a message box

1. Display the *CheckButton_Click* event handler, and then edit the *Try...Catch* code block so that it contains two additional lines of code above the *End Try* statement. The complete error handler should look like this:

```
Try
    TestImage.Image = System.Drawing.Bitmap.FromFile("e:\Road.jpg")
Catch
    MsgBox("Please insert the flash drive in drive E!")
Finally
    MsgBox("Error handler complete")
End Try
```

The *Finally* statement indicates to the compiler that a final block of code should be executed whether or not a run-time error is processed. To help you learn exactly how this feature works, I've inserted a *MsgBox* function to display a test message after the *Finally* statement. Although this simple use of the *Finally* statement is helpful for testing purposes, in a real program you'll probably want to use the *Finally* code block to update important variables or properties, display data, or perform other cleanup operations.

2. Remove the flash drive from drive E, and then click the Start Debugging button to run the program.

3. Click the Check Drive button.

The error handler displays a dialog box asking you to insert the flash drive in drive E.

4. Click OK.

The program executes the *Finally* clause in the error handler, and the following message box appears:

5. Click OK, insert the flash drive in drive E, and then click the Check Drive button again.

The file appears in the picture box as expected. In addition, the *Finally* clause is executed, and the Error Handler Complete message box appears again. As I noted earlier, *Finally* statements are executed at the end of a *Try...Catch* block whether or not there's an error.

6. Click OK, and then click the Close button on the form to terminate the program.

More complex *Try...Catch* error handlers

As your programs become more sophisticated, you might find it useful to write more complex *Try...Catch* error handlers that manage a variety of run-time errors and unusual error-handling situations. *Try...Catch* provides for this complexity by doing the following:

- Permitting multiple lines of code in each *Try, Catch*, or *Finally* code block.

- Using the *Catch* statement with particular *Exception* objects, which tests specific error conditions.

- Allowing nested *Try...Catch* code blocks, which can be used to build sophisticated and robust error handlers.

In addition, by using a special error-handling object named *Exception*, you can identify and process specific run-time errors and exceptions in your program. You'll investigate each of these error-handling features in the following section.

The *Exception* object

The Microsoft .NET Framework includes the *Exception* object to help you learn about the errors that occur in your programs. *Exception* provides you with information about the exception that occurred so that you can respond to it programmatically. The most useful *Exception* property is the *Message* property, which contains a short message about the error.

There are several different types of *Exception* objects. Table 13-2 provides a list of important *Exception* objects and what they mean.

TABLE 13-2 Important exception objects

Exception	Description
ArgumentException	Occurs when an argument passed to a method is not valid.
ArgumentOutOfRangeException	Occurs when an argument is passed to a method that is outside the allowable range.
ArithmeticException	Occurs when there is an arithmetic-related error.
DataException	Occurs when there is an error when accessing data by using ADO.NET.
DirectoryNotFoundException	Occurs when a folder can't be found.
DivideByZeroException	Occurs when an attempt is made to divide by zero.
EndOfStreamException	Occurs when an attempt is made to read past the end of a stream.
Exception	Occurs for any exception that is thrown. Other exceptions inherit from this object.
FileNotFoundException	Occurs when a file can't be found.
IndexOutOfRangeException	Occurs when an index is used that is outside the allowable range of an array.

Exception	Description
IOException	Occurs when there is an input/output error.
OutOfMemoryException	Occurs when there isn't enough memory.
OverflowException	Occurs when an arithmetic-related operation results in an overflow.
SecurityException	Occurs when there is a security-related error.
SqlException	Occurs when there is an error when accessing data in Microsoft SQL Server.
UnauthorizedAccessException	Occurs when the operation denies access.

So how do you know which exception types to use? That depends on your code. For example, in the exercise that we are working on, you have been using the *System.Drawing.Bitmap.FromFile* method. If you open the MSDN online documentation for *FromFile*, you will see an "Exceptions" section.

 Tip To quickly open up the MSDN documentation for *FromFile*, put your cursor in the *FromFile* text in Visual Studio and then press the F1 key. From here, click the "Image. FromFile Method (String)" topic.

The "Exceptions" section in the "Image.FromFile Method (String)" topic lists the following exceptions:

- *ArgumentException*

- *FileNotFoundException*

- *OutOfMemoryException*

With this information in hand, you can write code to handle common exceptions that take place when a programmer uses *FromFile*. As you write more code, you will discover additional *Exception* objects, and you can also learn about them by using the MSDN documentation. Even though there are many different *Exception* objects, you will use them in the same way described here and demonstrated in the following exercise, which uses two of the *Exception* objects above in a *Try...Catch* error handler to test for more than one run-time error condition.

Test for multiple run-time error conditions

1. In the *Button1_Click* event handler, edit the *Try...Catch* error handler so that it looks like the following code block. (The original *FromFile* statement is the same as the code you used in the previous exercises, but the *Catch* statements are all new.)

```
Try
    TestImage.Image = System.Drawing.Bitmap.FromFile("e:\road.jpg")
Catch ex As System.IO.FileNotFoundException 'if File Not Found error
    MsgBox("Check pathname and flash drive")
Catch ex As OutOfMemoryException 'if Out Of Memory error
    MsgBox("Is this really a photograph?", , ex.Message)
```

```
Catch ex As Exception
    MsgBox("Problem loading file", , ex.Message)
End Try
```

This code has three *Catch* statements. If the *FileNotFoundException* occurs during the file open procedure, the message Check Pathname And Disc Drive is displayed in a message box. If the *OutOfMemoryException* occurs—probably the result of loading a file that doesn't actually contain artwork—the message Is This Really A Photograph? is displayed. (I get this error if I accidentally try to open a Microsoft Word document in a picture box object by using the *FromFile* method.)

The final *Catch* statement handles all other run-time errors that could potentially occur during a file-opening process—it's a general catchall code block that prints a general error message inside a message box and a specific error message from the *Message* property in the title bar of the message box.

2. Click the Start Debugging button to run the program.

3. Remove the flash drive from the USB port (drive E).

4. Click the Check Drive button.

   The error handler displays the error message Check Pathname And Flash Drive in a message box. The first *Catch* statement works.

5. Click OK, and then click the Close button on the form to end the program.

6. Insert the flash drive again, and then use File Explorer or another tool to copy a second file to the flash drive that isn't an artwork file. For example, copy a Word document or a Microsoft Excel spreadsheet to the USB device.

   You won't open this file in Word or Excel, but you will try to open it (unsuccessfully, we hope) in your program's picture box object.

7. In the Code Editor, change the name of the Road.jpg file in the *FromFile* program statement to the name of the file (Word, Excel, or other) you copied to the flash drive in drive E.

   Using a file with a different format gives you an opportunity to test a second type of run-time error—an Out Of Memory exception, which occurs when Visual Basic attempts to load a file that isn't a photo or has too much information for a picture box.

8. Run the program again, and then click the Check Drive button.

   The error handler displays the following error message:

Notice that I have used the *Message* property to display a short description of the problem (Out Of Memory.) in the message box title bar. Using this property in your error handler can give the user a clearer idea of what has happened.

9. Click OK, and then click the Close button on the form to stop the program.

10. Change the file name back to Road.jpg in the *FromFile* method. (You'll use it in the next exercise.)

The *Catch* statement is very powerful. By using *Catch* in combination with the *Exception* object and *Message* property, you can write sophisticated error handlers that recognize and respond to several types of exceptions.

Raising your own errors

For testing purposes and other specialized uses, you can artificially generate your own run-time errors in a program with a technique called *throwing*, or *raising*, exceptions. To accomplish this, you use the *Throw* statement. For example, the following syntax uses the *Throw* statement to produce an exception and then handles the exception by using a *Catch* statement:

```
Try
    Throw New Exception("There was a problem")
Catch ex As Exception
    MsgBox(ex.Message)
End Try
```

When you learn how to write your own procedures, you can generate your own errors by using this technique and return them to the calling routine.

Specifying a retry period

Another strategy that you can use in an error handler is to try an operation a few times and then disable it if the problem isn't resolved. For example, in the following exercise, a *Try...Catch* block employs a counter variable named *Retries* to track the number of times the message Please Insert The Flash Drive In Drive E! is displayed, and after the second time, the error handler disables the Check Drive button. The trick to this technique is declaring the *Retries* variable at the top of the form's program code so that it has scope throughout all the form's event handlers. The *Retries* variable is then incremented and tested in the *Catch* code block. The number of retries can be modified by simply changing the "2" in the statement, as shown here:

```
If Retries <= 2
```

Use a variable to track run-time errors

1. In the Code Editor, scroll to the top of the form's program code, and directly below the *Public Class Form1* statement, type the following variable declaration:

    ```
    Dim Retries As Short = 0
    ```

    Retries is declared as a *Short* integer variable because it won't contain very big numbers. It's assigned an initial value of 0 so that it resets properly each time the program runs.

2. In the *CheckButton_Click* event handler, edit the *Try...Catch* error handler so that it looks like the following code block:

    ```
    Try
        TestImage.Image = System.Drawing.Bitmap.FromFile("e:\Road.jpg")
    Catch
        Retries += 1
        If Retries <= 2 Then
            MsgBox("Please insert the flash drive in drive E!")
        Else
            MsgBox("File Load feature disabled")
            CheckButton.Enabled = False
        End If
    End Try
    ```

    The *Try* block tests the same file-opening procedure, but this time, if an error occurs, the *Catch* block increments the *Retries* variable and tests the variable to be sure that it's less than or equal to 2. The number 2 can be changed to allow any number of retries—currently it allows only two run-time errors. After two errors, the *Else* clause is executed, and a message box appears indicating that the file-loading feature has been disabled. The Check Drive button is then disabled— that is, dimmed and rendered unusable for the remainder of the program.

3. Click the Start Debugging button to run the program.

4. Remove the flash drive from drive E.

5. Click the Check Drive button.

    The error handler displays the error message Please Insert The Flash Drive In Drive E! in a message box, as shown here. Behind the scenes, the *Retries* variable is also incremented to 1.

6. Click OK, and then click the Check Drive button again.

    The *Retries* variable is set to 2, and the message Please Insert The Flash Drive In Drive E! appears again.

7. Click OK, and then click the Check Drive button a third time.

   The *Retries* variable is incremented to 3, and the *Else* clause is executed. The message File Load Feature Disabled appears, as shown here:

8. Click OK in the message box.

   The Check Drive button is disabled on the form, as shown in the following illustration. Admittedly, the dimmed state of the button is a little subtle, but you'll see that the button does not work when you try to click it.

   The error handler has responded to the file load problem by allowing the user a few tries to fix the exception, and then it has disabled the misbehaving feature. (That is, the user can no longer click the button.) This disabling action stops future exceptions, although the program now does not function exactly as it was originally designed.

9. Click the Close button on the form to stop the program.

Using nested *Try...Catch* blocks

You can also use nested *Try...Catch* code blocks in your error handlers. For example, the following drive error handler uses a second *Try...Catch* block to retry the file open operation a single time if the first attempt fails and generates a run-time error:

```
Try
    TestImage.Image = System.Drawing.Bitmap.FromFile("e:\road.jpg")
Catch
    MsgBox("Insert the flash drive in drive E, then click OK!")
    Try
        TestImage.Image = System.Drawing.Bitmap.FromFile("e:\road.jpg")
    Catch
        MsgBox("File Load feature disabled")
        CheckButton.Enabled = False
    End Try
End Try
```

If the user inserts the flash drive into drive E as a result of the message prompt, the second *Try* block opens the file without error. However, if a file-related exception still appears, the second *Catch* block displays a message saying that the file load feature is being disabled, and the button is disabled.

In general, nested *Try...Catch* error handlers work well as long as you don't have too many tests or retries to manage. If you do need to retry a problematic operation many times, use a variable to track your retries, or develop a function containing an error handler that can be called repeatedly from your event handlers. (For example, you might locate it in a code module.)

Comparing error handlers with defensive programming techniques

Error handlers aren't the only mechanism for protecting a program against run-time errors. For example, the following program code uses the *File.Exists* method in the *System.IO* namespace of the .NET Framework to check whether a file exists on the flash drive in drive E before it's opened:

```
If File.Exists("e:\Road.jpg") Then
    TestImage.Image = System.Drawing.Bitmap.FromFile("e:\road.jpg")
Else
    MsgBox("Cannot find Road.jpg on drive E")
End If
```

This *If...Then* statement isn't an actual error handler because it doesn't prevent a run-time error from halting a program. Instead, it's a validation technique that some programmers call *defensive programming*. It uses a handy method in the .NET Framework class library to verify the intended file operation *before* it's actually attempted in the program code. And in this particular case, testing to see whether the file exists with the .NET Framework method is actually faster than waiting for Visual Basic to throw an exception and recover from a run-time error using an error handler. However, you might note that a few file-related errors could still potentially occur during the call to the *Bitmap.FromFile* function, such as an error related to file access permission.

Note To get the preceding program logic to work, the following statement must be included in the declarations section at the very top of the page or form's program code to make reference to the .NET Framework class library that's being invoked:

```
Imports System.IO
```

When should you use defensive programming techniques, and when should you use structured error handlers? The answer is that you should use a combination of defensive programming and structured error-handling techniques in your code. Defensive programming logic is usually the most efficient way to manage potential problems. As I mentioned earlier when discussing the *If...Then* code block, the *File.Exists* method is actually faster than using a *Try...Catch* error handler, so it also makes sense to use a defensive programming technique if performance issues are involved.

You should use defensive programming logic for errors that you expect to occur frequently in your program. Use structured error handlers for errors that you don't expect to occur very often. Structured error handlers are essential if you have more than one condition to test and if you want to provide the user with numerous options for responding to the exception. Structured error handlers also allow you to gracefully handle exceptions that you aren't even aware of.

The *Exit Try* statement

You've established a good foundation for error handling in this chapter. Now it is time to put them to work in your own applications. But before you move on, here is one more syntax option for *Try...Catch* code blocks that you might find useful: the *Exit Try* statement. *Exit Try* is a quick (although slightly abrupt) technique for exiting a *Try...Catch* code block prematurely. In this way *Exit Try* is similar to the *Exit For* statement that you learned about in Chapter 12, "Creative decision structures and loops," which allows you to leave a loop early.

Using the *Exit Try* syntax, you can jump completely out of the current *Try* or *Catch* code block. If there's a *Finally* code block, this code will be executed, but *Exit Try* lets you jump over any remaining *Try* or *Catch* statements that you don't want to execute.

The following sample routine shows how the *Exit Try* statement would work in the Windows desktop app that we have been experimenting with in this chapter. It first checks to see whether the *Enabled* property of the *TestImage* object is set to False, a flag that might indicate that the picture box isn't ready to receive input. If the picture box isn't yet enabled, the *Exit Try* statement skips to the end of the *Catch* code block, and the file load operation isn't attempted.

```
Try
    If TestImage.Enabled = False Then Exit Try
    TestImage.Image = System.Drawing.Bitmap.FromFile("e:\road.jpg")
Catch
    Retries += 1
    If Retries <= 2 Then
        MsgBox("Please insert the flash drive in drive E!")
    Else
        MsgBox("File Load feature disabled")
        CheckButton.Enabled = False
    End If
End Try
```

The example builds on the last error handler that you experimented with in this chapter. If you'd like to test the *Exit Try* statement, open the Code Editor in the Drive Handler project and enter the *If* statement that contains the *Exit Try* statement. You'll also need to use the Properties window to disable the picture box object on the form (that is, to set its *Enabled* property to False) before you run the app.

Summary

Congratulations! You've added the construction of error handlers to your set of fundamental programming techniques in Visual Basic. You learned how to manage run-time errors (or exceptions) using the *Try...Catch* error handler and how to use the *Exception* object and its *Message* property. In addition, you've learned how to build nested *Try...Catch* statements and use error handlers in combination with defensive programming techniques.

The error handling techniques that you've learned will apply equally to Windows Forms (Windows desktop) and Windows Store applications. The *Try...Catch* code block syntax is the same in both Windows platforms. As you move between the two environments, you'll simply find that the exception names are different from platform to platform. In addition, the controls and objects that you use in your apps are slightly different, so the types of exceptions that occur can have different characteristics.

In the next chapter, you'll return to data management issues, and you will learn more about using arrays and collections to handle different types of information, including collections provided by the .NET Framework. You'll also create a Windows Store app that tracks and sorts names by using a generic collection class.

CHAPTER 14

Using arrays, collections, and generics to manage data

After completing this chapter, you will be able to

- Manage data in arrays of variables.

- Reorder arrays using the *Array* class's *Sort* and *Reverse* methods.

- Use the *ProgressBar* control in a Windows Forms app to graphically depict how long a task is taking.

- Create your own collections to manage names, addresses, dates, and numeric values.

- Use a *For Each...Next* loop to cycle through collection members.

- Use generic collections in the .NET Framework to create strongly typed structures such as lists, queues, and hash tables.

Managing information in a Microsoft Visual Basic application is a very important task. As your programs become more substantial and information-rich, you'll need additional tools to store and process data. The most comprehensive approach to storing and retrieving large amounts of data is using databases and XML files, which you'll learn about later in the book. However, before you get there, there are some fundamental data-management techniques to learn.

In this chapter, you'll explore Visual Basic's core features related to arrays and collections. You'll learn how arrays are created and used, and you'll practice using arrays to store different types of data. You'll also learn how to redimension arrays and preserve the data in arrays when you decide to change an array's size. To demonstrate how large arrays can be processed, you'll use the *Sort* and *Reverse* methods in the Microsoft .NET Framework's *Array* class.

Sometimes, processing large arrays can take a little time. To help you manage the user's expectations in a Windows Forms app, you'll learn to use the *ProgressBar* control to give users an indication of how long a task is taking. You'll also learn how to create collections in a Windows Store app to store information and how to use generic collections to manage lists containing strongly typed values. Finally, you'll learn how to use a *For Each...Next* loop to work with the item in a collection. The techniques that you study will provide a solid introduction to LINQ and the data management concepts that you'll investigate later in the book.

Working with arrays of variables

In this section, you'll learn about arrays, an essential tool for storing lists of data during program execution. Arrays expand on the concept of variables by assigning a name to an entire set of values that are stored in-memory while a program runs. The developers of C, Pascal, BASIC, and other popular programming languages incorporated arrays into the earliest versions of these products to refer to a group of values by using one name and to reference the values individually or collectively.

Arrays can help you track related sets of values in ways that are impractical using traditional variables. For example, imagine creating a nine-inning baseball scoreboard in a program. To save and recall the scores for each inning of the game, you might be tempted to create two groups of 9 variables (a total of 18 variables) in the program. You'd probably name them something like *Inning1HomeTeam, Inning1VisitingTeam,* and so on, to keep them straight. Working with these variables individually would take considerable time and space in your program. But Visual Basic allows you to organize groups of similar variables into an array that has one common name and an easy-to-use index for referencing the items. For example, you can create a two-dimensional array (two units high by nine units wide) named *Scoreboard* to contain the scores for the baseball game. Let's review this fundamental concept and see how arrays can be put to use in a Windows-based application.

Creating an array

You create, or *declare*, arrays in program code just as you declare simple variables. As usual, the place in which you declare the array determines where it can be used, or its *scope*, as follows:

- If you declare an array locally in a routine, you can use it only in that routine.

- If you declare an array near the top of a class, you can use the array throughout the page or form.

- If you declare an array publicly in a code module, you can use it anywhere in the project.

When you declare an array, you typically include the information shown in Table 14-1 in your declaration statement.

TABLE 14-1 Syntax elements for an array declaration

Syntax elements in array declaration	Description
Array name	The name you'll use to represent your array in the program. In general, array names follow the same rules as variable names. (See Chapter 11, "Mastering data types, operators, and string processing," for more information about variables.)
Data type	The type of data you'll store in the array. In most cases, all the variables in an array are the same type. You can specify one of the fundamental data types, one of your own custom types, or if you're not yet sure which type of data will be stored in the array or whether you'll store more than one type, you can specify the *Object* type.

Syntax elements in array declaration	Description
Number of dimensions	The number of dimensions that your array will contain. Most arrays are one-dimensional (a list of values) or two-dimensional (a table of values), but you can specify additional dimensions if you're working with a complex mathematical model, such as a three-dimensional shape. The number of dimensions in an array is sometimes called the array's *rank*.
Number of elements	The number of elements that your array will contain. The elements in your array correspond directly to the array index, and each dimension includes its own number of elements. The first array index is always 0 (zero).

Note In Visual Basic 6 and earlier versions of Visual Basic, there was a technical difference between *fixed-size arrays*, which could hold a set number of elements, and *dynamic arrays*, which could resized during the execution of a program. However, in Visual Basic .NET, there is just one type of array (the resizable kind). The only real distinction is the timing that you choose to declare the number of elements. I'll discuss this distinction in the following sections.

Declaring an array with set elements

The basic syntax for an array with the number of elements set in advance is as follows:

```
Dim ArrayName(Dim1Index, Dim2Index, ...) As DataType
```

The following arguments are important:

- *Dim* is the keyword that declares the array. Use *Public* or other access modifier keywords instead if you place the array in a code module.

- *ArrayName* is the variable name of the array.

- *Dim1Index* is the upper bound of the first dimension of the array, which is the number of elements minus 1. (Specifying the number of elements is optional, but it is required if you want to set the number of elements during the declaration.)

- *Dim2Index* is the upper bound of the second dimension of the array, which is the number of elements minus 1. (Additional dimensions can be included if they're separated by commas.) Again, specifying the number of elements is optional.

- *DataType* is the corresponding data type that will be included in the array.

For example, to declare a one-dimensional string array named *Employees* that has room for 10 employee names (numbered 0 through 9), you can type the following in an event handler:

```
Dim Employees(9) As String
```

In a code module, the same array declaration looks like this when the *Public* keyword is used:

```
Public Employees(9) As String
```

You can also explicitly specify the lower bound of the array as zero by using the following code in an event handler:

```
Dim Employees(0 To 9) As String
```

This "0 to 9" syntax is included to make your code more readable—newcomers to your program will understand immediately that the *Employees* array has 10 elements numbered 0 through 9. However, the lower bound of the array must always be zero. You cannot use this syntax to create a different lower bound for the array.

Setting aside memory

When you create an array, Visual Basic sets aside room for it in memory. The following illustration shows conceptually how the 10-element *Employees* array is organized. The elements are numbered 0 through 9 rather than 1 through 10 because array indexes always start with 0.

Employees

To declare a two-dimensional array named *Scoreboard* that has room for two rows and nine columns of *Short* integer data, you can type the following statement in an event handler or at the top of the page or form:

```
Dim Scoreboard(1, 8) As Short
```

Using the syntax that emphasizes the lower (zero) bound, you can also declare the array as follows:

```
Dim Scoreboard(0 To 1, 0 To 8) As Short
```

After you declare such a two-dimensional array and Visual Basic sets aside room for it in memory, you can use the array in your program as if it were a table of values, as shown in the following illustration. (In this case, the array elements are numbered 0 through 1 and 0 through 8.)

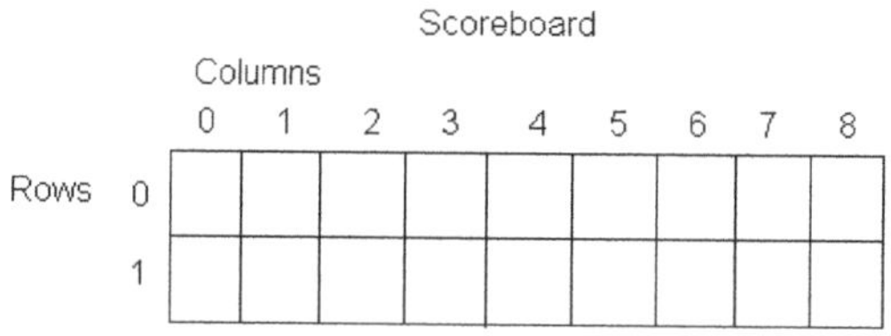

Working with array elements

To refer to an element of an array, you use the array name and an array index enclosed in parentheses. The index must be an integer or an expression that results in an integer. For example, the index could be a number such as 5, an integer variable such as *num*, or an expression such as *num-1*. (The counter variable of a *For...Next* loop is often used.) For example, the following statement assigns the value "Leslie" to the element with an index of 5—the sixth element—in the *Employees* array example in the previous section:

```
Employees(5) = "Leslie"
```

This statement produces the following result in our *Employees* array:

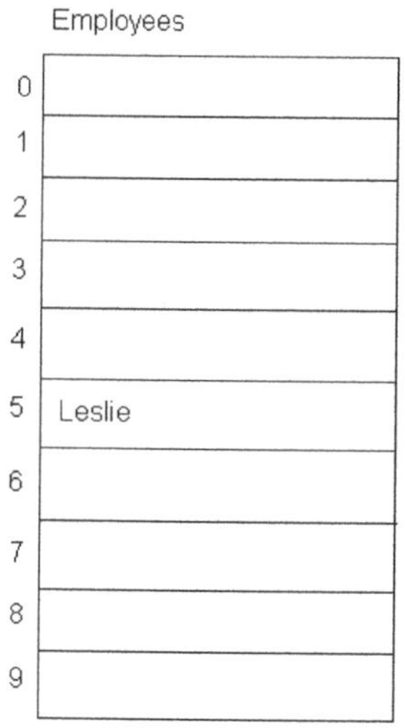

Similarly, the following statement assigns the number 4 to row 0, column 2 (the top of the third inning) in the *Scoreboard* array example in the previous section:

```
Scoreboard(0, 2) = 4
```

This statement produces the following result in our *Scoreboard* array:

```
                        Scoreboard
            Columns
                0   1   2   3   4   5   6   7   8
    Rows   0  [   ][   ][ 4 ][   ][   ][   ][   ][   ][   ]
           1  [   ][   ][   ][   ][   ][   ][   ][   ][   ]
```

You can use these indexing techniques to assign any array element.

Declaring an array and assigning initial values

It is also common for programmers to declare an array, set the number of elements, and assign the array initial values at the same time. This statement syntax is somewhat parallel to what you learned about assigning an initial value to a variable at the moment of declaration, and it is useful when you know in advance just how large an array needs to be and what its contents are.

To create an array in this way, you use what is known as an *array literal*. An array literal consists of a list of comma-separated values that are enclosed in braces ({}). When using this syntax, you can either supply the array type or let Visual Basic use *type inference* to determine what type the array should be. For example, to declare a one-dimensional array named *Musicians* of type *String* and fill it with six names, you would use the following syntax:

```
Dim Musicians() As String = {"Greg", "George", "Steve", "Eric", "Steve", "Mike"}
```

Note that the size of this array is determined automatically by Visual Basic when *Musicians* is declared. In addition, if you don't indicate an array data type, Visual Basic will use type inference to determine the right array data type for you. Obviously if all the values are the same type, it should be clear to the compiler what data type should be used for the array. But if there is a mixture of types, such as an assortment of integer, single, and double-precision numbers, Microsoft Visual Studio will pick a data type for the array that is large enough to accommodate all the values. In many cases, this will be the data type *Object* because *Object* variables (and arrays) are specifically designed to hold any type of data.

The following statement declares an array named *Investments* and uses an array literal to add four values to the array when it is created. Because no type is specified, Visual Basic evaluates the array elements and determines that in this case, the *Object* type is most appropriate.

```
Dim Investments() = {5000, 20350.50, 499.99, 10000}
```

Note If the compiler's *Option Infer* setting is set to On (or the *Option Infer On* statement is used in Visual Basic code), the *Double* type will be specified when the preceding statement is executed. See Chapter 2, "The Visual Studio Integrated Development Environment," for help adjusting this setting.

A multidimensional array can also be declared using array literals, although you need to list the elements in the proper order (that is, row 0 first, then row 1, row 2, and so on). For example, the following statement declares a two-dimensional array named *Box* and assigns four values to the array:

```
Dim Box = {{10, 20}, {50, 60}}
```

This array has two rows and two columns. Array element (0, 0)—that is, row 0, column 0—now contains a value of 10, and element (0, 1)—that is, row 0, column 1—now contains a value of 20. Also, notice that there are three sets of braces used in the declaration; these braces clarify which elements are being assigned and keep them in the proper order.

The following screen shot shows the Visual Studio Code Editor with the three examples of array literal declarations that I have shown in this section. Notice that the Code Editor is in debugging mode (or break mode) and that the Watch window is visible and shows the contents of the *Musicians* array. A *For...Next* loop is also being used to display the contents of the *Musicians* array in a XAML *TextBox* object named *ArrayContentTextBox*.

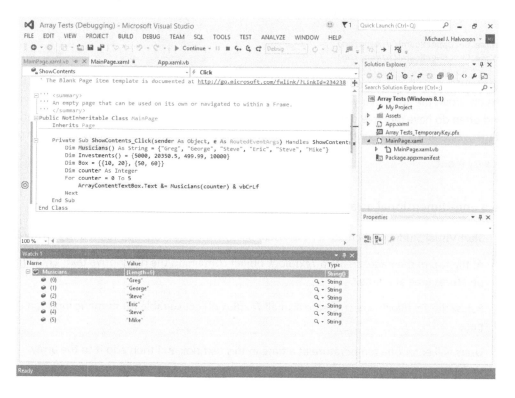

Creating an array to hold temperatures

The following exercise uses a one-dimensional array named *Temperatures* to record the daily high temperatures for a seven-day week. The Windows Store app demonstrates how you can use an array to store and process a group of related values on a page. The *Temperatures* array variable is declared at the top of the page, and then temperatures are assigned to the array by using an event handler that uses a variable named *count* for the array index. The array contents are then displayed on the page by using a *For...Next* loop and a text box object.

The *GetUpperBound* and *GetLowerBound* methods

To simplify working with the array, the Array Input program uses the *GetUpperBound* method supplied by the .NET Framework to check for the upper bound, or top index value, of the array. With *GetUpperBound*, you can process arrays without referring to the declaration statements that defined exactly how many values the array would hold.

The closely related *GetLowerBound* function, which confirms the lower index value, or lower bound, of an array, is also available to you. However, because all Visual Basic arrays have a lower bound of zero (0), the function almost always returns a value of 0. The "almost" qualification allows for the fact that the .NET Framework does technically support arrays that are not zero-based, although they are not typically used in Visual Basic. Such arrays are created with the *Array.CreateInstance* method, but the technique will not be demonstrated in this chapter.

The *GetUpperBound* and *GetLowerBound* methods have the syntax

```
ArrayName.GetUpperBound(dimension)
ArrayName.GetLowerBound(dimension)
```

where *ArrayName* is the name of an array that's been declared in the project and *dimension* is the dimension within the array that you want to determine a bounds for. (Yes, keep in mind that arrays can and often do have multiple dimensions!) When you are specifying the *dimension* argument, use an integer value and remember that the first dimension is 0, the second dimension is 1, and so on.

Let's try it out.

Use a one-dimensional array

1. Start Visual Studio, and create a new Visual Basic/Windows Store app named **My Array Input**.

2. At the top of the page, create a *TextBlock* object containing the descriptive text "Enter 7 temperatures (one at a time)".

3. Below the *TextBlock* object, create a small *TextBox* object suitable for numeric input on the page.

   Users will enter one temperature at a time in this text box and then add it to the array.

4.   Below the temperature text box, create two *Button* objects.

The first button object will add temperatures to the array. The second button object will display the entire contents of the array.

5.   Create a second (larger) *TextBox* object to the right of the objects you have created. Orient the text box vertically (with more height than width) so that it has room for a dozen rows or so of temperature data.

6.   Set the following properties for the five XAML Toolbox controls on the page:

Object	Property	Setting
TextBlock	Name	Directions
	Text	"Enter 7 temperatures (one at a time)"
	FontSize	16
TextBox	Name	TempInput
	Text	""
Button	Name	AddButton
	Content	"Add Temp to Array"
Button	Name	DisplayButton
	Content	"Display Array"
TextBox	Name	TempOutput
	Text	""

Your page should now look like this:

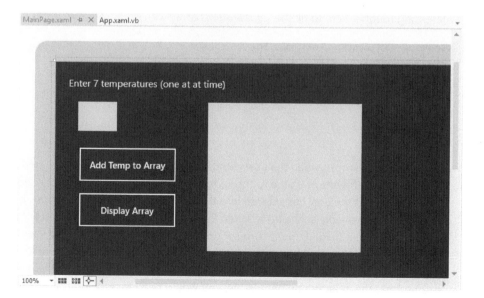

7. Double-click the *AddButton* object (the first button on the page).

8. Visual Studio creates an event handler named *AddButton_Click* and opens the MainPage.xaml. vb code-behind file in the Code Editor.

   Now you'll declare an array and a variable at the top of the page and then create the *AddButton_Click* event handler.

9. Scroll to the top of the Code Editor, and move the insertion pointer below the *Inherits Page* statement. Type the following two lines of code:

```
Dim Temperatures(0 To 6) As Single
Dim count As Short = 0
```

   The first statement creates an array named *Temperatures* (of the type *Single*) that contains seven elements numbered 0 through 6. Because the array has been declared at the top of the page, it is available for use (that is, it maintains its value) in all the event handlers in the page. A counter variable named *count* is also declared here and assigned a value of 0. (The 0 corresponds to the first element in the *Temperatures* array.) Counter variables are commonly used to step through an array. As you'll see below, another useful tactic for stepping through an array is a *For...Next* loop.

   Although this particular Visual Basic program is a Windows Store app, there is nothing unique about declaring an array in this development platform. The process is identical in a Windows Forms (Windows desktop) app or a Windows Phone app because arrays are a built-in feature of the Visual Basic language. You would just declare your array at the top of the form in a Windows Forms app, placing the declaration below the *Public Class Form1* statement.

10. Scroll back down to the *AddButton_Click* event handler in the Code Editor, and then enter the following routine there to fill the *Temperatures* array with data from the user:

```
Temperatures(count) = TempInput.Text
Directions.Text = "Enter " & _
    Temperatures.GetUpperBound(0) - count & " more temperatures"
If count = Temperatures.GetUpperBound(0) Then
    AddButton.IsEnabled = False
Else
    count = count + 1
End If
```

   This event handler runs when the user clicks the *AddButton* object. It is designed to add temperature values one at a time to the *Temperatures* array. The first line of code takes the temperature that the user has entered into the *TempInput* text box and assigns it to the array using the *count* variable as the array index. Because this variable is initialized with a value of 0 when the page is loaded, *count* corresponds to the first array index the first time the event handler is called. Note that the user can enter a temperature in Fahrenheit or Celsius and that the value can be an integer or a value with a decimal point, such as 74.5. (However, the code assumes that the input is a numeric value; you would need to add additional program logic to verify that the input is of the proper type if you are concerned that a user might intentionally try to crash the program.)

The second line of the event handler updates the text block object so that it displays the remaining number of temperatures that should be entered. This information is determined by evaluating the array with the *GetUpperBound* method, which returns the upper bound of the array. (The 0 value in parentheses after this method indicates that you are inquiring about the first dimension in the array.) The value returned by *GetUpperBound* will be 6 in this case, because the array has a lower bound of 0 and an upper bound of 6. The number of remaining temperature locations is calculated by subtracting the current array index (*count*) from the upper bound of the array. The text block is then configured with this information.

Near the bottom of the routine, the *count* variable is incremented by one in the *Else* clause of an *If...Then...Else* structure. This modification of the counter variable prepares the program to reference the next array element when the event handler is called again. However, when the array is full (when the *count* variable equals the upper bounds of the array), the *AddButton* object is disabled on the page, prohibiting additional storage. The user's only remaining option will be to display the contents of the array by using the Display Array button.

Now you need to create the program logic for the Display Array button, named *DisplayButton* in the project.

11. Display the MainPage.xaml page again in the Designer, and then double click the *DisplayButton* object on the page.

12. Visual Studio creates an event handler named *DisplayButton_Click* and opens the page's code-behind file again.

13. Type the following statements in the *DisplayButton_Click* event handler:

```
Dim i As Short
TempOutput.Text = ""
For i = 0 To Temperatures.GetUpperBound(0)
    TempOutput.Text &= Temperatures(i) & vbCrLf
Next
```

This event handler clears the *TempOutput* text box and then uses a *For...Next* loop to cycle through the elements in the array, adding each element in the array to the text box. The shortcut concatenation (&=) operator is used to combine the list of array elements with whatever is already in the text box. This means that you can click the button more than once, and each time you will see a fresh series of array values in the text box. You can examine these elements by using the direction keys, if some are not visible. As you have already seen in this book, the *vbCrLf* constant creates new lines so that the elements in the array are appropriately separated from one another.

A *For...Next* loop is a perfect tool to display the contents of an array when you know the number of elements in advance. This is because the loop's ending point can be readily set to the array's upper bound, a value that programmers can determine by using the *GetUpperBound* method.

14. Click the Save All button on the Standard toolbar to save the project. Specify the My Documents\Visual Basic 2013 SBS\Chapter 14 folder as the location.

   Now you'll run the program.

15. Click the Start button to run the Windows Store app.

16. Type the number **71** in the temperature box on the page, and then click the Add Temp To Array button.

   Your screen will look like this:

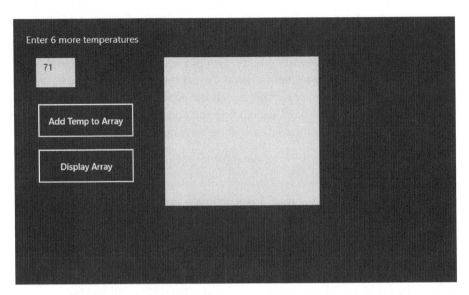

17. Replace 71 in the temperature box with the number **72**, and then click Add Temp To Array again.

18. Continue inserting temperatures in the array, using the text block at the top of the page to keep track of the remaining spaces in the *Temperatures* array.

   For testing purposes, I recommend that you use a simple series of temperature values that you can remember easily so that you can recall them when you display the array again (something like the series 71, 72, 73, 74, 75, 76, and 77). Be sure to click the Add Temp To Array button after each value.

   When you're finished with the sequence, you'll notice that the Add Temp To Array button is dimmed and no longer available. The array is full.

19. Now click Display Array to display the contents of the *Temperatures* array.

Your screen will look similar to this:

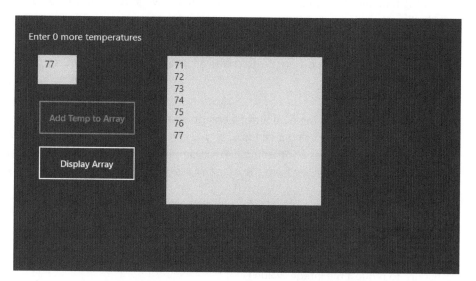

If you see these results, it means that your app has correctly stored the temperature information and that the *For...Next* loop is displaying it on the page appropriately. If you click Display Array again, the array contents will be displayed in the text box again.

Although this example didn't add more lines to the text box than could be displayed, you might want to plan for that situation. If you like, you can also add the following XAML markup to the *TempOutput* object in the XAML pane of the Designer, which will add a vertical scroll bar to the text box when the program runs:

```
ScrollViewer.VerticalScrollBarVisibility="Visible"
```

20. Close the program.

It's time to experiment with another fundamental array type.

Setting an array's size at runtime

As you have learned, arrays are well suited for managing lists of numbers, especially if you manipulate them with counter variables or a *For...Next* loop. But what if you're not sure how much array space you'll need before you run your program? For example, what if you want to let the user choose how many temperatures are entered into the Array Input program?

Visual Basic .NET arrays are designed to handle this type of computing scenario with ease. You simply leave out the size of the array when the array is declared, and then you use the *ReDim* statement to set the number of array elements when they are known at runtime. To create such an array, you would follow these basic steps:

1. Specify the name and type of the array in the program at design time, omitting the number of elements in the array. For example, to create an array named *Temperatures*, you type:

```
Dim Temperatures() As Single
```

2. Add code to determine the number of elements that should be in the array at run time. You can prompt the user by using a text box, or you can calculate the storage needs of the program by using properties or other logic. For example, the following statements in a Windows Forms app get the array size from the user and assign it to the *Days* variable of type *Short*:

```
Dim days As Short
days = InputBox("How many days?", "Create Array")
```

This logic shows off the simple but effective *InputBox* function, which is available only to Windows Forms apps. (In a Windows Store app, you would typically use a text box or App Bar feature to request the integer value.)

3. Use the integer variable in a *ReDim* statement to dimension the array, subtracting 1 because arrays in Visual Basic are zero-based. For example, the following statement sets the size of the *Temperatures* array at run time by using the *days* variable:

```
ReDim Temperatures(days - 1)
```

> **Important** With *ReDim*, you should not try to change the number of dimensions in an array that you've previously declared.

4. Use the *GetUpperBound* method to determine the upper bound in a *For...Next* loop, and process the array elements as needed. For example, you could do this:

```
For i = 0 to Temperatures.GetUpperBound(0)
    Temperatures(i) = InputBox(prompt, title)
Next
```

In the following exercise, you'll use the preceding steps to revise the Array Input program so that it can process any number of temperatures by using an array. The new program will be named Variable Elements Array, and you can load it into Visual Studio and examine it when you want to.

Use *ReDim* to change the size of an array

1. With the Array Input project still open, display the Code Editor and scroll to the top of the page where you originally declared the *Temperatures* array.

2. Remove *0 To 6* from the *Temperatures* array declaration so that the array is now resizable.

    The statement looks like the following:

    ```
    Dim Temperatures() As Single
    ```

3. Display the page in the Designer.

4. Change the *Text* property of the Directions text block to "Use Create Array text box and button to set number of array elements".

5. Click the *AddButton* object (the button containing the text Add Temp To Array), and in the Properties window, remove the check mark from the IsEnabled check box.

    You'll find this check box under the Common category if you fully expand it. By disabling this button when the program first starts, you will force the user to dimension the *Temperatures* array first. (After that step is done, the program will then reenable the button.)

6. Click the *DisplayButton* object (the button containing the text Display Array), and in the Properties window, remove the check mark from the IsEnabled check box.

    This button should also be disabled when the program first starts.

7. Create a new (small) text box object and button object on the page below the other objects in the program.

8. Name the text box *ArrayElements*, and remove the text from the text box.

    You'll use this text box to enter the number of elements that the array can hold. Because this text box is the first object on the page that you want the user to manipulate, you'll set its *TabIndex* property to 0 in the XAML markup so that the object gets the focus when the program runs. This technique, introduced in the book for the first time, is something that you can use whenever you want to draw the user's attention to an object on the page. And if you like, you can set the *TabIndex* property for other items so that they receive the focus next if the user presses the Tab key.

9. In the XAML markup for the new *ArrayElements* text box, insert the following markup:

    ```
    TabIndex="0"
    ```

10. Name the new button object that you added to the page *CreateArrayButton*, and change its *Content* property to Create Array.

Your updated page will look like this:

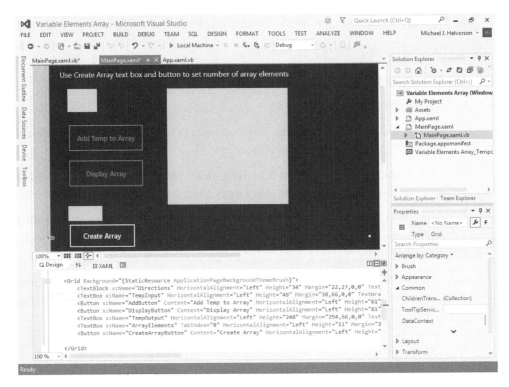

Now you'll add an event handler to redimension the *Temperatures* array.

11. Double-click the *CreateArrayButton* object in the Designer.

12. Visual Studio creates an event handler named *CreateArrayButton_Click* and opens the page's code-behind file.

13. Type the following statements in the *CreateArrayButton_Click* event handler:

```
Dim days As Short = 0
days = ArrayElements.Text
If days > 0 Then ReDim Temperatures(days - 1)
count = 0
TempOutput.Text = ""
Directions.Text = "Enter " & days & " temperatures (one at a time)"
TempInput.Focus(FocusState.Programmatic)
AddButton.IsEnabled = True
DisplayButton.IsEnabled = True
```

A new variable named *days* is declared and loaded with the number of array elements from the user's input in the *ArrayElements* text box. Then an *If...Then* decision structure is used to verify that the number of days is greater than zero. (Dimensioning an array with a number less than zero or equal to zero generates an error.) Because array index 0 is actually used to store the temperature for the first day, the *days* variable is decremented by 1 when dimensioning the array.

The count variable is then reset and the *TempOutput* text box is cleared. These actions are performed only to handle situations in which more than one array is created and filled with data in the program. An updated message is also printed in the *Directions* text box with the number of temperatures that need to be entered.

The routine then uses two new program statements, which are relatively straightforward. First, the input focus on the page is changed to the *TempInput* text box using the *Focus* method and the *FocusState.Programmatic* value. Use this technique with any XAML control on the page if you want to change the focus (that is, the insertion point or selection) to a specific item.

Next the *AddButton* and *DisplayButton* objects are enabled for input using the *IsEnabled* method. This is useful because, when the program starts, both buttons are in a disabled state. In addition, the *AddButton* object can be disabled by the *AddButton_Click* event handler.

Keep in mind that after the array is filled with data, the *CreateArrayButton_Click* event handler can redimension the array and prepare it for another round of temperatures.

Finally, it is important to note that the *AddButton_Click* and *DisplayArray_Click* event handlers that you built for the Fixed Array Temps program will run unmodified in this updated program. You have simply added a new text box and button to redimension the array. The features that add information to the array and change it work fine as they are.

14. Save your changes to disk.

The revised project is named Variable Elements Array in the My Documents\Visual Basic 2013 SBS\Chapter 14 folder.

15. Click the Start Debugging button to run the program.

The program runs, and this time the *AddButton* and *DisplayButton* objects are disabled.

16. Type the number **5** in the second text box to indicate that you plan to enter temperatures for five days.

17. Click the Create Array button.

18. Enter five temperatures, one by one, into the top text box. Click Add Temp To Array once for each new temperature.

This time you might try values with decimal places, such as **70.5**, **71**, **72.5**, **73**, and **73.5**.

19. When you've finished entering temperatures, click Display Array.

The program displays the five temperatures on the page. Your screen looks similar to the following illustration:

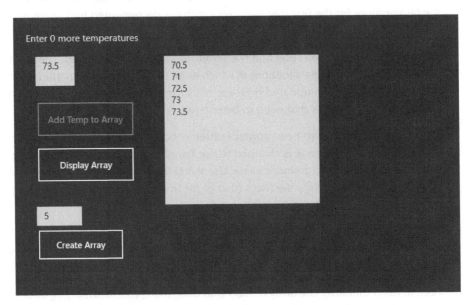

20. Continue experimenting with the Variable Elements Array program.

If you like, you can redimension the array again by putting a new number in the Create Array text box and clicking Create Array.

21. When you're finished, close the program.

You may discard your changes if you like, because I have created the Variable Elements Array project for you on disk.

Alright—you've practiced fundamental array operations in Visual Basic. Now we'll move on to some more sophisticated practices, including using *ReDim Preserve* and methods in the *Array* class of the .NET Framework.

Preserving array contents by using *ReDim Preserve*

In the previous exercise, you used the *ReDim* statement to specify the size of an array at run time. However, one potential shortcoming associated with the *ReDim* statement is that if you redimension an array that already has data in it, all the existing data in the array is lost. After the *ReDim* statement is executed, the contents of the array are set to their default value, such as zero or *null*. Depending on your outlook, this can be considered a useful feature for emptying the contents of arrays, or it can be an irksome feature that requires a workaround.

Fortunately, Visual Basic provides the *Preserve* keyword, which you use to retain the data in an array as much as possible when you change its dimensions. (However, if you use *ReDim* to create a smaller array, you will lose the data that no longer fits in the resized array.) The syntax for the *Preserve* keyword is as follows:

```
ReDim Preserve ArrayName(Dim1Elements, Dim2Elements, ...)
```

In such a *ReDim* statement, the array must continue to have the same number of dimensions and contain the same type of data. In addition, there's a caveat that you can resize only the last array dimension. For example, if your array has two or more dimensions, you can change the size of only the last dimension and still preserve the contents of the array. (Single-dimension arrays automatically pass this test, so you can freely expand the size of one-dimensional arrays by using the *Preserve* keyword.)

The following examples show how you can use *Preserve* to increase the size of the last dimension in an array without erasing any existing data contained in the array.

If you originally declared a string array named *Philosophers* by using the syntax:

```
Dim Philosophers() As String
```

you can redimension the array and add data to it by using code similar to the following:

```
ReDim Philosophers(200)
Philosophers(200) = "David Probst"
```

You can expand the size of the *Philosophers* array to 301 elements (0–300) and preserve the existing contents, by using the following syntax:

```
ReDim Preserve Philosophers(300)
```

Using *ReDim* for three-dimensional arrays

A more complex example involving a three-dimensional array uses a similar syntax. Imagine that you want to use a three-dimensional, single-precision, floating-point array named *MyCube* in your program. You can declare the *MyCube* array by using the following syntax:

```
Dim MyCube(,,) As Single
```

You can then redimension the array and add data to it by using the following code:

```
ReDim MyCube(25, 25, 25)
MyCube(10, 1, 1) = 150.46
```

after which you can expand the size of the third dimension in the array (while preserving the array's contents) by using the following syntax:

```
ReDim Preserve MyCube(25, 25, 50)
```

However, in this example, only the third dimension can be expanded—the first and second dimensions cannot be changed if you redimension the array by using the *Preserve* keyword. Attempting to change the size of the first or second dimension in this example produces a run-time error when the *ReDim Preserve* statement is executed.

Experiment a little with *ReDim Preserve*, and see how you can use it to make your own arrays flexible and robust.

Processing large arrays by using methods in the *Array* class

In previous sections, you reviewed the essential concepts about arrays and how they are used to store information in a Visual Basic program. In this section, you'll learn about powerful methods in the *Array* class of the .NET Framework, which allow you to quickly sort, search, and reverse the elements in an array. The sample program I've created demonstrates how these features work with larger arrays. You'll also learn how to use the *ProgressBar* control, a handy tool in the Windows Forms Toolbox designed to provide visual feedback in Windows desktop applications.

The *Array* class

When you create arrays in Visual Basic, you are using a base class that is defined by Visual Basic for implementing arrays within user-created programs. This *Array* class also provides a collection of methods that you can use to manipulate arrays while they are active in programs. The most useful methods include *Array.Sort, Array.Find, Array.Reverse, Array.Copy*, and *Array.Clear*. You can locate other interesting methods by experimenting with the *Array* class in the Code Editor (by using Microsoft IntelliSense) and by checking the MSDN resources online.

The *Array* class methods function much like the .NET Framework methods you have already used in this book; that is, they are called by name and (in this case) require a valid array name as an argument. They are also part of a namespace that is included automatically in Visual Basic programs.

For example, to sort an array of temperatures (such as the *Temperatures* array that you created in the previous exercise), use the following syntax:

```
Array.Sort(Temperatures)
```

You would make such a call after the *Temperatures* array had been declared and filled with data in the program. When Visual Basic executes the *Array.Sort* method, it uses a sorting routine to reorganize the array in alphanumeric order. After the sort is complete, the original array is ordered in ascending order, with the smallest value in array location 0 and the largest value in the last array location. With the preceding *Temperatures* example, the sort would produce an array of daily temperatures organized from coolest to hottest.

In the following exercise, you'll see how the *Array.Sort* and *Array.Reverse* methods can be used to quickly reorder a large array containing six-digit numbers randomly selected between 0 and 1,000,000. You'll also experiment with the *ProgressBar* control, which provides useful visual feedback for the user during long sorts or other time-consuming operations. This *ProgressBar* control is a component in the Windows Forms Toolbox designed for Windows desktop applications. (You can add something similar to your Windows Store apps if you use the XAML *ProgressBar* or *ProgressRing* controls, located in the XAML Toolbox for Windows Store apps.)

Use *Array* methods to sort an array of 3,000 elements

1. On the File menu, click Open Project, and then open the Array Class Sorts project, a Windows desktop app located in the My Documents\Visual Basic 2013 SBS\Chapter 14 folder.

2. Display the form if it is not already visible.

    The program's user interface looks like this:

    This form contains three command buttons and a sample text box for displaying array data. It also contains a progress bar object that will provide the user feedback during longer array operations. Visual feedback in a progress bar is especially useful when computations take longer than a few seconds to complete. This program begins to show such a delay when an array of 3,000 array elements or more is sorted.

3. Click the progress bar on the form.

    The *ProgressBar* object is selected on the form and is listed in the Properties window. I created the progress bar object by using the *ProgressBar* control on the Common Controls tab in the Windows Forms Toolbox. A progress bar is designed to display the progress of a computation by displaying an appropriate number of colored rectangles arranged in a horizontal progress bar. When the computation is complete, the bar is filled with rectangles. (A smoothing effect is applied so that the progress bar is gradually filled with a solid band of color—an especially attractive effect.) You've probably seen the progress bar many times while you downloaded files or installed programs within Windows. Now you can create one in your own programs!

    The important properties that make a progress bar work are the *Minimum*, *Maximum*, and *Value* properties, and these are typically manipulated using program code. (The other progress bar properties, which you can examine in the Properties window, control how the progress bar looks and functions.) You can examine how the *Minimum* and *Maximum* properties are set by looking at this program's *Form1_Load* event handler.

4. Double-click the form to display the *Form1_Load* event handler.

You see the following code:

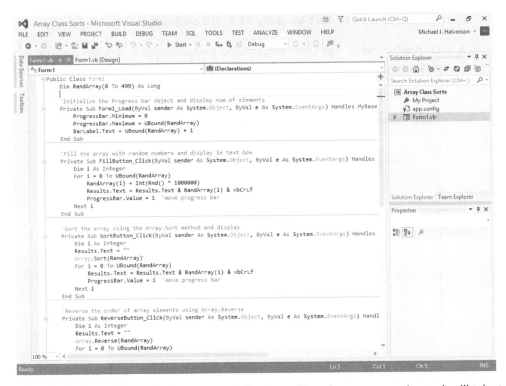

For a progress bar to display an accurate indication of how long a computing task will take to complete, you need to set relative measurements for the beginning and the end of the bar. This is accomplished with the *Minimum* and *Maximum* properties, which are set to match the first and the last elements in the array that we are building.

As I have noted, the first array element is always zero, but the last array element depends on the size of the array, so I have used the *GetUpperBound* method to return the top index value of the array and set the progress bar *Maximum* property accordingly. The array that we are manipulating in this exercise is *RandArray*, a *Long* integer array declared initially to hold 500 elements (0 to 499).

5. Click the Start Debugging button to run the program.

The program runs, and the Array Class Sorts form opens on the screen. In its *Form1_Load* event handler, the program declared an array named *RandArray* and dimensioned it with 500 elements. A progress bar object was calibrated to track a calculation of 500 units (the array size), and the number 500 appears to the right of the progress bar (the work of a label object named *BarMax* and the *GetUpperBound* method).

6. Click the Fill Array button.

The program loads *RandArray* with 500 random numbers (derived by the *Rnd* function, a member of the *VBMath* class), and displays the numbers in the text box. As the program processes the array and fills the text box object with data, the progress bar slowly fills with the color green. Your screen looks like this when the process is finished:

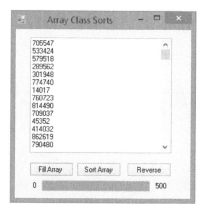

The code that produced this result is the *FillButton_Click* event handler, which contains the following program statements:

```
'Fill the array with random numbers and display in text box
Private Sub FillButton_Click(ByVal sender As System.Object, _
    ByVal e As System.EventArgs) Handles FillButton.Click
    Dim i As Integer
    For i = 0 To RandArray.GetUpperBound(0)
        RandArray(i) = Int(Rnd() * 1000000)
        Results.Text = Results.Text & RandArray(i) & vbCrLf
        ProgressBar.Value = i   'move progress bar
    Next i
End Sub
```

To get random numbers that are integers, I used the *Int* and *Rnd* functions together, and I multiplied the random number produced by *Rnd* by 1,000,000 to get whole numbers that are six digits or less. (The *Rnd* function is an alternative to the random number generator first described in Chapter 3, "Creating your first Windows Store application.") Assigning these numbers to the array is facilitated by using a *For...Next* loop with an array index that matches the loop counter (*i*).

Filling the array is an extremely fast operation; the slowdown (and the need for the progress bar) is caused by the assignment of array elements to the text box object one at a time. This involves updating a user interface component on the form 500 times, and the process takes a few seconds to complete. (In production code, it would be more typical to use the *StringBuilder* class in the .NET Framework to assemble strings in this manner. However, the example is instructional, and the delay provides a way for me to show off the *ProgressBar* control.) Because the progress bar object has been calibrated to use the number of array elements as its maximum, assigning the loop counter (*i*) to the progress bar's *Value* property allows the bar to display exactly how much of the calculation has been completed.

7. Click the Sort Array button.

The program follows a similar process to sort *RandArray*, this time using the *Array.Sort* method to reorder the array in ascending order. (The 500 elements are listed from lowest to highest.) Your screen looks like this:

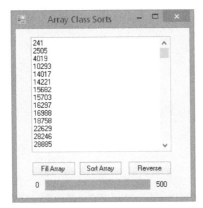

The code that produced this result is the *SortButton_Click* event handler, which contains the following program statements:

```
'Sort the array using the Array.Sort method and display
Private Sub SortButton_Click(ByVal sender As System.Object, _
    ByVal e As System.EventArgs) Handles SortButton.Click
    Dim i As Integer
    Results.Text = ""
    Array.Sort(RandArray)
    For i = 0 To RandArray.GetUpperBound(0)
        Results.Text = Results.Text & RandArray(i) & vbCrLf
        ProgressBar.Value = i  'move progress bar
    Next i
End Sub
```

This event handler clears the text box object when the user clicks the Sort Array button, and it then sorts the array by using the *Array.Sort* method described earlier. The sorting process is very quick. Again, the only slowdown is rebuilding the text box object one line at a time in the *For...Next* loop, a process that is reported by the *ProgressBar* object and its *Value* property. See how simple it is to use the *Array.Sort* method?

8. Click the Reverse button.

The program uses the *Array.Reverse* method to manipulate *RandArray*, reordering the array in backward or reverse order; that is, the first element becomes last and the last element becomes first.

Note This method does not always produce a sorted list; the array elements are in descending order only because *RandArray* had been sorted previously in ascending order by the *Array.Sort* method. (To examine the list more closely, use the scroll bars or the arrow keys.)

Your screen looks like this:

The code that produced this result is the *ReverseButton_Click* event handler, which contains the following program statements:

```
'Reverse the order of array elements using Array.Reverse
Private Sub ReverseButton_Click(ByVal sender As System.Object, _
    ByVal e As System.EventArgs) Handles ReverseButton.Click
    Dim i As Integer
    Results.Text = ""
    Array.Reverse(RandArray)
    For i = 0 To RandArray.GetUpperBound(0)
        Results.Text = Results.Text & RandArray(i) & vbCrLf
        ProgressBar.Value = i  'move progress bar
    Next i
End Sub
```

This event handler is identical to the *SortButton_Click* event handler, with the following exception:

```
Array.Sort(RandArray)
```

has become:

```
Array.Reverse(RandArray)
```

9. Click the Stop Debugging button to end the program.

10. Scroll to the top of the Code Editor, and locate the program statement that declares the *RandArray* array:

```
Dim RandArray(0 To 499) As Long
```

11. Replace 499 in the array declaration statement with **2999**.

    The statement now looks like this:

```
Dim RandArray(0 To 2999) As Long
```

12. Run the program again to see how declaring and filling an array with 3,000 elements affects program performance.

    Because processing 3,000 elements is much more work, Visual Basic takes a little while to update the text box object again and again as you fill, sort, and reverse *RandArray*. However, the progress bar keeps you posted, and you can see that with just a small change, you can adapt what you've learned in this chapter to different situations. (The secret was using the *GetUpperBound* method to report the size of the array to the program's event handlers, rather than hard-coding the upper bound at 499.)

Get your sort on

You can further experiment with this program by adding a *Randomize* statement to the *Form1_Load* event handler (to make the results truly random each time that you run the program) or by trying additional array sizes and array types. (For example, try an array size of 100, 800, 2,000, or 5,000 elements.)

If you try larger numbers, you'll eventually exceed the amount of data that the text box object can display, but it takes a while before you exceed the maximum array size allowed by Visual Basic.

If you want to focus on array operations without displaying the results, place a comment character (') before each line of code that manipulates a text box object to comment out the text box (but not the progress bar) portions of the program. You'll be amazed at how fast array operations run when the results do not need to be displayed on the form. (An array of 100,000 elements loads in just a few seconds.)

Working with collections

In this section, you'll learn about collections, a powerful mechanism for controlling data and objects that is closely related to the concept of arrays. Collections are part of the .NET Framework base class libraries, and the .NET Framework also provides a number of collections and collection-related tools that you can use to enhance your applications. You can use the Visual Studio Object Browser to search your system for collections, and this is one of the important ways to learn about operating system features and how you can access them.

In the .NET Framework, the *Collections* namespace is a component within the *System* namespace. *Collections* contains classes that you can use to work with lists of objects, as well as complex data structures. Collections have a lot in common with arrays conceptually, but you do not need to redimension a collection when you want to add additional items to it; you simply use the *Add* method (or one of the methods equivalent to *Add*).

Collections can be used to store simple lists of data, such as names, addresses, or dates. For some collections, you can assign a *key* to an item that you put into the collection so that you can quickly retrieve the object by using the key. Each collection in a program has its own name so that you can reference it as a distinct unit in the program code.

Table 14-2 shows some of the classes in the *Collections* namespace that can help you create and maintain lists and other structures in Visual Basic code. You can start using these classes when you understand the basic syntax of collections and how they are manipulated in Visual Basic.

TABLE 14-2 A few useful classes for maintaining lists in the *System.Collections* namespace

Class	Description
ArrayList	Simple list that functions like a dynamic array.
BitArray	Compact array of bit values, which are represented as Boolean values.
Dictionary	A list of key/value pairs that are organized based on the key.
Hashtable	List of key/value pairs that are organized based on the hash code of the key.
List	A basic list of values that can be accessed by an index.
Queue	List of values that is organized first in, first out.
SortedList	List of values sorted by one or more indices.
Stack	List of values that is organized last in, first out.

Creating collections and generic lists

Within the .NET Framework are many collections that you can access and manipulate in your programs. However, you can also create your own collections to track information and work with it in a systematic way. Although collections are sometimes created to hold objects, such as user interface controls, you can also use collections to store names, dates, and numeric values while a program is running. In this way, collections complement and expand upon the capabilities provided by arrays.

In the .NET Framework, some of the most useful collections are referred to as *generic collections*. Generic collections are defined in template form with the data type listed as an argument. This means that generic collections are data type specific, so they enforce type safety better than less structured collections of type *Object*. Therefore, when you retrieve an element from a generic collection that has not been specifically defined using the *Object* type, you do not have to determine its data type or convert it—its type is already authenticated. In addition, Microsoft claims that generic collections are faster in memory than other collections, so there is a speed benefit to using them.

The term *generic* might need some additional explanation. In essence, the term means that you declare a collection with a general-purpose template that identifies the structure of the collection.

The particular data type of the collection is included as an argument, and all of the standard data types in Visual Basic can be used. A common analogy that Microsoft offers for a generic collection declaration is a screwdriver set that contains a basic screwdriver tool with an assortment of removable heads used to customize the screwdriver. In this analogy, the basic screwdriver tool is the template that has many standard features and techniques associated with operating a screwdriver. However, within the tool set are also removable heads for different types of screws (slotted, crossed, starred, and so on). These removable heads are the various data type arguments that allow the generic screwdriver tool to be customized to fit a particular application. As a programmer, you simply use the tool in the way that you would normally use (or *call*) it. That is, the generic tool is easily customized to different situations.

This concept of generic templates, or coding techniques, is an important one in Visual Studio. Beyond collections, *generics*, or generic coding strategies, have been applied to how new classes, structures, interfaces, procedures, and delegates are defined and used. It is therefore important to understand the concept and begin to work with it as a Visual Basic programmer. By defining common features and functionality and then applying them to specific types and situations, you will save development time and reduce errors.

Declaring generic collections

The .NET Framework provides a number of generic collection classes in the *System.Collections.Generic* and *System.Collections.ObjectModel* namespaces. You can use these classes to declare generic collections that are powerful and very easy to use.

For example, to declare a generic list of items named *MyFavoriteCollection* in the *String* data type, you would use the following syntax:

```
Dim MyFavoriteCollection As New Generic.List(Of String)
```

A list is a basic collection of items, much like an array. In the Visual Studio documentation, you will sometimes see such a structure referred to as a *List (Of T)* where the letter *T* is a placeholder (or template) for an argument that specified the data type of the collection.

You could then add items to this list by using syntax like the following:

```
MyFavoriteCollection.Add("Rocking Chair")
```

Note that the *MyFavoriteCollection* list above will accept values only of type *String*. Other values, unless they can be represented in *String* format, will produce a run-time error when assigned to the collection. However, unlike a *String* array, which you experimented with earlier in the chapter, you do not need to know how many elements the list will contain when you declare it.

To create a generic list of *Integer* values, you would type:

```
Dim MyFavoriteIntegers As New Generic.List(Of Integers)
```

To create a generic *queue* (a first in, first out list of values), you would type a declaration in the following format. (In this case, note that I am indicating that the queue will hold *Date* values.)

```
Dim KeyGameDates As New Generic.Queue(Of Date)
```

To add items to this queue, you would use the *Enqueue* method. This sample syntax shows how you could add a value to the queue in *Date* format, which I am specifying using a literal date string. (The context of this example is that I am maintaining a sporting events calendar by adding specific dates to the *KeyGameDates* queue.)

```
KeyGameDates.Enqueue(#1/5/2014#)
```

The date in my North American cultural context is January 5, 2014. A literal date string like this is enclosed in pound (#) symbols and should be formatted according to the requirements of your culture and time zone.

To remove a date from this *KeyGameDates* queue, you would use the *Dequeue* method, in a manner similar to the following:

```
OutputTextBox.Text = KeyGameDates.Dequeue()
```

This particular statement copies the date value in the structure that is "next out" to the *OutputTextBox* object on a page. It is not necessary to use an index to extract data from a queue.

Sample app with generic list and background image

The following exercise shows you how to create a generic list that will hold the names of historic French men and French women. The generic list will be declared in the *String* type. The program is a Windows Store app written in Visual Basic that contains five XAML Toolbox controls: A *TextBlock* control that displays operating instructions; a *TextBox* control that accepts user input; two *Button* controls that load and display the list, respectively; and a *TextBox* control that displays the list contents.

The app displays the background image of a French castle (Chateau Fontainebleau, near Paris) by setting the page's *Background* and *ImageBrush* properties to a .jpg file that I preloaded into the project's Assets folder. The XAML markup that produces the photographic effect is in the MainPage. xaml file. It looks like this:

```
<Grid.Background>
    <ImageBrush ImageSource="ms-appx:/Assets/French_Castle.JPG"/>
</Grid.Background>
```

Background images are a hallmark of Windows Store apps, and you can use this technique to make your programs look very professional. Just be sure to preload the image into the Assets folder by using Solution Explorer.

Follow these steps to load and run the Historical Names Collection program.

Track names using a generic list

1. Click the Close Project command on the File menu.

2. Open the existing Windows Store app named Historical Names Collection in the My Documents\VB 2013 SBS\Chapter 14\Historical Names Collection folder.

3. Display the program user interface (MainPage.xaml) in the Designer.

   You'll see a page that looks like this:

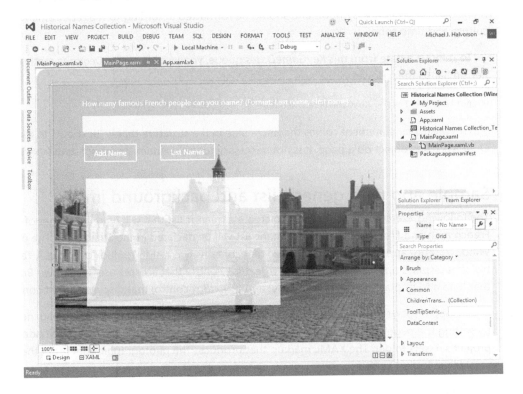

The following property settings have been made in the project:

Object	Property	Setting
Grid	Background/ImageBrush	ImageSource="ms-appx:/Assets/French_Castle.JPG"
TextBlock	Text	"How many famous French people can you name? (Format: Last name, First name)"
TextBox	Name	NameInput
	Text	""
Button	Name	AddButton
	Content	"Add Name"
Button	Name	ShowButton
	Content	"List Names"
TextBox	Name	OutputTextBox
	Text	""
	ScrollViewer.VerticalScrollBarVisibility	Visible

4. Open the MainPage.xaml.vb code-behind file in the Code Editor.

    The two event handlers in the project are visible in the Code Editor. At the top of the page, near the *Inherits Page* statement, you'll see the following comment and generic list declaration:

    ```
    'declare new generic collection of type String to hold names
    Dim FrenchNames As New  Generic.List(Of String)
    ```

    The *Dim* statement creates a new generic collection and indicates that the list structure will contain entries of type *String*. Because the declaration has been placed in the general declaration area for the page, the list has scope throughout all the page's event handlers.

5. Scroll down in the Code Editor to the *AddButton_Click* event handler.

    You'll see the following code:

    ```
    'add the name from the NameInput text box to the collection
    FrenchNames.Add(NameInput.Text)
    'clear the new name from the text box and keep cursor there
    NameInput.Text = ""
    NameInput.Focus(Windows.UI.Xaml.FocusState.Programmatic)
    ```

This event handler runs when the *AddButton* object is clicked on the page. It adds the name specified in the first text box to the list. The *Add* method is the simple technique to accomplish the task. Then I do a little housekeeping—I wipe the *NameInput* text box clean and prepare for entering a new name by keeping the cursor in the *NameInput* text box. This is accomplished using the *Focus* method, introduced earlier in the chapter.

6. Scroll down in the Code Editor to the *ShowButton_Click* event handler.

   You'll see the following code:

```
'determine how many names are in the collection and display a message
If FrenchNames.Count >= 2 Then
    OutputTextBox.Text = "There are " & FrenchNames.Count & " names: " & vbCrLf
    'sort names in alphabetical order
    FrenchNames.Sort()
ElseIf FrenchNames.Count = 1 Then
    OutputTextBox.Text = "There is 1 name:" & vbCrLf
End If
'then loop through collection, trim trailing spaces, and display
For Each Name As String In FrenchNames
    OutputTextBox.Text = OutputTextBox.Text & Name.TrimEnd & vbCrLf
Next
```

This event handler uses several methods of the generic list collection, including *Count*, *Sort*, and *TrimEnd*. The routine begins by using the *Count* property in an *If...Then* decision structure to see whether the *FrenchNames* list has at least two items in it. If so, a special message is printed containing the exact number of items, and then the list is sorted in alphabetical order using the *Sort* method.

If the *Count* method reveals that there is only one item in the list, a special message is printed indicating that this is the case. (Notice how the message uses the singular, and not the plural, tense.)

The last three lines of code in the routine are a *For Each...Next* loop, which has been used to display the French names. A *For Each...Next* loop is conceptually similar to a *For...Next* loop. The *For Each...Next* structure has been specifically designed to work with collections, and in this case, the *Name* variable is declared in the opening line of the loop. If the user has inadvertently added a space to the end of a name, that is trimmed by the second line. The results are displayed in the *OutputTextBox* text box, and the *vbCrLf* string constant is used to place each name on its own line.

Run the Historical Names Collection program

 Note The complete Historical Names Collection program is located in the My Documents\ VB 2013 SBS\Chapter 14\Historical Names Collection folder.

1. Click the Start Debugging button to run the program.

   The program displays its default user interface and background image. The cursor blinks in the top text box, ready to receive a name.

2. Type **Montesquieu** in the first text box.

   Your screen will look like this:

3. Click the Add Name button.

   Visual Basic adds the Enlightenment philosopher to the list and removes the name from the input box.

4. Click the List Names button.

   You'll see the following output:

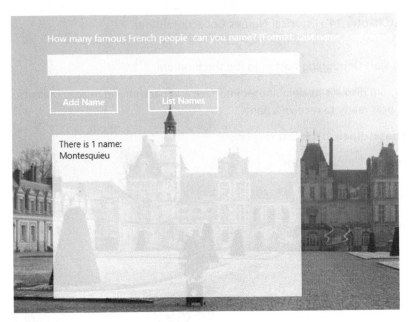

How many famous French people can you name? (Format: last name,

Add Name   List Names

There is 1 name:
Montesquieu

5. Now type the following name in the text box: **King Henri IV**.

6. Click Add Name.

7. Click List Names, and you'll see that the list has expanded. (The *If...Then...ElseIf* structure also displays a new header.)

Now you'll add a series of names to the list. After each name, be sure to click Add Name, because the program is designed to enter one name at a time. Feel free to use the following French names, or some of your own.

8. Add the following names, clicking Add Name after each: **Bonaparte, Napoleon**; **Ajenstat, François**; **Pitie, Jean-Christophe**; **Duby, Georges**; **Jeanne d'Arc**; **King Francis I**.

9. Click List Names.

The collection has grown, and now the list of names takes up much of the second text box. Notice that the program has sorted the list of names alphabetically, as well. This is the *Sort* method at work. Your program will look like this:

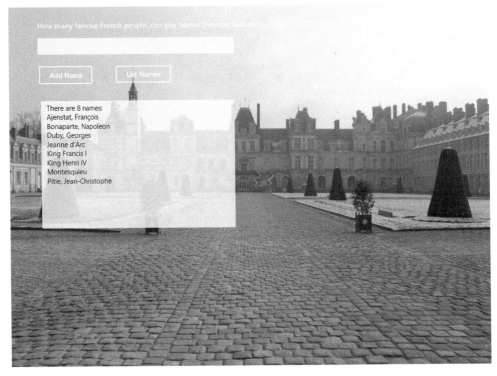

Feel free to experiment a little more with the program, adding additional names and listing them.

10. When you're finished, close the Windows Store app, and then save your changes and exit Visual Studio.

Congratulations—you've learned the basics about arrays and collections, and you've also learned to use generic structures in the .NET Framework, as well as *For Each...Next* loops to process information. These skills will be useful whenever you work with collections of data. As you become more familiar with classic computer science data structures and their uses (abstractions such as stacks, queues, dictionaries, hash tables, linked lists, and other structures), you'll find that the .NET Framework provides powerful tools to help you manage data in very innovative ways. You're off to a great start.

Summary

In this chapter, you learned how to use arrays, collections, and generic lists to manage information in a Visual Basic program. Although you began the chapter by reviewing fundamental techniques such as declaring and using one-dimensional arrays, you quickly moved to using the features of the .NET Framework to manage information, including methods in the *Array* class and generic templates in the *System.Collections.Generic* namespace.

The sample programs in this chapter demonstrated how to use arrays and collections in both Windows Forms and Windows Store applications. In a few circumstances, the techniques were different, because classes and methods in the .NET Framework sometimes differ in the two programming platforms. Fortunately, the fundamental techniques associated with arrays, collections, and generics are the same in all recent versions of the Visual Basic language.

In the next chapter, you'll continue working on fundamental data management techniques in Visual Basic, focusing on the Language Integrated Query (LINQ) tool in Visual Studio 2013.

CHAPTER 15

Innovative data management with LINQ

After completing this chapter, you will be able to

- Understand basic LINQ query syntax and fundamental data-extraction techniques.

- Use LINQ to retrieve data from arrays and collections.

- Use LINQ to retrieve data from XML documents.

In Microsoft Visual Studio, an important technology used for managing and retrieving data is known as *Language Integrated Query (LINQ)* (pronounced *link*). LINQ allows you to retrieve data in the same way from almost *any* data source, whether it is stored in arrays, collections, lists, databases, or Extensible Markup Language (XML) documents. If you've had any exposure to SQL statements that fetch information from structured tables in a database, you'll find that LINQ is similar in many respects.

In this chapter, you'll learn how to use LINQ to extract data from arrays and other structured lists and how to use the selected information efficiently in a program. You'll learn how to write LINQ *query expressions* in Visual Basic code and how to use essential LINQ keywords, including *From*, *Where*, and *Select*. After you learn the fundamentals of managing array and collection data with LINQ, you'll learn how to open XML documents in a program and how to use the data in XML documents as a source for LINQ queries.

LINQ tools and techniques

In the last chapter, you learned how to fill arrays and collections with data. The truth is, programmers spend a lot of time thinking about data and how best to make it available and move it from place to place in a program. The fundamental design concept behind LINQ is that it simplifies data retrieval for Visual Studio programmers from the many data containers that exist in a developer's world, including arrays, lists, collections, relational databases, XML documents, and other sources.

Broadly speaking, LINQ allows Visual Studio programmers to perform complex *queries* to retrieve data from a variety of data containers so that the information can be integrated into a Windows development project. Although this comprehensive definition of LINQ's capabilities might sound rather complicated, LINQ is really just a tool to select, or *extract*, information from one or more data sources. Like *Structured Query Language (SQL)*, LINQ was designed to help developers ask questions about valuable data collections that are typically too large or cumbersome to inspect manually (that is, item by item). For example, how many ski instructors at Alpine Ski House have worked at the ski school for 10 years or more? Or, how many books were published by Lucerne Publishing that earned more than $100,000 in gross sales over the past 12 months?

The questioning character of these data inquiries is where the term *query* comes from in LINQ. But it is not necessary to have extremely large data collections on hand to begin working with LINQ in your programs. In fact, most programmers don't realize how simple it is to get started with LINQ. As soon as you understand the fundamentals of basic LINQ query syntax, you can retrieve or filter data from common data sources, such as arrays or structured XML documents. In the following sections, you'll learn how to create basic LINQ expressions and how to get started with LINQ data selection in a Windows Store app.

Fundamental query syntax

Because the LINQ keywords that build a LINQ query are part of Visual Studio and the Visual Basic language, it is very easy to begin working with LINQ in code modules and event handlers. Each time that you create a LINQ expression query, you'll usually include the following keywords:

- **Dim**   When you build a LINQ query, you first need a storage variable to hold information related to elements in the query. Although the *Dim* keyword is not technically part of the LINQ syntax, it is often used to declare the variable that holds information returned by LINQ. In the following syntax, you'll see that no specific variable type is required with *Dim*, because LINQ uses something called an *anonymous type* to infer the data type automatically. An anonymous type is an object data type created automatically by Visual Basic and not given a name for the program to use. Just like an anonymous donor, who gives a gift but is not named in public records, an anonymous type provides an object that can be used in a program without the syntax that defines a type.

  The following line of code declares a variable named *queryData* to hold the results of a LINQ query. It also declares an iteration variable named *person* to represent each element of the data source individually. (Declaring the *person* variable is somewhat similar to declaring a counter variable for a *For...Next* loop.) The *Musicians* data source specified here will be discussed in the next section.

  ```
  Dim queryData = From person In Musicians
  ```

- **From**   In the preceding statement, you might also have noticed the *From* keyword. In a LINQ query, the *From* keyword is required to identify where the data you plan to use will come from. You can include more than one data source in a LINQ query, and this capability accounts for some of the power and flexibility of LINQ. In the following statement (which is simply copied from the preceding—you will include this statement only once in your code), the string array *Musicians* is specified as the data source for the query:

  ```
  Dim queryData = From person In Musicians
  ```

- **Where**   The optional *Where* clause filters the result returned by the LINQ query. You can include one or more *conditions*, or none at all. Typically, the iteration variable is used in a *Where* clause. For example, the following statement would filter the LINQ query so that only array elements that match the text "Robert" will be returned. Note that this statement uses the person iteration variable defined in the preceding *Dim* statement.

```
Where person = "Robert"
```

- **Select**   The *Select* clause is also optional; it allows you to return only selected fields or portions of the data source, to further refine your results. This is most effective when the data source that you are using has numerous fields or when you specify more than one data source and want to limit the results returned by the query.

There are many more options available for the *Select* clause, but the basic use of *Select* is quite straightforward. In the following example, a new LINQ query named *queryData* is declared that searches two string arrays (*WeekendInstructors* and *WeekdayInstructors*) to see whether there is any overlap between the two arrays. The iteration variables *person* and *teacher* represent each array element during the query; Visual Basic compares the arrays element by element, and if there is a match (if *person* is equal to *teacher*), that item is selected and stored with other matches in the *queryData* variable.

```
Dim queryData = From person In WeekendInstructors, teacher In WeekdayInstructors
    Where person = teacher
    Select person
```

> **Tip**   When you work in the Code Editor, you'll discover a time-saving feature associated with LINQ. Because LINQ is fully integrated into Visual Studio and the Visual Basic language, the IDE supplies IntelliSense to help you build your LINQ code block as soon as you specify the data source that you will be using with the *From* clause.

Extracting information from arrays

Now let's take a look at some program code to see how LINQ works in a Visual Basic event handler. The first data source you'll use with LINQ is an array of type *Double*. You'll also learn how to use a *For Each...Next* loop to display the results of a LINQ query in a program. The sample project that you will be working with is Linq Queries, a Windows Store app that uses three arrays, a generic collection, and a XAML document as data sources.

This application is based around activities at a fictitious ski school named Alpine Ski House, a business that offers downhill ski and snowboarding lessons during the winter months. The program is partially complete but requires that you complete the LINQ queries to extract information related to the business and its employees and students.

Build a query to extract numeric data from an array

1. Start Visual Studio, and open the Linq Queries program, a Windows Store app located in the My Documents\Visual Basic 2013 SBS\Chapter 15 folder.

   The ski school application already contains an array of type *Double* named *WeekRevenue*, which stores a week's worth of sales data for the company. In addition, there are two arrays of type *String* (*WeekdayInstructors* and *WeekendInstructors*), which contain the names of ski school instructors who work during the week and on the weekend.

   There is also an XML document file associated with the project that has been loaded into the Assets folder. This file contains the names of students in the school who are competing in the ski and snowboard racing program. The format of this document is typical of an XML file used for data in a Visual Basic program; it contains first name, last name, age, and gender fields for 24 students.

   The basic user interface for the Alpine Ski House app looks like this in the IDE. (Depending on how you have used the sample file in the past, the Add Name button may be active or dimmed; it does not matter which state the button is in.)

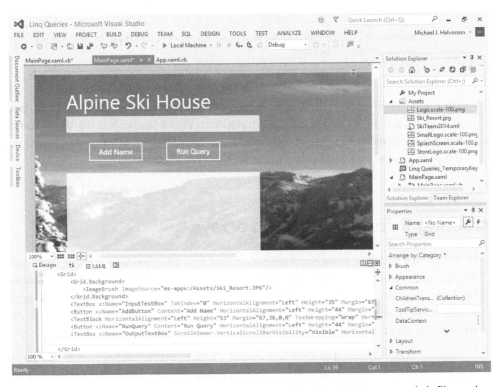

2. Because this program is all about data, begin by opening the MainPage.xaml.vb file, and examine the array and collection data sources provided at the top of the code-behind file in the Code Editor.

You'll see the following comments and declarations:

```
'declare array of type Double to hold a week's worth of ski school revenue
Dim WeekRevenue() As Double = {842.55, 340.05, 725.25, 680.43, 1120.38, 2675.99, 2175.64}
'declare two string arrays with instructor names
Dim WeekdayInstructors() As String = {"Bart", "Ken", "Maria", "Eve", "Claude", "Nikki"}
Dim WeekendInstructors() As String = {"Eve", "Allen", "Juan", "Larry", "Kim", "Al"}
'declare a generic collection list to hold student names input by user
Dim StudentNames As New Generic.List(Of String)
```

As the comments explain, these four *Dim* statements declare one array of type *Double* for sales revenue, two arrays of type *String* for instructor names, and a generic collection for student names that will be input by the user and stored in a list. These data sources will all be used as information providers for the LINQ queries that you will write in this program, and a fifth data source will be added (the XML document) when you complete that exercise. Note that the data samples are rather limited and for demonstration purposes only; a full-featured program would likely have much more substantial arrays, collections, and document files to store the records of a typical business.

Start your work with LINQ now by building your first expression, a retrieval query that runs when the user clicks Run Query on the page and which extracts information from the *WeekRevenue* array, based on a specific criteria.

Because this program is already partially complete, I have already created the *RunQuery_Click* event handler for you, a procedure that runs when the user clicks the Run Query button on the page.

3. In the Code Editor, scroll down in the MainPage.xaml.vb code-behind file to find the *RunQuery_Click* event handler.

4. Type the following code in the Code Editor, between *Private Sub* and *End Sub*. Lines two and three comprise a complete LINQ query.

```
OutputTextBox.Text = "Days with revenue greater than $500 this week" & vbCrLf & vbCrLf
Dim queryData = From dayrevenue In WeekRevenue
                Where dayrevenue > 500

For Each scanResult In queryData
    OutputTextBox.Text = OutputTextBox.Text & scanResult & vbCrLf
Next
```

Important By convention, I've placed a blank line after the LINQ query (that is, before the *For Each* loop) to clarify for the compiler that the query is complete. You should always include such a blank line in your LINQ code blocks.

The first line in this routine displays a message in *OutputTextBox* (the large text box on the page) describing what this particular LINQ query is doing. I will always begin queries in this chapter by setting up this simple text box banner, just to make it clear what you are seeing.

The next two statements define the LINQ query that analyzes the *WeekRevenue* array. The *Dim* keyword here creates a variable (*queryData*) to hold the results of the LINQ query. *WeekRevenue* is an array of type *Double* with entries that have been assigned when the array was initially dimensioned. The *dayrevenue* range variable is an iterative variable that represents each item in the *WeekRevenue* array as it is processed by the LINQ query.

The *Where* clause filters the results of the query, passing along only array items that are greater than 500. Keep in mind that additional conditions could be added to further refine the data returned by this query. This is the place in the query where you can be very specific with the range and type of information that you want to extract.

The final three lines of the event handler form a *For Each...Next* loop that steps through the *queryData* variable item by item and displays a separate line in the text box for each value returned. Only the items that are larger than 500 will appear in this particular query. (The information will allow the manager of the business to identify the days with the most-impressive sales figures.) Note that if no value exists in the data set that matches the criteria, the *For Each...Next* loop will not execute.

You'll run the program now to see how this LINQ query operates.

5. Click the Start Debugging button.

   The application launches and displays a page containing a winter photo, a descriptive label, two buttons, and two text boxes.

6. Click Run Query.

   Visual Basic loads the *RunQuery_Click* event handler and executes the LINQ expression to find array items that match the criteria you specified. Six matching items were found, and the *For Each...Next* loop displays each sales figure in the text box. Your screen should look like this:

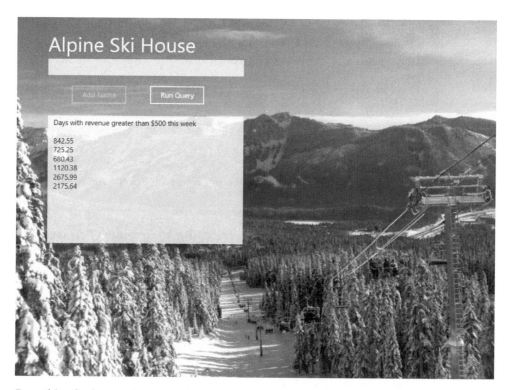

Everything looks good—your LINQ expression worked, and the financial figures were extracted as expected. It looks like they had a good week at the ski school!

7. Close the program, and return to the Visual Studio IDE.

You're off to a good start. You've learned a very fundamental use of LINQ: to search for numeric items that match a specific range or criteria within a single array or data collection. Now let's move on to something more interesting related to the *WeekRevenue* array. Let's try to narrow down the results that came back.

Build a query with a complex *Where* clause

1. In the Code Editor, scroll down to the *RunQuery_Click* event handler, and modify the *Where* clause in the LINQ query so that it looks like this. (The changes you need to make are formatted in bold.)

```
Where dayrevenue > 500 And dayrevenue < 1000
```

What's new is that I've added an *And* operator to the query, to join together two expressions in the existing *Where* clause. And in fact, with a little practice using Visual Studio's IntelliSense feature, you can find many other operators to expand your *Where* clauses and add additional complexity. In this case, what I am asking LINQ to do is evaluate the daily sales revenue figures item by item and retrieve only the items that have a value of greater than 500 but less than 1000.

2. Now modify the *OutputTextBox.Text* property containing our "documentation" banner in the event handler, so that it also reflects the change you made in the query. (Again, the change you should make is indicated in bold type.)

```
OutputTextBox.Text = "Days with revenue between $500 and $1000 this week" & vbCrLf &
vbCrLf
```

Now run the program again to see how LINQ works with the enhanced *Where* clause.

3. Click the Start Debugging button.

The application launches and displays the opening page for the Alpine Ski House business.

4. Click Run Query.

Visual Basic runs the *RunQuery_Click* event handler again, but this time only values between 500 and 1000 are returned. You'll see the following results:

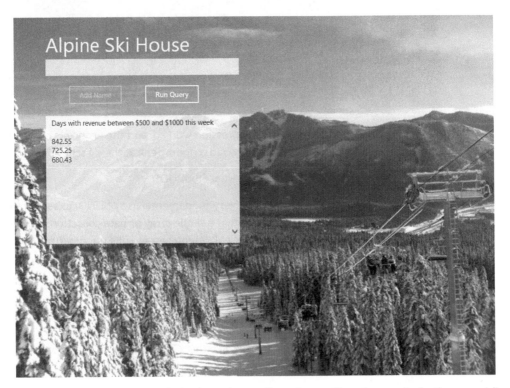

As you can see, a more detailed *Where* clause allowed us to filter the results further, providing more meaning and pinpointing important trends in the data.

5. Close the program, and return to the Visual Studio IDE.

Even these first steps with LINQ make it clear that there are numerous ways to extract information from a data source; it all depends on what you want to extract and the ways that you want to gather and combine information.

Now you'll see how LINQ works with queries designed for data that is in *String* format. This task offers us an opportunity to work with array data containing employee names. In addition, you'll have a chance to revisit some of the useful string-processing methods that you learned about in Chapter 11, "Mastering data types, operators, and string processing," such as *ToUpper*, *Contains*, and *TrimEnd*.

Use LINQ with string-processing methods to extract string data

1. In the Code Editor, display the *RunQuery_Click* event handler again within the Linq Queries program.

2. Now modify the LINQ query so that it extracts information from the *WeekendInstructors* array. This array of type *String* contains the first names of six ski instructors in the Alpine Ski House school. As you have already seen in the code-behind file, this array contains the following information:

```
Dim WeekendInstructors() As String = {"Eve", "Allen", "Juan", "Larry", "Kim", "Al"}
```

Now you'll modify the *RunQuery_Click* event handler so that it retrieves instructors whose names include the letters *Al*.

3. Change the event handler so that it looks like the following. (The elements that you need to modify are formatted again in bold.)

```
OutputTextBox.Text = "Names that include 'Al'" & vbCrLf & vbCrLf
Dim queryData = From person In WeekendInstructors
                Where person.Contains("Al")

For Each scanResult In queryData
    OutputTextBox.Text = OutputTextBox.Text & scanResult & vbCrLf
Next
```

As usual, the routine begins by setting the *OutputTextBox.Text* property to the purpose of the LINQ query. This serves as a reminder about what you are doing when you test the program.

In the second line, the *From* statement has been changed to query a new data source, the *WeekendInstructors* string array. The iteration variable has been changed to *person* in the *From* statement, and the lines that follow also use this variable to process information as it moves through the query. Remember that *person* is a placeholder variable akin to the counter variables you see in *For...Next* loops.

This time the *Where* clause has been modified to use the *Contains* method to filter the data, which is provided by the *String* class. *Contains* determines whether the specified string ("Al") occurs in the iteration variable (*person*), which stands for each element of the *WeekendInstructors* array as the query proceeds. If LINQ determines that "Al" is a part of an array element, the item is displayed in the *OutputTextBox* object.

Run the program now to see how LINQ works with the *Contains* method.

4. Click the Start Debugging button.

   The application launches and displays the opening page for the Alpine Ski House business.

5. Click Run Query.

   Visual Basic runs the *RunQuery_Click* event handler and extracts two names from the *WeekendInstructors* array based on the "Al" criteria given. You'll see these results:

Again we have a successful result. Both Allen and Al are indeed names that contain the string "Al". But wait a minute. This particular LINQ expression worked well because the capitalization pattern "Al" exactly matched two specific letter combinations in the array. But keep in mind that Visual Basic and the .NET Framework are sometimes case sensitive when it comes to comparing and sorting alphanumeric values. This means that you need to exercise some caution when extracting textual information with LINQ—you never know when some other capitalization pattern within the data source might be overlooked because a name included less-familiar capitalization schemes such as "AL", "al", or "aL".

So, is there a way to search more inclusively for strings by using techniques that you have already learned in this book?

The answer to this question is "yes." Recall that in Chapter 11 you were exposed to a variety of string-processing methods and techniques that are provided by the *System.String* namespace for just this reason. And fortunately, in LINQ, you can construct *Where* clauses that will combine several of these *String* methods together. Let's see how the *ToUpper, Contains,* and *TrimEnd* methods can be used to solve this problem and build a very interesting LINQ query.

6. Modify the *RunQuery_Click* event handler so that it appears like this (changed elements appear in bold):

```
OutputTextBox.Text = "Names that contain " & InputTextBox.Text & vbCrLf & vbCrLf
Dim queryData = From person In WeekendInstructors
                Where person.ToUpper.Contains(InputTextBox.Text.ToUpper.TrimEnd)

For Each person In queryData
    OutputTextBox.Text = OutputTextBox.Text & person & vbCrLf
Next
```

The main actor in this routine is the InputTextBox object (the first text box on the page), which will serve as a "Find" or "Search" text box in the program. Whatever text pattern the user enters into this text box, the LINQ query will attempt to locate within the *WeekendInstructors* array. If the user enters no search string at all in *InputTextBox*, all of the array elements will be extracted and displayed.

The important string-processing function within the routine is handled by the following statement:

```
Where person.ToUpper.Contains(InputTextBox.Text.ToUpper.TrimEnd)
```

Here the contents of the iteration variable *person* are converted to uppercase, and then that new string value is compared to the contents of *InputTextBox*, which the user has just entered. To make matters even more subtle, notice that I have also converted the contents of *InputTextBox* to uppercase and also removed any white space from the end of that value (this final adjustment facilitated by the *TrimEnd* method). The final trim is more important than you might think, because sometimes in user input or string operations extra blank spaces or carriage returns creep in and must be banished. (Note that you can also trim the beginning *and* the ending of a string by using the *Trim* method.)

The end result is that both the array items and the search string are temporarily converted to uppercase before the LINQ query is evaluated. (So when the name "Allen" in the array is evaluated, it temporarily becomes "ALLEN" for the comparison.) Just know that the change is not made to the actual array elements, but only to a copy of the elements that is being used by the *ToUpper* method.

Run the program now to see how the new text box feature and LINQ query works.

7. Click the Start Debugging button.

The application launches and displays its opening page.

8. Click Run Query.

Visual Basic runs the *RunQuery_Click* event handler. Because you didn't specify a search string in the *InputBox* text box, all of the array elements are extracted by the query. You'll see these results:

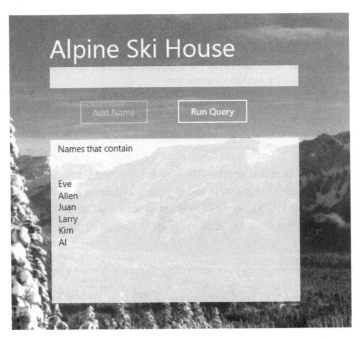

9. This is how the LINQ query was designed, so it is the expected (although somewhat unusual) functionality. Now try some specific search strings.

10. Type "l" (a lowercase *L*) in the text box, and then click Run Query.

Visual Basic searches for names in the array that contain the letter *L* (uppercase or lowercase). Your screen will look like this:

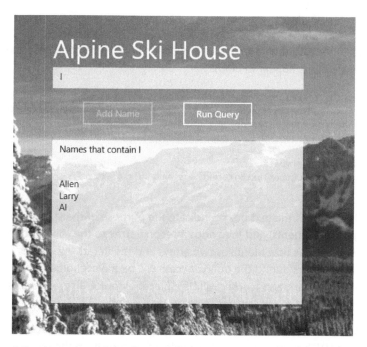

OK—that seems right, because both uppercase and lowercase letters seem to match the specified filter.

11. Now continue searching for letter patterns that you think might exist (or do not exist) in the *WeekendInstructors* array. Use patterns such as "e", "Al", "an", "Kim", "u", and so on.

    One by one, the program completes its LINQ queries with the filter values you specify. I find this interactive quality of LINQ very useful—you can use LINQ to create your own search features, assessing large or small data sources. This functionality is also impressive if you consider how much data that LINQ could search through if the array or data source were much larger. This is one fast query tool.

12. When you're finished, close the Linq Queries program and return to the IDE.

Now you'll practice using LINQ to extract information from two arrays at once. In this scenario, you'll compare the *WeekdayInstructors* array to the *WeekendInstructors* array and determine whether any of the ski school instructors are working in both groups.

Use LINQ to locate overlapping array elements

1. Display the Code Editor, and then modify the *RunQuery_Click* event handler so that it looks like this (changed elements appear in bold):

```
OutputTextBox.Text = "Instructors that work weekdays and weekends" & vbCrLf & vbCrLf
Dim queryData = From person In WeekendInstructors, teacher In WeekdayInstructors
                Where person = teacher
                Select person

For Each scanResult In queryData
    OutputTextBox.Text = OutputTextBox.Text & scanResult & vbCrLf
Next
```

This event handler modifies the text box to indicate the purpose of the LINQ query (to find overlapping array elements) and then adds a second array to the LINQ code block. Notice how the *From* clause now identifies two arrays and the iterative variables that will be used as placeholders during the query: *person* will be a placeholder for array elements in *WeekendInstructors*, and *teacher* will be a placeholder for array elements in *WeekdayInstructors*.

The *Where* clause filters the results so that only employees who appear in both of the arrays are returned by the LINQ query. (That is, where pairs of records from the two arrays share a common value.) However, the *Select* statement, used here for the first time, returns only the *person* array element. It is not desirable in this case to display the matching names twice in the *OutputTextBox* object—once is enough.

Run the program now to see how this LINQ query works.

2. Click the Start Debugging button.

The application launches and displays its opening page.

3. Click Run Query.

4. Visual Basic runs the LINQ program code and returns the instructor that works both weekends and weekdays for the ski and snowboard school. You'll see this result:

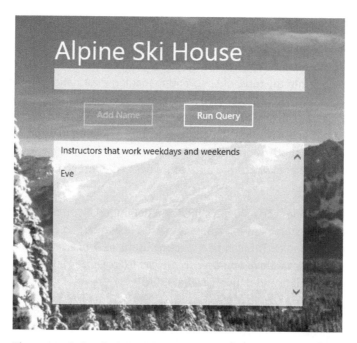

The query helped Alpine Ski House determine something that might not have been obvious at first: there is some overlap in their teaching shifts, and the instructor Eve is the only one who currently works both weekends and weekdays. The results would be even more impressive had the arrays contained hundreds or even thousands of elements.

5. Close the program, and display the IDE once more.

Using these techniques and ones that you just learned in the previous exercises, it is easy to see how you could refine this query by using a text box to allow for user-directed searches that compare several different arrays or data sources, and how you might use string-processing methods to search for different name or character patterns within the arrays. When you understand the meaning and flow of LINQ syntax and the basic LINQ elements, you can very quickly write your own sophisticated expressions.

LINQ debugging strategies

The Visual Studio IDE provides several tools that help you track down errors in your Visual Basic programs. As you get deeper into the topic of LINQ and managing information from different sources in your applications, the Visual Studio debugging tools will become especially useful. For example, you can use a DataTip or a Watch window to inspect the entire contents of a data source while your program is in break mode. If you place a *Stop* statement in a *For...Next* loop that processes an array or collection in some way, you can enter break mode and use the Step Into button on the Debug toolbar to watch the data container's contents change as you move through the loop.

Likewise, complex LINQ queries can be demystified and debugged if you place a *Stop* statement after the final *Select* statement in a query and use break mode to step through the remaining lines of the event handler. This can be especially useful in *For Each...Next* loops that process query variables, like the variables you used in the last exercise. The Locals window is also very useful when you evaluate and debug LINQ queries.

Finally, as you begin working with XML documents in Visual Basic applications, try using an XML *visualizer* to examine XML document structure and element formatting while you work on your program. A visualizer is represented by a small magnifying glass icon that appears in the Code Editor for certain program elements during break mode. If you see this tool next to a variable that contains XML data in your code, click the icon and you'll see a dialog box with helpful information about the document's contents.

For more information about fundamental debugging strategies and tools, see Chapter 9, "Debugging Applications" in my companion book *Start Here! Learn Microsoft Visual Basic 2012* (Microsoft Press, 2012).

Using LINQ with collections

As you learned in Chapter 14, "Using arrays, collections, and generics to manage data," collections also provide a helpful method for storing information in a Visual Basic program, and in many ways, collections really *surpass* the capabilities of arrays, in that they offer more built-in features and type-checking, and they can be configured to represent helpful data structures such as lists, queues, stacks, hash tables, and other entities.

Now that you understand the basic syntax of LINQ for using arrays, it will be simple for you to use collections as a data source. In the following exercise, you will use a generic collection of the *list* type to hold the names of new ski school students entering the Alpine Ski House program. We'll use the collection-management features developed in Chapter 14 to add names to a list collection by using the *InputTextBox* object on the page and the keyboard. The list of names that you create can be any size, but the query you construct is designed to process items of type *String*, and I am recommending that you enter your data in the *Lastname, Firstname* format. The LINQ query searches the entire list you enter and retrieves items that include the name "Smith".

> **Note** For more information about generic collections and using the list collection type in a program, see "Creating collections and generic lists" in Chapter 14. I recommend that you use a *generic* collection because it is more strongly typed and is therefore safer and easier to use.

Create a LINQ query that retrieves data from a generic collection

1. Display the Code Editor, and scroll to the top of the page to examine the declarations section of the MainPage.xaml.vb file, where the data sources in the program have been declared.

2. Locate the *StudentNames* variable, which is declared with the following *Dim* statement:

```
'declare a generic collection list to hold student names input by user
Dim StudentNames As New Generic.List(Of String)
```

StudentNames is a generic collection of the list type, designed to hold string values. It is currently empty, but the program will fill it with data using the *AddButton_Click* event handler, which runs when the user clicks the Add button on the page. You saw this routine in Chapter 14 when you were first working with collections in a Windows Store app. However, the purpose of this exercise is to show you how to extract data from a collection using LINQ. You'll do that in the following step.

3. Scroll down to the *RunQuery_Click* event handler, and modify it so that it contains the following lines code. (The updated elements appear in bold.)

```
OutputTextBox.Text = "New ski school students named Smith" & vbCrLf & vbCrLf
Dim queryData = From person In StudentNames
                Where person.ToUpper.Contains("SMITH")

For Each scanResult In queryData
    OutputTextBox.Text = OutputTextBox.Text & scanResult & vbCrLf
Next
```

The new event handler begins by modifying the *OutputTextBox* object so that it explains what the LINQ query does. In this case, the query has been designed to search for names in the list that match "SMITH." The *ToUpper* method is used to convert collection names to uppercase so that any pattern of uppercase and lowercase spelling of "Smith" will be a match.

That's all there is to the LINQ code in this simple example. Now you just need to make two property setting changes in the user interface. First, you'll enable the AddName button so that users can click it to enter names in the *StudentNames* list.

4. Display MainPage.xaml in the Designer, and then click the AddName button.

5. In the Properties window, expand the Common category, and add a check mark to the IsEnabled check box.

The *IsEnabled* property determines whether an object on the page is available for use or not. (Disabled objects appear dimmed and cannot have the focus.) To minimize confusion, I disabled this button earlier so that it would not be a distraction as you were completing the chapter's first exercises. But now that you want to use the text box and button for input, it's time to enable it and make it ready for use.

Next, you'll move the focus to the *InputTextBox* text box object when the program starts. This is an optional step, but establishing the focus is a helpful usability feature. Because this is the first user interface element that the user will interact with now, you might as well make it easy for them.

6. In the XAML pane of the Code Editor, locate the line of markup that defines the RunQuery button.

7. Select and move the markup element *TabIndex="0"* from its current location to the line of markup that defines the *InputTextBox* text box.

When you set the *TabIndex* property to "0" in the markup for an object, that object becomes the first object to receive the focus when the page loads. By moving the *TabIndex="0"* property setting now, you are making the first text box the object of attention when the program starts. (By the way, you can set the *TabIndex* property for addition items by following the pattern *TabIndex="1"*, *TabIndex="2"*, and so on. These property settings control the order in which objects get the focus when the user presses the Tab key.)

OK, perfect. Now run the program to see how the LINQ query extracts information from the *StudentNames* collection.

8. Click the Start Debugging button.

The application launches and displays its opening page. The cursor blinks in the *InputBox* text box, because it has been assigned the focus.

9. Type **Smith, Denise** in the text box, and then click Add Name.

10. Type **Smith Jr., Ronaldo** in the text box, and then click Add Name.

11. Type **Spencer, Phil** in the text box, and then click Add Name.

12. Type **Krebs, Peter J.** in the text box, and then click Add Name.

13. Type **Smith-Bates, Lorrin G.** in the text box, and then click Add Name.

Now you'll execute the LINQ query and see what names it returns.

14. Click Run Query.

Visual Basic processes the query expression and returns the names that include the alphanumeric pattern "SMITH." You'll see this result:

The query is working as expected and returns several variations of the name "Smith."

Because the *StudentNames* list is expandable, you can continue adding names to the collection, and you can run the LINQ query as many times as you would like. You might want to try different capitalization schemes, adding variations of the name "Smith" to the collection, such as "SMIth," "smith," "sMiTh," and so on.

15. When you're finished testing, close the program and display the IDE again.

Great work. We'll learn one more data retrieval technique in this chapter.

Using LINQ with XML documents

Arrays and collections are important sources of data for LINQ queries, but they represent only the beginning of what you can do with LINQ. Additional sources of data supported by LINQ include relational databases, Excel worksheets, products and search results from third-party providers such as Amazon and Google, and the topic of this section—XML documents.

An *XML document* is a structured text file that conforms to the specifications for XML. You can add an XML document to your program by including it in your project's Assets folder, or you can access such documents at runtime by locating them on the local system or in the cloud. As already discussed in this book, XAML files also conform to the general rules for XML documents, and they are in essence a special type of XML document designed to instantiate .NET objects in a Windows application.

Other than the initial declaration line, XML documents do not have a set list of predefined elements that they need to contain. Instead, they allow you to create your own names for elements in a document. The elements just need to conform to basic syntax rules for tagging and to fit together in a hierarchy under a single top-level element. In a Visual Basic application, you can use any hierarchical data structures that exist in XML documents, so it is beneficial to create and maintain them.

XML documents have several advantages over proprietary data formats, such as that used by Microsoft Access (.mdb format). First, XML is easily readable by humans, so special database tools are not required to open and understand XML data files. Second, XML is based on an open, public standard, and it has been adopted by Microsoft and other software publishers for information exchange and use on the web. Third, XML files are easily included in Visual Studio programming projects. Essentially, XML files are simply text files, so if you need an efficient, flexible data source in your project that can easily be updated and installed with your application, XML documents can be a good choice.

The XML document that you will use in this chapter is named SkiTeam2014.xml. The file is meant to represent information about a group of students in the Alpine Ski House business who are participating in the ski school's racing program. The file includes fields named *FirstName*, *LastName*, *Gender*, and *Age*. (This is the type of information that a ski school coordinator might use to register skiers for an age-based or gender-based competition.) Although the XML document contains only the information for 24 athletes now, it is the kind of file that could be expanded to contain hundreds or even thousands of records. This is just the type of information that a programmer might want to include in a programming project and that you can use to practice building LINQ queries.

You can find the SkiTeam2014.xml file in the My Documents\Visual Basic 2013 SBS\Chapter 15 folder on your hard disk. SkiTeam2014.xml is simply a text file, and you can edit the file in a text editor (such as Notepad or WordPad) or in the Visual Studio IDE, which is designed to open and edit XML documents. If you open SkiTeam2014.xml in Internet Explorer, the various document elements will appear in different colors, and the document's logical structure will be navigable via a collapsible/expandable tree.

The following illustration shows SkiTeam2014.xml in Visual Studio, which I loaded by opening the Assets folder in Solution Explorer and then double-clicking the SkiTeam2014.xml file.

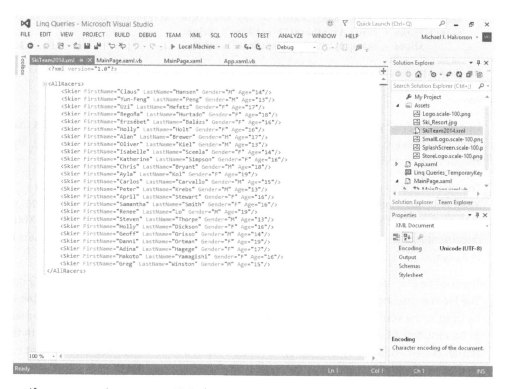

If you want to integrate an XML document into a Visual Basic project before the project is compiled, you need to include the document in the project's Assets folder. The procedure to add an XML document to the folder is the same as the process for adding electronic artwork, audio files, or video files to the Assets folder. You right-click the Assets folder in Solution Explorer, click Add | Existing Item, and then locate the XML document in the Add Existing Item dialog box. Because I have already completed this step for you, what remains is to write a LINQ query to extract information from the XML document. What you will create is a complex query that retrieves the first name and last name fields for every male student in the ski race program who is between the ages of 17 and 19, inclusive.

Create a LINQ query that retrieves data from an XML document

1. In the Code Editor, scroll to the *RunQuery_Click* event handler in the Linq Queries program.

2. Modify the procedure so that it contains the following code.

   (There are a lot of changes here. You might simply want to delete what is currently in the event handler and then retype everything below. Or you can just modify the statements in bold.)

   ```
   OutputTextBox.Text = "Male ski racers between 17 and 19, inclusive" & vbCrLf & vbCrLf

   Dim SkiRacingTeam = XElement.Load("Assets/SkiTeam2014.xml")
   Dim queryData = From skier In SkiRacingTeam.Descendants("Skier")
       Where (skier.Attribute("Gender").Value = "M") _
   ```

```
    And (skier.Attribute("Age").Value >= 17) And (skier.Attribute("Age").Value <= 19)
    Select FName = skier.Attribute("FirstName").Value,
           LName = skier.Attribute("LastName").Value

For Each scanResult In queryData
    OutputTextBox.Text &= scanResult.FName & " " & scanResult.LName & vbCrLf
Next
```

This code begins by setting the *OutputBox.Text* property to a descriptive label; in this case, you'll be retrieving male ski racers in the school who are between the ages 17 and 19, and this includes the boundary values of 17 and 19.

The second line of code is unique in this chapter—it is a *Dim* statement that uses the *XElement.Load* method to load the SkiTeam2014.xml document into the *SkiRacingTeam* variable. Notice how this statement relies on the fact that you have already inserted the XML document into the Assets folder in your project; the path name makes use of the Assets folder in its syntax.

The routine then declares a variable named *queryData* to hold the results of the LINQ query. The *From* clause indicates that the XML document stored in the *SkiRacingTeam* variable will be used as the source for the data and that the descendants of the top-level *Skier* element will all be included. (If you examine SkiTeam2014.xml again, you will see that it begins with the top-level element *Skier*.) A local iterative variable named *skier* is also used to represent each element in the XML document as the data is processed.

A long *Where* clause then filters the data such that only the ski racers who are male and between the ages of 17 and 19 (inclusive) appear in the final list. Notice how I use parentheses to separate the different components in the *Where* clauses, and how I use the *And* keyword to combine the three conditions of the *Where* clause. (The parentheses are simply used for clarity here.)

Visual Studio allows you to write fairly complex *Where* clauses with a variety of logical operators, including *And, Or, AndAlso, OrElse, Is*, and *IsNot*. You can also add in sophisticated clauses like *Order By, Distinct*, and *Aggregate* to further filter the results of a query.

For skier records that do match the gender and age filters, the *FirstName* and *LastName* elements for each ski racer are returned and displayed in the text box on the page. Note the particular syntax of the *Attribute* and *Value* properties; these allow XML data elements within the XML document hierarchy to be returned. The process is just a little more complicated than the array and collection processing work accomplished earlier in the chapter, because there is more structure in these XML documents than there was in the arrays and collection you used.

Finally, the items retrieved by the LINQ query are processed by a *For Each…Next* loop, which uses the *scanResult* variable to iterate over the results returned by the *queryData* variable, displaying a line in the text box for each male ski racer who is between 17 and 19. But…are there really any students in the XML document that fit this profile?

Run the program now to see what records (if any) are retrieved.

3. Click the Start Debugging button.

   The application launches and displays the familiar Alpine Ski House banner with its lively winter sports photograph.

4. Click Run Query.

   Visual Basic loads the *RunQuery_Click* event handler and executes the LINQ expression to extract male ski racers aged 17 to 19 from the SkiTeam2014.xml file. And what do you know, three matching names are found in the file, and they are displayed by the *For Each...Next* loop in the text box. Your screen should look like this:

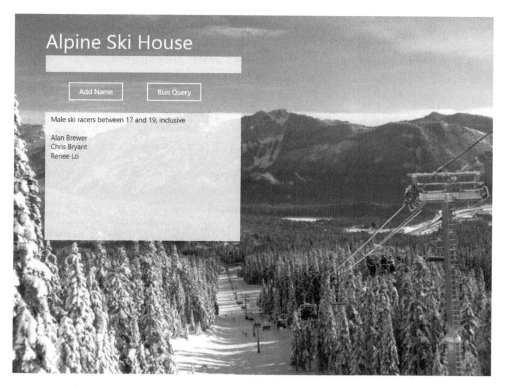

   As we saw, the XML document was pretty complex with its various fields and tags. However, the query had no problem immediately extracting just the data that we wanted to see. Such information would be useful for a race coordinator preparing heat sheets for weekend races. But the big picture is that LINQ queries and complex *Where* clauses can be extremely powerful when analyzing data. Imagine how powerful such a tool would be if there were hundreds or thousands of records in a business like Alpine Ski House?

5. Close the program, and return to the Visual Studio IDE.

6. Click the Save All button to save your changes to the project, and then exit Visual Studio.

You're finished working in Visual Basic for now. But excellent work with LINQ! You've learned valuable data management skills that you can expand in the future as needed. Indeed, you'll find that there is much more to learn about LINQ, and you can find this information in advanced Visual Basic and Visual Studio programming books, as well as specialized database books and forums on the Web. These fundamental steps are really just the beginning!

Summary

This chapter taught fundamental LINQ programming skills, including the syntax of LINQ expression queries, essential LINQ clauses such as *From*, *Where*, and *Select*, and how to work with three major data sources for LINQ queries: arrays, collections, and XML documents. You also learned how to integrate LINQ queries into a Windows Store app that managed different types of information for a fictitious ski and snowboarding school named Alpine Ski House.

As part of your work with LINQ, you retrieved weekly sales figures based on specific criteria, filtered employee records, combined string arrays and looked for overlapping elements, and extracted records from an XML document that matched a specific criteria. Working with data sources and tools is a fundamental task in computer programming, and as you continue working with Visual Basic, you'll have many opportunities to learn about connecting to data sources and processing data efficiently. You'll continue that work in this book in Part IV, "Database and web programming."

In the next chapter, you'll explore essential Visual Basic programming techniques related to object-oriented programming. Specifically, you'll learn how to inherit forms and classes and how to create your own classes with custom properties and methods.

CHAPTER 16

Object-oriented programming techniques

After completing this chapter, you will be able to

■ Use the Inheritance Picker to incorporate existing user interface elements into your projects.

■ Create your own base classes with custom properties and methods.

■ Derive new classes from base classes by using the *Inherits* statement.

■ Experiment with advanced concepts such as polymorphism and method overriding.

This book has explored fundamental Visual Basic programming skills, including designing the user interface, mastering language elements, working with data, and learning essential .NET Framework classes, objects, and methods. In this chapter, you'll pick up a core skill that is essential for engaging advanced topics. The skill is creating and deriving new classes, a technique associated with *object-oriented programming (OOP)*.

Object-oriented programming can be defined as a method of creating software in which all activity is centered around the manipulation of objects that are organized into a hierarchy. In this paradigm, a programmer uses classes to create objects and define their essential structure, like a contractor uses a blueprint to create buildings. In OOP, objects interact with one another by reading and setting properties, calling methods, and responding to events. Visual Basic 2013 is a fully object-oriented programming language, with features comparable to leading OOP languages such as C++, Java, and Python.

In this chapter, you'll learn the fundamental OOP concepts related to creating base classes with properties and methods and deriving new classes from base classes using the *Inherits* statement. You'll also get an introduction to important OOP concepts such as polymorphism and method overriding through step-by-step examples. Although this chapter will just touch on the advanced features of OOP in Visual Studio, what you learn will help you create and use your own classes, a fundamental skill that will make Visual Basic programming faster and more flexible for you. You will also develop skills that you will use later in this book, such as when you read and write records in XML data sources.

Inheriting a form by using the Inheritance Picker

In OOP syntax, *inheritance* means having one class receive the objects, properties, methods, and other attributes of another class. Visual Studio goes through this process routinely when it creates a new user interface for a project in the IDE. For example, you might have noticed that in the Windows Forms/Windows desktop platform, the first form that is created in a project (*Form1*) relies on the *System.Windows.Forms.Form* class for its definition and default values. In fact, this class is identified in the Properties window when you select the default form in the Designer, as shown in the following screen illustration:

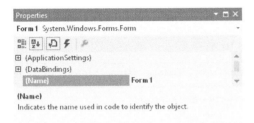

Although you might not have realized it, you've been using inheritance all along as a Visual Basic programmer. Inheritance is a key mechanism within the Visual Basic language, within the Windows operating system, and within the objects and methods of the Microsoft .NET Framework.

You'll also see program code related to inheritance in each Windows Store application that is created by Visual Studio. For example, consider this Blank Page template, which creates a new class named *MainPage* to hold objects in the user interface of a Visual Basic application:

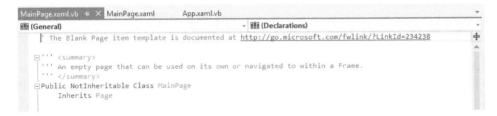

Near the top of this class definition is the relevant statement, *Inherits Page*, which instructs Visual Studio to derive the *MainPage* class from the *Page* base class. That is, the *MainPage* class inherits (or derives) its events, properties, and methods from the general definition of *Page*. Although there is some variation, the core concepts relating to creating and inheriting classes remains the same within the Visual Basic language.

Although this chapter is largely concerned with creating and using classes in a Windows Store app, the first exercise that I have prepared for you demonstrates something unique about the Visual Studio IDE when it is configured to edit a Windows Forms app. In this mode, you have access to a useful tool called the *Inheritance Picker*, which demonstrates in the clearest terms how inheritance works in a Visual Basic project. In addition, you can see up-close an important goal of object-oriented programming—to reuse and extend the functionality of existing objects and code.

Complete the following steps to build a Windows Forms dialog box and then inherit it in a project using the Inheritance Picker.

Inherit a simple dialog box

1. Start Visual Studio, and create a new Visual Basic Windows Forms Application project named **My Form Inheritance**.

2. Display the form in the project, and then use the *Button* control to add two button objects at the bottom of the form, positioned side by side.

3. Change the *Text* properties of the *Button1* and *Button2* buttons to "OK" and "Cancel," respectively.

4. Double-click OK to display the *Button1_Click* event procedure in the Code Editor.

5. Type the following program statement:

```
MsgBox("You clicked OK")
```

6. Display the form again, double-click the Cancel button, and then type the following program statement in the *Button2_Click* event procedure:

```
MsgBox("You clicked Cancel")
```

7. Display the form again, and set the *Text* property of the form to "Dialog Box."

   You now have a simple form that can be used as the basis of a dialog box in a program. With some customization, you can use this basic form to process several tasks—you just need to add the controls that are specific to your individual application.

8. Click the Save All button to save your project, and then specify the My Documents\Visual Basic 2013 SBS\Chapter 16 folder as the location.

   Now you'll practice inheriting the form. The first step in this process is building, or *compiling*, the project (creating an .exe or .dll file) because you can't open a form in the Windows Forms Designer if Visual Studio cannot create an instance of it. Note that each time the base form in a project is recompiled, changes made to the base form are passed to the derived (inherited) form.

9. Click the Build My Form Inheritance command on the Build menu.

   Visual Basic compiles your project and creates an .exe file.

10. Click the Add New Item command on the Project menu, and then click the Windows Forms category on the left side of the dialog box and the Inherited Form template in the middle of the dialog box.

The Add New Item dialog box looks as shown in the following screen shot:

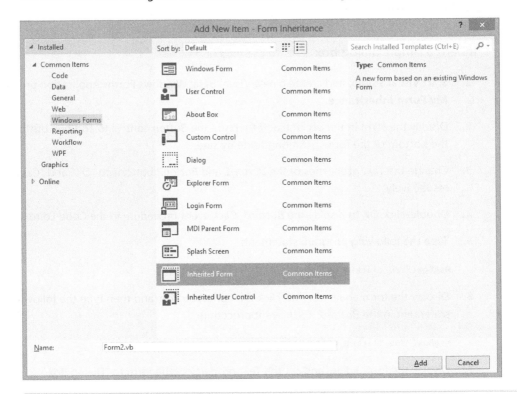

Note Most versions of Visual Basic Express do not include the Inherited Form template. If you are using Visual Basic Express and are looking for justification to upgrade to Visual Studio Professional, this lacuna might provide some. (In general, Professional and the other full versions of Visual Studio provide a number of additional templates that are useful.) At this point, you might want to simply review the sample project that I have included in the book's sample files and examine the code.

As usual, Visual Studio lists all the possible templates you could include in your projects, not just those related to inheritance. The Inherited Form template gives you access to the Inheritance Picker dialog box when a Windows Forms app is loaded.

You can also use the Name text box at the bottom of the dialog box to assign a name to your inherited form, although it is not necessary for this example. This name will appear in Solution Explorer and in the file name of the form on disk.

11. Click Add to accept the default settings for the new, inherited form.

Visual Studio displays the Inheritance Picker dialog box, as shown here:

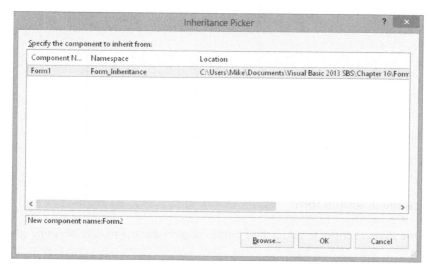

This dialog box lists all the inheritable forms in the current project. If you want to browse for another compiled form, click the Browse button and locate the .dll file on your system.

> **Note** If you want to inherit a form that isn't a component of the current project, the form must be compiled as a .dll file.

12. Click Form1 in the Inheritance Picker dialog box, and then click OK.

Visual Studio creates the Form2.vb entry in Solution Explorer and displays the inherited form in the Designer. Notice in the following screen shot that the form looks identical to the *Form1* window you created earlier except that the two buttons contain tiny icons, which indicate that the objects come from an inherited source.

It can be difficult to tell an inherited form from a base form (the tiny inheritance icons aren't that obvious), but you can also use Solution Explorer and the IDE tabs to distinguish between the forms.

Now you'll add a few new elements to the inherited form.

Customize the inherited form

1. Use the *Button* control to add a third button object near the middle of *Form2* (the inherited form).

2. Set the *Text* property for the button object to "Click Me!"

3. Double-click the Click Me! button.

4. In the *Button3_Click* event procedure, type the following program statement:

   ```
   MsgBox("This is the inherited form!")
   ```

5. Display *Form2* again, and then try double-clicking the OK and Cancel buttons on the form.

   Notice that you can't display or edit the event procedures or properties for these inherited objects without taking additional steps that are beyond the scope of this chapter. (Tiny "lock" icons indicate that the inherited objects are read-only.) However, you can add new objects to the form or customize it in other ways.

6. Enlarge the form.

   This works just fine. In addition to modifying the size, you can change the location and other display or operational characteristics of the form. Notice that if you use the Properties window to customize a form, the Object list box in the Properties window displays the form from which the current form is derived. Here's what the Properties window looks like in your project when *Form2* is selected:

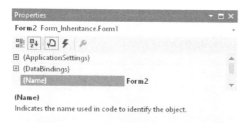

(Name)
Indicates the name used in code to identify the object.

Now set the startup object in your project to *Form2*.

7. Click the My Form Inheritance Properties command on the Project menu.

   The Project properties window appears.

8. On the Application tab, click the Startup Form list box, click *Form2*, and then close the Project properties window by clicking the Close button on the tab.

   There is no Save button in the Project Designer because Visual Studio saves your changes as you make them in the dialog box. Now run the new project.

9. Click the Start Debugging button.

   The inherited form opens, as shown here. (My version is shown slightly enlarged after following step 6 earlier in this exercise.)

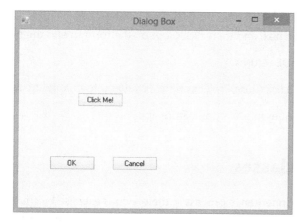

10. Click OK.

   The inherited form runs the event handler that it inherited from *Form1*, and the event handler displays the following message:

11. Click OK, and then click the Click Me! button.

Form2 displays the inherited form message, as shown here:

What this demonstrates is that *Form2* (the inherited form) has its own characteristics (a new Click Me! button and an enlarged size). *Form2* also uses two buttons (OK and Cancel) that were inherited from *Form1* and contain the code from *Form1*, as well as the exact visual representation of the buttons.

This means that you can redeploy the user interface and code features that you have previously created without cumbersome cutting and pasting. That is, you've encountered one of the main benefits of OOP—reusing and extending the functionality of existing objects (in this case, a form and its objects and properties). Further, you've learned to use the Visual Studio Inheritance Picker dialog box, which offers a handy way to select objects that you want to reuse in a Windows Forms app. However, as I noted earlier, this is currently available in the IDE only when a Windows Forms app is loaded. But not to worry; all of these procedures can all be accomplished with program code.

12. Click OK to close the message box, and then click Close on the form to end the program.

The program stops, and the IDE returns.

13. Save your changes, and then click Close Project on the File menu to unload the project.

It's time to work with OOP techniques in a Windows Store app.

Creating your own base classes

The Inheritance Picker managed the inheritance process in the previous exercise by creating a new class in your Windows Forms project named *Form2*. To build the *Form2* class, the Inheritance Picker established a link between the *Form1* class in the My Form Inheritance project and the new form. Here's what the new *Form2* class looks like in the Code Editor:

The *Button3_Click* event procedure that you added is also a member of the new class. But recall for a moment that the *Form1* class itself relied on the *System.Windows.Forms.Form* class for its fundamental behavior and characteristics. So the last exercise demonstrates that one derived class (*Form2*) can inherit its functionality from another derived class (*Form1*), which in turn inherited its core functionality from the base class (*Form*), which is a member of the *System.Windows.Forms* namespace in the Microsoft .NET Framework.

As you learned at the beginning of this chapter, Visual Studio provides the *Inherits* statement, which causes the current class to inherit the properties, methods, and variables of another class. To use the *Inherits* statement to inherit a form or a page, you must place the *Inherits* statement at the top of the form or page as the first statement in the class. Although you might choose to use the Inheritance Picker for this sort of work with forms in a Windows Forms app (which exists primarily to insert the *Inherits* statement in the derived class), it is required that you use *Inherits* in other contexts, including inheriting objects in Windows Store apps. You'll see an example of the *Inherits* statement a little later in this chapter.

Recognizing that classes are such a fundamental building block in Visual Basic programs, you might very well ask how new classes are created and how these new classes might be inherited down the road by subsequently derived classes. I devote the following sections to these possibilities, beginning with the syntax for creating classes in Visual Basic 2013.

Adding a new class to your project

Simply stated, a *class* in Visual Basic is a representation or blueprint that defines the structure of one or more objects. Creating a class allows you to define your own objects in a program—objects that have properties, methods, fields, and events, just like the objects that the Toolbox controls create in Visual Studio. To add a new class to your project, you click the Add Class command on the Project menu, and then you define the class by using Visual Basic program code.

In the following exercise, you'll build on the Alpine Ski House application that you started working with in Chapter 15, "Innovative data management with LINQ." You'll modify an existing Windows Store app named Skier Class that prompts the user for information about new ski racing students, including their first name, last name, age, and gender. You'll store this information in the properties of a new class named *Skier*, and you'll create a method in the class to determine which ski racing group the new student should belong to. This project will teach you how to create a new class and also how to use the new class in an event handler in your program.

Open and modify the Skier Class project

1. In Visual Studio, open an existing Windows Store Application project named Skier Class.

   I have partially created this demonstration program for you so that you do not need to spend time creating the various text block and text box objects on the page required for adding data to the new *Skier* class. This will allow you to focus on your OOP skills.

2. Display the MainPage.xaml page in the IDE.

   The user interface of the project looks like this:

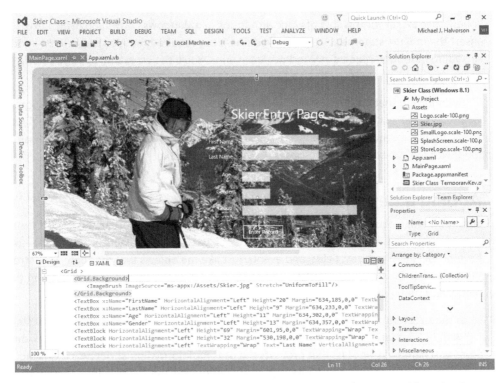

This is the basic user interface for a page that defines a new student record for a business application. The page isn't connected to a database, so only one record can be stored at a time.

Now you'll add a class to the project to store the information in the record.

3. Click the Add Class command on the Project menu.

Visual Studio displays the Add New Item dialog box, with the Class template selected, as shown here:

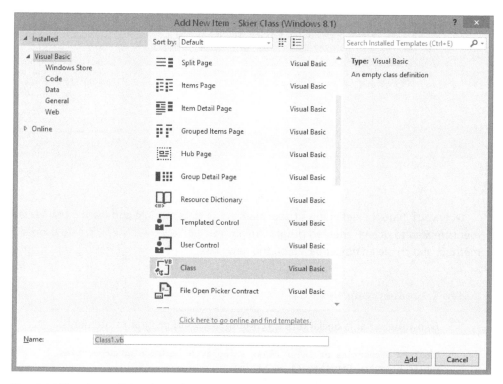

The Add New Item dialog box gives you the opportunity to name your class. Because you can store more than one class in a new class file, you might want to specify a name that is somewhat general. (There is not a one-to-one correspondence between class files and classes.) In this case, you are using a name (*Skier*) that just happens to be the name of the new file and the name of the new class.

4. Type **Skier.vb** in the Name box, and then click Add.

Visual Studio opens a blank class module in the Code Editor and lists a file named Skier.vb in Solution Explorer for your project, as shown here:

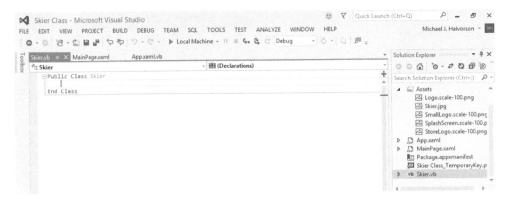

Now you'll type the definition of your class in the class module and learn a few Visual Basic statements related to object-oriented programming. You'll follow three steps: create properties, create a method, and create an object based on the new class.

Step 1: Create properties

Below the variable declarations, type the following program statements:

```
'Declare properties of Skier class using auto-implemented properties
Public Property FirstName() As String
Public Property LastName() As String
Public Property Age() As Short
Public Property Gender() As String
```

These statements create properties for your new class using types that fit the data that you are collecting for ski school students. The properties are declared using the *Public* keyword, because these values will be returned to the program through the class's property settings.

Some time ago in Visual Basic programming (Visual Basic versions 2008 and earlier), property definitions like this also required a *Get* block and a *Set* block to be defined next with program code. Now that syntax is optional and typically added only when you need to perform some additional operation related to defining a property value. In this case, the internal logic related to the properties can be auto-implemented, *and you don't need to add anything else.*

Now you'll create a new method named *Group*, which will determine the ski racing group that the ski school student will be assigned to.

Step 2: Create a method

1. Below the *Gender* property, type the following function definition:

```
Public Function Group() As String
    'Create a method for the Skier class named Group
    Dim notice As String = "" 'declare local string variable to hold result
    Select Case Age  'use Select Case and Age property to group by age
        Case Is <= 12
            notice = "not assigned (too young for team)"
        Case 13 To 16
            If Gender.ToUpper = "M" Then 'use Gender property to group by sex
                notice = "Blue Storm"
            ElseIf Gender.ToUpper = "F" Then
                notice = "Pink Storm"
            End If
        Case 17 To 19
            If Gender.ToUpper = "M" Then
                notice = "Blue Lasers"
            ElseIf Gender.ToUpper = "F" Then
                notice = "Pink Lasers"
            End If
        Case Is >= 20
            notice = "Not assigned (too old for team)"
    End Select

    Return notice 'method returns message in notice variable
End Function
```

To create a method in the class that performs a specific action, you add a function or a *Sub* procedure to your class. You can create methods that require (or do not require) arguments to accomplish their work. In this case, I have created a function named *Group* that will return a short message of type *String* indicating which ski racing group the new ski school student will be placed in. The following paragraphs describe the function, which uses a *Select Case* decision structure to determine where the students will be assigned.

The function places each student in a group based on age and gender. Because the ski racing program contains an element of danger and is designed for teenage athletes, only ski school students between the ages of 13 and 19, inclusive, are allowed into the program. As a result, the *Select Case* structure needs to determine which of four groups the eligible students fall in, displaying an appropriate message for students who don't fit the program. (Students between the ages of 1 and 12 are too young to be assigned to a team, and students aged 20 and over are too old to be assigned to a team.) Within the *Select Case* clauses is additional program logic to determine whether the student applicant is a boy or a girl. This gender determination is based on the letters "M" (for male) and "F" (for female), which the user enters into the Gender text box on the page. I also use the *ToUpper* method from the *String* class to provide some string conversion if the user enters the letter "m" or "f" on the page. (However, I do assume that the user enters the "m" or "f" letters in the *Gender* text box; additional input masking could be done here to force an entry in the proper format.)

The four potential groups are Blue Storm (for boys between the ages of 13 and 16), Pink Storm (for girls between the ages of 13 and 16), Blue Lasers (for boys between the ages of 17 and 19), and Pink Lasers (for girls between the ages of 17 and 19). The created text for each sub-group is held temporarily in the *notice* string variable. However, at the end of the function, this value is returned to the program via the *Return* keyword.

Note that this function uses the *Age* and *Gender* properties, which are maintained by the *Skier* class. For the function to work as designed, these properties should be filled with the appropriate data for the ski school student before the *Group* method is called. I wrote the method in this way to demonstrate that objects can and often do use their own properties and methods to accomplish their work. However, you need to design your methods so that there is sufficient error handling and type checking when you deal with user input. In the next step, I show you one way that you might do this before the *Group* method is actually used.

Your class definition is finished, and in the Code Editor, the *Skier* class now looks like the following:

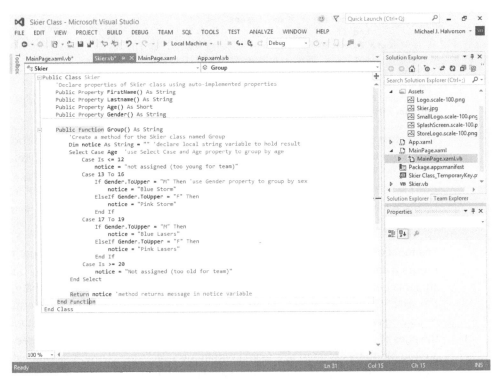

2. Click Save All to save your changes, and return to MainPage.xaml.vb, where you can use the new class in an event handler.

Step 3: Create an object based on the new class

1. In the Code Editor, scroll down in the MainPage.xaml.vb code-behind file to find the *EnterButton_Click* event handler.

    Because this program is already partially complete, I have already created the *EnterButton_Click* event handler for you, a procedure that runs when the user clicks the Enter Record button on the page.

2. Type the following code in the Code Editor, between *Private Sub* and *End Sub*:

```
'Declare new SkiRacer object of type Skier
Dim SkiRacer As New Skier
'Set properties of SkiRacer object using text boxes for input
SkiRacer.FirstName = FirstName.Text
SkiRacer.LastName = LastName.Text
If (Age.Text <> Nothing) Then SkiRacer.Age = Age.Text
SkiRacer.Gender = Gender.Text
'Display the race group skier is in using call to Group method of SkiRacer object
GroupBox.Text = SkiRacer.LastName & " in group: " & SkiRacer.Group()
```

This routine stores the values entered by the user in an object named *SkiRacer* that's declared as type *Skier*. The *New* keyword indicates that you want to immediately create a new instance of the *SkiRacer* class. You've declared variables often in this book—now you get to declare one based on a class you created yourself!

The routine then begins setting properties in the new object by using values that the user has entered in text boxes on the page. The *FirstName* property of the *SkiRacer* object is assigned a string value from the *FirstName* text box on the page, and the *LastName* property of the *SkiRacer* object is assigned a string value from the *LastName* text box. The *Age* property is then assigned after a little type checking—a value is assigned as long as the user has entered some value into the Age text box on the page. (There is still more error-handling that could be done, because if the user intentionally enters a text value here rather than a number, the assignment will generate an exception.)

After the *Gender* property of the *SkiRacer* object is set from the Gender text box, the *Group* method of the *SkiRacer* object is called. The result is displayed along with some formatting information in the *GroupBox* text box on the page.

As you can see, this part of the program is quite straightforward. After you define a class in a class module, it's a simple matter to use it in an event handler.

3. Click the Save All button to save your changes.

4. Click the Start Debugging button to run the program.

    The user interface for the Alpine Ski House new skier page appears, ready for your input.

5. Type **Dan** in the First Name text box, and type **Jump** in the Last Name text box.

6. Type **17** in the Age text box, and type **M** in the Gender text box.

7. Click Enter Record.

Visual Basic processes the information using the new *SkiRacer* object and assigns Dan Jump to the Blue Lasers ski racing group. Your page looks similar to this:

The class is working perfectly, and the skier has been assigned to the expected group. Now modify the data to see how the *Select Case* statement handles the other group assignments.

8. Change the Age text box to **15**, and then click Enter Record.

The program revises the group assignment. Accounting for Dan Jump's modified age of 15, the *Skier* class assigns him to the Blue Storm ski racing team.

9. Type **Anne** in the First Name text box, and type **Weiler** in the Last Name text box.

10. Type **19** in the Age text box, and type **F** in the Gender text box.

11. Click Enter Record.

The program changes each of the property settings in the *SkiRacer* object and then assigns Anne Weiler to the Pink Lasers ski racing team. Your page looks like this:

Skier Entry Page

First Name   Anne

Last Name   Weiler

Age   19

Gender   F

Group   Weiler in group: Pink Lasers

Enter Record

12. Change the Age text box to **13**, and then click Enter Record.

The program revises the group assignment for Anne Weiler to the Pink Storm racing team.

The *Select Case* structure is still working properly. Now try some input conditions in which no ski racing team should be assigned by the *Group* method of the *Skier* class.

13. Change the Age text box to **8**, and then click Enter Record.

The program displays the message Weiler In Group: Not Assigned (Too Young For Team). This is the expected result, because 8 years old is currently too young for the teenage ski racing program at Alpine Ski House school.

14. Remove the number entirely from the Age text box, and then click Enter Record.

The program detects that there is no value in the Age text box and does not assign a value to the *Age* property in the *SkiRacer* class. When the *Group* method runs, the *Select Case* statement assigns no value to the *Banner* variable, and the Group text box on the page displays Weiler In Group: Not Assigned (Too Young For Team). This is also the expected result; an incomplete student record results in no group assignment.

Now make one final test.

15. Type **Dylan** in the First Name text box, and type **Miller** in the Last Name text box.

16. Type **35** in the Age text box, and type **m** in the Gender text box. (Take care to type a lower-case *m*.)

17. Click Enter Record.

The *Select Case* structure evaluates the record for Dylan Miller and determines that he is too old to be placed on a racing team in this program. You'll see the following output:

18. Continue experimenting with different data scenarios in the Skier Class program. When you're finished experimenting with the new class, close the program and return to the Visual Studio IDE.

The development environment returns. Great work!

Inheriting a base class

Just as pages in the user interface can inherit their attributes from the *Page* class, you can also inherit classes that you (or another programmer) have created in a project. The mechanism for inheriting a base (parent) class is to use the *Inherits* statement. You can then add additional properties or methods to the derived (child) class to distinguish it from the base class. If this sounds a bit abstract, let's try an example based on the previous exercise.

In the following task, you'll modify the My Skier Class project so that it stores information about ski students and their administrative status in the Alpine Ski House ski school. First, you'll add a second user-defined class, named *Student*, to the *Skier* class module. This new class will inherit the *FirstName*, *LastName*, *Age*, and *Gender* properties, and the *Group* method, from the *Skier* class. However, it will also add two new properties named *Balance* and *Certificate*, to maintain additional information about students in the ski school.

Use the *Inherits* keyword

1. Click the Skier.vb class tab at the top of the Code Editor to display the Skier class.

2. Scroll to the bottom of the Code Editor so that the insertion point is below the *End Class* statement.

   As I mentioned earlier, you can include more than one class in a class module, as long as each class is delimited by *Public Class* and *End Class* statements. You'll create a second class named *Student* in this class module, and you'll use the *Inherits* keyword to incorporate the method and properties you defined in the *Skier* class.

3. Type the following class definition in the Code Editor:

```
Public Class Student
    Inherits Skier
    Public Property Balance As Double
    Public Property Certificate As Boolean
End Class
```

   The *Inherits* statement links the *Skier* class to this new class, incorporating all of its variables, properties, and methods. If the *Skier* class were located in a separate module or project, you could identify its location by using a namespace designation, just as you identify classes when you use the *Imports* statement at the top of a program file that uses classes in the .NET Framework class libraries. Basically, I've defined the *Student* class as a special type of *Skier* class—in addition to the *FirstName*, *LastName*, *Age*, and *Gender* properties, the *Student* class has a *Balance* property that records the amount of money the student currently owes for instruction (if any) and a *Certificate* property that records whether or not the student has received an end-of-season ski school participant certificate.

   The new *Balance* property is declared with the *Double* type, which is suitable for financial balances. The new *Certificate* property is declared with the *Boolean* type, a True or False value indicating whether or not the certificate has been issued.

   Now you'll use the new class in the *EnterButton_Click* event handler.

4. Display the *EnterButton_Click* event handler in MainPage.xaml.vb.

   Rather than create a new variable to hold the *Student* class, I'll just modify the program so that the *SkiRacer* variable is now derived from the *Student* class rather than from the *Skier* class. This way I can use the existing code and simply add a few lines to fill the new *Balance* and *Certificate* properties with data.

5. Modify the *EnterButton_Click* event handler as follows. (The statements in bold are the ones that you need to change.)

```
'Declare new SkiRacer object of type Student
Dim SkiRacer As New Student
'Set properties of SkiRacer object using text boxes for input
SkiRacer.FirstName = FirstName.Text
SkiRacer.LastName = LastName.Text
If (Age.Text <> Nothing) Then SkiRacer.Age = Age.Text
SkiRacer.Gender = Gender.Text

SkiRacer.Balance = 121.95
SkiRacer.Certificate = False

'Display balance skier owes school using Balance property and ToString(currency)
GroupBox.Text = SkiRacer.LastName & " owes " & SkiRacer.Balance.ToString("C")
```

   In this example, I've removed the use of the *Group* method and I have modified the information that is displayed in the *GroupBox* text box so that the current balance (if any) that is owed by the student in the ski school is displayed. I display the *Balance* property of the *SkiRacer* object using the *ToString* method, which can be used to display currency formatting appropriate for the culture defined for your system. (The "C" character requests the currency formatting.)

   Although I have assigned a value of False to the *Certificate* property, I am not using that value specifically in the program code. However, it would be a simple matter to create an *If...Then...Else* structure that displays an appropriate message for the user based on the value maintained by the *Certificate* property.

   Now you'll run the program.

6. Click the Start Debugging button to run the program.

   The familiar Skier Entry Page for Alpine Ski House opens on the screen, ready for your input.

7. Type **Modesto** in the First Name text box, and type **Estrada** in the Last Name text box.

8. Type **18** in the Age text box, and type **M** in the Gender text box.

9. Click Enter Record.

   Visual Basic processes the information using the enhanced *SkiRacer* object and assigns the values you entered along with the new *Balance* and *Certificate* properties. Your page looks similar to this:

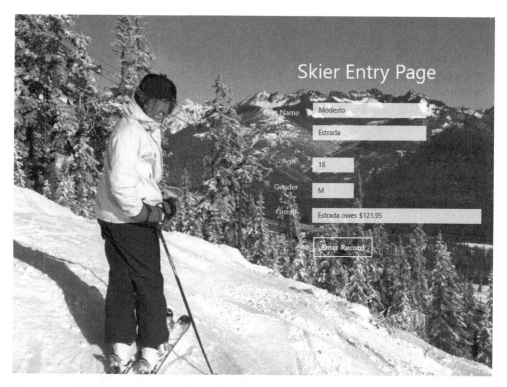

The value of 121.95 assigned to the *Balance* property now appears in the Group text box on the page, formatted for currency in a United States cultural context. (On my computer, the amount appears as $121.95.) The new *Student* class is working as expected.

10. Continue to experiment with a few more values if you like, and when you're finished, close the Windows Store app.

11. When the IDE returns, consider modifying the *EnterButton_Click* event handler a little on your own to experiment with the *SkiRacer* class and its various properties and methods.

    For example, consider adding additional methods and properties to the new class and then using these members in the MainPage.xaml.vb code-behind file.

12. When you're finished experimenting, save your changes and close the Skier Class project.

You now have the ability to create your own base classes and to derive new classes from existing classes using the *Inherits* statement.

Polymorphism

In addition to creating base classes and inheriting classes, there are a few more concepts related to object-oriented programming that you should learn about as you move into intermediate and advanced Visual Basic programming topics. You'll see them in professional-level books about Visual Studio programming, and they build on the concepts that you've just experimented with. In this section, you'll learn about polymorphism and overriding methods and procedures, two mechanisms that extend the power of inheritance.

Polymorphism describes a method of programming in which you treat an object in one class as if it were from a parent class or another class in the inheritance hierarchy. The term comes originally from the natural sciences, in which closely related variations among different organisms or species are understood to be related and thus *polymorphic*. One example is the variation among blood types in humans, which has persisted over thousands of years and yet has not led to an appreciable advantage or disadvantage among peoples in terms of natural selection. The difference in eye color among humans is also an example of polymorphism.

In object-oriented programming, polymorphism is a type of inheritance that allows you to create more elegant and maintainable code. Polymorphism creates closer relationships among objects, ideally reducing programming errors and allowing you to write fewer lines of code overall, because many of the objects rely on one another for their attributes and functionality.

Microsoft sometimes describes polymorphism by using the following creative illustration: Imagine that there are two classes in a Visual Basic program named *Flea* and *Tyrannosaur*. And imagine further that through an *Inherits* statement the *Flea* and *Tyrannosaur* classes gain many of their essential attributes from *Animal*, a base class containing common animal behaviors and characteristics.

Now, here's the polymorphism part. Imagine that to perform the act of chewing, the *Flea* and *Tyrannosaur* classes *override* (that is, replace and enhance) the *Animal* class's *Bite* method so that each creature can bite with its own unique characteristics. The flea and tyrannosaur actually do have some things in common, but they chew in unique ways. To accomplish their work they replace the *Animal* class's *Bite* method with an enhanced definition of *Bite*. In Visual Basic terms, the replacement is facilitated by a process called *method overriding*.

In fact, to continue the example, polymorphism occurs whenever a replacement *Bite* method is defined in any class derived from *Animal*. With polymorphism, the caller doesn't have to know what class an object actually belongs to before calling the property or method. It just needs to verify the hierarchical relationship between the objects.

Syntax for overriding methods and properties

As you learned earlier in this chapter, a derived class inherits properties and methods from a base class. This is true whether the base class is one that you have just created or whether the base class is a well-known entity in the .NET Framework. But, if you decide that an inherited method or property needs to function differently in the derived class, Visual Basic allows you to override the original method or property.

Although the process might sound complicated, overriding methods and properties can be accomplished using just a few Visual Basic keywords in the definition for the base class and in the call to the base class's methods and properties. The following keywords facilitate overloading and polymorphism in Visual Basic:

- **Overridable** A keyword that allows a method or property in a class to be overridden by a derived class.

- **Overrides** A keyword that, when used in a derived class, overrides a method or property defined as *Overridable* in the base class.

- **NotOverridable** A keyword that stops a method or property from being overridden in an inherited class. (Public methods are *NotOverridable* by default.)

- **MustOverride** A keyword that forces a derived class to override the method or property.

You'll see the *Overridable* and *Overrides* keywords used in the exercise below.

Referring to the base class with *MyBase*

There is one final thing. When you are creating a new class that is derived from an existing class, it is useful to reference the base class in a programmatic way. To assist with this type of reference, Visual Studio provides the *MyBase* keyword, which refers (or points to) the base class of the current instance of a class. You can also use the *Me* keyword to explicitly refer to members of the local (derived) class.

MyBase is typically used to access base class members that are overridden or *shadowed* (partially hidden from view) in a derived class. You can also use the syntax *MyBase.New* to explicitly call a base class constructor from a derived class constructor. (A *constructor* is simply a procedure named *New* that Visual Basic calls when a new instance of a class or structure is created. Constructors do basic initialization work and get an object ready for use.)

Experimenting with polymorphism

The following step-by-step example demonstrates how polymorphism and method overriding work in a Visual Basic program. In this example, you'll build a Windows Store app that calculates the amount of discount that ski school students receive when they register online for classes. The typical discount is 8.5% for new students that register online and 14% for continuing students. Currently, the Alpine Ski House ski school also allows continuing students who register online to combine the two discounts.

In the Polymorphism project that follows, the first discount rate will be computed using a new class named *BaseDiscount*. The *BaseDiscount* class contains the method *FindDiscount*, which computes the total dollar amount of the discount when the cost of ski school tuition is passed to it as an argument. The *BaseDiscount* class is quite simple, as inheritable objects should typically be in programs. The class is used to create a new object in the *TestButton_Click* event handler named *WebDeal2014*. This object is passed to a *Sub* procedure named *ViewSavings*, which actually calls the *FindDiscount* method and displays the applicable discount in a text box object on the page.

What makes this a polymorphism demonstration is the second class that is defined in the program, named *DeepDiscount*. This class is derived from the *BaseDiscount* class, but it uses the *Overrides* keyword to create a replacement method named *FindDiscount*, which will change the functionality of the base class and compute the discount pricing that occurs when students both register online and are returning for additional instruction in the program.

To make typing in the program code relatively simple for you in this exercise, I will direct you to declare the program's constants, classes, *Sub* procedure, and *TestButton_Click* event handler all in the same MainPage.xaml.vb file. I have also included plenty of comments in the code so that you can see what is taking place.

Calculate discount rates using method overriding

1. On the File menu, click New Project.

2. Choose Visual Basic/Windows Store under Templates, and then verify that the Blank App (XAML) template is selected.

3. Type **My Polymorphism** in the Name text box, and then click OK to open and configure the new project.

   Visual Studio creates the new Windows Store project with the appropriate support files.

4. Right-click the MainPage.xaml file in Solution Explorer, and then select View Designer.

   A blank page opens in the Designer.

5. Change the magnification percentage in the Designer's Zoom box to 100%.

6. Click the XAML *TextBlock* control in the Toolbox, and then create a text label near the top of the page to display a title for the program.

7. Set the *Text* property of the text block object to "**Ski School Tuition Discounts**", and change the *FontSize* property to **48**.

8. Position the text block object so that it is in the upper-left corner of the page.

9. Create a *Button* control on the page and a large, rectangular *TextBox* control next to it.

10. Change the *Name* property of the button object to "**TestButton**", and change the *Content* property to "**Show Discounts**".

11. Change the *Name* property of the text box object to "**Output**", and delete the contents of the *Text* property so that the text box object appears empty.

    Now you'll add a background image to the *Grid* object on the page. (You'll use another ski photo from my collection.) Insert the image by setting the grid's *Background* property, as shown in Steps 12-14.

12. In Solution Explorer, add an existing image to the Assets folder named Mountain.jpg.

You'll find this photo file in the My Documents\Visual Basic 2013 SBS\Chapter 16 folder.

13. Now display the XAML tab of the Code Editor, and add the following XAML markup just below the *<Grid>* tag in the MainPage.xaml file.

14. Type the following markup to load the image onto the page:

```
<Grid>
    <Grid.Background>
        <ImageBrush ImageSource="ms-appx:/Assets/Mountain.jpg" Stretch="UniformToFill"/>
    </Grid.Background>
```

The first *<Grid>* tag might need to be modified slightly so that it looks like what I have shown. As you learned in the past few chapters, this technique allows you to display an attractive graphical image as the backdrop of your page, which is a compelling effect.

Now you'll add program code defining constants, two new classes, a *Sub* procedure, and an event handler for the button object on the page. Rather than create the classes and procedure in a separate file or module, you'll simply enter all of the program code at the bottom of the MainPage.xaml.vb file.

15. Below the lines that define the *OnNavigatedTo* procedure (that is, beneath that procedure's *End Sub* statement), type the following lines of Visual Basic code:

```
' Declare a constant for 8.5% base discount for ski school
Public Const webRateDiscount As Double = 0.085
' Declare a constant for 14% returning student discount
Public Const returnStudentDiscount As Double = 0.14

Public Class BaseDiscount
    'Declare new BaseDiscount class that contains FindDiscount method.
    'Using Overridable keyword during method declaration allows for method overriding
    Overridable Function FindDiscount(ByVal CashValue As Double) As Double
        Return CashValue * webRateDiscount 'determine basic discount for student
    End Function
End Class

Public Class DeepDiscount
    ' Declare new DeepDiscount class which modifies a method in the BaseDiscount class
    Inherits BaseDiscount  'Inherits keyword must be first statement in class
    Private initialDiscount As Double  'declare local variable to hold calculation

    'This modified FindDiscount method will override the same method in the base class
    'when the Overrides keyword is used
    Overrides Function FindDiscount(ByVal CashValue As Double) As Double
        'Use of the MyBase keyword here refers to the base class of current instance.
        'That calculation is the first, but then second discount is added to it
        initialDiscount = MyBase.FindDiscount(CashValue)
        'Goal is to return the total "deep discount" (or multiple discount value)
        Return (returnStudentDiscount * CashValue) + initialDiscount
    End Function
End Class
```

```
'The ViewSavings procedure calculates the amount of money saved on ski school
'tuition and displays the value in the Output text box on the page.
'The procedure takes two arguments, an object of the BaseDiscount type and
'a tuition value that should be discounted.

Sub ViewSavings(ByVal Item As BaseDiscount, ByVal SaleAmount As Double)
    'Note the polymorphism support: Although the first argument calls for an object
    'of type BaseDiscount, an object of type DeepDiscount also works.
    Dim taxAmount As Double
    taxAmount = Item.FindDiscount(SaleAmount)
    Output.Text = Output.Text & "On " & SaleAmount.ToString("C") & _
        " tuition, the amount saved was " & taxAmount.ToString("C") & vbCrLf
End Sub

Private Sub TestButton_Click(sender As Object, e As RoutedEventArgs) Handles
TestButton.Click
    'Declare objects related to new classes
    Dim WebDeal2014 As New BaseDiscount
    Dim ReturnStdBargain2014 As New DeepDiscount

    'Call ViewSavings procedure to determine discount on $150 ski school tuition.
    'The first call uses the regular Web registration discount rate
    ViewSavings(WebDeal2014, 150)
    'The second call adds the web discount to the returning student discount
    ViewSavings(ReturnStdBargain2014, 150)
End Sub
```

16. Click the Save All button to save your changes, and specify the My Documents\Visual Basic 2013 SBS\Chapter 16 folder as the location.

   Now you'll run the Windows Store app.

17. Click Start Debugging.

   The program loads and displays its basic user interface, featuring a snowy mountain scene, a text block object, a text box, and a button.

18. Click Show Discounts.

   Visual Basic declares two variables based on the *BaseDiscount* and *DeepDiscount* classes, named *WebDeal2014* and *ReturnStdBargain2014*, respectively. These variables are passed to the *ViewSavings* procedure and used to calculate the student tuition discounts for a $150 class session. The two discounts are displayed in the text box. For students who register online for a $150 ski school class, the discount is $12.75. For students who register online for a class and are also returning students in the program, the combined discount is $33.75.

Your screen will look like this:

Ski School Tuition Discounts

Show Discounts

On $150.00 tuition, the amount saved was $12.75
On $150.00 tuition, the amount saved was $33.75

19. Close the program, and quit Visual Studio.

You're finished writing code in this chapter.

Using inheritance and method overriding, you have created a program that defines its own classes and modifies them to perform useful work. This functionality has been achieved through some fairly simple keywords, including *Overridable*, *Overrides*, *Inherits*, and *MyBase*.

The underlying concepts of object-oriented programming are more complex, but with the necessary practice, they will help you write impressive real-world applications. Professional programmers use polymorphism in a variety of contexts to create elegant and highly maintainable code.

Summary

This chapter introduced object-oriented programming terminology and fundamental techniques. We covered creating base classes with custom properties and methods, deriving new classes from base classes, and experimenting with advanced concepts such as polymorphism and method overriding. There is more to learn about OOP and its usefulness in Visual Basic applications. You will continue working with custom classes and their uses in Chapter 18, "Data access for Windows Store apps."

In the Part IV, "Database and web programming," you will continue your introduction to Visual Studio development skills with a discussion of database programming and creating web applications using ASP.NET. In Chapter 17, "Database controls for Windows desktop apps," you'll survey the useful wizards and controls that allow a Windows Forms app to connect to an Access database.

Database and web programming

Database controls for Windows desktop apps

After completing this chapter, you will be able to

- Use the Data Source Configuration Wizard to establish a connection to a database and build a dataset.

- Use the Dataset Designer and the Data Sources window to examine dataset members and create bound objects on forms.

- Bind Windows Forms controls to an Access database and create datacentric applications by using dataset and data navigator objects.

- Write SQL statements to filter and sort dataset information with the Visual Studio Query Builder tool.

As a programmer with some experience in software development, you already know that working with data is a core activity in information management. In Part III, "Visual Basic programming techniques," you spent considerable time working with data-processing concepts, including managing data types, processing strings, using arrays and collections, and writing LINQ expression queries. In Part IV, "Database and web programming," you'll work specifically with data sources in Windows Forms and Windows Store apps, and you'll learn how to expand your coding skills to the web platform with ASP.NET.

In this chapter, you'll learn how to bind controls to a database in a Windows Forms (Windows desktop) application. You'll use the Data Source Configuration Wizard to establish a connection to a Microsoft Access database on your system, and you'll create a dataset that represents a subset of useful fields and records from a database table. You'll use the Dataset Designer and Data Sources window to examine dataset members and create bound objects on your forms. You'll also use the *TextBox* and *MaskedTextBox* controls to present database information to your user, and you'll learn to write Structured Query Language (SQL) SELECT statements that filter datasets (and therefore what your user sees and uses) in interesting ways.

This chapter deals specifically with data access in Windows Forms applications and introduces ADO.NET, the most popular data model for database programming in Visual Studio 2013. In Chapter 18, "Data access for Windows Store apps," you'll learn how to use XML documents as data sources in Windows Store programs created in Visual Basic 2013. I designed these chapters to be read sequentially; Chapter 18 extends the discussion about using data sources that I begin in this chapter and moves the conversation to a new platform.

Database programming with ADO.NET

A *database* is an organized collection of information stored in one or more files. You can create powerful databases by using any of a variety of database products, including Access, Microsoft SQL Server, and Oracle. You can also store and transmit database information by using Extensible Markup Language (XML), a file format designed for exchanging structured data over the Internet and in other settings.

Creating and maintaining databases has become an essential task for all major corporations, government institutions, nonprofit agencies, and most small businesses. Rich data resources—for example, customer addresses, manufacturing inventories, account balances, employee records, donor lists, and order histories—have become the lifeblood of the business world.

You can use Microsoft Visual Studio 2013 to create new databases, but Visual Studio 2013 is primarily designed for displaying, analyzing, and manipulating the information in existing databases or XML files. ADO.NET, first introduced in Microsoft Visual Studio .NET 2002, is still the standard data model for database programming in Visual Studio 2013. ADO.NET has been improved over the years to work with a large number of data access scenarios, and it has been carefully optimized for Internet use. For example, it uses the same basic method for accessing local, client-server, and Internet-based data sources, and XML is tightly integrated into ADO.NET.

Fortunately, most of the database applications that programmers created using earlier versions of Microsoft Visual Basic and ADO.NET still function very well, and the basic techniques for accessing a database are mostly the same in Visual Basic 2013. However, there is a supplementary model for database management in Visual Studio called the Entity Framework, first shipped with Visual Studio 2010. The Entity Framework does not replace ADO.NET but offers a data model for working with information that is some ways richer and more flexible than ADO.NET. That is, the Entity Framework is not a radically new way of accessing information but is really an extension of ADO.NET and its functionality. For this reason, it is very important to learn the ADO.NET object model, both for its current practicality and its future potential.

Database terminology

An underlying theme in the preceding section is that database programmers are often faced with new technologies to decode and master, a reorientation often initiated by the terms *new paradigm* or *new database model*. Although continually learning new techniques can be a source of frustration, the rapid pace of change can be explained partially by the relative newness of distributed and multiple-tier database application programming in Windows, as well as technical innovations, security needs, and web programming challenges that are beyond the control of the Visual Studio development team.

In this chapter, we'll be starting at the beginning, and with database programming more than almost any other subject, you really need to be exposed to topics *step by step*. Let's start by understanding some basic database terminology. I expect that you'll know some of this information, but it is included so that we have some agreement from the start about key terms.

A *field* (also called a *column*) is a category of information stored in a database. Typical fields in a faculty member database might contain ID numbers, the names of faculty members, email addresses, business phone numbers, and department names. All the information about a particular faculty member is called a *record* (also called a *row*). When a database is created, information is entered in a *table* of fields and records.

Records correspond to rows in the table, and fields correspond to columns, as shown in the following faculty database (*Faculty.accdb*) in Access 2010:

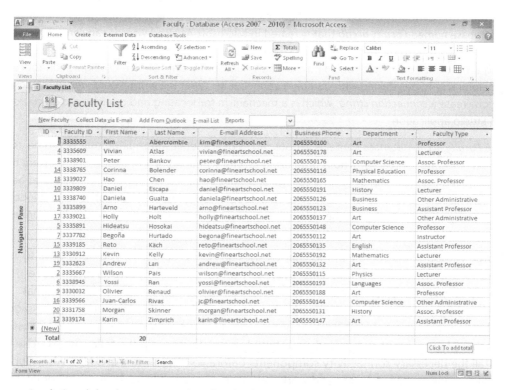

A *relational database* can consist of multiple linked tables. In general, most of the databases that you connect to from Visual Studio will probably be relational databases that contain multiple tables of data organized around a particular theme.

In ADO.NET, various objects are used to retrieve and modify information in a database. First, a *connection* is made, which specifies connection information about the database and creates something for other controls and components to bind to. Next, the Data Sources Configuration Wizard creates a *dataset*, which is a representation of one or more database tables that you plan to work with in your program. (You don't manipulate the actual data, but rather a copy of it.) The Data Sources Configuration Wizard also adds an *XML schema file* to your project and associates a *table adapter* and *data navigator* with the dataset to handle retrieving data from the database, posting changes, and moving from one record to the next in the dataset. You can then bind information in the dataset to controls on a form by using the Data Sources window or *DataBindings* property settings.

Although in this chapter we will be experimenting with this process in a Windows Forms application, you can also bind dataset information to Windows Presentation Foundation (WPF) client applications, Windows Store applications, web applications (via ASP.NET), and Windows Phone applications. However, in some platforms (such as the Windows Store environment), the Data Sources Configuration Wizard cannot be used to establish a dataset connection.

Working with an Access database

In the following sections, you'll learn how to use the ADO.NET data access technology in Visual Basic 2013. You'll get started by using the Data Source Configuration Wizard to establish a connection to a database named *Faculty.accdb* that I created in Microsoft Access. Wizards can sometimes get a bad rap for being rather simplistic (and as I've noted, they don't work in all platforms), but if you are writing a Windows Forms app, you'll find that the Visual Studio Data Source Configuration tool is a very helpful way to get started with database connections. What the wizard does well in this case is help you create a *connection string*, which is a mechanism for locating and opening a data source in a Visual Studio application.

The *Faculty.accdb* database contains various tables of academic information that would be useful for an administrator or teacher who is organizing faculty schedules or workloads, or important contact information for the employees at a college or school. You'll learn how to create a dataset based on a table of information in the *Faculty* database, and you'll display this information on a Windows form. When you've finished, you'll be able to put these skills to work in your own database projects.

Note Although the sample in this chapter uses an Access database, you don't have to have Access installed. However, a few Microsoft connectivity components might be required on your computer to work with Access files, depending on how your system has been configured. If you try to complete the exercises below and receive an error message indicating that Microsoft.Jet.OLEDB is not registered on your computer or that the Access database format is not recognized, you should complete step 1 in the following exercise to install the necessary connectivity components before you work with ADO.NET. Also, if you want to open the file in Access and work with it, you'll need to have Access 2007 or later installed on your system.

Establish a connection by using the Data Source Configuration Wizard

1. Make sure that you have Access 2007 or later installed. If you don't have Access 2007 installed, download and install the 2007 Office System Driver: Data Connectivity Components from *http://microsoft.com*.

2. Start Visual Studio, and then create a new Visual Basic Windows Forms Application project named **My ADO Faculty Form**.

   A new project opens in the Integrated Development Environment (IDE).

3. On the Project menu, click the Add New Data Source command.

   The Data Source Configuration Wizard starts in the development environment, as shown in the following screen shot:

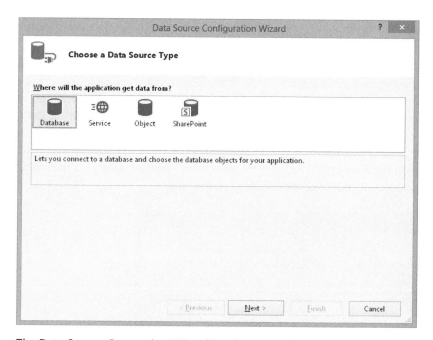

The Data Source Connection Wizard is a feature within the Visual Studio IDE that automatically prepares your Visual Basic program to receive database information. The wizard prompts you for the type of database that you will be connecting to (a local or remote database, web service, custom data object that you have created, or Microsoft SharePoint site), establishes a connection to the data, and then creates a dataset or data entity within the program to hold specific database tables and fields. The result is that the wizard opens the Data Sources window and fills it with a visual representation of each database object that you can use in your program.

4. Click the Database icon (if it is not already selected) in the Data Source Configuration Wizard, and then click Next.

   The wizard displays a screen prompting you to choose a database model for your application and the connection that your program will make to the database information.

5. Click Dataset, and then click Next to select the dataset model.

   The wizard now displays a screen that helps you establish a connection to your database by building a connection string. A connection string contains the information that Visual Studio needs to locate and open a database. This includes the file or network-based location of the database and also potentially sensitive data such as a user name and password. For this reason, the connection string is treated carefully within the Data Source Connection Wizard, and you should take care to protect it from unauthorized access as you copy your source files from place to place.

6. Click the New Connection button.

   The first time that you click the New Connection button, the Choose Data Source dialog box opens, prompting you to select the database format that you plan to use. If you see the Add Connection dialog box instead of the Choose Data Source dialog box, it simply means that your copy of Visual Studio has already been configured to favor a particular database format. No problem; simply click the Change button in the Add Connection dialog box, and you'll see the same thing that first-time wizard users see, except that the title bar reads Change Data Source. In this example, I'll assume that you haven't selected a data source format; in that case, your screen looks like the following screen shot:

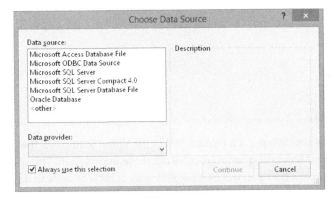

   The Change/Choose Data Source dialog box is the place where you select your preferred database format, which Visual Studio uses as the default format. In this chapter, you'll select the Access format, but note that you can change the database format to one of the other choices at any time. (Periodically, the list of available data sources changes.) You can also establish more than one database connection—each to a different type of database—within a single project.

7. Click Microsoft Access Database File, and then click Continue (or OK).

   The Add Connection dialog box opens, as shown in the following screen shot:

Now you'll specify the location and connection settings for your database so that Visual Studio can build a valid connection string.

8. Click Browse.

   The Select Microsoft Access Database File dialog box opens, which functions like an Open dialog box.

9. Browse to the My Documents\Visual Basic 2013 SBS\Chapter 17 folder, click the Faculty.accdb database, and then click Open.

   You have selected the Access database that I built to demonstrate how database fields and records are displayed within a Visual Basic program. The Add Connection dialog box opens again with the path name recorded. I don't restrict access to this file in any way, so a user name and password are not necessary with Faculty.accdb. However, if your database requires a user name, a password, or both, you can specify it now in the User Name and Password boxes. These values are then included in the connection string.

10. Click the Test Connection button.

    Visual Studio attempts to open the specified database file with the connection string that the wizard has built for you. If the database is in a recognized format and the user name and password entries (if any) are correct, you see the message shown here:

Note If you get a message that says Unrecognized Database Format, you might not have Access 2007 or later installed. If you don't have Access 2007 or later installed, you might need to download and install the 2007 Office System Driver: Data Connectivity Components, or a later tool, from Microsoft.com. (See step 1 of this procedure.) Close Visual Studio, install the required driver, restart Visual Studio, and then complete these steps again.

11. Click OK to close the message box, and then click OK to close the Add Connection dialog box.

Visual Studio displays the Data Source Configuration Wizard again.

12. Click the plus sign (+) next to the Connection String item in the dialog box to display your completed connection string.

Your wizard page looks similar to the following:

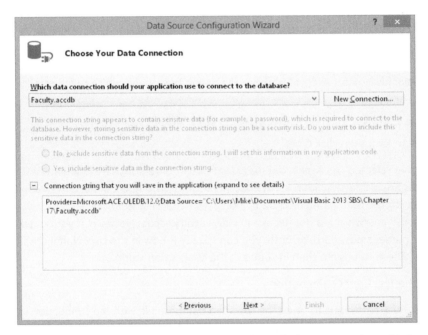

The connection string identifies a *provider* (also called a *managed provider*) named Microsoft. ACE.OLEDB.12.0, which is an underlying database component that understands how to connect to a database and extract data from it. The two most popular providers offered by Visual Studio are Microsoft OLE DB and SQL Server, but third-party providers are available for many of the other popular database formats.

13. Click the Next button.

The wizard displays an alert message indicating that a new local database (or local data file) has been selected that is not in the current project, and you are asked whether the database should be copied to your project folders. (This message appears only the first time that you make a connection to a local database file. If you are repeating this exercise, you probably won't see the message.)

In a commercial application that uses a database, you might want to control how this works a little more carefully. (To learn more about your options, you would click the Help button or press F1.)

14. Click No to avoid making an extra copy of the database at this time.

You are not commercially distributing this project; it is only a sample program, and an extra copy is not needed.

The Data Source Configuration Wizard now asks you the following question: Do You Want To Save The Connection String To The Application Configuration File? Saving the connection string is the default selection, and in this example, the recommended string name is *FacultyConnectionString*. You usually want to save this string within your application's default configuration file, because if the location of your database changes, you can edit the string in your configuration file (which is listed in Solution Explorer), as opposed to tracking down the connection string within your program code and recompiling the application.

15. Click Next to save the default connection string.

You are now prompted to select the subset of database objects that you want to use for this particular project, as shown in the following dialog box:

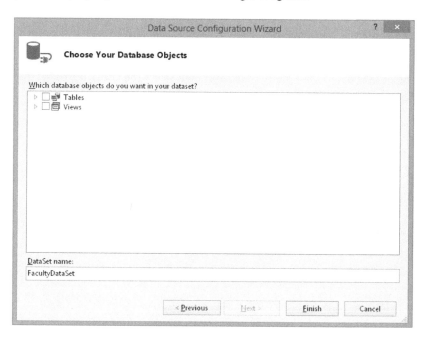

Note Visual Studio allows you to use just part of a database or to combine different databases—a useful feature when you're working to build datacentric applications.

The items you select in this dialog box are referred to within the project as *database objects*. Database objects can include tables of fields and records, database views, stored procedures, functions, and other items unique to your database. In this way, database programming in Visual Studio fits nicely into the object-oriented programming paradigm you've already been exposed to in this book.

The collective term for all the database objects that you select is a *dataset*. In this project, the dataset is assigned the default name *FacultyDataSet*, which you can adjust in the DataSet Name box.

Important The dataset you create now only *represents* the data in your database— if you add, delete, or modify database records in the dataset, you don't actually modify the underlying database tables until you issue a command that writes your changes back to the original database. Database programmers call this kind of arrangement a *disconnected data source*.

16. Click the arrow next to the Tables node to expand the list of the tables included in the *Faculty.accdb* database.

    In this case, there is only one table listed, named *Faculty*, which we'll use in our sample program.

17. Click the arrow next to the Faculty node, and then select the check boxes for the *Last Name* and *Business Phone* fields.

    You'll add these two fields to the *FacultyDataSet* dataset. The wizard page looks like the following screen shot:

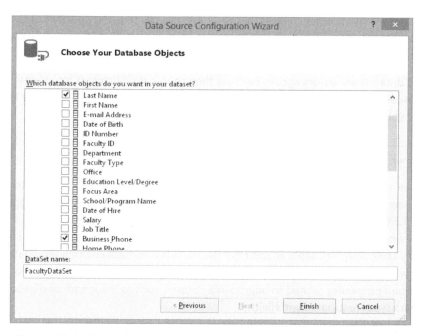

18. Click the Finish button to complete and close the Data Source Configuration Wizard.

Visual Studio finishes the tasks of adding a database connection to your project and configuring the dataset with the selected database objects.

19. Click the Save All button on the Standard toolbar to save your changes. Specify the My Documents\Visual Basic 2013 SBS\Chapter 17 folder as the location.

20. If Solution Explorer is not currently visible, open it now to display the major files and components contained in the ADO Faculty Form project.

Solution Explorer looks like this:

In addition to the standard Solution Explorer entries for a project, you see a new file named FacultyDataSet.xsd. This file is an XML schema that describes the tables, fields, data types, and other elements in the dataset that you have just created. The presence of the schema file means that you have added a *typed dataset* to your project. (Typed datasets have a schema file associated with them, but untyped datasets don't.)

Typed datasets are advantageous because they enable the Microsoft IntelliSense feature of the Visual Studio Code Editor, and they give you specific information about the fields and tables you're using.

21. Right-click the FacultyDataSet.xsd schema file in Solution Explorer, and then click View Designer.

You see a visual representation of the tables, fields, and data adapter commands related to your new dataset in a visual tool called the *Dataset Designer*. The Dataset Designer contains tools for creating components that communicate between your database and your application—what database programmers call *data access layer components*. You can create and modify table adapters, table adapter queries, data tables, data columns, and data relationships with the Dataset Designer. You can also use the Dataset Designer to review and set important properties related to objects in a dataset, such as the length of database fields and the data types associated with fields.

22. Click the *Last Name* field, and then press F4 to highlight the Properties window.

23. Click the *MaxLength* property. Your screen looks similar to the following screen shot:

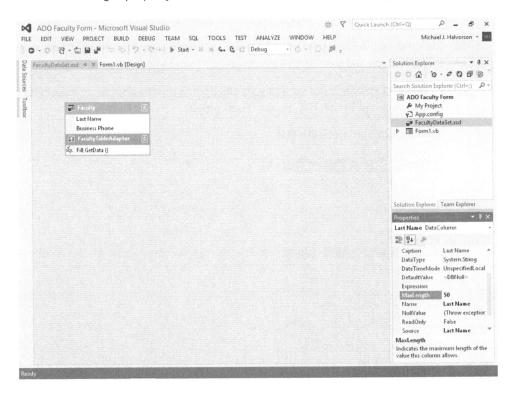

Here the Dataset Designer is shown with an active dataset named *FacultyDataSet*, and the Properties window shows that the *MaxLength* property is set to allow for a maximum of 50 characters in the *Last Name* field. Although this length seems sufficient to display the longest conceivable last names in a database, you can adjust this property (and others too) if you find that the underlying database settings are inadequate for your application.

Setting the Dataset Designer aside for a moment, let's continue building the sample database application in the Data Sources window.

The Data Sources window

The Data Sources window is a useful and timesaving feature of the Visual Studio 2013 IDE. Its purpose is to display a visual representation of the datasets that have been configured for use within your project and to help you bind these datasets to controls in the user interface. Remember that a dataset is just a temporary representation of database information in your program and that each dataset contains only a subset of the tables and fields within your entire database file—that is, only the items that you selected while using the Data Source Configuration Wizard. The dataset is displayed in a hierarchical (tree) view in the Data Sources window, with a root node for each of the objects that you selected in the wizard. Each time you run the wizard to create a new dataset, a new dataset tree is added to the Data Sources window, giving you potential access to a wide range of data sources and views within a single program.

If you have been following the instructions for selecting fields in the *Faculty* table of the *Faculty* database, you have something interesting to display in the Data Sources window now. To prepare for the following exercises and display the Data Sources window, display the form again (click the Form1.vb [Design] tab), point to the Other Windows submenu on the View menu, and then click the Data Sources command. When the Data Sources window is open, expand the *Faculty* table so that you can see the two fields that we selected. Your Data Sources window should look like this now:

Across the top of the window are four helpful tools that allow you to work with datasets. From left to right, these toolbar buttons allow you to add a new data source to your project, edit the selected dataset in the Dataset Designer, add or remove dataset fields with the wizard, and refresh the dataset.

The easiest way to display the information in a dataset on a form (and therefore for your users) is to drag objects from the Data Sources window to the Windows Forms Designer. (This is the Designer you used in earlier chapters, but I am calling it the *Windows Forms Designer* here to distinguish it from the Dataset Designer.)

In the remainder of this chapter, you'll experiment with dragging individual fields of data to the Windows Forms Designer to bind controls to select fields in the *Faculty* database. Give it a try now.

Use the Data Sources window to create database objects on a form

1. In the Data Sources window, click the arrow next to the *Faculty* node to display the available fields in *FacultyDataSet* (if you have not already done so).

   Your Data Sources window looks like the previous screen shot. In Visual Studio, you can display individual fields or an entire table of data by simply dragging the desired database objects onto your form.

2. Click the *Last Name* field, which contains the name of each instructor in the *Faculty* database. An arrow appears to the right of the *Last Name* field in the Data Sources window. If the arrow does not appear, make sure that the Form1.vb [Design] tab is active in the Designer window, and then click *Last Name* again.

3. Click the *Last Name* arrow.

   Clicking this arrow displays a list of options related to how a database field is displayed on the form when you drag it, as shown in the following screen shot:

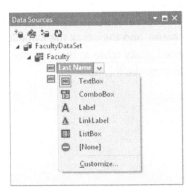

   Although I haven't discussed it yet, most of the controls on the Common Controls tab of the Toolbox have the built-in ability to display database information. In Visual Studio terminology, these controls are called *bound controls* when they are connected to data-ready fields in a dataset. Binding data to controls is an important topic in all Windows programming platforms. You'll learn how to bind XAML controls to XML data in a Windows Store app in Chapter 18.

   The list of controls you see now is a group of common options for displaying string information from a database, but you can add additional controls to the list (or remove items) by clicking the Customize command. In this case, you'll simply use the *TextBox* control, the default bound control for string data.

4. Click *TextBox* in the list.

    The list collapses, and Visual Studio registers your selection.

5. Now drag the *Last Name* field to the middle of the form in the Windows Forms Designer.

    As you drag the field over the form, a plus sign (+) below the pointer indicates that adding this database object to a form is a valid operation. When you release the mouse button, Visual Studio creates a data-ready text box object and places a professional-looking navigation bar at the top of the form. The form looks something like this (your Data Sources window might be in a different location):

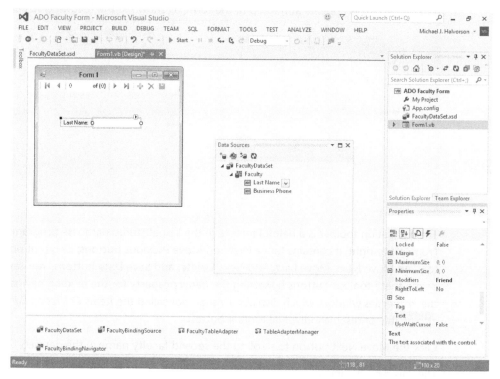

Visual Studio has actually created two objects for this *Last Name* field: a descriptive label object containing the name of the field and a bound text box object that will display the contents of the field when you run the program. Below the form in the component tray, Visual Studio has also created several objects to manage internal aspects of the data access process, including the following:

- **FacultyDataSet** The dataset that you created with the Data Source Configuration Wizard to represent fields in the *Faculty* database.

- **FacultyBindingSource** An intermediary component that acts as a conduit between the *Faculty* table and bound objects on the form.

- *FacultyTableAdapter* and *TableAdapterManager* Intermediary components that move data between *FacultyDataSet* and tables in the underlying *Faculty* database.

- *FacultyBindingNavigator* A component that provides navigation services and properties related to the navigation toolbar and the *Faculty* table.

Now you'll run the program to see how all these objects work.

6. Click the Start Debugging button on the Standard toolbar.

   The ADO Faculty Form program runs in the IDE. The text box object is loaded with the first *Last Name* record in the database (Abercrombie), and a navigation toolbar with several buttons and controls appears at the top of the form, as shown in the following screen shot:

   The navigation toolbar is a helpful feature in the Visual Studio database programming tools. From left to right, it contains Move First and Move Previous buttons; a current position indicator; and Move Next, Move Last, Add New, Delete, and Save Data buttons. You can change or delete these toolbar buttons by setting the *Items* property for the binding navigator object in the Properties window, which displays a visual tool called the *Items Collection Editor*. You can also enable or disable individual toolbar buttons.

7. Click the Move Next button to scroll to the second faculty name in the dataset.

   The Pais record appears.

8. Continue scrolling through the dataset one record at a time. As you scroll through the list of names, notice that the position indicator keeps track of where you are in the list of records.

9. Click the Move First and Move Last buttons to move to the first and last records of the dataset, respectively.

10. Delete the last record from the dataset (Skinner) by clicking the Delete button when the record is visible.

    The record is deleted from the dataset, and the position indicator shows that there are now 19 records remaining. (Lan has become the last and current record.) Your form looks like this:

As I mentioned earlier, the dataset represents only the subset of tables from the *Faculty* database that have been used in this project—the dataset is a disconnected image of the database, not the database itself. Accordingly, the record that you deleted has been deleted only from the dataset that is loaded in memory while the program is running. However, to verify that the program is actually working with disconnected data and is not modifying the original database, you'll stop and restart the program now.

11. Click the Close button on the form to end the program.

    The program terminates, and the IDE returns.

12. Click Start Debugging to run the program again.

    When the program restarts and the form loads, the navigation toolbar shows that the dataset contains 20 records, as it did originally. That is, it works as expected.

13. Click the Move Last button to view the last record in the dataset.

    The record for Skinner appears again. This final faculty name was deleted only from memory and has reappeared because the underlying database still contains the name.

14. Click the Close button again to close the program.

Well done. Without writing any program code, you have built a simple database application that displays specific information from a database. Setting up the dataset has taken many steps, but the dataset is now ready to be used in many ways in the program.

Although I selected only one table and one field from the *Faculty* database to reduce screen clutter and focus our attention, you will probably want to select a much wider range of objects from your databases when you build datasets using the Data Source Configuration Wizard. As you can see, it is not necessary to create bound objects for each dataset item on a form—you can decide which database records you want to use and display.

Using toolbox controls to display database information

As I mentioned earlier, Visual Studio can use a variety of the controls in the Visual Studio Toolbox to display database information. You can bind controls to datasets by dragging fields from the Data Sources window (the easiest method), and you can create controls separately on your forms and bind them to dataset objects at a later time. This second option is an important feature, because occasionally you will be adding data sources to a project after the basic user interface has been created.

The procedure I'll demonstrate in this section handles that situation, while giving you additional practice with binding data objects to controls within a Visual Basic application. You'll create a masked text box object on your form, configure the object to format database information in a useful way, and then bind the *Business Phone* field in *FacultyDataSet* to the object.

Bind a masked text box control to a dataset object

1. Display the form in the Windows Forms Designer.

2. Using the Properties window, change the *Text* property of the form to **Faculty Contacts**.

3. Open the Toolbox, click the *MaskedTextBox* control on the Common Controls tab, and then create a masked text box object on the form below the *Last Name* label and text box.

    As you might recall from Chapter 12, "Creative decision structures and loops," the *MaskedTextBox* control is similar to the *TextBox* control, but it gives you more ability to regulate or limit the information entered by the user into a program. The input format for the *MaskedTextBox* control is adjusted by setting the *Mask* property.

    In this exercise, you'll use *Mask* to prepare the masked text box object to display formatted phone numbers from the *Business Phone* field. (By default, phone numbers in the *Faculty* database are stored without the spacing, parentheses, or dashes of North American phone numbers, but you want to see this formatting in your program.)

4. Click the smart tag in the upper-right corner of the masked text box object, and then click the Set Mask command.

    Visual Studio displays the Input Mask dialog box, which lists a number of predefined formatting masks. Visual Studio uses these masks to format output in the masked text box object, as well as input received from users.

5. Click the Phone Number input mask, and then click OK.

    The masked text box object now appears with input formatting guidelines for the country and language settings stored within Windows. (These settings might vary from country to country, but for me, it looks like a North American telephone number with area code.)

6. Change the *Name* property of the masked text box object to **BizPhoneMasked**.

7. Add a Label control to the left of the new masked text box object, and set its *Text* property to **Phone:** (including the colon).

The first descriptive label was added automatically by the Data Sources window, but we need to add this one manually.

8. Adjust the spacing between the two labels and text boxes so that they are aligned consistently. When you're finished, your form looks similar to the following:

Now you'll bind the *Business Phone* field in *FacultyDataSet* to the new masked text box object. The process is easy—you simply drag the *Business Phone* field from the Data Sources window onto the object that you want to bind to the data—in this case, the *BizPhoneMasked* object.

9. Display the Data Sources window if it is not visible, and then drag the *Business Phone* field onto the *BizPhoneMasked* object.

When you drag a dataset object onto an object that already exists on the form (what we might call the *target object*), a new bound object is not created. Instead, the *DataBindings* properties for the target object are set to match the dragged dataset object in the Data Sources window.

After this dragging operation, the masked text box object is bound to the *Business Phone* field, and the masked text box object's *Text* property contains a small database icon in the Properties window (a sign that the object is bound to a dataset).

10. Verify that the *BizPhoneMasked* object is selected on the form, and then press F4 to highlight the Properties window.

11. Scroll to the *DataBindings* category within the Properties window, and then click the arrow to expand it.

Visual Studio displays the properties typically associated with data access for a masked text box object. Your Properties window looks similar to the following:

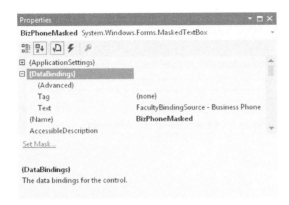

The noteworthy bound property here is the *Text* property, which has been set to FacultyBindingSource – Business Phone as a result of the dragging operation. (Note that the tiny database icon does not appear here; it appears only in the *Text* property at the bottom of the alphabetical list of properties.) In addition, if you click the arrow in the *Text* property now, you'll see a representation of the masked text box object. (This useful visual display allows you to quickly change the data source that the control is bound to, but don't adjust that setting now.)

12. Click the form to close any open Properties window panels.

13. Click the Start Debugging button to run the program.

Visual Studio runs the program in the IDE. After a moment, the two database fields are loaded into the text box and masked text box objects, as shown in the following screen shot:

Importantly, the masked text box object correctly formats the phone number information so that it is in the expected format for North American phone numbers.

14. Click the Move Next button a few times.

Another important feature is also demonstrated here: The two dataset fields scroll together, and the displayed faculty names match the corresponding business phone numbers recorded in the *Faculty* database. This synchronization is handled by the *FacultyBindingNavigator* object, which keeps track of the current record for each bound object on the form.

15. Click the Close button to stop the program, and then click the Save All button to save your changes.

You've learned to display multiple database fields on a form, use the navigation toolbar to browse through a dataset, and format database information with a mask. Very well done!

However, before you leave this chapter, take a moment to filter your dataset by using a few SQL statements.

SQL statements and filtering data

You have used the Data Source Configuration Wizard to extract just the table and fields you wanted from the *Faculty* database by creating a custom dataset named *FacultyDataSet*. In addition to this filtering, you can further organize and fine-tune the data displayed by bound controls by using SQL statements and the Visual Studio Query Builder. This section introduces these tools.

For Visual Basic users who are familiar with Access or SQL Server, filtering data with SQL statements is nothing new. But the rest of us need to learn that *SQL statements* are commands that extract, or *filter*, information from one or more structured tables in a database. The reason for this filtering is simple: Just as web users are routinely confronted with a bewildering amount of data on the Internet (and use clever search keywords in their browsers to locate just the information they need), database programmers are routinely confronted with tables containing tens of thousands of records that need refinement and organization to accomplish a particular task. The SQL SELECT statement is one traditional mechanism for organizing database information. By chaining together a group of these statements, programmers can create complex search directives, or *queries*, that extract only the data that is needed from a database.

Realizing the industry-wide acceptance of SQL, Visual Studio offers several mechanisms for using SQL statements. You have already been introduced to a close cousin of SQL, *Language-Integrated Query (LINQ)*, which allows Visual Basic programmers to write SQL-styled queries directly within Visual Basic code. Chapter 15, "Innovative data management with LINQ," introduced that tool and explored how to extract information from arrays, collections, and generic lists.

In the following exercise, I'll demonstrate a second mechanism related to SQL, a powerful feature in the IDE called *Query Builder*. Query Builder is a visual tool that helps programmers construct database queries based on SQL syntax. In the following example, you'll use Query Builder to further organize your *FacultyDataSet* dataset by sorting it alphabetically.

Create SQL statements with Query Builder

1. On the form, click the *Last_NameTextBox* object (the first bound object that you created to display the last names of faculty members in the *Faculty* database).

2. Click the smart tag in the upper-right corner of the *Last_NameTextBox* object, and then click the Add Query command.

The Add Query command is available when a bound object, such as *Last_NameTextBox*, is selected in the Designer. The Search Criteria Builder dialog box opens, as shown in the following screen shot:

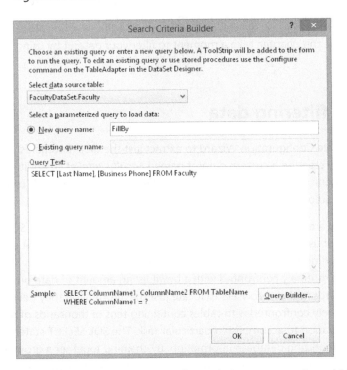

This dialog box helps you organize and view your queries, which are created by the Query Builder and consist of SQL statements. (However, a full discussion of SQL syntax is beyond the scope of this book.) The table that your query will filter and organize by default (*FacultyDataSet.Faculty*) is selected in the Select Data Source Table box, near the top of the dialog box. You'll recognize the object hierarchy format used by the table name, which is read as "the *Faculty* table within the *FacultyDataSet* dataset." If you had other tables to choose among, they would be in the list box displayed when you click the Select Data Source Table arrow.

3. Type **SortLastNames** in the New Query Name box.

    This text box assigns a name to your query and forms the basis of toolbar buttons added to the form. (For easy access, the default arrangement is that new queries are assigned to toolbar buttons within the application you are building.)

4. Click the Query Builder button in the dialog box to open the Query Builder tool.

The Query Builder allows you to create SQL statements by typing them directly into a large SQL statement text box or by clicking list boxes and other visual tools.

5. In the *Last Name* row representing the *Last Name* field in your dataset, click the cell under Sort Type, and then click the arrow to display the Sort Type list box.

Your screen looks like this:

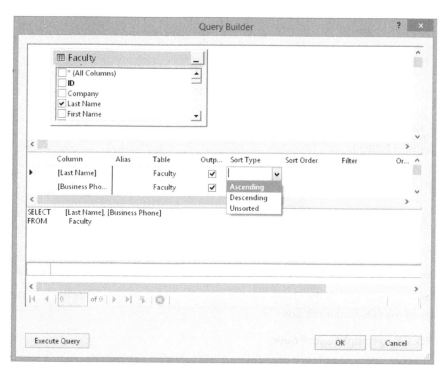

6. In the Sort Type list box, click Ascending.

You'll sort records in the *Last Name* field in ascending order.

7. Click the SQL statement text box below the grid pane to update the Query Builder window.

A new clause (ORDER BY [Last Name]) is added to the SQL statement box, and your screen looks like this:

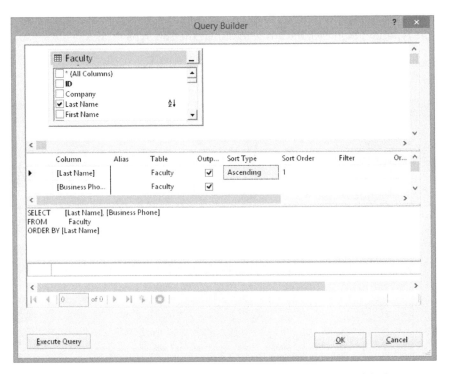

This is the strength of the Query Builder tool—it automatically builds the SQL statements for you in the SQL statement box.

8. Click OK to complete your query.

Visual Studio closes the Query Builder and displays your new query in the Search Criteria Builder dialog box. The name of the query (*SortLastNames*) is listed, as well as the SQL statements that make up the sort.

9. Click OK to close the Search Criteria Builder dialog box, and then configure the *Last_NameTextBox* object to list names in ascending alphabetical order.

The process has also created a *SortLastNamesToolStrip* object in the component tray below the form. The Designer and component tray now look like this:

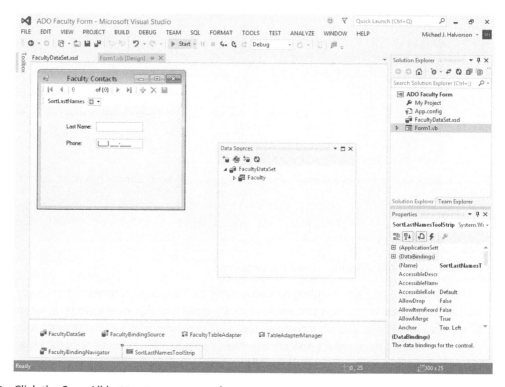

10. Click the Save All button to save your changes.

11. Click the Start Debugging button to run the program.

Visual Studio loads the form and displays the first record for two dataset objects.

12. Click the SortLastNames button on the new toolbar.

Your new SQL statement sorts the *Last Name* records in the dataset and displays the records in their new order. The first record is still Abercrombie, but now the second and third names are Atlas and Bankov, respectively. Such a sort would be useful to provide more systematic access to the records in the database. Rather than displaying the records as they were entered in the database (with no apparent order), an alphabetical sort provides the user with something more tangible.

13. Click the Move Last button on the toolbar.

Now Zimprich appears, as shown in the following screen shot:

Because the names are listed alphabetically from A to Z, Zimprich is now last in the list of faculty members.

14. Scroll through the remainder of the records, and then verify that it is now in ascending alphabetical order.

15. Click the Close button to end the program.

You're on your way with building custom queries by using SQL statements and Query Builder. This tool will be especially helpful if you want to quickly add some SQL queries to your database application. Database programming is a complex topic, but you have learned fundamental techniques that will help you build datacentric applications—highly personalized collections of data that benefit the user and his or her computing needs—in Visual Basic.

Summary

This chapter has offered an introduction to database programming in Visual Basic with Windows Forms and the ADO.NET data model. ADO.NET is the standard data access technology for Visual Studio programmers; it is a fundamental building block for Visual Basic programs that connect to local and remote databases. You began your work with ADO.NET by using the Data Source Connection Wizard to connect to a local Access database on your system. You learned how to create a dataset that represents the fields and records of a database table and how to use the Dataset Designer and Data Sources window to create bound objects on the forms of a Windows desktop application. You also learned how to use SQL SELECT statements and the Query Builder tool to filter database information.

In the next chapter, you'll build on these important skills by connecting to XML documents in a Windows Store application. You'll move beyond wizards and visual tools, and you'll explore fundamental data management techniques within Visual Basic code. Although the techniques are somewhat different in a Windows Store app that organizes data assets in a different manner, you'll still be binding data to objects on the page—an essential skill that you also explored in this chapter.

CHAPTER 18

Data access for Windows Store apps

After completing this chapter, you will be able to

- Bind XAML controls to data in a Windows Store application.

- Use the *XDocument* and *XElement* classes in the *System.Xml.Linq* namespace.

- Read and write records in XML data sources.

- Use LINQ to search and filter XML documents.

In this chapter, you'll continue working with data in a Visual Studio 2013 application. In Chapter 17, "Database controls for Windows desktop apps," you learned how to establish a connection to a database by using the Data Source Configuration Wizard and how to bind Windows Forms controls to an Access database and extract records. Accessing data is conceptually similar in a Windows Store app, although the process of binding data to XAML controls is somewhat different. You'll learn the syntax in this chapter, and the information that you access will come from classes, collections, and XML documents.

Windows Store apps often use XML documents as the source of their information when they need database information. This is because XML documents have some important advantages over proprietary database formats, such as Microsoft Access.

First, XML is based on an open, public standard that has been adopted by Microsoft and other software publishers for information exchange. Second, XML files are easily created within an application or downloaded via the Windows Store. Because your project is installed and updated via the web, data access is typically much more involved than simply accessing records from a local database. Third, XML files have a well-understood hierarchy and tagging format that is easily integrated into a Visual Studio programming project. Finally, the ADO.NET database framework has been optimized for XML data sources and syntax.

This chapter teaches you how to bind XAML controls to data in a Windows Store application and how to read, search, and write to XML documents—a major source of data on the Windows platform.

Data binding in XAML

The first skill to learn when working with data in a Windows Store app is *binding* data to XAML controls on the page. Binding means establishing a connection between a user interface control and a data object that has been included or referenced in the project. You typically bind Windows Store controls to data by using XAML markup while you are designing the user interface for your application.

After the data binding has been established, the control on the page will change automatically whenever the data object is updated. In addition, your program can send changes made to the data in bound controls back to the original data source so that a Windows Store application can interact with and update local files stored on the user's system or files stored on the Internet.

A variety of data sources

The data for a Windows Store app can exist in several locations. In some cases, the Visual Studio developer will be involved with locating and loading the files directly, and in some cases, Windows will handle most of the details about where the files are located and how they are stored.

If your app works with local files on the computer, you can access these resources by using XML-related objects and methods in ADO.NET (discussed later in this chapter) or by loading the files directly via one of the file picker tools provided by the .NET Framework. You can also access live data on the Internet, such as RSS feeds or Bing Maps, using API calls in Windows Web Services.

You should also know that Windows will store the data associated with your application in different locations. If you build an application that is enabled for *roaming*, meaning that the settings and files can be kept in sync across multiple devices, Windows will handle where the information is stored in the cloud and how it is accessed. When your program has *app data* that is specific to a particular user or session, such as confidential information or user preferences, Windows will store the information securely in the system registry and various local files. When the user runs the program again, this information will be loaded automatically.

Although the potential range of data sources and connections goes well beyond the scope of this chapter, most data in a Windows Store app can be packaged as an instance of a class or by using a data template so that the data can be displayed on a page using bound controls. You'll see how this works in the exercises that follow.

Binding elements

Every data binding includes the following elements:

- A *binding source* that is an object with data that you want to access or display. Typically, a property in the data object is the source of the data.

- A *binding target* that is a control in the user interface that displays data. A property in the control is typically set as the binding target, such as the *Text* property of the *TextBox* control.

- A *binding object* that transfers the data between the binding source and binding target and that can also reformat the data by using a converter, if required.

The data binding is expressed in XAML markup as a *markup extension*. Markup extensions are used in XAML when there is a need to identify an attribute that is not simply a literal value. The name of a data source fits this definition; another typical usage for markup extension is when you want to specify a static resource such as a built-in text style in Visual Studio to format an object on the page.

A pair of curly braces, "{" and "}", indicate that the specified XAML is a markup extension. This syntax will force the XAML processor to evaluate the given attribute and insert the resource specified when the program runs. One of the most common reference words used in markup extension is *Binding*, which indicates that the control is a binding target and that a binding object will specify how the data binding will take place.

For example, the following XAML defines a *TextBox* control named *OutputTextBox* on the page of a Windows Store app. Notice that the *Text* property of this control uses a markup extension reference to indicate that the control is a binding target in the application.

```
<TextBox x:Name="OutputTextBox" Text="{Binding}" FontSize="28" IsReadOnly="True"
         TextWrapping="Wrap" AcceptsReturn="True" Margin="12,51,1001,637"
         ScrollViewer.VerticalScrollBarVisibility="Auto" />
```

When data binding is specified in XAML as shown in the preceding example, additional properties can also be set to control how the binding functions in the program. For example, the following XAML shows how one might configure the *Text* property for data binding and also specify that the data access be *TwoWay* (indicating that both the target and the source will be updated when either changes), and that the text displayed will be additionally formatted by the *Converter1* style within a *StaticResource* dictionary.

```
Text="{Binding Mode=TwoWay, Converter={StaticResource Converter1}}"
```

The Visual Studio documentation on MSDN provides several examples of how binding objects can be specified using the various properties and methods in the *Binding* class. See *http://msdn.microsoft.com/en-us/library/windows/apps/windows.ui.xaml.data.binding.aspx.*

In the following exercise, you will see how the *TextBox* control defined in the preceding example can be bound to a class in a Visual Basic program.

Binding a control to a class

In Chapter 16, "Object-oriented programming techniques," you learned how to create your own base classes with custom properties and methods and how to use the new classes using method overriding and other techniques. Those skills will come in handy in this exercise, where you will use a custom base class named *Student* to hold registration information for a ski school. The Visual Basic class will have four properties that hold data about the student and skiing course that they are enrolled in, including *Student*, *ClassName*, *StartDate*, and *Instructor*. You'll learn how to bind this class to a *TextBox* control on the page so that the control can display information from a linked source.

Although the example doesn't demonstrate how to connect to an XML data source or an entire collection of records, this first exercise is a steppingstone toward that goal. When you know how to bind a XAML control to a data object (such as an instance of the *Student* class), you can use similar techniques to bind to any type of data in a Windows Store app.

Bind a data source to a *TextBox* control

1. Start Visual Studio, and open the Data Binding program, a Windows Store app located in the My Documents\Visual Basic 2013 SBS\Chapter 18 folder.

    This demonstration program already contains *TextBox* and *ListBox* controls, defined with XAML markup, to show how binding works in different data access scenarios. The binding source in this example is the *Student* class, a custom class that is defined in the MainPage.Xaml.vb code-behind file.

    The basic user interface for the Data Binding app looks like this in the IDE:

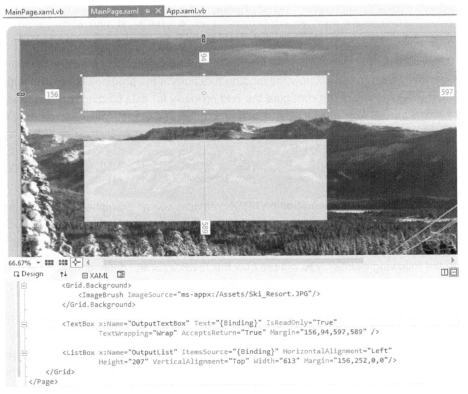

    Now look at the XAML code that produces the *Grid* background image and the *TextBox* control. (You'll examine the *ListBox* control in the next exercise.)

2. Open the XAML tab of the Code Editor, and examine the markup for the page.

    You'll see the following statements:

```
<Grid.Background>
        <ImageBrush ImageSource="ms-appx:/Assets/Ski_Resort.JPG"/>
</Grid.Background>

<TextBox x:Name="OutputTextBox" Text="{Binding}" IsReadOnly="True"
        TextWrapping="Wrap" AcceptsReturn="True" Margin="156,94,597,589"/>
```

The first block of markup simply sets the *ImageSource* property for the *Grid* background image. We used this syntax in earlier chapters; recall that to make it work you need to load the image file into the project's Assets folder (which I've done for you). The Ski_Resort.jpg image gives the application a wintry feel.

Now examine the second set of lines, which define the *OutputTextBox* object. Notice in particular the text box's *Text* property, which is set to *{Binding}*. This bit of markup extension prepares the text box for a data connection when the program runs. In effect, the XAML defines the *OutputTextBox* object as the binding target for a data source.

You have two options for specifying the binding source. First, you can set the *Binding.Source* property in the text box's XAML to specify (by name) the data object in the program that is the source of the information. Alternatively, you can set the text box object's *DataContext* property, which is the preferred method if you are making more than one connection to the data source in the program. I'll use the second method in this program, and I'll set the *DataContext* property to the *Student* class using program code.

3. Open the MainPage.xaml.vb code-behind file in the Code Editor.

    This is the location of the program's constructor and custom class used for data access. First, look at how the *Student* class is defined using Visual Basic code:

```
'A public class that provides a data source (with 4 properties) for bound controls.
Public Class Student
    Public Sub New()
    End Sub

    Public Sub New(ByVal studentName As String, ByVal classTitle As String,
        ByVal sessionDate As DateTime, ByVal teacher As String)
        Student = studentName
        ClassName = classTitle
        StartDate = sessionDate
        Instructor = teacher
    End Sub

    'These properties contain student name, course, start date, & instructor.
    Public Property Student As String
    Public Property ClassName As String
    Public Property StartDate As DateTime
    Public Property Instructor As String
    ' The following statement overrides the ToString method.
    Public Overloads Overrides Function ToString() As String
        Return Student + " enrolled in " + ClassName + "; Begins: " _
            + StartDate.ToString("d") + "; Instructor: " + Instructor
    End Function
End Class
```

The *Student* class is a new class created just for this program and its data requirements. The class defines four public properties, and it creates a *ToString* method override to display the data. The properties are *Student, ClassName, StartDate,* and *Instructor.* I'm using typical class and property procedure syntax for the declaration; you can learn more about these Visual Basic keywords in Chapter 16.

4. Scroll up in the Code Editor to display the *Public Sub New* procedure.

You'll see the following program statements, followed by a block of comments:

```
' Constructor
Public Sub New()
    InitializeComponent()

    ' Sample 1: Bind a TextBox control to the Student class to display
    ' one student record.
    ' Sets DataContext property of text box to new student record with name,
    ' course, start date, and instructor fields.
    OutputTextBox.DataContext = New Student("Kim Akers", "Intermediate Skiing",
        New DateTime(2015, 2, 5), "Hamlin")
```

This *New* procedure runs when the program is launched, providing a simple way to test the program code that binds the *TextBox* control to data in the *Student* class. Recall from Chapter 16 that this procedure is called a constructor. A *constructor* is simply a procedure named *New* that Visual Basic calls when a new instance of a class or structure is created. Constructors do basic initialization work and get an object ready for use.

The statement related to data access here is the final statement (broken into two lines), which sets the *DataContext* property of the text box object to a new instance of the *Student* class. As noted earlier, the *DataContext* property provides a simple way to specify the data source that is used for data binding.

A typical use of *DataContext* is to set it to point directly to a data source object. This data source object might be an instance of a class such as the *Student* class used here. Alternatively, you might create a data source as an observable collection (which I'll do in the next exercise) so that the data context allows modifications made to the data to travel back to the linked collection.

The *DataContext* property is most convenient when you want to bind several different properties on the same object to a shared data source. However, you can also leave the *DataContext* property undefined, leaving binding directives to other statements, such as the *Binding.Source* keyword.

In its entirety, the two-line statement that we just examined defines a new data object (a class named *Student*), fills the object with data, and then identifies the data object as the binding source for the *TextBox* control on the page. However, it would be just as simple to assign another kind of data object to the *TextBox* control—you are limited only by the capability of the *TextBox* control to display data.

Finally, note the comment block consisting of twelve lines at the bottom of the *Sub New* procedure. This is the sample code for the next exercise you'll work on. I've just commented it out here to avoid distraction right now.

You'll run the program now to see how data binding works.

5. Click the Start Debugging button.

The application launches and displays a page containing a ski resort image, a text box, and a list box. The *Sub New* procedure runs immediately and produces the following result:

As you can see, Visual Basic created the *Student* class, filled the class with the information for one student, bound the class to the *TextBox* control, and displayed the information on the screen. In each example that you work with in this chapter, the *TextBox* control will use the *ToString* method as the source of the content that is displayed. Close the program, and return to the Visual Studio IDE.

You're off to a good start. You've learned a very fundamental use of data binding—establishing a connection between a control on the page and a custom class that contains data. Now you'll bind a *ListBox* control to an entire collection of student records.

Using a collection as a source of data

Now that you know how data binding works, it is time for a more typical example of data binding in a Windows Store app. Building on a skill you learned in Chapter 14, "Using arrays, collections, and generics to manage data," you'll learn how to bind a generic collection to a *ListBox* control in this section.

The generic collection type we'll use in this exercise is a list known as an *ObservableCollection*, because it implements the *INotifyCollectionChanged* and *INotifyPropertyChanged* interfaces. These interfaces send change notification events to bound controls when an item in the collection is modified or when a property of the collection is modified, respectively. In Visual Studio 2013, not all data objects send this type of notification to bound controls, so *ObservableCollection* is especially handy. However, you can implement the *INotifyPropertyChanged* interface yourself for a binding source if you ever need to. For more information, see the section "Change notification" in the topic "Data binding overview," at *http://msdn.microsoft.com/en-us/library/windows/apps/hh758320.aspx*.

The sample code that I want you to examine and run is also located in the Data Binding project, which should be loaded in Visual Studio now if you completed the previous exercise.

Bind an observable collection to a *ListBox* control

1. Display the MainPage.xaml file again in the Code Editor so that you can see the XAML that defines the *ListBox* object on the page that will be the binding target for the observable collection.

   You'll see the following markup:

   ```
   <ListBox x:Name="OutputList" ItemsSource="{Binding}" HorizontalAlignment="Left"
            Height="287" VerticalAlignment="Top" Width="655" Margin="156,252,0,0"/>
   ```

   Recall that a XAML *ListBox* control is a user interface tool that displays a list of items in a rectangular box on the screen. Unlike the *TextBox* control, the items in a *ListBox* control can be accessed individually and modified, removed, or sorted. You can also add new items to a *ListBox* control at run time.

   In this bit of markup, I am naming the control *OutputList* (so that I can reference it in Visual Basic code) and I am setting the *ItemsSource* property to *{Binding}*, which establishes *OutputList* as the binding target. (You'll find that most of the XAML controls that can be assigned a collection of objects have an *ItemsSource* property.) Like the previous exercise, I'll set the binding source for the data connection by setting the *ListBox* control's *DataContext* property to the instance of the observable collection *AllStudents*.

2. Display the MainPage.xaml.vb code-behind file in the Code Editor.

   Now you'll see how the observable collection is defined, and you'll uncomment the program code to fill the collection with data.

3. Locate the *Public AllStudents* program statement near the middle of the file.

   You'll see the following code:

   ```
   'A public generic collection used for Sample 2 to store student data.
   Public AllStudents As New ObservableCollection(Of Student)()
   ```

   This statement creates a new public observable collection named *AllStudents* to store student records in the ski school. The collection will contain records of type *Student*—that is, records that each match the structure of the *Student* class you created in the first exercise. (Because you are still in the same program, that class is still defined, unchanged, in the MainPage.xaml. vb file.) Here you can see the advantage of creating your own classes, if it was not already obvious—you can create custom data records that are easily combined into collections of almost any size.

   The only code that remains is the block that fills the collection with data and then sets the *DataContext* property of the *ListBox* object to the *AllStudents* collection. Because this is a simple demonstration program, I will just be using the *AllStudents* collection's *Add* method to add four records to the data object. But in a full-featured program, you could use input controls to prompt the user for student records, validate them, and then add them to the collection. You could also load information from a text file or database into the collection.

4. Locate the *Public Sub New* procedure near the top of the file.

   You'll see the following code:

   ```
   ' Constructor
      Public Sub New()
         InitializeComponent()

         ' Sample 1: Bind a TextBox control to the Student class to display
         ' one student record.
         ' Sets DataContext property of text box to new student record with name,
         ' course, start date, and instructor fields.
         OutputTextBox.DataContext = New Student("Kim Akers", "Intermediate Skiing",
            New DateTime(2015, 2, 5), "Hamlin")

         ' Sample 2: Bind a ListBox control to a collection of student records.
         ' To run this sample, uncomment the following code, which adds 4 student
         ' records to the collection in the format required by Students class.
         ' AllStudents.Add(New Student("Walter Harp", "Beginning Snowboarding",
         '    New DateTime(2014, 1, 15), "Khan"))
         'AllStudents.Add(New Student("Toni Poe", "Advanced Ski Racing",
         '    New DateTime(2014, 1, 8), "Hanson"))
         'AllStudents.Add(New Student("Paul Cannon", "Beginning Nordic",
         '    New DateTime(2015, 1, 13), "Khan"))
         'AllStudents.Add(New Student("Sunil Uppal", "Beginning Nordic",
         '    New DateTime(2015, 1, 13), "Khan"))
         'OutputList.DataContext = AllStudents    'this line assigns collection to list box

      End Sub
   ```

This is the routine that runs when the Windows Store app is launched. Currently, just the data binding code connecting the *TextBox* control to the *Student* class is active. However, now you'll activate (or uncomment) the Visual Basic code related to Sample 2, which fills the *AllStudents* collection with data and binds it to the *ListBox* control.

5. Uncomment the nine lines of code in this procedure that begin with a single quotation mark ('). The first line I want you to uncomment begins with *'AllStudents.Add*. The last line begins with *'OutputList.DataContext*.

   To uncomment a line of code, you simply remove the single quotation mark from the beginning of the line. If you are using the default VB keyboard setup, you can also select a group of commented lines and press Ctrl+K followed by Ctrl+U to uncomment the lines. (You can also comment-out a collection of selected lines by pressing Ctrl+K followed by Ctrl+C.)

   The *New Sub* procedure should look like this when you are finished:

```
MainPage.xaml.vb  + X   MainPage.xaml        App.xaml.vb
MainPage                                     - ۞ New

        ' Constructor
        Public Sub New()
            InitializeComponent()

            ' Sample 1: Bind a TextBox control to the Student class to display
            ' one student record.
            ' Sets DataContext property of text box to new student record with name,
            ' course, start date, and instructor fields.
            OutputTextBox.DataContext = New Student("Kim Akers", "Intermediate Skiing", _
                New DateTime(2015, 2, 5), "Hamlin")

            ' Sample 2: Bind a ListBox control to a collection of student records.
            ' To run this sample, uncomment the following code, which adds 4 student
            ' records to the collection in the format required by Students class.
            AllStudents.Add(New Student("Walter Harp", "Beginning Snowboarding", _
                New DateTime(2014, 1, 15), "Khan"))
            AllStudents.Add(New Student("Toni Poe", "Advanced Ski Racing", _
                New DateTime(2014, 1, 8), "Hanson"))
            AllStudents.Add(New Student("Paul Cannon", "Beginning Nordic", _
                New DateTime(2015, 1, 13), "Khan"))
            AllStudents.Add(New Student("Sunil Uppal", "Beginning Nordic", _
                New DateTime(2015, 1, 13), "Khan"))
            OutputList.DataContext = AllStudents    'this line assigns collection to list box

        End Sub
```

Each of the Visual Basic program statements assigns a student record to the *AllStudents* collection. The *New DataTime* syntax adds the date of the first ski school class to the collection in *DateTime* format, which is more flexible than simply storing the date in a *String* variable. The final statement completes the data connection process, using the list box's *DataContext* property to set the *AllStudents* collection as the binding source.

You'll run the program now to see how binding to a collection works.

6. Click the Start Debugging button.

   The app starts and displays a page containing a ski resort image, a text box, and a list box. The *Sub New* procedure runs and produces the following result:

Kim Akers enrolled in Intermediate Skiing; Begins: 2/5/2015; Instructor: Hamlin

Walter Harp enrolled in Beginning Snowboarding; Begins: 1/15/2014; Instructor: Khan

Toni Poe enrolled in Advanced Ski Racing; Begins: 1/8/2014; Instructor: Hanson

Paul Cannon enrolled in Beginning Nordic; Begins: 1/13/2015; Instructor: Khan

Sunil Uppal enrolled in Beginning Nordic; Begins: 1/13/2015; Instructor: Khan

The four student records in the collection appear in the list box object. This means that Visual Basic created the *Student* class, used the class to define an observable collection named *AllStudents*, filled the collection with data, bound the collection to the *ListBox* control, and successfully displayed the information by using the *ToString* method.

7. Click each item in the list box individually.

Because list box items are kept distinct, each of the items can be selected and manipulated individually, which makes this a good control to display lists of data.

It would now be a relatively simple task to write individual event handlers that added or removed items from the collection, disabled items, or rearranged the list. (Each event handler could be tied to a user interface control, such as a button object.) The key mechanisms for creating these features are the *ListBox* control's *SelectionChanged* event, which fires when an item in the list box is selected, and the *SelectedIndex* property, which contains information about the item selected.

Because you have bound an observable collection to the list box, any changes that you make to the items in the list can also be sent back to the *AllStudents* data object, if you prefer. To accomplish this, one change you would need to make is to set the *Mode* property of the binding object to *TwoWay*. However, you will also need to allow for the data source to be updated by actions that are independent of the user's interaction with the *ListBox* control. (That is, you can assume that your application is the only way that items are added to or removed from a data source.)

8. Close the program.

9. When the Visual Studio IDE reappears, save your changes and close the Data Binding project.

You've seen how data binding works in a Windows Store app and, hopefully, some of the potential of this powerful ADO.NET technology. Now you'll learn more about using XML documents in a Windows Store app.

Accessing data in XML documents

In Chapter 15, "Innovative data management with LINQ," you learned a little about XML documents and how they can be used as a source of data for LINQ queries. Now it's time to experiment a little more with XML and to see how XML documents can be read, searched, and written by a Windows Store app.

An *XML document* is a simply a structured text file that conforms to the open XML specifications established by the World Wide Web Consortium (W3C). XML documents do not have a set list of predefined elements that they need to contain. Instead, they allow you to create your own names and structure for elements in a document. The elements just need to conform to basic syntax rules for tagging (enclosing items with < and > tags) and to fit together in a hierarchy under a single top-level element. In Visual Studio, you can add an XML document to a project by including it in your project's Assets folder.

XML files are essentially just text files, so they are relatively small in size when compared to relational databases that hold the same content. This makes XML files efficient to work with and exchange over the web. The format's popularity has led Microsoft to integrate XML support into ADO.NET and the Visual Studio languages, and since Visual Studio 2008, XAML markup, which is closely related to XML, has been a feature of application development for Windows. In the remainder of this chapter, you'll work with two simple XML documents. You'll practice fundamental data access skills, including reading an XML file, searching for information in XML files, and writing to an XML file. You'll use the Visual Studio *System.Xml.Linq* namespace to assist you with these efforts.

Reading an XML file

With the advent of Language Integrated Query (LINQ), working with XML document has become even easier in a Visual Studio program. Two helpful classes in the *System.Xml.Linq* namespace that provide useful functionality are *XDocument* and *XElement*. You'll use both classes in this chapter.

XDocument allows you to store a complete in-memory copy of an XML document in your program. After you load the document into memory, you can display its contents, search for specific items with LINQ, or add new items to the document. *XDocument* even has a *Save* method that allows you to save the changed in-memory version of the XML document to disk.

The following Visual Basic code demonstrates how to load an XML document named Students.xml into memory, storing the document's contents in a new object named *Students*.

```
Dim Students As XDocument = XDocument.Load("Assets/Students.xml")
```

Note that the preceding statement assumes that the Students.xml file has already been added to the project's Assets folder, making it available for use throughout the project. And because the *Students* object is of type *XDocument*, it has access to all of the properties and methods of the *XDocument* class. (You'll see a few of these used in the exercises that follow.)

The *XElement* class complements *XDocument*, allowing you to load just a portion of an XML document into memory. For example, you could create an *XElement* object containing just one tagged element, or you could create an *XElement* object that holds a large portion of an XML document in memory for some processing purpose.

The following program statement creates a new *XElement* object named *xe* that contains beginning and ending LASTNAME tags and the string value "Lyon":

```
Dim xe As XElement = New XElement("LASTNAME", "Lyon")
```

This creates the equivalent of the following XML markup:

```
<LASTNAME>Lyon</LASTNAME>
```

In the exercise that follows, you'll open the XML Document Data project, a Windows Store app written in Visual Basic. The project contains six code samples that demonstrate how XML documents are read, searched through, and written—the most common database programming tasks in a Windows Store application. You will uncomment the various code samples as you work your way through the remaining sections of this chapter.

The first exercise demonstrates how you can open an XML document in a Windows Store app and then display its entire contents—including tags—in a text box object on the page. This first exercise is simply meant to show the structure of the XML document and to show you how easy it is to display such a file in a program. However, you'll more typically suppress the XML tags, and I'll do this in most of the subsequent exercises.

Open an XML document and display its contents

1. Start Visual Studio, and open the XML Document Data program, a Windows Store app located in the My Documents\Visual Basic 2013 SBS\Chapter 18 folder.

   This demonstration program already contains a *TextBox* control named *OutputTextBox*, a *Button* control named *XmlTestButton*, a code-behind file containing data access routines, two XML files in the Assets folder, and a background image for the page.

The basic user interface for the XML Document Data app looks like this in the IDE:

The XAML for the *Button* and *TextBox* controls is very straightforward; however, you should note that the *TextBox* control is not bound to a data source in this particular example. (You learned how that ADO.NET technology works in the last exercise.)

When the user clicks the *XmlTestButton* control, an event handler named *XmlTestButton_Click* fires, which runs the data access routines I've developed for you in the code-behind file. The output of the data access routines is always displayed in the *OutputTextBox* object so that you can see how the XML data is loaded and processed by the program.

2. Open the MainPage.xaml.vb code-behind file in the Code Editor.

This is the location of six routines or samples that demonstrate how to read, display, search through, and write XML documents. The first routine is uncommented and ready for use. (The other samples are commented, and you will uncomment them in future exercises.)

You'll see the following Visual Basic code near the top of the code-behind file:

```
'SAMPLE 1: Opening an XML document in a text box.
'  This code loads an XML document into the Students object and displays it
'  in a text box, complete with tags.

OutputTextBox.Text = "All content in the XML file including tags:" & vbCrLf & vbCrLf
Dim Students As XDocument = XDocument.Load("Assets/Students.xml")
OutputTextBox.Text &= Students.ToString
```

The first line displays an explanatory header at the top of the text file. The second line declares an *XDocument* object named *Students* to hold the contents of the Students.xml file. The third line assigns the content of the *Students* object to the *OutputTextBox* object so that it appears on the page with the header. The *ToString* method is used to convert the XML data to *String* format.

Note that this code simply displays the contents of the XML document in the text box—tags and all. Accordingly, it is useful primarily for testing purposes and to demonstrate how easy it is to work with and display XML document content in a program.

3. Click Start Debugging to run the program.

4. Click the Display Data button.

Visual Studio loads the XML document into the *Students* object and displays it in the text box. Your page will look like this:

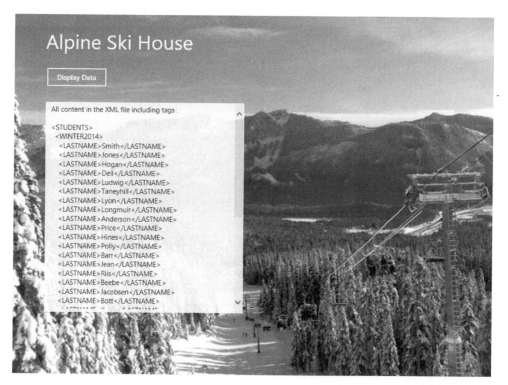

The Students.xml file contains the last names of students in the Alpine House ski school who are scheduled to take classes during the Winter 2014 term. Tags appear around the various structural headings and names, and you can use the scroll bars to view the entire document. This is the data that you will be working with in the next few exercises.

5. Close the program.

Now you'll learn how to display records in an XML document without the tags. This task can be accomplished in several ways, but perhaps the most straightforward approach is to use LINQ, the data extraction tool you learned to use in Chapter 15. Because LINQ is built into Visual Studio and the Visual Basic programming language, it has a compact coding structure and also provides IntelliSense to help you work with database records.

You'll use LINQ in the following exercise to display all of the records in the Students.xml document that are surrounded by <LASTNAME></LASTNAME> tags.

Read a selection of tagged XML elements

1. Open the MainPage.xaml.vb code-behind file, if it is not currently visible in the Code Editor.

   The *XmlTestButton_Click* event handler is the most dominant routine in the MainPage.xaml.vb file, and you'll see that it contains six data access code blocks written in Visual Basic. Because all six of these sections use the *OutputTextBox* object to display database information on the page, I designed them to be run and tested one at a time. Accordingly, the procedure you'll follow in this exercise and those that follow is to uncomment the block that you want to run and test and to comment-out the blocks that you are no longer using.

    Note By *uncomment,* I simply mean to remove the comment character (') from the beginning of each line in the routine. *Comment-out* means to place a comment character (') at the beginning of each line, effectively hiding the code from the compiler and rendering it inactive.

2. Comment out the first block (Sample 1) in the *XmlTestButton_Click* event handler, and then uncomment the second block (Sample 2).

   Remember that you can comment out a block if you select it and press Ctrl+K, followed by Ctrl+C. You can uncomment a block if you select it and press Ctrl+K, followed by Ctrl+U.

   After you're finished, you'll see the following code for Sample 2, which demonstrates how to read a selection of tagged records from an XML document:

```
'SAMPLE 2: Display a selection of records from an XML document using LINQ.
'  In the following LINQ query, all of the tagged items that match LASTNAME
'  are displayed in a text box. Note the exact capitalization of LASTNAME!

OutputTextBox.Text = "Last Names of all Students in program" & vbCrLf & vbCrLf
Dim Students As XDocument = XDocument.Load("Assets/Students.xml")
Dim query = From person In Students.Descendants("LASTNAME")
            Select person.Value

For Each item In query
    OutputTextBox.Text &= item & vbCrLf
Next
```

Chapter 15 discusses the syntax for LINQ query expressions in detail, but as a review, recall that most LINQ queries use *Dim* to declare a storage variable to hold the results of the query, and in this case, I've used *query*. LINQ is in essence a data extraction tool, and the elements of a LINQ query systematically extract the specified elements from a data source. Here the data source is the XML document stored in the *Students* data object, and the records that I want to extract are all of the tagged items or "nodes" identified by the LASTNAME element.

There is no specific *Where* clause in this LINQ query. All of the LASTNAME records are returned by the *Select* statement and stored in the *person* variable. A *For Each...Next* loop then displays the names one by one in the *OutputTextBox* object.

Be advised that operations involving XML and LINQ are case sensitive, so you must identify the LASTNAME element in this routine by using all capital letters. (This is because the tags in the Students.xml file are coded in all capital letters.)

3. Click Start Debugging to run the program.

4. Click the Display Data button.

Visual Studio loads the XML document into the *Students* object and then uses LINQ to extract and display the specified LASTNAME records. Your page will look like this:

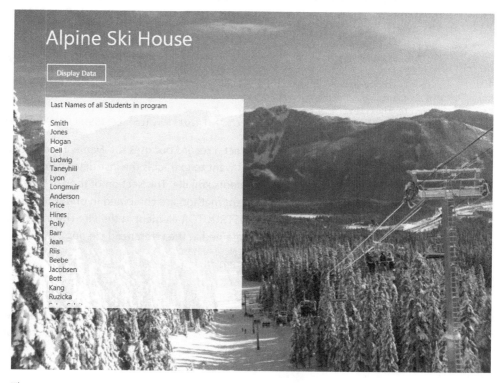

There are 32 names in the Students.xml file. You can examine the names that are not currently visible by using the vertical scroll bar in the text box. (Recall that the scroll bars won't appear until you touch the text box or hover the mouse over it.)

As the preceding illustration shows, the LINQ query extracted a selection of tagged items from the XML document and displayed them on the page. You can now use this technique to read and manipulate many types of elements from XML documents. The only thing that you will need is some practice writing expressions that navigate the sometimes-complex hierarchy of an XML data source.

5. Close the program.

In the next exercise, you'll learn how to reference XML elements that are located a little deeper in the structure of an XML document. The key syntax item that you'll work with in Sample 3 is the *Element* method, which is provided by both the *XDocument* and *XElement* classes. The *Element* method allows you to access child elements within the specified XML document's structure.

Use the *Element* property to locate child elements in an XML hierarchy

1. Display the MainPage.xaml.vb code-behind file again.

2. Comment out the second block (Sample 2) in the *XmlTestButton_Click* event handler, and then uncomment the third block (Sample 3).

This exercise demonstrates how you can use the *Element* method of the *Students* data object to reference individual elements within an XML data tree. The Sample 3 code looks like this:

```
'SAMPLE 3: Display XML elements nested in a more complex XML hierarchy.
'  This example displays an instructor scheduled to work in Winter 2015 in Students.xml.

OutputTextBox.Text = "Instructors scheduled to work in Winter 2015" & vbCrLf & vbCrLf
Dim Students As XDocument = XDocument.Load("Assets/Students.xml")
OutputTextBox.Text = OutputTextBox.Text & _
Students.Element("STUDENTS").Element("WINTER2015").Element("INSTRUCTOR").Value
```

This routine does not use LINQ to extract a record but uses the *Element* method and the *Value* property. The individual element that I want to extract is the instructor name that appears in the WINTER2015 section of the Students.xml file. This section of the file is near the end of the document. Three calls to the *Element* method are combined in one statement to navigate down the XML data tree to the first INSTRUCTOR element in the file. The *Value* property is then used to return the text that is contained in the referenced element.

3. Click Start Debugging to run the program.

4. Click the Display Data button.

Visual Studio displays the banner message, loads the XML document, and uses the *Element* method to locate the first INSTRUCTOR record. The Alpine Ski House instructor for Winter 2015 (Hamlin) is displayed in the text box.

Your screen will look like this:

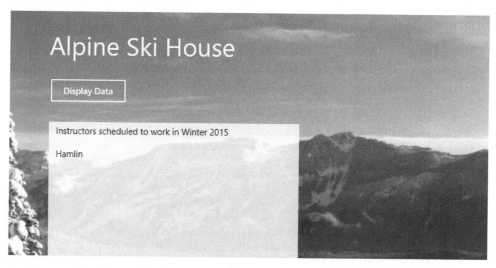

As the preceding illustration shows, you can extract an element from an XML document that is deep within its structure by using successive calls to the *Element* method. You simply need to know the structure of the XML container that you are referencing.

This syntax also offers an alternative to using LINQ to read data from an XML document. However, LINQ is much more effective at extracting information when you have a more complex retrieval criteria. This is especially true when you are trying to extract a series of elements that match a criteria.

5. Close the program.

In the next exercise, you'll see another example of LINQ's impressive extraction capabilities.

Searching for items in an XML file

The LINQ tool is designed specifically for extracting or *searching* within XML files for information. In particular, LINQ can go behind simply locating particular headings in an XML data source—it can also search within the XML tags to extract specific information based on multiple search criteria. As you learned in Chapter 15, this capability allows you to ask sophisticated questions about your data, such as "How many books were published by Lucerne Publishing that earned more than $100,000 in gross sales over the past 12 months?" or "How many female ski students do we have in the program that are between the ages of 16 and 17, inclusive?"

The key to asking these types of questions with LINQ is the *Where* clause, which can specify additional filtering of the query data. You can also use the *Attribute* method, which identifies specific attributes within an XML data hierarchy.

The following exercise, Sample 4 in the XML Document Data project, uses LINQ to search the SkiTeam2014.xml document for the answer to the question posed above: "How many female ski students do we have in the program that are between the ages of 16 and 17, inclusive?"

The SkiTeam2014.xml document was first used in Chapter 15 in this book. (Although here you will be using different LINQ queries.) I have added this document to the XML Document Data project's Assets folder so that you have an additional data container to work with. This is what the contents of the SkiTeam2014.xml document look like:

```xml
<?xml version="1.0"?>

<AllRacers>
    <Skier FirstName="Claus" LastName="Hansen" Gender="M" Age="14" />
    <Skier FirstName="Yun-Feng" LastName="Peng" Gender="M" Age="13"/>
    <Skier FirstName="Uzi" LastName="Hefetz" Gender="F" Age="17"/>
    <Skier FirstName="Begoña" LastName="Hurtado" Gender="F" Age="18"/>
    <Skier FirstName="Erzsébet" LastName="Balázs" Gender="F" Age="16"/>
    <Skier FirstName="Holly" LastName="Holt" Gender="F" Age="16"/>
    <Skier FirstName="Alan" LastName="Brewer" Gender="M" Age="17"/>
    <Skier FirstName="Oliver" LastName="Kiel" Gender="M" Age="13"/>
    <Skier FirstName="Isabelle" LastName="Scemla" Gender="F" Age="14"/>
    <Skier FirstName="Katherine" LastName="Simpson" Gender="F" Age="16"/>
    <Skier FirstName="Chris" LastName="Bryant" Gender="M" Age="18"/>
    <Skier FirstName="Ayla" LastName="Kol" Gender="F" Age="19"/>
    <Skier FirstName="Carlos" LastName="Carvallo" Gender="M" Age="15"/>
    <Skier FirstName="Peter" LastName="Krebs" Gender="M" Age="13"/>
    <Skier FirstName="April" LastName="Stewart" Gender="F" Age="16"/>
    <Skier FirstName="Samantha" LastName="Smith" Gender="F" Age="16"/>
    <Skier FirstName="Renee" LastName="Lo" Gender="M" Age="19"/>
    <Skier FirstName="Steven" LastName="Thorpe" Gender="M" Age="13"/>
    <Skier FirstName="Holly" LastName="Dickson" Gender="F" Age="16"/>
    <Skier FirstName="Geoff" LastName="Grisso" Gender="M" Age="14"/>
    <Skier FirstName="Danni" LastName="Ortman" Gender="F" Age="19"/>
    <Skier FirstName="Adina" LastName="Hagege" Gender="F" Age="17"/>
    <Skier FirstName="Makoto" LastName="Yamagishi" Gender="F" Age="16"/>
    <Skier FirstName="Greg" LastName="Winston" Gender="M" Age="15"/>
</AllRacers>
```

Use LINQ to extract specific information from an XML data source

1. Display the MainPage.xaml.vb code-behind file in the Code Editor.

2. Comment out the third block (Sample 3) in the *XmlTestButton_Click* event handler, and then uncomment the fourth block (Sample 4).

   The Sample 4 program code looks like this when the section has been uncommented and made ready for use. Note that I've indented the *Where, And*, and *Select* clauses a little to make the code a little more readable and to match LINQ syntax conventions.

```
'SAMPLE 4: Use LINQ to search creatively in an XML document.
'  This query searches the SkiTeam2014.xml file for female skiers
'  between 16 and 17 (inclusive) that are in the XML document.

OutputTextBox.Text = "Female ski school students between 16 and 17" & vbCrLf & vbCrLf
Dim xdoc As XDocument = XDocument.Load("Assets/SkiTeam2014.xml")
Dim query = From skier In xdoc.Descendants("Skier")
    Where (skier.Attribute("Gender").Value = "F") _
    And (skier.Attribute("Age").Value >= 16) And (skier.Attribute("Age").Value <= 17)
    Select FName = skier.Attribute("FirstName").Value,
           LName = skier.Attribute("LastName").Value

For Each skier In query
    OutputTextBox.Text &= skier.FName & " " & skier.LName & vbCrLf
Next
```

This Visual Basic routine displays a header, opens the SkiTeam2014.xml file, and executes a LINQ query to extract specific information from the data source. (The *query* variable holds an expression tree that defines the query.)

You should recognize the *From* clause, which indicates that the descendants of the *<Skier>* element will be used as the source for the data search. A long *Where* clause filters the XML such that only the ski school students who are female and between the ages of 16 and 17 (inclusive) will appear in the query results. Notice how I use optional parentheses to clearly separate the different components in the *Where* clauses, how I used the *Attribute* method to identify specific elements in each record, and how I use the *And* keyword to combine different parts of the *Where* clause.

For skier records that do match the gender and age filters, the *FirstName* and *LastName* attributes for each ski racer are returned and displayed in the text box on the page. The process is a little more complex than the examples used earlier in the chapter, because we are searching for specific trends in the data.

Finally, the items retrieved by the LINQ query are processed by a *For Each...Next* loop, which steps through the *query* results item by item, displaying a line in the text box for each female ski school student who is between 16 and 17.

Let's see how many students fit these particular search criteria.

3. Click Start Debugging to run the program.

4. Click the Display Data button.

Visual Studio displays the header, loads the XML data source, and then uses LINQ to search for a subset of records and document elements. Your screen will look like this:

As the preceding illustration shows, nine student names were returned by the search query. This is information that would have been rather tedious to gather had we examined the file manually and tried to count the students by looking at the raw XML data.

Now imagine how powerful this search tool could be if you had thousands of records in an XML document that you wanted to examine in a Windows Store app?

5. Close the program.

In the following exercise, you'll see how to make changes to an XML document that is loaded in memory.

Writing to an XML file

Writing to an XML file means modifying the XML data container that is stored in memory and (optionally) saving those changes to disk. As a programmer, you might decide to write to an XML file when your user attempts to update a student or employee record or when you want to add entirely new records to your XML-based data store.

Visual Studio handles modifying XML data through a variety of mechanisms. In the following exercises, you'll learn how to update an element in an XML data object by using the *Element* and *SetValue* methods. You'll also create a new node in an XML document by creating a new *XElement* object for the node, specifying the content of the node, and then using the *Add* method to add the node to the XML document. These are essential skills as you work with and build XML data stores in memory.

Finally, there might be times that you want to save a modified XML document from computer memory back to disk so that the changes are saved permanently. This can be accomplished using the *Save* method for an XML data object that has been declared using the *XDocument* class. However, I don't demonstrate this method in the following procedure. (I want to preserve the XML sample files for you in an unmodified state.)

You'll begin by modifying an element in the in-memory copy of an XML document.

Modify an element in an XML document

1. Display the MainPage.xaml.vb code-behind file in the Code Editor.

   You're still working in the XML Document Data program, a Windows Store app written in Visual Basic. This time you'll return to experiments with the Students.xml document. You'll learn how to modify the first record in the XML document that is surrounded by the <LASTNAME></LASTNAME> tags.

2. Comment out the fourth block (Sample 4) in the *XmlTestButton_Click* event handler, and then uncomment the fifth block (Sample 5).

   The Sample 5 program code looks like this when the section has been uncommented and made ready for use:

   ```
   'SAMPLE 5: Modify an element in the in-memory copy of an XML Document.
   '  This code shows how to change the LASTNAME field in the first record in the XML file
   '  from Smith to George. The final line displays the name so you can verify the change.

   Dim xdoc As XDocument = XDocument.Load("Assets/Students.xml")
   xdoc.Element("STUDENTS").Element("WINTER2014").Element("LASTNAME").SetValue("George")
   OutputTextBox.Text = xdoc.Element("STUDENTS").Element("WINTER2014").Element("LASTNAME").
   Value
   ```

   This routine uses three *Element* methods to reference the first LASTNAME record in the Students.xml document. The second line of code uses the *SetValue* method to change the name stored in that location from "Smith" to "George." The third line uses the *Value* property to display the modified record. (Type the entire statement on one line—it just wraps here due to the book's margins.) What we're hoping to see is the name "George" in the text box on the page—not "Smith."

   This routine is very short—it displays no header or other information in the text box. All we're hoping to see there is the modified name "George."

   Let's see how this basic write operation works on the in-memory copy of Students.xml.

3. Click Start Debugging to run the program.

4. Click the Display Data button.

Visual Studio executes the event handler, loads the XML document into memory, and modifies the first LASTNAME record that it finds. Your screen will look like this:

The program worked as intended. The output in the text box is simply "George," nothing more, nothing less. This means that the code is working.

Here we used just *XDocument* and *XElement* object syntax. As you can see, it is just as easy to modify an XML element in memory as it is to display an XML element.

5. Close the program.

In the following exercise, you'll see how to create a new node of XML data and how to add it to the XML document that is stored in memory.

Create a new node with data and add it to an XML document

1. Display the MainPage.xaml.vb code-behind file one final time.

2. Comment out the fifth block (Sample 5) in the *XmlTestButton_Click* event handler, and then uncomment the sixth block (Sample 6).

The Sample 6 program code looks like this after it has been readied for use:

```
'SAMPLE 6: Add to an XML Document by creating a new node.
'  To create a new XML "node" and add it to the end of the LASTNAME section, do this:
'  Load XML document into Students variable. Create a new XElement object to hold
'  the new node, and assign the LASTNAME value "Lyon" to the node.
'  Use Add method to add the new node to the end of the LASTNAME section.
'  Display modified XML document in the text box (with tags) to verify change.

Dim Students As XDocument = XDocument.Load("Assets/Students.xml")
Dim xe As XElement = New XElement("LASTNAME", "Lyon")
Students.Element("STUDENTS").Element("WINTER2014").Add(xe)
OutputTextBox.Text = Students.ToString
```

This routine begins with the declaration of the *Students* object (of type *XDocument*) and loads the Students.xml file into the object. Then a new node is declared named *xe*, which is of type *XElement*. Data is also assigned to the new node in the second line. In this case, the node conforms to the format of a LASTNAME element, and the name "Lyon" is assigned to the node.

In the third line of code, the new *xe* object is added to the *Students* data object via the *Add* method. As you'll see in a moment, the *Add* method directs Visual Studio to add the node not to the end of the document but to the end of the <WINTER2014> section.

Finally, the entire contents of the modified in-memory copy of the Students.xml document are displayed in the *OutputTextBox* object on the page. This will allow you to examine the XML file and see how it has been changed.

3. Click Start Debugging to run the program.

4. Click the Display Data button.

Visual Studio loads the Students.xml document into memory, creates the *xe* node containing new XML data, adds the node to the in-memory copy of the XML document, and displays the entire document in the text box on the page. Notice that the routine displays all of the document's XML tags too, so you can see what the new node looks like in context.

5. Scroll to the bottom of the text box.

Your screen will look like this:

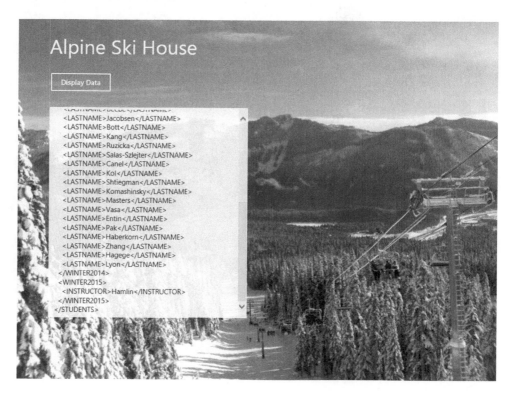

At the end of a long list of <LASTNAME></LASTNAME> elements, you will see the <LASTNAME>Lyon</LASTNAME> node. This is the new addition to the XML document that was created in this exercise. Something that is important to notice as well is that the new element is not placed at the end of the file, but at the end of the <WINTER2014> section. That is, Visual Studio not only modified the XML document, but it knew where to put the information.

6. Close the program, save your changes, and then close Visual Studio.

You're finished working with Windows Store data access concepts for now.

A user interface for data entry

Although this chapter focused on fundamental skills related to binding data to XAML controls and manipulating the contents of XML documents, you can begin to see how these building blocks can be used in more sophisticated Visual Basic programs to receive input from the user, manipulate it in memory, and store it permanently on disk via XML documents or another mechanism.

For example, recall the user interface for data entry that you developed along with custom classes in Chapter 16, which provided several fields for receiving input from the user and displaying output:

This type of front end could be ideal for gathering student or employee information in a Windows Store application. You could take the information gathered by such a page and store it in an observable collection declared according to the parameters of a class that you defined to hold student records. You could then bind this collection to controls in the user interface, and you could use LINQ to extract interesting information from the collection.

Finally, you could store the contents of the collection in an XML document, which you might load, modify, and save back to disk as needed in your program. It might also be nice to supplement the *TextBox* and *Button* controls you see in the preceding illustration with the *CommandBar* and *Flyout* controls you learned about in Chapter 9, "Exploring Windows 8.1 design features: Command bar, flyout, tiles, and touch." The decision is really up to you!

Summary

This chapter has offered an introduction to fundamental data access techniques in Windows Store applications. First, you learned how to bind XAML controls to classes and data collections in a Windows Store app. You learned how to configure the necessary binding elements in a project, how to use the *Binding* class in XAML markup, and how to write Visual Basic code to manage a variety of data access tasks.

You also learned more about using XML documents in a Windows Store app, including how to read and display XML data elements, how to extract XML data with LINQ, and how to modify XML documents with methods in the *XDocument* and *XElement* classes. These essential skills will prepare you to make the most of XML data sources in your programs. Learning data access with XML is an important skill to acquire, because XML has achieved worldwide acceptance and is highly suited for transactions over the web. The ADO.NET database framework has also been optimized for XML data sources and syntax.

In the next chapter, you'll learn about the web development options in Visual Studio 2013. You'll explore several ADO.NET programming models, including Web Forms, ASP.NET MVC, Web Pages with Razor syntax, and HTML5/JavaScript. You'll also create a car loan calculator website that demonstrates how server controls are used, how to write Visual Basic event handlers, and how to handle typical web development scenarios in ASP.NET and Visual Basic.

CHAPTER 19

Visual Studio web development with ASP.NET

After completing this chapter, you will be able to

- Understand ASP.NET 4.5.1, Microsoft's newest web development framework.

- Evaluate leading ASP.NET web development platforms, including Web Forms, ASP.NET MVC, Web Pages (with Razor), and HTML5/JavaScript.

- Build a sample car mortgage application using Web Forms.

- Add server controls and event handlers to a Web Forms project.

- Display database records and customize a website template.

The topic of creating Visual Studio 2013 applications for the web deserves an entire book on the subject. Actually, the topic deserves several books. But rather than simply forwarding you on to other sources of information, I want to give you an overview of the exciting web technologies available in Visual Studio 2013 and offer a walkthrough of the powerful Web Forms development platform. I think you'll be quite impressed with what you can accomplish with just a few hours' work in Web Forms, and you'll find many conceptual similarities to developing apps in the Windows Forms and Windows Store models.

This chapter begins with an introduction to ASP.NET 4.5.1, an extension of the .NET Framework, and continues with a survey of the web projects that you can create in Visual Studio 2013, including Web Forms, ASP.NET MVC, Web Pages (with Razor), and a programming model that uses HTML5 and JavaScript.

Although a complete description of ASP.NET isn't possible here, you should find enough material to help you make some basic decisions about which platform to investigate when you decide to design Visual Studio applications for the web. In most cases, you'll be using the Visual Basic and .NET Framework skills that you have learned and practiced throughout this book.

Inside ASP.NET

ASP.NET is a *web application framework* designed to create dynamic webpages and websites for the Internet. ASP.NET was first released in 2002 with Microsoft Visual Studio.NET version 1.0. Subsequent versions of ASP.NET have been aligned with new releases of the .NET Framework and Visual Studio. Following this general pattern, Visual Studio 2013 released with ASP.NET 4.5.1 as its web development interface, which corresponded to the release of the .NET Framework 4.5.1. The two libraries are designed to be used together.

One of the goals of ASP.NET was to simplify web development by providing a programming model that was similar to what developers were already doing on the Windows platform. ASP.NET achieved this by allowing developers to build pages composed of controls, similar to the way that Windows Forms applications were created in the Visual Studio IDE. A Web Forms control, such as a button or label, functioned similarly to a Windows Forms button. In both cases, there were customizable properties, methods, events, and code-behind files that worked according to the general principles of object-oriented programming in Visual Studio. This included the ability to use the entire Visual Basic language and reference objects in the ASP.NET Framework, just as developers had used these features for Windows programming and the .NET Framework. However, while Windows Forms controls are rendered on the screen, ASP.NET Web Forms controls produce segments of *HTML* and *JavaScript* that form pages sent to a browser on the user's computer or handheld device.

Like the .NET Framework, ASP.NET is built on the Windows *Common Language Runtime* (CLR), which allows Visual Studio developers to write ASP.NET programs using any supported *.NET language*, including Visual Basic. Using ASP.NET, you can create a website that displays a user interface, processes data, and provides many of the commands and features that a standard application for Windows might offer. However, the website that you create is viewed in a web browser, such as Internet Explorer, Google Chrome, Mozilla Firefox, Apple Safari, or a mobile device such as Windows Phone 8, an Android smartphone, or an Apple iPhone.

ASP.NET websites are typically stored on one or more *web servers*, which use Microsoft Internet Information Services (IIS) to display the correct webpages and handle most of the computing tasks required by the website. This distributed strategy allows your websites to potentially run on a wide range of Internet-based or stand-alone computers—wherever your users and their rich data sources are located.

 Note When you use Visual Studio, the websites that you create can also be located and run on a local computer that does not require IIS, giving you more options for development and deployment. This is a fine point about developing and testing your application that I will pick up later in the chapter.

The following sections describe the most important web development opportunities available to Visual Basic 2013 developers, including Web Forms, ASP.NET MVC, Web Pages (with Razor), and HTML5 with JavaScript.

Web Forms

ASP.NET Web Forms lets you build dynamic websites or web applications using a familiar drag-and-drop, event-driven model. You create pages by dragging Toolbox controls onto a design surface. Because this model has been available for some time, dozens of controls and components are available, including a data access model that is similar to what developers have used with Windows Forms. Many Visual Studio and web developers are familiar with this model and its strengths.

The Web Forms framework targets developers who have used Visual Studio before and are comfortable with declarative and control-based programming, including Windows Forms and Windows Presentation Foundation (WPF). The Web Forms model provides a designer-driven development paradigm, so it's popular with developers looking for a rapid application development (RAD) approach to web development. Web Forms is also a good fit for traditional desktop programmers who do not have that much experience in HTML and JavaScript. One potential shortcoming of this model is that ASP.NET sends a considerable amount of content to the user's browser to enable its rich collection of controls and features. Web programming models like ASP.NET MVC and Web Pages (with Razor) were developed in part to create web applications that have a smaller footprint.

To create an ASP.NET Web Forms application with Visual Basic in Visual Studio 2013, you select the New Project command from the File menu. Under Templates, you select Web and then ASP.NET Web Application. In the New ASP.NET Project dialog box, select Web Forms and click Create Project.

You can also create a website with the Web Forms model, the approach that will be taken later in this chapter. The following screen shot shows the New ASP.NET Project dialog box with the Web Forms project type selected. This is the project type that you select when you want to create a web application using the Web Forms model.

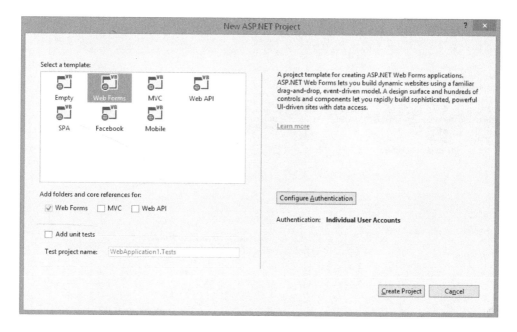

ASP.NET MVC

ASP.NET MVC is an alternative framework for creating web applications that first appeared in 2009. Because it came after Web Forms, the new framework was designed to address what were perceived as some of the limitations of Web Forms, including the way that HTML was rendered for webpages, the combination of business logic and user-interface presentation code in code-behind files, and the way that Web Forms applications were tested. The Model-View-Controller (MVC) architecture was selected for this framework (which had existed since the 1970s) because it had a built-in structure that separated the business logic layer of a web application from its presentation layer. Accordingly, an ASP.NET MVC application requires a developer to build a web application as a composite of three roles: Model, View, and Controller.

In this programming scenario, a *model* represents the business objects in the application, a *view* renders the user interface to display information, and a *controller* handles requests from the user and manages application logic and flow. The requests are mapped to methods in classes, and these methods receive user input and provide other functionality. Many software developers are already familiar with this programming model and will therefore find it easy to use, especially when it is integrated with the powerful features of the .NET Framework and ASP.NET object libraries. The separation of business logic from presentation code is especially useful. The current version of ASP.NET MVC is version 5.

To create an ASP.NET MVC application with Visual Basic in Visual Studio 2013, you select the New Project command from the File menu. Under Templates, you select Web and then ASP.NET Web Application. In the New ASP.NET Project dialog box, select MVC and click Create Project.

The following screen shot shows the New ASP.NET Project dialog box with the MVC project type selected:

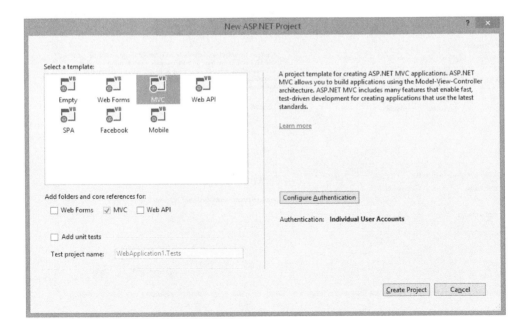

Web Pages (with Razor)

In 2011, Microsoft released a free web development tool named WebMatrix, a cloud-connected application that allows developers to build dynamic websites using templates and open-source content from information management systems such as Drupal and WordPress. WebMatrix was also designed to be compatible with ASP.NET and Visual Studio 2010. It provided an easy-to-learn web development tool that offered an alternative and enhancement to the Web Forms and ASP.NET MVC models. To differentiate WebMatrix tools from Web Forms and ASP.NET MVC, the new model was called ASP.NET Web Pages in the Visual Studio 2012 and Visual Studio 2013 products. The technology is rapidly evolving and attracting adherents, especially those who have some experience with HTML, Visual Basic, and Visual C#. The current release is version 3.

In the Web Pages model, you create dynamic webpages that have the .VBHTML (for Visual Basic) or .CSHTML (for C#) extension. These are essentially HTML files within in-line code written in either the Visual Basic or Visual C# language. In-line code means that there is no absolute requirement for separate code-behind files in a Web Pages project, as you would see in a Web Forms or Windows Store application (although typically, developers create separate code files just like any other .NET application). The in-line coding approach is often called "Web Pages with Razor syntax" because the in-line code follows certain syntax rules. You can tell the difference between HTML markup and the Razor code in a Web Page file by the '@' character that appears before the Visual Basic or Visual C# code. These Razor instructions are typically used to send instructions to the web server.

Razor is technically a *view engine*—that is, a pluggable module that implements template syntax within the ASP.NET MVC platform. As a result, Web Pages with Razor should really be understood as an extension of ASP.NET MVC. It allows you to create optimized HTML for webpages with a minimum of code. Rather than tedious hand-coding or potentially confusing user interface and code-behind files, the Razor syntax allows you to create the needed HTML markup with a modified version of Visual Basic or Visual C# syntax. All of this is available to you within the familiar Visual Studio 2013 IDE.

You can learn more about the WebMatrix web development tool at *http://www.microsoft.com/web/*. However, the support for Web Pages with Razor is now built into Visual Studio 2013. To create an ASP.NET Web Pages application with Visual Basic in Visual Studio, you select the New Web Site command from the File menu. Under Templates, select Visual Basic, and then select ASP.NET Web Site (Razor v3). Click OK to configure the new Web Pages project. Visual Studio will create a boilerplate website that is ready to go, with an assortment of .VBHTML files ready for customizing in Solution Explorer.

The following screen shot shows the New Web Site dialog box with the ASP.NET Web Site (Razor v3) project type selected:

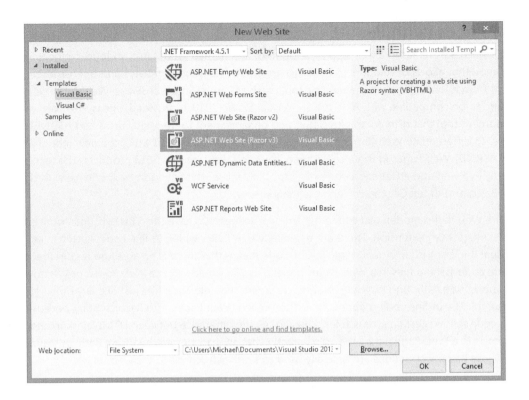

HTML5 and JavaScript

You have spent considerable time in this book learning how to write Windows Store applications. An excellent question might now be: Is there an easy way for me to create web applications that look and behave like tile-based Windows Store apps but that run in an Internet browser? And while we're at it, here's a follow-up: Is there a simple way to write a Visual Basic application in Visual Studio that runs in Windows 8.1 *and* a variety of web browsers and handheld devices, such that no converting, upgrading, or porting is required?

Unfortunately, the short answer to both of these questions is: "No."

It is not possible (yet) to simply upgrade or recompile a Windows Store application for use on the web or to create an application like Windows Calculator that automatically runs on Windows 8.1, Windows Phone 8, and web servers. The reason is that the Windows, Phone, and web platforms are considerably different, and the needs of browser-based or mobile applications are simply much different than traditional desktop computers and laptops running Windows 8.1. This is not to say that there aren't many similarities and common tools used for creating Windows, Phone, and web-based applications, but the Holy Grail of developing one project in Visual Studio and deploying it automatically to a variety of platforms is still a ways off.

So, in Visual Studio 2013, you develop core code, data stores, and user interface assets and then adapt them to different operating environments using libraries and classes in the .NET Framework. If you want to create a web application that actually looks and operates like a Windows Store app, with tile-based features and a similar user interface, you should create a Windows Store app using JavaScript, a programming language specifically designed for use with web browsers.

Like Visual Basic, JavaScript is one of the primary languages for Visual Studio development. However, JavaScript also has an incredible heritage as a web-based development tool. If you create a Windows Store app in Visual Studio and select one of the JavaScript templates, you can create controls and features that are directly connected to Windows 8.1 and .NET Framework services. This is made possible because Windows Store apps designed with JavaScript use resources in the Windows Library for JavaScript (WinJS). This web development option is typically called "Windows Store app with HTML5 and JavaScript."

In such a Windows 8.1 project, JavaScript code is embedded directly into the HTML of webpages. This code is also allowed to interact with the browser's Document Object Model (DOM), which can represent HTML and other browser objects. The DOM enables webpages to implement typical HTML5 features such as animations, transitions, text color changes, and text effects.

The JavaScript language uses a syntax similar to that of C and supports language constructs such as *if...else* and *do...while*. JavaScript also supports various data types, including *Array* and *Object*. Best of all, you can use the templates and controls that you've become familiar with in Windows Store apps, all within the familiar setting of the Visual Studio 2013 IDE. However, you do need to switch languages, essentially taking a break from Visual Basic and moving into JavaScript for the sake of retaining Windows Store-type features and tools. It's not the end of the world, even for Visual Basic diehards like myself.

To create a Windows Store application for the web with JavaScript, you start Visual Studio 2013 and select the New Project command from the File menu. Under Templates, select Other Languages and then select JavaScript. Click Windows Store, and then click the new project template that you want to open. (The list of templates is identical to what you see under Visual Basic/Windows Store apps.) Specify a project name, and then click OK to open the new web application.

The following screen shot shows the New Project dialog box with the JavaScript/Windows Store/Navigation App template selected:

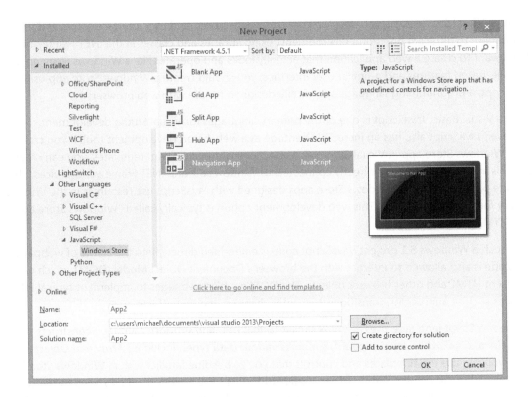

Building a Web Forms website with ASP.NET

After a review of some of the leading Visual Studio web development technologies, the best way to get started with ASP.NET is to get some hands-on experience. In the exercises that follow, you'll create a simple car loan calculator with the Web Forms development model described earlier in this chapter. You'll create a website that will determine the monthly payments for an automobile purchase, display a table of data from a database, and display a help page when needed.

You'll begin the process by verifying that Visual Studio is properly configured for ASP.NET programming, and then you'll review the essential steps for creating a Web Forms website. (You can create either websites or web applications with the Web Forms model, but we'll try the more comprehensive website approach here.)

Next, you'll move on to creating the project with Visual Studio, which entails creating several ASP.NET pages, using Toolbox controls, writing code, testing, and other familiar tasks.

Software requirements for ASP.NET development

Before you get started, take a moment to understand the software requirements for what follows. To begin ASP.NET programming, you need to have Visual Studio 2013 Professional, Premium, or Ultimate installed. You also need to be running Windows 8.1.

If you don't have one of the full retail versions of Visual Studio, you can install a product known as Visual Studio Express 2013 for Web at *http://www.microsoft.com/express/web/*. This free tool contains almost all the features described in this chapter. (I'll point out any differences as we go.) If you are using Visual Studio Express 2013 for Web, be sure to adjust the settings to Expert by clicking the Tools menu, clicking Settings, and then clicking Expert Settings. This will ensure that the steps in this chapter more closely match your software. When the differences between these editions of the software don't matter, I'll simply refer to the product as Visual Studio.

Something quite helpful here is that Visual Studio includes its own local web server for Internet development, so setting up and configuring a separate web server with Microsoft Internet Information Services (IIS) and the .NET Framework is not required. Having a local web server makes it easy to create and test your ASP.NET websites, and you'll see it described below as the ASP.NET Development Server.

In Visual Studio, you can create and run your website in one of three of the following locations:

- Your own computer (via the ASP.NET Development Server).

- An HTTP server that contains IIS and related components.

- An FTP site (a remote file server). This option is for distribution only. Visual Studio can copy a website to an FTP site, but it must then be deployed to an HTTP server that contains IIS and related components.

The first location is the option we'll use in this book because it requires no additional hardware or software. In addition, when you develop your website on the local file system, all the website files are stored in one location. When you've finished testing the application, you can deploy the files to a web server of your choosing.

Essential steps

To create a website in Visual Studio 2013, you click the New Web Site command on the File menu, and then use the Visual Studio IDE to build one or more webpages that will collectively represent your website. Each webpage consists of the following two pieces:

- A Web Forms page, which contains HTML, ASP.NET markup, and controls to create the user interface.

- A code-behind file, which is a code module that contains Visual Basic code that relates directly to the Web Forms page.

This division is conceptually much like the Windows Forms and Windows Store platforms you've been working with already in this book—there's a user interface component and a code module component. The code for both of these components can be stored in a single .aspx file, but typically the Web Forms page code is stored in an .aspx file and the code-behind file is stored in an .aspx.vb file.

In addition to webpages, websites can contain code modules (.vb files), HTML pages (.htm files), configuration information (Web.config files), global web application information (Global.asax files), cascading style sheet (CSS) information, scripting files (JavaScript), master pages, image files, and other components. You can use the Web Designer and Solution Explorer to switch back and forth between these components quickly and efficiently.

Webpages vs. Windows Forms

What are the important differences between webpages and Windows Forms? To begin with, webpages offer a slightly different programming paradigm than Windows Forms. Whereas Windows Forms use a Windows-based application window as the primary user interface for a program, a website presents information to the user through one or more webpages with supporting program code. These pages are viewed through a web browser, and you can create them by using the Web Designer.

Like a Windows Form, a webpage can include text, graphic images, buttons, list boxes, and other objects that are used to provide information, process input, or display output. However, the basic set of controls that you use to create a webpage is not the set on the Common Controls tab of the Toolbox. Instead, ASP.NET websites must use controls on one of the tabs in the Web Forms Toolbox, including Standard, Data, HTML, and many others. Each of the Web Forms controls has its own unique methods, properties, and events, and although there are many similarities between these controls and Windows Forms controls, there are also several important differences. For example, the Windows Forms *DataGridView* control is called *GridView* in Web Forms and has different properties and methods.

Many webpage controls are *server controls*, meaning that they are controlled by the web server. Server controls have an "asp" prefix in their tag. HTML controls (located on the HTML tab of the Web Forms Toolbox) are *client controls* by default, meaning that they run only within the user's browser. However, for now, you simply need to know that you can use server controls, HTML controls, or a combination of both in your website projects.

Server controls

Server controls are more capable than HTML controls and function in many ways like the Windows Forms controls. Indeed, many of the server controls have the same names as the Windows Forms controls and offer many of the same properties, methods, and events. In addition to simple controls such as *Button*, *TextBox*, and *Label*, more sophisticated controls such as *Chart*, *FileUpload*, *LoginView*, and *RequiredFieldValidator* are provided on a number of tabs in the Toolbox. The screen shot on the following page shows a sample of the server controls in the Web Forms Toolbox. (AJAX Extensions, Dynamic Data, and Reporting controls are not shown.) This impressive collection of controls is one of the main reasons web developers like working with Web Forms applications.

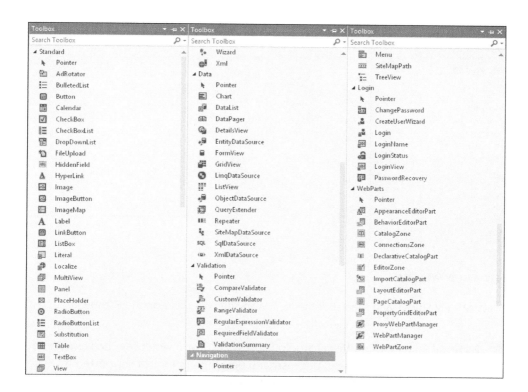

HTML controls

The HTML controls are a set of older user interface controls that are supported by all web browsers and conform closely to the early HTML standards developed for managing user interface elements on a typical webpage. They include *Button, Text*, and *Checkbox*—useful basic controls for managing information on a webpage that can be represented entirely with HTML code. Indeed, you might recognize these controls if you've coded in HTML before. However, although they're easy to use and have the advantage of being a common denominator for web browsers, they're limited by the fact that they have no ability to maintain their own state. (That is, the data that they contain will be lost between views of a webpage unless you write code to manage the state.) The next screen shot shows the HTML controls offered on the HTML tab of the Toolbox when the Web Designer is loaded:

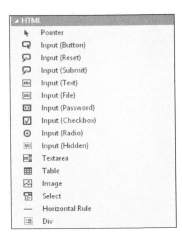

Create a new website

1. Start Visual Studio, and then click the New Web Site command on the File menu.

> **Note** If you are using Visual Studio Express 2013, you won't see the New Web Site command on the File menu, because web development is not supported by that product. But don't worry, you can get the necessary software by downloading Visual Studio Express 2013 for Web at *http://www.microsoft.com/express/web/.* Do that now, and return to this step when you are ready to go.

Although you might have seen the New Web Site command before, we haven't used it yet in this book. This command prepares Visual Studio to build a website. You see a New Web Site dialog box similar to the following:

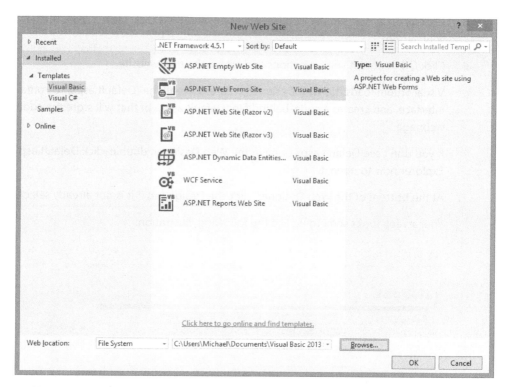

In this dialog box, you can select a variety of website templates (including a Web Forms site), the location for the website (local file system, HTTP server, or FTP site), and the programming language that you want to use (Visual Basic or Visual C#).

You can also identify the version of the .NET Framework that you want to target with your web application. (Version 4.5.1 offers the most recent features, but there are times that you might need to design specifically for platforms with an earlier version of the .NET Framework. However, the Express product does not provide the option of targeting a specific version of the .NET Framework.)

2. In the New Web Site dialog box, verify that Visual Basic is the selected language and that ASP. NET Web Forms Site is the selected template.

3. In the Web Location list box, make sure that File System is selected.

4. Click the Browse button, browse to the My Documents\Visual Basic 2013 SBS folder, and then edit the Folder path so that it is My Documents\Visual Basic 2013 SBS**My Chapter 19**.

Because a Visual Studio website takes up an entire folder, you'll create a new folder for your project with the "My" prefix. Although you have been specifying the folder location for projects *after* you have built the projects in this book, in web development, projects are typically saved up front.

5. Click Open to confirm the location selection, and then click Yes to create the new folder on your system.

6. Click OK to accept your selections and create the new website.

   Visual Studio loads the Web Designer, creates a webpage (Default.aspx) to contain the user interface, and creates a code-behind file (Default.aspx.vb) that will store the code for your webpage.

   If you don't see Default.aspx open in the Web Designer, double-click Default.aspx in Solution Explorer now to open it.

7. At the bottom of the Web Designer, click the Design tab if it is not already selected.

   Your screen looks something like the following illustration:

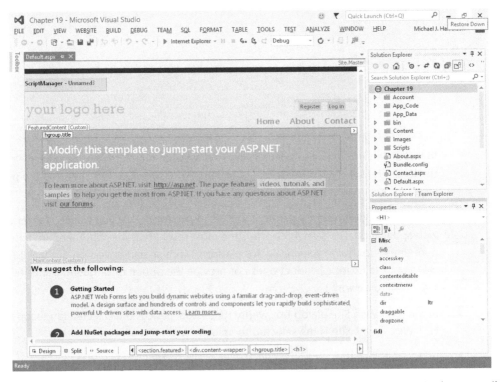

   Unlike the Windows Forms Designer, the Web Designer displays the webpage in three possible views in the IDE, and three tabs at the bottom of the Designer (Design, Split, and Source) allow you to change your view of the webpage.

   The Design tab shows you approximately how your webpage will look when a web browser displays it. When the Design tab is selected, a basic template page with the words Modify This Template To Jump-Start Your ASP.NET Application appears in the Designer, and you can add controls to your webpage and adjust how objects on the page are arranged.

On the Source tab, you can view and edit the HTML and ASP.NET markup that are used to display the webpage in a web browser. The Split tab offers a composite view of the Design and Source tabs. Because you are used to seeing XAML markup and a Windows Store page in the Designer in Split view, the overall look of the Web Designer will be somewhat familiar to you.

A few additional differences between the Windows Forms Designer and the Web Designer are worth noting at this point. The Toolbox now contains several collections of controls used exclusively for web programming. Solution Explorer also contains a different list of project files for the website you're building, as shown in the preceding screen shot. In particular, notice the Default.aspx file in Solution Explorer; this file contains the user interface code for the active webpage. Nested under the Default.aspx file, you'll find the code-behind file named Default. aspx.vb. A configuration file named Web.config and a master page file named Site.master are also listed.

 Tip When you close your new website and exit Visual Studio, note that you open the website again by clicking the Visual Studio File menu and then clicking the Open Web Site command. Websites are not opened by using the Open Project command on the File menu.

Now you're ready to add some text to the webpage by using the Web Designer.

Using the Web Designer

Unlike a Windows Form, a webpage can have text added directly to it when it is in the Web Designer. In Source view, the text appears within HTML and ASP.NET tags somewhat as it does in the Visual Studio Code Editor. In Design view, the text appears in top-to-bottom fashion within a grid as it does in a word processor such as Microsoft Word, and you'll see no HTML tags. In the next exercises, you'll type text in Design view, edit it, and then make formatting changes by using buttons on the Formatting toolbar. Manipulating text in this way is usually much faster than adding a *Label* control to the webpage to contain the text. You'll practice entering the text for your car loan calculator in the following exercise.

Add text in Design view

1. Click the Design tab, if it is not currently selected, to view the Web Designer in Design view.

   A faint rectangle appears at the top of the webpage, near the template text Modify This Template To Jump-Start Your ASP.NET Application. The template text is there to show you how text appears on a Web Form and where you can go to get additional information about ASP.NET. You'll also notice that your webpage has Home, About, and Contact tabs, as well as Register and Log In fields, which are provided for you as part of your default page.

2. Position your insertion point at the end of the text Jump-Start Your ASP.NET Application.

   A blinking I-beam appears at the end of the line.

3. Press the Backspace key to remove Modify This Template To Jump-Start Your ASP.NET Application. You should also delete the period at the beginning of the line.

4. Type **Car Loan Calculator** in place of the text you deleted.

   Visual Studio displays the title of your webpage exactly as it will appear when you open the website in your browser.

5. Delete the paragraph beginning with To Learn More About ASP.NET..., and in its place, type the following sentence:

   Enter the required information and click Calculate!

   Now you'll use the Formatting toolbar to format the title with italic formatting.

6. Right-click the Standard toolbar in Visual Studio to display the list of toolbars available in the IDE.

7. If you do not see a checkmark next to Formatting in this list, click Formatting to add the Formatting toolbar.

   The Formatting toolbar now appears in the IDE if it was not already visible. Notice that it contains a few features not usually found on a text formatting toolbar.

8. Select the text Car Loan Calculator. Before you can format text in the Web Designer, you must select it.

9. Click the Italic button on the Formatting toolbar.

   Your screen looks like this:

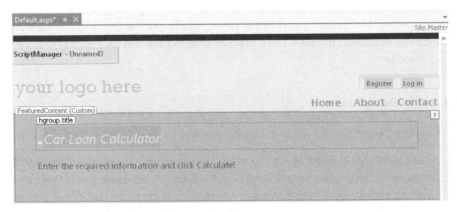

Now, you'll examine the HTML and ASP.NET markup for the text and formatting you entered.

View the HTML and ASP.NET markup for a webpage

1. Click the Source tab at the bottom of the Designer.

The Source tab displays the actual HTML and ASP.NET markup for your webpage. To see more of the markup, you might want to resize a few programming tools temporarily and use the document scroll bars. The markup looks like the following screen shot. Your markup might have some differences.

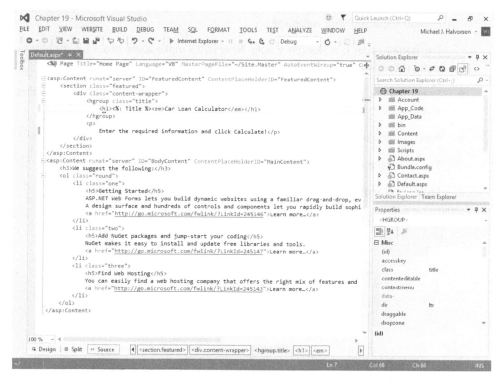

A webpage is made up of page information, scripting code, cascading style sheet (CSS) information, HTML tags, ASP.NET tags, image references, objects, and text. The @ *Page* directive contains information about the language you selected when creating the web application, the name of any code-behind file, and any inherited forms.

HTML and ASP.NET tags typically appear in pairs so that you can see clearly where a section begins and ends. For example, the *<h1>* tag identifies the beginning of a major heading, and the *</hi>* tag identifies the end. Notice that the Car Loan Calculator text appears within *<em></em>* tags to make the text italic. Below the Car Loan Calculator text, the second line of text you entered is displayed.

> **Important** Remember that the Source tab is an actual editor, so you can change the text that you entered by using standard text editing techniques. If you know something about HTML and ASP.NET, you can add other tags and content as well.

2. Examine the line *<h1><%: Title %>Car Loan Calculator</h1>*.

The *<%: Title %>* tag in this line directs the web browser to place the title of the page at the beginning of the line (before the words Car Loan Calculator) when the page is loaded. (The *Title* value is currently assigned the string "Home Page" by markup at the top of the page.)

3. Because you don't want that particular label on your page anymore, select the tag *<%: Title %>* and then press Del.

4. Now click the Design tab to display your webpage again in Design view, and see how the change impacted your webpage.

The page header is no longer visible. Now you'll make some room for content by deleting the instructions in the *MainContent* section of the webpage.

5. Select the line We Suggest The Following:, as well as all of the content in the three numbered steps below.

6. Press Del to delete the boilerplate information.

This will make room for new content.

7. Press Enter eight times to make room for text and controls on the page.

Your screen should look like this:

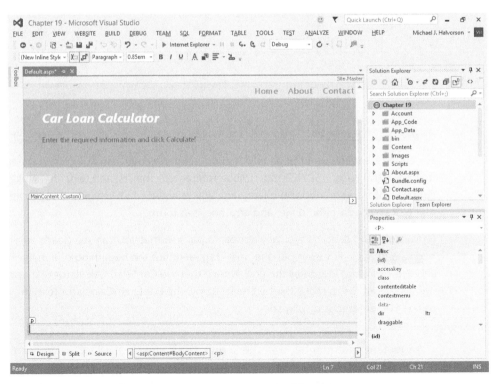

Now you'll open the Toolbox, if it is not visible, and add some new content.

Adding server controls to a website

In the following exercise, you'll add *TextBox*, *Label*, and *Button* controls to the main page in the car loan calculator. Although these controls are located in the Web Forms Toolbox, they're very similar to the Windows Forms controls of the same name that you've used throughout this book. (I'll cover a few of the important differences as they come up.) The most important thing to remember is that in the Web Designer, controls are inserted at the insertion point if you double-click the control name in the Toolbox. After you add the controls to the webpage, you'll set property settings for the controls.

Use *TextBox*, *Label*, and *Button* controls

1. Click to place the insertion point at about the third line from the top in the *MainContent* section that you just cleared and filled with eight lines.

    Because controls are placed at the insertion point, you need to place the cursor in a specific location before double-clicking a control in the Toolbox.

     Tip By default, the Web Designer positions controls relative to other controls. This is an important difference between the Web Designer and the Windows Forms Designer. The Windows Forms Designer allows you to position controls wherever you like on a form. You can change the Web Designer so that you can position controls wherever you like on a webpage (called *absolute positioning*); however, you might get different behavior in different web browsers.

2. Open the Toolbox, and display the Standard tab, if it isn't already visible.

3. Double-click the *TextBox* control on the Standard tab of the Toolbox to create a text box object at the insertion point on the webpage.

    Notice the *asp:textbox#TextBox1* text that appears above the text box object. The "asp" prefix indicates that this object is an ASP.NET server control. (This text disappears when you run the program.)

4. Click below the text box object to place the insertion point on the next line.

5. Double-click the *TextBox* control again to add a second text box object to the webpage.

6. Repeat steps 4 and 5 to create a third text box object below the second text box.

    Now you'll use the *Label* control to insert labels that identify the purpose of the text boxes.

7. Click to the right of the first text box object to place the insertion point at the right edge of the text box.

8. Press the Spacebar key twice to add two blank spaces, and then double-click the *Label* control in the Toolbox to add a label object to the webpage.

9. Repeat steps 7 and 8 to add label objects to the right of the second and third text boxes.

10. Click to the right of the third label object to place the insertion point to the right of the label, and then press Enter.

11. Click below the third text box object, and then double-click the *Button* control to create a button object near the bottom page.

    The *Button* control, like the *TextBox* and *Label* controls, is very similar to its Windows Forms counterpart. Your screen looks like this:

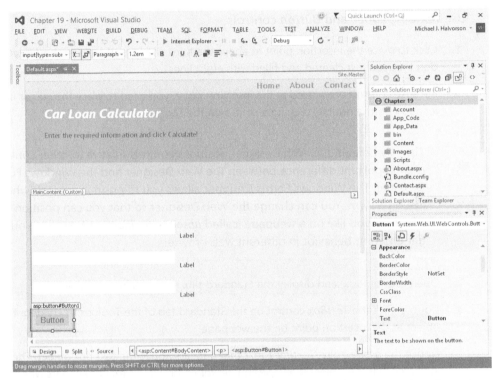

    Now you'll set a few properties for the seven new controls you have created on the webpage. If it is not already visible, open the Properties window by pressing F4. As you set the properties, you'll notice one important difference between webpages and Windows Forms—the familiar *Name* property has been changed to *ID* in Web Forms. Despite their different names, the two properties perform the same function.

12. Set the following properties for the objects on the webpage:

Object	Property	Setting
TextBox1	*ID*	AmountTextBox
TextBox2	*ID*	InterestTextBox
TextBox3	*ID*	PaymentTextBox

Object	Property	Setting
Label1	ID	AmountLabel
	Text	"Loan Amount"
Label2	ID	InterestLabel
	Text	"Interest Rate (for example, 0.09)"
Label3	ID	PaymentLabel
	Text	"Monthly Payment"
Button1	ID	CalculateButton
	Text	"Calculate"

Your webpage looks like this:

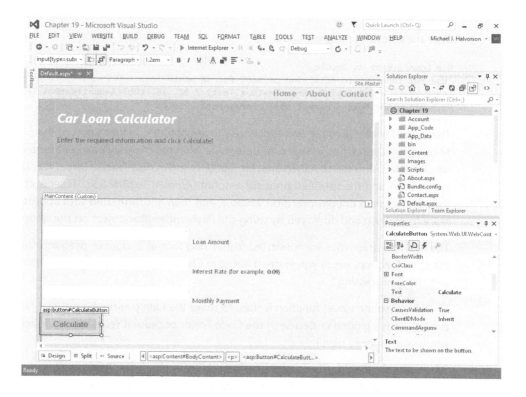

Writing event handlers for webpage controls

You write default event handlers for controls on a webpage by double-clicking the objects on the webpage and typing the necessary program code in the Code Editor. Although the user will see the controls on the webpage in his or her own web browser, the actual code that's executed will be located on the local test computer or a web server, depending on how you configured your project for development and how it is eventually deployed.

For example, when the user clicks a button on a webpage that is hosted by a web server, the browser sends the button click event back to the server, which processes the event and sends a new webpage back to the browser. Although the process seems similar to that of Windows Forms, there's actually a lot going on behind the scenes when a control is used on an ASP.NET webpage!

In the following exercise, you'll practice creating the default event handler for the *CalculateButton* object on the webpage.

Create the *CalculateButton_Click* event handler

1. Double-click the Calculate button on the webpage.

    The code-behind file (Default.aspx.vb) opens in the Code Editor, and the *CalculateButton_Click* event handler appears.

2. Type the following program code:

    ```
    Dim LoanPayment As Double
    'Use Pmt function to determine payment for 36-month loan
    LoanPayment = Pmt(CDbl(InterestTextBox.Text) / 12, 36, CDbl(AmountTextBox.Text))
    PaymentTextBox.Text = Format(Abs(LoanPayment), "$0.00")
    ```

    This event handler uses the *Pmt* function, a financial function that's part of the *Microsoft.VisualBasic* namespace, to determine what the monthly payment for a car loan would be by using the specified interest rate (*InterestTextBox.Text*), a three-year (36-month) loan period, and the specified principal amount (*AmountTextBox.Text*). The result is stored in the *LoanPayment* double-precision variable, and then it is formatted with appropriate monetary formatting and displayed by using the *PaymentTextBox* object on the webpage.

    The two *Text* properties are converted from string format to double-precision format by using the *CDbl* function, which you learned about in Chapter 11, "Mastering data types, operators, and string processing."

    The *Abs* (absolute value) function is used to make the loan payment a positive number. (*Abs* currently has a jagged underline in the Code Editor because it relies on the *System.Math* class, which you'll specify next.)

    Why make the loan payment appear as a positive number? The *Pmt* function returns a negative number by default (reflecting money that's owed), but I think negative formatting looks strange when it isn't part of a balance sheet, so I'm converting it to positive.

    Notice that the program statements in the code-behind file are just regular Visual Basic code—the same stuff you've been using throughout this book. Basically, the process feels similar to creating a Windows-based application in a RAD environment.

3. Scroll to the top of the Code Editor, and then enter the following program statement as the first line of the file:

    ```
    Imports System.Math
    ```

The *Abs* function isn't included in Visual Basic by default, but it is part of the *System.Math* class in the .NET Framework and can be more easily referenced in your project by the *Imports* statement. Web applications can make use of the .NET Framework class libraries just as Windows applications can.

The Code Editor looks like this:

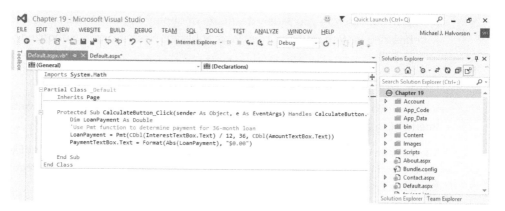

4. Click the Save All button on the Standard toolbar.

That's it! You've entered the program code necessary to run the car loan calculator and make your webpage interactive. Now you'll build and run the project and see how it works. You'll also learn a little bit about security settings within Internet Explorer, a topic closely related to web development.

Build and view the website

1. Click the Start Debugging button on the Standard toolbar.

   Visual Studio starts the ASP.NET Development Server, which runs ASP.NET applications locally (on your own computer) so that you can test this application. A status balloon appears at the bottom of your screen and lets you know the local Uniform Resource Locator (URL) on your computer that has been established. You also might see a message about debugging:

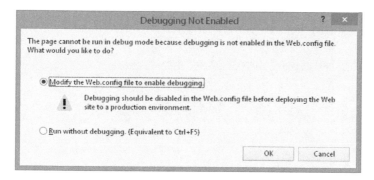

The potentially confusing Debugging Not Enabled dialog box is not a major concern. Visual Studio is indicating only that the Web.config file in your project does not currently allow debugging (a standard security feature). Although you can bypass this dialog box each time that you test the application within Visual Studio by clicking the Run Without Debugging button, I recommend that you modify the Web.config file now.

> **Important** Before you widely distribute or deploy a real website, be sure to disable debugging in Web.config to keep your application safe from unauthorized tampering.

2. If you do see this dialog box, click OK to modify the Web.config file.

Visual Studio modifies the file, builds your website, and displays the opening webpage in Internet Explorer (or your default browser).

The car loan calculator looks like the following screen shot. (I'm using Internet Explorer for the browser.) If your browser window does not appear, you might need to select it on the Windows taskbar.

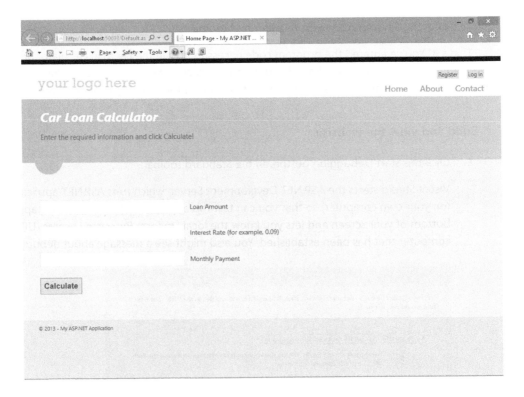

Important If you are using Internet Explorer, you might see an Information Bar at the top of Internet Explorer now indicating that intranet settings are turned off by default. This warning is designed to protect you from rogue programs or unauthorized access. An intranet is a local network (typically a home network or small workgroup network), and because Visual Studio uses intranet-style addressing when you test websites built on your own computer, you're likely to see this warning message. To suppress the warning temporarily, click the Information Bar and then click Don't Show Me This Again. To remove intranet warnings more permanently, click the Internet Options command on the Tools menu of Internet Explorer, click the Security tab, and then click Local Intranet. Click the Sites button, and clear the checkmark from Automatically Detect Intranet Network in the Local Intranet dialog box. However, exercise caution whenever you disable security warnings, because they are meant to protect you.

Now, let's get back to testing our webpage.

3. Type **18000** in the Loan Amount text box, press Tab, and then type **0.09** in the Interest Rate text box.

   You'll compute the monthly loan payment for an $18,000 loan at 9 percent interest for 36 months.

4. Click the Calculate button.

   Visual Basic calculates the payment amount and displays $572.40 in the Monthly Payment text box. Your screen looks like this:

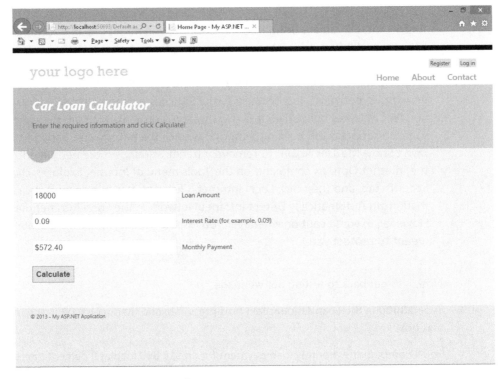

Your program is working correctly.

Now that you're in the default website template, take a moment to look around the application and see what else the default template provides you.

5. Click the About link in the upper-right corner of the website.

    The default text for the current About page appears. This is content that you can quickly customize. (And you'll see how to in a moment.)

6. Click the Contact link in the upper-right corner of the website.

    Basic boilerplate contact information appears, which you can also customize for your business.

7. Click the Log In link.

    You'll see a basic Log In screen template, as shown in the following illustration:

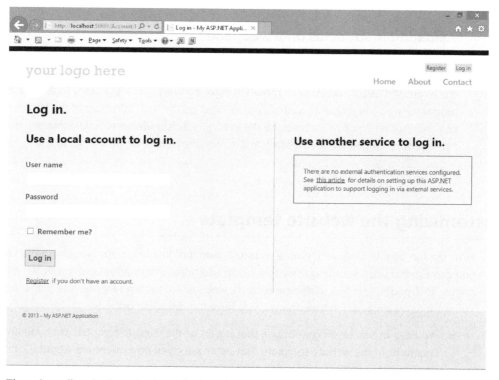

8. There is really a lot here in the default website template. As noted earlier, the multitude of controls and handy features of the default website template are a few of the reasons that developers like using the Web Forms model to build websites and write web applications.

9. Close your browser window.

You're finished testing your website for now. When your web browser closes, your program is effectively ended. As you can see, building and viewing a website is basically the same as building and running a Windows-based application, except that the website is executed in the browser. You can even set break points and debug your application just as you can in a Windows application.

Curious about installing a website like this on an actual web server? The basic procedure for deploying websites is to copy the .aspx files and any necessary support files for the project to a properly configured virtual directory on a web server running IIS and the .NET Framework. There are a couple of ways to perform deployment in Visual Studio. To get started, click Copy Web Site on the Website menu, or click Publish Web Site on the Build menu. For more information about your options, see "ASP.NET Deployment Content Map" in the Visual Studio Help documentation. To find a hosting company that can host ASP.NET web applications, you can check out *http://www.asp.net*.

Customizing the website template

Now the fun begins! Only very simple websites consist of just one webpage. Using the Web Designer, you can expand your website quickly to include additional information and resources, including HTML pages, XML pages, text files, database records, web services, login sessions, site maps, and more. If you want to create additional webpages, you have the following options:

- You can use an existing webpage that is part of the website template that you are using. For example, in the website template that you have open now, there are About, Contact, and Log In pages that you can customize quickly.

- You can create a new webpage by using the HTML Page template or the Web Form template. You select these templates by using the Add New Item command on the Website menu. After you create the page, you add text and objects to the page by using the Web Designer or HTML.

- You can add a webpage that you have already created by using the Add Existing Item command on the Website menu, and then customize the page in the Web Designer. You use this method if you want to include one or more webpages that you have already created in a tool such as Microsoft Blend for Visual Studio. (However, if you add pages that rely on external style sheets or other resources, you'll need to add those items to the project as well.)

In the following exercise, you'll display the About webpage supplied by the template that you are using, and you will customize it with some information about how the car loan calculator application works.

Customize the About.aspx webpage

1. Display Solution Explorer, and then double-click the About.aspx file.

   Visual Studio displays About.aspx in the Designer, and it displays a line of placeholder text (Your App Description Page.).

2. Delete the placeholder text and the lines below it, and then type the following information:

Car Loan Calculator

The Car Loan Calculator website was developed for the book Microsoft Visual Basic 2013 Step by Step, by Michael Halvorson (Microsoft Press, 2013). The website is best viewed using Microsoft Internet Explorer. To learn more about how this ASP.NET Web Forms application was created, read Chapter 19 in the book.

Operating Instructions:

Type a loan amount, without currency symbol or commas, into the Loan Amount box.

Type an interest rate in decimal format into the Interest Rate text box. Do not include the "%" sign. For example, to specify a 9% interest rate, type "0.09".

Note that this loan calculator assumes a three-year, 36-month payment period.

Click the Calculate button to compute the basic monthly loan payment that does not include taxes or other fees.

3. Use the Italic button on the Formatting toolbar to add italics to the book title *Microsoft Visual Basic 2013 Step by Step.*

4. Use the Bold button on the Formatting toolbar to add bold formatting to the Operating Instructions heading, as shown here:

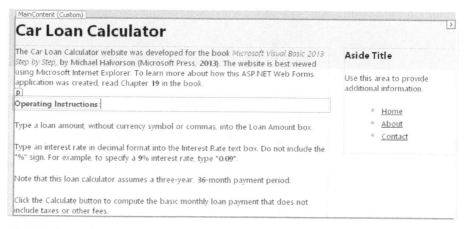

5. Click the Save All button on the Standard toolbar to save your changes.

6. Click the Start Debugging button.

   Visual Studio builds the website and displays it in Internet Explorer.

7. Click the Home tab on the webpage.

   Visual Studio displays the Home page for your website, the car loan calculator.

8. Compute another loan payment to experiment further with the loan calculator.

   If you want to test another set of numbers, try entering **20000** for the loan amount and **0.075** for the interest rate. The result should be $622.12.

9. Now click the About tab to view the About webpage with instructions for your program.

   Internet Explorer displays the About page on the screen. Your browser looks something like this:

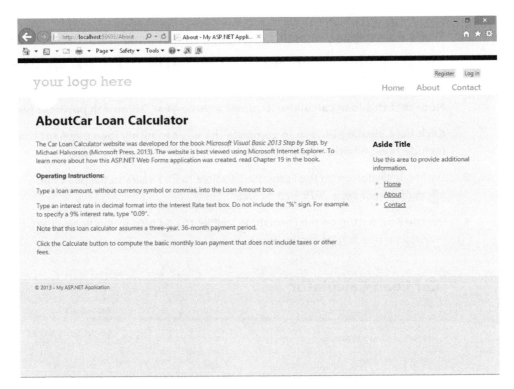

10. Read the text, and then click the Back button in Internet Explorer.

    Just like any website, this one lets you click the Back and Forward buttons to jump from one webpage to the next.

11. Close Internet Explorer to close the website.

You've added a simple About page to your website, and you have experimented with moving from one page to the next. Pretty cool so far. Now try something more sophisticated that shows how far you can take your website if you choose to include information from a database.

Displaying database records on a webpage

Accessing the web is a daily activity for many (and soon most?) people on our planet. A typical scenario in web-based computing is using a web browser to access large amounts of information. Often, the sheer quantity of information that needs to be accessed on commercial websites far exceeds what a developer can realistically prepare for by using basic text documents. In these cases, web programmers add database objects to their websites to display tables, fields, and records of database information, and they connect these objects to a secure database residing in the cloud.

Visual Studio 2013 makes it easy to display the database information that is stored on a database server, and there are many mechanisms for doing this. As your computing needs grow, you can use Visual Studio to process orders, handle security, manage customer information profiles, and create new database records—all from the web. If you choose to use the Web Forms model, the platform can deliver this power very effectively.

For example, the Web Forms *GridView* control is easily accessible in the Toolbox, and it can be used to display database tables containing dozens or thousands of records on a webpage without any program code. You'll see how this works in the following exercise, which adds a webpage containing loan contact data to the Car Loan Calculator project.

Add a new webpage for database information

1. With the Car Loan Calculator website still loaded into the Designer, click the Add New Item command on the Website menu.

   Visual Studio displays a list of components that you can add to your website.

2. Click the Web Form template (the first item in the list), type **FacultyLoanLeads.aspx** in the Name text box, and then click Add.

   Visual Studio adds a new webpage to your website. You'll customize it with some text and server controls.

3. Click the Design tab to switch to Design view.

4. Enter the following text at the top of the webpage:

   The following grid shows instructors who want loans and their contact phone numbers:

5. Press Enter twice to add two blank lines below the text.

> **Note**   Remember that webpage controls are added to webpages at the insertion point, so it is always important to create a few blank lines when you are preparing to add a control.

Next, you'll display two fields from the *Faculty* table of the *Faculty.accdb* database by adding a *GridView* control to the webpage. *GridView* presents information on a webpage by establishing a grid of rows and columns to display data as you might see it in a program such as Microsoft Excel or Microsoft Access. *GridView* can be used to display almost any type of tabular data, including text, numbers, dates, or the contents of an array.

Note that I'm using the same Access database table I used in Chapter 17, "Database controls for Windows desktop apps," so that you can see how similar data access is in ASP.NET. In a more sophisticated project, it is likely that you would use SQL databases to store data. ASP.NET handles these formats very well, too.

Add a *GridView* control

1. With the new webpage open and the insertion point in the desired location, double-click the *GridView* control on the Data tab of the Web Forms Toolbox.

   Visual Studio displays the GridView Tasks list box and adds a grid view object named *GridView1* to the webpage. The grid view object currently contains placeholder information.

   If the GridView Tasks list is not visible, click the *GridView1* object's smart tag to display the list.

2. In GridView Tasks, click the Choose Data Source arrow, and then click the <New Data Source> option.

3. Visual Studio displays the Data Source Configuration Wizard, a tool that you used in Chapter 17 to establish a connection to a database and select the tables and fields that will make up a dataset.

   Your screen looks like this:

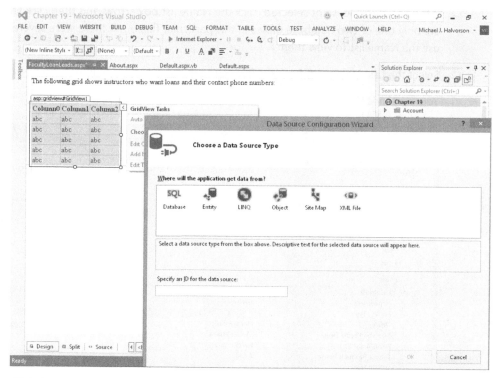

4. Click the SQL Database icon, type **Faculty** in the Specify An ID For The Data Source box, and then click OK.

   You are now prompted to specify the location of the database on your system.

5. Click the New Connection button.

6. Click Microsoft Access Database File under Data Source, and then click Continue.

7. In the Add Connection dialog box, click the Browse button, and then select the Faculty.accdb file in the My Documents\Visual Basic 2013 SBS\Chapter 17 folder. Click Open.

8. Click OK in the Add Connection dialog box.

9. Click Next in the Choose Your Data Connection dialog box to confirm the Faculty.accdb file you've selected.

10. Click Next in the Save The Connection String dialog box.

    You are now asked to configure your data source with an SQL-type *Select* statement—that is, to select the table and fields that you want to display on your webpage. Here, you'll use two fields from the *Faculty* table. (Remember that in Visual Studio, database fields are often referred to as *columns*, so you'll see the word *columns* used in the IDE and the following instructions.)

11. If the *Faculty* table is not selected, click the Name list box arrow, and then click Faculty. (There are only one or two database tables in this particular file, but if there were several, you could use the Name list to view them.)

12. Select the Last Name and Business Phone check boxes in the Columns list box.

Your screen looks like this:

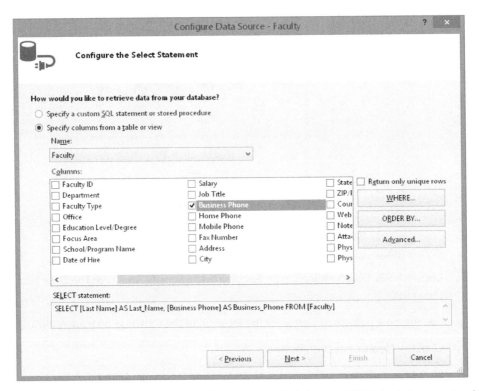

As you make selections in this dialog box, you are building an SQL Select statement, which you can see at the bottom of the dialog box.

13. Click Next to see the Test Query screen.

14. Click the Test Query button to see a preview of your data.

You'll see a preview of actual *Last Name* and *Business Phone* fields from the database. This data looks as expected, although if we were preparing this website for wider distribution, we would take the extra step of formatting the Business Phone column so that it contains standard spacing and phone number formatting.

15. Click Finish.

Visual Studio closes the wizard and adjusts the number of columns and column headers in the grid view object to match the selections that you have made. However, it continues to display placeholder information ("abc") in the grid view cells.

16. With the GridView Tasks list still open, click the Auto Format command.

17. Click the Professional scheme.

The AutoFormat dialog box looks like this:

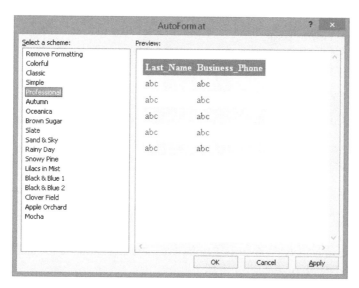

The ability to format, adjust, and preview formatting options quickly is a great feature of the *GridView* control.

18. Click OK, and then close the GridView Tasks list by clicking on the webpage.

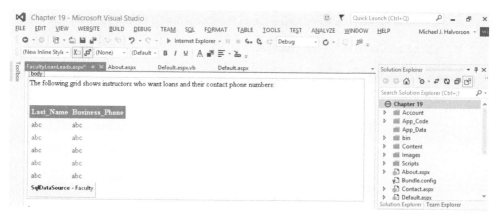

19. Save your changes to the project.

Now, you'll add a hyperlink on the first webpage (or Home page) that will display this page when the user wants to see the database table. You'll create the hyperlink with the *HyperLink* control, which has been designed to allow users to jump from the current page to a new one with a simple mouse click.

How does the *HyperLink* control work? The *HyperLink* control is located in the Standard Toolbox. When you add a *HyperLink* control to your webpage, you set the text that will be displayed on the page by using the *Text* property, and then you specify the desired webpage or resource to jump to (either a URL or a local path) by using the *NavigateUrl* property. That's all there is to it.

Add a hyperlink to the Home page

1. Click the Default.aspx tab at the top of the Designer.

   The Home page for your website opens in the Designer.

2. Click below the Calculate button object to place the insertion point after that object.

3. Double-click the *HyperLink* control on the Standard tab of the Toolbox to create a hyperlink object at the insertion point.

4. Select the hyperlink object, and then set the *Text* property of the object to "Display Loan Prospects."

   We'll pretend that your users are bank loan officers (or well-informed car salespeople) looking to sell auto loans to university professors. Display Loan Prospects will be the link that they click to view the selected database records.

5. Set the *ID* property of the hyperlink object to "ProspectsLink".

6. Click the *NavigateUrl* property, and then click the ellipsis button in the second column.

   The Select URL dialog box opens.

7. Click the FacultyLoanLeads.aspx file in the Contents Of Folder list box, and then click OK.

8. Click Save All to save your changes.

Your link is finished, and you're ready to test the website and *GridView* control in your browser.

Test the final Car Loan Calculator website

1. Click the Start Debugging button.

   Visual Studio builds the website and displays it in the default browser.

2. Enter **8000** for the loan amount and **0.08** for the interest rate, and then click Calculate.

   The result is $250.69. Whenever you add to a project, it is always good to go back and test the original features to verify that they have not been modified inadvertently. Your screen looks like the following screen shot.

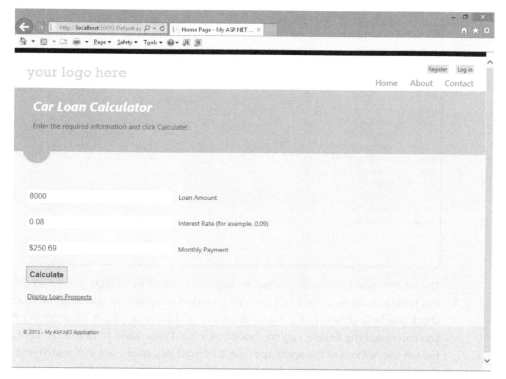

The new hyperlink (Display Loan Prospects) is visible at the bottom of the webpage.

3. Click Display Loan Prospects to load the database table.

Internet Explorer loads the *Last Name* and *Business Phone* fields from the *Faculty.accdb* database into the grid view object. Your webpage looks something like this:

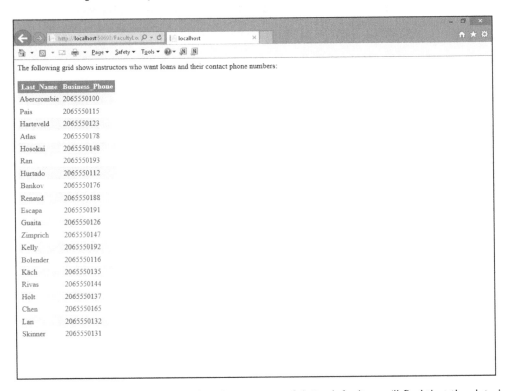

The information is nicely formatted and appears useful. By default, you'll find that the data in this table cannot be sorted, but you can change this option by selecting the Enable Sorting check box in GridView Tasks. If your database contains many rows (records) of information, you can select the Enable Paging check box in GridView Tasks to display a list of page numbers at the bottom of the webpage (like a list that you might see in a search engine that displays many pages of "hits" for your search).

4. Click the Back and Forward buttons in Internet Explorer.

As you learned earlier, you can jump back and forth between webpages in your website, just as you would in any professional website.

5. When you're finished experimenting, close Internet Explorer to close the website.

You've added a table of custom database information to your website.

Editing document and site master properties

Here are two last ASP.NET skills to enhance your website and send you off on your own explorations with Web Forms.

You might have noticed while testing the Car Loan Calculator website that Internet Explorer displayed "Home Page" in the title bar and window tab when displaying your website. Your program also displays the template title "My ASP.NET Application" at the bottom of the window in a copyright message. You might want to change these and other default settings within your project.

First, you can customize what Internet Explorer and other browsers display in the title bar by setting the *Title* property of the *DOCUMENT* object for the webpage. Give this a try now.

Set the *Title* property

1. With the Default.aspx webpage open in Design view, click the *DOCUMENT* object in the Object list box at the top of the Properties window.

    Each webpage in a website contains a *DOCUMENT* object that holds important general settings for the webpage. However, the *DOCUMENT* object is not selected by default in the Designer, so you might not have noticed it. One of the important properties for the *DOCUMENT* object is *Title*, which sets the title of the current webpage in the browser.

2. Set the *Title* property to **Car Loan Calculator**.

The change does not appear on the screen, but Visual Studio records it internally. Now, change the title of your application in something called the *site master* page.

Edit the site master page title

1. Double-click the Site.master file in Solution Explorer to edit the master page in the Designer.

    Visual Studio displays the master page for editing. The master page is a template that provides default settings for your website and lets you adjust characteristics such as appearance, banner titles, logo, menus, and links. For example, you can click smart tags associated with the website's menu items and adjust them.

    Your screen looks like this:

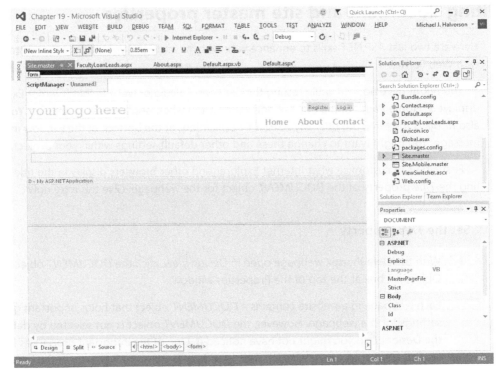

2. Delete the text Your Logo Here.

Although a logo is an attractive feature, you won't add one right now.

Type **Time for a new car?** in the area where the logo message was.

At the bottom of the page, change the copyright message to **Trey Research**.

3. Click the Start Debugging button.

Visual Studio opens Internet Explorer and loads the website. Now a more useful title bar and banner message appears, as shown in the following screen shot:

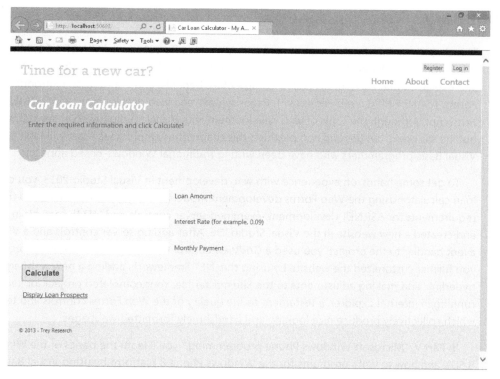

Now that looks better.

4. Close Internet Explorer, and then update the *Title* property for the new loan prospects page that you added so that it matches the pattern of the other webpages on your site.

5. When you're finished experimenting with the Car Loan Calculator, save your changes and close Visual Studio.

Summary

This chapter explored web programming with Visual Studio 2013 and ASP.NET 4.5.1, Microsoft's framework for web development. The chapter surveyed the leading web platforms in Visual Studio and explained that each model has its complexities, benefits, and enthusiasts. I introduced Web Forms, ASP.NET MVC, Web Pages (with Razor syntax), and web development with HTML5 and JavaScript. Although the topic of web development with Visual Studio deserves several books to fully outline the opportunities and complexities, this chapter has emphasized what will look familiar to Visual Basic programmers who have been writing traditional Windows-based apps.

To get some hands-on experience with web development in Visual Studio 2013, you created a car loan calculator using the Web Forms development model and Designer. You examined the software requirements for ASP.NET development, examined server controls and HTML controls in the Toolbox, and created a new website in the Visual Studio IDE. After adding server controls and a Visual Basic event handler to the project, you used a *GridView* control to display Access database records, and you further customized the website by using the .NET Framework, adding a new webpage, adding a hyperlink, and making adjustments to the Site.master file. Your completed project looked very good running in Internet Explorer, a testament to the quality of the Web Forms controls and template, which collectively produce nice looking and handsomely formatted webpages.

In Part V, "Microsoft Windows Phone programming," you'll learn the basics of the Windows Phone 8 SDK and how to write programs for the Windows Phone 8 platform by using Visual Basic 2013 and the Visual Studio IDE.

Microsoft Windows Phone programming

CHAPTER 20

Introduction to Windows Phone 8 development

After completing this chapter, you will be able to

- Describe the development opportunities in the Windows Phone 8 platform.

- Identify the key features and attributes of the Windows Phone ecosystem.

- Evaluate the Windows Phone Store.

- Install the Windows Phone SDK 8.0 and 8.0.1 toolkits.

- Understand differences and similarities between the Windows Phone 8 platform and the Windows Store platform.

Are you ready to give Windows Phone programming a try? In this chapter, you'll learn about the requirements and opportunities presented by the Windows Phone 8 platform for Visual Basic programmers.

While most introductory and intermediate books about Visual Basic do not discuss mobile phone programming, the opportunities presented by this emerging platform are simply too important to pass up. In particular, the Visual Studio 2013 development team has worked hard to narrow the gap between Windows 8.1 desktop development and Windows Phone 8 development. If you've become comfortable writing Windows Store apps using the tools in this book, you'll be amazed at how quickly you can begin writing your own Phone apps with Visual Studio and the Windows Phone SDK 8.0.

In this chapter, you'll get an overview of the features and capabilities presented by the Windows Phone 8 platform. You'll identify key hardware characteristics in the Windows Phone *ecosystem*, and you'll explore the impressive marketing opportunities tendered by the Windows Phone Store. You'll learn how to install the Windows Phone SDK 8.0 on your system and how to verify that Visual Studio is ready for Phone app development. Finally, you'll see how Windows Phone development compares to and contrasts with Windows Store app development. While creating a Windows Phone app is not simply a matter of porting your Windows Store app to the Phone platform, you'll discover that there are many similarities and shared techniques between the two environments.

This chapter is essentially a warm-up act. The material that you learn here will prepare you for hands-on development work in Chapter 21, "Creating your first Windows Phone 8 application." Note that a registered Windows Phone 8 device is not required to complete the exercises in Chapters 20 and 21, although if you have such a phone (as I do), you can use it to think creatively about Windows Phone development.

Opportunities in the Windows Phone 8 platform

In 2007, the consumer marketplace for mobile phones and applications exploded into a revenue-generating machine with the advent of smartphones. While the new smartphone devices rapidly created large and enthusiastic followings, the real revolution for mobile phone customers and software developers became the *public marketplace* that developed for mobile phone apps. Suddenly developers could reach a worldwide audience of millions with their phone programs, and customers could use the multitude of applications to turn their smartphones into full-featured tools, gaming devices, and media players, shifting their daily computing experience from the desktop to the cloud.

Microsoft responded to this revolution by abandoning the Windows Mobile platform and redoubling its efforts to create a smartphone platform that would compete with, and surpass, anything that had been released yet by Apple or Google. Their contribution in 2010 was the Windows Phone 7 platform, which presented a redesigned user interface and architecture based on recent developments in the Zune, Xbox, and Windows environments. In particular, the new Windows Phone 7 platform required that phone hardware manufacturers meet an aggressive new set of hardware requirements for mobile phones, including a standard set of buttons and features. To make the system easy for Windows developers to accept, Microsoft chose the Visual Studio development platform as the primary tool for creating Windows Phone apps.

When Microsoft released the Windows 8 operating system in Fall 2012, it revised and enhanced its phone platform as well, introducing Windows Phone 8. The two Windows platforms shared the design guidelines for user interface construction—a tile-based layout that I have referred to in this book as "the Windows Store application guidelines."

The Windows Phone 8 platform is a very impressive entry into the highly competitive smartphone marketplace. Windows Phone 8 devices are currently manufactured by Nokia, HTC, Samsung, and Huawei. Since late 2012, several million Windows Phone 8 devices have been sold by carriers in the United States, such as Verizon, T-Mobile, AT&T, and Sprint. (In Europe, a leading carrier selling Windows Phone 8 devices is France Telecom Orange.)

Although Android and iPhone devices still outsell Windows Phone, the Windows Phone 8 platform has been a success, and there is a significant business opportunity now for Windows Phone developers. In particular, those developers with Visual Studio and either Visual Basic or Visual C# experience will find that their current programming skills provide an excellent foundation for Windows Phone development.

Note As this book went to press in Fall 2013, Microsoft had just announced the availability of Windows Phone 8 Update 3. This Windows Phone operating system update includes a new Driving Mode feature, improved Internet sharing, support for 1080p devices with 5- and 6-inch screens, and numerous performance enhancements. However, there are few, if any, changes that developers need to make to current Windows Phone 8 apps to make them compatible with Windows Phone 8 Update 3. A new version of the Windows Phone SDK is available (version 8.0.1), and instructions are provided later in this chapter for installing it. The exercises in this book are compatible with Windows Phone 8 Update 3 and Windows Phone SDK 8.0.1.

Key Windows Phone 8 features

Because Windows Phone 8 apps and Windows Store apps share the same user interface guidelines, the two platforms have many common features. For example, the following screen shot from my HTC Windows Phone 8 device shows the Phone Start page with its familiar tile-based layout. This is the place where apps are launched with a tap on the app tile, a very familiar concept for Windows Store users.

In addition, notice how the Phone Start page tiles have a solid color background and white lettering on top, just like the live tiles in a Windows Store application. In fact, you've already learned how to design tiles like these in Chapter 9, "Exploring Windows 8.1 design features: Command bar, flyout, tiles, and touch."

Windows Phone apps also place a premium on touch and gestures, just like the specs recommend for Windows Store apps. In fact, other than Bluetooth devices and voice commands (a cool feature of the Windows Phone), there is no other way to provide user input on a Windows smartphone than touch—everything is about using gestures such as tap, double-tap, pan, flick, hold, pinch, and stretch.

Hardware requirements

The Windows Phone 8 hardware requirements specify that all phones have a power button, a touch screen that supports at least four simultaneous touch points, a volume control with *rocker switch*, a camera button, a back button, a start button, and a search button. The start button must be centrally located in the bottom center of the device and should be marked with a Windows Start page logo. The search button should be on the lower-right side and be labeled with a Search charm (magnifying glass icon). The back button should be on the lower-left side and labeled with a left-pointing arrow. By requiring all of these hardware input controls and labels, the Windows Phone ecosystem provides a reliable environment for both users and programmers.

In addition, there are some important hardware requirements for Windows Phone 8 devices that impact how the phone can be used by developers. The camera must be capable of capturing 5-megapixel images (minimum), Bluetooth connectivity is required, Wi-Fi capability is required, and a number of environmental sensors are required, including GPS, an accelerometer, a compass, a light sensor, a proximity sensor, and a gyro. These sensors are among the most exciting hardware features of Windows Phone, capable of producing amazing special effects in applications. A Windows Phone 8 app developed in Visual Studio and Visual Basic is capable of interacting with all these hardware features.

Integration and collaboration

An impressive feature of the Windows Phone 8 platform is the ability for Phone apps and users to be highly interactive, encouraging communication and collaboration in unprecedented ways. Windows Phone allows you to manage personal contacts, phone messages, text messages, voice mail, and email in one location and then store all related communications in the cloud so that they can be accessed from any location.

The People hub supports meeting and collaboration spaces called Rooms and Groups, as well as connectivity with social networking apps such as Facebook and Twitter. Office apps for Windows Phone provide productivity tools and integration with Outlook, Word, Excel, and PowerPoint projects. Windows SkyDrive allows users to share and preserve information in the cloud and sync it with other desktop and laptop systems.

The Phone's Calendar app allows you to share your calendar with friends and work colleagues and sync it with Windows, Google, and iPhone devices. The Music + Videos hub allows you to listen to your music, watch videos, subscribe to podcasts, and create playlists. If you add an Xbox Music Pass, you can download or stream music from a global catalog containing millions of songs.

You can also pin live tiles on the Start page and customize how your phone looks and operates so that contacts, applications, music, websites, directions, games, photos, documents, and more are at your fingertips. If you pin a tile representing a person on the Start page, you will quickly be able to see their most recent social media posts, tweets, and photos related to an individual in an instant.

Along with social media updates, you'll also see new texts, emails, and incoming calls from the person you're following. Whenever you need to access the Internet, Windows Phone 8 launches a feature-rich version of the Internet Explorer 10 browser, supported by the Bing search engine.

And yes, you can also make telephone calls with Windows Phone devices!

The Windows Phone Store

Because the Windows Phone Store provides a new and potentially profitable way of selling and distributing Windows Phone 8 applications to a wide audience, this section provides an overview of what the Windows Phone Store is and how you can use it to reach customers for Windows Phone apps. There is a compelling business incentive for developing Windows Phone apps that is similar to the opportunity presented by the Windows Store for Windows 8.1 developers.

What is the Windows Phone Store?

The Windows Phone Store is an electronic marketplace that allows consumers to search for and acquire Windows Phone applications. You can access the Windows Phone Store from a Windows-based computer using the Windows Phone application or a web browser (*http://www.windowsphone.com*), but the Store is accessed on a Windows Phone through the Store app. This hub for purchasing and downloading Phone programs was previously known as the Windows Phone Marketplace, and it serves customers with Windows Phone 7 and Windows Phone 8 devices.

The Windows Phone Store is designed much like the Windows Store. The difference, of course, is that the Windows Phone store is designed to merchandize, sell, and install Windows Phone apps. In this way, it is similar to Apple's App Store for iPhone and the Google Play store that sells apps for Android.

The Windows Phone Store allows software developers to monetize Phone applications, either by charging for the Phone app or by including advertising in the Phone app. Apps that are downloaded from the Windows Phone Store are certified and ready to run. The details about downloading, deploying, and updating the application are handled by the Windows Phone Store automatically.

Accessing the Windows Phone Store

The Windows Phone Store is designed for customers who already have a Windows Phone. However, if you don't yet have a Windows Phone and you want to learn more about the phones or applications that are available, you can visit it from a Windows-based computer or device by visiting the website *http://www.windowsphone.com*.

The following screen shot shows what the Windows Phone Store looks like when you visit it from a Windows-based computer using Internet Explorer:

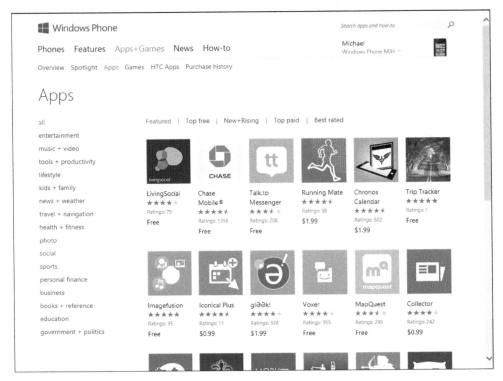

Across the top of the screen are tabs that allow customers to search for available Windows Phones, applications, games, and other information. Because I am a registered Windows Phone customer and user, my particular phone and user name are shown in the upper-right corner of the screen. (I have an HTC phone running Windows Phone 8.0. The screen resolution of this particular device is 720×1280.) I can access the Windows Phone Store from my smartphone, but it is also convenient to access the Store through my Windows 8.1 desktop. This allows me to manage settings, look at installed photos and other media, and review application purchases.

As you can see in the preceding illustration, in the Windows Phone Store some of the apps are sold for a price and others are free. Free applications sometimes display advertisements as a way to gain revenue or are used to support existing products or services, such as a restaurant app, a sports-team app, or an app that provides access to a financial institution. Another feature of the App marketplace is the rating system that shows customer satisfaction with a particular app.

When you select a particular application in the Windows Phone Store, you'll see a details page similar to the following screen:

The app listing page is the place where software vendors get a chance to sell their product and describe the benefits. It is tremendously important to present your Phone app in the best possible light in this location. The application name, logo, description, customer rating, price, and screen illustrations are all important factors in making a good impression on your audience. As people purchase or download your app, the rating system (based on five possible stars for the highest level of customer satisfaction) will become especially important to customers, because there are often several products in the marketplace that provide similar services.

Here is what the Store app icon looks like on a Windows Phone 8 device. (You'll see the Store tile in the middle of the following screen.)

You launch the Store app by tapping the Store tile on the Windows Phone Start page. Inside the Store, you'll see product categories much like the ones you've already examined in the Windows desktop version of the Store, including apps, games, music, and podcasts. Because the Phone has less real estate on the screen, you'll typically see just one column of text in an app.

You can search for Phone apps in the Store by using the Search charm as you would in the Windows Store. In the following illustration, you'll see that I've located the MapQuest Phone app and have displayed its Details page. This page contains an icon, app title, size (2 MB), customer rating, and Install button.

Installing a Windows Phone app from the Windows Phone Store is extremely simple. You just click the Install button, and within moments, the app will be deployed on your Phone, ready for use. A reliable cellular or Wi-Fi connection is required to download the app and (often) to gather data for the app while the program runs.

How much money do developers make?

Windows Phone apps can be distributed free via the Windows Phone Store or sold for a price. Microsoft follows a revenue-sharing model to pay software developers for the apps that they sell in the Windows Phone Store. Currently, the revenue sharing rate is 70% of net revenues for the software developer and 30% of net revenues for Microsoft. (Net revenues means gross sales receipts less applicable taxes and country surcharges.) This revenue sharing model might change over time.

A setting known as a *price tier* sets the fee for the Windows Phone app that you sell in the Windows Phone Store. For example, typical price tiers in the United States for Windows Phone 8 apps are $0.99, $1.49, $1.99, and $2.99. Local and country taxes are also added to this amount when the user makes a purchase.

Windows Phone Dev Center gives you the option to customize your app's price for each country that you sell in. When you register as a Windows Phone developer, you will be given a developer account that tracks your sales and shows you your incoming revenue stream, as well as account information so that you can get paid electronically. There are interesting debates currently on the MSDN forums about whether it is more profitable to sell Phone apps for a fee or make money by advertising or selling in-product services directly from your Windows Phone app. You can also offer users a free trial of your application, which gets them using your product, and then ask for payment after a set period of time.

Planning ahead for certification

Microsoft recommends that you review the certification requirements carefully for Windows Phone apps before you begin serious development work on your project so that you aren't surprised by the necessary steps. For the most part, these steps are simply good development practices that will make your programs robust and high quality. Microsoft is enforcing high standards so that customers come to trust the Windows Phone Store and all of the software distributed through it.

A list of certification requirements is maintained by Microsoft on the Microsoft Developer Network (MSDN) in the Windows Phone Development Center. The certification requirements are updated periodically, and they are designed to keep poorly constructed applications and inappropriate content out of the Store. In this way, the Windows Phone Store requirements are similar to the Windows Store app requirements that you read about in Chapter 1, "Visual Basic 2013 development opportunities and the Windows Store."

The current list of certification requirements can be found on MSDN at: *http://msdn.microsoft.com/ en-us/library/windowsphone/develop/hh184843.aspx*. You'll see the following certification categories listed on MSDN:

- App policies for Windows Phone

- Content policies for Windows Phone

- App submission requirements for Windows Phone

- Technical certification requirements for Windows Phone

- Additional requirements for specific app types for Windows Phone

The next section in this chapter describes the Windows Phone Software Development Kit (SDK) (version 8.0) that you need to write Windows Phone 8 apps. When this SDK is installed and a Windows Phone project is loaded in Visual Studio, the Project menu in the IDE will have an Open Store Test Kit command that you can use to evaluate your Windows Phone 8 app against the certification requirement list. This is a very helpful tool with comprehensive tests that will help you get your Phone app ready for submission. You should review this list of requirements before you get too far along in your development effort.

You will also need to register as a Windows Phone developer before you submit an application for certification. There is an annual fee for being a Windows Phone developer, although it is a relatively minimal cost, and it is free if you are a student or teacher receiving software through Microsoft DreamSpark, an educational program that supports teaching and research. The registration provides some helpful development tools and your own personal dashboard to track your Phone apps and earnings.

Working with Windows Phone SDK 8.0

If you have Visual Studio 2013 Professional, Premium, or Ultimate, you should already have the software that you need to write your first Windows Phone 8 apps. These retail editions of Visual Studio contain the necessary templates, emulators, and support files to enable Windows Phone 8 development. However, you may need to run setup again to install the necessary files. (The Windows Phone 8.0 SDK is an optional feature installed at setup.)

To find out if you have the files that you need, start Visual Studio, and then select the New Project command from the File menu. If you don't see the Windows Phone category under Visual Basic, you'll need to modify your Visual Studio installation. The easiest way to do this is to open Control Panel, select Programs, and then Programs and Features. Double-click Microsoft Visual Studio 2013 to modify the program's features. When Visual Studio setup starts, select Windows Phone 8.0 SDK under Optional Features to Install. You'll see the following screen:

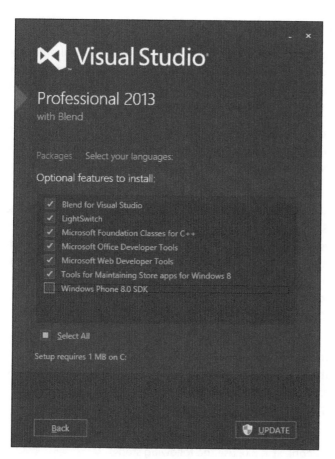

If you are still using Visual Studio 2012 or if you have Visual Studio Express 2013 for Windows, you will need to download the Windows Phone SDK 8.0 to prepare your computer for Windows Phone 8 development. In addition, you will need to download the Windows Phone SDK 8.0 if you have a retail edition of Visual Studio 2013 but would also like to develop apps for Windows Phone 7.5. (Visual Studio 2013 supports Windows Phone 8, but not Windows Phone 7 unless you download the SDK.) The following section describes how to download the SDK if you need it.

Downloading the SDK

The Windows Phone SDK 8.0 includes an Express edition of Visual Studio and all of the tools that you need to develop apps for Windows Phone 8.0 and Windows Phone 7.5. The product is configured this way to lower the requirements necessary to create Phone apps and to make the product suitable for students learning programming in the context of Phone apps.

If you have a retail edition of Visual Studio 2012 or Visual Studio 2013, the SDK will not install the Express product but instead will install the necessary libraries, templates, and emulators to configure your version of Visual Studio for Phone app development. The download also includes Blend Express for Windows Phone.

On the Microsoft website, you will also see information about the newest Windows Phone SDK, named Windows Phone SDK 8.0.1. This version of the SDK supports Windows Phone 8 Update 3, which is a Phone operating system update scheduled for Fall 2013. SDK 8.0.1 does not offer new APIs for developers, but it supports new 1080p devices with 5- and 6-inch screens and provides software emulators for these devices. From the developer point of view, there is not much difference between SDK 8.0 and SDK 8.0.1, and it does not matter which SDK you use when you complete the exercises in this book. I will refer to both, collectively, as the Windows Phone SDK 8.0.

 Note The Windows Phone SDK 8.0 toolkit does not run well in a virtual machine environment. The reason is that the emulator application, which simulates a Windows Phone 8 device within Visual Studio, is actually itself a virtual machine. So things get really slow, and this configuration for your computer is not recommended.

To download the Windows Phone SDK 8.0, use the following steps.

Get the SDK

1. Open a web browser, and go to the following website: *https://dev.windowsphone.com/en-us/downloadsdk*.

2. Under SDK 8.0, click Download.

3. Follow the instructions for installation that appear on the screen.

   As newer versions of the SDK become available, you might need to reinstall the SDK or modify the techniques described in this section or the exercises that follow. Obviously, Microsoft has invested a lot in Windows Phone and will continue to refine and revise the product.

4. After the installation is complete, you might want to consider purchasing an annual Windows Phone Dev Center subscription.

An annual subscription entitles a developer to submit an unlimited number of paid apps to the Windows Phone Store and up to 100 free apps. As I noted earlier, registration is a relatively low-cost endeavor, and it is free if you are a DreamSpark student.

Alternatively, you can complete Chapters 20 and 21 in this book and then decide whether Windows Phone development is for you. It is not necessary to purchase an annual subscription to complete the exercises that I have prepared for you. However, you will need to get a subscription before you can publish applications on the Windows Phone Store.

Now verify that you're ready to start Windows Phone programming.

5. Start Visual Studio 2013.

You should see a Windows Phone template when you create a new project.

6. On the File menu, click New Project.

7. Under Templates, select Visual Basic and then select the Windows Phone category.

You should see a collection of Windows Phone templates, as shown in the following screen shot:

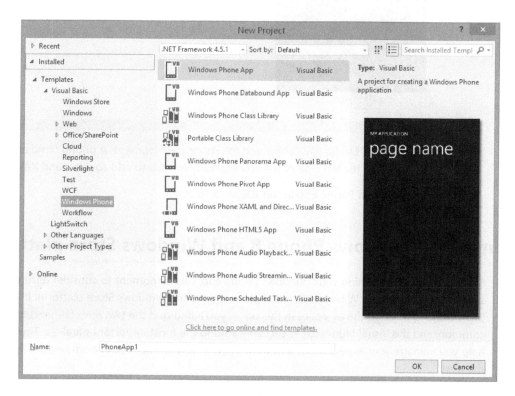

8. Click Windows Phone App (Visual Basic), and click OK.

If the necessary libraries and support files are installed, Visual Studio 2013 will configure your system for Windows Phone 8 programming, and you'll see the following screen:

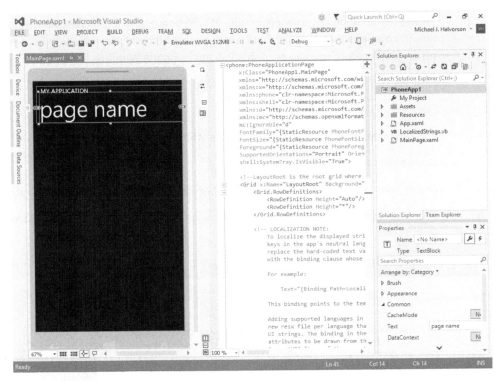

This is the Visual Studio IDE configured for Phone development. A phone template appears in the Designer on the left side of the screen, ready for you to add controls and XAML markup.

You'll create your first Phone app in this IDE in Chapter 21.

Comparing Windows Phone 8 and Windows Store platforms

Before you begin designing your Windows Phone app, take a moment to consider differences and similarities between the Windows Phone 8 platform and the Windows Store platform. If you have been working through the exercises in this book, you'll find that the two environments have a lot in common, and the Visual Studio IDE is certainly among the most important parallels. These lists will help you manage your expectations and transfer your development skills from one environment to the next.

Differences

There was once a time when software developers expected that porting an application from one hardware platform to the next should entail little more than configuring a few settings and then recompiling the program for a new environment. This holy grail is tempting to hope for, but very unrealistic. In terms of Windows Phone 8, the platform certainly has much in common with Windows Store development, but it is also its own unique hardware environment. Some of the major differences Windows Store developers will find when writing applications for Windows Phone include the following:

- **User interface**   The Phone screen is obviously much smaller than a laptop or desktop computer screen, and the Phone's screen resolution is different. Accordingly, applications will need a complete user interface redesign when being ported to the Windows Phone platform, and new Phone apps will need to adapt creatively to the Phone interface, which features panorama views, hubs, and other unique content styles. Multiple columns do not work well on a Windows Phone—there is not enough space to display them.

- **XAML controls and namespaces**   Although XAML is used to define the user interface of a Windows Phone app (and therefore it makes the "similarities" list below), the XAML controls in a Windows Phone app are different than in a Windows Store app (although many have the same names), and accordingly, they have slightly different properties and methods. This is because the XAML controls needed to be optimized for the Phone environment, its design, and its space constraints. So XAML markup cannot easily be reused if you are porting a Windows Store app to the Windows Phone 8 platform. The same is also true for the namespaces in Windows Phone libraries. You'll find that the Phone namespaces have different names, and this even applies to the pages that you use for an application's user interface. For example, *Page* is the root page element for a Windows Store app, but in a Windows Phone app, the root element is *PhoneApplicationPage*.

- **Hardware**   A major advantage of the Windows Phone platform is the exciting hardware that smartphone manufactures are required to include in Windows Phone 8 devices. You'll want to take advantage of some of this hardware, which includes a camera, Bluetooth connectivity, GPS, an accelerometer, a compass, a proximity sensor, and so on. This is simply not the case with Windows desktop devices—you can't know for sure what type of hardware your Windows Store app will have access to, so you can't be quite so bold in your programming. Even in a case when there is a shared hardware device between platforms, such as a camera device that is commonly found on newer Windows desktops and laptops, the development technique for accessing the feature is different. Both Windows Store apps and Windows Phone apps support capturing images and video, but the APIs that you use are different.

- **Designed solely for touch**   Although it is required for Windows Store apps to support touch and gestures if the user's computer is designed to support these features, many (or most?) computers running Windows 8 and Windows 8.1 still do not fully support touch-based input. However, touch is typically the only physical mechanism for input on a Windows Phone, so the apps must be designed primarily for touch. This means that the program code that you have written for other types of input won't work "as is" in your Windows Phone app. You'll also need to get used to new types of events and event handlers in your code.

- **Application lifecycle**   Although there are similarities to how Windows Phone apps start, run, go dormant, and terminate, the APIs that Windows Store apps and Windows Phone apps call to manage the lifecycle of an application are somewhat different. One reason for this is that relatively limited system resources exist in the Windows Phone environment compared to the relatively expansive space of a (newer) Windows 8.1 desktop computer. A new term to learn related to lifecycle management on a Windows Phone device is *tombstoning*, an application state in which a dormant Phone app is shut down to free up system resources. However, when a tombstoned Phone app is activated by the user again, the program needs to open and run as if it had never been terminated. (That is, the application state needs to be preserved.)

- **Background processing**   By design, a Windows Phone 8 device will typically run only one application at a time to prevent battery loss. This is a lesson that Microsoft learned after watching Android users constantly complain that they were running out of battery power because they had inadvertently enabled multitasking on their smartphones. For this reason, a Windows Phone app will run only one application at a time, and developers will need to approach multitasking in a different way than you might in a Windows Store app. However, in some circumstances a kind of limited multitasking is allowed; for example, you can play music on the Phone's speaker from one application while using another application. Or you can browse the web while making a phone call.

- **Windows Runtime APIs**   Although both Windows Phone and Windows Store apps have access to the extensive Windows Runtime API libraries, there are differences in how these classes are used. System tasks and contracts are different, local storage is different, networking is different, and Toast notifications are different.

- **Testing**   As you will see in Chapter 21, the procedures for testing a Windows Phone app are somewhat different than a Windows Store app. Essentially, you test a Phone app in a software emulator that functions like a real Windows Phone. However, because the emulator is a piece of software that shows input on the screen in Visual Studio, it does not have a touch interface or buttons that you can press like a Windows Phone does. Alternatively, you can use your own Windows Phone for testing during the development process. The only requirement is that you register with Microsoft as a Phone developer. After you do so, you can unlock your phone so that it can download an app that has not been certified yet.

- **User expectations**   Most significantly, user expectations are simply different for smartphone apps. The platform calls for new and innovative *mobile* solutions. Customers want to find Wi-Fi hotspots when they're out walking around, they want to stay connected with their friends via social media, they want to use the sensors on their phones to react to their environment, and they want to share media and track their phone's data usage. They want to start a task and then complete it on their laptop or desktop. For this reason, new ideas and solutions are required.

Similarities

The preceding list of differences between platforms might seem a little daunting at first, but there really is a lot of good news for Windows Store programmers who are hoping to become productive quickly with Windows Phone 8 development. Some of the major similarities you'll find between Windows Store and Windows Phone 8 development include the following:

- **Visual Studio development environment** As you've already seen, the Visual Studio IDE can be configured easily for Windows Phone 8 development, and the SDK that you need is actually free at this time. Within Visual Studio, most of the tools that you will use to write Windows Phone programs are the ones that you have already been using. The Designer, the Code Editor, Solution Explorer, and the Properties window are all similar to the Properties window you see during Windows Store app development. You create applications using the same object-oriented programming model, and the process of creating, building, and debugging solutions is the same.

- **XAML markup** Building on the success of Windows Presentation Foundation (WPF) and Windows Store app development, the user interface for Windows Phone apps is designed using XAML markup. As you know now, XAML is an XML-based markup language that uses a hierarchy of elements to describe an application's design and to instantiate .NET objects. This is all done in the Visual Studio IDE using the Code Editor and the Properties window. (You can also use Blend for Visual Studio to create the XAML markup for your Phone app and your Windows Store app.)

- **XAML controls** Both the Windows Store controls and the Windows Phone 8 controls are based on the Windows 8.1 design guidelines, which aim to reduce screen clutter and unnecessary interface "chrome," such as menu bars, toolbars, persistent scroll bars, and dialog boxes. Accordingly, you'll find that most of the Windows Phone controls have familiar names and functionality, even if the specific properties, methods, and events are slightly different, and you need to use them in different ways in the smaller ecosystem of the Phone.

- **.NET Framework** Although some of the Windows Runtime APIs are different when you write Windows Phone 8 apps, you'll find that most of the familiar .NET Framework libraries and classes work without modification when you use them in a Windows Phone application. The skills you've developed to declare collections and arrays, process strings, compute mathematical formulas, and so on will work mostly unchanged in Windows Phone apps because Windows Phone programming is part of the .NET family of Windows technologies.

- **Visual Basic language** Visual Basic 2013 is the same core language in Windows Phone 8 development as it is in Windows Store development. This is because the Windows Phone SDK 8.0 is a toolkit that configures Visual Studio for Phone programming, and Visual Basic (along with Visual C#) is a core language in the Visual Studio product. This means that the fundamental language skills that you have developed, such as using types, declaring variables, writing event handlers, using structures and loops, managing data with LINQ, creating classes and property procedures, and so on, are all fundamental activities that you can continue in Windows Phone 8 apps.

- **Data access** Data access tools and techniques in a Windows Phone 8 application are similar to what you have learned already for Windows Store apps. You can use ADO.NET, XML documents, collections, LINQ, and so on in your projects. At the very technical level, the APIs used in Windows Phone 8 apps are a subset of the APIs available to Windows Store applications, and they don't provide support for temporary data storage and a few other advanced features.

- **Live tiles** As you have seen in this chapter, the Windows Phone Start page makes use of colorful application tiles just like the Windows 8.1 Start page. Both platforms also support live tiles, which periodically update the content on tiles with useful information. (However, the process for sending live tiles updates is somewhat different.) You can design the tiles necessary for both platforms using tools in the Visual Studio IDE.

- **Portable class libraries** Although some of the code in a Windows Phone project needs to be unique to that application, there are also times when code can be shared between a Windows Store app and a Windows Phone app. In Visual Studio, this is facilitated by creating a portable class library containing the shared code. Basically, what you do is write your Visual Basic code in classes that contain the logic and structures that you want to share across multiple platform s, and then you build managed assemblies that encapsulate that logic. Portable class libraries let you build assemblies that will work without modification on Windows Store, Windows Forms, WPF, ASP.NET, Silverlight, Windows Phone 7, Windows Phone 8, and Xbox 360 platforms.

- **Windows Phone Store** From a business point of view, the merchandizing, sales, distribution, and update model provided by the Windows Phone Store is very similar to what is provided by the Windows Store. For a Windows Store app developer, this business model is familiar and the certification requirements are similar.

- **Windows usability** It is worth pointing out the obvious convergence and synergy now in the marketplace between the Windows 8.1 and Windows Phone 8 platforms. These tools work very well together, and users are often active in both environments, beginning a task on the desktop, adding something on the Phone, and then viewing it later on a Surface tablet. If you have experience writing Windows Store apps and designing programs for Windows 8.1 users, that experience will be of great help to you as you create Windows Phone apps.

In summary, the Windows Store and Windows Phone 8 platforms provide a common feature set and complementary business model, which allows for a significant amount of code and asset reuse when building solutions for both platforms. However, there are significant differences between the two environments, especially in relation to how the unique hardware characteristics of the Phone are leveraged in a Windows Phone app. These differences mean that you will need to create a separate user interface for both platforms and that, in most cases, the interfaces will require their own XAML markup, controls, and event handlers. However, most significantly, Windows Phone 8 offers an exciting platform for entirely new types of applications. As you design them, you will be able to take your Visual Basic and Visual Studio coding skills with you!

Summary

This chapter introduced Windows Phone 8 development opportunities for Visual Basic 2013 programmers, including the Windows Phone Store, an exciting marketing and distribution point for software developers who want to create smartphone applications. You've learned about the unique features of the Windows Phone 8 ecosystem, how the Windows Phone Store operates, how the Windows Phone SDK 8.0 toolkit is installed, and what the major differences and similarities are between Windows Phone and Windows Store app development.

In Chapter 21, you'll use Visual Studio and the Windows Phone SDK 8.0 to write a Windows Phone 8 application from scratch, leveraging the skills and techniques that you've learned throughout this book.

Creating your first Windows Phone 8 application

After completing this chapter, you will be able to

- Use Visual Studio tools to build the user interface for a Windows Phone app.

- Use essential XAML controls in the Windows Phone Toolbox.

- Write Visual Basic event handlers for touch events in Windows Phone.

- Test your app in the Visual Studio Phone Emulator.

- Manage Windows Phone life-cycle states, such as *Activated* and *Deactivated*.

A s you learned in Chapter 20, "Introduction to Windows Phone 8 development," the Visual Studio 2013 IDE is ready to help you build Windows Phone applications. If you've completed that chapter and have worked through the Windows Store programming content in this book, you're ready to build your first Windows Phone 8 app right now.

In this chapter, you'll learn how to create a mobile phone application that keeps score on the golf course as you play a real or imagined 18-hole round. If you have no particular interest in golf, don't worry about it—I've selected this smartphone app because the concept lends itself to walking around outdoors, which is what I like to do with my Windows Phone. A golf-scoring app also needs to be able to deactivate when it is not in use and activate again when you're ready to record a score. This feature requirement is typical of smartphone apps, and it will give me a chance to teach you how to use the *PhoneApplicationService* class and the *Activated* and *Deactivated* event handlers.

You'll begin your work by creating a new Windows Phone 8 project and exploring a Visual Studio IDE that is configured for Phone programming. Then you'll learn how to use XAML controls in the Windows Phone Controls Toolbox, how to set properties and create event handlers, and how to declare global variables in a Windows Phone application. Next, you'll learn how to manage life-cycle events in a Windows Phone application, including launching, activation, deactivation, and closing events. Finally, you'll learn how to test your Phone app using the Visual Studio Phone Emulator.

Note that a Windows Phone is not required to complete the exercises in this chapter. You just need the Windows Phone SDK 8.0 toolkit, which is included in Visual Studio 2013 Professional, Premium, and Ultimate. You can also download the toolkit manually. (For more information, see Chapter 20.)

Creating a Windows Phone project

Visual Studio 2013 provides several templates for Windows Phone 8 app development, which you can examine in the New Project dialog box when you open a new Windows Phone project. The selection of Phone app templates is somewhat parallel to what you see in the New Project dialog box for a Windows Store app, in that there is a basic, default template and also templates that have embedded controls, such as the Windows Phone Panorama App template, which uses the *Panorama* control to create an application workspace that is scrollable and similar to what you see in commercial Windows Phone 8 apps.

Of particular interest is the Windows Phone Audio Playback template, which lets you play music in the background from a Phone app. This template exploits a special service on the Phone platform that allows background playback even after the app has been deactivated. (This is useful because typically, Windows Phone apps don't run in the background.)

In the following exercise, you'll start building the Golf Caddy Windows Phone 8 app by first creating a new Phone project and then using XAML controls to build the user interface.

Create a new Windows Phone project

1. Start Visual Studio 2013.

2. On the Visual Studio File menu, click New Project.

3. Under Templates, select Visual Basic and then select the Windows Phone category.

   You'll see a collection of Windows Phone templates. (If you don't, it could be that the Windows Phone SDK 8.0 toolkit is not installed. See Chapter 20 for a discussion about how to configure your system properly for Windows Phone 8 development.)

4. Click Windows Phone App (Visual Basic) template.

   This is the basic (default) Windows Phone app template, with plenty of useful template code but no special controls or features.

5. In the Name text box, type **My Golf Caddy**, and then click OK.

   Visual Studio creates a new Windows Phone 8 project named My Golf Caddy and prepares the IDE for Windows Phone programming. (Throughout this chapter, you'll simply see Golf Caddy in the title bar, the name of the sample files project.) Your screen will look like this:

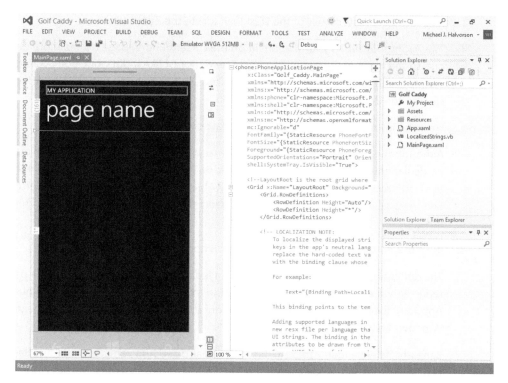

What you see here looks a lot like the standard IDE setup for a Windows Store or Windows Forms app, except that the Designer on the left side of the screen contains a preview of the Windows Phone user interface rather than a page with traditional desktop proportions.

Notice that the Code Editor is also displayed in the middle of the IDE. Because there is a little more room on the screen (the Phone app's user interface is not as big as a Windows Store app), some developers like to display the Code Editor on the right side of the Designer.

In Solution Explorer, you will also see the familiar App.xaml and MainPage.xaml files, as well as the Assets folder that contains tiles and other image files. These three project elements are all included in Windows Store projects coded in Visual Basic, but the contents of each item are slightly different.

Now you'll look around the Visual Studio IDE a little more to see what else looks familiar.

Explore the Visual Studio IDE

1. On the left side the IDE, locate the Toolbox, Device, Document Outline, and Data Sources windows.

   By default, these items are all in the docked position. Each tool performs a similar function in the IDE when you are creating a Windows Phone app. You'll use the Toolbox in the next exercise.

2. Near the lower-left corner of the Designer, locate the Zoom tool.

   The Zoom tool allows you to zoom in on the current Phone page (to see more detail) or zoom out (to see more of the page). This tool functions just like it did when you created Windows Store apps. The current value of the Zoom tool is 67%, but you can select a different value by clicking the Zoom tool's drop-down button.

3. Near the lower-right corner of the IDE, locate the Properties window.

   Although the controls, properties, and events in a Windows Phone app are unique to this particular environment, the Properties window functions like it does in the Windows Store platform. You can set properties by using XAML markup or by using the Properties window. Before you can set a property, you must select the relevant control in the Designer or in XAML markup.

4. In Solution Explorer, click the tree expansion node next to the App.xaml file.

   The default contents of App.xaml are displayed in the Code Editor. This file is a partial class representing global project settings and resources. It has the same name and purpose as the App.xaml file in a Windows Store application, but the contents of App.xaml are different in a Windows Phone app.

   Beneath the expanded App.xaml file, you will also see App.xaml.vb, the Visual Basic code-behind file that, when combined with App.xaml, will make a complete class in your project. App.xaml.vb contains default Visual Basic code provided by the Windows Phone template that defines the App class, initializes various components, and provides event handlers for life-cycle events in the flow of your program, such as launching and deactivating. You'll add code to this file to manage the application state later in the chapter.

5. In Solution Explorer, click the tree expansion node next to the MainPage.xaml file.

   Visual Studio displays the entry for the MainPage.xaml.vb file. MainPage.xaml is currently visible in the Designer—it contains the default template's user interface for the Phone application. The MainPage.xaml.vb code-behind file works just like its namesake in a Windows Store application—it imports necessary namespaces, defines the partial class *MainPage*, and provides space for event handlers that respond to interaction with the XAML objects defined on the page in MainPage.xaml.

Now you'll edit the default Windows Phone template in the Designer. You'll use the Designer and Properties windows to make changes to the *PhoneApplicationPage* element in the App.xaml file. The *PhoneApplicationPage* class is equivalent to the *Page* class in a Windows Store app.

Adjust settings in *PhoneApplicationPage*

1. Click the Page Name text block object at the top of the Windows Phone page in the Designer.

    Visual Studio highlights the XAML markup for a *TextBlock* control in the App.xaml file that contains the words "page name." This is the default banner heading for the basic Windows Phone template, and it is easy to customize by directly editing the XAML in App.xaml or by using the Properties windows when the *TextBlock* object is selected.

2. In the Properties window, change the *Text* property of the selected *TextBlock* object to **Golf Caddy**.

    Visual Studio updates the App.xaml file and the page in the Designer, with the new heading.

3. Click the MY APPLICATION text block object above the new Golf Caddy object that you just modified.

    Visual Studio highlights the XAML markup for a second text block object in the App.xaml file.

4. Use the Properties window to change the *Text* property of this object to **Score Master**.

    Your Windows Phone page will now look like this in the Designer:

    Just like in a Windows Store app, you can set properties by using XAML markup directly or by using the Properties window.

Now you'll add a Windows Phone *Image* control to the user interface.

Add an *Image* control to the page

1. Right-click the Assets folder in Solution Explorer, point to the Add command, and then click Existing Item.

2. In the Add Existing Item dialog box, browse to the My Documents\Visual Basic 2013 SBS\ Chapter 21 folder and click Golf Course, a JPEG file containing the image of a golf course green and flag.

3. Click Add to add the photo to your project's Assets folder.

   As you learned in Windows Store development, when a file has been added to the Assets folder it becomes part of the project you are working on, and it will be included when your project is packaged for distribution via the Windows Phone Store.

4. Now open the Windows Phone Toolbox, and examine the controls that you can use to create smartphone apps.

   Your Toolbox will look like this:

The controls in the Windows Phone Toolbox share many of the names and characteristics of Windows Store controls, and they are based on .NET classes and XAML. However, the Phone controls are stored in a different namespace and maintain a different set of methods, properties, and events. You'll also see some controls that are unique to the Windows Phone Toolbox, such as *Panorama*.

5. Click the *Image* control, and then create an *Image* object on the page in the Designer that takes up about three-quarters of the page.

   This object will provide a colorful background picture for our Golf Caddy smartphone app. You should size the image so that it takes up the complete application area provided by the Phone app template below the Golf Caddy text block. The image control will snap into place when you drag the control's sides to the edge of the template.

6. With the new image object selected, return to the Properties windows, and then open the Common category for the *Image* control.

7. Click the *Source* text box, and then click GolfCourse.jpg.

   A photo of a golf course fills the image object in the Designer.

8. Set the *Stretch* property to Fill.

9. Adjust the spacing of the image so that it takes up the entire application area on the page beneath the Golf Caddy text block.

   Notice that the template design preserves a very thin ribbon of space around the border of the Windows Phone page. I recommend that you leave this space black, because the template design is preserving a thin ribbon of black around the display to show the current time and other information.

10. In the Properties window, change the *Name* property of the image object to **GolfImage**.

    Naming your objects is also an important step in Windows Phone programming, and it is a requirement if you will be referring to an object in the MainPage.xaml.vb code-behind file. (That's not the case here, but it will be for other objects.)

    Your page should look like this:

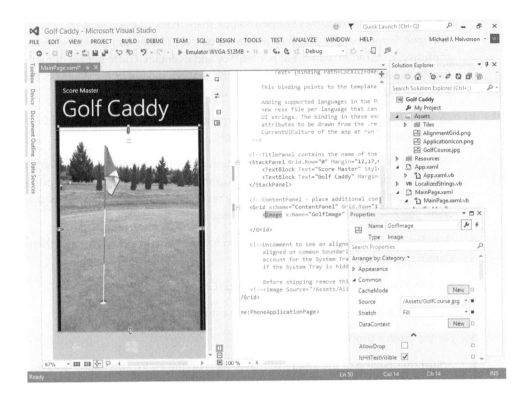

Designing the Golf Caddy user interface

Now you'll add the user interface controls that make up the Golf Caddy Phone app. This program is designed to keep score for an 18-hole golf round as an alternative to using a printed scorecard and pencil. Accordingly, the program should be easy to use and it should have interface tools that are simple to operate via touch. I selected this particular program for this chapter because it is obviously a *mobile* app—you wouldn't carry a desktop or laptop around the golf course to keep score, would you?

The Golf Caddy program will use a *TextBlock* control (*TotalTextBlock*) to display the current score as it builds through the 18-hole golf round. Each time that the score for a new hole is entered in the Phone app, the *TotalTextBlock* object will be updated to reflect the rolling score.

The app will also use a *TextBox* control named *HoleScore* to receive numeric input from the user and add it to the total. Next to the *HoleScore* text box there will be an unnamed label that describes the text box, as well as a *Button* control named *ScoreHoleButton* that runs an event handler to record the score when the user presses the button. There is also a *TextBlock* control named *CurrentHoleTextBlock*, which displays the hole being played, and a second *Button* control named *NewRoundButton* that the user will press when (and if) they want to reset the score and start a new round of golf. Launching the program from the Start page will also reset the app and begin a new round of golf.

The completed user interface will look like the page in the following illustration:

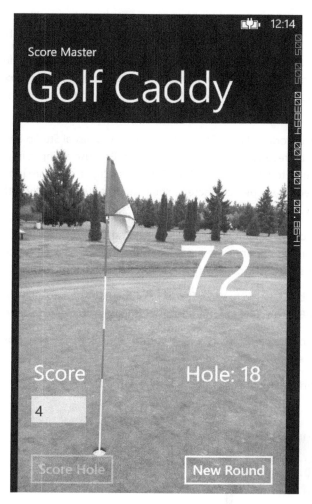

Perform the following exercises to complete the user interface for the Golf Caddy Phone app.

Add three *TextBlock* controls and a *TextBox*

1. Click the *TextBlock* control in the Toolbox, and then create an oversized text block object near the middle of the page. Name the text block **TotalTextBlock**, and set its *FontSize* property to **120**. Set the *Text* property to **"0"**, and center-align the text that appears in the text block.

2. Click the *TextBlock* control in the Toolbox again, and below the new *TotalTextBlock* object, create another text block object that will display the number of the current hole being played. Name this object **CurrentHoleTextBlock**. Set the *Text* property to "**Hole: 1**", and set the *FontSize* property to **36**.

3. Create another *TextBlock* control on the left side of the page (across from the *CurrentHoldTextBlock*), and set its *Text* property to "**Score**". Change the object's *FontSize*

property to **36**. You don't need to name this object because it won't be used in the code-behind file. It simply serves as a label for the text box object that you'll create in the next step.

4. Below the text block containing "Score", create a small *TextBox* control that contains enough room to display a two or three-digit number. Name the object **HoleScoreTextBox**, and set its *InputScope* property to Number. Remove the text that is currently in the text box so that it is empty.

   The *InputScope* property, introduced here for the first time, gives Visual Studio a hint about what type of input might be received by the text box object. Because all input in a Windows Phone app happens through touch input, Windows Phone displays a software input panel (SIP) to help the user enter the needed characters. You'll get this automatically with the *TextBox* and *PasswordBox* controls.

   You can change the look of the default Phone SIP by setting the *TextBox* control's *InputScope* property. A number of common options are provided in the Properties window for *InputScope*. I'm making it easier for Golf Caddy users now by specifying Number.

5. Below the new text box object, in the lower-left corner of the page, create a new *Button* control named **RecordScoreButton**. Change the button's *Content* property to "**Score Hole**."

6. In the lower-right corner of the page, create a new *Button* control named **NewRoundButton**. Change the button's *Content* property to "**New Round**."

   Nice work. Your user interface will look like this in the Designer:

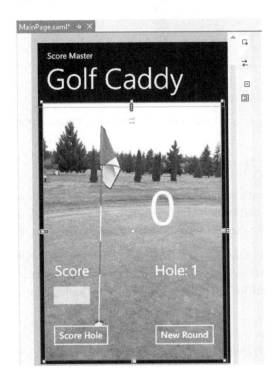

If you look in the Code Editor now, you'll see XAML markup that defines the layout and content of the objects that you just created, and you can make property or spacing adjustments if you want.

7. Click the Save All command on the File menu to save your additions to the Golf Caddy project. Specify the My Documents\Visual Basic 2013 SBS\Chapter 21 folder as the location.

The Save All command saves everything in your project—the project file, the pages, the code-behind files, the assets, and other related components in your Windows Phone 8 application.

Writing the code

Now you're ready to write the code for the Golf Caddy program. In the following steps, you'll create a code module for a few global variables, and then you'll create event handlers for the *RecordScoreButton* and *NewRoundButton* objects. You'll use the same Visual Basic language that you have worked with throughout this book.

Use the Code Editor

1. Click Add Module on the Project menu to create a new code module in the project.

2. With the Module template selected in the Add New Item dialog box, click Add.

Visual Studio adds a code module named Module1.vb to the project, and the files appears in Solution Explorer with the other project files. The module is also visible now in the Code Editor.

You'll use this code module to declare two global variables so that they can be referenced in both MainPage.xaml.vb and App.xaml.vb. The first variable (*TotalScore*) will be a short integer variable that holds the golfer's score as it builds from hole to hole. The second variable (*CurrentHole*) will also be a short integer variable. *CurrentHole* tracks the number of holes played. When the program is launched, *TotalScore* is reset to 0, and *CurrentHole* is reset to 1. These global variables will also be used to save and restore state information when the application is deactivated and activated.

> **Note** In this program, the number of holes played will always be 18, although an enhanced version of the program could prompt the user for a number of interesting options related to the golf round, including the number of holes to be played, the name of the golf course, the par rating, the golfer's name, the date, and so on. These options would typically be set and stored on a separate settings page in your Phone app, and they could be stored between rounds by using methods in the *IsolatedStorageSettings* class. (See "Life cycle management with the *IsolatedStorageSettings* class," later in this chapter.)

3. Type the following code between the *Module* and End *Module* statements:

```
'Global variables for the Golf Caddy Phone app
Public TotalScore As Short = 0
Public CurrentHole As Short = 1
```

4. Click the Save All button on the toolbar, and then click the Close button on the Module1.vb tab to close the code module.

Now you'll create event handlers for the two button objects.

5. In the Designer, click the button containing Score Hole (the *RecordScoreButton* object), and then click the Event Handler (lightning bolt) button in the Properties window.

6. The list of events supported by the *Button* object appears in the Properties window, as shown in the following screen:

Notice that the list of supported *Button* events is different than what you would see for the *Button* control in a Windows Store application. This is because the *Button* control has been optimized for Windows Phone 8 development.

Pause to think about how user input works in a Windows Phone app. There is no traditional mouse, keyboard, or light pen here; all of the input is touch-based. For this reason, Windows Phone programmers are often eager to exploit the *Tap*, *DoubleTap*, *Drag*, and *Hold* gestures, which you'll see listed in the collection of supported events for the *Button* control. However, you'll also see a number of events that seemingly relate to mouse input, such as *Click*, *DoubleClick*, *MouseMove*, *MouseWheel*, and so on. Why would these mouse input events still be listed for the Windows Phone *Button* control?

The answer is that mouse input is still used as a convenient model for event handling in Windows Phone programming, even though a physical mouse is not actually used for input. After all, there is a lot of code out there that processes mouse clicks to manage input controls. The designers at Microsoft thought that it would be just fine to continuing using *Click* and *DoubleClick* events as the primary events that a *Button* control waits for, even though the mobile phone user is actually *touching* the phone screen and not using a mouse.

Accordingly, the two event handlers you'll write in this chapter will wait for the *Click* event, which takes place when the user presses the button objects on the screen. As you write your own Windows Phone programs, you'll want to expand you list of supported events to *Hold*, *Drag*, and other gestures.

7. Double-click the *Click* event in the Properties windows for the *RecordScoreButton* object.

Visual Studio opens the *RecordScoreButton_Click* event handler in the Code Editor.

8. Type the following Visual Basic code:

```
'add score from current hole to total and display
TotalScore = TotalScore + HoleScoreTextBox.Text
TotalTextBlock.Text = TotalScore

'determine if there are any holes left to play
If CurrentHole = 18 Then
    'stop if 18th hole finished; disable Score Hole button, await new round
    RecordScoreButton.IsEnabled = False
Else
    'if not finished yet, move to next hole and await a new score
    CurrentHole = CurrentHole + 1
    CurrentHoleTextBlock.Text = "Hole: " & CurrentHole
End If
```

This event handler runs when the user clicks the Score Hole button, indicating that they have typed a number into the *HoleScoreTextBox* object and want to move on to the next hole. The tasks that this routine completes are very straightforward: The hole score in the text box is added to the overall total and stored in the *TotalScore* global variable. This number is also displayed in the oversized *TotalTextBlock* object on the page so that the running total is visible.

The routine then tests to see where the golfer is in his or her round on the course. If they were playing the 18th and final hole and just recorded that score, the routine disables the *RecordScoreButton* object so that no more scores can be added, and the round is complete. The user can then take their time viewing the page with its attractive graphic and final score. When they are finished with their work, they can close the application by clicking the Back button, or they can start a new game by clicking the New Round button.

However, if the round is not complete, the event handler increments the global variable *CurrentHole* and displays the new hole number on the page by using the *CurrentHoleTextBlock* object. The *Else* clause manages this process once for each hole that the golfer plays. By contrast, the *Then* clause is executed only once during the entire round—when the 18th hole is complete.

Now you'll create the event handler for the New Round button.

9. In the Designer, click the *NewRoundButton* object, and then display the event list in the Properties window.

10. Double-click the *Click* event in the Properties window to create the event handler.

Visual Studio opens the *RecordScoreButton_Click* handler in the Code Editor.

11. Type the following code:

```
'reset the game, variables, and user interface
TotalScore = 0
TotalTextBlock.Text = TotalScore
CurrentHole = 1
CurrentHoleTextBlock.Text = "Hole: 1"
RecordScoreButton.IsEnabled = True
```

This routine is executed when the golfer is ready for a new game. The global variable *TotalScore* is reset to 0, and *CurrentHole* is reset to 1. The text block objects on the page are reset to display the same initial settings that the user saw when they first launched the program. Finally, the *RecordScoreButton* object is enabled so that it can be used again to enter scores.

12. Click the Save All button to save your changes.

You've added enough features to run and test your application. However, the process is a little different than with a Windows Store or Windows Forms app. You'll use the Visual Studio Windows Phone Emulator.

Testing Windows Phone apps

The Visual Studio commands for running, testing, and debugging Windows Phone apps are similar to the commands you have used for other application types in Visual Studio 2013. The only major difference is that for the majority of tests you will be running your application using the Windows Phone Emulator software, a virtual machine that simulates the Phone platform. This will give you a sense of how your application looks and functions before you test the app on an actual Windows Phone.

Remember that before your Windows Phone app can be published and distributed on the Windows Phone Store, it needs to be formally registered with Microsoft, and it also needs to pass various certification tests. That is, Microsoft will not let you distribute your Windows Phone app until it has been certified. The exception is that if you register as a Windows Phone developer with Microsoft and pay for an annual subscription, you will be allowed to unlock your Windows Phone 8 device and use it to run and test your Phone apps.

Before this takes place, you'll want to do all of your major testing with the Windows Phone Emulator software. You'll try that now.

Use the Windows Phone Emulator

1. Click the Start button on the Standard toolbar.

   Notice that the Start button has the name of a Windows Phone Emulator in it. For example, my version of Visual Studio has an emulator named "WVGA 512MB" listed next to the Start button. (A standard hardware specification that should simulate the minimum of what all authorized Windows Phone 8 device manufacturers are using.) You can select a different emulator by using the Start button drop-down list box.

   Because this emulator is an actual virtual machine, it will take Visual Studio a little while to launch it and to display your running app. Be patient. The first thing that you see will be the emulator window on the screen with a sample Windows Phone Start page in it. You'll see typical simulated tiles and features. This is what my emulator looked like shortly after I launched the program:

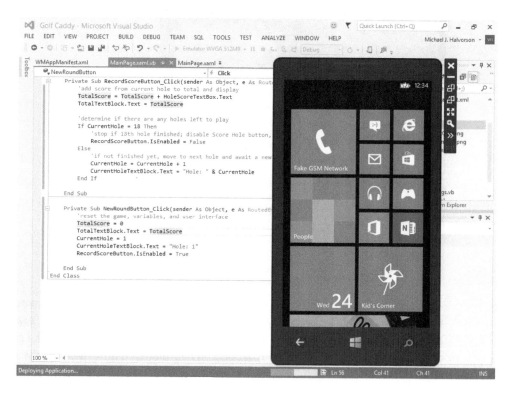

Don't get carried away here—you won't be able to start touching the emulator and operating the Phone as if it were an actual touch device. However, the emulator has been designed to work with mouse clicks on a desktop development system. You can click the Back, Windows, or Search buttons, and you can drag in the user interface to scroll. You will also be able to click the buttons in the Golf Caddy user interface with the mouse to test them.

The Golf Caddy app will start automatically. When the program appears in the emulator, it will look like this:

The user interface looks nice. It is ready to receive input for an 18-hole golf game. But notice that in addition to the Golf Caddy app, a few additional things are visible. For example, you can see a phone-charging icon in the status bar at the top of the page, and the current system time is also visible (1:15). Some debugging information is also visible on the page in the upper-right corner.

Now you'll test the app's behavior.

2. Click the text box object below the Score label.

   Windows Phone displays the software input panel for numeric input.

3. Click the number 4, your simulated score for the first hole.

   Your screen will look like this:

4. Click the background of the Golf Caddy app.

   The SIP disappears.

5. Click the Score Hole button.

   The app updates the *TotalScore* variable and text block and moves to hole #2.

   Your screen looks like this:

The oversized score number is the most important user interface feature in this program. It will allow the user to see at a glance how they are doing.

Now you'll enter information for the rest of the holes in the 18-hole round. For simplicity, you'll use a score of 4 for all 18 holes, although you could easily enter different values with the handy numeric key pad.

6. Click Score Hole repeatedly until you complete the 18th hole.

7. As you click the scores, imagine that you are playing golf and shooting a pretty great round right now. (The typical par rating for a full-length golf course is 72.) Of course, this would take about four hours to complete, and while you played the round, you would likely deactivate the phone now and then or switch to other tasks.

After hole 18, the Golf Caddy app will look like this:

Notice that the Score Hole button is now disabled. But you can continue with another round by clicking the New Round button on the page. Try it now.

8. Click New Round.

The Golf Caddy app resets the global variables, displays 0 for the score, and enables the Score Hole button. Your app is ready for another round.

In just a few minutes, you have created a basic smartphone app that uses interface controls and presents information in an attractive way. As you can see, the process is quite similar to writing a Windows Store application—only the testing is different.

Now you'll close the Golf Caddy app. In the emulator, you can do this by simply clicking the Close button on the emulator toolbar or the Stop Debugging button on the Visual Studio toolbar.

9. Click the Close button on the emulator now.

The emulator closes, and the Visual Studio IDE returns.

Of course, the procedure for closing (or terminating) a Windows Phone app is much different for the user who is actually operating a Windows phone. There are several options here—some actions that close (or terminate) an app, and some that merely deactivate (or suspend) an app, holding it in memory until the user ultimately returns to the program or until the app is *tombstoned* by the Windows Phone OS and removed from memory. (Recall that *Tombstoning* is the forced closure of a deactivated app by the phone, which happens when there is no longer enough memory to keep the program in a suspended state.)

Tombstoning and other application life cycle issues will be discussed in the next section.

Application life cycle considerations

If you are not that familiar with Windows Phone hardware buttons and operating procedures, you should know that there are several ways that a user might choose to open, close, or deactivate a Windows Phone application. This makes sense, of course—the ability to rapidly switch from one application to the next is a real benefit of a Windows Phone, and there are many ways to do it. Stop to consider how often this type of rapid-fire switching happens during a typical phone session: a user might display a webpage on their phone, only to stop to send a text message (maybe related to the content they just viewed in a browser); then they might stop to take an incoming phone call, quickly open the contacts list, run the calculator app to add something, and then send an email message, which sends the user off on another web browser session to gather more data. As those of us who have smartphones know, this entire session might take just a few minutes!

Rapid switching among applications like this brings up an important topic for Windows Phone developers that we need to investigate now—life cycle management considerations. In particular, I want to introduce you to the programming issues related to deactivation, activation, launching, and closing apps in the Windows Phone 8 ecosystem.

Closing or deactivating?

For a Windows Phone user, it might seem like terminating (closing an app) and deactivating (suspending an app) are really very similar actions. And in truth, they should seem quite similar to the user. However, it turns out that closing and deactivating applications are two related but distinct events in the life cycle of a Windows Phone app.

A Windows Phone app is terminated when any of the following occurs:

- The user presses the Back button when the app is running. (This is the de facto "close" button on a Windows Phone.)

- The user presses the Start button and launches another application.

- The phone runs out of battery power and shuts down.

- A deactivated app in memory is tombstoned by the operating system to save memory.

A Windows Phone app is deactivated when any of the following occurs:

- The user switches away from the application without closing it.

- The application that the user is using launches another application (or the user clicks a link or URL in a program).

- The user receives an incoming phone call.

- The lock screen appears after a period of inactivity on the Phone.

Remember that the Windows Phone environment does not support true multitasking. To save battery life, the system's scarcest resource, the phone provides only limited background task support to applications that are deactivated and still in memory. However, while in suspension, the data and page details of a deactivated app are preserved in the system. All of this is by design.

The thing to remember is that the software developer can't know for sure when or if a suspended application will be activated again. Deactivated apps remain in memory until they are tombstoned by the operating system, the app is activated again, or the system is shut down. By default, a Windows Phone 8 device can keep up to eight deactivated apps in a suspended app stack in memory, but after that, the apps are unloaded from memory to free up system resources.

Why does this internal state management matter to the programmer? It matters because the developer needs to meet the expectations of the user related to the data in their application. If the user was truly finished with the application and closed it, there is no expectation that the details of the last session should be visible when the app is launched again. Consider this example: When you use a calculator app on a smartphone and you launch the program after a long period of inactivity, you don't really expect the last calculation you made in that app days ago to still be there. But you might expect that the calculator still has data in it if you are using the app and simply shift away from it for five minutes while you take a phone call.

Visual Studio provides tools and .NET Framework APIs to help you manage life-cycle states in your program so that an application that is temporarily deactivated by the user can be activated again with no data loss. Much of this is done for you automatically; in Windows Phone 8, the system automatically preserves application data and page data for up to eight apps that have been suspended. (This "resume" feature is an improvement over Windows Phone 7.1, which didn't preserve application data automatically—it had to be saved programmatically by your application.) However, you might still want to preserve data in your apps and reload it to guard against the potential problem of tombstoning. It really matters what type of application you are creating. For example, a user might not care that calculator data is no longer visible, but they might expect that text messages or calendar information is always visible in an app—whenever they come back to it.

In the following section, you'll be introduced to the *PhoneApplicationService* class, which can help you save and restore application data during periods of suspension.

The *PhoneApplicationSerivce* class

The *PhoneApplicationService* class provides a way to monitor and respond to the various life-cycle states that a Windows Phone application is going through. When you create a new Windows Phone 8 project in Visual Studio, the templates automatically create *PhoneApplicationService* resources for you in the App.xaml and App.xaml.vb files. Let's check these resources out in the following exercise.

Examine Windows Phone life-cycle states

1. With the Golf Caddy project still loaded in Visual Studio, display the App.xaml file in the XAML tab of the Code Editor.

   Near the end of the file, you'll see the following XAML markup:

   ```
   <Application.ApplicationLifetimeObjects>
       <!--Required object that handles lifetime events for the application-->
       <shell:PhoneApplicationService
           Launching="Application_Launching" Closing="Application_Closing"
           Activated="Application_Activated" Deactivated="Application_Deactivated"/>
   </Application.ApplicationLifetimeObjects>
   ```

   Do you see the event names *Launching*, *Closing*, *Activated*, and *Deactivated*? Your Phone app defines these for you in App.xaml and creates event handlers so that you can add code to manage what happens during the four life-cycle states. During launching, it is sometimes useful to load saved application data. During closing, it makes sense to do final cleanup and save any application data that has not been saved yet. However, be advised that you can't be sure that an app will actually execute its closing event handler, because it might be tombstoned by the operating system before then. This makes the activated and deactivated states of critical importance.

   The activated event gives you a place to restore data that you saved when the application was deactivated. Note that during the deactivation process, you are given only a few seconds to store information, so it is important that any code you place here works quickly and efficiently. As noted earlier, Windows Phone handles some of this saving for you automatically via its "resume" feature.

2. Now open the App.xaml.vb file in the Code Editor.

   You'll see the following lines that reference the *PhoneApplicationService* event handlers in the code-behind file. These are the default event handlers.

   ```
   ' Code to execute when the application is launching (eg, from Start)
   ' This code will not execute when the application is reactivated
   Private Sub Application_Launching(ByVal sender As Object, ByVal e As LaunchingEventArgs)
   End Sub
   ```

```
' Code to execute when the application is activated (brought to foreground)
' This code will not execute when the application is first launched
Private Sub Application_Activated(ByVal sender As Object, ByVal e As ActivatedEventArgs)
End Sub

' Code to execute when the application is deactivated (sent to background)
' This code will not execute when the application is closing
Private Sub Application_Deactivated(ByVal sender As Object, ByVal e As
DeactivatedEventArgs)
End Sub

' Code to execute when the application is closing (eg, user hit Back)
' This code will not execute when the application is deactivated
Private Sub Application_Closing(ByVal sender As Object, ByVal e As ClosingEventArgs)
End Sub
```

The Windows Phone app template created these empty procedures for you, and you can add code to them to manage state information if you feel that your app would benefit from that information.

Let's run the Golf Caddy app again to see whether preserving state information would be useful. However, first you're going to set a special debugging option so that your program will automatically be tombstoned the moment the app is deactivated. This is not the typical behavior, because an app can reside suspended in memory for some time after it has deactivated. Remember that the Windows Phone 8 device will store up to eight deactivated apps in memory before it begins tombstoning programs on the stack. (Further, the user can display the list of apps in the stack by holding down the Back button.)

3. Click Golf Caddy Properties on the Project menu, and then click the Debug category.

4. Select the Tombstone Upon Deactivation While Debugging check box.

    Visual Studio will now let you test what your app will look like when it is deactivated, tombstoned, and then activated again. The question is: Will it preserve the current score in your golf round? Or will the global variables and information on the page be lost?

5. Click the Start Debugging button to run the Golf Caddy app in the emulator.

6. When the app appears, enter a score of **4** for the first hole, and enter **5** for the second hole.

    Your screen will look like this:

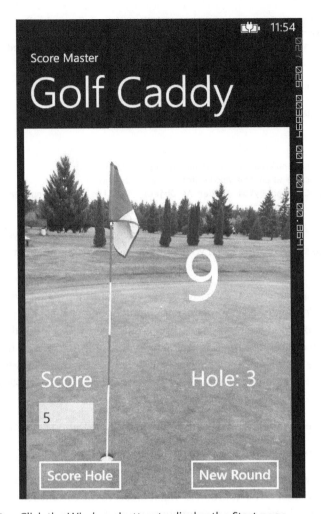

7. Click the Windows button to display the Start page.

Under normal operating conditions, this would simply deactivate your app, and you could activate it again by clicking the Back button. But Visual Studio has tombstoned your app, simulating a condition in which more recent deactivated apps have pushed your app out of the suspended app stack.

8. Click the Back button.

Visual Studio resets the application page, and your data has been lost. Your screen looks like this:

This is not an ideal situation, because it means that a few holes into the 18-hole golf round the user might lose their score. This data loss would happen if they switched away to a number of different programs at some point during the round, which is fairly typical if you consider how tempting it is to take a phone call, check the calendar, add a contact, or take a photo during the golf round.

Although this is a simple demonstration program, is there anything that can be done to prevent this potential data loss?

The answer, of course, is "yes!"

9. Close the program by clicking the Close button on the emulator toolbar.

With the potential problem clearly outlined, you'll now add event handlers for the deactivation and activation events. And you'll edit the MainPage.xaml.vb file to restore key user interface settings.

Handle deactivation and activation states

1. Display the App.xaml.vb file again in the Code Editor.

2. In the *Application_Deactivated* event handler, type the following code:

```
If PhoneApplicationService.Current.State.ContainsKey("Score") Then
    PhoneApplicationService.Current.State("Score") = TotalScore
Else
    PhoneApplicationService.Current.State.Add("Score", TotalScore)
End If
If PhoneApplicationService.Current.State.ContainsKey("Hole") Then
    PhoneApplicationService.Current.State("Hole") = CurrentHole
Else
    PhoneApplicationService.Current.State.Add("Hole", CurrentHole)
End If
```

This handler is executed when the operating system notifies the Windows Phone app that it is time to deactivate. Although Windows Phone can restore suspended applications that are activated rather quickly, the *PhoneApplicationService* class offers a few useful methods and properties to save information in the event of tombstoning and more significant data loss.

In the preceding code, I am using the key values of "Score" and "Hole" to save important state information, just in case the app is tombstoned. Because I can't be sure whether the app has been deactivated in the past, I am creating the "Score" and "Hole" keys only if they do not already exist. In this case, the only values from the program that I am saving are the global variables *TotalScore* and *CurrentHole*, which are the essential data resources related to the golf round that is underway.

3. In the *Application_Activated* event handler, type the following code:

```
If PhoneApplicationService.Current.State.ContainsKey("Score") Then
    TotalScore = PhoneApplicationService.Current.State("Score")
End If
If PhoneApplicationService.Current.State.ContainsKey("Hole") Then
    CurrentHole = PhoneApplicationService.Current.State("Hole")
End If
'Global variables TotalScore and CurrentHole then used to restore
'Golf Caddy UI settings when MainPage is loaded
```

This handler is the other half of the *Application_Deactivated* routine—it restores data to the program that has been saved using the "Score" and "Hole" keys. However, the data restoration happens only if the "Score" and "Hole" keys exist. As the final comment notes, the user interface will be updated by the *MainPage* constructor.

Now you'll return to the MainPage.xaml.vb file and use the global variables *TotalScore* and *CurrentHole* to restore the user interface settings on the Golf Caddy page.

4. Display the MainPage.xaml.vb file in the Code Editor.

    At the bottom of the constructor (the code between *Public Sub New()* and *End Sub*, which runs each time that the MainPage.xaml file is loaded, type the following code:

    ```
    'Update the Golf Caddy UI using global variables (important if app was tombstoned)
    TotalTextBlock.Text = TotalScore
    CurrentHoleTextBlock.Text = "Hole: " & CurrentHole
    ```

    In my constructor, I placed these three lines as the last program statements before the *End Sub* statement.

    These lines of Visual Basic code will be executed each time that the MainPage.xaml file is loaded. They will update the *Text* property for two important text blocks on the page. When the program first starts, only the initial startup values are displayed. But if the program has been tombstoned in the middle of a round and then reactivated, the global variables will contain the current golf score and hole.

    Now you'll run the program again.

5. Click the Start Debugging button to run the Windows Phone app in the emulator.

6. When the app appears, enter a score of **7** for the first hole, and enter **6** for the second hole.

    Your screen will look like this:

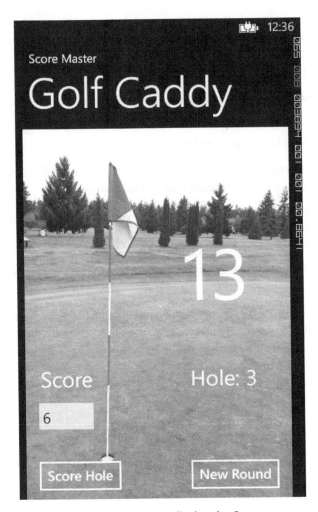

7. Click the Windows button to display the Start page.

   Windows Phone tombstones the program, because the Tombstone check box is still selected in the Properties window.

8. Click the Back button.

   Visual Studio resets the application page, and this time your application data has been preserved. The total score of 13 appears again, and the Golf Caddy app indicates that you are still on hole number 3. You can test the restoration by adding a new score to the text box.

9. Type **3** in the text box, and click Score Hole.

Your screen shows a total score of 16. This means that the value was saved—even after a tombstoning event. The current hole has also been incremented to 4. Your screen looks like this:

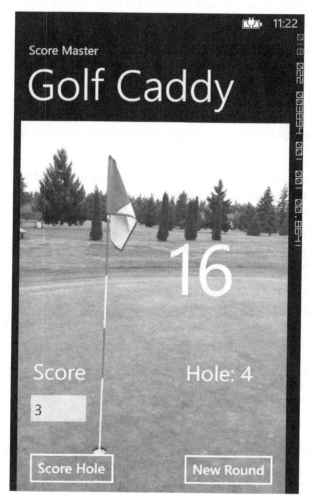

10. Close the program in the emulator.

The Visual Studio IDE returns.

11. Click Golf Caddy Properties on the Project menu, and then click the Debug category.

12. Remove the checkmark from the Tombstone Upon Deactivation While Debugging check box.

You're finished doing Windows Phone life cycle programming for now.

Life cycle management with the *IsolatedStorageSettings* class

A useful exercise for you in the future might be to return to the *Application_Deactivated* event handler in App.xaml.vb and see what other variables and properties you think would be useful to save with key values in the Golf Caddy program. I preserved the essential values by saving the *TotalScore* and *CurrentHole* variables. But you might also want to save the contents of the current hole text box, or another value or property in the program.

As you write more sophisticated Windows Phone applications, you might also find that the *IsolatedStorageSettings* class provides a helpful mechanism to store information a little deeper in the system during closing operations. This is the approach that you would take if you wanted to save some information when an app is closed and terminated that you can display again when the app is launched anew. In such a scenario, the issue is not recovering from a deactivation or tombstoning event, but saving settings during the execution of a program that you might want to restore when the application is started.

The *IsolatedStorageSettings* class provides methods to help you save what I would call "small amounts of data" at application closing—that is, the contents of a few key variables, a short list of important names, or perhaps a small collection of key numeric values. Alternatively, if you want to save large amounts of user data, you would want to open and update an XML document or even use an SQL Server database. Chapter 18, "Data access for Windows Store apps," describes how to work with XML documents in the context of a XAML user interface.

Although a full implementation of the *IsolatedStorageSettings* class goes beyond the scope of this chapter, here is a possible *Application_Launching* event handler that you could add to the Golf Caddy program. It loads the "Score" key that you used in the previous example with the contents of the *TotalScore* variable:

```
Private Sub Application_Launching(ByVal sender As Object, ByVal e As LaunchingEventArgs)
    If IsolatedStorageSettings.ApplicationSettings.Contains("Score") Then
        TotalScore = IsolatedStorageSettings.ApplicationSettings("Score")
    End If
End Sub
```

You can see that the syntax of this event handler is very similar to the *Application_Activated* event handler you wrote earlier in this chapter. Here is what the matching *Application_Closing* event handler might look like that defines the "Score" key used in the preceding example:

```
Private Sub Application_Closing(ByVal sender As Object, ByVal e As ClosingEventArgs)
    IsolatedStorageSettings.ApplicationSettings("Score") = TotalScore
    IsolatedStorageSettings.ApplicationSettings.Save()
End Sub
```

In both cases, the *IsolatedStorageSettings* class is used. Note that both of these event handlers require the following *Imports* statement at the top of the App.xaml.vb file to function properly:

```
Imports System.IO.IsolatedStorage
```

With the addition of the *IsolatedStorageSettings* class, you now have the ability to manage the complex life-cycle demands of a Windows Phone 8 application. The ability to handle tombstoning and activation states will make your smartphone apps much more durable during actual operating conditions.

Setting options in the Window Phone manifest file

Like a Windows Store application, a Windows Phone 8 application has a manifest file that contains important application settings, capabilities, and packaging information. This file is named WMAppManifest.xml. You can use the Manifest Designer in Visual Studio to customize the manifest in several useful ways.

You'll see the file listed in Solution Explorer under the My Project node. If it is not visible, you might need to click the Show All Files command on the Project menu. Try opening this manifest file now.

Edit the Windows Phone app manifest

1. Click Show All Files on the Project menu if the option is not already selected.

    This option shows some of the hidden files in the project, including hidden project or system files in Solution Explorer.

2. Open the My Project Node in Solution Explorer, and double-click the WMAppManifest.xml file.

3. Visual Studio displays the file in the Manifest Designer, as shown in the following illustration:

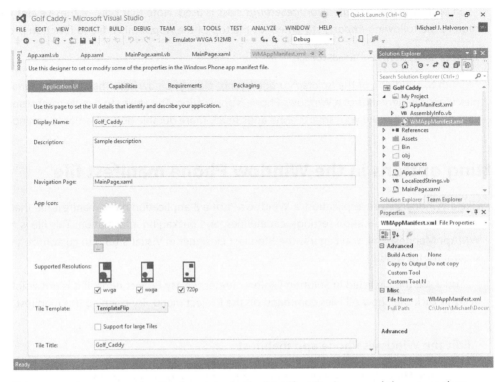

4. Take some time to examine the four tabs in the Manifest Designer and the pages they represent.

   On the Application UI tab, you'll see the name of the application that is displayed on the Phone Start page as well as files and application icons for your app. You can create custom tiles for your app using the steps found in Chapter 9, "Exploring Windows 8.1 design features: Command bar, flyout, tiles, and touch." There are slightly different tiles required for a Windows Phone project, but the concept and design tools are the same.

   On the Capabilities tab, you'll see a list of the various capabilities and permissions that you can give to your Windows Phone app. Security is a concern for Windows Phone applications, so you don't want to allow your app to access sensitive information or hardware on the system that it is not entitled to. Likewise, the Requirements tab identifies the hardware requirements of your application. For example, there are check boxes that allow you to enable Near Field Communication, the front camera, the rear camera, a magnetometer, and a gyroscope.

   On the Packaging tab, you'll see software publisher information, as well as a list of the supported languages for your application.

5. After you make your changes to the Windows Phone manifest file, click the Save All button on the toolbar.

6. Close the Manifest Designer.

7. Close the Golf Caddy Phone app, and then close Visual Studio.

You're finished working with Visual Studio 2013 in this chapter—and this book!

Summary

This chapter described how to create a Windows Phone app with Visual Studio 2013 and the Windows Phone SDK 8.0 toolkit. The development process has much in common with Windows Store app development in Visual Basic. You added XAML Toolbox controls to a page, set properties, wrote program code, tested the application, and managed important life-cycle events, such as *Deactivated* and *Activated*.

While creating the Golf Caddy application, you practiced using the *TextBlock* control, the *Button* control, the *Image* control, and the *TextBox* control. You also learned how to declare global variables, write event handlers, and manage application life-cycle states. Finally, you tested your Windows Phone app using the Visual Studio Emulator software.

You've covered a lot of ground with Visual Basic app development in Visual Studio 2013. You started out creating a Windows Store app, explored the Windows Forms and console app models (the Windows desktop), web programming with Web Forms (ASP.NET), and now you've completed a Windows Phone 8 app walkthrough. You've learned fundamental techniques for each development platform, and you've also learned beginning and intermediate Visual Basic programming skills along the way—the coding fundamentals upon which great Windows applications can be built. I wish you the best of luck as you continue your work with Visual Basic and Visual Studio!

Index

Symbols

A

Q

R

About the author

 MICHAEL HALVORSON is the author or co-author of more than 35 books, including *Start Here! Learn Microsoft Visual Basic 2012*, *Microsoft Visual Basic 2010 Step by Step*, *Microsoft Office XP Inside Out*, and *Microsoft Visual Basic 6.0 Professional Step By Step*. He has been the recipient of numerous non-fiction writing awards, including the Computer Press Best How-to Book Award (Software category) and the Society for Technical Communication Excellence Award (Writing category). Halvorson earned a bachelor's degree in Computer Science from Pacific Lutheran University in Tacoma, Washington, and master's and doctoral degrees in History from the University of Washington in Seattle. He was employed at Microsoft Corporation from 1985 to 1993, and he has been an advocate for Visual Basic programming since the product's original debut at Windows World in 1991. Halvorson is currently an associate professor at Pacific Lutheran University. You can learn more about his books and ideas at *http://michaelhalvorsonbooks.com*.

How to download your ebook

Thank you for purchasing this Microsoft Press title. Your companion PDF eBook is ready to download from our official distributor's site on oreilly.com.

To download your eBook, go to http://aka.ms/PressEbook
and follow the instructions.

Please note: You will be asked to create a free online account and enter the access code below.

ACCESS CODE:

NZTVBDG

Microsoft Visual Basic 2013 Step by Step

Your PDF eBook allows you to:

- search the full text
- print
- copy and paste

Best yet, you will be notified about free updates to your eBook.

If you ever lose your eBook file, you can download it again just by logging in to your account.

Need help? Please contact:
mspbooksupport@oreilly.com
or call 800-889-8969.